THE BROTHERHOOD PRAYER BOOK
Second Revised Edition

EMMANUEL PRESS

Labia sacerdotis custodient scientiam. Mal. 2:7

Copyright © 2007 Benjamin T. G. Mayes
Published by Emmanuel Press
11155 Hubbard Rd., Kansas City, KS 66109, USA
www.emmanuelpress.us

All rights reserved. Unless specifically noted, no part of this publication may be reproduced, stored in a retrieval system, or transmitted, in any form or by any means, electronic, mechanical, photocopying, recording, or otherwise, without the prior permission of Benjamin T. G. Mayes.

The liturgical texts and melodies in this work are in the public domain. The introductions, artwork, typesetting, layout, and all other parts of this work are protected by copyright.

Artwork by Edward Riojas, 10385 Byron Center Ave., Byron Center, MI 49315, USA. Artwork copyright © 2007 Emmanuel Press.

Manufactured in the United States of America

ISBN 978-1-934328-01-9

> Behold, how good and how pleasant it is for brethren
> to dwell together in unity!
> *Psalm 133:1*

Table of Contents

The Calendar..4
Feasts and Commemorations...6
Introduction to the First Edition..10
Introduction to the Second Revised Edition..12
    Gregorian Musical Notation..15
    Introduction to the Daily Offices..19
    Introduction to the Chants..22
    How the Psalm-Text is Accented..25
    How to Sing the Accented Psalm-Text..26
The Ordinary..30
    Vigils (Matins)..30
    Morning Prayer (Lauds)..38
    Midday Prayer (Prime, Terce, Sext, None)....................................47
    Evening Prayer (Vespers)...56
    Night Prayer (Compline)..63
    Ordo Officii ad Completorium...76
    Die Nachtgebet (Komplet)...85
Lectionaries..95
    The Psalter Distributed over Seven Days......................................95
    The Psalter Distributed over Four Weeks......................................97
    The Psalter Distributed over Thirty-One Days.............................98
    Daily Lectionary..99
Common Tones..104
The Psalmody...114
    Alleluia Antiphons...114
    Canticles...118
    The Psalter..138
The Propers..349
    Weekday Propers...349
    Seasonal Propers..389
    Saint's Day Propers...506
    Common of Saints..534
The Seven Penitential Psalms with the Great Litany............................570
Litany of the Holy Sacrament of the Altar...584
The Itinerarium (Prayer Before Travel)..587
Collects for All Occasions...591
Psalms Appropriate for Life's Various Situations.................................605
Preparation for Private Absolution...609
Indices...620

The Calendar

Advent Sunday
    The Advent Season — four weeks
Ember Days in Advent — Wednesday, Friday, and Saturday after Advent 3
CHRISTMAS DAY — THE FEAST OF THE NATIVITY OF OUR LORD
                                                                           December 25
The Circumcision and the Name of Jesus..January 1
The Epiphany of Our Lord..January 6
    The Epiphany Season — one to six weeks
The Transfiguration of Our Lord
Septuagesima Sunday
Sexagesima Sunday
Quinquagesima Sunday
Ash Wednesday — the first day of Lent
    Lententide — forty-six days
Invocavit — First Sunday in Lent
Ember Days in Lent — Wednesday, Friday, and Saturday after Invocavit
Reminiscere — Second Sunday in Lent
Oculi — Third Sunday in Lent
Laetare — Fourth Sunday in Lent
Judica — Passion Sunday — Fifth Sunday in Lent
Palmarum — Sixth Sunday in Lent
Monday of Holy Week
Tuesday of Holy Week
Wednesday of Holy Week
Maundy Thursday
Good Friday
Holy Saturday — Easter Eve

EASTER DAY — THE FEAST OF THE RESURRECTION OF OUR LORD
    The Easter Season — forty days
Easter Monday
Easter Tuesday
Quasimodogeniti — First Sunday after Easter
Misericordias Domini — Second Sunday after Easter
Jubilate — Third Sunday after Easter
Cantate — Fourth Sunday after Easter [2]
Rogate — Fifth Sunday after Easter
Rogation Days — Monday, Tuesday, and Wednesday before Ascension (Lesser Litany Days)
The Ascension of Our Lord
Exaudi — The Sunday after the Ascension
WHITSUNDAY — THE FEAST OF PENTECOST
Monday of Whitsun-Week
Tuesday of Whitsun-Week
Ember Days in Pentecost — Wednesday, Friday, and Saturday after Whitsunday
The Feast of the Holy Trinity
    The Trinity Season — from twenty-two to twenty-seven weeks

Feasts and Commemorations

Feasts are listed with capital letters. The propers for Feasts are listed in the Seasonal Propers or the Saint's Day Propers (pp. 389-533) and are used in all the offices of that day where propers are called for. Commemorations are in lower-case letters, and are usually commemorated after Morning Prayer, while the propers for the offices are taken from the Seasonal Propers (pp. 389-505). One may also use the Common of Saints (pp. 534-569) to treat a Commemoration as a Feast.

JANUARY
1 THE CIRCUMCISION AND THE NAME OF JESUS
2 J. K. Wilhelm Loehe, *Pastor*
6 THE EPIPHANY OF OUR LORD
10 Basil the Great of Caesarea, Gregory of Nazianzus, and Gregory of Nyssa, *Bishops and Doctors*
18 Confession of St. Peter
20 Sarah, *Holy Woman*
24 Timothy, *Bishop and Martyr*
25 THE CONVERSION OF ST. PAUL
26 Titus, *Bishop and Confessor*
27 John Chrysostom, *Bishop and Doctor*

FEBRUARY
2 THE PRESENTATION OF OUR LORD & THE PURIFICATION OF MARY
5 Jacob (Israel), *Patriarch (Holy Man)*
10 Silas, *Fellow worker of St. Peter and St. Paul (Holy Man)*
13 Aquila, Priscilla, Apollos, *Saints*
14 Valentine, *Martyr*
15 Philemon and Onesimus, *Martyrs*
16 Philip Melanchthon (birth), *Doctor*
18 Martin Luther, *Pastor and Doctor*
23 Polycarp of Smyrna, *Bishop and Martyr*
24 ST. MATTHIAS — APOSTLE

MARCH
7 Perpetua and Felicitas, *Martyrs*
17 Patrick, *Missionary to Ireland*
19 Joseph, *Guardian of Jesus (Holy Man)*
25 THE ANNUNCIATION
31 Joseph, *Patriarch (Holy Man)*

April
6 Lucas Cranach and Albrecht Dürer
20 Johannes Bugenhagen, *Pastor*
21 Anselm of Canterbury, *Doctor*
24 Johann Walter, *Kantor*
25 ST. MARK—EVANGELIST

May
1 ST. PHILIP AND ST. JAMES—APOSTLES
2 Athanasius of Alexandria, *Bishop and Doctor*
4 Friedrich Wynecken, *Pastor and Missionary*
5 Frederick the Wise, *Christian Ruler (Holy Man)*
7 C. F. W. Walther, *Pastor and Doctor*
9 Job, *Holy Man*
11 Cyril and Methodius, *Missionaries to the Slavs*
21 Emperor Constantine, *Christian Ruler (Holy Man)*, and Helen, *Mother of Constantine (Holy Woman)*
24 Esther, *Holy Woman*
25 Bede the Venerable, *Doctor*
31 THE VISITATION (NEW DATE)

June
1 Justin, *Martyr*
5 Boniface of Mainz, *Bishop and Missionary to the Germans*
11 Barnabas, *Apostle*
12 The Ecumenical Council of Nicaea, A.D. 325 *(Doctors)*
14 Elisha, *Prophet (Doctor)*
24 THE NATIVITY OF ST. JOHN THE BAPTIST
25 PRESENTATION OF THE AUGSBURG CONFESSION
26 Jeremiah, *Prophet (Doctor)*
27 Cyril of Alexandria, *Bishop and Confessor*
28 Irenaeus of Lyons, *Bishop and Martyr*
29 ST. PETER AND ST. PAUL—APOSTLES

July
2 THE VISITATION (OLD DATE)
6 Isaiah, *Prophet (Doctor)*
16 Ruth, *Holy Woman*
20 Elijah, *Prophet (Doctor)*
21 Ezekiel, *Prophet (Doctor)*
22 ST. MARY MAGDALENE
25 ST. JAMES THE ELDER—APOSTLE

28 Johann Sebastian Bach, *Kantor*
29 Mary, Martha, and Lazarus of Bethany, *Saints*
30 Robert Barnes, *Martyr*
31 Joseph of Arimathea, *Holy Man*

August
3 Joanna, Mary of Cleopas, Mary of Zebedee, and Salome, *Holy Women*
10 Lawrence, *Martyr and Deacon*
[15 THE DORMITION OF ST. MARY, THE MOTHER OF GOD]
16 Isaac, *Patriarch (Holy Man)*
17 Johann Gerhard, *Doctor*
19 Bernard of Clairvaux, *Doctor*
20 Samuel, *Prophet and High Priest (Holy Man)*
24 ST. BARTHOLOMEW — APOSTLE
27 Monica, *Mother of Augustine (Holy Woman)*
28 Augustine of Hippo, *Bishop and Doctor*
29 THE BEHEADING OF SAINT JOHN THE BAPTIST

September
1 Joshua, *Holy Man*
2 Hannah, *Holy Woman*
3 Gregory the Great, *Bishop and Doctor*
4 Moses, *Patriarch (Doctor)*
5 Zacharias and Elizabeth, *Saints*
[8 THE NATIVITY OF THE BLESSED VIRGIN MARY]
[14 HOLY CROSS DAY]
16 Cyprian of Carthage, *Bishop and Martyr*
21 ST. MATTHEW — APOSTLE, EVANGELIST
22 Jonah, *Prophet (Doctor)*
29 ST. MICHAEL AND ALL ANGELS
30 Jerome, *Translator of Holy Scripture (Doctor)*

October
7 Henry Melchior Muhlenberg, *Pastor*
9 Abraham, *Patriarch (Holy Man)*
11 Philip the Deacon, *Holy Man*
17 Ignatius of Antioch, *Bishop and Martyr*
18 ST. LUKE — EVANGELIST
23 St. James of Jerusalem, *Apostle*
25 Dorcas (Tabitha), Lydia, and Phoebe, *Holy Women*
26 Philipp Nicolai, Johann Heerman, and Paul Gerhardt, *Hymnwriters (Pastors)*

28 ST. SIMON AND ST. JUDE—APOSTLES
31 THE FESTIVAL OF THE REFORMATION

November
1 ALL SAINTS' DAY
8 **Johannes von Staupitz,** *Luther's Father Confessor (Pastor)*
9 **Martin Chemnitz (birth),** *Pastor and Doctor*
11 **Martin of Tours,** *Bishop*
14 **Emperor Justinian,** *Christian Ruler and Confessor of Christ (Holy Man)*
19 **Elizabeth of Hungary (or: of Thuringia),** *Holy Woman*
23 **Clement of Rome,** *Bishop*
29 **Noah,** *Patriarch (Holy Man)*
30 ST. ANDREW—APOSTLE

December
4 **John of Damascus,** *Doctor and Hymnwriter*
6 **Nicholas of Myra,** *Bishop*
7 **Ambrose of Milan,** *Doctor, Bishop, and Hymnwriter*
13 **Lucia,** *Martyr and Virgin*
17 **Daniel the Prophet and the Three Young Men,** *Confessors*
19 **Adam and Eve,** *Saints*
20 **Katharina von Bora Luther,** *Holy Woman*
21 ST. THOMAS—APOSTLE
25 CHRISTMAS DAY—THE FEAST OF THE NATIVITY OF OUR LORD
26 ST. STEPHEN—MARTYR
27 ST. JOHN—APOSTLE, EVANGELIST
28 THE HOLY INNOCENTS—MARTYRS
29 **David,** *King of Israel and Psalmwriter (Doctor)*

Introduction to the First Edition

Within the last two decades, the Lutheran Church in the United States, and perhaps all Christendom in North America, has seen two tendencies in worship. One tendency is to make worship as accessible as possible to modern man, for the sake of mission. This tendency has led to wholesale or partial abandonment of historic western liturgical forms and has often neglected liturgical song, making worship music the business of a band or song leader. Music and text have striven for *simplicity*.

The other tendency has perhaps arisen as a result of this simplification of the liturgy. Awakened by the excesses of the former tendency, many have sought meaning and edification in the classical liturgical forms of the Lutheran Church. As the Lutheran liturgical heritage is rooted firmly in western catholic liturgy, they have sought to re-appropriate for themselves everything edifying, everything beautiful, everything solemn from the history of our church. Whereas the former tendency strives for *simplicity*, the latter tendency strives for *transcendence and reverence*. It is out of this latter, liturgical tendency within the Lutheran Church, and the Lutheran Church—Missouri Synod in particular, that this prayer book has been born. While I was studying abroad in Oberursel, Germany, I came across a book entitled *Breviarium Lipsiensae: Tagzeitengebete,* published by the Evangelical Lutheran Prayer Brotherhood *(Evangelisch-Lutherische Gebetsbrüderschaft),* a group at that time under the leadership of Bishop Emeritus Jobst Schoene of the Independent Evangelical Lutheran Church of Germany (SELK). I was fortunate enough to purchase this *Breviarium* for myself and to attend a retreat of the *Brüderschaft*.

Upon returning to the United States, I began to pray and chant the liturgy from this *Breviarium* with Michael Frese, a fellow student at Concordia Theological Seminary—Fort Wayne, Ind. and now pastor in Adell, Wis., who had likewise spent a year in Oberursel. It was at Rev. Frese's instigation that a new project was undertaken. His goal was to produce for our English-speaking brethren a Lutheran, liturgical resource on a par with the German *Breviarium*. For the next two years, the two of us went to work, using the *Breviarium* as well as other sources. Rev. Frese did publicity and much of the conversion of propers from German to English, while I served as general editor and musician. Finally, after two years, the work is done.

We have chosen to use classical, Jacobean English for the prayer book. The text of the Psalms and Canticles is from the King James Version. The text of the propers conforms to that of *The Lutheran Hymnal* (St. Louis: Concordia, 1941) and other works which use classical English. This has been done for several reasons. First, new English translations of the Bible appear constantly. No matter what version we would choose, no one knows whether that version will be widely used in as little as ten years. The King James, on the other hand, has been a classic of the English language for 400 years. It will never go any more out of style than it is now. In addition, the King James, unlike modern English Bibles, is in the public domain. Its classic language often preserves nuances in the biblical languages which are lost in modern English, such as the difference between the 2nd person singular and plural (thou and ye). Finally, many other prayer books already exist which make use of modern English. We recommend these works to those who lack the patience to learn classical English and who prefer not to look up unknown words in a dictionary, as may be required when using this book.

The music chosen for this prayer book is Gregorian Chant. It has been chosen due to its beauty, antiquity, and reverence. The music is high in aesthetic value. No other form of music has been the carrier of Sacred Writ for so long a time. Experience teaches that Gregorian Chant imposes very little of a foreign mood on the text of Holy Scripture, making it conducive to reverence. Yet the music in this book is not simple. It requires practice in order to perform it well. But this too can have a salutary effect on the one who uses it. To spend lengths of time practicing liturgical song makes sense if that song is seen as a sacrifice of praise and thanksgiving to God. To spend such time on a kind of music inaccessible to most outsiders may not make sense to some, but it *does* makes sense if God the Holy Trinity is confessed and believed as the proper object of the utmost of human talent.

Gregorian musical notation has been chosen as the means of conveying the music of this prayer book. While there are many arguments why modern musical notation would have been preferable, the arguments for the Gregorian notation prevailed. First of all, Gregorian notation takes up about half the space that modern notation would take. In addition, Gregorian musical symbols have been developed over the centuries which have no exact equivalent in modern musical notation. Modern notation is especially suited for polyphonic music (such as a four-part hymn), while Gregorian notation is especially suited for monophonic music (such as chanting). Experience also teaches that those who already know how to read modern music can learn Gregorian notation without difficulty. And for those who cannot read modern music, it is immaterial what notation is used.

We have done our best to note our sources. Some of the Saint's Day Propers have been selected by Rev. Frese and myself from Holy Scripture according to ancient patterns. We have aimed at a full sanctoral section which, nevertheless, is fully in harmony with the Confessions of the Evangelical Lutheran Church. Thus, invocation of the saints has been removed when appropriating ancient sources, but the praises of the saints have been retained (see Apology 21:4). In doing so, we have the precedent of the Lutheran editors of the liturgy contained in Lucas Lossius' *Psalmodia* (Wittenberg, 1569), who corrected some of the ancient liturgical hymns and texts so that they would agree with the Scriptures.

May the Lord grant His blessing to all those who use this book! May these words preach Christ—the only hope and salvation of us, and of all the saints.

The Rev. Benjamin T. G. Mayes
The Rev. Michael N. Frese
on the feast of St. Bartholomew
August 24, 2004

INTRODUCTION TO THE SECOND REVISED EDITION

The welcome which the *Brotherhood Prayer Book* received since its publication in late 2004 has far surpassed our expectations. After less than two years, the looming end to the first print run of the *Brotherhood Prayer Book*, the many corrections posted at www.llpb.us, and the desire to produce a prayer book more complete with music and rubrics has led us to create this second revised edition of the *Brotherhood Prayer Book*.

The *Brotherhood Prayer Book*, since it lacks the Scripture readings and meditations needed for services, is not a "breviary," technically speaking. We think of it more as a "choral service book." It can also be used by choirs and pastors as a source book for enriching a traditional Matins, Vespers, or Compline service. Some have asked, "Where did you get all this?" Except for the hymns, all the liturgical music in both the 1st and 2nd editions was arranged by the undersigned. Vigils is our own adaptation of medieval Matins. *Ordo Officii ad Completorium* and *Die Nachtgebet* are straight from Walter Heinz Bernstein, *Breviarium Lipsiensae Tagzeitengebete* (Allgäu, 1988) (the *Leipzig Breviary*). Note: The Psalms in Latin Compline have been changed in this edition to match the traditional Vulgate text as found in the *Leipzig Breviary*. The seven-day Psalm schedule is from *The Anglican Breviary* (Mt. Sinai, NY: Frank Gavin Liturgical Foundation, 1955; reprint, Irvine, CA: Daniel Lula, 1998). The four-week Psalm schedule is from the *Leipzig Breviary*. The 31-day Psalm schedule is from the Common Service, as found for example in the *Evangelical Lutheran Hymn-Book* (St. Louis: Concordia Publishing House, 1914). The Psalm-prayers are from Neale and Littledale's *Commentary on the Psalms* (London: Joseph Masters & Co., 1874-1883; reprint, Denver, 1999). These 19th-century editors gathered prayers and comments from ancient liturgies and service books. Thus, many of the Psalm-prayers are from the Mozarabic Breviary, but there are some also from various medieval writers. The Psalm-tones and Canticle-tones are from Otto Brodde,

"Evangelische Choralkunde," in *Leiturgia: Handbuch des evangelischen Gottesdienstes*, vol. 4 (Kassel: Johannes Stauda-Verlag, 1961), 475-476, 489. Antiphons for Psalms and their melodies were translated and arranged from the *Leipzig Breviary*. The hymns are in the public domain and were taken from *The English Hymnal* (1906) and *The Lutheran Hymnal* (St. Louis: Concordia Publishing House, 1941). The Common Service was the source of much of the seasonal propers (Appointed Psalms, Gospel, Epistle, and Collect); Seasonal Invitatory, Antiphons, and Responsory; and the Collects for All Occasions. The Common Service also provided the textual material for Morning and Evening Prayer. The Antiphons in the Propers (especially for the Benedictus and Magnificat) were often taken from the *Leipzig Breviary* and *The Anglican Breviary*. For many of the saints' days, the Rev. Michael N. Frese chose new antiphons based on the appointed readings for the day. In the second edition, these antiphons especially presented a struggle: where to find music for them? In the end, the undersigned composed new melodies based on ancient melodies in the *Antiphonale Romanum pro diurnis horis* (Rome, 1912). At the end of the BPB, the Litany and Itinerarium are from the *Leipzig Breivary,* and the text of the Commandments and their explanations in the Confession-Mirror is from Martin Luther's *Small Catechism*, in *Concordia Triglotta: The Symbolical Books of the Ev. Lutheran Church, German-Latin-English* (St. Louis: Concordia Publishing House, 1921), 539-543.

Perhaps the biggest change from the 1st edition is the additional music. Gregorian music has been included for responsories and for Magnificat Antiphons. The musical basis of my work has been the *Leipzig Breviary* and the *Antiphonale Romanum pro Diurnis Horis*. I have composed new music for antiphons on the Magnificat for the following liturgical days: Advent 1, Advent 3, Sunday After New Year, Baptism of Our Lord, Epiphany 3, Trinity 25, Trinity 26, Trinity 27, St. Andrew, St. Thomas, Conversion of St. Paul, the Presentation of Our Lord and the Purification of Mary, St. Matthias, St. Mark, St. Mary Magdalene, St. James the Elder, St. Bartholomew, Holy Cross Day, St. Matthew, St. Michael and All Angels, St. Luke, SS. Simon and Jude, Reformation, All Saints, Common of the B.V.M., Common of the Holy Angels, and the Day of Humiliation and Prayer. For this edition, we have placed all the liturgical texts and music which we created for this book into the public domain. With the addition of the materials that were previously in the public domain, this means that the liturgical texts and music of the *BPB* 2nd edition are all in the public domain. The typesetting, layout, artwork, and introductions, however, are not in the public domain.

Other changes include the following. The 2nd ed. of the *BPB* is graced by the beautiful art of Mr. Edward Riojas. We have added rubrics based on the questions we've received and on the learned experience of the Lutheran Liturgical Prayer Brotherhood. Marginal page numbers are included in the 2nd edition, which refer back to the BPB, 1st ed. This will allow a group using both editions to "be on the same page." We have included the non-movable Feasts of the Church Year in the "Feasts and Commemorations" calendar. Brackets indicate where our calendar differs from that of the *Lutheran Service Book* (St. Louis: Concordia Publishing House, 2006). Liturgical role abbreviations have been added to the liturgies to avoid confusion. Gregorian Invitatories and Venite have been adapted from Lucas Lossius, *Psalmodia* (Wittenberg: Johann Schwertel, 1569) and added to Vigils. The rubrics regarding Psalm-prayers have been changed to reflect the actual practice of the LLPB and the general usage of Western Christendom. Readings at Midday Prayer have been added for the festival half of the Church Year. We have included alternate Compline hymns and additional hymns for the Church Year from Sydney H. Nicholson, *Hymns Ancient and Modern: A Plainsong Hymnbook* (London: Wm. Clowes and Sons, Ltd., 1932). We have included the Flexible Psalm Schedule on p. [62], relying on ancient Lutheran practice (see Graff, *Auflösung* I 206). The daily Lectionary from the Common Service takes the place of the Lectionary included in the 1st edition. In response to requests, we have added suggested seasonal Psalm Tones from the *Evangelisch-Lutherisches Kirchengesangbuch* of the Independent Evangelical Lutheran Church (SELK) of Germany. The Lection Tones now show what marks can be used to prepare a text for chanting. More settings of the Benedicamus from Lucas Lossius have been added. The Canticles and Psalms have remained unchanged from the 1st ed. As noted above, new public domain hymns from the *Plainsong Hymnbook* have been added. The hymn indices list the sources of our hymns. We give thanks to the Rev. Mark Buetow, whose work has been incorporated into these indices. Finally, new Canticle Antiphons for Ember Days, full propers for the Beheading of John the Baptist (Aug. 29) from *The Anglican Breviary,* and a Prayer for the Church and Her Pastors after the Collects for All Occasions have been added.

Again, may the Lord grant His blessing to all who use this book! May these words and this music proclaim Christ—the only hope and salvation of us, and of all the saints.

The Rev. Benjamin T. G. Mayes

Gregorian Musical Notation

Four note lines are the basis for the musical notation.

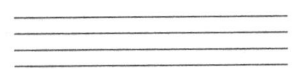

In addition, there are two movable key signatures: the C-clef and the F-clef.

In the examples above, the first C clef shows us that the fourth line from the bottom is a C. The first F clef shows us that the fourth line from the bottom is an F. These note names, however, should be considered *relative* pitches, not absolute. For example, an "A" on the Gregorian staff above does not have to match an "A" on a piano. The placement of the clef is determined by the *mode* (key) and the range of the particular piece of music.

The Notes

In the following examples, the modern equivalents of gregorian notations have been included. As usual, in connected groups of notes, the left note is sung first, then the right note. The only exception is the *Pes*, whose notes are on top of one another. Here the lower note is sung first, then the upper note. The notes are categorized as follows (time durations are relative):

A) Simple Neumes: *Punctum*, *Virga*, and *Apostropha* are single notes with an equal value, which can be varied according to the text.

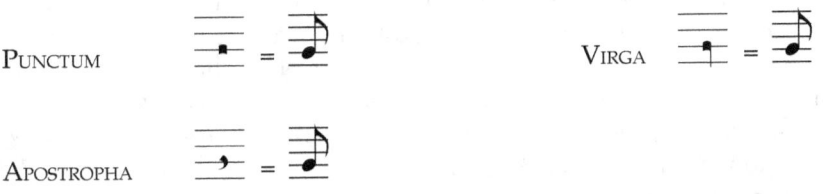

B) Repeated Neumes (Conjunctures) The notes of this group double or triple the value of the Simple Neumes. A glottal stop of the individual notes is not implied, but a corresponding emphasis of breath may be observed.

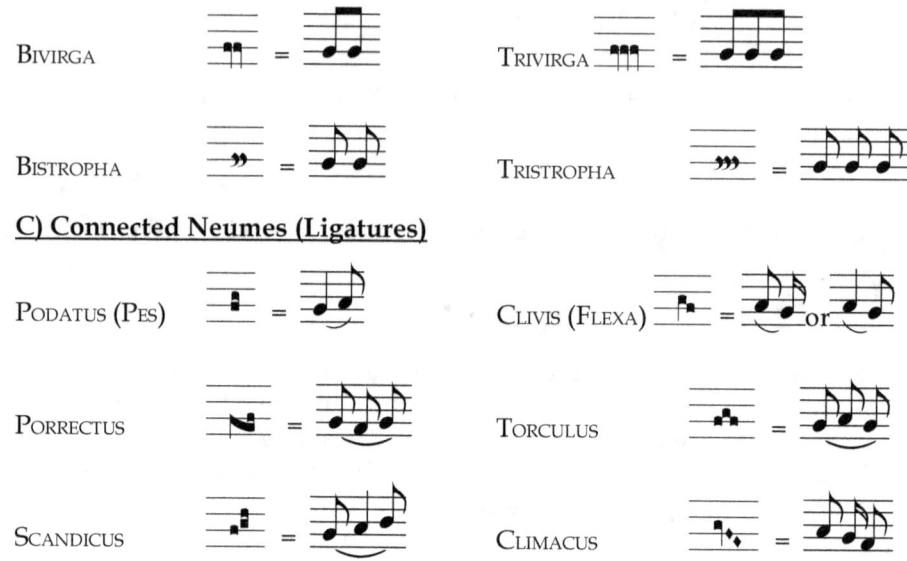

C) Connected Neumes (Ligatures)

For the *Podatus,* note that the two notes are not sung equally, but instead, the first note is longer than the second. The *Clivis* can be sung as two short tones, but also two longer tones may be needed. If its first note is to be long, this will be indicated by an additional mark. The *Porrectus,* a figure of three tones, is sung quickly. The *Torculus,* another figure of three tones, consists of notes of equal value, whose first note can be slightly emphasized. The *Scandicus* is likewise a figure of three tones whose notes are sung with equal value. For the *Climacus,* the first and last tones of the figure are longer.

D) Ornamental Neumes

For the rendition of the ornamental neumes, greater freedoms are required. They are often placed at the liberty of the singer, which is also made more difficult by the fact that in the ancient manuscripts, often no real notes are indicated, but instead symbols are included, or a note is given a deviating printed form. By this it is indicated that an ornamentation is to be performed which can scarcely ever be recorded in concrete notes. The ornamental neumes also have an *ad libitum* character to them. The *Quilisma* is this kind of a figure, usually made up of three printed notes, of which the middle is printed as notched or serrated. The figure of the *Oriscus* demands special attention, first, because it can be observed as an independent tonal symbol, as in certain figures which already have an ornamental character; second, it causes a rhythmic change in the notes preceding it. Such a varying character of a figure which is always printed the same allows the conclusion: for its rendition, the interpreter is allowed greater freedoms than can be described in words or notes. Therefore the suggestions for rendition are just that—suggestions which include just *one* possible rendition.

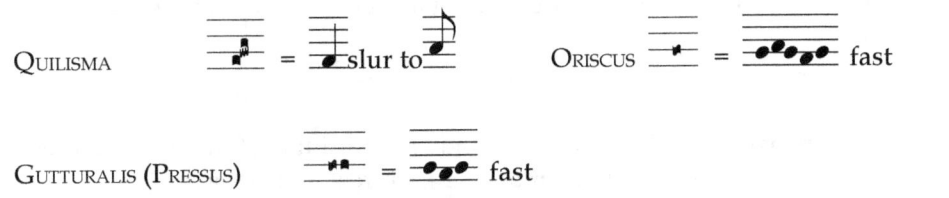

[10]

E) Half-vocalized Neumes (Liquiescents) The second tone of the *Cephalicus* and the *Eptaphonus* are sung so softly, they are almost inaudible, as a "grace note" would be in modern musical notation.

Assisting Symbols

Even choral notation requires additional symbols, in order to fix certain views of interpretation.

Punctum Mora

This symbol, which can stand after one or two notes, doubles their length. This symbol is used most often at the end of phrases. Usually, the dot indicates a phrase, a melodic unit, but it also can mean an effect similar to a *ritardando*, especially at the end of a sentence. It can be held longer or shorter depending on its placement in relation to the whole.

Episem Transversum (a small horizontal line above or below a note or group of notes)

The similarity of this symbol with the *tenuto* marking of modern musical notation is apparent. The rendition, also, of the *episem* is basically the same as for the *tenuto*. The *episem* indicates an intensification of the note, perhaps also its broadening. However, it should not be considered and used as a rhythmic symbol.

The Pauses belong to the assisting symbols also. In contrast to modern notation, pauses in choral (gregorian) notation exist only in the form of vertical lines of various lengths.

1. A short line on the top line of the staff indicates an optional breath mark.

2. A somewhat longer line on the second and third line of the staff requires a longer pause, perhaps equivalent to an eighth-rest in modern music.

3. A line from the top to the bottom line of the staff (bar line) indicates a proper pause which must appear to organize and form the music conceptually. It would be musically logical to prepare for such a pause while still singing by means of relaxing the volume and the tempo.

4. The double bar line belongs only hypothetically to the pause symbols, since it indicates the end of a piece of music, but also the change of choirs or persons (as in the responsories).

Among the assisting symbols, the small, additional letters *(litterae)* which stand above certain notes must also be reckoned. These symbols (derived originally from unlined manuscripts) refer in this book only to the length and shortness of the tones. These symbols are used: *c (cito, celeriter)* for a quick rendition of the notes, and *t (tenere)* for a held rendition, for which effect the *episem,* which approximates the *t,* can also be used.

For these symbols as for others, the rule holds: they are to be rendered with artistic delicacy; a schematic handling is inappropriate.

Introduction to the Daily Offices

Liturgical Roles

In the daily offices, there are these roles:

The **Officiant (O.)** (pastor, *Vorbeter*): He is active in the Opening Sentences, in the Explanation of the Scripture Reading, in the Prayer section (Kyrie, Our Father, Responsive Prayer, Salutation, Collects), and in the Blessing. In addition, at Compline he takes over the Blessing at the beginning of the office, the Confiteor, and the Confiteor's closing versicle. If there is no lector, the officiant then takes over the Reading as well. He or the lector may ring a bell as a signal for the choir/congregation to stand.

The **Congregation (A.)** (All): It sings the hymn (perhaps responsively: Congregation I — Congregation II, or choir — congregation) and the other congregational chants, and possibly also the antiphons. It responds in the responsorial chants: Opening Sentences, Responsory, Kyrie, Our Father, Responsive Prayer (Preces), Salutation, and Benedicamus, and concludes the Collects and Blessings with "Amen." In the Psalmody and Canticle, a trained congregation will be able to take over the role of Choir II.

The **Choir (I. & II.)**: It sings (divided into two choirs, or responsively with the congregation) Psalms, stanzas of the Hymn, and the Canticle, as well as the Antiphons, perhaps also the Responsory. If there is no choir, the congregation's chants can take the place of the choir parts.

The **Cantor (C.)** (Lead Singer): He sings the intonation in the Psalmody, Responsory, Hymn, Versicle, Canticle, and Benedicamus, as well as in the congregation's chants, if these are executed without organ accompaniment. He leads the singing of Choir I; Choir II has its own cantor.

The **Lector (L.)** (Reader): He takes over the Reading and may read an Explanation or Meditation. If there is no cantor, the lector or the officiant may take over his tasks. He or the officiant may ring a bell as a signal for the choir/congregation to stand.

[12]

The **Schola (S.)**: One or two singers who form a *favorit* choir with the cantor in Choir I. It is active in the Responsories and Benedicamus.

Liturgical Space

Considering the predominantly antiphonal manner of responsive singing in the Daily Offices (Choir I over against Choir II), it is desirable that an *over-against* come to expression in the spatial arrangement. The Prayer Offices are, in the rule, executed without the use of the altar.

Those participating in the Daily Offices can be arranged in the liturgical space as follows:

Where the choir area (the area between the altar and the nave) allows it, the congregation gathers in two halves which sit across from each other, facing each other. (Cf. diagram A.)

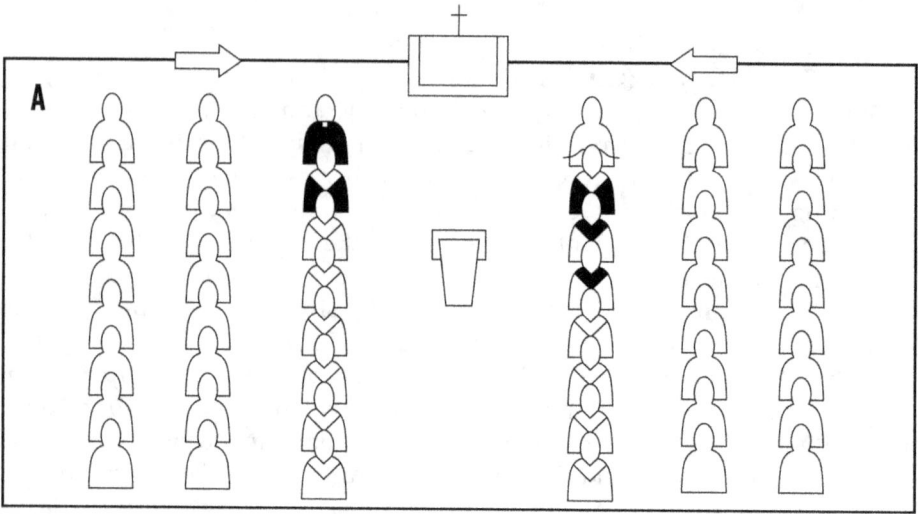

Where there is no sufficient choir area, the congregation sits in the nave (in the pews), the choir perhaps in the first rows. For antiphonal singing, choir and congregation are each divided into two groups by the center aisle. The officiant and the lector are located in the front row (officiant — left, lector — right). (Cf. diagram B.)

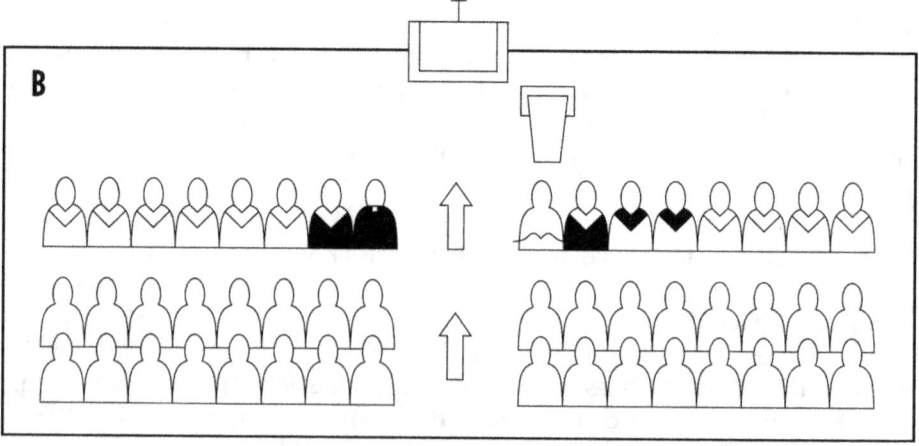

For churches with small choir areas, or when a large congregation is present, officiant, lector, cantor, and choir (possibly also part of the congregation) sit in the choir area as in A.; the congregation sits in the nave. (Cf. diagram C.)

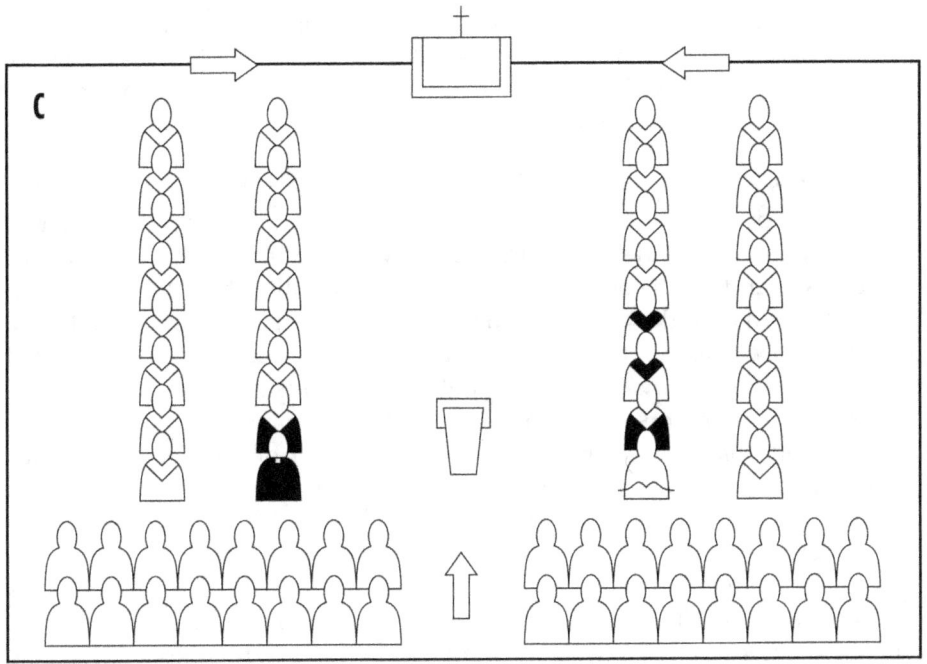

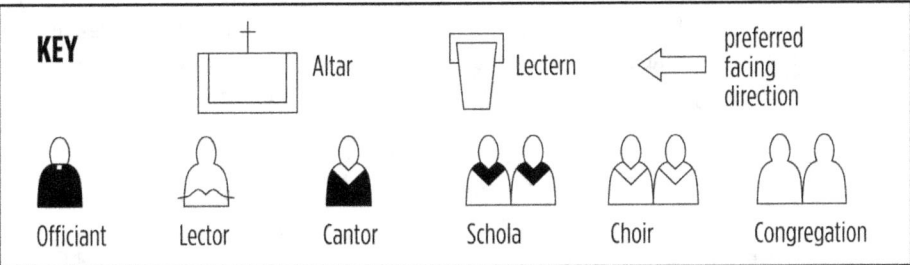

The place of the lector can be determined by the placement of the lectern. The preceding should be applied appropriately for spaces without an altar. Officiant and cantor perform their functions, in the rule, at their seats; for the Readings, the lector moves to the lectern or to the steps of the choir area or altar and turns to the congregation. The officiant gives the blessing at the steps of the choir area or altar, facing the congregation.

The *Introitus* is a simple processional ceremony which may be used by the choir to enter the sanctuary at all offices except the first morning office of the day (either Vigils or Lauds), and may be used to leave the sanctuary at all offices. They form two lines outside of the sanctuary and at a signal from the officiant enter the sanctuary in pairs. The two members of each pair reverence the altar and greet each other by bowing before proceeding to their places in the choir area opposite one another, remaining standing. The choir may exit in the following manner. Members of each choir come in pairs before the altar, reverence the altar, and then exit the sanctuary. Outside the sanctuary they bow to each other and depart, meditating upon the Word of God just heard and sung.

Liturgical Posture

All persons with a special function (officiant, cantor, lector) stand during the parts executed by them. Otherwise they take the posture of the choir to which they belong, or the congregation with which they alternate. The lector moves to the lectern, if one is present, for his function; the officiant moves to face the congregation for the blessing; all others remain in their places. At major (festival) Offices, an officiant who is a pastor may move to the altar for the Prayers and perhaps the Opening Sentences.

If incense is used at Vespers, incense is put on the coals before the beginning of the Office. The officiant may move during the versicle and put incense on the coals again. He may also cense the altar during the Magnificat.

For the Opening Sentences, Responsory, Office Hymn, Canticle, Benedicamus, and Blessing, and also for those portions of the Prayers where one does not kneel, all stand. For the Psalmody, Reading, Explanation, and other Hymns, all sit. According to circumstances, one kneels either during all of the Prayers (from the Kyrie to the Collects), or during the Responsive Prayers and the adjoining Collects, or only for the Silent Prayers and Collects. At Compline, one may kneel also for the Confiteor.

INTRODUCTION TO THE CHANTS

Antiphonal Psalmody

The Psalmody and the Canticles are sung antiphonally, that is, responsively by whole verse on the part of two groups (half-choirs: Choir I and Choir II). The Psalm-Tones, according to their musical structure, are set up for this kind of antiphonal responsive singing. It is inadvisable to sing the Psalmody responsorially, that is, responsively between officiant and congregation, officiant and choir, or cantor and choir. The Psalm, always being preceded by the Antiphon, is intoned by the cantor, i.e. he sings the first few notes in order to establish the tonality and tempo. If need be, it could be intoned by a few voices of the choir—perhaps three boys or men. The cantor intones in such a way that the *tuba* (the repeated reciting tone) does not lie under F nor above C.

Antiphonal Psalmody is, furthermore, to be divided by whole verse:

each half-choir sings one whole Psalm-verse, in the middle of which (at the star *) a breathing pause is made. It contradicts the musical structure of the Psalmody to sing responsively by half-verse, so that one choir would always begin a verse, increasing musical tension, and the other would end the verse, releasing musical tension.

The Antiphon belongs to the Psalmody. As a theme-verse, it improves the understanding of the Psalm and often links it to the Church Year. The choice of a Psalm-tone is based on the tonality of the Antiphon.

The Psalmody consists of:
Antiphon
Psalm
Gloria Patri (Glory be to the Father...)
Antiphon repeated

The Psalm is sung according to one of the eight Psalm-tones, whose structure (demonstrated on the model of the 8th Psalm-tone) is as follows:

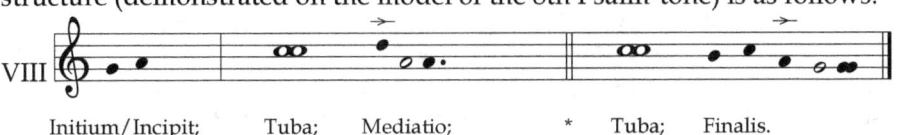

Initium/Incipit;   Tuba;   Mediatio;   *   Tuba;   Finalis.

The *initium/incipit* (entry form) connects the final tone of the Antiphon with the *tuba* (reciting tone) of the Psalm. Therefore it is always and only sung after the Antiphon, not at the *Gloria Patri*. The *tuba* is the tone, repeated according to the number of syllables of the half-verse, on which the main part of the text is sung. The *mediatio* is the middle cadence at the end of the first half-verse. The *finalis* is the final cadence at the end of the second half-verse. According to the number of syllables in the cadence, extra tones (printed as hollow notes in the music) are inserted. At the middle cadence of the 2nd, 4th, 5th, and 8th Psalm tones, if the last syllable is accented, the note following the accented note must sometimes be abruptly omitted *(mediatio correpta)*. There is no *finalis correpta*. Example:

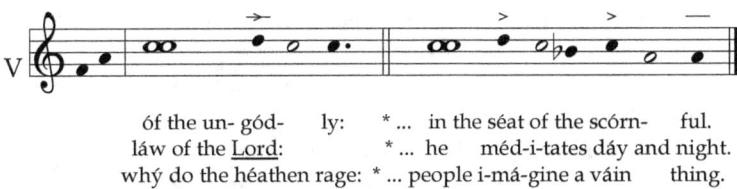

óf the un- gód-   ly: * ... in the séat of the scórn-   ful.
láw of the <u>Lord</u>:   * ... he   méd-i-tates dáy and night.
whý do the héathen rage: * ... people i-má-gine a váin   thing.

For the recitation of the Psalms, grammatical punctuation (comma, semicolon) in the Psalm-verse never means a breath mark and must never interrupt the flow of speech. For some long half-verses, the *flexa* (†) is used as a breath mark; the last one or two syllables before the *flexa* are sung on a lower note. (If more than one syllable is to be sung on the lower tones, the accented syllable is marked with a circumflex ^.) In Psalm-tones 2, 3, 5, and 8, the tone is dropped a minor 3rd from the *tuba;* in Psalm-tones 1, 4, 6, and 7, the tone is dropped a Major 2nd. The *flexa* occurs only in the first half-verse. Example:

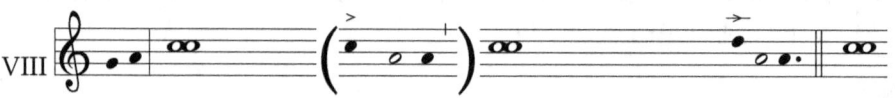

redemption unto his peo-   ple, †   he hath commanded...
maketh glad the hêart of man, †   and oil to make...

The execution of the Psalmody and Canticles is as follows:

Antiphon: Cantor intones until the star *. Whole choir continues and sings the Antiphon to the end.

Psalm: Cantor intones the first half of the first verse with the *initium*, in order to set the tempo of recitation. Choir I sings the second half of the first verse. Choir II sings the second verse without the *initium*. Choir I sings the third verse without *initium*. Choir II sings the fourth verse, etc. Each half-choir begins singing its verse when the other half-choir has finished, with no intervening pause. This means that the choir must take a breath before the other has finished singing. Verses are divided musically, not canonically. For example, Psalm 69:2 and 4 are divided into two liturgical verses.

Gloria Patri: Choir I or II sings "Glory be to the Father..." on the same Psalm-tone. Choir II or I (the other choir, as the case may be) sings "As it was in the beginning...Amen." Note: Missouri Synod custom is that the whole choir sings the *Gloria Patri* in unison.

Antiphon repeated: The whole choir repeats the Antiphon without intonation of the cantor.

The cantor leads the choir and the choir leads the congregation. The **organ**, especially if not located in the choir area, is less suited to the role of leading the gregorian prayer offices. If there is a choir organ present, it can, beyond prelude and postlude, take over the functions of a figural choir, can intone and accompany congregational hymns and chants, and with a large congregation can support the singing in a restrained manner.

A **figural choir** can execute the Psalms, Responsory, and Canticle with polyphony. The figural choir can also take over individual stanzas of the Office Hymn, or alternate stanzas in other hymns and chants. In the Psalmody, the opportunity to perform several Psalms should especially be observed. In the Canticle, a figural execution together with the unison singing of the congregation is not recommended. Here an alternation by whole verse of the figural choir and congregation may be appropriate.

How the Psalm-Text is Accented

1. The Psalm verses are divided into two parts by means of an asterisk * according to conceptual parallelism. The enumeration of Psalm verses in modern editions of the Bible does not necessarily follow conceptual parallelism. In this Psalter, a "whole verse" is a *liturgical* verse of two parts (or three).
2. If a verse is long and can be divided into three parts according to conceptual parallelism, a dagger † divides parts one and two (which together constitute the first half-verse) and the asterisk * divides parts two and three. There is never a division of the second half-verse.
3. If both half-verses must be subdivided, each one becomes its own whole verse, divided by the asterisk *.
4. Next, the last two stressed syllables of each half-verse are accented. The gregorian Psalm-tones are matched with the text of the Psalm according to stressed syllables. Stressed syllables must be sung on stressed notes, and likewise, unstressed syllables must be sung on unstressed notes.
5. Latin most often stresses the 2nd-last or 3rd-last syllable of each half-verse. E.g. Psalm 119:105 "Lucerna pedibus meis vérbum túum, * et lumen sémitae méae." English, however, often stresses the last syllable of the half-verse. E.g. "Thy word is a lamp únto my féet, * and a light únto my páth." Thus in order to use English text with the gregorian Psalm-tones, certain rules of accenting must be followed.
6. Accenting is begun from the end of the half-verse. If possible, the 2nd-last or 3rd-last syllable of each half-verse is accented.
7. The last syllable is not accented if the 3rd-last syllable can be accented. Wrong: "I will live and práise the Lórd." Right: "I will líve and práise the Lord."
8. The 4th-last syllable is not accented as the final accent of the half-verse. Wrong: "as lóng as I live."
9. If the last and 4th-last syllables are stressed, they are accented. Instead of an accent mark on the last syllable, underlining is used. Right: "as lóng as I <u>live</u>."
10. Next, the 2nd-, 3rd- or 4th-last syllable before the final accent is marked with an accent. This is the "penultimate accent."
11. The last syllable before the final accent is not accented. Wrong: "I was glád whén they said." Right: "I was glád when they <u>said</u>." Right: "I was

[16]

gláḋ when they sáid to me."
12. The best accenting for gregorian Psalm-tones is ´ - ´ - . E.g. "of his péoples' práises." Nevertheless, unstressed syllables should not be accented, if at all possible.
13. A dot · may be placed before the 3rd syllable preceding the final accent. This has been done in the Gospel canticles, since the inflection of the melismatic canticle tones often begin at that point. E.g. "My soul · doth mágnifý the Lord."
14. When the ending "-ed" is to be pronounced as a separate syllable, add a hyphen (-) to make that clear. E.g. "Bless-ed." For clarity, mark silent letters by printing them in italics. E.g. "Ev*e*ry."
15. Syllables ending in "r" can often be counted as two syllables. E.g. "fíre-", "devóur-". When this is done, place a hyphen (-) after the word.
16. Words like "answeredst" and "saidst" are difficult to pronounce. In the 2nd person singular, simple past, a consonant cluster occurs which is nearly impossible to pronounce. In these situation it is perhaps best to pronounce the final "st" as a separate syllable. E.g. "answered-st" and "said-st".
17. Pronunciation of other common words: "saith"—seth (one syllable), "shew"—show.
18. From these rules, the following English accenting patterns appear:
    ´ - ´ -   foréver. Ámen.
    ´ - - ´ - -   unspéakable óracles.
    ´ - - ´   óut of the <u>womb.</u>
But these should be avoided:
    ´ - - - ´ -
    ´ - - - ´   morning and évening to re<u>joice</u>. (*Here the following would be better*: and évening tó rejoice.)
    ´ - ´   Father and tó the Són
    ´ - ´ - - -   and tó the Hóly Spirit
    ´ ´

How to Sing the Accented Psalm-Text to the Accented Psalm-Tones

1. If the half-verse of the Psalm-tone has one accent, this accent corresponds to the final accent of the Psalm-text. If more than one syllable follows the final accent of the Psalm-text, the extra syllable is sung on the hollow note. Hollow notes are not whole notes. They have the same length as black notes.

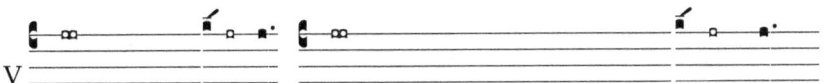

But thóu art hó- ly * I cry in the daytime, bút thou héarest not; *

2. If a half-verse of the Psalm-tone has one accent with leading tones (e.g., the first half of tone IV), the tone-accent corresponds to the final text-accent, and the leading tones are sung to the corresponding number of syllables before the final text-accent. The second-last (penultimate) text-accent is ignored.

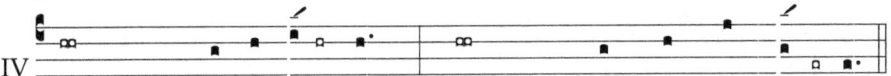

... O Lord, Gód of our fá- thers * ... my vows before thém that féar him.

3. If a half-verse of the Psalm-tone has two accents (e.g., tone VII), these correspond to the two text-accents. If more than one syllable follows an accented syllable in the text, the extra syllables are sung on the hollow notes.

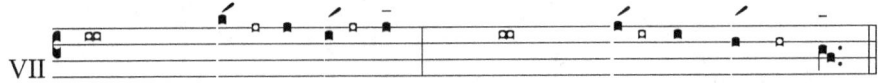

... in the great cón- gre-gá- tion * ... brought me ínto the dúst of death.

4. Whenever the final text-accent falls on the last syllable of a half-verse (stressed *ultima*), that syllable is <u>underlined</u> instead of being indicated by an accent mark. At the end of the first half-verse *(mediatio)*, there are two manners of handling the stressed *ultima*. In Psalm-tones II, IV, V, and VIII, the stressed *ultima* falls on the same note as the accent. In this case, the last note of the *mediatio* falls out and is not sung *(mediatio correpta)*.

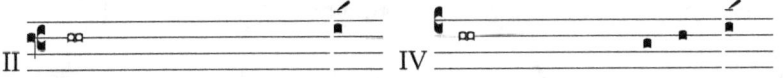

Our fathers trústed in <u>thee</u>: *   Our fathers trústed in <u>thee</u>: *

5. In some Psalm-tones, the stressed *ultima* falls on the last note of the *mediatio* (e.g., tone I). In this case, the penultimate tone-accent corresponds to the penultimate text-accent. The final tone-accent is disregarded.

[18]

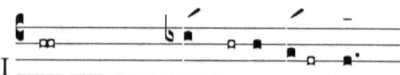

Our fathers trúst- ed in thee: *

6. At the end of the second half-verse *(conclusio)*, there are three manners of handling the stressed *ultima*. If the *conclusio* has one accent with leading tones, the stressed ultima may fall on the same note as the tone-accent does (e.g., tone IV). In this case, the *ultima* is slurred.

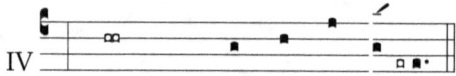

... upon your béd and be still—.

7. If the *conclusio* has one accent with leading tones, the stressed *ultima* may also fall on the last note of the *conclusio* (e.g. tone I and III). In this case, the leading tones and accented note are sung to the corresponding number of syllables before the stressed *ultima*. The tone-accent is disregarded.

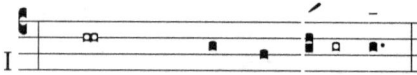

... upon your béd and be   still.

8. If the *conclusio* has two accents, the stressed *ultima* may fall on the last note or note-cluster (e.g., tone V and VII). In this case, the penultimate tone-accent corresponds to the penultimate text-accent. The final tone-accent is disregarded.

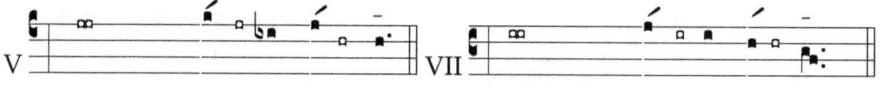

... upon your béd   and be   still.   ... upon your béd and be   still—.

9. The tones of the beginning formula *(initium)* are sung on the first verse of the Psalm and on every verse of the Gospel Canticles *(Benedictus, Magnificat,* and *Nunc Dimittis)*. The *initium* is also sung on the antiphon, if the antiphon is sung to the Psalm-tone.

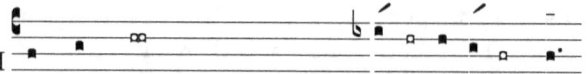

My God, my God, why hast thóu forsáken me? * (Ps. 22:1)

BUT COMPARE:

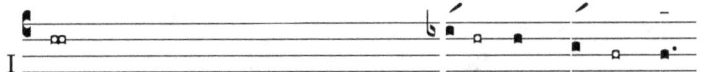

O my God, I cry in the daytime, bút thou héarest not; * (Ps. 22:2)

10. The dagger (†) marks the *flexa*, dividing the first half-verse. The last syllable before the dagger is lowered from the reciting tone to the last tone of the *initium*. If the 3rd-last syllable before the dagger is accented (marked with a circumflex ^), the last two syllables before the dagger are lowered.

[19]

... like a potsherd; † and my tongue ... ... eat and be sâ-tis-fied: † they shall ...

THE ORDINARY

✠ *denotes an appropriate place to make the sign of the cross. Whenever the Gloria Patri is said or chanted, one may bow. At the Name of Jesus the head may be bowed. O: = Officiant. A: = All. C: = Cantor. L: = Lector. I. & II. = Choir I & Choir II. S: = Schola.*

THE ORDER OF VIGILS

Vigils, known in the Middle Ages as Matins, is a late night or early morning service of Psalms and readings. Its distinguishing feature is its three nocturnes, each nocturne consisting of Psalmody, a Reading, and a Responsory.

At the first morning office of the day, all take their places quietly. At a signal from the officiant, all rise.

Then shall be said or chanted the Versicles here following. (O., A.)
℣. O Lord, open Thou my lips.
(At this versicle, a cross may be marked with the thumb upon the lips.)
℟. And my mouth shall show forth Thy praise.
℣. Make haste, O God, to ✠ deliver me.
℟. Make haste to help me, O Lord.
A. Glory be to the Father and to the Son : and to the Holy Ghost. As it was in the beginning, is now and ever shall be : world without end. Amen. Alleluia!
Instead of Alleluia, from Septuagesima to Easter Eve:
Praise to Thee, O Christ, King of eternal Glory!

The Invitatory

May be omitted except on Sundays and Feasts. First the Invitatory is sung twice, being intoned by the cantor the first time and continued by all after the *. Next, Psalm 95 is sung, interspersed with repetitions of the Invitatory according to the following order. When the Invitatory is repeated, it is sung by all, without intonation by the cantor. (Proper Invitatories are found on pp. 389-569. Or an antiphon may be used as the Invitatory. If sung according to a Psalm-tone, the entire Invitatory is repeated at each interval.)

Invitatory: See pp. 389-569. (C., A.)
Psalm 95 *Venite, exsultemus*

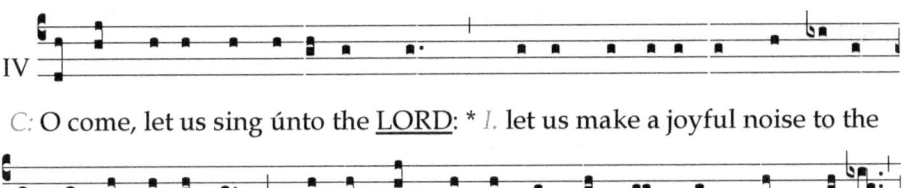

C: O come, let us sing únto the LORD: * *I.* let us make a joyful noise to the rock of óur salvátion. *II.* Let us come before his presence wíth thanksgíving, * and make a joyful noise ún- to hím with psalms.

The entire Invitatory is repeated.

I. For the LÓRD is a gréat God, * and a great Kíng a-bóve all gods. *II.* In his hand are the deep pláces óf the earth: * the strength of the hílls is his ál-so.

The second half of the Invitatory is repeated.

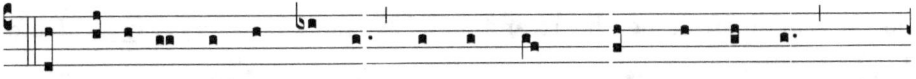

I. The sea is his, ánd he máde it: * and his hands fórmed the drý land. *(Kneel.)*

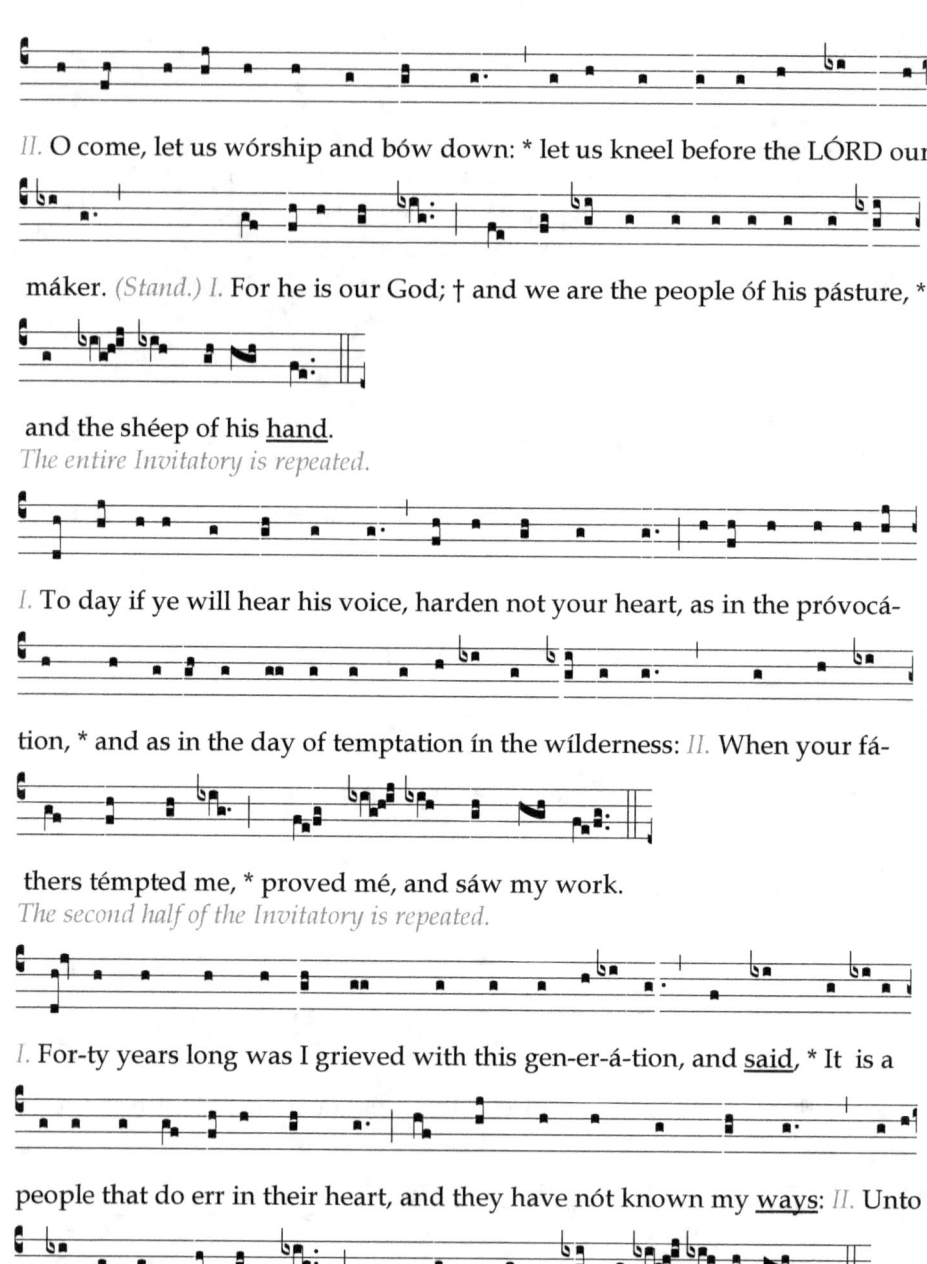

II. O come, let us wórship and bów down: * let us kneel before the LÓRD our máker. *(Stand.)* *I.* For he is our God; † and we are the people óf his pásture, * and the shéep of his <u>hand</u>.
The entire Invitatory is repeated.

I. To day if ye will hear his voice, harden not your heart, as in the próvocá-tion, * and as in the day of temptation ín the wílderness: *II.* When your fá-thers témpted me, * proved mé, and sáw my work.
The second half of the Invitatory is repeated.

I. For-ty years long was I grieved with this gen-er-á-tion, and <u>said</u>, * It is a people that do err in their heart, and they have nót known my <u>ways</u>: *II.* Unto whom I swáre in my <u>wrath</u> * that they should not en-ter ín-to my <u>rest</u>.
The entire Invitatory is repeated.

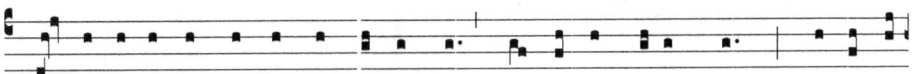

I. Glo-ry be to the Fáther and tó the Son * and tó the Hóly Ghost. *II.* As it was

in the beginning, is now, and éver sháll be, * wórld with-out énd. A- men.
The second half of the Invitatory is repeated; thereafter the entire Invitatory.

The Hymn
Intoned by cantor; continued by all after the first phrase of the first stanza. May be sung in alternation between choirs I and II. (May be omitted except on Sundays and Feasts)

(sit)
The 1st Nocturne
Psalmody: *(C., I., II.) One or more Psalms are prayed, each with its own antiphon. See One-Week Psalm Schedule.*
(sit) **Reading**: *(L.) From the Holy Scriptures. After the reading:*
  L: **But thou, O Lord, have mercy upon us.** A: **Thanks be to thee, O Lord.**
(stand) **Responsory**: *(C., S., A.) A Responsory from the propers (pp. 389-569) may be used.*
Silent Prayer: *The Lord's Prayer and other prayers may be prayed.*

The 2nd Nocturne
Psalmody: *(C., I., II.) One or more Psalms are prayed, each with its own antiphon. See One-Week Psalm Schedule.*
(sit) **Reading**: *(L.) From a Church Father. After the reading:* L: **Here ends the reading.**
(stand) **Responsory**: *(C., S., A.) A weekday Responsory from the weekday propers (349-388) may be used.*
Silent Prayer: *The Lord's Prayer and other prayers may be prayed.*

The 3rd Nocturne
Psalmody: *(C., I., II.) One or more Psalms are prayed, each with its own antiphon. See One-Week Psalm Schedule.*
(Sit) **Reading**: *(L.) From the Holy Scriptures, usually the Gospels. After the reading:*
  L: **But thou, O Lord, have mercy upon us.** A: **Thanks be to thee, O Lord.**

(stand) **Responsory**: *On Sundays and Feasts not in penitential seasons, the Te Deum shall be sung. On other days a hymn stanza may be sung.*

Te Deum

(This arrangement of the Te Deum may be sung according to a Psalm-tone.)
C., I., II:

We praise Thee, O God; we acknowledge Thée to bé the Lord. * All the earth doth worship Thee, the Father éverlásting.

To Thee all angels cry aloud, the heavens and all the pówers there<u>in</u>; * to Thee cherubim and seraphim contínua̋llý do cry:

(Bow for the Triple Holy) Holy, holy, holy, Lord Gód of Sábaoth! * Heaven and earth are full of the majesty óf Thy glóry.

[22] The glorious company of the Apóstles práise Thee; * the goodly fellowship of the próphets práise Thee;

The noble army of mártyrs práise Thee; * the holy Church throughout all the world dóth acknówledge Thee:

The Father of an infinite mâjesty; † Thine adorable trúe and ónly Son, * also the Holy Ghóst, the Cómforter.

Thou art the King of Glóry, O <u>Christ</u>. * Thou art the everlasting Són of the Fáther.

(Bow) When Thou tookest upon Thee tó delíver man, * Thou didst humble Thyself to be born óf a vírgin. *(Stand)*

When Thou hadst overcome the shárpness of <u>death</u>, * Thou didst open the kingdom of heaven to áll belíevers.

Thou sittest at the ríght hand of <u>God</u> * in the glory óf the Fáther.

We belíeve that Thóu shalt come * to bé our judge.

(Genuflect) We therefore pray Thee, hélp Thy sérvants * whom Thou hast redeemed wíth Thy précious blood. *(Stand)*

Make them to be númbered wíth Thy saints * in glory éverlásting.

O Lord, save Thy people and bléss Thine héritage. * Govern them and lift them úp foréver.

Day by day we mágnify <u>Thee</u>. * And we worship Thy name ever, wórld without <u>end</u>.

Vouchsafe, O Lord, to keep us this dáy without <u>sin</u>. * O Lord, have mercy upon us, have mércy upón us.

O Lord, let Thy mercy be upon us, as our trúst is in <u>Thee</u>. * O Lord, in Thee have I trusted; let me never bé confóunded.

OR: **Te Deum noted**
(This arrangement of the Te Deum may be sung in alternation between two choirs. The Cantor intones up to the asterisk.)

C: We praise Thee, O God; * *I.* we acknowledge Thee to be the Lord.

II. All the earth doth worship Thee, the Father everlasting. *I.* To Thee all

angels cry aloud, the heavens and all the powers therein. *II.* To Thee cheru-

bim and seraphim: continu-al-ly do cry: *I. Ho-ly, II. Ho-ly, I. & II.* **Ho-ly,**

Lord God of Saba-oth! *I.* Heaven and earth are full of the majesty of Thy

glory. *II.* The glori-ous company of the Apostles praise Thee; *I.* The good-

ly fellowship of the prophets praise Thee; *II.* The noble army of martyrs

praise Thee; *I.* The ho-ly Church throughout all the world doth acknow-

ledge Thee: *II.* The Father of an in-fin-ite majesty; *I.* Thine a-dor-a-ble true and only Son, *II.* Al-so the Holy Ghost, the Comforter. *I.* Thou art the

King of Glory, O Christ. *II.* Thou art the ev-er-lasting Son of the Father.

I. When Thou tookest upon Thee to de-liv-er man, Thou didst humble Thyself to be

born of a virgin. II. When Thou hadst overcome the sharpness of death,

Thou didst open the kingdom of heaven to all believers. *I.* Thou sittest at

the right hand of God in the glory of the Father. *II.* We believe that Thou

shalt come to be our judge. *I. We therefore pray Thee, help Thy servants: whom*

Thou hast redeem-ed with Thy precious blood. II. Make them to be number-ed

with Thy saints: in glory ev-er-lasting. *I.* O Lord, save Thy people: and

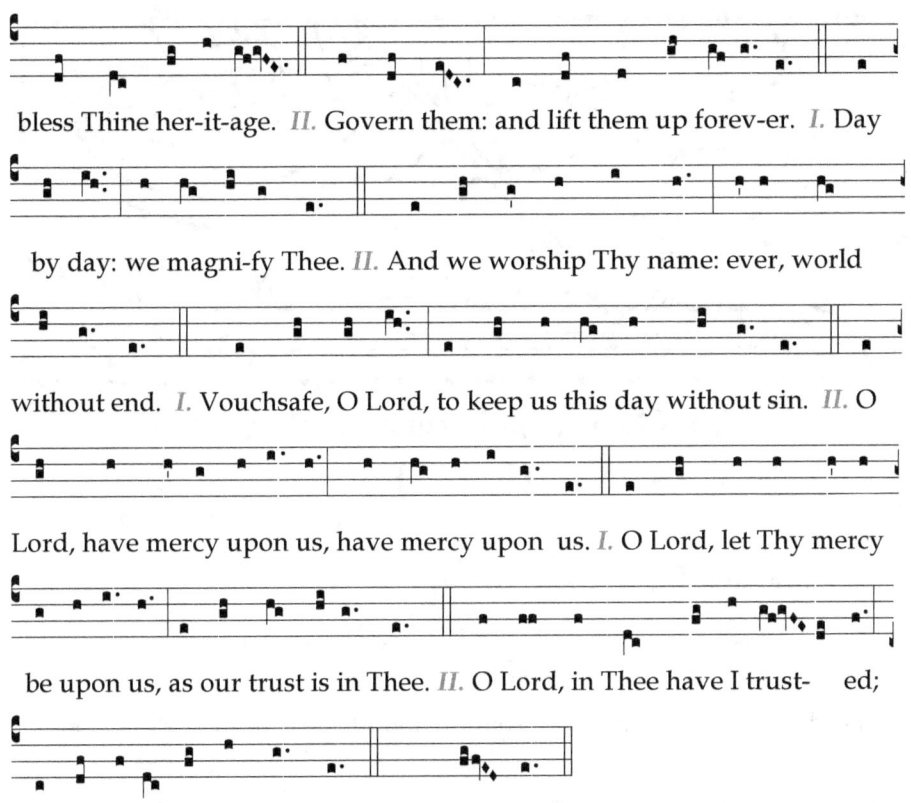

bless Thine her-it-age. *II.* Govern them: and lift them up forev-er. *I.* Day by day: we magni-fy Thee. *II.* And we worship Thy name: ever, world without end. *I.* Vouchsafe, O Lord, to keep us this day without sin. *II.* O Lord, have mercy upon us, have mercy upon us. *I.* O Lord, let Thy mercy be upon us, as our trust is in Thee. *II.* O Lord, in Thee have I trust- ed; let me never be confounded. *I. & II.* A- men.

Silent Prayer: *The Lord's Prayer and other prayers may be prayed.*

Morning Prayer may follow immediately with the versicle "Make haste O God..." If Morning Prayer does not follow immediately, Vigils ends with the Salutation, "Let us pray," the Collect of the Day, the Salutation, the Benedicamus, and the Blessing.

The Order of Morning Prayer
(Lauds)

At the first morning office of the day, all take their places quietly. At a signal from the officiant, all rise. If Vigils has already been prayed, the office begins with the versicle **Make haste***. (O., A.)*

℣. O Lord, open Thou my lips. ℟. And my mouth shall show forth Thy praise.
(At this versicle, a cross may be marked with the thumb upon the lips.)

℣. Make haste, O God, to ✠ deliver me.   ℟. Make haste to help me, O Lord.

Glory be to the Father and to the Son: and to the Holy Ghost. As it was

in the beginning, is now and ever shall be: world without end.   Amen.

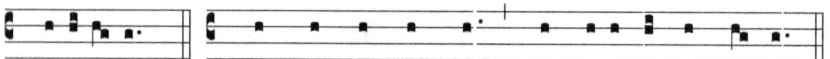

Al-le-lu-ia!   *Or:* **Praise to Thee, O Christ, King of e-ter-nal Glory!**
          (Used instead of Alleluia from Septuagesima to Easter Eve.)

The Psalmody

(C., I., II.) One or more Psalms shall be said or chanted. At the end of each Psalm the Gloria Patri (Glory be...) shall be said or chanted. An Antiphon shall be used before and after each Psalm. After the repeated Antiphon, a period of silence may be observed, during which the Psalm-prayer may be prayed silently. Each Antiphon and Psalm is intoned by the Cantor up to the asterisk (*). All may be seated during the Psalmody and rise at the Gloria Patri.

The Lection

Sit. The Reading or Readings shall then be read.
L: A reading from _____ , the _____ chapter.

After the Reading may be said or chanted:

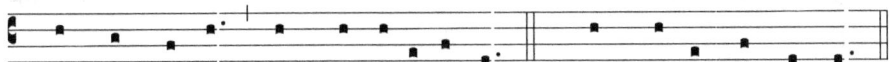

L: But Thou, O Lord, have mercy upon us.   A: Thanks be to Thee, O Lord!

The Responsory

[26]

(C., S., A.) Stand. After the Lection a Responsory (from the Propers, pp. 349-569) shall be said or chanted.

(O. or L.) Then may follow a sermon or reading from the fathers, in which case all sit.

The Hymn

(C., A.) Stand. The first phrase of the Hymn is intoned by the cantor. Hymns proper to the day or season are included in the Propers (pp. 349-569). Other Hymns may be used.

The Canticle

*Then, all standing, shall be said or chanted **the Versicle** (C., A.).   An **Antiphon** (C., A.) shall then be said or chanted before **the Canticle** (C., I., II.).   After the Gloria Patri, the **Antiphon** shall be repeated (A.).   On Sundays or Feast Days, the Antiphon may also be said or chanted after every other verse of the Benedictus. Versicles and antiphons proper to the day or season can be found in the Weekday Propers, the Seasonal Propers, or the Saints' Day Propers (pp. 349-569).*

Example: *Versicle on Sunday (from Weekday Propers)*

℣. The LORD reigneth, he is clothed with majes-   ty.
℟. The LORD is clothed with strength, wherewith he hath girded him-   self.

Luke 1:68-79 *Benedictus*
The raised dot indicates the third syllable before the final accent and is helpful for use with the more intricate Canticle Tones.

Antiphon for the Benedictus (see the Propers, pp. 349-569).
✠ Bless-ed be the · Lord Gód of Ísrael; * for he hath visited and · redéemed his péople,
And hath raised up an horn of · salvátion fór us * in the house of · his sérvant Dávid;
As he spake by the mouth of · his hóly próphets, * which have · been sínce the wórld began:
That we should be · saved fróm our énemies, * and from the hand · of áll that háte us;
To perform the mercy pro · mised tó our fáthers, * and to remember · his hóly cóvenant;
The oath which he sware to · our fáther Ábraham, * that he · would gránt unto <u>us</u>,
That we being delivered out of the · hánd of our énemies * might · serve hím without <u>fear</u>,
In holiness and right · eousnéss befóre him, * all · the dáys of our <u>life</u>.
And thou, child, shalt be called the proph · et óf the Híghest: * for thou shalt go before the face of the · Lórd to prepáre his ways;
To give knowledge of salvation · únto his péople * by the · remíssion óf their sins,
Through the tend · er mércy óf our God; * whereby the dayspring from on high · hath vísited <u>us</u>,
[27] To give light to them that sit in darkness and in · the shádow of <u>death</u>, * to guide our feet · ínto the wáy of peace.

Glory be to the · Fáther and tó the Son * · and tó the Hóly Ghost.
As it was in the beginning, is now, · and éver sháll be, * · wórld without énd. Amen.
Antiphon repeated.

The Prayers

(O., A.) It is appropriate to kneel for the prayers. On Sundays, Feasts, and in Eastertide all may stand. The officiant intones up to the asterisk (*).

The Kyrie

Kyri-e ele-ison!   *   Christ-e ele-ison! Kyri-e ele-ison!

The Lord's Prayer

Our Father who art in heaven, * Hallowed be Thy name; Thy kingdom come;

Thy will be done on earth as it is in heaven; Give us this day our daily bread;

And forgive us our trespasses, as we forgive those who trespass against us;

And lead us not into temptation; But deliver us ☩ from evil; For Thine is

the kingdom and the power and the glory forever and ever. Amen.

Then may be said the Suffrages. It is appropriate to use the Suffrages in penitential seasons (e.g., Advent weekdays, Pre-lent, Lent, Ember Days, and any other days of fasting). [28]

℣. I said, O Lord, be merciful ûn-..to ....me;
℟. Heal my soul; for I have sinned against.............................Thee.
℣. Return, O Lôrd, ...how ....long?
℟. And let it repent Thee concerning Thy ser-......................vants.
℣. Let Thy mercy, O Lord, be upon..us,
℟. According as we hôpe ....in...............thee.
℣. Let Thy priests be clothed with rîgh-...................teous-...........ness,
℟. And let Thy saints shôut...for ....joy.
℣. O Lord, save our ru-..lers;
℟. Let the King hear us whên.................................we ....call.
℣. Save Thy people and bless Thine inhêr-..................i-..............tance;
℟. Feed them also and lift them up forev-...............................er.
℣. Remember Thy congrega-...tion,
℟. Which Thou hast purchased ....of ....<u>old</u>.
℣. Peace be withîn...thy ....walls,
℟. And prosperity within thy pâ-...........................la-...............ces.
℣. Let us pray for our absent breth-..ren.
℟. O Thou, our God, save Thy servants that trûstin ....Thee.
℣. Let us pray for the broken-hearted and the cap-....................tives.
℟. Redeem Israel, O God, out of all his trou-..........................bles.
℣. Send them help from the Sanctua-...ry
℟. And strengthen them out of Zi-..on.

The Salutation

If the officiant is an ordained pastor, the first Salutation shall be used. If a layman is serving as officiant, the second Salutation shall be used.

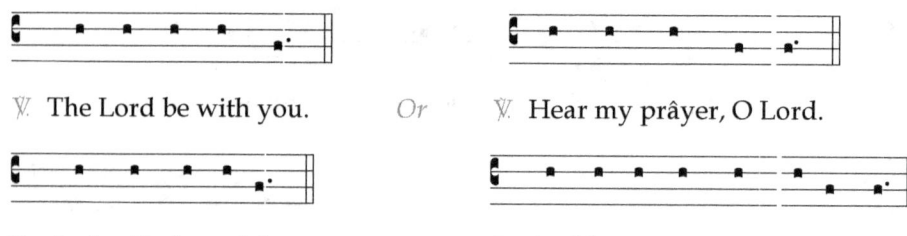

℣. The Lord be with you.   *Or*   ℣. Hear my prâyer, O Lord.

℟. And with thy spirit.   ℟. And let my cry come ûnto Thee.

℣. Let us pray.

(O.) *Then shall be said or chanted the Collect for the Day, other Collects, and the Collect for Grace. A total of 3, 5, or 7 Collects shall be prayed. After each Collect the Congregation shall say or chant:* **Amen**. [29]

The Collect for Grace
O: O Lord, our heavenly Father, almighty and everlasting God, who hast safely brought us to the beginning òf this day : defend us in the same with Thy mighty power and grant that this day we fall into no sin, neither run into any kind of dangèr; but that all our doings, being ordered by Thy governance, may be righteous in Thy sight; through the merits of Jesus Christ, our Saviòr; who liveth and reigneth with Thee and the Hòly Ghost : ever one God, world without end.
A: **Amen**.

The Salutation
If the officiant is an ordained pastor, the first Salutation shall be used. If a layman is serving as officiant, the second Salutation shall be used.

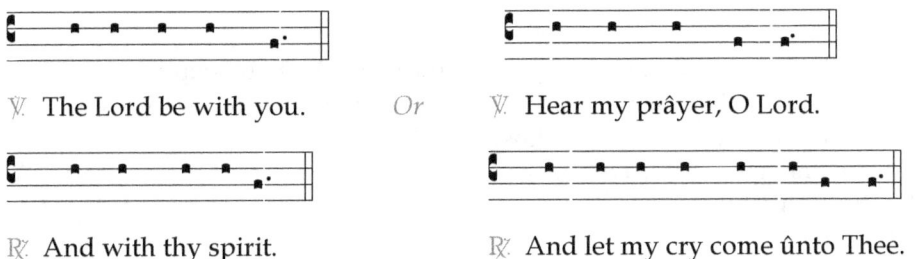

℣. The Lord be with you.   *Or*   ℣. Hear my prâyer, O Lord.

℟. And with thy spirit.   ℟. And let my cry come ûnto Thee.

The Benedicamus
(C. & S., A.) *If chanted according to the melody here given, the Benedicamus may be sung three times.*

 *Outside of Eastertide*

℣. Bless   we   the   Lord.   ℟. Thanks   be   to God.

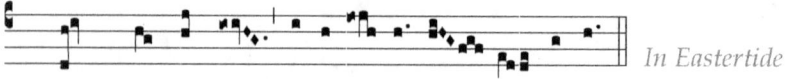 *In Eastertide*

℣ Bless we the Lord, al-le-lu-ia, al- le- lu-ia.
℟ Thanks be to God, al-le-lu-ia, al- le- lu-ia.

[30] ## The Benediction

If a layman is serving as officiant, the Benediction shall be omitted. The Benediction, if chanted, is sung softly on one tone. The congregation kneels. The pastor stands to give the Benediction.

O: The grace of our Lord Jesus Christ and the love of God and the communion of the Holy Ghost ✠ be with you all.
A: Amen.

Silent Prayer.

The Commemoration of Saints and the Departed

(O., A.) After a morning office (Vigils, Morning Prayer, or Prime), the names of the saints and departed, whom the Church or community commemorates, may be named. Thereafter are said one or more of the following versicles and a collect.

O: Today we remember *name*, the *title/office*.

℣ Precious in the sight of the Lord; ℟ Is the death of His saints.
℣ Remember them which have the rule over you, who have spoken unto you the Wôrd of God; ℟ Whose faith follow, considering the end of their conversation. *(Commemoration of pastors or doctors)*
℣ Jesus Chrîst the same; ℟ Yesterday, and today, and forever.

O: Let us pray.

Commemoration of St. Mary. Almighty God, who didst exalt the lowly Virgin Mary bý Thy grace : give us ever humble heàrts, that we may never fail of Thy grace; through Jesus Christ, Thy Son, oùr Lord, who liveth and reigneth with Thee and the Hòly Ghost : ever one God, world without end. Amen.
Commemoration of a Martyr. Almighty God, who didst give Thy servant *N.* boldness to confess the Name of our Savior Jesus Christ before the rulers of this world, and courage to die fòr this faith : Grant that we likewise may ever be ready to give a reason for the hope that is in ùs, and to suffer

gladly for His sake; through the same, Jesus Christ, Thy Son, oùr Lord, who liveth and reigneth with Thee and the Hòly Ghost : ever one God, world without end. Amen.

Commemoration of a Confessor. O God, who makest us glad with the yearly feast of Saint N., Thý confessor : mercifully grant, that, as we now observe his (her) heavenly birthdày, so we may follow him (her) in all virtuous and godly living; through Jesus Christ, Thy Son, oùr Lord, who liveth and reigneth with Thee and the Hòly Ghost : ever one God, world without end. Amen.

Commemoration of a Doctor. O God, who hast endowed Thy servant N. with clarity of faith and holinèss of life: Grant us to keep with steadfast minds the faith which he tàught, and in his fellowship to be made partakers of eternal glory; through Jesus Christ, Thy Son, oùr Lord, who liveth and reigneth with Thee and the Hòly Ghost : ever one God, world without end. Amen.

Commemoration of a Bishop or Pastor. Accept, O Lord, our thanksgiving this day for Thy sèrvant N. : and grant that all ministers and stewards of Thy mysteries may afford to Thy faithful people, by word and examplè, the instruction which is of Thy grace; through Jesus Christ, Thy Son, oùr Lord, who liveth and reigneth with Thee and the Hòly Ghost : ever one God, world without end. Amen. [31]

Commemoration of a Virgin. Graciously hear us, O God of oùr salvation : that, like as we do rejoice in the festival of blessed N., Thy holy virgìn, so we may learn to follow her in all godly and devout affections; through Jesus Christ, Thy Son, oùr Lord, who liveth and reigneth with Thee and the Hòly Ghost : ever one God, world without end. Amen.

Commemoration of a Holy Woman. Graciously hear us, O God of oùr salvation : that, like as we do rejoice in the festival of blessed N., Thy holy womàn, so we may learn to follow her in all godly and devout affections; through Jesus Christ, Thy Son, oùr Lord, who liveth and reigneth with Thee and the Hòly Ghost : ever one God, world without end. Amen.

Commemoration of a Holy Man. O almighty God, who hast called us to faith in Thee, and hast compassed us about with so great a clòud of witnesses : Grant that we, encouraged by the good examples of Thy Saints, and especially of Thy servant N., may persevere in running the race that is set before ùs, until at length, through Thy mercy, we with them attain to Thine eternal joy; through Him who is the author and finisher of our faith, Thy Son Jesus Chrìst our Lord. Amen.

After each office may be said privately the evangelical commemoration of the Blessed Virgin Mary:

Antiphon. **Blessed is the womb that bore Thee, Lord Jesus, and the breasts which nursed Thee! : Yea, blessed are those who hear the Word of God and keep it!** *(In Eastertide:* **Alleluia.***) (Lk. 11:27-28, according to Luther's translation)*

℣. Behold, a virgin shall conceive and bear a Son. *(In Eastertide:* **Alleluia.***)*

℞. And shall call His name Immanuel. *(In Eastertide:* **Alleluia.***)*

Let us pray. Almighty God, who hast dealt wonderfully with Thy handmaiden, the Virgin Mary, and hast chosen her to be the mother of Thy Son and hast graciously made known that Thou regardest the poor and lowly and the despised, grant us grace in all humility and meekness to receive Thy Word with hearty faith and so to be made one with Jesus Christ, Thy Son, òur Lord, who liveth and reigneth with Thee and the Hòly Ghost : ever one God, world without end. Amen.

THE ORDER OF MIDDAY PRAYER
(PRIME, TERCE, SEXT, NONE)

(O, A.)

℣. Make haste, O God, to ✠ deliver me.   ℟. Make haste to help me, O Lord.

Glory be to the Father and to the Son: and to the Holy Ghost. As it was in the beginning, is now and ever shall be: world without end. Amen.

Al-le-lu-ia!   *Or:* **Praise to Thee, O Christ, King of e-ter-nal Glory!**
(Used instead of Alleluia from Septuagesima to Easter Eve.)

The Hymn

(C., A.) The first phrase of the Hymn is intoned by the cantor. Suggested Hymns for specific times of the day are provided. Other Hymns may be used.

At Prime (before midmorning). **Jam lucis orto sidere.** *5th c., trans. by J. M. Neale*

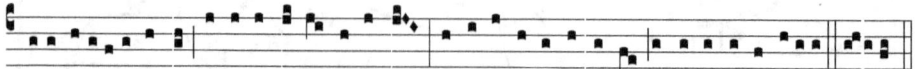

1. Now that the daylight fills the sky, / We lift our hearts to God on high, / That He, in all we do or say, / Would keep us free from harm to-day:
2. Would guard our hearts and tongues from strife; / From anger's din would hide our life; / From all ill sights would turn our eyes; / Would close our ears from vanities:
3. Would keep our inmost conscience pure; / Our souls from folly would secure; / Would bid us check the pride of sense / With due and holy abstinence.
4. So we, when this new day is gone, / And night in turn is drawing on, / With conscience by the world unstained / Shall praise His name for victory gained.
5. All laud to God the Father be; / All praise, eternal Son, to Thee; / All glory, as is ever meet, / To God the holy Paraclete. Amen.

[33]   *At Terce (midmorning).* **Nunc Sancte nobis Spiritus.** *4th c., trans. by J. M. Neale*

1. Come Holy Ghost, with God the Son / And God the Father, ever one; / Shed forth Thy grace within our breast, / And dwell with us a ready guest.
2. By every power, by heart and tongue, / By act and deed, Thy praise be sung; / Inflame with perfect love each sense, / That others' souls may kindle thence.
3. O Father, that we ask be done, / Through Jesus Christ, thine only Son, / Who, with the Holy Ghost and Thee, / Doth live and reign eternally. Amen

At Sext (midday). **Rector potens, verax Deus.** *4th c., trans. by J. M. Neale*

1. O God of truth, O Lord of might, / Who orderest time and change aright, / And send'st the early morning ray, / And light'st the glow of perfect day:
2. Extinguish Thou each sinful fire, / And banish every ill desire; / And while Thou keep'st the body whole, / Shed forth Thy peace upon the soul.
3. O Father, that we ask be done, / Through Jesus Christ, Thine only Son; / Who, with the Holy Ghost and Thee, / Doth live and reign eternally. Amen.

At None (midafternoon). **Rerum Deus tenax vigor.** *4th c., trans. by J. M. Neale*

1. O God, Creation's secret force, / Thyself unmoved, all motion's source, / Who from the morn till evening ray / Through all its changes guid'st the day:
2. Grant us, when this short life is past, / The glorious evening that shall last; / That, by a holy death attained, / Eternal glory may be gained.
3. O Father, that we ask be done, / Through Jesus Christ, Thine only Son; / Who, with the Holy Ghost and Thee, / Doth live and reign eternally. Amen.

The Psalmody

(C., I., II.) One or more Psalms shall be said or chanted. At the end of each Psalm the Gloria Patri (Glory be…) shall be said or chanted. An Antiphon shall be used before and after each Psalm. After the repeated Antiphon, a period of silence may be observed, during which the Psalm-prayer may be prayed silently. Each Antiphon and Psalm is intoned by the Cantor up to the asterisk (*). All may be seated during the Psalmody and rise at the Gloria Patri.

The Lection [34]

Sit. The Reading or Readings shall then be read. Other readings besides those given below may be used.
L: A reading from _____, the ____ chapter.

Suggested Readings Through the Year:
Sunday—1 Tim. 6:15-16
To the King of kings, and Lórd of lords: who only hath immortality, dwelling in the light which no man can approach únto; whom no man hath seen, nor cán see: / to Him be honor and power everlasting, Ámen.
Monday—John 17:24
These words spake Jesus, and lifted up his eyes to heaven, and <u>said</u>: "Father, I will that they also, whom thou hast given me, be with me where I <u>am</u>; / that they may behold my glory, which thou hast gíven me: / for thou lovedst me before the foundation óf the world."
Tuesday—Matt. 5:3-10
Jesus opened his mouth, and taught his disciples, sáying: "Blessed are the poor in spírit, / for theirs is the kingdom of héaven. Blessed are théy that mourn: / for they shall be cómforted. Blessed áre the meek: / for they shall inherit the <u>earth</u>. Blessed are they which do hunger and thirst after ríghteousness: / for they shall be <u>filled</u>. Blessed are the mérciful: / for they shall obtain mércy. Blessed are the púre in heart: / for they shall see <u>God</u>. Blessed are the péacemakers: / for they shall be called the children of <u>God</u>. Blessed are they which are persecuted for righteousness' <u>sake</u>: / for theirs is the kingdom of héaven."
Wednesday—John 1:14
And the Word was made flesh, and dwelt amóng us: and we beheld his glory, the glory as of the only begotten of the Fáther, / full of gráce and truth.
Thursday—John 6:51
Jesus said, "I am the living bread which came down from héaven: if any man eat of this bread, he shall live for éver, / and the bread that I will give is my flesh, which I will give for the life of the <u>world</u>."
Friday—John 14:27
Jesus said to his discíples: "Peace I leave with you, my peace I give unto <u>you</u>; / not as the world giveth, give I únto you. Let not your heart be tróubled: / neither let it bé afraid."
Saturday—1 Tim. 3:16
And without controversy great is the mystery of gódliness: God was manifest in the flesh, justified in the Spírit, / seen of angels, preached unto the Géntiles: believed on in the <u>world</u>, / received up into glóry.

Festival Half of the Church Year
Advent—Jer. 23:6
In his days Judah shall be saved, and Israel shall dwell sáfely; and this is his Name whereby he shall be <u>called</u>: / The Lord our Ríghteousness.

Christmas—Heb. 1:10
Unto the Són he saith: Thou, Lord, in the beginning hast laid the foundation óf the earth; / and the heavens are the works of thine <u>hands</u>.
Epiphany—Isa. 60:4
Lift up thine eyes round abóut and see: all they gather themselves together, they cóme to thee: / thy sons shall come from far, and thy daughters shall be nursed at thy <u>side</u>.
Lent—Isa. 55:7
Let the wicked forsake his way, and the unrighteous mán his thoughts: and let him return unto the Lord, and he will have mercy upón him; / and to our God, for he will abundantly párdon.
Passiontide—Jer. 17:18
Let them be confounded that persecute me, but let not me be confóunded: let them be dismayed, but let not me be dis<u>mayed</u>; / bring upon them the day of evil, and destroy them with double destruction, O Lórd our God.
Eastertide—1 Cor. 15:20
Now is Christ risen from the dead, and become the first fruits of thém that slept; For since by man came death, by man came also the resurrection óf the dead; / For as in Adam all die, even so in Christ shall all be máde alive.
Ascensiontide—Acts 1:4
And being assembled together wíth them, he commanded them that they should not depart from Jerúsalem, but wait for the Promise of the Fáther, / which, saith he, ye have héard of me. For John truly baptized with wáter; / but ye shall be baptized with the Holy Ghost not many days <u>hence</u>.
Pentecost—Acts 2:10
Jews and proselytes, Cretes and Arábians, we do hear them speak in our <u>tongues</u> / the wonderful wórks of God.

After the Reading may be said or chanted:

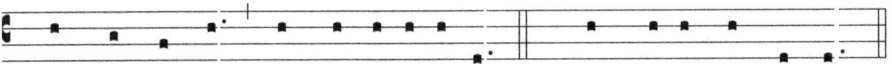

L: But Thou, O Lord, have mercy upon us. A: Thanks be to Thêe, O Lord!

The Responsory [35]

(C., S., A.) Stand. After the Lection the Responsory (from the Propers, pp. 349-569) shall be said or chanted.

(O. or L.) Then may follow a sermon or reading from the fathers, in which case all sit.

The Prayers

(O., A.) Kneel. On Sundays, Feasts, and in Eastertide, all may stand. The officiant intones up to the asterisk (*).

The Kyrie

Kyri-e ele-ison!   * Christe ele-ison! Kyri-e ele-ison!

The Lord's Prayer

Our Father who art in heaven, * Hallowed be Thy name; Thy kingdom come;

Thy will be done on earth as it is in heaven; Give us this day our daily bread;

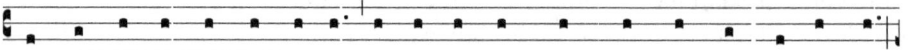

And forgive us our trespasses, as we forgive those who trespass against us;

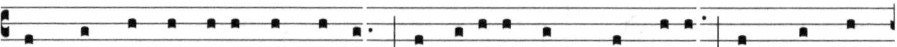

And lead us not into temptation; But deliver us ✠ from evil; For Thine is

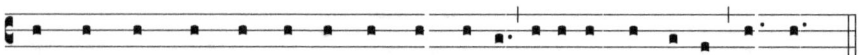

the kingdom and the power and the glory forever and ever. Amen.

(O., A.) *Then shall be said or chanted* **The Versicle**. *See the Propers (pp. 349-569).* [36]

Example: Versicle on Sunday (from the Weekday Propers).

℣. The LORD is my shepherd; I shâll not want.

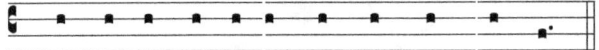

℟. He maketh me to lie down in green pastures.

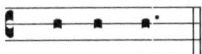

℣. Let us pray.

Then shall be said or chanted the **Collect for the Day** *(O.), the* **Da Pacem** *(C., A.) with its Versicle and Collect (O., A.), and the* **Weekday Collect** *(O.) with its preceding Antiphon (C., A.) and Versicle (O., A.). After each Collect shall be said or chanted:* **Amen** *(A.). See the Weekday Propers (pp. 349-388).*

The Salutation
If the officiant is an ordained pastor, the first Salutation shall be used. If a layman is serving as officiant, the second Salutation shall be used.

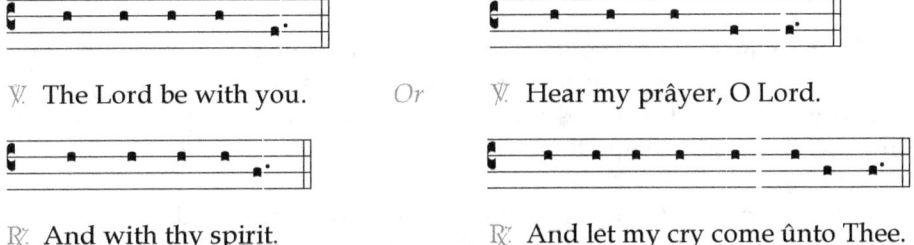

℣. The Lord be with you.   *Or*   ℣. Hear my prâyer, O Lord.

℟. And with thy spirit.   ℟. And let my cry come ûnto Thee.

The Benedicamus
(C. & S., A.) If chanted according to the melody here given, the Benedicamus may be sung three times.

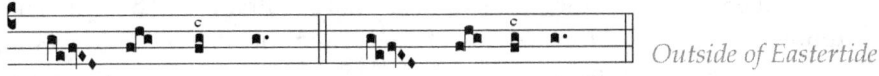

Outside of Eastertide

℣. Bless we the Lord. ℟. Thanks be to God.

 *In Eastertide*

℣. Bless we the Lord, al- le-lu-ia.
℟. Thanks be to God, al- le-lu-ia.

[37]
The Benediction

(O.) If a layman is serving as officiant, the Benediction shall be omitted. The Benediction, if chanted, is sung softly on one tone. The congregation kneels. The pastor stands to give the Benediction.

℣. The grace of our Lord Jesus Christ and the love of God and the communion of the Holy Ghost ✠ be with you all.
℟. Amen.

Silent Prayer.

Morning Suffrages
For use as the Prayers at Prime.

℣. O Lord, ℟. Have mercy upon us.
℣. O Christ, ℟. Have mercy upon us.
℣. O Lord, ℟. Have mercy upon us.

Our Father who art in heaven; * Hallowed be Thy name; Thy kingdom come; Thy will be done on earth as it is in heaven; Give us this day our daily bread; And forgive us our trespasses, as we forgive those who trespass against us; And lead us not into temptation; But deliver us from evil. Amen.

I believe in God the Father Almighty, * Maker of heaven and earth; And in Jesus Christ, His only Son, our Lord; Who was conceived by the Holy Ghost, Born of the Virgin Mary; Suffered under Pontius Pilate, Was crucified, dead, and buried; He descended into hell; The third day He rose again from the dead; He ascended into heaven, And sitteth on the right hand of God the Father Almighty; From thence He shall come to judge the quick and the dead. I believe in the Holy Ghost; The holy Christian Church; The communion of saints; The forgiveness of sins; The resurrection of the body; And the life everlasting. Amen.

℣. Unto Thee have I crîed, O Lord:
  ℟. And in the morning shall my prayer come before Thee.
℣. Let my mouth be filled with Thy <u>praise</u>:
  ℟. And with Thine honor âll the day.
℣. O Lord, hide Thy face from my <u>sins</u>:
  ℟. And blot out all mine inîquities.
℣. Create in me a clean hêart, O God:
  ℟. And renew a right spirit within me.
℣. Cast me not away from Thy presence:
  ℟. And take not Thy Holy Spirit from me.
℣. Restore unto me the joy of Thy salvation:
  ℟. And uphold me with Thy free Spirit.
℣. Vouchsafe, O Lôrd, this day:
  ℟. To keep us without <u>sin</u>.
℣. Have mercy upon us, O <u>Lord</u>:
  ℟. Have mercy upon us.
℣. O Lord, let Thy mercy be upon us:
  ℟. As our trust is in <u>Thee</u>.
℣. Hear my prâyer, O Lord:
  ℟. And let my cry come ûnto Thee.
[℣. The Lord be with you:
  ℟. And with thy spirit.]

℣. Let us pray.

(O.) Then shall be said or chanted the Collect for the Day, other collects, and the Collect here following. A total of 3, 5, or 7 collects shall be prayed. After each collect the Congregation shall say or chant: **Amen**.

We give thanks unto Thee, heavenly Father, through Jesus Christ, Thy dear Son, that Thou hast kept us this night from all hàrm and danger : and we pray Thee that Thou wouldst keep us this day also from sin and every evìl, that all our doings and life may please Thee. For into Thy hands we commend ourselves, our bodies and souls, and all things. Let Thy holy angel be with us that the wicked Foe may have no power over us. Amen.

The office continues with the Salutation and Benedicamus on p. 53.

The Order of Evening Prayer
(Vespers)

(O., A.)

℣. Make haste, O God, to ✠ deliver me.   ℟. Make haste to help me, O Lord.

Glory be to the Father and to the Son: and to the Holy Ghost. As it was

in the beginning, is now and ever shall be: world without end. Amen.

Al-le-lu-ia!   *Or:* Praise to Thee, O Christ, King of e-ter-nal Glory!
(Used instead of Alleluia from Septuagesima to Easter Eve.)

The Psalmody

(C., L., II.) One or more Psalms shall be said or chanted. At the end of each Psalm the Gloria Patri (Glory be...) shall be said or chanted. An Antiphon shall be used before and after each Psalm. After the repeated Antiphon, a period of silence may be observed, during which the Psalm-prayer may be prayed silently. Each Antiphon and Psalm is intoned by the Cantor up to the asterisk (*). All may be seated during the Psalmody and rise at the Gloria Patri.

The Lection

Sit. The Reading or Readings shall then be read.
L: **A reading from _____ , the _____ chapter.**
After the Reading may be said or chanted:

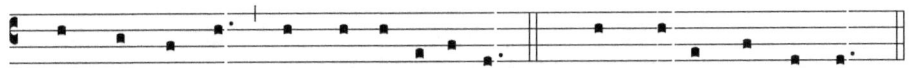

L: **But Thou, O Lord, have mercy upon us.**   A: **Thanks be to Thee, O Lord!**

The Responsory

(C., S., A.) Stand. After the Lection a Responsory (from the Propers, pp. 349-569) shall be said or chanted.

(O. or L.) Then may follow a sermon or reading from the fathers, in which case all sit.

The Hymn

(C., A.) Stand. The first phrase of the Hymn is intoned by the cantor. Hymns proper to the day or season are included in the Propers (pp. 349-569). Other Hymns may be used.

The Canticle

*Then, all standing, shall be said or chanted the Versicle (C., A.). An **Antiphon** (C., A.) shall then be said or chanted before the Canticle (C., I., II.). After the Gloria Patri, the **Antiphon** shall be repeated (A.). At 1st and 2nd Vespers (i.e., Vespers of the Eve or of the Day) of Sundays and Feast Days, the Antiphon may also be said or chanted after every other verse of the Magnificat. Versicles and antiphons proper to the day or season can be found in the Weekday Propers, the Seasonal Propers, or the Saints' Day Propers (pp. 349-569).*

*Example: **Versicle on Sunday through Friday** (from the Weekday Propers)*

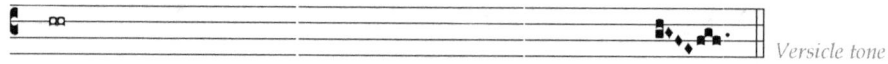
Versicle tone

℣. Let my prayers be set forth before Thee as in-   cense:
℟. And the lifting up of my hands as the evening sacri-fice.

Luke 1:46-55 *Magnificat*
(The raised dot indicates the third syllable before the final accent and is helpful for use with the more intricate Canticle Tones.)

Antiphon for the Magnificat (see the Propers, pp. 349-569).
✠ My soul · doth mágnifý the Lord, * and my spirit hath rejoiced · in Gód my Sáviour.
For · he háth regárded * the low estate · of hís handmáiden:
For, · behóld, from hénceforth * all generations · shall cáll me bléss-ed.
For he that is mighty · hath dóne to mé great things; * · and hóly ís his name.
And his mercy is · on thém that féar him * from generation · to génerátion.
He hath · shewed stréngth with his <u>arm</u>; * he hath scattered the proud in the ima · ginátion óf their hearts.
He hath put down · the míghty fróm their seats, * and exalt · ed thém of lów degree.
He hath filled the · húngry with góod things; * and the rich he hath · sent émpty a<u>way</u>.
He hath holpen · his sérvant Ísrael, * in remem · brance óf his mércy;
As he · spake tó our fáthers, * to Abraham, and to · his séed for éver.
Glory be to the · Fáther and tó the Son * · and tó the Hóly Ghost.
As it was in the beginning, is now, · and éver sháll be, * · wórld without énd. Amen.
Antiphon repeated.

The Prayers

(O., A.) It is appropriate to kneel for the prayers. On Sundays, Feasts, and in Eastertide all may stand. The officiant intones up to the asterisk (*).

The Kyrie

Kyri-e ele-ison! * Christe ele-ison! Kyri-e ele-ison!

The Lord's Prayer

Our Father who art in heaven, * Hallowed be Thy name; Thy kingdom come;

Thy will be done on earth as it is in heaven; Give us this day our daily bread;

And forgive us our trespasses, as we forgive those who trespass against us;

And lead us not into temptation; But deliver us ✠ from evil; For Thine is

the kingdom and the power and the glory forever and ever. Amen.

[41] *Then may be said the Suffrages. It is appropriate to use the Suffrages in penitential seasons (e.g., Advent weekdays, Pre-lent, Lent, Ember Days, and any other days of fasting).*

℣. I said, O Lord, be merciful ûn-..to ....me;
℟. Heal my soul; for I have sinned against...............................Thee.
℣. Return, O Lôrd, ...how ....long?
℟. And let it repent Thee concerning Thy ser-........................vants.
℣. Let Thy mercy, O Lord, be upon...us,
℟. According as we hôpe ....in...............thee.
℣. Let Thy priests be clothed with rîgh-...................teous-............ness,
℟. And let Thy saints shôut...for ....joy.
℣. O Lord, save our ru-...lers;
℟. Let the King hear us whên..............................we ....call.
℣. Save Thy people and bless Thine inhêr-..................i-.............tance;
℟. Feed them also and lift them up forev-.......................................er.
℣. Remember Thy congrega-...tion,
℟. Which Thou hast purchased ....of ....<u>old</u>.
℣. Peace be withîn...thy ....walls,
℟. And prosperity within thy pâ-..........................la-............ces.
℣. Let us pray for our absent breth-..ren.
℟. O Thou, our God, save Thy servants that trûstin ....Thee.
℣. Let us pray for the broken-hearted and the cap-......................tives.
℟. Redeem Israel, O God, out of all his trou-............................bles.
℣. Send them help from the Sanctua-..ry
℟. And strengthen them out of Zi-...on.

The Salutation

If the officiant is an ordained pastor, the first Salutation shall be used. If a layman is serving as officiant, the second Salutation shall be used.

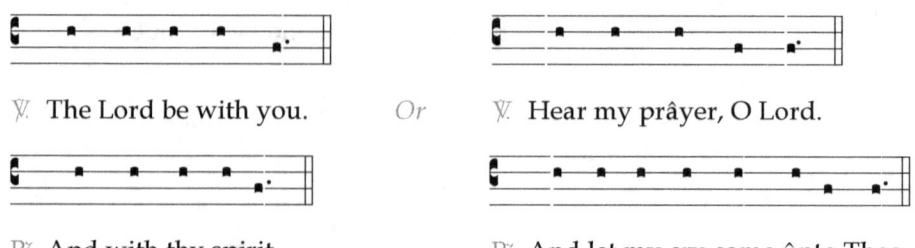

℣. The Lord be with you.   *Or*   ℣. Hear my prâyer, O Lord.

℟. And with thy spirit.   ℟. And let my cry come ûnto Thee.

℣. Let us pray.

Then shall be said or chanted the Collect for the Day, other collects, and the Collect for Peace. A total of 3, 5, or 7 collects shall be prayed. After each collect the Congregation shall say or chant: **Amen**. [42]

The Collect for Peace
O: O God, from whom all holy desires, all good counsels, and all just works dò proceed : give unto Thy servants that peace which the world cannòt give; that our hearts may be set to obey Thy commandments, and also that we, being defended by Thee from the fear of our enemies, may pass our time in rest and quietness; through the merits of Jesus Christ, our Saviòr; who liveth and reigneth with Thee and the Hòly Ghost : ever one God, world without end.

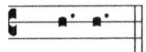

A: Amen.

The Salutation
If the officiant is an ordained pastor, the first Salutation shall be used. If a layman is serving as officiant, the second Salutation shall be used.

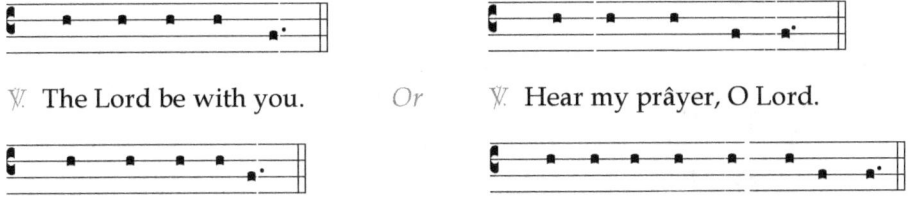

℣. The Lord be with you.   *Or*   ℣. Hear my prâyer, O Lord.

℟. And with thy spirit.   ℟. And let my cry come ûnto Thee.

The Benedicamus

(C. & S., A.) If chanted according to the melody here given, the Benedicamus may be sung three times.

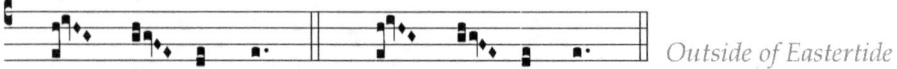 *Outside of Eastertide*

℣. Bless we the Lord. ℟. Thanks be to God.

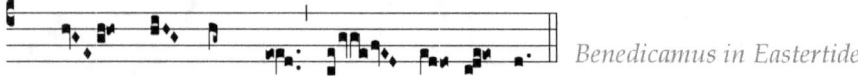 *Benedicamus in Eastertide*

℣. Bless we the Lord, al- le- lu- ia.
℟. Thanks be to God, al- le- lu- ia.

The Benediction

If a layman is serving as officiant, the Benediction shall be omitted. The Benediction, if chanted, is sung softly on one tone. The congregation kneels. The pastor stands to give the Benediction.

[43]   O: **The grace of our Lord Jesus Christ and the love of God and the communion of the Holy Ghost ✠ be with you all.**

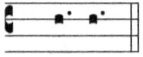

A: **Amen.**

Silent Prayer.

The Order of Night Prayer
(Compline)

L: Brethren, pray for God's blessing!

O: The Lord Almighty grant us a quiet night, and peace at the last.

A: Amen.

The Brief Lesson at Compline never varies: 1 Pt. 5:8.

L: Brethren: Be sober, be vîgilant: because your adversary, the devil,

as a roaring lion, walketh about, seeking whom he may devour-; / whom

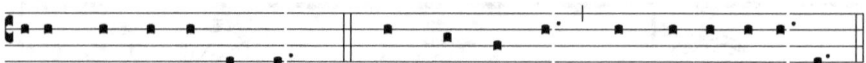
resist steadfast in the Faith.   But Thou, O Lord, have mercy upon us.

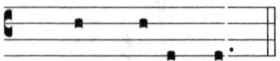
A: Thanks bê to God.

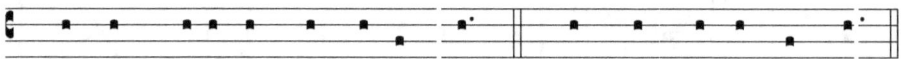
O: Our help ✣ is in the Name of the Lord.   *A:* Who made heaven and earth.

[45]
The Confiteor

Kneel. If the officiant is an ordained pastor, the following form shall be used. The confiteor *may be sung on one note.*

O: I confess to Almighty God, before the whole company of heaven, and to you, brethren, that I have sinned exceedingly in thought, word, and deed, *(he strikes his breast thrice, saying:)* **by my fault, by my own fault, by my own most grievous fault. Wherefore I ask you to pray for me to the Lord our God.**

A: **Almighty God have mercy upon thee, forgive thee thy sins, and bring thee to everlasting life.**
O: Amen.

A: **I confess to Almighty God, before the whole company of heaven, and to thee, father, that I have sinned exceedingly in thought, word, and deed,** *(they strike their breast thrice, saying:)* **by my fault, by my own fault, by my own most grievous fault. Wherefore I ask thee to pray for me to the Lord our God.**

O: Almighty God have mercy upon you, forgive you your sins, and bring you to everlasting life.
A: **Amen.**

O: The Almighty and merciful Lord grant us pardon, ✣ absolution, and remission of our sins.
A: **Amen.**

+ + +

If an ordained pastor be not present, the following form shall be used, the choir (and congregation) speaking (or singing on one note) all parts together:

A: **I confess to Almighty God, before the whole company of heaven, and to you, brethren, that I have sinned exceedingly in thought, word, and deed,** *(they strike their breast thrice, saying:)* **by my fault, by my own fault, by my own most grievous fault. Wherefore I pray God Almighty to have mercy on me, forgive me all my sins, and bring me to everlasting life.**

The Almighty and merciful Lord grant us pardon, ✠ absolution, and remission of our sins. Amen.
All stand. (O., A.)

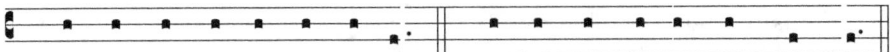

℣. Turn us, then, O God our Savior. ℟. And let thine anger cease from us.
(And during this ℣. all may make the sign of the cross with the thumb over the left breast.)

[46]

℣. Make haste, O God, to ✠ deliver me. ℟. Make haste to help me, O Lord.

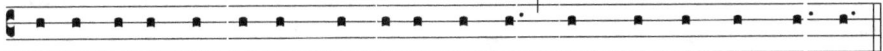

Glory be to the Father, and to the Son, and to the Holy Ghost. As it was

in the beginning, is now, and ever shall be, world without end. Amen.

Al-le-lu-ia!   Praise to Thee, O Christ, King of e-ter-nal Glory!
(Instead of Alleluia, from Septuagesima to Easter Eve.)

The Psalmody

(C., I., II.) The three Psalms for Compline are, as a rule, Psalms 4, 91, and 134. Other Psalms may be used. At the end of each Psalm the Gloria Patri (Glory be...) shall be said or chanted. The Antiphon shall be used before and after the Psalmody

as a whole. Each Antiphon and Psalm is intoned by the Cantor up to the asterisk (*). All may be seated during the Psalmody and rise at the last Gloria Patri.

Ant. Have mercy upon me, O Lord: * and hear my prayer.

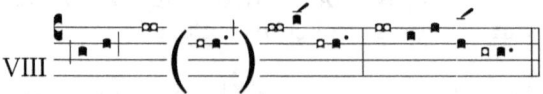
VIII

Psalm 4 *Cum invocarem*
1 |Hear me| when I call, O God of my rîghteousness: † thou hast enlarged me when Í was / ín distress; * have mercy upón / me, and héar my prayer.
2 O ye sons of men, how long will ye turn my glóry / ínto shame? * how long will ye love vanity, and seek / áfter léasing?
3 But know that the LORD hath set apart him that is gódly / fór himself: * the LORD will hear when / Í call únto him.
4 Stand in áwe, and / sín not: * commune with your own heart upon your béd, / and be still.
5 Offer the sacrifíces of / ríghteousness, * and put thy trúst / in the LORD.
6 There be many that say, Who will shéw us / ány good? * LORD, lift thou up the light of thy counte- / nánce upón us.
7 Thou hast put gládness / ín my heart, * more than in the time that their córn / and their wíne increased.
8 I will both lay me dówn in / péace, and sleep: * for thou, LORD, only makest me / dwéll in sáfety.
**Glory be to the Fáther and / tó the Son * and / tó the Hóly Ghost.
As it was in the beginning, is now, and éver / sháll be, * wórld / without énd. Amen.**

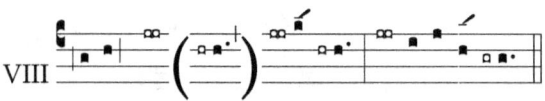
VIII

Psalm 91 *Qui habitat*
1 |He that| dwelleth in the secret place óf the / móst High * shall abide under the shadow óf / the Almíghty.
2 I will say of the LORD, He is my refuge ánd my / fórtress: * my God; in hím / will I trust.
3 Surely he shall deliver thee from the snáre of the / fówler, * and from the / nóisome péstilence.
4 He shall cover thee with his feathers, † and under his wíngs shalt thou / trust: * his truth shall be thy / shíeld and búckler.

5 Thou shalt not be afraid for the térror by / night; * nor for the arrow that flí- / eth by day;
6 Nor for the pestilence that wálketh in / dárkness; * nor for the destruction that wást- / eth at nóonday.
7 A thousand shall fall at thy side, † and ten thousand át thy / ríght hand; * but it shall / nót come nígh thee.
8 Only with thine éyes shalt / thóu behold * and see the rewárd / of the wícked.
9 Because thou hast made the LORD, which ís my / réfuge, * even the most High, thy / hábitátion;
10 There shall no évil be- / fáll thee, * neither shall any plague come / nígh thy dwélling.
11 For he shall give his angels chárge over / thee, * to kéep / thee in áll thy ways.
12 They shall bear thee úp in their / hands, * lest thou dash thy / fóot agáinst a stone.
13 Thou shalt tread upon the líon and / ádder: * the young lion and the dragon shalt thou / trámple únder feet.
14 Because he hath set his love upon me, therefore will Í de- / líver him: * I will set him on high, because / hé hath knówn my name.
15 He shall call upon me, and I will ânswer him: † I will be wíth him in / tróuble; * I will deliver / hím, and hónour him.
16 With long life will I sátisfy / him, * and shew him / mý salvátion.
Glory be to the Fáther and / tó the Son * and / tó the Hóly Ghost.
As it was in the beginning, is now, and éver / sháll be, * wórld / without énd. Amen.

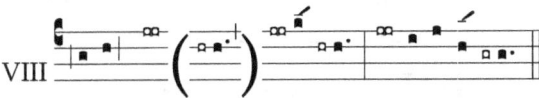

VIII

Psalm 134 *Ecce, nunc*

1 |Behold,| bless ye the LORD, all ye sérvants / óf the LORD, * which by night stand in the hóuse / of the LORD.
2 Lift / úp your hands * in the sanctuá- / ry, and bléss the LORD.
3 The LORD that made héaven and / earth * bless thee / óut of Zíon.   [48]
Glory be to the Fáther and / tó the Son * and / tó the Hóly Ghost.
As it was in the beginning, is now, and éver / sháll be, * wórld / without énd. Amen.
Ant. repeated

Ant. Have mercy upon me, O Lord: * and hear my prayer.

The Little Chapter

Sit. The Little Chapter at Compline never varies: Jer. 14:9.

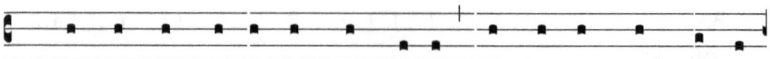

L: Thou, O Lord, art in the midst of us, and we are called by thy

Name; * leave us not, O Lord our God. A: Thanks be to God.

The Responsory

Stand. (C., S., A.)

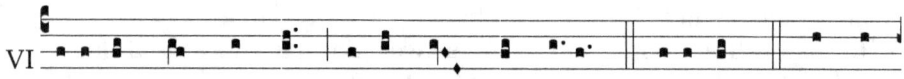

℟. Into thy hands, O Lord, ‡ I commend my spirit. ℟. Into thy... ℣. For thou

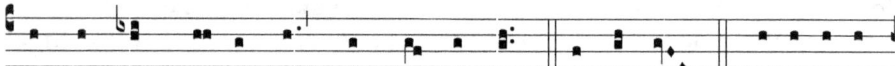

hast redeemed us, O Lord, thou God of truth. ‡ I commend... Glory be to

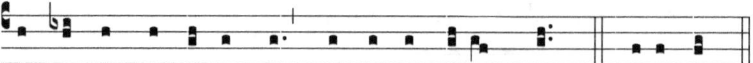

the Father and to the Son: and to the Holy Ghost. ℟. Into thy...

The Hymn

(C., A.) See pp. 73-75 for hymns in Christmastide, Epiphanytide, Lent, Eastertide, Ascensiontide, Whitsuntide, and feasts of Apostles.

Te lucis ante terminum. *Before 8th c., trans. by J. M. Neale.* Sundays and Feasts:

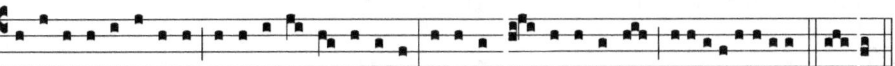

Weekdays:

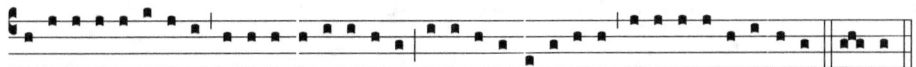

[49]

1. To Thee, before the close of day, / Creator of the world, we pray / That with Thy wonted favor, Thou / Wouldst be our Guard and Keeper now.
2. From all ill dreams defend our eyes, / From nightly fears and fantasies: / Tread under foot our ghostly foe, / That no pollution we may know.
3. O Father, that we ask be done / Through Jesus Christ, Thine only Son, / Who, with the Holy Ghost and Thee, / Shall live and reign eternally. Amen.

The Gospel Canticle

Then shall be said or chanted the **Versicle** *(C., A.), and the* **Antiphon** *(C., A.). Then shall be said or chanted the* **Canticle** *(C., I., II.). After the Gloria Patri, the* **Antiphon** *shall be repeated (A.). On Feast Days, the Antiphon also may be said or chanted after every verse of the Nunc Dimittis.*

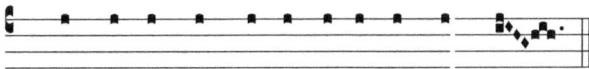

℣. Keep us, O Lord, as the apple of thine eye.
℟. Hide us under the shadow of thy   wings.

[50] *Antiphon for Nunc Dimittis:*

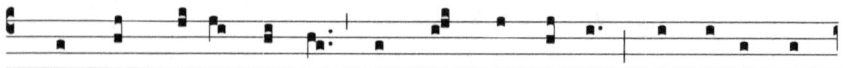

Guide us * waking, O Lord, and guard us sleeping: That awake we

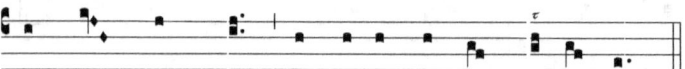

may watch with Christ and asleep we may rest in peace.

III — Sundays & Feasts

III — Weekdays

Luke 2:29-32 *Nunc dimittis*

✠ |Lord, now| lettest thou thy / sérvant depárt in peace: * accórd- / ing tó thy word;
|For mine| eyes have seen / thý Salvátion: * which thou hast prepared before the fáce of / all péople;
|A Light| to / líghten the Géntiles: * and the Glory of Thy péo- / ple Ísrael.
|Glory| be to the / Fáther and tó the Son * and tó / the Hóly Ghost.
|As it| was in the beginning, is now, and / éver sháll be, * wórld with- / out énd. Amen.
Antiphon repeated.

The Prayers

(O., A.) It is appropriate to kneel for the prayers. On Sundays, Feasts, and in Eastertide all may stand. The officiant intones up to the asterisk (*).

The Kyrie

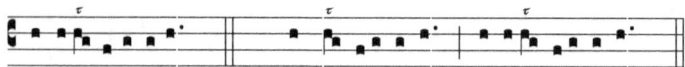

Kyri-e ele-ison! * Christe ele-ison! Kyri-e ele-ison!

The Lord's Prayer

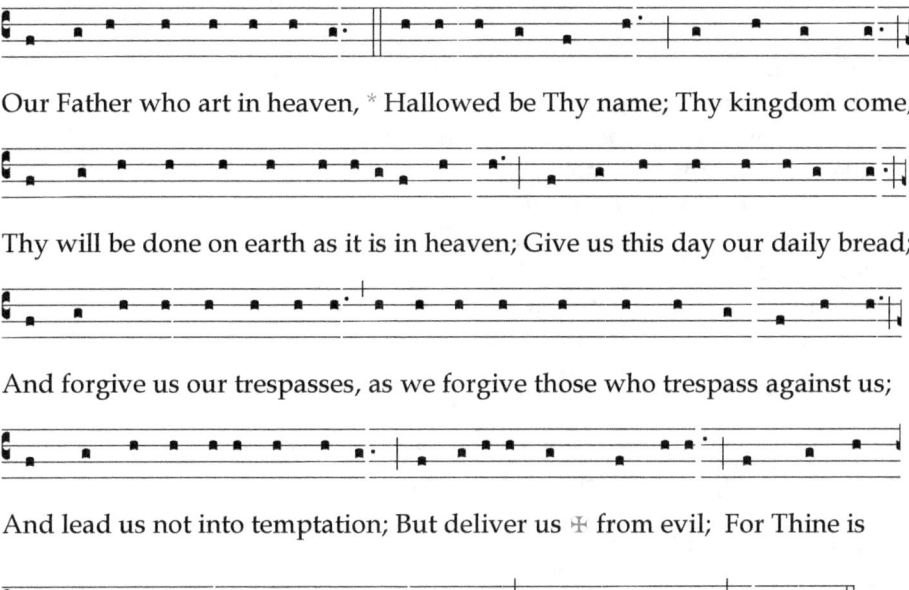

Our Father who art in heaven, * Hallowed be Thy name; Thy kingdom come;

Thy will be done on earth as it is in heaven; Give us this day our daily bread;

And forgive us our trespasses, as we forgive those who trespass against us;

And lead us not into temptation; But deliver us ✠ from evil; For Thine is

the kingdom and the power and the glory forever and ever. Amen.

The Apostles' Creed *(Sung on one note).*

I believe in God the Father Almighty, * Maker of heaven and earth.

And in Jesus Christ, His only Son, our Lord; Who was conceived by the Holy Ghost, Born of the Virgin Mary; Suffered under Pontius Pilate, Was crucified, dead, and buried; He descended into hell; The third day He rose again from the dead; He ascended into heaven, And sitteth on the right hand of God the Father Almighty; From thence He shall come to judge the quick and the dead.

I believe in the Holy Ghost; The holy Christian Church; The communion of saints; The forgiveness of sins; The resurrection of the body; And the life ✠ everlasting. Amen.

℣. Vouchsâfe, ...O.......Lord,
  ℟. to keep us this night with-.............out ....<u>sin</u>.
℣. O Lord, have mercy upon ....us;
  ℟. have mercy upon ....us.
℣. O Lord, let thy mercy be upon ....us.
  ℟. As our trust is ....in ....<u>thee</u>.
℣. Hear my prâyer, ...O.......Lord.
  ℟. And let my cry come ûn-...to ....thee.

If the officiant is an ordained pastor, the Salutation shall be used. If a layman is serving as officiant, the Salutation shall be omitted.

[℣. The Lord be with you. ℟. And with thy spirit.]

[52] **The Collect of the Office** *(On one tone.)*
O: Let us pray. Visit, we beseech thee, O Lord, this habitation, and drive far from it all snares of the enemy: let thy holy angels dwell herein, to preserve us in peace; and let thy blessing be always upon us. Through Jesus Christ, Thy Son our Lord, who liveth and reigneth with thee, in the unity of the Holy Ghost, ever one God, world without end.
A: Amen.

The Salutation
(O., A.) If the officiant is an ordained pastor, the first Salutation shall be used. If a layman is serving as officiant, the second Salutation shall be used.

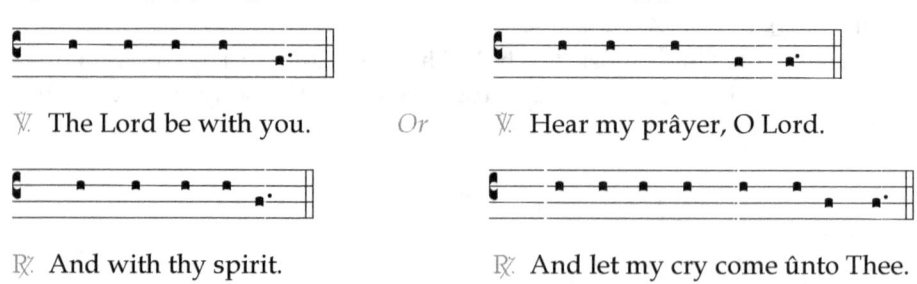

℣. The Lord be with you.   *Or*   ℣. Hear my prâyer, O Lord.

℟. And with thy spirit.   ℟. And let my cry come ûnto Thee.

The Benedicamus

(C. & S., A.) If chanted according to the melody here given, the Benedicamus may be sung three times.

℣. Bless we the Lord. ℟. Thanks be to God.

The Benediction

If a layman is serving as officiant, the Benediction shall be omitted. The congregation kneels. The Benediction, if chanted, is sung softly on one tone. The pastor stands to give the Benediction.

O: The almighty and merciful Lord, the Father, the ✠ Son, and the Holy Ghost, bless us and keep us.
A: Amen.

Silent Prayer.

Other Compline Hymns

Hymn in Christmastide, Epiphanytide, Whitsuntide, and on Feasts of Apostles.
Salvator mundi Domine. *Trans. by Copeland and others*

1. O Savior, Lord, to Thee we pray, / Who hast preserved us through the day. / Protect us through the coming night, / And ever save us by Thy might.
2. Be with us now, in mercy nigh, / And spare Thy servants when they cry; / Our sins blot out, our prayers receive, / Thy light throughout our darkness give.
3. To Thee who dost our hearts renew, / With fervent prayer we humbly sue, / That pure in thought and free from stain / We from our beds may rise again.
4. O Lord, the Virgin-born, to Thee / Eternal praise and glory be, / Whom with the Father we adore / And Holy Ghost forevermore. Amen.

Hymn in Lent I - IV.

Christe, qui lux es et dies. *Latin, 6th cent., trans. by Wm. J. Copeland and others*

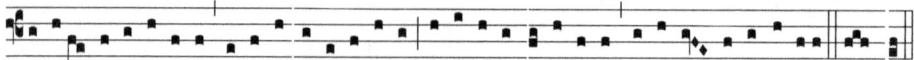

1. O Christ, who art the Light and Day, / Thou drivest darksome night away! / We know Thee as the Light of light / Illuminating mortal sight.
2. All-holy Lord, we pray to Thee, / Keep us tonight from danger free; / Grant us, dear Lord, in Thee to rest, / So be our sleep in quiet blessed.
3. And while the eyes soft slumber take, / Still be the heart to Thee awake, / Be Thy right hand upheld above / Thy servants resting in Thy love.
4. Yea, our Defender, be Thou nigh, / To bid the powers of darkness fly; / Keep us from sin, and guide for good / Thy servants purchased by Thy blood.
5. Remember us, dear Lord, we pray, / While in this mortal flesh we stay: / 'Tis Thou who dost the soul defend / Be present with us to the end.
6. Blest Three in One and One in Three, / Almighty God, we pray to Thee, / That Thou wouldst now vouchsafe to bless / Our fast with fruits of righteousness.
7. All laud to God the Father be; / All praise, eternal Son, to Thee; / All glory, as is ever meet, / To God the Holy Paraclete. Amen.

Hymn in Passiontide.

Cultor Dei memento. *Pruduntius, c. 400, trans. by T. A. Lacey*

1. Servant of God, remember / The stream thy soul bedewing, / The grace that came upon thee / Anointing and renewing.
2. When kindly slumber calls thee, / Upon thy bed reclining, / Trace thou the cross of Jesus, / Thy heart and forehead signing.
3. The cross dissolves the darkness, / And drives away temptation; / It calms the wavering spirit / By quiet consecration.
4. Begone, begone, the terrors / Of vague and formless dreaming; / Begone, thou fell deceiver, / With all thy boasted scheming.
5. Begone, thou crooked serpent, / Who, twisting and pursuing, / By fraud and lie preparest / The simple soul's undoing;
6. Tremble, for Christ is near us, / Depart, for here He dwelleth, / And this, the sign thou knowest, / Thy strong battalions quelleth.
7. Then while the weary body / Its rest in sleep is nearing, / The heart will muse in silence / On Christ and His appearing.

8. To God, eternal Father, / To Christ, our King, be glory, / And to the Holy Spirit, / In never-ending story. Amen.

Hymn in Eastertide. **Jesu, Salvator saeculi.** *Trans. by W. J. Copeland*

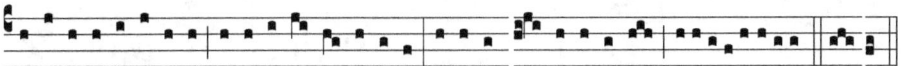

1. Jesus, the world's redeeming Lord, / The Father's coeternal Word, / Of light invisible true Light, / Thine Israel's keeper day and night;
2. Our great Creator and our Guide, / Who times and seasons dost divide, / Refresh tonight with quiet rest / Our limbs by daily toil opprest:
3. That while in this frail house of clay / A little longer here we stay, / Our weary flesh may take its sleep, / Our souls in Thee their vigils keep.
4. We pray Thee, while we dwell below, / Preserve us from our ghostly foe; / That he may ne'er victorious be / O'er those so dearly bought by Thee.
5. O Lord of all, with us abide / In this our joyful Eastertide; / From every weapon death can wield / Thine own redeemed forever shield.
6. All praise be Thine, O risen Lord, / From death to endless life restored; / All praise to God the Father be / And Holy Ghost eternally. Amen.

Ordo Officii ad Completorium

Lector: **Jube, domne, be-ne-di-ce-re.**

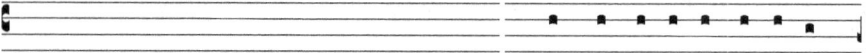

Hebdomodarius (qui anglice dicitur "officiant"): **Noctem quietam, et finem**

perfectum concedat nobis Dominus om-ni-po-tens. *Alii:* **Amen.**

Lectio Brevis: 1 Pt. 5:8.

L: **Fratres: Sobri-i estote, et vi-gi-la-te: quia adversari-us vester di-abolus**

tamquam le-o rugi-ens circu-it, quaerens quem devoret / cui re-sisti-te

fortes in fi-de.

L: Tu autem, Domine, mi-se-re-re nobis. *A:* De-o grâ-ti-as.

L: Adjutori-um nostrum in nomine ✠ Dômini. *A:* Qui fe-cit caelum et terram.

Confessio in Choro

H: Confiteor Deo omnipotenti et vobis, fratres: quia peccavi nimis cogitatione, verbo, et opere: mea culpa, mea culpa, mea maxima culpa. Ideo precor vos, fratres, orare pro me ad Dominum Deum nostrum.
A: **Misereatur tui omnipotens Deus / et, dimissis peccatis tuis, perducat te ad vitam aeternam.**
H: Amen.

A: **Confiteor Deo omnipotenti et tibi, pater (frater): quia peccavi nimis cogitatione, verbo, et opere: mea culpa, mea culpa, mea maxima culpa. Ideo precor te, pater (frater), ora pro nos ad Dominum Deum nostrum.**

H: Misereatur vestri omnipotens Deus / et, dimissis peccatis vestris, perducat vos ad vitam aeternam. [54]

A. **Amen.**

[*Si vocatus et ordinatus minister ecclesiae adest, sic dicit:* **Indulgentiam, absolutionem, et remissionem peccatorum nostrorum tribuat nobis omnipotens et misericors Dominus.**
A. **Amen.**]

+ + +

Confessio extra Chorum

Si unus vel duo recitent officium, ita fit confessio:
A: Confiteor tibi, sancte Deus, quia peccavi nimis cogitatione, verbo et opere: mea culpa, mea culpa, mea maxima culpa. Memento mei non secundum delicta mea / sed secundum misericordiam tuam magnam / et dimitte mihi culpam meam propter Jesum Christum. Amen.
A: Si confiteamur peccata nostra, fidelis est Deus et justus / ut remittat nobis peccata nostra et emundet nos ab omni iniquitate. Amen.

(H., A.)

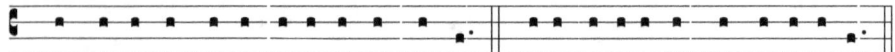

℣. Converte nos Deus sa-lu-ta-ris noster. ℟. Et a-verte i-ram tu-am a nobis.

Ingressus

℣. De-us ✠ in ad-ju-to-ri-um me-um in-tende. ℟. Do-mi-ne, ad adjuvandum

me festina.

Glo-ri-a Pa-tri et Fi-li-o   et Spi-ri-tu-i Sancto.   Sic-ut er-at in

princi-pi-o, et nunc et semper, et in sae-cu-la sae-cu-lo-rum. Amen.

Al-le-lu-ia!   Laus ti-bi, Do-mi-ne, Rex ae-ternae glo-ri-ae!
(*Sic dicitur Alleluia ad omnes Horas, praeter quam a Vesperis Sabbati ante Dominicam I Quadragesimae usque ad Completorium Feriae IV Majoris Hebdomadae inclusive; tunc enim dicitur: Laus tibi, etc.*)

Psalmodia

(*C., A.*) *Psalmi 4 (Cum invocarem), 91 (Qui habitat), et 134 (Ecce nunc benedicite) recitantur cum Gloria Patri etc. sub una antiphona:*

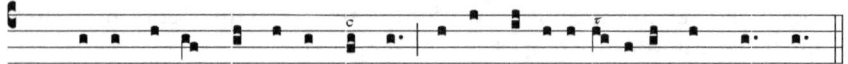

Ant. Mi-se-re-re * mi-hi Do-mi-ne, et ex-au-di o-ra-ti-o-nem me-am.

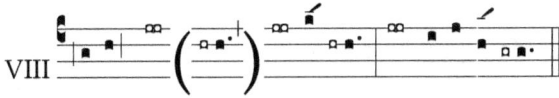

Psalmus 4 *Cum invocarem*

|Cum in-| vocarem, exaudivit me Deus iustitiae / méae, * In tribulatione dila- / tasti míhi.

Miserere / méi * et exaudi orati- / onem méam.

Filii hominum, usquequo gravi / córde? * Ut quid diligitis vanitatem et quaeri- / tis mendácium?

Et scitote quoniam mirificavit Dominus sanctum / súum; * Dominus exaudiet me cum clamave- / ro ad éum.

Irascimini, et nolite peccare; † quae dicitis in cordibus / véstris, * in cubilibus vestris / compungímini.

Sacrificate sacrificium iustitiae et sperate in / Dómino. * Multi dicunt: Quis ostendit / nobis bóna?

Signatum est super nos lumen vultus tui, / Dómine. * Dedisti laetitiam in / corde méo.

A fructu frumenti, vini, et olei / súi, * mul- / tiplicáti sunt.

In pace in id- / ípsum * dormiam et / requiéscam;

Quoniam tu, Domine, singulariter / ín spe * con- / stituísti me.

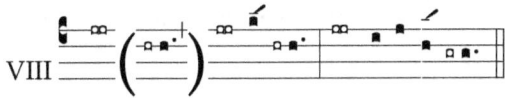

Psalmus 91 *Qui habitat*

Qui habitat in adiutorio Al- / tíssimi, * in protectione Dei caeli / commorábitur.

Dicet Domino: Susceptor meus es tu et refugium / méum; * Deus meus, spera- / bo in éum.

Quoniam ipse liberabit me de laqueo ven- / ántium * et a / verbo áspero.

Scapulis suis obumbrabit / tíbi, * Et sub pennis e- / ius sperábis.

Scuto circumdabit te ver- / itas éius; * Non timebis a timo- / re noctúrno;

A sagitta volante in die, a peste perambulante in / ténebris, * Ab incursu, et daemonio me- / ridiáno.

Cadent a latere tuo mille, et decem milia a dextris / túis; * Ad te autem non ap- / propinquábit.

Verumtamen oculis tuis consider- / ábis * Et retributionem peccator- / um vidébis.

Quoniam tu es, Domine, spes / méa; * Altissimum posuisti refu- / gium túum.

Non accedet ad te / málum, * et flagellum non appropinquabit taberna- /

culo túo,
Quoniam angelis suis mandavit de / te, * Ut custodiant te in omnibus / viis túis.

[56] In manibus por- / tábunt te, * Ne forte offendas ad lapidem / pedem túum.
Super aspidem et basiliscum ambu- / lábis, * Et conculcabis leonem / et dracónem.
Quoniam in me speravit, liberabo / éum; * Protegam eum, quoniam cognovit / nomen méum.
Clamabit ad me, et ego exaudiam eum; † Cum ipso sum in tribulati- / óne; * Eripiam eum et glorifi- / cabo éum.
Longitudine dierum replebo / éum, * Et ostendam illi salu- / tare méum.

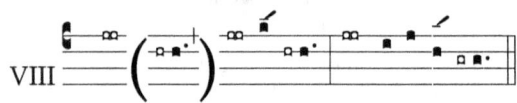

Psalmus 134 *Ecce, nunc*
Ecce nunc benedicite / Dóminum, * omnes / servi Dómini:
Qui statis in domo / Dómini, * In atriis domus Dei nostri.
In noctibus extollite manus vestras in / sáncta, * Et benedi- / cite Dóminum.
Benedicat te Dominus ex / Síon, * Qui fecit cae- / lum et térram.
Gloria Patri et / Fílio * et Spiri- / tui Sáncto.
Sicut erat in principio, et nunc, et / sémper * et in saecula saecu- / lorum. Ámen.

Ant. repetita

Ant. Mi-se-re-re * mi-hi Do-mi-ne, et ex-au-di o-ra-ti-o-nem me-am.

Capitulum (Jer. 14:9)

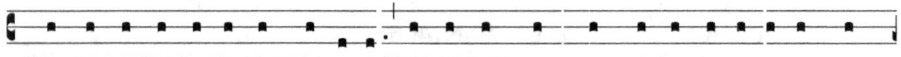

L. Tu autem in nobis es, Domine: et nomen sanctum tuum invocatum est

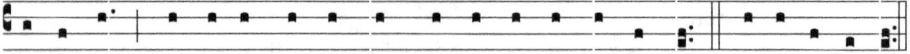

super nos / ne de-re-linquas nos, Do-mi-ne, De-us noster. ℟ De-o gra-ti-as.

Reponsorium Breve

(C., S., A.)

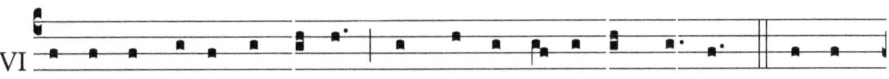

℟. In ma-nus tu-as, Do-mi-ne, ‡ commendo spi-ri-tum me-um. ℟. In ma-

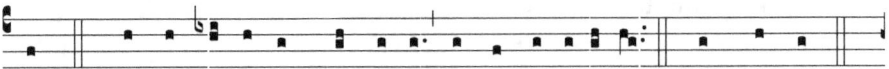

nus... ℣. Re-de-mis-ti nos, Do-mi-ne, De-us ver-i-ta-tis. ‡ Commendo...

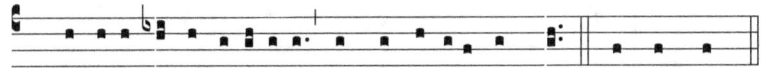

℣. Glo-ri-a Pa-tri et Fi-li-o et Spir-i-tu-i Sancto. ℟. In ma-nus...

Hymnus

[57]

(C., A.)
Dominica/Festa:

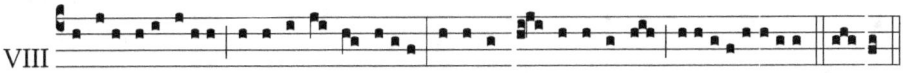

Feriae:

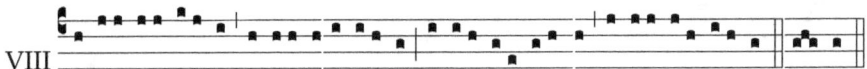

1. Te lucis ante terminum / Rerum creator poscimus, / Ut solita clementia / Sis praesul ac custodia.
2. Procul recedant somnia / Et noctium phantasmata, / Hostemque nostrum comprime, / Ne polluantur corpora.
3. Praesta, Pater piissime, / Patrique compar Unice / Cum Spiritu paracleto / Nunc et per omne saeculum. Amen.

Versiculum
(C., A.)

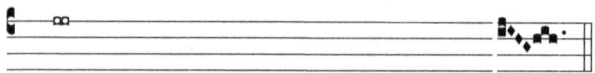

℣. Custodi nos Domine ut pupillam ocu- li.
℟. Sub umbra alarum tuarum protege nos.

Canticum Simeonis, Luc. 2:29-32
(C., I., II.)

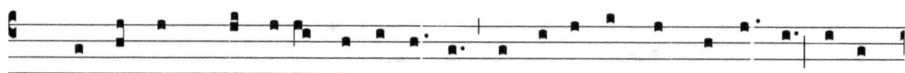

Ant. Sal-va nos * Do-mi-ne, vi-gi-lantes, cus-to-di nos dor-mi-en-tes: ut vi-

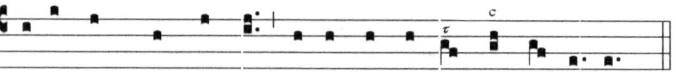

gi-le-mus cum Christo, et re-qui-es-ca-mus in pa-ce.

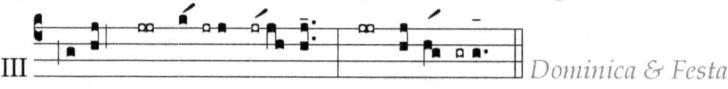

III — Dominica & Festa

III — Feriae

Luc. 2:29-32

☩ | Nunc di-| mittis servum / tuum Dómine: * secundum verbum tuum / in páce.
| Quia | viderunt / oculi méi: * saluta- / re túum.
| Quod par-| asti / ante fáciem: * omnium pop- / ulórum.
| Lumen | ad revelati- / onem géntium: * et gloriam plebis tu- / ae Ísrael.
| Glori-| a / Patri et Fílio * et Spiritu-/ i Sáncto.
| Sicut | erat in principio, et / nunc et sémper, * et in saecula saeculor- / um. Ámen.

Ant. repetita.

Preces
(H., A.)

[58]

Kyri-e ele-ison! * Christe ele-ison! Kyri-e ele-ison!

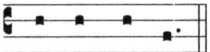

Pa-ter nos-ter...

(dicitur secreto): **qui es in coelis, Sanctificetur nomen tuum, Adveniat regnum tuum, Fiat voluntas tua sicut in coelo et in terra, Panem nostrum quotidianum da nobis hodie, Et dimitte nobis debita nostra, sicut et nos dimittimus debitoribus nostris,**

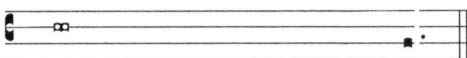

℣. Et ne nos inducas in tentatio- nem,
℟. Sed libera nos ✠ a ma-..............lo.

(Preces sequentes omittuntur in Dominicis et Festis.)

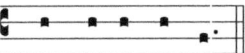

Cre-do in De-um...

(dicitur secreto): **Patrem omnipotentem, creatorem coeli et terrae. Et in Jesum Christum, Filium eius unicum, Dominum nostrum, qui conceptus est de Spiritu sancto, natus ex Maria virgine, passus sub Pontio Pilato, crucifixus, mortuus et sepultus, descendit ad inferna, tertia die resurrexit a mortuis, ascendit ad coelos, sedet ad dexteram Dei Patris omnipotentis. Inde venturus est judicare vivos et mortuos. Credo in Spiritum sanctum, unam sanctam Ecclesiam catholicam, sanctorum communionem, remissionem peccatorum,**

[59]

℣. Carnis resurrectio-................................... .nem
℟. et vitam ✠ aeter-................................... .nam.
℣. Dignare, Domine, nocte is-........................ta.
℟. Sine peccato nos custodi-......................re.
℣. Miserere nostri, Dô-...........................mi- ne.
℟. Miserere nos-...tri.
℣. Fiat misericordia tua, Domine, sû-...per nos.
℟. Quemadmodum speravimus in ....te.
℣. Domine, exaudi orationem me-...............am.
℟. Et clamor meus ad te vên-................i-...at.
(Si vocatus et ordinatus minister ecclesiae adest, sic dicit:)
[℣. Dominus vobis-....................................... .cum.
℟. Et cum spiritu tu-................................o.]

H: Oremus. Visita, quaesumus, Domine, habitationem istam, et omnes insidias inimici ab ea longè repelle : Angeli tui sancti habitent in ea, qui nos in pace custodìant; et benedictio tua sit super nos semper. Per Dominum nostrum Jesum Christum, Filium tuùm; qui tecum vivit et regnat in unitate Spiritus Sàncti Deus : per omnia saecula saeculorum.
A: Amen.

(Si vocatus et ordinatus minister ecclesiae adest, sic dicit:)
[℣. Dominus vobiscum.
℟. Et cum spiritu tuo.]

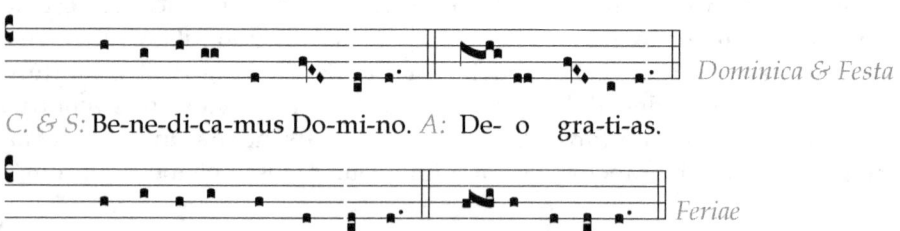

C. & S: Be-ne-di-ca-mus Do-mi-no. A: De- o gra-ti-as. Dominica & Festa

C. & S: Be-ne-di-ca-mus Do-mi-no. A: De- o gra-ti-as. Feriae

Benedictio

H: Benedicat et custodiat nos omnipotens et misericors Dominus: Pater, et Filius, ✠ et Spiritus Sanctus.
A: Amen.

DIE NACHTGEBET
(COMPLET)

Der Lektor bittet um den Lesesegen:

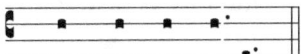

L: Herr, gib den Segen.

Praeses chori [oder Hebdomodarius]:

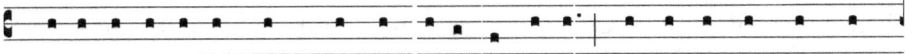

P: Ei-ne ge-ru-hi-ge Nacht und ein se-li-ges Ende / ver-lei-he uns der HErr,

der All-mäch-ti-ge. ℟ Amen.

Lektion (1. Pe. 5:8-9)
L: Brüder, seid nüchtern und wachet: denn euer Widersacher, der Teufel, gehet umher wie ein brüllender Löwe und suchet, welchen er verschlinge / dem widerstehet fest im Glauben. Du aber HErr, erbarme Dich unser.
℟ GOtt sei ewig Dank.

℣ Unsere Hilfe ✠ stehet im Namen des HErren.
℟ Der Himmel und Erde gemacht hat.

Confiteor
Der Hebdomodarius spricht das Sündenbekenntnis:
H: Ich bekenne GOTT, dem Allmächtigen und euch, Brüder, daß ich oft und viel gesündigt habe mit Gedanken, Worten und Werken — durch meine Schuld, durch meine Schuld, durch meine übergroße Schuld —. Darum bitte ich euch, Brüder, daß ihr für mich betet zu GOTT, unserm HErren.

A: Der allmächtige GOTT erbarme sich deiner, Er vergebe dir deine Sünden und führe dich zum ewigen Leben. H: Amen.

A: Wir bekennen GOTT, dem Allmächtigen und dir, Bruder, daß wir oft und viel gesündigt haben mit Gedanken, Worten und Werken — durch unsre Schuld, durch unsre Schuld, durch unsre übergroße Schuld —. Darum bitten wir dich, Bruder, daß du für uns betest zu GOTT, unserm HErren.

H: Der allmächtige GOTT erbarme sich euer, Er vergebe euch eure Sünde und führe euch zum ewigen Leben. A: Amen.

H: Nachlaß, Lossprechung und Vergebung unsrer Sünden schenkt uns der allmächtige und barmherzige HErr. A: Amen.

+ + +

Wenn einer oder zwei die Complet beten, kann das Confiteor gemeinsam mit folgenden Worten gebetet werden:
Ich bekenne Dir, heiliger GOTT, daß ich oft und auf mancherlei Weise gegen Dich gesündigt habe mit Gedanken, Worten und Werken – durch meine Schuld, durch meine Schuld, durch meine übergroße Schuld –. Gedenke mein nicht nach meinen Sünden, sondern nach Deiner großen Barmherzigkeit und vergib mir meine Schuld um JESU CHRISTI willen. Amen.

Einer spricht:
Wenn wir unsre Sünden bekennen, dann ist GOTT treu und gerecht, daß Er uns die Sünde vergibt und reinigt uns von aller Untugend. ℟. Amen.

+ + +

(H., A.)
℣. Tröste uns, GOTT, unser Heiland.
℟. Und laß ab von Deiner Ungnade über uns.

Ingressus

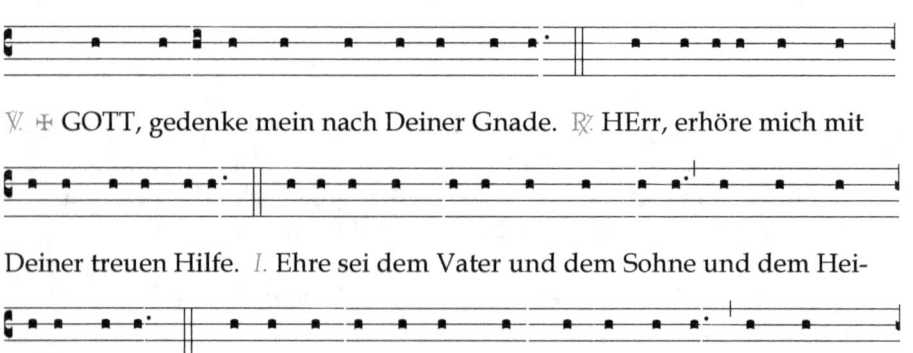

℣. ✠ GOTT, gedenke mein nach Deiner Gnade. ℟. HErr, erhöre mich mit Deiner treuen Hilfe. *I.* Ehre sei dem Vater und dem Sohne und dem Heiligen Geiste. *II.* Wie es war im Anfang, jetzt und immerdar, und von

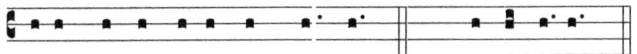

Ewigkeit zu Ewigkeit. Amen. *I./II.* Hal-le-lu-ja.

(In den Fasten: Lob sei Dir, HErr, Du König der ewigen Herrlichkeit.*)*

Psalmodie

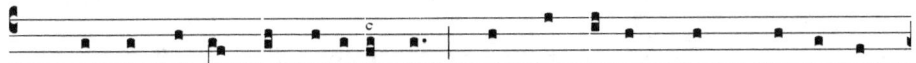

Ant. Sei mir gnädig und erhöre mich, 'wenn ich 'ru-fe : GOTT, 'meiner Ge-

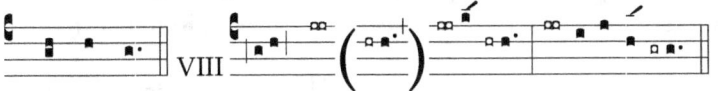

'rechtigkeit. *(Ps. 4, 91, 134)*

PSALM 4
Erhöre mich, 'wenn ich 'rufe: * GOTT, 'meiner Ge'rechtigkeit.
Der Du mich tröstest in 'meinen 'Ängsten: * sei mir gnädig und er'höre 'mein Gebet.
Ihr Herren, wie lange soll meine Ehre ge'schändet 'werden: * wie habt ihr das Eitle so lieb und die 'Lüge so 'gerne.
Erkennet doch, daß der HErr Seine Heiligen 'wunderbar 'führet: * der HErr höret, wenn ich 'ihn an'rufe.
Zürnet 'ihr, so 'sündigt nicht: * redet mit eurem Herzen auf eurem Lager 'und seid 'stille.
'Opfert, was 'recht ist: * und hoffet 'auf den 'HErren.
Viele sagen – wer wird uns Gutes 'sehen 'lassen: * HErr, laß über uns das Licht Deines 'Antlitzes 'leuchten.
'Du er'freust mein Herz: * ob jene auch viel 'Wein und Korn 'haben.
Ich liege und schlafe 'ganz mit 'Frieden: * denn alleine Du, HErr, hilfst mir, daß ich 'sicher 'wohne.

PSALM 91
Wer unter dem Schirm des 'Höchsten 'sitzet: * und unter dem Schatten des All'mächtigen 'bleibet.
Der spricht zu dem Herren meine Zuver'sicht und 'meine Burg: * mein GOTT, auf 'den ich 'hoffe.

Denn Er errettet dich vom 'Stricke des 'Jägers: * und von der ver'derblichen 'Seuche.

Er wird dich mit Seinen 'Fittichen 'decken: * und Zuflucht wirst du unter Seinen 'Flügeln 'haben.

Seine Wahrheit ist Schîrm und Schild, † daß du nicht erschrecken mußt vor dem 'nächtlichen 'Grauen: * vor den Pfeilen, die des 'Tages 'fliegen.

Vor der Pest, 'die im 'Finstern schleicht: * vor der Seuche, die am 'Mittag ver'derben bringt.

Wenn auch tausend fallen zu deiner Seite † und zehntausend zu 'deiner 'Rechten * so wird es doch 'dich nicht 'treffen.

Ja, du wirst es mit eigenen 'Augen 'sehen: * und schauen, wie den Gott'losen ver'golten wird.

Denn der Herr is 'deine 'Zuversicht: * der Höchste ist 'deine 'Zuflucht.

Es wird dir kein 'Übel be'gegnen: * und keine Plage wird sich deinem 'Hause 'nahen.

Denn Er hat Seinen 'Engeln be'fohlen: * daß sie dich behüten auf allen 'Deinen 'Wegen.

Daß sie dich auf den 'Händen 'tragen: * und du deinen Fuß nicht an 'einen Stein 'stößest.

Über Löwen und Ottern 'wirst du 'gehen: * und junge Löwen und Drachen 'nieder'treten.

Er liebet Mich, darum will ICH ihn erretten + er kennet Meinen Namen, darum will 'ICH ihn 'schützen: * er rufet Mich an, darum will ICH 'ihn er'hören.

ICH bin 'bei ihm 'in der Not: * ICH will ihn herausreißen und zu 'Ehren 'bringen.

ICH will ihn sättigen mit 'langem 'Leben: * und will ihm 'zeigen 'Mein Heil.

PSALM 134

Wohlan, lobet den HErren, alle 'Knechte des 'HErren: * die ihr stehet des Nachts im 'Hause des 'Herren.

Hebet eure Hände 'auf im 'Heiligtum: * und 'lobet den 'HErren.

Der HErr segne 'dich aus 'Zion: * der Himmel und 'Erde ge'macht hat.

Ehre sei dem Vater 'und dem 'Sohne: * und dem 'Heiligen 'Geiste.

Wie es war im Anfang, 'jetzt und 'immerdar: * und von Ewigkeit zu 'Ewigkeit. 'Amen.

Antiphon wiederholen.

Kapitel

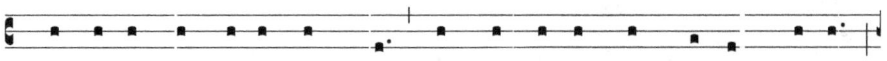

L: Du bist ja doch unter uns, HErr: und wir heißen nach Deinem Namen /

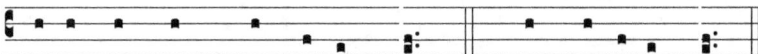

verlaß uns nicht, HErr, unser GOTT. ℟ GOTT sei ewig Dank. *(Jer. 14:9)*

Responsorium Br.

VI

℟ HErr, Du bist meine Stärke ‡ in Deine Hände befehle ich meinen Geist.

℟ HErr... ℣ Du hast mich erlöset, HErr, Du treuer GOTT. ‡ in Deine...

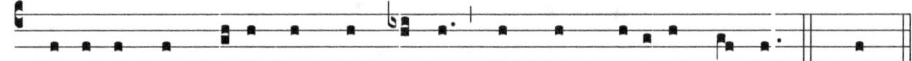

℟ Ehre sei dem Vater und dem Sohne : und dem Heiligen Geiste. ℟ HErr...

Hymnus

Am Sonntag im Winter VIII

Am Sonntag im Sommer IV

1. Dich vor dem Untergang des Lichts, / der Dinge Schöpfer, rufen wir: / daß mit gewohnter Milde Du / als Wächter gegenwärtig seist.
2. Laß Träume fern von hinnen fliehn / samt allem Wahngebild der Nacht: / dämpf unsres Widersachers List / und halt die Leiber unbefleckt.
3. Almächtger Vater, das verleih / durch JESUM CHRISTUM, unsern HErrn: / der mit Dir selbst in Ewigkeit / regiert zusamt dem Heilgen Geist. Amen.

An Werktagen im Sommer **II**

An Werktagen im Winter **VIII**

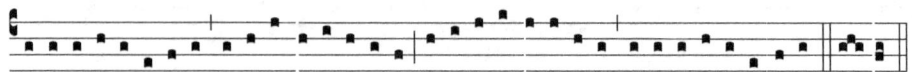

1. JESU, Erlöser aller Welt, / des höchsten Vaters ewig Wort, / des unsichtbaren Lichtes Licht, / der Deinen Wächter Tag und Nacht.
2. Der allem Form und Wesen gibt, / den Unterschied der Zeiten setzt; / erquicke Du durch Ruh der Nacht / die Leiber von der Arbeit müd.
3. Dich flehen wir in Demut an / mach uns vom Widersacher frei: / daß er nicht Macht hab zu verführn, / die Du erkauft mit Deinem Blut.
4. Solang im schlafestrunknen Leib / wir bleiben eine kurze Zeit: / laß unser Fleisch dann also ruhn, / daß unser Herz vom Schlaf nichts weiß.
5. O milder König, JESU CHRIST, / Dir und dem Vater sei die Ehr / zusamt dem Tröster, Heilgen Geist, / jetzt und in alle Ewigkeit. Amen.

Am Samstag im Sommer **VII**

Am Samstag im Winter **IV**

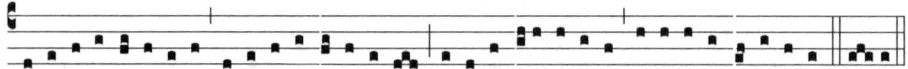

1. HErr GOTT, Du Schöpfer aller Ding, / der Pole Lenker, DU gibst Zier / dem Tage in des Lichtes Glanz, / der Nacht im Schlaf nach Deiner Huld.
2. Damit die Ruh den matten Leib / dem Brauch der Arbeit wieder geb, / den müden Sinn erheitere, / ihn lös von Angst und Traurigkeit.
3. Da nun der Tag vergangnen ist, / die Nacht beginnt, so bitten wir: / steh uns Gebundnen immer bei, / die jetzt Dir singen Dankes Lied.
4. Dich preise unsres Wesens Grund, / Dich lob der Wohllaut unsrer Stimm, / Dich liebe keusche Liebe recht, / Dich bete nüchtern an das Herz.
5. Damit, wenn tiefe Dunkelheit / der Nacht den lichten Tag beschließt, / der Glaub nichts weiß von Finsternis, / die Nacht ihm leuchte wie der Tag.
6. Laß unser Herz nicht müde sein, / mit Gnad bedecke alle Schuld: / des keuschen Glaubens Nüchternheit, / sie kühle unrer Träume Glut.
7. Vom bösen Trachten frei gemacht, / des Herzens Tiefe träum von Dir: /

daß nicht durch bösen Feindes List / die Angst aufjag die Ruhenden.
8. So bitten wir den Einen GOTT: / den Vater, Sohn und beider Geist: / den Flehenden allmächtig helf / durch alles die Dreieinigkeit. Amen.

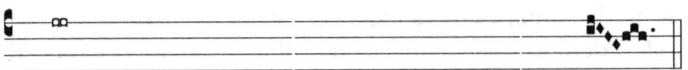

℣. Behüte uns, HErr, wie einen Augapfel im Au- ge.
℟. Beschirme uns unter dem Schatten Deiner Flügel.

Canticum Simeonis

Ant. Bewahre uns, HErr, wenn wir wachen, behüte uns, 'wenn wir 'schlafen :

auf daß wir wachen mit CHRISTO und ' ruhen in 'Frieden.

IIIa

✠ HErr, nun läßt Du Deinen Diener in 'Frieden 'fahren: * wie 'Du ge'saget hast.
Denn meine Augen haben Deinen 'Heiland ge'sehen: * welchen Du bereitet hast vor 'allen 'Völkern.
Ein Licht zu er'leuchten die 'Heiden: * und zum Preise Deines 'Volkes 'Israel.
Ehre sei dem Vater 'und dem 'Sohne: * und dem 'Heiligen 'Geiste.
Wie es war im Anfang, 'jetzt und 'immerdar: * und von Ewigkeit zu 'Ewigkeit. 'Amen.
Antiphon wiederholen.

Orationes
(H., A.)

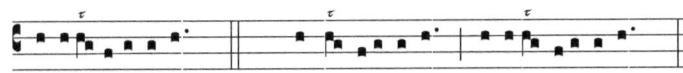

Kyri-e ele-ison! * Christe ele-ison! Kyri-e ele-ison!

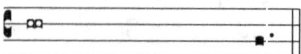

Vater unser im Himmel
(*still:* geheiligt werde dein Name; dein Reich komme; dein Wille geschehe, wie im Himmel, so auf Erden; unser tägliches Brot gib uns heute; und vergib uns unsere Schuld, wie auch wir vergeben unsern Schuldigern)

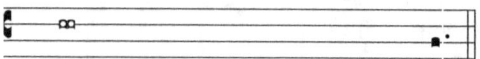

℣. Und führe uns nicht in Versuchung.
℟. Sondern erlöse uns ✠ von dem Bösen.

+++

Apostolicum und Preces entfallen an Sonn- und Festtagen.

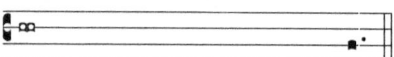

Ich glaube an GOTT den Vater,
(*still:* den Allmächtigen, Schöpfer Himmels und der Erden. Und an Jesus Christus, Gottes eingebornen Sohn, unsern Herrn, der empfangen ist von dem Heiligen Geist, geboren von der Jungfrau Maria, gelitten unter Pontius Pilatus, gekreuziget, gestorben und begraben, niedergefahren zur Hölle, am dritten Tage auferstanden von den Toten, aufgefahren gen Himmel, sitzend zur Rechten Gottes, des allmächtigen Vaters, von dannen er kommen wird, zu richten die Lebendigen und die Toten. Ich glaube an den Heiligen Geist, *eine* heilige christliche Kirche, die Gemeinde der Heiligen, Vergebung der Sünde)
℣. Auferstehung des Fleisches. ℟. Und ein ewiges ✠ Leben. Amen.
℣. O HErr, bewahre uns in 'dieser Nacht. ℟. Nach Deiner Gnade ohne Sünde.
℣. Sei uns 'gnädig, HErr. ℟. Sei uns gnädig.
℣. Deine Güte, HErr, sei 'über uns. ℟. Wie wir auf dich hoffen.
℣. HErr, höre 'mein Gebet. ℟. Und laß mein Schreien zu Dir kommen.

+++

H: Der HErr sei mit euch. ℟. Und mit deinem Geiste.

H: Lasset uns beten.

Am Sonntag:
Wir bitten Dich, HErr, suche gnädig heim dieses Haus und vertreibe alle List des Feindes: laß Deine heiligen Engel bei uns wohnen und un in Frieden bewahren / und Dein Segen sei allezeit über uns. Durch Jesum Christum,

deinen Sohn, unsern Herrn, der mit Dir und dem Heiligen Geiste lebt und regiert von Ewigkeit zu Ewigkeit. ℟ Amen.

Am Montag
Herr GOTT, dem der Tag und die Nacht gehört: laß, wenn die Finsternis kommt, die Sonne der Gerechtigkeit uns aufgehen / und das Dunkel unheiliger Gedanken vertreiben. Durch... ℟ Amen.

Am Dienstag
Allmächtiger, ewiger GOTT, wir denken des Nachts an Deinen Namen: und bitten Dich, treibe alle Finsternis der Sünde aus unseren Herzen / und führe uns zu dem wahren Lichte JESUS CHRISTUS. Der mit Dir und dem Heiligen Geiste lebt und regiert von Ewigkeit zu Ewigkeit. ℟ Amen.

Am Mittwoch
Wir bitten Dich, HErr, schenke uns eine ruhige Nacht und bewahre uns vor der Gewalt des Teufels: damit wir in Deinem Frieden schlafen / und wenn der Tag anbricht, Deinen Namen preisen. Durch... ℟ Amen.

Am Donnerstag
HErr GOTT, Du wachest über uns, damit uns die Schrecken der Nacht nicht bedrohen: bewahre uns durch himmlischen Schutz / und sei Du in unseren Herzen, wenn wir schlafen. Durch... ℟ Amen.

Am Freitag
HErr JESUS CHRISTUS, Du Erlöser aller Menschen: Du hast uns mit Deinem teuren Blute erkaufet / schenke uns, so mit dem Leibe zu ruhen, daß wir im Glauben allezeit mit Dir wachen. Der Du mit dem Vater und dem Heiligen Geiste lebst und regierst von Ewigkeit zu Ewigkeit. ℟ Amen.

Am Samstag
Wache über uns HErr, und bewahre uns vor allem Übel an Leib und Seele: verleihe gnädig, daß wir in dieser Nacht sicher unter Deinem Schutze ruhen / und wenn dann unser letzter Abend kommt, laß uns einschlafen in Frieden, daß wir erwachen zu Deiner Herrlichkeit. Durch... ℟ Amen.

H: Der HErr sei mit euch. *A:* Und mit deinem Geiste.

Am Sonntag

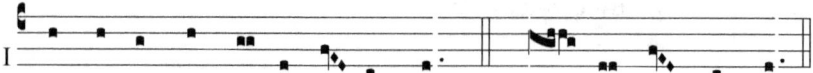

C: Las-set uns den HErren be- ne- dein. A: GOTT sei Preis und Lob.

An Werktagen

C: Las-set uns den HErren be- ne- dein. A: GOTT sei Preis und Lob.

H: Es segne und behüte uns der allmächtige und barmherzige Herr, ✠ der Vater und der Sohn und der Heilige Geist. ℟ Amen.

THE PSALTER DISTRIBUTED OVER SEVEN DAYS

The BPB is set up most fully for four services a day: Morning Prayer, Midday Prayer, Evening Prayer, and Compline. Those who want to use the one-week schedule must re-use the same texts for various purposes. Midday Prayer is used four times per day. In this case, the four times are called "Prime, Terce, Sext, and None."

Readings: At Sext, use the reading from p. 50-51. At Prime, Terce, and None, use a verse from Sunday's Gospel or the Gospel of the Feast.

The Responsory: At Sext, use the weekday responsory from pp. 349-388. At Prime, use the seasonal or Saint's Day responsory from pp. 389-569. At Terce and None, use a short hymn of your choice (or omit the responsory).

The Prayers: At Prime, use the Morning Suffrages on p. 54. (This replaces the entire The Prayers section on pp. 52-53. At Terce and None, use only the Kyrie, Lord's Prayer, Seasonal or Saint's Day versicle (pp. 389-569), and the Collect for the Day. At Sext, use the Collect for the Day, the *Da Pacem* and the other collect with its antiphon and versicle from the Weekday Propers, pp. 349-388.

During penitential seasons: Psalm 51 *Miserere mei*, takes the place of the first Psalm of Lauds. The displaced Psalm from Lauds is then used as the first Psalm of Prime on Sunday or the last Psalm (weekdays) in addition to Prime's other Psalms. As the fourth Psalm at Lauds (the OT canticle), the canticle in parentheses replaces the normal canticle.

On feasts and in Eastertide: Dan. 3:35-68 replaces the fourth Psalm (the OT canticle) at Lauds.

SUGGESTED TIMETABLE FOR COMMUNITIES USING THE ONE-WEEK SCHEDULE:

Weekday Schedule: Vigils & Lauds 5:10; Prime 7:00; Breakfast & Reading; Terce 8:15; Holy Eucharist 8:30; Little Chapter & Work Period; Sext 12:00; Dinner; Rest Period or Reading; None 2:30; Work Period; Vespers 6:00; Supper & Free time; Compline 8:30; Silence.

Sunday Schedule: As on weekdays except as follows: Terce 8:30; Holy Eucharist 10:00; Coffee Hour & Dinner; Sext & None prayed privately or at an announced time.

	Sun.	Mon.	Tues.	Wed.	Thurs.	Fri.	Sat.
VIGILS	I: 1-3 II: 8-9 III: 10-11	I: 14-15, 17 II: 18 III: 20, 21, 30	I: 35 II: 37 III: 38, 39	I: 45, 46 II: 48, 49 III: 50, 51	I: 62, 66 II: 68 III: 69	I: 78:1-31 II: 78:32-72 III: 79, 81, 83	I: 105 II: 106 III: 107
LAUDS	93, 100, 63, Dan. 3:35-68 (Dan. 3: 29-34, 67); 148	47, 5, 29, 1Chr. 29: 10-13 (Isa. 12:1-6); 117	96, 43, 67, Tob. 13:1-10 (Isa. 38:10 -20); 135	97, 65, 101, Judt. 16:15-21 (1Sam. 2: 1-10); 146	98, 90, 36, Jer. 31:10-14 (Ex. 15: 1-18); 147:1-11	99, 143, 85, Isa. 45:15-25 (Hab. 3:2-11); 147:12-20	149, 92, 64, Sir. 36:1-16 (Deut. 32: 1-43); 150
PRIME	118 or 54 or 100; 119i-ii, iii-iv; [Athan. Creed]	24, 19	25	26, 52, 53	23, 72	22	94, 108
TERCE	119v-vi, vii-viii, ix-x	27, 28	40	54, 55	73	80, 82	102
SEXT	119xi-xii, xiii-xiv, xv-xvi	31	41, 42	56-58	74	84, 87	104
NONE	119xvii-xviii, xix-xx, xxi-xxii	32, 33	44	59, 60	75, 76	89	109
VESP.	110-115	116, 120-122	123-127	128-132	133, 136-138	139-142	144-145
COMP.	4, 91, 134	6, 7	12, 13, 16	34, 61	70-71	77, 86	88, 103

The Psalter Distributed over Four Weeks

The Four-Week Psalm Schedule begins anew at Week 1 on the 1st Sunday of Advent and on Easter.

Wk 1	Morning Prayer	Daytime Prayer	Evening Prayer
Sun.	1, 2, 93, 148-150	119:1-48	110-112
Mon.	Ex. 15:1-18; 5, 17, 29	10	7, 125
Tue.	1Sam. 2:1-10; 35	28, 30	13, 16, 129
Wed.	67, 25	40	62, 97, 133
Thur.	Jdt. 16:15-21; 6, 98, 99	56, 57	31
Fri.	51, 22	80	71, 141
Sat.	Dan. 3:29-34,67; 38, 95	20, 21	73

Wk 2	Morning Prayer	Daytime Prayer	Evening Prayer
Sun.	3, 8, 100, 148-150	119:49-96	113-115
Mon.	Dt. 32:1-18; 18	12, 15	11, 14, 126
Tue.	Dt. 32:19-43; 36, 85, 135	45	39, 41, 130
Wed.	67, 50, 92	52, 53	64, 101, 137
Thur.	Isa. 38:10-20; 42, 43	60, 61	34, 140
Fri.	51, 69	81, 82	87, 144
Sat.	Dan. 3:35-68; 105	23, 24	103, 142

Wk 3	Morning Prayer	Daytime Prayer	Evening Prayer
Sun.	9, 63, 148-150	119:97-136	116, 120-121
Mon.	1Chr. 29:10-13; 32, 47, 70	19	33, 127
Tue.	Isa. 12:1-6; 37	54, 75	59, 131
Wed.	67, 65, 88, 146	55	89
Thur.	Isa. 45:15-25; 66, 90	72	79, 139
Fri.	51, 78:1-16, 143	78:17-31	78:32-72
Sat.	Tob. 13:1-7; 106	27	104

Wk 4	Morning Prayer	Daytime Prayer	Evening Prayer
Sun.	118, 148-150	119:137-176	122-124
Mon.	Hab. 3:2-11; 46, 96, 117	26, 48	49, 128
Tue.	Hab. 3:12-19; 44	94	77, 132
Wed.	67, 74	58, 83	136, 138
Thur.	Jer. 31:10-14; 68	76	109
Fri.	51, 108, 147	84	102
Sat.	Sir. 36:1-19; 107	86	145

Compline Every Day: 4, 91, 134

The Psalter Distributed over Thirty-One Days

In months having thirty days the psalms for the the thirty-first day are to be read on the thirtieth day; in the morning, Pss. 146, 147; in the evening, Pss. 148-150. On the twenty-eighth of February Pss. 140-144 are to be read in the morning, Pss. 145-150 in the evening.

Morning	Evening	Morning	Evening	Morning	Evening
1. 1-4	5-8	12. 64, 65	66-68	23. 112-115	116-118
2. 9-11	12-17	13. 69	70-72	24. 119:1-40	119:41-88
3. 18	19-22	14. 73	74-76	25. 119:89-128	119:129ff.
4. 23-25	26-30	15. 77	78	26. 120-125	126-132
5. 31, 32	33, 34	16. 79, 80	81-83	27. 133-135	136-139
6. 35	36, 37	17. 84, 85	86-88	28. 140, 141	142, 143
7. 38	39-41	18. 89	90-92	29. 144	145
8. 42-44	45-48	19. 93-95	96-100	30. 146	147
9. 49	50, 51	20. 101, 102	103, 104	31. 148	149, 150
10. 52-54	55-57	21. 105	106		
11. 58, 59	60-63	22. 107	108-111		

A Flexible Psalm Schedule

According to old Lutheran custom, the Psalms may be recited in canonical order from 1-109 at Matins (or Lauds) and in order from 110-150 at Vespers. In addition, one may profitably choose to leave out Psalms 4, 91, and 134 from recitation at Matins and Vespers and to use these Psalms at Compline; also to use the Old Testament Canticles at Midday Prayer; and to leave out Ps. 119 from recitation at Vespers and use it at Midday Prayer on Sundays.

Daily Lectionary
Lessons for Morning and Evening throughout the Year

These Lessons may be used at Matins and Vespers, or at Morning and Evening Prayer, on the days of the week. The Lessons appointed for days between the *Fourth Sunday in Advent* and the *First Sunday after Epiphany* are to be omitted when the days for which they are appointed do not occur. When there are not six *Sundays after Epiphany,* the Lessons for the week after the *First Sunday* may be omitted one year; and those which follow another *Sunday,* the second year; and so on: in order that in the course of several years all the Lessons provided may be read. The Lessons appointed for the days from the *Twentieth Sunday after Trinity* to the end of the year are to be read in every year, and those appointed for the weeks before the *Twentieth Sunday after Trinity* are to be omitted so far as necessary to this end. (In this Table the first Lesson is for the morning, and the second for the evening of each day.) The Lessons for Sundays and Feast Days are found in the Propers (389-569).

1st Sunday in Advent			Fri.	Luke 1:67-80	Is. 7:1-17
Mon.	Matt. 11:25-30	Gen. 3:1-24	Sat.	Matt. 1:1-17	Mic. 5:1-5
Tues.	Acts 3:22-26	Gen. 9:1-19			
Wed.	Col. 1:15-29	Gen. 22:1-19	*Christmas*		
Th.	Heb. 1:1-4	Gen. 49:1-28	Dec. 27.	John 1:15-18	Mic. 4:1-8
Fri.	Heb. 2:1-4	Num. 24:14-25	Dec. 28.	Luke 2:15-20	Is. 32:1-8
Sat.	Eph. 3:1-12	Deut. 18:15-19	Dec. 29.	Luke 2:22-24	Is. 46:3-13
			Dec. 30.	Luke 2:25-32	Is. 49:1-13
2nd Sunday in Advent			Dec. 31.	Matt. 2:13-15	Is. 55:1-13
Mon.	Acts 17:16-34	1 Chr. 17:1-27	Jan. 2.	Matt. 2:16-18	Is. 42:1-9
Tues.	1 John 4:9-16	2 Chr. 7:11-22	Jan. 3.	Matt. 2:19-23	Is. 61:1-11
Wed.	Col. 1:1-8	Is. 11:1-10	Jan. 4.	Matt. 3:1-12	Is. 56:1-8
Th.	Phil. 2:12-18	Jer. 23:2-8	Jan. 5.	Luke 3:1-9	Is. 12:1-6
Fri.	Phil. 3:12-16	Jer. 30:1-22			
Sat.	Col. 3:1-11	Jer. 33:14-26	*Epiphany*		
			Mon.	Luke 3:10-14	Gen. 1:1-31
3rd Sunday in Advent			Tues.	Luke 3:15-20	Gen. 2:1-25
Mon.	Heb. 10:35-39	Is. 2:1-5	Wed.	Mark 1:1-8	Gen. 4:1-26
Tues.	Lk. 21:5-24	Is. 24:21-25:5	Th.	Mark 1:9-11	Gen. 5:1-32
Wed.	Luke 12:35-59	Is. 25:6-10	Fri.	Luke 3:21-22	Gen. 6:9-22
Th.	James 5:7-11	Is. 26:1-21	Sat.	Luke 3:23-38	Gen. 7:1-24
Fri.	Luke 1:1-25	Is. 51:1-16			
Sat.	Luke 1:26-38	Is. 52:1-12	*1st Sunday after Epiphany*		
			Mon.	John 1:29-34	Gen. 8:1-22
4th Sunday in Advent			Tues.	John 1:35-42	Gen. 11:1-9
Mon.	Matt. 1:18-25	Is. 40:1-11	Wed.	John 1:43-51	Gen. 12:1-20
Tues.	Luke 1:39-45	Mal. 3:1-7	Th.	Luke 4:1-13	Gen. 13:1-18
Wed.	Luke 1:46-56	Mal. 4:1-6	Fri.	Mark 1:12-15	Gen. 14:8-24
Th.	Luke 1:57-66	Is. 28:14-19	Sat.	Matt. 4:12-17	Gen. 15:1-21

2nd Sunday after Epiphany
Mon.	Matt. 4:18-25	Gen. 17:1-22
Tues.	Matt. 5:1-9	Gen. 18:1-33
Wed.	Matt. 5:27-48	Gen. 19:1-29
Th.	Matt. 6:1-23	Gen. 21:1-8
Fri.	Matt. 7:1-14	Gen. 24:1-28
Sat.	Matt. 7:24-29	Gen. 24:29-67

3rd Sunday after Epiphany
Mon.	Matt. 8:14-22	Gen. 25:19-34
Tues.	Matt. 8:28-34	Gen. 27:1-45
Wed.	Matt. 9:9-17	Gen. 27:46-28:22
Th.	Matt. 9:27-38	Gen. 29:1-20
Fri.	Matt. 10:1-16	Gen. 31:1-18
Sat.	Matt. 10:17-11:1	Gen. 32:3-32

4th Sunday after Epiphany
Mon.	Matt. 11:11-24	Gen. 33:1-20
Tues.	Matt. 12:1-21	Gen. 35:1-21
Wed.	Matt. 12:22-50	Gen. 37:1-36
Th.	Matt. 13:1-23	Gen. 39:1-23
Fri.	Matt. 14:1-36	Gen. 40:1-23
Sat.	Matt. 15:1-20	Gen. 41:1-37

5th Sunday after Epiphany
Mon.	Matt. 15:29-39	Gen. 41:38-57
Tues.	Matt. 16:1-12	Gen. 42:1-38
Wed.	Matt. 16:21-28	Gen. 43:1-34
Th.	Matt. 17:9-27	Gen. 44:1-34
Fri.	Matt. 19:1-15	Gen. 45:1-28
Sat.	Matt. 20:17-34	Gen. 46:1-34

6th Sunday after Epiphany
Mon.	Matt. 21:10-46	Gen. 47:1-31
Tues.	Matt. 23:1-39	Gen. 48:1-22
Wed.	Mark 1:16-45	Ex. 1:1-22
Th.	Mark 2:1-28	Ex. 2:1-25
Fri.	Mark 3:1-35	Ex. 3:1-22
Sat.	Mark 5:1-20	Ex. 4:1-31

Septuagesima Sunday
Mon.	Mark 5:21-43	Ex. 5:1-23
Tues.	Mark 6:1-29	Ex. 6:1-13
Wed.	Mark 6:30-56	Ex. 11:1-10
Th.	Mark 7:1-30	Ex. 12:1-28
Fri.	Mark 8:10-9:1	Ex. 12:29-42
Sat.	Mark 9:2-32	Ex. 13:1-22

Sexagesima Sunday
Mon.	Mark 10:1-31	Ex. 14:1-31
Tues.	Mark 10:32-52	Ex. 15:1-21
Wed.	Mark 11:1-33	Ex. 15:22-16:36
Th.	Mark 12:13-44	Ex. 17:1-16
Fri.	Luke 4:14-44	Ex. 19:1-25
Sat.	Luke 5:12-39	Ex. 20:1-23

Quinquagesima Sunday
Mon.	Luke 6:1-35	Ex. 24:1-25:9
Tues.	Luke 6:33-49	Ex. 31:18-32:35
Wed.	Luke 7:1-10	Ex. 33:1-23
Th.	Luke 7:18-8:3	Ex 34:1-10
Fri.	Luke 8:16-56	Ex. 34:27-35
Sat.	Luke 9:1-27	Ex. 40:1-38

1st Sunday in Lent (Invocavit)
Mon.	Luke 9:28-62	Num. 3:5-13
Tues.	Luke 10:1-22	Num. 10:11-36
Wed.	Luke 10:38-11:13	Num. 11:1-35
Th.	Luke 11:29-36	Num. 12:1-15
Fri.	Luke 11:37-54	Num. 13:1-25
Sat.	Luke 12:1-34	Num. 13:26-33

2nd Sunday in Lent (Reminiscere)
Mon.	Luke 13:1-17	Num. 14:1-45
Tues.	Luke 14:25-35	Num. 16:1-22
Wed.	Luke 15:11-32	Num. 16:23-50
Th.	Luke 16:10-18	Num. 20:1-29
Fri.	Luke 17:1-10	Num. 20:1-29
Sat.	Luke 18:1-8	Num. 21:1-22:1

3rd Sunday in Lent (Oculi)
Mon.	Luke 18:15-30	Num. 22:2-41
Tues.	Luke 19:1-40	Num. 23:1-30
Wed.	Luke 20:1-21:4	Num. 24:1-13
Th.	Luke 21:37-22:38	Num. 27:12-23
Fri.	Luke 22:39-71	Deut. 5:1-33
Sat.	Luke 23:1-25	Deut. 8:1-20

4th Sunday in Lent (Laetare)
Mon.	Luke 23:26-56	Deut. 9:1-29
Tues.	Matt. 26:1-35	Deut. 10:1-22
Wed.	Matt. 26:36-75	Deut. 11:1-32
Th.	Matt. 27:1-38	Deut. 28:1-14
Fri.	Matt. 27:39-66	Deut. 28:15-68
Sat.	Mark 14:1-31	Deut. 34:1-12

5th Sunday in Lent (Judica)
Mon.	Mark 14:32-72	Jer. 2:1-19
Tues.	Mark 15:1-19	Hosea 13:9-14
Wed.	Mark 15:20-47	Zeph. 3:1-8
Th.	John 12:1-19	Micah 3:9-12
Fri.	John 12:20-50	Is. 66:1-9
Sat.	John 13:16-38	Zech. 9:1-17

Palm Sunday (Palmarum)
Mon.	John 18:1-18	Jer. 7:1-15
Tues.	John 18:19-40	Is. 50:4-11
Wed.	John 19:1-12	Jer. 11:18-23
Th.	John 19:13-24	Zech. 3:1-10
Fri.	John 19:25-37	Lam. 2:8-15
Sat.	John 19:38-42	Is. 52:13-15

Easter
Easter Mon.
Tues.	Matt. 28:1-15	Eze. 17:22-24
Wed.	John 20:1-18	Haggai 2:20-23
Th.	Luke 24:1-12	Zech. 6:9-15
Fri.	Luke 24:36-49	Eze. 17:22-24
Sat.	Mark 16:9-14	Is. 44:21-28

1st Sunday after Easter (Quasimodo Geniti)
Mon.	John 21:1-25	Jonah 1:1-16
Tues.	John 2:12-25	Jonah 1:17-2:10
Wed.	John 3:22-36	Jonah 3:1-10
Th.	John 4:1-27	Jonah 4:1-11
Fri.	John 4:28-38	Is. 33:2-6
Sat.	John 4:39-45	Is. 42:10-17

2nd Sunday after Easter (Misericordias Domini)
Mon.	John 5:1-17	Micah 2:12-13
Tues.	John 5:18-30	Is. 30:19-26
Wed.	John 5:31-47	Jer. 3:11-19
Th.	John 6:16-29	Eze. 34:1-11
Fri.	John 6:30-40	Eze. 34:12-22
Sat.	John 6:41-59	Eze. 34:23-31

3rd Sunday after Easter (Jubilate)
Mon.	John 6:60-71	Eze. 36:1-15
Tues.	John 7:1-13	Eze. 36:16-32
Wed.	John 7:14-24	Eze. 36:33-38
Th.	John 7:25-36	Haggai 2:2-9
Fri.	John 7:37-53	Zech. 2:1-13
Sat.	John 8:1-11	Zech. 11:1-17

4th Sunday after Easter (Cantate)
Mon.	John 8:12-20	Zech. 12:1-14
Tues.	John 8:21-29	Is. 65:1-7
Wed.	John 8:30-45	Is. 65:8-16
Th.	John 9:1-13	Jer. 8:4-13
Fri.	John 9:14-34	Zech. 8:18-23
Sat.	John 9:35-41	Is. 49:22-26

5th Sunday after Easter (Rogate)
Mon.	John 10:1-5	Amos 9:8-15
Tues.	John 10:6-10	Is. 4:2-6
Wed.	Matt. 28:16-20	Is. 29:18-24

Ascension Day
Fri.	Luke 24:50-53	Micah 7:7-13
Sat.	Acts 1:12-26	Micah 7:14-20

Sunday after Ascension (Exaudi)
Mon.	John 10:17-21	Zech. 13:7-9
Tues.	John 10:22-31	Zech. 14:1-21
Wed.	John 10:32-42	Is. 66:10-24
Th.	John 11:1-27	Jer. 46:27-28
Fri.	John 11:28-44	Is. 32:9-20
Sat.	John 11:45-57	Is. 57:15-21

Whitsunday
Whitmonday
Tues.	Acts 2:14-36	Eze. 47:1-12
Wed.	Acts 2:37-47	Is. 45:18-21
Th.	John 14:1-22	Is. 45:22-25
Fri.	John 15:1-25	Jer. 9:23-26
Sat.	John 16:31-17:26	Is. 44:6-8

Trinity Sunday
Mon.	Acts 3:1-21	Josh. 1:1-18
Tues.	Acts 4:1-37	Josh. 3:1-17
Wed.	Acts 5:1-42	Josh. 4:1-24
Th.	Acts 6:1-15	Josh. 6:1-27
Fri.	Acts 7:1-60	Josh. 8:1-35
Sat.	Acts 8:1-40	Josh. 9:1-27

1st Sunday after Trinity
Mon.	Acts 9:1-43	Josh. 10:1-15
Tues.	Acts 10:1-33	Josh. 11:1-23
Wed.	Acts 11:1-30	Josh. 23:1-16
Th.	Acts 12:1-25	Josh. 24:1-31
Fri.	Acts 13:1-52	Judg. 2:1-23
Sat.	Acts 14:1-28	Judg. 6:1-40

2nd Sunday after Trinity
Mon.	Acts 15:1-41	Judg. 7:1-25
Tues.	Acts 16:1-40	Judg. 13:1-25
Wed.	Acts 17:1-15	Judg. 14:1-20
Th.	Acts 18:1-28	Judg. 15:1-20
Fri.	Acts 19:1-41	Judg. 16:4-31
Sat.	Acts 20:1-38	1 Sam. 1:1-28

3rd Sunday after Trinity
Mon.	Acts 21:1-39	1 Sam. 2:1-21
Tues.	Acts 21:40-22:29	1 Sam. 3:1-21
Wed.	Acts 22:30-23:35	1 Sam. 4:1-22
Th.	Acts 24:1-27	1 Sam. 5:1-12
Fri.	Acts 25:1-27	1 Sam. 7:1-17
Sat.	Acts 26:1-32	1 Sam. 8:1-22

4th Sunday after Trinity
Mon.	Acts 27:1-44	1 Sam. 9:1-27
Tues.	Acts 28:1-31	1 Sam. 10:1-27
Wed.	Rom. 1:1-15	1 Sam. 12:1-25
Th.	Rom. 1:16-32	1 Sam. 13:1-14
Fri.	Rom. 2:1-29	1 Sam. 15:1-35
Sat.	Rom. 3:1-31	1 Sam. 16:1-23

5th Sunday after Trinity
Mon.	Rom. 4:1-25	1 Sam. 17:1-58
Tues.	Rom. 5:1-6:2	1 Sam. 18:1-21
Wed.	Rom. 6:12-18	1 Sam. 19:1-24
Th.	Rom. 7:1-25	1 Sam. 20:1-42
Fri.	Rom. 8:1-11	1 Sam. 22:1-23
Sat.	Rom. 13:1-7	1 Sam. 24:1-22

6th Sunday after Trinity
Mon.	Rom. 14:1-15:3	1 Sam. 26:1-25
Tues.	Rom. 15:14-33	1 Sam. 28:3-25
Wed.	Rom. 16:1-27	1 Sam. 31:1-13
Th.	1 Cor. 1:10-31	2 Sam. 1:1-27
Fri.	1 Cor. 2:1-16	2 Sam. 5:1-25
Sat.	1 Cor. 4:6-5:5	2 Sam. 6:1-23

7th Sunday after Trinity
Mon.	1 Cor. 5:9-6:20	1 Chr. 16:1-43
Tues.	1 Cor. 7:1-40	2 Sam. 7:1-29
Wed.	1 Cor. 8:1-13	2 Sam. 12:1-23
Th.	1 Cor. 9:1-23	2 Sam. 15:1-15
Fri.	1 Cor. 10:14-33	2 Sam. 16:5-35
Sat.	1 Cor. 11:1-22	2 Sam. 18:1-13

8th Sunday after Trinity
Mon.	1 Cor. 12:12-31	2 Sam. 19:1-23
Tues.	1 Cor. 14:1-40	1 Chr. 21:1-30
Wed.	1 Cor. 15:58-16:24	1 Chr. 22:1-19
Th.	2 Cor. 1:1-24	1 Chr. 28:1-21
Fri.	2 Cor. 2:1-3:3	1 Chr. 29:1-23
Sat.	2 Cor. 6:11-7:16	2 Chr. 1:1-13

9th Sunday after Trinity
Mon.	2 Cor. 8:1-24	1 Kgs. 3:16-28
Tues.	2 Cor. 9:1-15	1 Kgs. 4:22-34
Wed.	2 Cor. 10:1-18	1 Kgs. 5:1-18
Th.	2 Cor. 11:1-18	2 Chr. 3:1-17
Fri.	2 Cor. 12:19-13:13	1 Kgs. 7:1-12
Sat.	Gal. 1:1-24	1 Kgs. 8:1-66

10th Sunday after Trinity
Mon.	Gal. 2:1-21	1 Kgs. 9:1-28
Tues.	Gal. 3:1-14	1 Kgs. 10:1-29
Wed.	Gal. 4:8-20	1 Kgs. 11:1-43
Th.	Gal. 5:1-15	1 Kgs. 12:1-33
Fri.	Gal. 6:11-18	1 Kgs. 13:1-34
Sat.	Eph. 6:1-9	1 Kgs. 14:1-31

11th Sunday after Trinity
Mon.	Eph. 6:18-24	1 Kgs. 16:29-17:24
Tues.	Phil. 1:12-2:4	1 Kgs. 18:1-46
Wed.	Phil. 2:19-30	1 Kgs. 19:1-21
Th.	Phil. 3:1-11	1 Kgs. 21:1-29
Fri.	Phil. 4:1-3	1 Kgs. 22:52-2 Kgs. 1:17
Sat.	Phil. 4:8-23	2 Kgs. 2:1-25

12th Sunday after Trinity
Mon.	Col. 2:1-23	2 Kgs. 4:1-44
Tues.	Col. 3:18-4:18	2 Kgs. 5:1-27
Wed.	1 Thess. 1:1-10	2 Kgs. 6:1-23
Th.	1 Thess. 2:1-20	2 Kgs. 6:24-7:20
Fri.	1 Thess. 3:1-13	2 Kgs. 8:1-15
Sat.	1 Thess. 4:8-12	2 Kgs. 9:1-37

13th Sunday after Trinity
Mon.	1 Thess. 5:12-28	2 Kgs. 10:1-36
Tues.	1 Tim. 1:1-20	2 Chr. 22:1-12
Wed.	1 Tim. 2:1-15	2 Chr. 23:1-21
Th.	1 Tim. 3:1-16	2 Chr. 24:1-27
Fri.	1 Tim. 4:1-16	2 Kgs. 14:1-29
Sat.	1 Tim. 5:1-25	2 Kgs. 15:1-38

14th Sunday after Trinity
Mon.	1 Tim. 6:1-21	Is. 6:1-13
Tues.	2 Tim. 1:1-18	Amos 7:7-17
Wed.	2 Tim. 2:1-26	2 Kgs. 16:1-20
Th.	Titus 1:1-16	2 Kgs. 17:1-23
Fri.	Titus 2:1-10	2 Kgs. 18:1-37
Sat.	Titus 2:15-3:3	2 Kgs. 19:1-37

15th Sunday after Trinity
Mon.	Titus 3:8-15	2 Kgs. 20:1-21
Tues.	Phlm. 1-25	2 Kgs. 21:1-26
Wed.	Heb. 1:1-14	2 Chr. 34:1-33
Th.	Heb. 2:5-3:6	2 Chr. 35:20-36:10
Fri.	Heb. 4:4-5:14	Jer. 22:1-30
Sat.	Heb. 6:1-20	Jer. 25:1-14

16th Sunday after Trinity
Mon.	Heb. 7:1-28	Jer. 37:1-21
Tues.	Heb. 8:1-13	Jer. 38:1-28
Wed.	Heb. 9:1-10	Jer. 32:1-44
Th.	Heb. 9:16-28	Jer. 39:1-18
Fri.	Heb. 10:1-34	Jer. 29:1-23
Sat.	Heb. 11:1-7	Dan. 1:1-21

17th Sunday after Trinity
Mon.	Heb. 11:17-40	Dan. 3:1-30
Tues.	Heb. 12:1-17	Dan. 4:1-37
Wed.	Heb. 13:1-25	Dan. 5:1-30
Th.	James 1:1-15	Dan. 5:31-6:28
Fri.	James 2:1-13	Ezra 1:1-11
Sat.	James 2:14-26	Ezra 3:1-13

18th Sunday after Trinity
Mon.	James 3:1-18	Ezra 4:1-24
Tues.	James 4:1-5:6	Haggai 1:1-15
Wed.	James 5:12-20	Ezra 5:1-17
Th.	1 Peter 3:1-7	Ezra 6:1-22
Fri.	1 Peter 3:15-22	Ezra 7:1-28
Sat.	1 Peter 5:1-5	Ezra 8:31-9:15

19th Sunday after Trinity
Mon.	1 John 1:1-10	Neh. 1:1-11
Tues.	1 John 2:1-17	Neh. 2:1-20
Wed.	1 John 5:1-3	Neh. 4:1-23
Th.	1 John 5:10-21	Neh. 8:1-18
Fri.	2 John 1-13	Neh. 9:1-38
Sat.	3 John 1-14	Zech. 8:1-23

20th Sunday after Trinity
Mon.	Mark 4:1-41	Is. 43:1-13
Tues.	Luke 13:18-35	Is. 41:1-20
Wed.	Matt. 13:31-58	Hab. 2:1-4
Th.	Matt. 16:13-20	Is. 63:7-19
Fri.	2 Cor. 3:10-4:18	Is. 64:1-12
Sat.	2 Cor. 5:1-21	Is. 5:1-7

21st Sunday after Trinity
Mon.	Eph. 1:1-23	Micah 6:1-8
Tues.	Eph. 2:1-22	Is. 58:1-14
Wed.	Eph. 4:7-21	Is. 59:1-21
Th.	Eph. 4:29-32	Jer. 31:1-22
Fri.	Eph. 5:10-14	Jer. 31:23-40
Sat.	Eph. 5:22-33	Is. 48:1-22

22nd Sunday after Trinity
Mon.	Matt. 18:1-22	Micah 4:9-5:1
Tues.	Mark 9:33-50	Is. 49:14-21
Wed.	Luke 17:20-37	Is. 2:10-21
Th.	Rom. 8:24-39	Is. 63:1-6
Fri.	Mark 12:1-12	Joel 2:1-11
Sat.	Matt. 25:14-30	Joel 2:12-27

23rd Sunday after Trinity
Mon.	1 Cor. 3:1-23	Joel 3:1-13
Tues.	Matt. 19:16-30	Joel 3:14-21
Wed.	Luke 14:12-15	Obad. 1-21
Th.	Mark 13:1-37	Nah. 1:1-14
Fri.	Rom. 9:1-33	Nah. 1:15-3:19
Sat.	Rom. 10:1-21	Is. 10:5-27

24th Sunday after Trinity
Mon.	Rom. 11:1-36	Is. 13:1-22
Tues.	2 Thess. 1:11-2:17	Is. 13:1-27
Wed.	2 Thess. 3:1-18	Is. 47:1-15
Th.	2 Tim. 3:1-17	Dan. 2:27-45
Fri.	2 Tim. 4:1-22	Dan. 7:1-28
Sat.	Matt. 24:1-14	Dan. 9:1-27

25th Sunday after Trinity
Mon.	Matt. 24:29-51	Dan. 11:36-12:13
Tues.	Matt. 22:23-33	Eze. 38:1-23
Wed.	1 Cor. 15:11-50	Eze. 39:1-29
Th.	Heb. 3:7-4:13	Is. 43:14-25
Fri.	Heb. 11:8-16	Is. 33:17-24
Sat.	Heb. 12:18-29	Eze. 37:1-14

26th Sunday after Trinity
Mon.	1 Peter 1:1-12	Zeph. 3:9-20
Tues.	1 Peter 1:13-2:10	Is. 34:1-17
Wed.	1 Peter 4:1-7	Is. 35:1-10
Th.	1 Peter 4:12-19	Is. 54:1-17
Fri.	2 Peter 1:1-15	Is. 60:7-22
Sat.	2 Peter 2:1-22	Is. 62:1-12

27th Sunday after Trinity
Mon.	2 Peter 3:1-18	Is. 65:17-25
Tues.	Jude 1-25	Eze. 37:15-28
Wed.	1 John 2:18-29	Hab. 3:1-19
Th.	1 John 3:1-12	Is. 40:27-31
Fri.	1 John 3:19-24	Jer. 14:7-9
Sat.	1 John 4:1-8	Mal. 3:7-18

Common Tones

The following are instructions and music for making use of the features of this book.

*A*NTIPHONS *(refrains), unlike the Psalms, are divided with a **colon**, to mark the midway point of the verse, and are pointed with accents. Longer antiphons in the propers are divided into multiple verses. Antiphons may be sung to their proper melodies (if such are provided) or according to the tone of the Psalm or canticle. The asterisk * in the antiphons indicates the point at which the choir/congregation joins the cantor in singing the antiphon.*

*P*SALMS AND *C*ANTICLES *are divided with an asterisk *. Psalms, together with Canticles from the Old Testament and Apocrypha as well as the Athanasian Creed (when chanted), are referred to collectively as "Psalmody." The "Gospel Canticles" are the Benedictus, the Magnificat, and the Nunc Dimittis (from Luke 1-2).*

For the Psalmody, the Initium/Incipit (pick-up notes) are sung by the cantor only on the first verse (and on the Antiphon, if the Antiphon is sung according to the Psalm tone instead of its proper melody). For the Gospel Canticles, the Initium/Incipit is sung on every verse (and on the Antiphon, if the Antiphon is sung according to the Psalm tone instead of its proper melody).

Sometimes the text is too short to accommodate all the parts of the Psalm tone. In these cases the cadence (Mediatio or Finalis) takes precedence, then the Tuba, then the Incipit.

Example 1: Magnificat on Sunday

☦ |My| soul / doth mágnifý the Lord, * |and| my spirit hath rejoiced in Gód / my Sáviour.
For / he háth regárded * |the| low estate of hís / handmáiden:
For, / behóld, from hénceforth * |all| generations shall cáll / me bléss-ed.
|For| he that is mighty / hath dóne to mé great things; * |and| hó- / ly ís his name.

On the first and fourth verses there is enough text to be able to sing the Incipit. On the second and third verses, however, the Incipit is omitted since there is not enough text to sing it.

Example 2: Benedictus on Tuesday

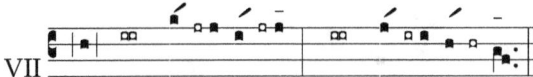
VII

|To| give light to them that sit in darkness and in the / shádow of <u>death</u>, * to guide our feet / ínto the wáy of peace.
|Glo- | ry be to the / Fáther and tó the Son * and / tó the Hóly Ghost.
|As| it was in the beginning, is now, and / éver sháll be, * - / wórld without énd. Amen.

The last half-verse of the Gloria Patri does not have enough text for a Tuba, and so instead begins directly with the Finalis. [71]

Psalm Tones
Each Psalm tone used in this book is given below. Above each tone are instructions on how the Psalm is pointed when the last syllable of each half-verse is stressed (indicated in the text by underlining).

If last syllable is <u>stressed</u>: <u>inflect at first áccent</u> * <u>inflect at first áccent</u>

I

If last syllable is <u>stressed</u>: <u>hold on G</u> * <u>inflect at second-last syllable</u>

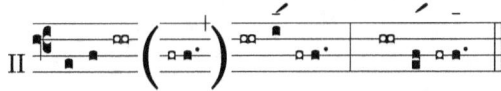
II

If last syllable is <u>stressed</u>: <u>inflect at first áccent</u> * <u>inflect at first áccent</u>

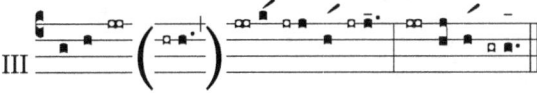
III

If last syllable is <u>stressed</u>: <u>hold on B</u> * <u>inflect at first áccent and slur</u>

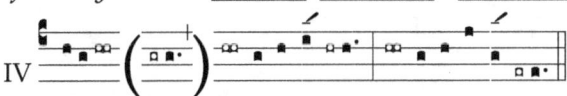
IV

If last syllable is <u>stressed</u>: <u>hold on D</u> * <u>inflect at first áccent</u>

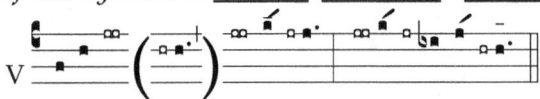
V

If last syllable is <u>stressed</u>: <u>inflect at first áccent * slur</u>

If last syllable is <u>stressed</u>: <u>inflect at first áccent * inflect at first áccent</u>

If last syllable is <u>stressed</u>: <u>hold on D * slur</u>

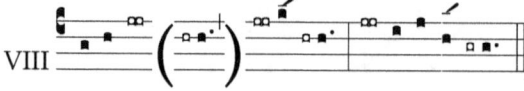

If last syllable is <u>stressed</u>: <u>inflect 1 syllable before first áccent * inflect at 3rd-last syllable</u>

If last syllable is <u>stressed</u>: <u>inflect at second-last syllable * inflect at first áccent</u>

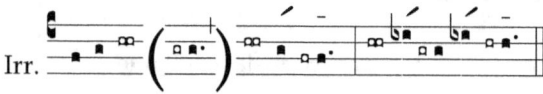

Canticle Tones

The canticle tones, more difficult than the Psalm tones, may be used with the Benedictus, Magnificat, or Nunc Dimittis on Sundays and Feasts.

The Gloria Patri (*Glory Be...*)

The raised dots in the text below indicate the third syllable before the final accent. Since some of the canticle tones (e.g. II, IV, VIII) begin their inflection at this point, the raised dot facilitates chanting.

Glory be to the ·Fáther and tó the Son * ·and tó the Hóly Ghost.
As it was in the beginning, is now, ·and éver shall be, * ·wórld without énd. Amen.

Psalm Tones in Modern Musical Notation [73]

Glory be to the / Fáther and tó the Son * - and / tó the Hóly Ghost.
As it was in the beginning, is now, and / éver shall be, * - wórld / without énd. Amen.

Glory be to the Fáther and / tó the Son * and tó the / Hóly Ghost.
As it was in the beginning, is now, and éver / shall be, * world without / énd. Amen.

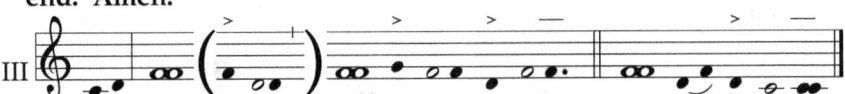

Glory be to the / Fáther and tó the Son * and tó / the Hóly Ghost.
As it was in the beginning, is now, and / éver shall be, * wórld with- / out énd. Amen.

Glory be to the Fá-/ ther and tó the Son * -/ and tó the Hóly Ghost.
As it was in the beginning, is now, and / éver sháll be, * -/ wórld without
   énd. Amen.

Glory be to the Fáther and / tó the Son * and / tó the Hóly Ghost.
As it was in the beginning, is now, and éver / sháll be, * -/ wórld without
   énd. Amen.

Glory be to the / Fáther and tó the Son * - and / tó the Hóly Ghost.
As it was in the beginning, is now, and / éver sháll be, * - wórld / without
   énd. Amen.

Glory be to the / Fáther and tó the Son * and / tó the Hóly Ghost.
As it was in the beginning, is now, and / éver sháll be, * -/ wórld without
   énd. Amen.

Glory be to the Fáther and / tó the Son * and / tó the Hóly Ghost.
As it was in the beginning, is now, and éver / sháll be, * wórld / without
   énd. Amen.

[74]

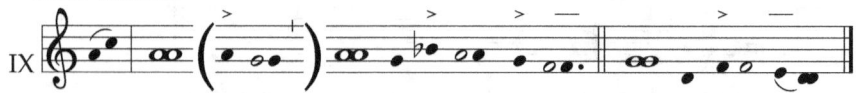

Glory be to / the Fáther and tó the Son * and tó / the Hóly Ghost.
As it was in the beginning, is now, / and éver sháll be, * wórld with-/ out
   énd. Amen.

Glory be to the Fáther and / tó the Son * and / tó the Hóly Ghost.
As it was in the beginning, is now, and éver / sháll be, * -/ wórld without
   énd. Amen.

Seasonal Psalm Tones

These tones may be used when the Brotherhood Prayer Book does not specify any tone, such as for the Benedictus in the Seasonal Propers, Saint's Day Propers, and Common of Saints. Or, the seasonal tone may be used with all the Psalms, responsories, canticles, etc. in a given season, as a way to help learn the tones. The tone arrangement suggested here is not ancient, but rather comes from the Evangelisch-Lutherisches Kirchengesangbuch, *the hymnal of the Independent Evangelical Lutheran Church of Germany. This book, in turn, is dependent on the 20th-century* Evangelisches Kirchengesangbuch. *Notice that only tones I, IV, V, and VIII are used.*

Season	Tone
Advent	IV
Christmas	V
Epiphany	V
Sundays after Epiphany	VIII
Pre-Lent	VIII
Lent	IV
Easter	V
Pentecost	V
Trinity	V
Trinity 1-15	I
Trinity 16-end	VIII
Day of Prayer and Repentance	IV
Martyrs and Apostles	VIII
Feasts of Mary	I
Feasts of John the Baptist	I
Feasts of Angels	V
Commemorations of the Reformation	VIII
All Saints	VIII
Thanksgiving and Harvest Festival	VIII
Dedication of a Church	VIII
Votive Divine Services	IV
Ordination	VIII

Responsories *are pointed with accents and may be sung to one of the Psalm-tones or Canticle-tones. The cantor intones the Responsory up to the midway point of the ℟. verse (marked with the symbol ‡). After the symbol ‡, the schola (a favorit choir from Choir I) may sing with him the rest of the ℟. verse. The ℟. verse is then repeated by all (Choir I & II) . The cantor (and schola) then sing the ℣. verse, after which all respond by singing the last half of the ℟. verse. The cantor (and schola) then sing the first half of the Gloria Patri:* **Glory be to the Father and to the Son : and to the Holy Ghost.** *The rest of the Gloria Patri is not sung. Finally, the entire ℟. verse is repeated by all.*

Hymns *proper to certain feasts or seasons of the church year are given. Other appropriate hymns may be substituted. The cantor intones the first phrase of the first stanza of the hymn. All join him thereafter. Hymns may also be sung responsively between Choir I and Choir II stanza by stanza, with both Choirs singing the doxological stanza.*

1st and 2nd Vespers: *For some Sundays and feasts, two sets of propers are given, one for Vespers of the eve of the Sunday or feast (1st Vespers) and one for Vespers on the day of the Sunday or feast (2nd Vespers). If only one set of propers is given, it may be used at both 1st and 2nd Vespers.*

Readings: *For Sundays and feasts, the Gospel and Epistle readings are listed. These are read as the (final) reading at Morning Prayer and Evening Prayer respectively. All readings may be chanted according to the following formulas. (The symbols |, /, ¿, and accent marks may be used to point texts for chanting.)*

Lection Tones At Morning Prayer and Evening Prayer

This is the Fléxa | And this is the Métrum /   And this is the Púnctum.

¿Can one ask a Quéstion?   The Correptum is stressed at the <u>end</u>.

L: But Thou, O Lord, have mercy upon us.   *A:* Thanks be to Thee, O Lord!

At Midday Prayer and Compline

This is the Fléx- a: And this is the Métrum /   And this is the Púnctum.

¿Can one ask a Quéstion?   The Correptum is stressed at the <u>end</u>.

L: But Thou, O Lord, have mercy upon us.   *A:* Thanks be to Thee, O Lord!

[76] COLLECTS

The Collect of the Day (that is, the Collect proper to today's feast day or the previous Sunday) is used as the first Collect at each office. Collects are pointed with a grave accent (`). Using the Collect for Christmas Day as a model, the manner of chanting Collects is given below. Note the two kinds of cadence: Metrum and Flexa. The Metrum is indicated by the grave accent followed by a colon. The Flexa is indicated by the grave accent followed by any other punctuation.

Metrum

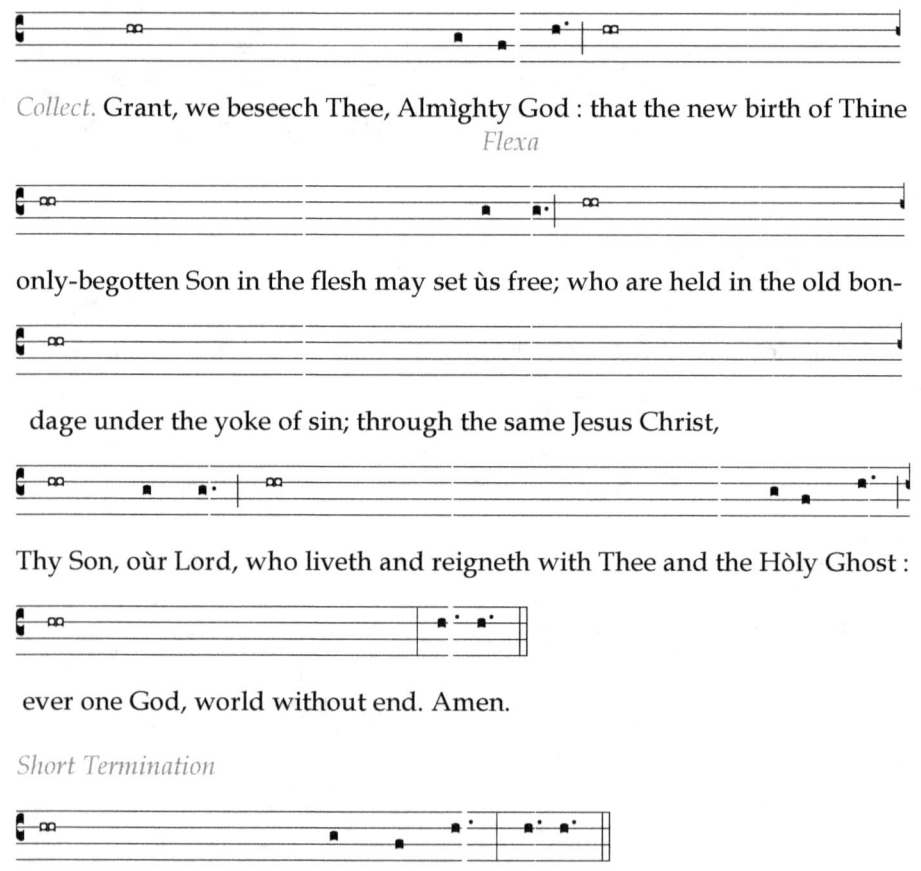

Collect. **Grant, we beseech Thee, Almìghty God : that the new birth of Thine**

Flexa

only-begotten Son in the flesh may set ùs free; who are held in the old bon-

dage under the yoke of sin; through the same Jesus Christ,

Thy Son, oùr Lord, who liveth and reigneth with Thee and the Hòly Ghost :

ever one God, world without end. Amen.

Short Termination

through the same Jesus Christ, our Lord. Amen.

Benedicamus

The following settings of the Benedicamus may be used ad libitum. *See also p. 450.*

High Feasts not in Eastertide.

A   *Lucas Lossius*

℣. Bless   we the Lord.
℟. Thanks be to God.

Feasts not in Eastertide.

B   *Lucas Lossius*

℣. Bless   we   the Lord.
℟. Thanks be   to God.

Sundays.

C   *Lucas Lossius*

℣. Bless   we the Lord.
℟. Thanks be to God.

Another for Sundays.

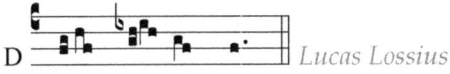
D   *Lucas Lossius*

℣. Bless   we the Lord.
℟. Thanks be to God.

The Psalmody

PRONUNCIATION: *Pronounce the ending "-ed" as a separate syllable only when it is separated by a hyphen (e.g.* **bless-ed**). *Unvoiced letters are printed in italics (e.g. "*continu*a*lly*" *is pronounced "con-tin-yul-ly.") Sometimes a letter has been marked as silent in order to facilitate pronunciation. The word* **saith** *is pronounced as one syllable: "seth." The word* **shew** *is pronounced just like its modern equivalent: "show."*

The Gloria Patri is sung after every Psalm and canticle, unless otherwise marked:
Glory be to the Fáther and tó the Son * and tó the Hóly Ghost.
As it was in the beginning, is now, and éver shálll be, * wórld without énd. Amen.

An alternate Gloria Patri:
Glory be to the Fáther and tó the Son * and to the Hóly Spírit.
As it was in thé begínning * is now and will be foréver. Ámen.

ALLELUIA ANTIPHONS FOR EACH OF THE PSALM TONES
These antiphons may be used for Psalmody on Sunday at Morning Prayer and Midday Prayer. They may also be used as the antiphons for all Psalmody during Eastertide.

TONE I

Ant.1 Al-le— lu-ia, * al-le-lu-ia.

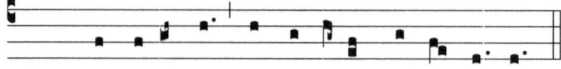

Ant.2 Al- le-lu- ia, * al- le-lu-ia, al- le- lu- ia.

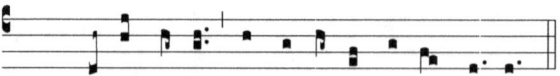

Ant.3 Al- le-lu- ia, * al- le-lu-ia, al- le- lu- ia.

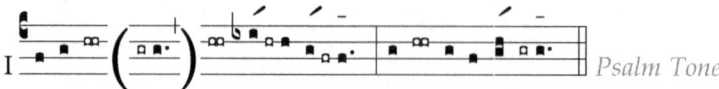

TONE II

Ant.4 Al- le-lu- ia, * al- le-lu-ia.

Ant.5 Al- le-lu- ia, * al- le-lu-ia,   al- le-lu-ia, al- le-lu-ia.

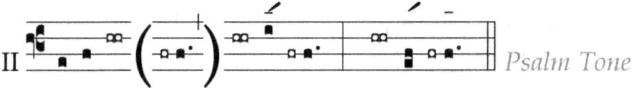

II *Psalm Tone*

TONE III

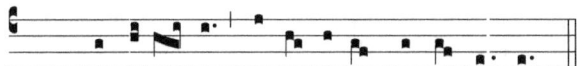

Ant.6 Al- le-lu- ia, * al- le- lu-ia,   al- le- lu- ia.

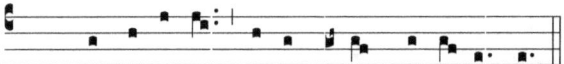

Ant.7 Al- le-lu- ia, * al- le- lu-ia,   al- le- lu- ia.

III *Psalm Tone*

TONE IV

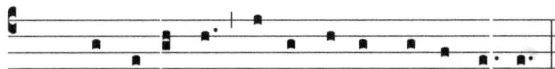

Ant.8 Al- le-lu- ia, * al- le- lu-ia,   al- le- lu- ia.

Ant.9 Al- le-lu- ia, * al- le- lu-ia,   al- le- lu- ia, al- le- lu- ia.

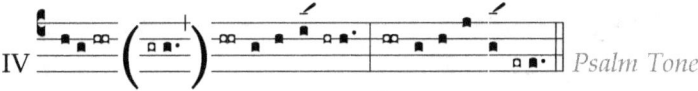

IV *Psalm Tone*

[78]

TONE V

Ant.10 Al- le-lu- ia, * al- le- lu-ia, al- le- lu- ia, al- le- lu- ia.

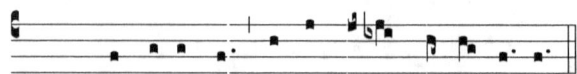

Ant.11 Al- le-lu- ia, * al- le- lu-ia, al- le- lu- ia.

TONE VI

Ant.12 Al- le-lu- ia, * al- le- lu-ia, al- le- lu- ia.

Ant.13 Al- le-lu- ia, * al- le- lu- ia,   al- le- lu- ia, al- le- lu- ia.

TONE VII

Ant.14 Al-le-lu-ia, * al-le-lu-ia, al- le- lu- ia.

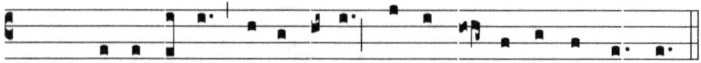

Ant.15 Al-le-lu-ia, * al-le-lu-ia, al- le- lu- ia, al- le- lu- ia.

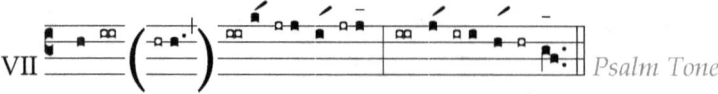

TONE VIII

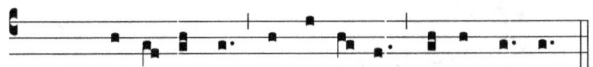

Ant.16 Al- le- lu- ia, * al- le- lu-ia,   al- le- lu- ia.

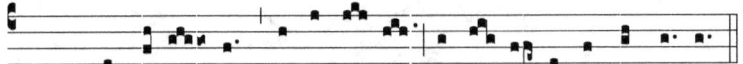

Ant.17 Al- le-lu- ia, * al- le- lu- ia,   al- le- lu- ia, al- le- lu- ia.

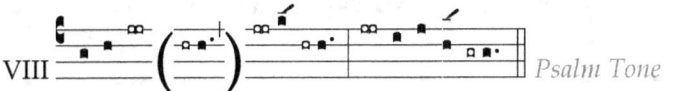

VIII   *Psalm Tone*

TONE IX *(Peregrinus)*

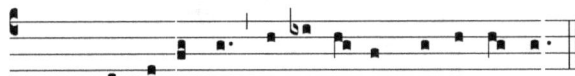

Ant.18 Al- le-lu- ia, * al- le- lu-ia,   al- le- lu- ia.

IX   *Psalm Tone*

TONUS IRREGULARIS

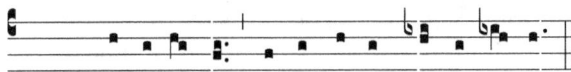

Ant.19 Al- le-lu- ia, * al- le- lu-ia,   al- le- lu- ia.

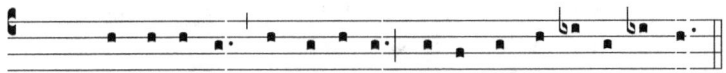

Ant.20 Al- le-lu- ia, * al- le- lu-ia,   al- le- lu- ia, al- le- lu- ia.

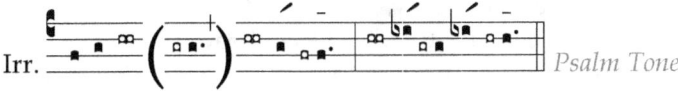

Irr.   *Psalm Tone*

CANTICLES

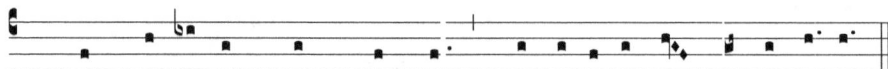

Ant. The Lórd is my stréngth and song: * and he is become mý salvátion.

Irr.

Exodus 15:1-18 *Cantemus Domino*

I will sing unto the LORD, for he hath tríumphed / glóri*ous*ly: * the horse and his rider hath he thrown / ínto the <u>sea</u>.

The LÓRD is my / stréngth and song, * and he is become / mý salvátion:

He is my God, and I will prepare him an hábi- / tátion; * my father's God, and / Í will exált him.

The LÓRD is a / mán of war: * the / LÓRD is his <u>name</u>.

Pharaoh's chariots and his host hath he cast ínto / the <u>sea</u>: * his chosen captains also are / drówned in the Réd sea.

The dépths have / cóvered them: * they sank into the / bóttom ás a stone.

Thy right hand, O LORD, is become glóri*ous* in / pówer: * thy right hand, O LORD, hath dashed in / píeces the énemy.

And in the greatness of thine excellency thou hast overthrown them that rose úp a- / gáinst thee: * thou sentest forth thy wrath, which con- / súmed them as stúbble.

And with the blast of thy nostrils the waters were gathered together, † the floods stood úpright / ás an heap, * and the depths were congealed in the / héart of the <u>sea</u>.

The enemy said, I will pursue, I will overtake, Í will di- / víde the spoil; * my lust shall be satis- / fíed upón them;

Í will / dráw my sword, * my / hánd shall destróy them.

Thou didst blow with thy wínd, the sea / cóvered them: * they sank as lead in the / míghty wáters.

Who is like unto thee, O LÓRD, a- / móng the gods? * who is like thee, glorious in holiness, fearful in praises, / dóing wónders?

Thou stretch-edst óut thy / ríght hand, * - / the earth swállowed them.

Thou in thy mercy hast led forth the people which thóu hast / re<u>deem</u>ed: * thou hast guided them in thy strength unto thy holy / hábitátion.

The people shall héar, and / bé afraid: * sorrow shall take hold on the inhabitants of / Pálestína.

Then the dukes of Edom shall bê amazed; † the mighty men of Moab, trembling shall take hóld up- / ón them; * all the inhabitants of / Cánaan shall mélt away.

Fear and dread shall fáll up- / ón them; * by the greatness of thine arm they shall be as / stíll as a <u>stone</u>;

Till thy people pass óver, / O <u>LORD</u>, * till the people pass over, which / thóu hast púrchased.

Thou shalt bring them in, and plant them in the mountain of thíne in- / héritance, * in the place, O LORD, which thou hast made for / thée to dwéll in,

In the Sanctuary, O Lord, which thy hánds have es- / táblished. * The LORD shall reign for / éver and éver. [82]

Glory be to the Fáther and / tó the Son * and / tó the Hóly Ghost.

As it was in the beginning, is now, and éver / sháll be, * - / wórld without énd. Amen.

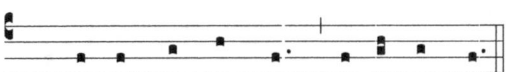

Ant. Ascríbe ye gréatness: * únto our <u>God</u>.

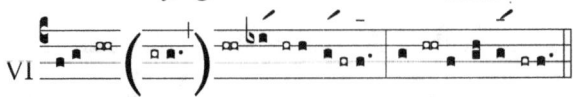

Deuteronomy 32:1-18 *Audite caeli*

Give ear, O ye / héavens, and Í will speak; * and hear, O earth, the wórds / of my <u>mouth</u>.

My doctrine shall / dróp as the <u>rain</u>, * my speech shall distíl / as the <u>dew</u>,

As the small rain up- / ón the ténder herb, * and as the shów- / ers upón the grass:

Because I will publish the / náme of the <u>LORD</u>: * ascribe ye greatness ún- / to our <u>God</u>.

He is the Rock, his / wórk is pérfect: * for all his / wáys are júdgment:

A God of truth and with- / óut iníquity, * - / júst and ríght is he.

They have corrupted themselves, † their spot is not the / spót of his chíldren: * they are a perverse and crooked / géneratión.

Do ye thus requite the LORD, O foolish people and unwise? † is not he thy father / thát hath bóught thee? * hath he not made thee, / ánd estáblished thee?

Re- / mémber the dáys of old, * consider the years of many / generatións:

Ask thy father, and / hé will shéw thee; * thy elders, and / théy will téll thee.

When the most High divided to the nations their inhéritance, † when he separated the / sóns of Ádam, * he set the bounds of the people according to the number of the chíl- / dren of Ísrael.

For the LORD'S portion / ís his péople; * Jacob is the lot of / hís inhéritance.

He found him / ín a désert land, * and in the waste / hówling wílderness;

He led him about, / hé instrúcted him, * he kept him as the / ápple óf his eye.

As an eagle stirreth up her nest, fluttereth over her young, / spréadeth abróad her wings, * taketh them, béar- / eth them ón her wings:

So the LORD a- / lóne did léad him, * and there was / nó strange gód with him.

He made him ride on the high / pláces óf the earth, * that he might eat the / íncrease óf the fields;

And he made him to suck honey / óut of the <u>rock</u>, * and oil óut / of the flínty rock;

Butter of kine, and milk of sheep, with fât of lambs, † and rams of the breed of Bashan, and goats, with the fat of / kídneys of <u>wheat</u>; * and thou didst drink the pure blóod / of the <u>grape</u>.

But Jeshu- / rún waxed fát, and kicked: * thou art waxen fat, thou art grown thick, thou art có- / vered with fátness;

Then he forsook / Gód which máde him, * and lightly esteemed the Rock of / hís salvátion.

They provoked him to jealou- / sý with stránge gods, * with abominations provoked they / hím to ánger.

They sacrificed unto / dévils, nót to God; * to gods / whóm they knéw not,

To new gods / thát came néwly up, * whom your / fáthers féared not.

Of the Rock that begat thee thou / árt unmíndful, * and hast forgotten / Gód that fórmed thee.

[83] **Glory be to the / Fáther and tó the Son * - and / tó the Hóly Ghost.**

As it was in the beginning, is now, and / éver shíll be, * - wórld / without énd. Amen.

120

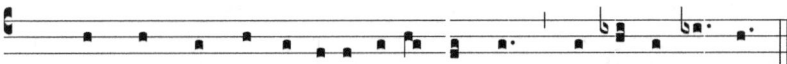

Ant. The Lord will be merciful únto his land: * ánd to his péople.

Irr.

Deuteronomy 32:19-43 *Vidit Dominus*

And when the LORD saw it, hé ab- / hórred them, * because of the provoking of his sons, and / óf his dáughters.

And he said, I will hide my fâce from them, † I will see whát their / énd shall be: * for they are a very froward generation, children in / whóm is no faith.

They have moved me to jealousy with thát which / ís not God; * they have provoked me to anger / wíth their vánities:

And I will move them to jealousy with those which are nót a / péople; * I will provoke them to anger with a / fóolish nátion.

For a fire is kindled ín mine / ánger, * and shall burn / únto the lówest hell,

And shall consume the éarth with her / íncrease, * and set on fire the foundations / óf the móuntains.

I will heap míschiefs up- / ón them; * I will spend mine / árrows upón them.

They shall be burnt with hunger, † and devóured with / búrning heat, * and with / bítter destrúction:

I will also send the teeth of béasts up- / ón them, * with the poison of / sérpents óf the dust.

The sword without, and terror within, † shall destroy both the young man ánd the / vírgin, * the suckling also with the / mán of gray hairs.

I said, I would scatter them ínto / córners, * I would make the remembrance of them to / céase from amóng men:

Were it not that I feared the wráth of the / énemy, * lest their adversaries should be- / háve themselves strángely,

And lest they should sáy, Our / hánd is high, * and the / LÓRD hath not dóne all this.

For they are a nation vóid of / cóunsel, * neither is there any under- / stánding ín them.

O that they were wise, that they únder- / stóod this, * that they would con- / síder their látter end!

How should one cháse a / thóusand, * and two put ten / thóusand to flight,

Except their Róck had / sóld them, * and the / LÓRD had shút them up?

For their rock is nót as / óur Rock, * even our enemies themselves / béing júdges.

For their vine is of the víne of / Sódom, * and of the fields / óf Gomórrah:

Their grápes are / grápes of gall, * their / clústers are bítter:
Their wine is the póison of / drágons, * and the cruel / vénom of <u>asps</u>.

[84] Is not this laid úp in / stóre with me, * and sealed up a- / móng my tréasures?

To me belongeth véngeance, and / récompence; * their foot shall / slíde in due <u>time</u>:

For the day of their calámity / ís at hand, * and the things that shall come up- / ón them make <u>haste</u>.

For the LORD shall júdge his / péople, * and repent himself / fór his sérvants,

When he seeth that their pówer / is <u>gone</u>, * and there is / nóne shut úp, or left.

And he shall say, Whére are / their <u>gods</u>, * their rock in / whóm they trústed,

Which did eat the fat of their sácri- / fíces, * and drank the wine of / théir drink ófferings?

Let them rise úp and / hélp you, * and be / yóur protéction.

See now that I, éven / Í, am he, * and there / ís no gód with me:

I kill, and I make alive; I wóund, and / I <u>heal</u>: * neither is there any that can deliver / óut of my <u>hand</u>.

For I lift up my hánd to / héaven, * and say, I / líve for éver.

If I whet my glítter- / ing <u>sword</u>, * and mine hand take / hóld on júdgment;

I will render vengeance tó mine / énemies, * and will reward / thém that háte me.

I will make mine árrows / drúnk with blood, * and my sword / sháll devóur flesh;

And that with the blood of the slain and óf the / cáptives, * from the beginning of revenges up- / ón the énemy.

Rejoice, O ye nations, wíth his / péople: * for he will avenge the / blóod of his sérvants,

And will render vengeance to his ádver- / sáries, * and will be merciful unto his land, / ánd to his péople.

Glory be to the Fáther and / tó the Son * and / tó the Hóly Ghost.

As it was in the beginning, is now, and éver / sháll be, * - / wórld without énd. Amen.

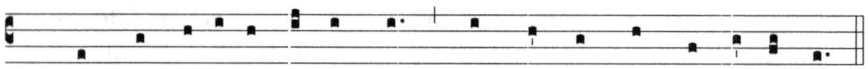

Ant. My heart rejóiceth ín the Lord: * who bringeth lów, and lífteth up.

1 Samuel 2:1-10 *Exultavit cor meum*
My heart re- / jóiceth ín the LORD, * mine horn is ex- / álted ín the LORD:
My mouth is enlarged / óver mine énemies; * because I rejoice in / thý salvátion.
There is none holy as the LORD: † for there is / nóne besíde thee: * neither is there any / róck like óur God.
Talk no more so ex- / céeding próudly; * let not arrogancy come / óut of your <u>mouth</u>:
For the LORD is a / Gód of knówledge, * and by him / áctions are <u>weighed</u>.
The bows of the mighty / mén are bróken, * and they that stumbled are / gírded with <u>strength</u>.
They that were full have hired / óut themsélves for bread; * and / théy that were húngry ceased:
So that the barren / háth born séven; * and she that hath many children / ís waxed féeble.
The LORD killeth, and / máketh a<u>live</u>: * he bringeth down to the / gráve, and bríngeth up.
The LORD maketh / póor, and máketh rich: * he bringeth / lów, and lífteth up.
He raiseth up the poor / óut of the <u>dust</u>, * and lifteth up the beggar / fróm the dúnghill,
To set / thém among prínces, * and to make them inherit the / thróne of glóry:
For the pillars of the / éarth are the <u>LORD'S</u>, * and he hath set the / wórld upón them.
He will keep the feet of his saints, † and the wicked shall be / sílent in dárkness; * for by strength shall / nó man pre<u>vail</u>.
The adversaries of the LORD shall be / bróken to píeces; * out of heaven shall he / thúnder upón them:
The LORD shall judge the ends of the earth; † and he shall give strength / únto his <u>king</u>, * and exalt the horn of / hís anóinted.
Glory be to the / Fáther and tó the Son * and / tó the Hóly Ghost.
As it was in the beginning, is now, and / éver sháll be, * - / wórld without énd. Amen.

[85]

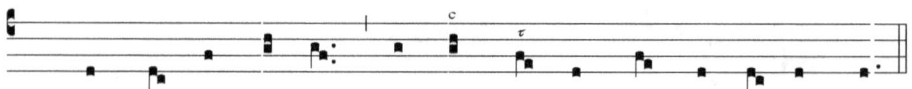

Ant. Now thérefore, our <u>God</u>: * we thank thee and práise thy glór*i*ous name.

1 Chronicles 29:10-13 *Benedictus es, Domine Deus Israel*
Bless-ed be thou, LORD God of Isra- / él our fáther, * for év- / er and éver.

Thine, O LORD, is the greatness, and the power, and the glory, and the victory, / ánd the májesty: * for all that is in the heaven and / ín the éarth is thine;

Thine is the / kíngdom, O <u>LORD</u>, * and thou art exalted as / héad above <u>all</u>.

Both riches and / hónour cóme of thee, * and thou / réignest óver all;

And in thine hand is / pówer and <u>might</u>; * and in thine hand it is to make great, and to give / stréngth unto <u>all</u>.

Now therefore, our / Gód, we thánk thee, * - and / práise thy glórious name.

Glory be to the / Fáther and tó the Son * - and / tó the Hóly Ghost.

As it was in the beginning, is now, and / éver sháll be, * - wórld / without énd. Amen.

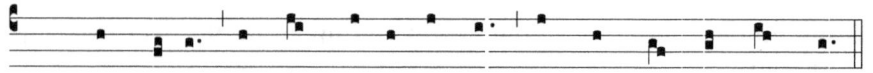

Ant. Thine anger * is túrned awáy, O Lord: and thou cóm-for-teds*t* <u>me</u>.

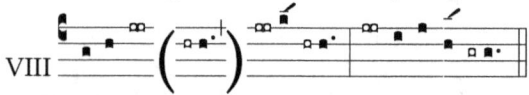

Isaiah 12:1-6 *Confitebor tibi*
O LORD, I will praise thee: † though thou wast angry with me, thine ánger is / túrned away, * and thou cóm- / fort-edst <u>me</u>.

Behold, God is mý salv- / átion; * I will trust, and nót / be a<u>fraid</u>:

For the LORD JEHOVAH is my stréngth and my / <u>song</u>; * he also is become / mý salvátion.

[86] Therefore with joy shall ye draw water out of the wélls of salv- / átion. * And in that dáy / shall ye <u>say</u>,

Praise the LORD, call upôn his name, † declare his doings amóng the / péople, * make mention that his náme / is exálted.

Sing unto the LORD; for he hath done éxcellent / <u>things</u>: * this is / knówn in áll the earth.

Cry out and shout, thou inhabitánt of / Zíon: * for great is the Holy One of

Israel / ín the mídst of thee.
Glory be to the Fáther and / tó the Son * and / tó the Hóly Ghost.
As it was in the beginning, is now, and éver / sháll be, * wórld / without énd. Amen.

Ant. Thou wilt recóver mé, O Lord: * and máke me to <u>live</u>.

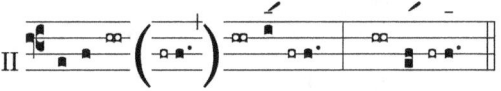

Isaiah 38:10-20 *Quaesivi residuum*

I said in the cutting off of my days, † I shall go to the gátes of the / <u>grave</u>: * I am deprived of the résidue / óf my years.

I said, I shall not see the LORD, even the LORD, in the lánd of the / líving: * I shall behold man no more with the inhábitants / óf the world.

Mine age is departed, and is removed from me ás a / shépherd's tent: * I have cut off like a wéaver / my <u>life</u>:

He will cut me off with píning / síckness: * from day even to night wilt thou máke an / énd of me.

I reckoned till morning, that, as a lion, so will he bréak all my / <u>bones</u>: * from day even to night wilt thou máke an / énd of me.

Like a crane or a swallow, so díd I / chátter: * I did móurn as / a <u>dove</u>:

Mine eyes fail with lóoking / úpward: * O LORD, I am oppressed; únder- / táke for me.

What shall I say? he hath both spoken unto me, and himsélf hath / dóne it: * I shall go softly all my years in the bítterness / óf my soul.

O Lord, bý these things / mén live, * and in all these things is the lífe of my / spírit:

So wilt thóu re- / cóver me, * and máke me / to <u>live</u>.

Behold, for peace I had great bîtterness: † but thou hast in love to my soul delivered it from the pít of cor- / rúption: * for thou hast cast all my síns be- / hínd thy back.

For the grave cannot praise thee, death can not célebrate / <u>thee</u>: * they that go down into the pit cannot hópe for / thy <u>truth</u>.

The living, the living, he shall praise thee, ás I / dó this day: * the father to the children sháll make / knówn thy truth.

The LORD was ready to save me: † therefore we will sing my songs tó the stringed / ínstruments * all the days of our life in the hóuse of / the <u>LORD</u>.

Glory be to the Fáther and / tó the Son * and tó the / Hóly Ghost.

[87] As it was in the beginning, is now, and éver / sháll be, * wórld without / énd. Amen.

Ant. In the LORD * shall all the seed of Is-ra-él be júst-i-fied: ánd shall gló-ry.

Isaiah 45:15-25 *Vere tu es Deus*

Verily thou art a God that / hídest thyself, * O God of Isra- / él, the Sáviour.
They shall be ashamed, and also con- / fóunded, áll of them: * they shall go to confusion together that are má- / kers of ídols.
But Israel shall be saved in the LORD with an ever- / lásting salvátion: * ye shall not be ashamed nor confounded / wórld without end.
For thus saith the LORD that cre- / áted the héavens; * God himself that formed the / éarth and máde it;
He hath established it, he created it nôt in vain, † he formed it to / bé inhábited: * I am the LÓRD; / and there ís none else.
I have not spoken in secret, in a dark / pláce of the earth: * I said not unto the seed of Jacob, / Séek ye mé in vain:
I the / LÓRD speak ríghteousness, * I declare / thíngs that are right.
As- / sémble yoursélves and come; * draw near together, ye that are escáped / of the nátions:
They have no knowledge that set up the wood of their / gráven ímage, * and pray unto a / gód that cánnot save.
- / Téll ye, and bríng them near; * yea, let them take cóun- / sel togéther:
Who hath de- / cláred this from áncient time? * who hath tóld / it from thát time?
Have not Î the LORD? † and there is no God / élse besíde me; * a just God and a Saviour; there is / nóne besíde me.
Look unto me, and be ye saved, all the / énds of the earth: * for I am Gód, / and there ís none else.
I have / swórn by myself, * the word is gone out of my mouth in righteousness, / ánd shall nót return,
That unto me / évery knée shall bow, * - / évery tóngue shall swear.
Surely, shall one say, in the LORD have I righteousness and strength: † even to / hím shall men come; * and all that are incensed against / hím shall bé ashamed.
In the LORD shall all the seed of Isra- / él be jústified, * - / ánd shall glóry.

Glory be to the / Fáther and tó the Son * - and / tó the Hóly Ghost.
As it was in the beginning, is now, and / éver shálle be, * - wórld / without énd. Amen.

[88]

Ant. My people shálle be sátisfied: * with my góodness, sáith the Lord.

IV

Jeremiah 31:10-14 *Audite verbum Domini*
Hear the word of the LORD, / Ó ye nátions, * and declare it in the / ísles afar óff, and say,
He that scattered Isra- / él will gáther him, * and keep him, as / a shépherd dóth his flock.
For the LORD háth / redeemed Jácob, * and ransomed him from the hand of him that was / strónger than he.
Therefore they shall come and sing in the / héight of Zíon, * and shall flow together to / the góodness óf the LORD,
For wheat, and for wíne, / and for óil-, * and for the young of / the flóck and óf the herd:
And their soul shall be as a / wátered gárden; * and they shall not sor- / row ány móre at all.
Then shall the virgin rejóice / in the dance, * both young men / and óld togéther:
For I will turn their mourning into joy, / ánd will cómfort them, * and make them re- / joice fróm their sórrow.
And I will satiate the soul of the / príests with fátness, * and my people shall be satisfied with / my góodness, sáith the LORD.
Glory be to the Fá- / ther and tó the Son * - / and tó the Hóly Ghost.
As it was in the beginning, is now, and / éver shálle be, * - / wórld without énd. Amen.

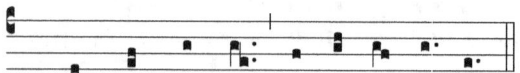

Ant. In wráth, O Lord: remémber mércy.

IV

Habakkuk 3:2-11 *Domine audivi*

O LORD, I have heard thy / spéech, and wás afraid: * O LORD, revive thy work in the / mídst of the <u>years</u>,

In the mídst / of the yéars make known; * in wrath / remémber mércy.

Gód / came from Témam, * and the Holy / One fróm mount Páran.

His glory cóv- / ered the héavens, * and the earth was / fúll of his <u>praise</u>.

And his brightness was âs the light; † he had horns coming óut / of his <u>hand</u>: * and there was the hid- / ing óf his pówer.

Before him / wént the péstilence, * and burning coals went / fórth at his <u>feet</u>.

He stood, and méa- / sured the <u>earth</u>: * he beheld, and drove a- / súnder the nátions;

And the everlasting mountains were scattered, † the per- / pétu*a*l hílls did bow: * his ways / are éverlásting.

I saw the tents of Cushan / ín afflíction: * and the curtains of the land of Mi- / di-án did trémble.

Was the LORD displeased a- / gáinst the rívers? * was thine anger / agáinst the rívers?

Was thy / wráth agáinst the sea, * that thou didst ride upon thine horses and thy char- / *i*ots óf salvátion?

Thy bow was / máde quite náked, * according to the oaths of the tribes, / éven thy <u>word</u>.

Thou didst cleave the / éarth with rívers. * The mountains saw / thee, ánd they trémbled:

The overflowing of the / wáter pássed by: * the deep uttered his voice, and lift- / ed úp his hánds on high.

The sun and moon stood still in their habitation: † at the light of thine ár- / rows they <u>went</u>, * and at the shining of thy / glíttering <u>spear</u>.

Glory be to the Fá- / ther and tó the Son * - / and tó the Hóly Ghost.

As it was in the beginning, is now, and / éver sháll be, * - / wórld without énd. Amen.

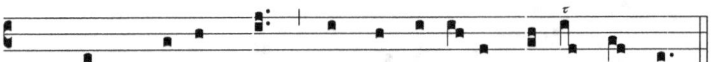

Ant. Thou wéntest forth: * for the salvation óf thy péople.

Habakkuk 3:12-19 *In fremitu*

Thou didst march through the land in / índignátion, * thou didst thresh the / héathen in ánger.

Thou wentest forth for the salvation / óf thy péople, * even for salvation with / thíne anóinted;

Thou wound-edst the head out of the / hóuse of the wícked, * by discovering the foundation / únto the neck.

Thou didst strike through with his staves the head of his vîllages: † they came out as a / whírlwind to scátter me: * their rejoicing was as to de- / vóur the poor sécretly.

Thou didst walk through the / séa with thine hórses, * through the / héap of great wáters.

When I heard, my / bélly trémbled; * my lips / quívered át the voice:

Rottenness entered into my bones, † and I / trémbled ín myself, * that I might rest in the / dáy of tróuble:

When he cometh up / únto the péople, * he will in- / váde them wíth his troops.

Although the fig tree / sháll not blóssom, * neither shall / frúit be ín the vines;

The labour of the / ólive shall fail, * and the / fíelds shall yíeld no meat;

The flock shall be cut / óff from the fold, * and there shall be no / hérd in the stalls:

Yet I will re- / jóice in the LORD, * I will joy in the God of / mý salvátion.

The LORD God is my strength, † and he will make my / féet like hínds' feet, * and he will make me to walk up- / ón mine high pláces.

Glory be to the / Fáther and tó the Son * and / tó the Hóly Ghost.

As it was in the beginning, is now, and / éver sháll be, * - / wórld without énd. Amen.

[90]

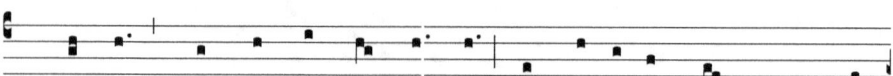

Ant. O Lord, * thou art gréat and glórious: wonderful in strength, ánd in-

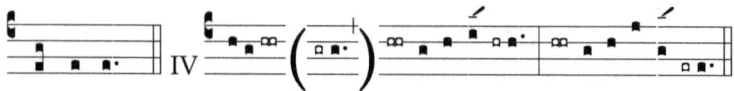

vín-ci-ble.

Judith 16:15-21 *Hymnum cantabo Domino*
I will sing unto the Lórd / a new song: * O Lord, thou art great and glorious, wonderful in / strength, ánd invíncible.
Let all / créatures sérve thee: * for thou / spákest, and théy were made,
Thou didst send forth thy spirit, and / ít creáted them, * and there is none / that cán resíst thy voice.
For the mountains shall be moved from their foundations with the waters, † the rocks shall melt as wáx / at thy présence: * yet thou art merciful / to thém that féar thee.
For all sacrifice is too little for a sweet savour ûnto thee, † and all the fat is not sufficient for / thý burnt óffering: * but he that feareth the Lord / is gréat at áll times.
Woe to the nations that rise up a- / gáinst my kíndred! * The Lord Almighty will take vengeance of them in / the dáy of júdgment,
In putting fire and wórms / in their flesh; * and they shall feel them, / and wéep for éver.
Glory be to the Fá-/ ther and tó the Son * -/ and tó the Hóly Ghost.
As it was in the beginning, is now, and / éver sháll be, * -/ wórld without énd. Amen.

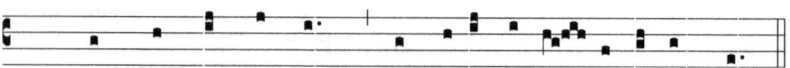

Ant. Práise the Lórd of might: * and extol the év- erlásting King.

Tobit 13:1-7 *Magnus es Domine*
Bless-ed be God that / líveth for éver, * and bless-ed / bé his kíngdom.
For he doth scourge, and hath mercy: † he leadeth down to hell, and / bríngeth úp again: * neither is there any that / cán avóid his hand.
Confess him before the Gentiles, ye / chíldren of Ísrael: * for he hath

scattered / ús amóng them.
There de- / cláre his gréatness, * and extol him before / áll the líving:
For / hé is our Lord, * and he is the God our / Fáther for éver.
And he will scourge us for / óur iníquities, * and will have / mércy again,
And will gather us / óut of all nátions, * among whom / hé hath scáttered us.
If ye turn to him with your whole heart, and / wíth your whóle mind, * and deal up- / ríghtly befóre him,
Then will / hé turn únto you, * and will not / híde his fáce from you.
Therefore see what he will dô with you, † and confess him / wíth your whóle mouth, * and praise the Lord of might, and extol the / éverlásting King.
In the land of my captivity / dó I práise him, * and declare his might and majesty to a / sínful nátion. [91]
O ye sinners, turn and do / jústice befóre him: * who can tell if he will accept you, and have / mércy ón you?
I will extôl my God,† and my soul shall praise the / Kíng of héaven, * and shall re- / jóice in his gréatness.
Glory be to the / Fáther and tó the Son * and / tó the Hóly Ghost.
As it was in the beginning, is now, and / éver sháll be, * - / wórld without énd. Amen.

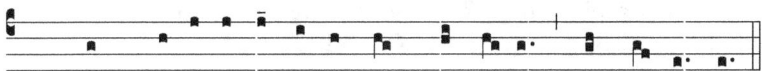

Ant. Have mercy upon us, Ó Lord Gód of all: * ánd behóld us.
(Do not repeat in verse 1.)

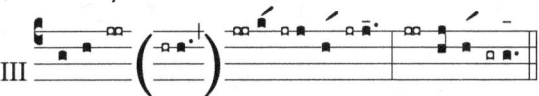

Sirach 36:1-16 *Miserere nostri Deus*
[Have mercy upon us, O Lord God of all, / ánd behóld us:] * and send thy fear upon all the nations that séek / not áfter thee.
Lift up thy hand a- / gáinst the strange nátions, * and let them sée / thy pówer.
As thou wast sanctified in / ús befóre them: * so be thou magnified among thém / befóre us.
And let them know thee, as / wé have knówn Thee, * that there is no God but ón- / ly thóu, O God.
Shew new signs, and make / óther strange wónders: * glorify thy hand and thy right arm, that they may set fórth / thy wóndrous works.

Raise up indig- / nátion, and póur out wrath: * take away the adversary, and destróy / the énemy.
Make the time short, re- / mémber the cóvenant, * and let them declare thy / wónderful works.
Let him that escapeth be consumed by the / ráge of the fíre-; * and let them perish that oppréss / the péople.
Smite in sunder the heads of the rulers of the / héathen, that say, * There is none / óther but we.
Gather all the tribes of / Jácob togéther, * and inherit thou them, as fróm the / begínning.
O Lord, have mercy upon the people that is / cálled by thy name, * and upon Israel, whom thou hast námed / thy fírstborn.
O be merciful / únto Jerúsalem, * thy holy city, the / pláce of thy rest.
Fill Sion with thine un- / spéakable óracles, * and thy people wíth / thy glóry.
Give testimony unto those that thou hast possessed / fróm the begínning, * and raise up prophets that have / béen in thy name.
Reward / thém that wáit for thee, * and let thy prophets bé / found fáithful.
O Lord, hear the prayer / óf thy sérvants, * according to the blessing of Aaron óver / thy péople,
That all they which dwell up- / ón the éarth may know * that thou art the Lórd, the / etérnal God.
Glory be to the / Fáther and tó the Son * and tó / the Hóly Ghost.
As it was in the beginning, is now, and / éver sháll be, * wórld with- / out énd. Amen.

Ant. The three children stood up * in the mídst of the fíre-: and opening

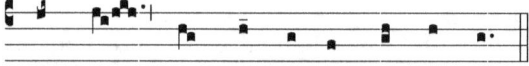

their mouth said, Bléssed art thóu, O Lord.

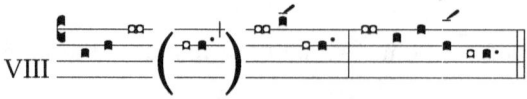

VIII

Daniel 3:29-34, 67 *Benedictus es, Domine*
Bless-ed art thou, O Lord Gód of our / fáthers: * and to be praised and exalted above / áll for éver.
And bless-ed is thy glórious and / hóly name: * and to be praised and

exalted above / áll for éver.

Bless-ed art thou in the temple of thine hóly / glóry: * and to be praised and exalted above / áll for éver.

Bless-ed art thou that beholdest the depths, † and sittest upón the / chérubim: * and to be praised and exalted above / áll for éver.

Bless-ed art thou on the glorious thróne of Thy / kíngdom: * and to be praised and exalted above / áll for éver.

Bless-ed art thou in the firmamént of / héaven: * and above all to be praised and glori- / fíed for éver.

O give thanks unto the Lord, because hé is / grácious: * for his mercy endúr- / eth for éver.

Glory be to the Fáther and / tó the Son * and / tó the Hóly Ghost.

As it was in the beginning, is now, and éver / sháll be, * wórld / without énd. Amen.

Ant. The three children at the king's command * were cast in-to the furnace,

fearing not the fláme of fíre-: but saying, Bléss-ed be Gód. (Ál-le-lú-ia).

[93]

Daniel 3:35-68 *Benedicite omnia opera*

O all ye works of the Lord, / bléss ye the <u>Lord</u>: * praise and exalt him above áll / for éver.

O ye heavens, / bléss ye the <u>Lord</u>: * praise and exalt him above áll / for éver.

O ye angels of the Lord, / bléss ye the <u>Lord</u>: * praise and exalt him above áll / for éver.

O all ye waters that be above the heaven, / bléss ye the <u>Lord</u>: * praise and exalt him above áll / for éver.

O all ye powers of the Lord, / bléss ye the <u>Lord</u>: * praise and exalt him above áll / for éver.

O ye sun and moon, / bléss ye the <u>Lord</u>: * praise and exalt him above áll / for éver.

O ye stars of heaven, / bléss ye the <u>Lord</u>: * praise and exalt him above áll / for éver.

O every shower and dew, / bléss ye the <u>Lord</u>: * praise and exalt him above áll / for éver.

O all ye winds, / bléss ye the Lord: * praise and exalt him above áll / for éver.

O ye fire and heat, / bléss ye the Lord: * praise and exalt him above áll / for éver.

O ye winter and summer, / bléss ye the Lord: * praise and exalt him above áll / for éver.

O ye dews and storms of snow, / bléss ye the Lord: * praise and exalt him above áll / for éver.

O ye nights and days, / bléss ye the Lord: * praise and exalt him above áll / for éver.

O ye light and darkness, / bléss ye the Lord: * praise and exalt him above áll / for éver.

O ye ice and cold, / bléss ye the Lord: * praise and exalt him above áll / for éver.

O ye frost and snow, / bléss ye the Lord: * praise and exalt him above áll / for éver.

O ye lightnings and clouds, / bléss ye the Lord: * praise and exalt him above áll / for éver.

O let the / éarth bless the Lord: * praise and exalt him above áll / for éver.

O ye mountains and little hills, / bléss ye the Lord: * praise and exalt him above áll / for éver.

O all ye things that grow on the earth, / bléss ye the Lord: * praise and exalt him above áll / for éver.

O ye fountains, / bléss ye the Lord: * praise and exalt him above áll / for éver.

O ye seas and rivers, / bléss ye the Lord: * praise and exalt him above áll / for éver.

O ye whales, and all that move in the waters, / bléss ye the Lord: * praise and exalt him above áll / for éver.

O all ye fowls of the air, / bléss ye the Lord: * praise and exalt him above áll / for éver.

O all ye beasts and cattle, / bléss ye the Lord: * praise and exalt him above áll / for éver.

O ye children of men, / bléss ye the Lord: * praise and exalt him above áll / for éver.

O Israel, / bléss ye the Lord: * praise and exalt him above áll / for éver.

O ye priests of the Lord, / bléss ye the Lord: * praise and exalt him above áll / for éver.

O ye servants of the Lord, / bléss ye the Lord: * praise and exalt him above áll / for éver.

O ye spirits and souls of the righteous, / bléss ye the Lord: * praise and exalt him above áll / for éver.

O ye holy and humble men of heart, / bléss ye the Lord: * praise and exalt him above áll / for éver.

O Ananias, Azarias, and Misael, / bléss ye the Lord: * praise and exalt him above áll / for éver.

For he hath de- / lívered ús from hell, * and saved us fróm / the hánd of death,

And delivered us out of the midst of the / fúrnace and búrning flame: * even out of the midst of the fire hath hé / delívered us. [94]

O give thanks unto the Lord because / hé is grácious: * for his mercy endúreth / for éver.

O all ye that worship the Lord, bless the God of gods, / práise him, and gíve him thanks: * for his mercy endúreth / for éver.

Let us bless the Father and the Son and the / Hóly Spírit, * let us praise and exalt him above áll / for éver.

(The Glory Be is omitted).

Athanasian Creed *Quicunque vult*

Whoéver / wíll be saved * shall, above all else, / hóld the cátholic faith.

Which faith, except everyone keeps whóle and / úndefiled, * without doubt he will / pérish etérnally.

And the catholic fâith is this, † that we worship one God in three persons and three pérsons / ín one God, * neither confusing the persons nor di- / víding the súbstance.

For there is one person óf the / Fáther, * another of the Son, and another of the / Hóly Spírit.

But the Godhead of the Father, of the Son, and of the Holy Spírit / ís all one: * the glory equal, the majesty / cóetérnal.

Such as the Father is, súch is the / Son, * and such is the / Hóly Spírit.

The Father uncreated, † the Son úncre- / áted, * and the Holy Spirit / úncreáted.

The Father incomprehênsible, † the Son incómpre- / hénsible, * and the Holy Spirit in- / cómprehénsible.

The Father eternal, † the Són e- / térnal, * and the Holy / Spírit etérnal.

And yet they are not thrée e- / térnals * but / óne etérnal.

As there are not three uncreated nor three incómpre- / hénsibles * but one uncreated and one in- / cómprehénsible.

So likewise the Father is almighty, † the Són al- / míghty, * and the Holy / Spírit almíghty.
And yet they are not thrée al- / míghties * but / óne almíghty.
So the Father is God, the Son is God, and the Holy Spírit is / <u>God</u>. * And yet they are not / thrée Gods but óne God.
So likewise the Father is Lord, the Son Lord, and the Hóly / Spírit Lord. * And yet they are not / thrée Lords but óne Lord.
For as we are compelled bý the / Chrístian truth * to acknowledge every person by himself to / bé both Gód and Lord,
So we cannot bý the / cátholic faith * say that there are three / Góds or three <u>Lords</u>.
The Fáther is / máde of none, * neither created / nór begótten.
The Son is of the Fáther a- / <u>lone</u>, * not made nor created / bút begótten.
The Holy Spirit is of the Fáther and / óf the Son, * neither made nor created nor begotten / bút procéeding.
So there is one Father, not three Fathers; † óne Son, not / thrée Sons; * one Holy Spirit, not three / Hóly Spírits.

[95] And in this Trinity none is before or áfter an- / óther; * none is greater or / léss than anóther;
But the whole three persons are coeternal together and coequal, † so that in all things, as ís a- / fóresaid, * the Unity in Trinity and the Trinity in Unity / ís to be wórshipped.
He, thérefore, that / wíll be saved * is compelled thus to / thínk of the Trínity.
Furthermore, it is necessary to everlásting sal- / vátion * that he also believe faithfully the incarnation of / óur Lord Jésus Christ.
For the right faith is that we belíeve and con- / <u>fess</u> * that our Lord Jesus Christ, the Son of / Gód, is Gód and Man;
God of the substance of the Father, begótten be- / fóre the worlds; * and man of the substance of his mother, / bórn in the <u>world</u>;
Perfect Gód and / pérfect Man, * of a reasonable soul and human / flésh subsísting.
Equal to the Father as tóuching his / Gódhead * and inferior to the Father as / tóuching his mánhood;
Who, although hé is / Gód and Man, * yet he is not / twó but óne Christ:
One, not by conversion of the Gódhead / ínto flesh * but by taking the / mánhood ínto God;
One altogether, not by confúsion of / súbstance * but by uni- / tý of pérson.
For as the reasonable soul and flésh is / óne man, * so God and / Mán is óne Christ;
Who suffered for our salvation, † descénded / ínto hell, * rose again the /

thírd day fróm the dead.
He ascended into heaven, † He sits at the right hand of the Father, Gód Al- / míghty, * from whence he will come to judge the / líving ánd the dead.
At whose coming all men will rise again wíth their / bódies * and will give an ac- / cóunt of their ówn works.
And they that have done good will go into life éver- / lásting; * and they that have done evil, into ever- / lásting fíre-.
This is the catholic faith which, except a man believe faithfullý and / fírmly, * He / cánnot be <u>saved</u>.

[96]

The Psalter

Ant. Bless-ed is the man * that doth méd-i-tate dáy and night: in the Láw of

the Lord.

Psalm 1 *Beatus vir*

1 Bless-ed is the man that walketh not in the counsel of the ungodly, † nor standeth in the / wáy of sínners, * nor sitteth in the seat / óf the scórnful.
2 But his delight is in the / láw of the LORD; * and in his law doth he méd- / itate dáy and night.
3 And he shall be like a tree planted by the / rívers of wáter, * that bringeth forth his frúit / in his séason;
His leaf also / sháll not wíther; * and whatsoever he dó- / eth shall prósper.
4 The un- / gódly are nót so: * but are like the chaff which the wind / driveth a<u>way</u>.
5 Therefore the ungodly shall not / stánd in the júdgment, * nor sinners in the congregation / óf the ríghteous.
6 For the LORD knoweth the / wáy of the ríghteous: * but the way of the ungód- / ly shall pérish.
Glory be to the / Fáther and tó the Son * - and / tó the Hóly Ghost.
As it was in the beginning, is now, and / éver sháll be, * - wórld / without énd. Amen.

138

Psalm-prayer. Make us, O Lord, like a most fruitful tree, planted in Thy garden; and vouchsafe that we, being watered by the showers of Thy grace, may bring forth to Thee plenteousness of fruit in due season; through Jesus Christ our Lord, who liveth and reigneth with Thee and the Holy Ghost, ever one God, world without end. Amen.

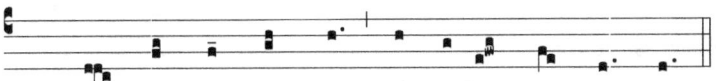

Ant. Sérve the Lórd with fear: * and rejóice with trémbling.

Psalm 2 *Quare fremuerunt*

1 — Why / dó the héathen rage, * and the people imá- / gine a váin thing?
2 The kings / óf the earth sét themselves, * and the rulers take counsel together, against the LORD, and against his a- / nóinted, sáying,
3 Let us break their / bánds asúnder, * and cast a- / wáy their córds from us.
4 He that sitteth in the / héavens shall <u>laugh</u>: * the Lord shall have them / ín derísion.
5 Then shall he speak unto / thém in his <u>wrath</u>, * and vex them in his / sóre displéasure.
6 Yet / háve I sét my king * upon my holy / híll of Zíon. [97]
7 I will declare the decree: † the LORD hath / sáid unto <u>me</u>, * Thou art my Son; this day have / Í begótten thee.
8 Ask of me, and I shall give thee the heathen for / thíne inhéritance, * and the uttermost parts of the earth for / thý posséssion.
9 Thou shalt break them with a / ród of íron; * thou shalt dash them in pieces like a / pótter's véssel.
10 Be wise now / thérefore, Ó ye kings: * be instructed, ye / júdges óf the earth.
11 — / Sérve the LÓRD with fear, * and re- / jóice with trémbling.
12 Kiss the Son, lest he be angry, † and ye perish from the way, when his wrath is kindled / bút a líttle. * Bless-ed are all they that / pút their trúst in him.
Glory be to the / Fáther and tó the Son * - and / tó the Hóly Ghost.
As it was in the beginning, is now, and / éver shálll be, * - wórld / without énd. Amen.

Psalm-prayer. Break in sunder, O Lord, we beseech Thee, the chains of our sins; that, taking upon us Thy light yoke and easy burden, we may serve

Thee, with fear and reverence, all the days of our life; through Jesus Christ our Lord, who liveth and reigneth with Thee and the Holy Ghost, ever one God, world without end. Amen.

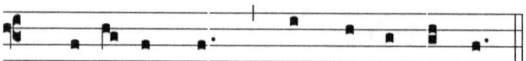

Ant. Aríse, O LORD: * sáve me, Ó my God.

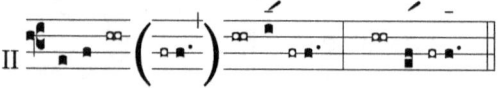

Psalm 3 *Domine, quid*
1 LORD, how are they incréased that / tróuble me! * many are they that rise úp a- / gáinst me.
2 Many there be which sáy of my / soul, * There is no hélp for / hím in God.
3 But thou, O LORD, árt a / shíeld for me; * my glory, and the lifter úp of / mine head.
4 I cried unto the LÓRD with my / voice, * and he heard me óut of his / hóly hill.
5 I láid me / dówn and slept; * I awaked; for the LÓRD sus- / táined me.
6 I will not be afraid of ten thóusands of / péople, * that have set themselves agáinst me / róund about.
7 Arise, O LORD; save me, Ô my God: † for thou hast smitten all mine enemies upón the / chéek bone; * thou hast broken the teeth óf the un- / gódly.
8 Salvation belongeth únto the / LORD: * thy blessing is upón thy / péople.
Glory be to the Fáther and / tó the Son * and tó the / Hóly Ghost.
As it was in the beginning, is now, and éver / sháll be, * wórld without / énd. Amen.

Psalm-prayer. Pour forth, O Lord, Thy blessing upon Thy people, that being fortified by Thy Resurrection, we may not be afraid of ten thousands of the adversaries that have set themselves against us round about; who livest and reignest with the Father and the Holy Ghost, ever one God, world without end. Amen.

[98]

Ant. Have mercy * upón me, O Lord: and héar my prayer.

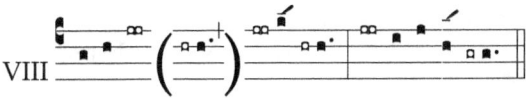

Psalm 4 *Cum invocarem*

1 Hear me when I call, O God of my rîghteousness: † thou hast enlarged me when Í was / ín distress; * have mercy upón / me, and héar my prayer.
2 O ye sons of men, how long will ye turn my glóry / ínto shame? * how long will ye love vanity, and seek / áfter léasing?
3 But know that the LORD hath set apart him that is gódly / fór himself: * the LORD will hear when / Í call únto him.
4 Stand in áwe, and / sín not: * commune with your own heart upon your béd, / and be <u>still</u>.
5 Offer the sacrifíces of / ríghteousness, * and put your trúst / in the <u>LORD</u>.
6 There be many that say, Who will shéw us / ány good? * LORD, lift thou up the light of thy counten- / ánce upón us.
7 Thou hast put gládness / ín my heart, * more than in the time that their córn / and their wíne increased.
8 I will both lay me dówn in / péace, and sleep: * for thou, LORD, only makest me / dwéll in sáfety.
Glory be to the Fáther and / tó the Son * and / tó the Hóly Ghost.
As it was in the beginning, is now, and éver / sháll be, * wórld / without énd. Amen.

Psalm-prayer. Hear us, we beseech thee, O Lord, and have mercy upon us in our tribulations; and, as Thou alone art glorious over the people, give spiritual gladness to us, who look for the hope of Thine eternal kingdom; through Jesus Christ our Lord, who liveth and reigneth with Thee and the Holy Ghost, ever one God, world without end. Amen.

Ant. Hearken unto the vóice of my <u>cry</u>: * my Kíng and my <u>God</u>.

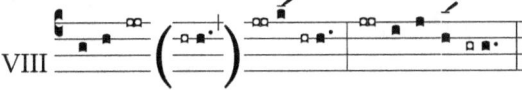

Psalm 5 *Verba mea*

1 Give éar to my / wórds, O LORD, * consider my / méditátion.
2 Hearken unto the voice of my cry, my Kíng, and my / <u>God</u>: * for unto thée / will I <u>pray</u>.
3 My voice shalt thou hear in the mórning, O / <u>LORD</u>; * in the morning will I

direct my prayer unto thée, / and will lóok up.

4 For thou art not a God that hath pléasure in / wíckedness: * neither shall / évil dwéll with thee.

[99] 5 The foolish shall not stánd in thy / <u>sight</u>: * thou hatest all workers / óf iníquity.

6 Thou shalt destroy thém that speak / léasing: * the LORD will abhor the bloody / ánd decéitful man.

7 But as for me, I will come into thy house in the multitude óf thy / mércy: * and in thy fear will I worship toward thy / hóly témple.

8 Lead me, O LORD, in thy righteousness becáuse of mine / énemies; * make thy way / stráight befóre my face.

9 For there is no fáithfulness / ín their mouth; * their inward part is / véry wíckedness;

Their throat is an ópen / sépulchre; * they / flátter wíth their tongue.

10 Destróy thou / thém, O God; * let them fall by / théir own cóunsels;

Cast them out in the multitude of théir trans- / gréssions; * for they have re- / bélled agáinst thee.

11 But let all those that put their trust in thee rejoice: † let them ever shout for joy, because thóu de- / féndest them: * let them also that love thy name be jóy- / ful in <u>thee</u>.

12 For thou, LORD, wilt bléss the / ríghteous; * with favour wilt thou compass / hím as wíth a shield.

Glory be to the Fáther and / tó the Son * and / tó the Hóly Ghost.

As it was in the beginning, is now, and éver / sháll be, * wórld / without énd. Amen.

Psalm-prayer. O merciful Lord, who understandest the groaning of the contrite heart before it is expressed; make us, we pray Thee, the temple of the Paraclete, to the end that we, trusting in Thee, may be compassed with the shield of celestial mercy; through Jesus Christ our Lord, who liveth and reigneth with Thee and the same Holy Ghost, ever one God, world without end. Amen.

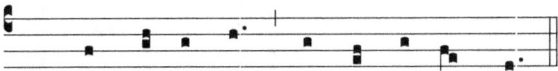

Ant. Sáve me, O Lord: * fór Thy mércy's sake.

Psalm 6 *Domine, ne in furore*

1 O LORD, rebuke me not / ín thine ánger, * neither chasten me in thy / hót displéasure.
2 Have mercy upon me, O / LÓRD; for Í am weak: * O LORD, heal me; / fór my bónes are vexed.
3 My soul is / álso sore vexed: * - but / thóu, O LÓRD, how long?
4 Return, O LORD, de- / líver my soul: * oh save me / fór thy mércies' sake.
5 For in death there is no re- / mémbrance of thee: * in the grave / whó shall gíve thee thanks?
6 I am weary with my groaning; † all the night make / Í my béd to swim; * I water my / cóuch with my tears.
7 Mine eye is con- / súmed becáuse of grief; * it waxeth old because of / áll mine énemies.
8 Depart from me, all ye workers / óf iníquity; * for the LORD hath heard the vóice / of my wéeping.
9 The LORD hath heard my / súpplicátion; * the LÓRD / will recéive my prayer.
10 Let all mine enemies be a- / shámed and sore vexed: * let them return and bé / ashamed súddenly.
Glory be to the / Fáther and tó the Son * - and / tó the Hóly Ghost.
As it was in the beginning, is now, and / éver sháll be, * - wórld / without énd. Amen.

Psalm-prayer. O Christ, Son of the Living God, whose beauty in Thy passion departed for very heaviness and was worn away because of all Thine enemies; heal the wounds of our hearts, that Thy grace being confirmed in us, we may so put our trust in Thy passion as to find our glory in Thy Resurrection; who livest and reignest with the Father and the Holy Ghost, ever one God, world without end. Amen.

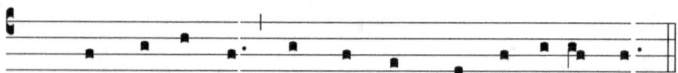

Ant. Sáve me, O <u>God</u>: from all them that pérsecute <u>me</u>.

VI

Psalm 7i *Domine, Deus meus*
1 O LORD my God, in / thée do I pút my trust: * save me from all them that persecute me, / ánd delíver me:
2 Lest he tear my soul like a lion, rending / ít in píeces, * while there is nóne / to delíver.
3 O LORD my God, if / Í have dóne this; * if there be iní- / quity ín my hands;
4 If I have rewarded evil unto him that / wás at péace with me; * (yea, I have delivered him that without cause / ís mine énemy:)
5 Let the enemy persecute my / sóul, and táke it; * yea, let him tread down my life upon the earth, and lay mine / hónour ín the dust.
6 Arise, O LORD, in thine anger, † lift up thyself because of the / ráge of mine énemies: * and awake for me to the judgment that thou / hást commánded.
7 So shall the congregation of the people / cómpass thée about: * for their sakes therefore retúrn / thou on <u>high</u>.
8 The LORD shall judge the people: † judge me, O LORD, according / tó my ríghteousness, * and according to mine integrity / thát is ín me.
9 Oh let the wickedness of the wicked come to an end; but es- / táblish the <u>just</u>: * for the righteous God trí- / eth the héarts and reins.
Glory be to the / Fáther and tó the Son * - and / tó the Hóly Ghost.
As it was in the beginning, is now, and / éver sháll be, * - wórld / without énd. Amen.

[101]

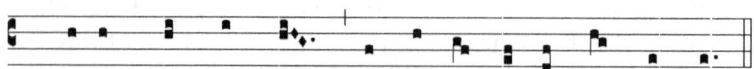

Ant. Í will práise the LORD: * ac-cording tó his ríghteousness.

VII

Psalm 7ii *Justum adjutorium*
10 My de- / fénce is of <u>God</u>, * which saveth the / úpright in <u>heart</u>.
11 God / júdgeth the ríghteous, * and God is angry with the / wícked évery

day.
12 If he turn not, / hé will whét his sword; * he hath bent his bow, and / máde it réady.
13 He hath also prepared for him the / instruménts of death; * he ordaineth his arrows against the / pérsecútors.
14 Behold, he travaileth with iníquity, † and / háth conceived míschief, * and / bróught forth fálsehood.
15 He made a / pít, and dígged it, * and is fallen into the / dítch which he made.
16 His mischief shall return up- / ón his ówn head, * and his violent dealing shall come down up- / ón his ówn pate.
17 I will praise the LORD according / tó his ríghteousness: * and will sing praise to the / náme of the LÓRD most high.
Glory be to the / Fáther and tó the Son * and / tó the Hóly Ghost.
As it was in the beginning, is now, and / éver shálll be, * - / wórld without énd. Amen.

Psalm-prayer. O God, that searchest the heart and triest the reins, deliver us from them that persecute us: and grant us, through the expectation of Thy judgment, such firm trust of heart that we may never recompense to our enemies evil for evil; through Jesus Christ our Lord, who liveth and reigneth with Thee and the Holy Ghost, ever one God, world without end. Amen.

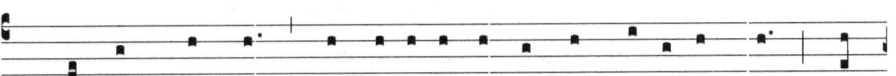

Ant. O LORD our Lord, * how excellent is thy náme in áll the earth!: who

hast set thy glory a-bóve the héavens. *(Do not repeat in verse 1).*

Psalm 8 *Domine, Dominus noster*
1 [O LORD our Lord, how excellent is thy / náme in áll the earth! * who hast set thy glory / abóve the héavens.]
2 Out of the mouth of babes and sucklings hast thou ordained strength becáuse / of thine énemies, * that thou mightest still the enemy / ánd the avénger.
3 When I consider thy heavens, the wórk / of thy fíngers, * the moon and the

[102]
    stars, which / thóu hast or<u>dained</u>;
4 What is man, that thou art mínd- / ful of <u>him</u>? * and the son of man, that thou / vísitest <u>him</u>?
5 For thou hast made him a little lower / thán the ángels, * and hast crowned him with / glóry and hónour.
6 Thou madest him to have dominion over the wórks / of thy <u>hands</u>; * thou hast put all things / únder his <u>feet</u>:
7 All / shéep and óxen, * yea, and the / béasts of the fíeld-;
8 The fowl of the air, and the físh / of the <u>sea</u>, * and whatsoever passeth through the / páths of the <u>seas</u>.
9 O LORD our / Lórd, how éxcellent * is / thy náme in áll the earth!

Glory be to the Fá- / ther and tó the Son * - / and tó the Hóly Ghost.
As it was in the beginning, is now, and / éver sháll be, * - / wórld without énd. Amen.

Psalm-prayer. We beseech Thy Name, O Lord, which is great, wonderful, and holy, that as Thou didst create the beasts of the field for the service of man, so Thou wouldst cause man to delight in the service of Thee; through Jesus Christ our Lord, who liveth and reigneth with Thee and the Holy Ghost, ever one God, world without end. Amen.

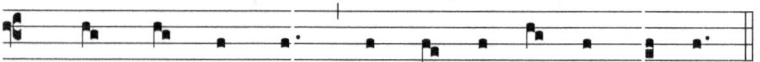

Ant. Thóu hast main<u>tained</u>: * my ríght and my cáuse, O Lord.

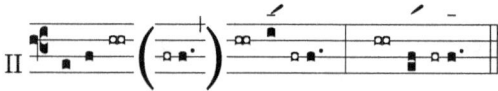

Psalm 9i *Confitebor tibi*
1 I will praise thee, O LORD, wíth my / whóle heart; * I will shew forth all thy márvel- / lous <u>works</u>.
2 I will be glád and re- / jóice in thee: * I will sing praise to thy náme, O / thóu most High.
3 When mine enemíes are / túrned back, * they shall fall and perish át thy / présence.
4 For thou hast maintained my ríght and my / <u>cause</u>; * thou satest ín the throne / júdging right.
5 Thou hast rebuked the heathen, † thou hast destróyed the / wícked, * thou hast put out their name for éver and / éver.
6 O thou enemy, destructions are come to a perpetual end: † and thou hást destroyed / cíties; * their memorial is perished / wíth them.

7 But the LORD shall endúre for / éver: * he hath prepared his thróne for / júdgment.
8 And he shall judge the wórld in / ríghteousness, * he shall minister judgment to the péople in / úprightness.
9 The LORD also will be a refuge fór the op- / pressed, * a refuge in tímes of / tróuble.
10 And they that know thy name will pút their / trúst in thee: * for thou, LORD, hast not forsaken thém that / séek thee.
Glory be to the Fáther and / tó the Son * and tó the / Hóly Ghost.
As it was in the beginning, is now, and éver / sháll be, * wórld without / énd. Amen.

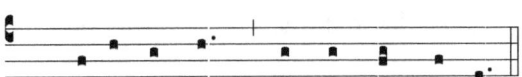

[103]

Ant. Aríse, O LORD: * lét not mán prevail.

Psalm 9ii *Psallite Domino*
11 Sing praises to the LORD, which / dwélleth in Zíon: * declare among the péo- / ple his dóings.
12 When he maketh inquisition for blood, / hé remémbereth them: * he forgetteth not the crý / of the húmble.
13 Have mercy upon me, O LORD; † consider my trouble which I suffer of / thém that háte me, * thou that liftest me up / fróm the gátes of death:
14 That I may shew forth all thy praise in the gates of the / dáughter of Zíon: * I will rejoice in / thý salvátion.
15 The heathen are sunk down in the / pít that they made: * in the net which they hid is their / ówn foot táken.
16 The LORD is known by the judgment which he / éxecúteth: * the wicked is snared in the wórk / of his ówn hands.
17 The wicked shall be / túrned into hell, * and all the nations / thát forget God.
18 For the needy shall not alway / bé forgótten: * the expectation of the poor shall not pér- / ish for éver.
19 Arise, O LORD; / lét not mán prevail: * let the heathen be / júdged in thy sight.
20 — / Pút them in féar, O LORD: * that the nations may know them- / sélves to bé but men.
Glory be to the / Fáther and tó the Son * - and / tó the Hóly Ghost.

As it was in the beginning, is now, and / éver shall be, * - wórld / without énd. Amen.

Psalm-prayer. Open, O merciful Lord, Thine ears to our prayers, Thou who never forsakest them that trust in Thee: so that we, being lifted up from the gates of perpetual death, may be able safely to escape the snares of the Tempter; through Jesus Christ our Lord, who liveth and reigneth with Thee and the Holy Ghost, ever one God, world without end. Amen.

Ant. Arise, O LORD; * O Gód, lift úp thine hand: forget nót the húmble.

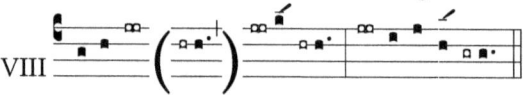

Psalm 10 *Ut quid, Domine*

1 Why standest thóu afar / óff, O LORD? * why hidest thou thyself in / tímes of tróuble?
2 The wicked in his pride doth pérse- / cúte the poor: * let them be taken in the devices that they / háve imágined.
3 For the wicked boasteth óf his / héart's desire, * and blesseth the covetous, whom the / LÓRD abhórreth.
4 The wicked, through the pride of his countenance, will nót seek / áfter God: * God is / nót in áll his thoughts.
5 His ways are always grievous; † thy judgments are far above óut of his / sight: * as for all his enemies, he / púffeth át them.
6 He hath said in his heart, Í shall / nót be moved: * for I shall never be / ín advérsity.
7 His mouth is full of cursing ánd de- / céit and fraud: * under his tongue is mís- / chief and vánity.
8 He sitteth in the lurking places of the víllages: † in the secret places doth he múrder the / ínnocent: * his eyes are privily / sét agáinst the poor.
9 He lieth in wait secretly as a lion în his den: † he lieth in wáit to / cátch the poor: * he doth catch the poor, when he draweth him ín- / to his net.
10 He croucheth, and húmbleth him- / self, * that the poor may fáll / by his stróng ones.
11 He hath said in his heart, Gód hath for- / gótten: * he hideth his face; he will / néver sée it.
12 Arise, O LORD; O Gód, lift / úp thine hand: * forget / nót the húmble.
13 Wherefore doth the wícked con- / témn God? * he hath said in his heart,

Thou wilt / nót requíre it.
14 Thou hast seen it; for thou beholdest míschief and / spite, * to re- / quíte it wíth thy hand:
The poor committeth himsélf unto / thee; * thou art the helper / óf the fátherless.
15 Break thou the arm of the wicked ánd the / évil man: * seek out his wickedness / tíll thou fínd none.
16 The LORD is King for éver and / éver: * the heathen are perished óut / of his land.
17 LORD, thou hast heard the desire óf the / húmble: * thou wilt prepare their heart, thou wilt / cáuse thine éar to hear:
18 To judge the fatherless ánd the op- / pressed, * that the man of the earth / máy no móre oppress.
Glory be to the Fáther and / tó the Son * and / tó the Hóly Ghost.
As it was in the beginning, is now, and éver / sháll be, * wórld / without énd. Amen.

Psalm-prayer. We pray Thee, O Lord, to preserve us unhurt from the works of Antichrist; to the end that we, deserting him and acknowledging Christ the Lord, may follow Thee by our faith, and may glorify Thee by good works; through the same, our Lord Jesus Christ, who liveth and reigneth with Thee and the Holy Ghost, ever one God, world without end. Amen.

[105]

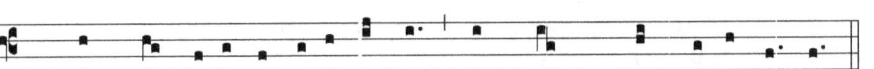

Ant. The LORD is in his hóly témple: * the LORD'S thróne is in héaven.

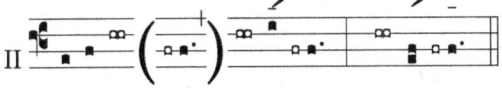

Psalm 11 *In Domino confido*
1 In the LORD put Î my trust: † how sáy ye / tó my soul, * Flee as a bird tó your / móuntain?
2 For, lo, the wicked bênd their bow, † they make ready their árrow up- / ón the string, * that they may privily shoot at the úpright / in heart.
3 If the foundátions / bé destroyed, * what cán the / ríghteous do?
4 The LORD is in his hóly / témple, * the LORD'S thróne is in / héaven:
His eyes behóld, his / éyelids try, * the chíldren / of men.
5 The LORD trieth the / ríghteous: * but the wicked and him that loveth violence hís soul / háteth.
6 Upon the wicked he shall rain snares, fire and brimstone, and an hórrible /

témpest: * this shall be the pórtion / óf their cup.

7 For the righteous LORD lóveth / ríghteousness; * his countenance doth behóld the / úpright.

Glory be to the Fáther and / tó the Son * and tó the / Hóly Ghost.

As it was in the beginning, is now, and éver / sháll be, * wórld without / énd. Amen.

Psalm-prayer. Let Thy merciful eyes, O Lord, vouchsafe to look upon our low estate; and protect us with the armour of faith, that we, being preserved from the arrows of the wicked, may be able to keep truth and righteousness; through Jesus Christ our Lord, who liveth and reigneth with Thee and the Holy Ghost, ever one God, world without end. Amen.

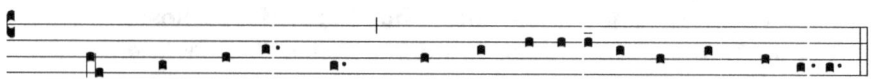

Ant. Thou shált presérve them: * from this generation, O Lórd, for éver.

Psalm 12 *Salvum me fac*

1 Help, LORD; for the gód- / ly man céaseth; * for the faithful fail from among the / chíldren of <u>men</u>.

2 They speak vanity every one / wíth his néighbour: * with flattering lips and with a double / héart do they <u>speak</u>.

3 The LORD shall cut / óff all fláttering lips, * and the tongue / that spéaketh próud things:

4 Who have said, With our / tóngue will wé prevail; * our lips are our own: / whó is lord óver us?

5 For the op- / préssion óf the poor, * for the sigh- / ing óf the néedy,

Now will Í / arise, sáith the LORD; * I will set him in safety from him / that púffeth át him.

6 The words of the / LÓRD are púre words: * as silver tried in a furnace of earth, / púrified séven times.

7 Thou shalt kéep / them, O <u>LORD</u>, * thou shalt preserve them from this gene- / rátion for éver.

8 The wicked / wálk on évery side, * when the vilest / mén are exálted.

Glory be to the Fá- / ther and tó the Son * - / and tó the Hóly Ghost.

As it was in the beginning, is now, and / éver shálll be, * - / wórld without énd. Amen.

Psalm-prayer. Have mercy, most holy Father, on our infirmity, and grant to us to receive and to hold fast Thy words in a pure heart, that we may be able to turn away from the flattering speeches of Thine enemies; through Jesus Christ our Lord, who liveth and reigneth with Thee and the Holy Ghost, ever one God, world without end. Amen.

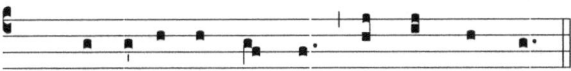

Ant. Consíder and héar me: * O Lórd, my God.

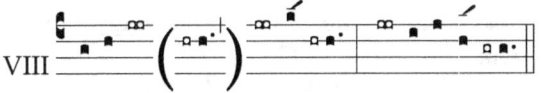
VIII

Psalm 13 *Usquequo, Domine*
1 How long wilt thou forget me, O LÓRD? for / éver? * how long wilt thou / híde thy fáce from me?
2 How long shall I take counsel în my soul, † having sorrow in mý heart / dáily? * how long shall mine enemy be ex- / álted óver me?
3 Consider and héar me, O / LÓRD my God: * lighten mine eyes, lest I / sléep the sléep of death;
4 Lest mine enemy say, I have prevailed a- / gáinst him; * and those that trouble me re- / jóice when Í am moved.
5 But I have trusted ín thy / mércy; * my heart shall rejoice in / thý salvátion.
6 I will sing únto the / LORD, * because he hath dealt bounti- / fúlly wíth me.
Glory be to the Fáther and / tó the Son * and / tó the Hóly Ghost.
As it was in the beginning, is now, and éver / sháll be, * wórld / without énd. Amen.

Psalm-prayer. Turn not away, O Almighty God, Thy face from us, lest our adversaries should be exalted over us; but so kindle our souls into the joy of Thy salvation that we may escape the sleep of the second death; through Jesus Christ our Lord, who liveth and reigneth with Thee and the Holy Ghost, ever one God, world without end. Amen.

[107]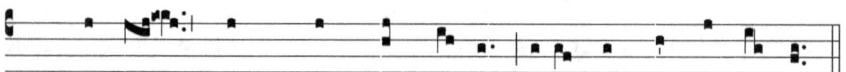

Ant. The Lord * looked dówn from héaven: upon the chíldren of men.

VIII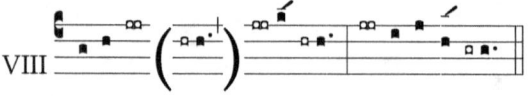

Psalm 14 *Dixit insipiens*

1 The fool hath said in his heart, There îs no God. † They are corrupt, they have done abóm*i*nable / <u>works</u>, * there is / nóne that dóeth good.
2 The LORD looked down from heaven upon the chíldren of / <u>men</u>, * to see if there were any that did understánd, / and seek <u>God</u>.
3 They are all gone aside, they are all together bécome / fílthy: * there is none that dó- / eth good, nó, not one.
4 Have all the workers of iniquity no knowledge? † who eat up my people ás they eat / <u>bread</u>, * and call / nót upón the LORD.
5 There were théy in / gréat fear: * for God is in the generation / óf the ríghteous.
6 Ye have shamed the cóunsel / óf the poor, * because the LÓRD / is his réfuge.
7 Oh that the salvation of Israel were come out of Zion! † when the LORD bringeth back the captivity óf his / péople, * Jacob shall rejoice, and Ís- / rael sháll be glad.

Glory be to the Fáther and / tó the Son * and / tó the Hóly Ghost.
As it was in the beginning, is now, and éver / sháll be, * wórld / without énd. Amen.

Psalm-prayer. Vouchsafe, O Lord, to look down from Thy holy heaven upon the children of men, and grant us to know the way of peace; that we, being set free from the hard captivity of vice, may enjoy the habitations of the heavenly Jerusalem; through Jesus Christ our Lord, who liveth and reigneth with Thee and the Holy Ghost, ever one God, world without end. Amen.

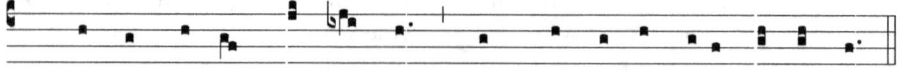

Ant. He that wórketh ríghteousness: * shall dwell in Thy hóly híll, O Lord.

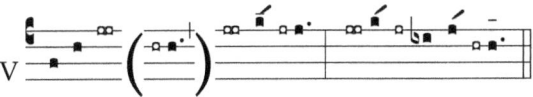

Psalm 15 *Domine, quis habit*
1 LORD, who shall abide in thy táber- / nácle? * who shall dwell / ín thy hóly hill?
2 He that walketh uprightly, and wórketh / ríghteousness, * and speaketh the / trúth in his <u>heart</u>.
3 He that backbiteth not with his tongue, † nor doeth evil tó his / néighbour, * nor taketh up a reproach a- / gáinst his néighbour.
4 In whose eyes a vile person is contemned; † but he honoureth thém that / féar the LORD. * He that sweareth to his own / húrt, and chángeth not.
5 He that putteth not out his money to ûsury, † nor taketh reward agáinst the / ínnocent. * He that doeth these things shall / néver be <u>moved</u>. [108]
Glory be to the Fáther and / tó the Son * and / tó the Hóly Ghost.
As it was in the beginning, is now, and éver / sháll be, * - / wórld without énd. Amen.

Psalm-prayer. Grant to us, merciful God, to enter Thy church without spot, and turn us away from doing evil to our neighbors; that while we observe all things according to Thy precepts, we may not be afflicted by Thy punishments forever; through Jesus Christ our Lord, who liveth and reigneth with Thee and the Holy Ghost, ever one God, world without end. Amen.

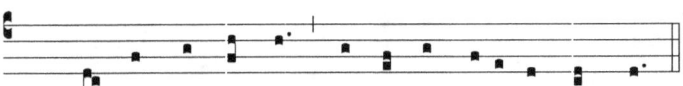

Ant. Presérve me, O <u>God</u>: * for in thée do I pút my trust.
(Do not repeat in verse 1)

Psalm 16 *Conserva me*
1 [- Pre- / sérve me, O <u>God</u>: * for in thée / do I pút my trust.]
2 O my soul, thou hast said unto the LORD, / Thóu art my <u>Lord</u>: * my goodness ex- / téndeth nót to thee;
3 But to the saints / thát are ín the earth, * and to the excellent, in whom is / áll my de<u>light</u>.
4 Their sorrows shall be multiplied that hasten after anôther god: † their drink offerings of blood will / Í not óffer, * nor take up their names / ínto

my <u>lips</u>.
5 The LORD is the portion of mine inheritance / ánd of my <u>cup</u>: * thou main- / táinest my <u>lot</u>.
6 The lines are fallen unto me in / pléasant pláces; * yea, I have a / góodly héritage.
7 I will bless the LORD, who hath / gíven me cóunsel: * my reins also instruct me ín / the night séasons.
8 I have set the LORD / álways befóre me: * because he is at my right hand, / Í shall nót be moved.
9 Therefore my heart is glad, and my / glóry rejóiceth: * my flesh ál- / so shall rést in hope.
10 For thou wilt not / léave my sóul in hell; * neither wilt thou suffer thine Holy One to / sée corrúption.
11 Thou wilt shew me the pâth of life: † in thy presence is / fúlness of <u>joy</u>; * at thy right hand there are pléa- / sures for évermore.
Glory be to the / Fáther and tó the Son * - and / tó the Hóly Ghost.
As it was in the beginning, is now, and / éver sháll be, * - wórld / without énd. Amen.

Psalm-prayer. Preserve, O Lord, them that put their trust in Thee, and conform our will to Thine; that we, enlightened by the joy of Thy Resurrection, may be made glad at Thy right hand with all Thy saints; who livest and reignest with the Father and the Holy Ghost, ever one God, world without end. Amen.

[109]
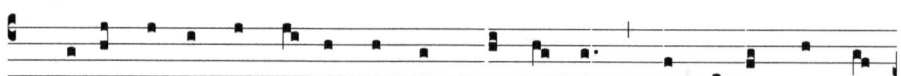

Ant. I will behold thy face in ríghteousnéss, O Lord: * and awáke with thy
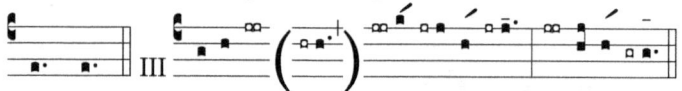
líkeness.

Psalm 17 *Exaudi, Domine*
1 Hear the right, O LORD, attend / únto my <u>cry</u>, * give ear unto my prayer, that goeth not óut / of féigned lips.
2 Let my sentence come / fórth from thy présence; * let thine eyes behold the thíngs that / are équal.
3 — / Thóu hast próved mine heart; * thou hast visited / mé in the <u>night</u>;
Thou hast tried me, and / shált find nóthing; * I am purposed that my móuth

/ shall nót transgress.
4 Con- / cérning the wórks of men, * by the word of thy lips I have kept me from the paths óf the / destróyer.
5 Hold up my / góings ín thy paths, * that my fóot- / steps slíp not.
6 I have called upon thee, for thou wilt / héar me, O <u>God</u>: * incline thine ear unto mé, / and héar my speech.
7 Shew thy marvellous lovingkindness, O thou that savest / bý thy right <u>hand</u> * them which put their trust in thee from those that rise úp / agáinst them.
8 Keep me as the / ápple óf the eye, * hide me under the shá- / dow óf thy wings,
9 From the wicked / thát oppréss me, * from my deadly enemies, who cóm- / pass mé about.
10 They are in- / clósed in their ówn fat: * with their móuth they / speak próudly.
11 They have now / cómpassed us ín our steps: * they have set their eyes bowing / dówn to the <u>earth</u>;
12 Like as a lion that is / gréedy óf his prey, * and as it were a young lion lurking in sé- / cret pláces.
13 Arise, O LORD, disap- / póint him, cást him down: * deliver my soul from the wicked, / whích is thy <u>sword</u>:
14 From men which are thy hand, O LORD, † from men of the world, which have their / pórtion ín this life, * and whose belly thou fillest wíth thy / hid tréasure:
They are / fúll of chíldren, * and leave the rest of their súb- / stance tó their babes.
15 As for me, I will behold thy / fáce in ríghteousness: * I shall be satisfied, when I awáke, with / thy líkeness.
Glory be to the / Fáther and tó the Son * and tó / the Hóly Ghost.
As it was in the beginning, is now, and / éver sháll be, * wórld with- / out énd. Amen.

Psalm-prayer. Keep us, O Lord, as the apple of Thine eye, lest the whirlwind of carnal concupiscence should injure the eyes of our innocence: guard us under the shadow of Thy wings, that we may not be seduced by the allurements of those pleasures that lie in wait for us; that we, who, up to this day, stand firm by the help of Thy grace, may, when Thy glory shall appear, be satisfied with it; through Jesus Christ our Lord, who liveth and reigneth with Thee and the Holy Ghost, ever one God, world without end. Amen.

[110]

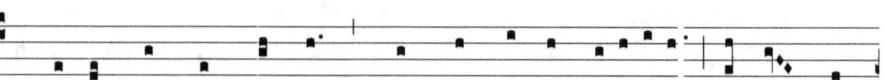

Ant. I will lóve Thee, O <u>Lord</u>: * Thou who art my Deliverer, my Gód, and

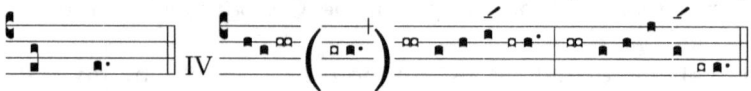

my <u>Strength</u>.

Psalm 18i *Diligam te*

1 I will lóve / thee, O LÓRD, my strength. * 2 The LORD is my rock, and my fortress, / and mý delíverer;

My God, my strength, in whóm / I will <u>trust</u>; * my buckler, and the horn of my salvation, / and mý high tówer.

3 I will call upon the LORD, who is / wórthy tó be praised: * so shall I be / sáved from mine énemies.

4 The sorrows / óf death cómpassed me, * and the floods of ungodly men / máde me a<u>fraid</u>.

5 The sorrows of hell / cómpassed mé about: * the snares / of déath prevénted me.

6 In my distress I called upon the LORD, and cried ún- / to my <u>God</u>: * he heard my voice out of his temple, and my cry came before him, even / ínto his <u>ears</u>.

7 Then the earth / shóok and trémbled; * the foundations also of the hills moved and were shaken, be- / cáuse he was <u>wroth</u>.

8 There went up a smoke out of his nostrils, † and fire out of his / móuth devóured: * coals / were kíndled bý it.

9 He bowed the heavens / álso, ánd came down: * and darkness was / únder his <u>feet</u>.

10 And he rode upon a / chérub, ánd did fly: * yea, he did fly upon the / wíngs of the <u>wind</u>.

11 He made dárk- / ness his sécret place; * his pavilion round about him were dark waters and thick / clóuds of the <u>skies</u>.

12 At the brightness that was befóre / him his thíck clouds passed, * - / háil stones and cóals of fire.

13 The LORD also thundered in the heavens, and the / Híghest gáve his voice; * - / háil stones and cóals of fire.

14 Yea, he sent out his ár- / rows, and scáttered them; * and he shot out lightnings, and dis- / cómfited <u>them</u>.

15 Then the channels of wá- / ters were <u>seen</u>, * and the foundations of the / wórld were discóvered

At / thý rebúke, O LORD, * at the blast of the / bréath of thy nóstrils.
Glory be to the Fá- / ther and tó the Son * - / and tó the Hóly Ghost.
As it was in the beginning, is now, and / éver sháll be, * - / wórld without énd. Amen.

[111]

Ant. The LÓRD rewárded me: * according tó my ríghteousness.

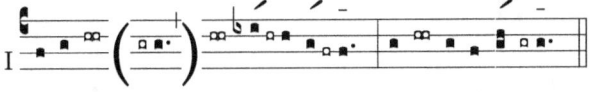

Psalm 18ii *Misit de summo*

16 He sent from a- / bóve, he tóok me, * he drew me out of / mány wáters.
17 He delivered me from my strong ênemy, † and from / thém which háted me: * for they / wére too stróng for me.
18 They prevented me in the day of / mý calámity: * but the / LÓRD was my stay.
19 He brought me forth also / ínto a lárge place; * he delivered me, because he de- / líghted in me.
20 The LORD rewarded me according / tó my ríghteousness; * according to the cleanness of my hands hath he / récompénsed me.
21 For I have kept the / wáys of the LORD, * and have not wickedly de- / párted fróm my God.
22 For all his judgments / wére befóre me, * and I did not put away his / státutes fróm me.
23 I was also / úpright befóre him, * and I kept myself from / míne iníquity.
24 Therefore hath the LORD recompensed me according / tó my ríghteousness, * according to the cleanness of my hánds / in his éyesight.
25 With the merciful thou wilt / shéw thyself mérciful; * with an upright man thou wilt shéw / thyself úpright;
26 With the pure thou wilt / shéw thyself pure; * and with the froward thou wilt shéw / thyself fróward.
27 For thou wilt save the af- / flícted péople; * but wilt / bríng down hígh looks.
28 For thou wilt / líght my cándle: * the LORD my God will enlíght- / en my dárkness.
29 For by thee I have / rún through a troop; * and by my God have I leaped / óver a wall.
30 As for God, his way is perfect: † the / wórd of the LÓRD is tried: * he is a buckler to all / thóse that trúst in him.

Glory be to the / Fáther and tó the Son * - and / tó the Hóly Ghost.
As it was in the beginning, is now, and / éver shálll be, * - wórld / without énd. Amen.

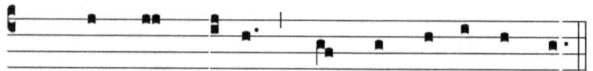

Ant. The LORD líveth: * and bléss-ed bé my rock.

VIII

Psalm 18iii *Quoniam quis Deus*

31 For who is Gód save the / LORD? * or who is a róck / save our God?
32 It is God that gírdeth / mé with strength, * and maketh / mý way pérfect.
33 He maketh my féet like / hínds' feet, * and setteth me upón / my high pláces.
34 He téacheth my / hánds to war, * so that a bow of steel is / bróken bý mine arms.
35 Thou hast also given me the shield of thy salvation: † and thy right hand hath hólden me / up, * and thy gentle- / néss hath máde me great.

[112] 36 Thou hast enlarged mý steps / únder me, * that my féet / did not slip.
37 I have pursued mine enemies, and óver- / táken them: * neither did I turn again till théy / were consumed.
38 I have wounded them that they were not áble to / rise: * they are fallen ún- / der my feet.
39 For thou hast girded me with strength únto the / báttle: * thou hast subdued under me those that rose / úp agáinst me.
40 Thou hast also given me the nécks of mine / énemies; * that I might destroy / thém that háte me.
41 They cried, but there was nóne to / sáve them: * even unto the LORD, but he án- / swered them not.
42 Then did I beat them small as the dúst be- / fóre the wind: * I did cast them out as the dírt / in the streets.
43 Thou hast delivered me from the strivings of the people; † and thou hast made me the héad of the / héathen: * a people whom I have not / knówn shall sérve me.
44 As soon as they hear of me, they sháll o- / béy me: * the strangers shall submít / themselves únto me.
45 The stróngers shall / fáde away, * and be afraid out of / théir close pláces.
46 The LORD liveth; and bléss-ed / bé my rock; * and let the God of my salvation / bé exálted.

47 It is God thát a- / véngeth me, * and subdueth the / péople únder me.

48 He delivereth me from mine ênemies: † yea, thou liftest me up above those that rise úp a- / gáinst me: * thou hast delivered me / fróm the víolent man.

49 Therefore will I give thanks unto thee, O LORD, amóng the / héathen, * and sing praises ún- / to thy <u>name</u>.

50 Great deliverance giveth he to his king; † and sheweth mercy to hís a- / nóinted, * to David, and to his / séed for évermore.

Glory be to the Fáther and / tó the Son * and / tó the Hóly Ghost.

As it was in the beginning, is now, and éver / sháll be, * wórld / without énd. Amen.

Psalm-prayer. O most merciful God, foundation of our hope, and refuge in our affliction, preserve us from our enemies, and from the snares of death, that we, being delivered from the multitude of our afflictions, may most devoutly give thanks to Thy holy Name, with the purity of innocence; through Jesus Christ our Lord, who liveth and reigneth with Thee and the Holy Ghost, ever one God, world without end. Amen.

[113]

Ant. The statutes óf the Lórd are right: * re-jói-cing the <u>heart</u>.

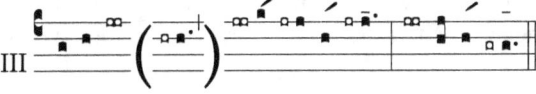

III

Psalm 19 *Caeli enarrant*

1 The heavens declare the / glóry of <u>God</u>; * and the firmament shéweth / his hándywork.

2 Day unto day / úttereth <u>speech</u>, * and night unto night shéw- / eth knówledge.

3 There is no / spéech nor lánguage, * where their / vóice is not <u>heard</u>.

4 Their line is gone / óut through áll the earth, * and their words to the / énd of the <u>world</u>.

In them hath he set a tabernacle for the sun, † 5 which is as a bridegroom coming / óut of his chámber, * and rejoiceth as a stróng man / to rún a race.

6 His going forth is from the end of the heaven, † and his circuit / únto the énds of it: * and there is nothing híd from / the héat thereof.

7 The law of the LORD is perfect, con- / vérting the <u>soul</u>: * the testimony of the LORD is sure, making wíse / the símple.

8 The statutes of the LORD are right, re- / jóicing the <u>heart</u>: * the commandment of the LORD is pure, en- / líghtening the <u>eyes</u>.
9 The fear of the LORD is clean, en- / dúring for éver: * the judgments of the LORD are true and righteous ál- / togéther.
10 More to be desired are they than gold, / yéa, than much fíne gold: * sweeter also than honey ánd / the hóneycomb.
11 Moreover by them / ís thy sérvant warned: * and in keeping of them thére / is gréat reward.
12 Who can under- / stánd his érrors? * cleanse thou mé / from sécret faults.
13 Keep back thy servant also / fróm presúmptuous sins; * let them not have domín- / ion óver me:
Then shall / Í be úpright, * and I shall be innocent from the gréat / transgréssion.
14 Let the words of my mouth, and the meditation of my heart, be ac- / céptable ín thy sight, * O LORD, my strength, and mý / redéemer.
Glory be to the / Fáther and tó the Son * and tó / the Hóly Ghost.
As it was in the beginning, is now, and / éver sháll be, * wórld with- / out énd. Amen.

Psalm-prayer. Most gracious God, who didst proceed from the virginal shrine to liberate us, and didst thus at length ascend to the right hand of the Father: we beseech Thy boundless mercy, that we, being converted to Thy law, illuminated by Thy commandments, made wise by Thy testimonies, may be cleansed from our secret faults, and delivered from our enemies; who livest and reignest with the same Father and the Holy Ghost, ever one God, world without end. Amen.

[114]

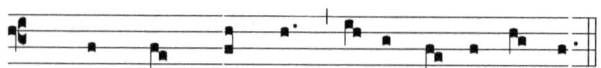

Ant. The LORD héar thee: * in the dáy of tróuble. *(Do not repeat in verse 1)*

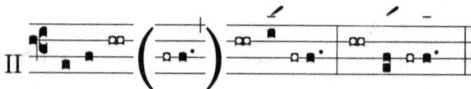

Psalm 20 *Exaudiat te Dominus*
1 [The LORD hear thee in the dáy of / tróuble;] * the name of the God of Jácob de- / fénd thee;
2 Send thee help from the sánctu- / áry, * and strengthen thee óut of / Zíon;
3 Remember áll thy / ófferings, * and accept thý burnt / sácrifice.
4 Grant thee according tó thine / ówn heart, * and fulfil áll thy / cóunsel.
5 We will rejoice in thy salvation, † and in the name of our God we will set

úp our / bánners: * the LORD fulfil áll thy pe- / títions.
6 Now know I that the LORD saveth hís a- / nóinted; * he will hear him from his holy heaven with the saving stréngth of his / ríght hand.
7 Some trust in chariots, and sóme in / hórses: * but we will remember the náme of the / LÓRD our God.
8 They are brought down and fallen: † but we are risen, ánd stand / úpright. * 9 Save, LORD: let the king héar us / whén we call.
Glory be to the Fáther and / tó the Son * and tó the / Hóly Ghost.
As it was in the beginning, is now, and éver / sháll be, * wórld without / énd. Amen.

Psalm-prayer. Fulfill, O Lord, our petitions, and accept us as a burnt-offering well-pleasing to Thee: that we, having overthrown the chariots of our enemies, may rejoice in the protections of Thy salvation; who livest and reignest with the Father and the Holy Ghost, ever one God, world without end. Amen.

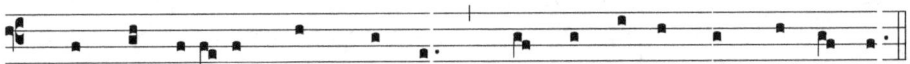

Ant. In Thine etérnal stréngth, O Lord: * Thine appointed Kíng shall re-joice.

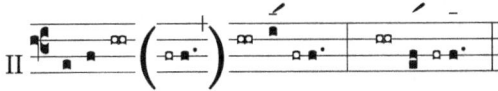

Psalm 21 *Domine, in virtute*
1 The king shall jóy in thy / stréngth, O LORD; * and in thy salvation how gréatly shall / hé rejoice!
2 Thou hast given him his héart's de- / síre-, * and hast not withholden the requést of / his lips.
3 For thou preventest him with the bléssings of / góodness: * thou settest a crown of pure góld on / his head.
4 He asked life of thee, and thou gávest it / him, * even length of days for éver and / éver.
5 His glory is great in thý sal- / vátion: * honour and majesty hast thou láid up- / ón him.
6 For thou hast made him most bléss-ed for / éver: * thou hast made him exceeding glad with thy / cóuntenance.
7 For the king trústeth / ín the LORD, * and through the mercy of the most High hé shall / nót be moved.
8 Thine hand shall find out áll thine / énemies: * thy right hand shall find out thóse that / háte thee.

9 Thou shalt make them as a fiery oven in the time of thine anger: † the LORD shall swallow them úp in his / <u>wrath</u>, * and the fire sháll de- / vóur them.

10 Their fruit shalt thou destróy from the / <u>earth</u>, * and their seed from among the chíldren / of <u>men</u>.

11 For they intended évil a- / gáinst thee: * they imagined a mischievous device, which they are not áble / tó perform.

12 Therefore shalt thou máke them / túrn their back, * when thou shalt make ready thine arrows upon thy strings agáinst the / fáce of them.

13 Be thou exalted, LORD, ín thine / ówn strength: * so will we sing and práise thy / pówer.

Glory be to the Fáther and / tó the Son * and tó the / Hóly Ghost.

As it was in the beginning, is now, and éver / sháll be, * wórld without / énd. Amen.

Psalm-prayer. Destroy the fruit of Thine enemies, O Lord, from the earth, and their seed from among the children of men, because they will not confess Thee, the one Christ, Son of God and Son of Man, to the end that Thy cross, which is to the Jews a stumbling-block, and to the Greeks foolishness, may direct both those peoples to the rule of faith, and may join them to Thee, to be crowned by Thine hand forever; who livest and reignest with the Father and the Holy Ghost, ever one God, world without end. Amen.

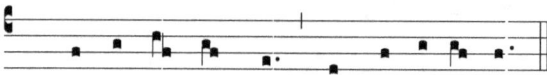

Ant. Bé not fár from Me: * for tróuble is <u>near</u>.

Psalm 22i *Deus, Deus meus*

1 My God, my God, why hast / thóu forsáken me? * Why art thou so far from helping me, and from the wórds / of my róaring?

2 O my God, I cry in the daytime, / bút thou héarest not; * and in the night season, and / ám not sílent.

3 But / thóu art hóly, * O thou that inhabitest the práis- / es of Ísrael.

4 Our fathers / trústed in <u>thee</u>: * they trusted, and thou / dídst delíver them.

5 They cried unto thee, and / wére delívered: * they trusted in thee, and were / nót confóunded.

6 But I am a / wórm, and nó man; * a reproach of men, and despised / óf the péople.

7 All they that see me / láugh me to scorn: * they shoot out the lip, they sháke / the head, sáying,
8 He trusted on the LORD that he / wóuld delíver him: * let him deliver him, seeing he de- / líghted ín him.
9 But thou art he that took me / óut of the womb: * thou didst make me hope when I was up- / ón my móther's breasts. [116]
10 I was cast upon / thée from the womb: * thou art my God from my / móther's bélly.
11 Be not far from me; for / tróuble is near; * - for / thére is nóne to help.
Glory be to the / Fáther and tó the Son * - and / tó the Hóly Ghost.
As it was in the beginning, is now, and / éver sháll be, * - wórld / without énd. Amen.

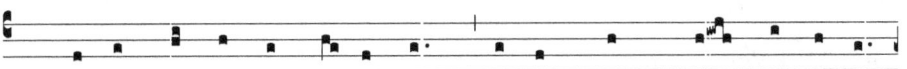

Ant. Be not thou fár from mé, O LORD: * O my strength, háste thee to hélp

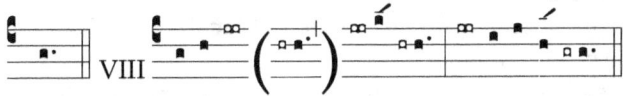

me.

Psalm 22ii *Circumdederunt*
12 Many búlls have / cómpassed me: * strong bulls of Bashan / háve besét me round.
13 They gaped upón me / wíth their mouths, * as a ravening and a / róaring líon.
14 I am poured óut like / wáter, * and all my / bónes are óut of joint:
My héart is like / wax; * it is melted in the mídst / of my bówels.
15 My strength is dried up like a potsherd; † and my tongue cléaveth / tó my jaws; * and thou hast brought me ín- / to the dúst of death.
16 For dogs have cômpassed me: † the assembly of the wicked háve in- / clósed me: * they pierced my hánds / and my feet.
17 Í may tell / áll my bones: * they look and / stáre upón me.
18 They part my gárments a- / móng them, * and cast lots up- / ón my vésture.
19 But be not thou fár from / mé, O LORD: * O my strength, háste / thee to hélp me.
20 Deliver my sóul from the / sword; * my darling from the / pówer óf the dog.
21 Save me fróm the / líon's mouth: * for thou hast heard me from the hórns

/ of the únicorns.
Glory be to the Fáther and / tó the Son * and / tó the Hóly Ghost.
As it was in the beginning, is now, and éver / sháll be, * wórld / without énd. Amen.

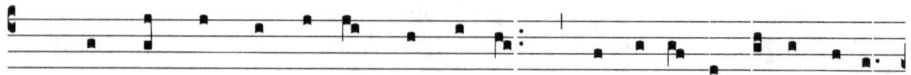

Ant. The Lord hath not despísed nor abhorred: * the affliction óf the Afflíc-

ted.

Psalm 22iii *Narrabo nomen*

22 I will declare thy name / únto my bréthren: * in the midst of the congregation wíll / I práise thee.

23 Ye that fear the LORD, praise him; † all ye the seed of Jacob, / glórify him; * and fear him, all ye the séed / of Ísrael.

24 For he hath not despised nor abhorred the affliction of the afflicted; † neither hath he / híd his fáce from him; * but when he cried ún- / to hím, he heard.

25 My praise shall be of thee in the great / cóngregátion: * I will pay my vows before thém / that féar him.

26 The meek shall eat and be sâtisfied: † they shall praise the / LÓRD that séek him: * your heart shall líve / for éver.

27 All the ends of the world shall remember and turn / únto the LORD: * and all the kindreds of the nations shall wórship / befóre thee.

28 For the / kíngdom ís the LORD'S: * and he is the governor amóng / the nátions.

29 All they that be fat upon earth shall eat and worship: † all they that go down to the dust shall / bów befóre him: * and none can keep alíve / his ówn soul.

30 A / séed shall sérve him; * it shall be accounted to the Lord for a gén- / erátion.

31 They shall come, and shall declare his righteousness unto a / péople that sháll be born, * that hé / hath dóne this.

Glory be to the / Fáther and tó the Son * and tó / the Hóly Ghost.
As it was in the beginning, is now, and / éver sháll be, * wórld with- / out énd. Amen.

Psalm-prayer. God, that art the source of mercy, who for us didst descend into the womb of the Virgin; wast nailed to the cross; didst behold Thy garments divided; didst rise Victor from hell; we beseech Thee that Thou, remembering this Thy conversation among us, wouldst free Thy people from the mouth of the lion, as Thou didst once deliver our fathers that hoped in Thee; who livest and reignest with the Father and the Holy Ghost, ever one God, world without end. Amen.

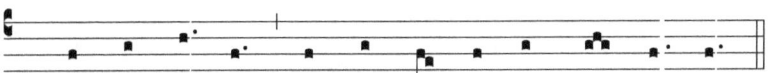

Ant. Ín green pástures: * the Lord my Shépherd shall féed me.

Psalm 23 *Dominus regit me*
1 The LORD is my shepherd; I shâll not want. † 2 He maketh me to lie / dówn in green pástures: * he leadeth me besíde / the still wáters.
3 He re- / stóreth my soul: * he leadeth me in the paths of righteousness / fór his náme's sake.
4 Yea, though I walk through the valley of the shadow of death, I will / féar no évil: * for thou art with me; thy rod and thy / stáff they cómfort me.
5 Thou preparest a table before me in the presence / óf mine énemies: * thou anointest my head with oil; my cup / rúnneth óver.
6 Surely goodness and mercy shall follow me all the / dáys of my life: * and I will dwell in the house of the / LÓRD for éver.
**Glory be to the / Fáther and tó the Son * - and / tó the Hóly Ghost.
As it was in the beginning, is now, and / éver shall be, * - wórld / without énd. Amen.**

Psalm-prayer. Shepherd us, O Lord, with the sweet rod and staff of Thy Word, that we may obtain a place in Thine eternal habitation, and be filled with the plenitude of the celestial banquet; through Jesus Christ our Lord, who liveth and reigneth with Thee and the Holy Ghost, ever one God, world without end. Amen.

Ant. He that hath clean hands * ánd a púre heart: shall ascend into the híll

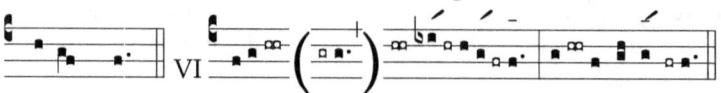

of the Lord.

Psalm 24 *Domini est terra*
1 The earth is the LORD'S, and the / fúlness thereof; * the world, and / théy that dwéll therein.
2 For he hath founded / ít upón the seas, * and established / ít upón the floods.
3 Who shall ascend into the / híll of the LORD? * or who shall stand / ín his hóly place?
4 He that hath clean hands, / ánd a púre heart; * who hath not lifted up his soul unto vanity, nor / swórn decéitfully.
5 He shall receive the / bléssing fróm the LORD, * and righteousness from the God of / hís salvátion.
6 This is the generation of / thém that séek him, * that seek thy / fáce, O Jácob.
7 Lift up your heads, O ye gates; † and be ye lift up, ye / éverlásting doors; * and the King of / glóry shall come in.
8 Who is this / Kíng of glóry? * The LORD strong and mighty, the LORD mígh- / ty in báttle.
9 Lift up your heads, O ye gates; † even lift them up, ye / éverlásting doors; * and the King of / glóry sháll come in.
10 Who is this / Kíng of glóry? * The LORD of hosts, he is the / Kíng of glóry.
Glory be to the / Fáther and tó the Son * - and / tó the Hóly Ghost.
As it was in the beginning, is now, and / éver sháll be, * - wórld / without énd. Amen.

Psalm-prayer. O God, the establisher of the world, to whom all the fulness of the earth is obedient: restore us to innocency of life, that Thou going before us, we may ascend to the hill of sanctification; through Jesus Christ our Lord, who liveth and reigneth with Thee and the Holy Ghost, ever one God, world without end. Amen.

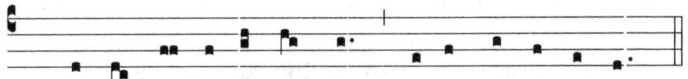

Ant. O my Gód, I trúst in Thee: * let me nót be ashamed.

Psalm 25i *Ad te, Domine, levavi*
1 Unto thee, O LORD, do I lift up my soul. † 2 O my / Gód, I trúst in thee: * let me not be ashamed, let not mine enemies / tríumph óver me.
3 Yea, let none that wait on / thée be ashamed: * let them be ashamed which trans- / gréss without cause.
4 — / Shéw me thy wáys, O LORD; * - / téach me thy paths.
5 Lead me in thy truth, and teach me: † for thou art the God of / mý salvátion; * on thee do / Í wait áll the day.
6 Remember, O LORD, thy tender mercies and thy / lóvingkíndnesses; * for they have been / éver of old.
7 Remember not the sins of my youth, nor / mý transgréssions: * according to thy mercy remember thou me for thy / góodness' sáke, O LORD.
Glory be to the / Fáther and tó the Son * - and / tó the Hóly Ghost.
As it was in the beginning, is now, and / éver sháll be, * - wórld / without énd. Amen.

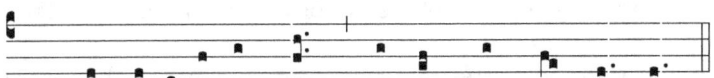

Ant. The sécret óf the LORD: * is with thém that féar him.

Psalm 25ii *Dulcis et rectus*
8 — Good and / úpright ís the LORD: * therefore will he teach / sínners ín the way.
9 The meek will he / guíde in júdgment: * and the méek / will he téach his way.
10 All the paths of the LORD are / mércy and truth * unto such as keep his covenant and his / téstimónies.
11 For thy / náme's sake, O LORD, * pardon mine iniqui- / tý; for ít is great.
12 What man is he that / féareth the LORD? * him shall he teach in the / wáy that hé shall choose.
13 His / sóul shall dwéll at ease; * and his seed shall in- / hérit the earth.

14 The secret of the LORD is with / thém that féar him; * and he will shéw / them his cóvenant.

Glory be to the / Fáther and tó the Son * - and / tó the Hóly Ghost.

As it was in the beginning, is now, and / éver sháll be, * - wórld / without énd. Amen.

[120]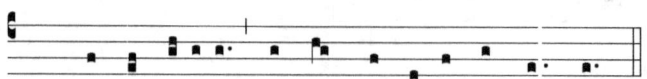

Ant. Redeem Ísraél, * O God: out of áll his tróubles.

IV

Psalm 25iii *Oculi mei*

15 Mine eyes are / éver tóward the LORD; * for he shall pluck my feet / óut of the <u>net</u>.

16 Turn thee unto me, and have mér- / cy upón me; * for I am deso- / late ánd afflícted.

17 The troubles of my héart / are en<u>larged</u>: * O bring thou me out / of mý distrésses.

18 Look upon mine af- / flíction ánd my pain; * and for- / gíve all my <u>sins</u>.

19 Consider mine enemies; for / théy are mány; * and they hate me / with crúel hátred.

20 O keep my soul, / ánd delíver me: * let me not be ashamed; for / I pút my trúst in thee.

21 Let integrity and uprightness preserve me; / fór I wáit on thee. * 22 Redeem Israel, O God, out / of áll his tróubles.

Glory be to the Fá- / ther and tó the Son * - / and tó the Hóly Ghost.

As it was in the beginning, is now, and / éver sháll be, * - / wórld without énd. Amen.

Psalm-prayer. Deliver us, O most merciful God, from all our miseries, for we lift up our souls unto Thee; remember not, we pray Thee, the sins of our youth and our former ignorance; and if we have through negligence offended Thee, do Thou, of Thy mercy, pardon us; through Jesus Christ our Lord, who liveth and reigneth with Thee and the Holy Ghost, ever one God, world without end. Amen.

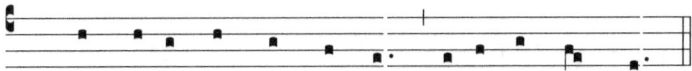

Ant. Thy loving-kíndness, O Lord: * ís befóre mine eyes.

Psalm 26 *Judica me, Domine*

1 Judge me, O LORD; for I have walked in / míne intégrity: * I have trusted also in the LORD; therefore / Í shall nót slide.
2 Examine me, O / LÓRD, and próve me; * try my / réins and my heart.
3 For thy lovingkindness / ís befóre mine eyes: * and I have / wálked in thy truth.
4 I have not / sát with vain pérsons, * neither will I go ín / with dissémblers.
5 I have hated the congregation of / évil dóers; * and will not sít / with the wícked.
6 I will wash mine hands in / ínnocency: * so will I compass thine / áltar, O LORD:
7 That I may publish with the / vóice of thanksgíving, * and tell of / áll thy wóndrous works.
8 LORD, I have loved the habit- / átion óf thy house, * and the place where thine / hónour dwélleth.
9 Gather not my / sóul with sínners, * nor my / lífe with blóody men:
10 In whose / hánds is míschief, * and their right / hánd is fúll of bribes.
11 But as for me, I will walk in / míne intégrity: * redeem me, and be mér- / ciful únto me.
12 My foot standeth / ín an éven place: * in the congregations / wíll I bléss the LORD.
Glory be to the / Fáther and tó the Son * - and / tó the Hóly Ghost.
As it was in the beginning, is now, and / éver sháll be, * - wórld / without énd. Amen.

[121]

Psalm-prayer. Redeem us, O Lord, and have mercy upon us, that our voice may praise Thee in the Church, and our lips may bless Thee among the people: purge our reins and prove our hearts by Thy love; and cut off from us all pleasures, and stop the influx of evil thoughts; through Jesus Christ our Lord, who liveth and reigneth with Thee and the Holy Ghost, ever one God, world without end. Amen.

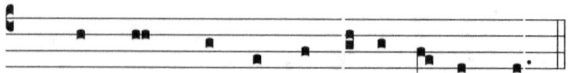

Ant. My light * and my sal-va-tion is the Lord.

Psalm 27 *Dominus illuminatio*

1 The LORD is my light and my sal- / vátion; whom sháll I fear? * the LORD is the strength of my life; of whóm / shall I bé afraid?
2 When the wicked, even mine enemies and my foes, came upon me to / éat up my <u>flesh</u>, * - they / stúmbled and <u>fell</u>.
3 Though an host should encamp against me, my / héart shall not <u>fear</u>: * though war should rise against me, in this will / Í be cónfident.
4 One thing have I desired of the LORD, that will I seek after; † that I may dwell in the house of the LORD all the / dáys of my <u>life</u>, * to behold the beauty of the LORD, and to enquire / ín his témple.
5 For in the time of trouble he shall hide me in his pavilion: † in the secret of his tabernacle / sháll he híde me; * he shall set me / úp upón a rock.
6 And now shall mine head be lifted up above mine enemies round about me: † therefore will I offer in his tabernacle sacri- / fíces of <u>joy</u>; * I will sing, yea, I will sing praises / únto the <u>LORD</u>.
7 Hear, O LORD, when I / crý with my <u>voice</u>: * have mercy also upón / me, and ánswer me.
8 When thou saidst, / Séek ye my <u>face</u>; * my heart said unto thee, Thy / fáce, LORD, wíll I seek.
9 Hide / nót thy face fár from me; * put not thy servant a- / wáy in ánger:
- / Thóu hast béen my help; * leave me not, neither forsake me, O God of / mý salvátion.
10 When my father and my / móther forsáke me, * then the / LÓRD will táke me up.
11 — / Téach me thy wáy, O LORD, * and lead me in a plain path, becáuse / of mine énemies.
12 Deliver me not over unto the will of mine ênemies: † for false witnesses are risen / úp agáinst me, * and such as / bréathe out crúelty.
13 I had fainted, un- / léss I hád believed * to see the goodness of the LORD in the lánd / of the líving.
14 Wait on the LORD: be of good courage, and he shall / stréngthen thine <u>heart</u>: * - wáit, / I say, ón the LORD.

[122] **Glory be to the / Fáther and tó the Son * - and / tó the Hóly Ghost.
As it was in the beginning, is now, and / éver sháll be, * - wórld / without**

énd. Amen.

Psalm-prayer. O God, our light and defence, remove from us the night of sorrow and ignorance; give us the light of truth and knowledge, that all our hope may remain fixed on Thee, and that all the assembly of them that would seek to hurt us may be brought to nought. Grant that we may be set on the rock, that, being made strong in Christ, in Him we may be lifted up in charity, by whom we are edified in faith; through the same Jesus Christ our Lord, who liveth and reigneth with Thee and the Holy Ghost, ever one God, world without end. Amen.

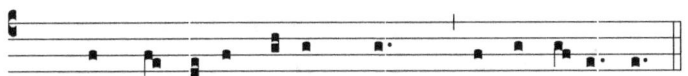

Ant. The Lord ís the sáving Strength: * of Hís anóinted.

Psalm 28 *Ad te, Domine*
1 Unto thee will I / crý, O LÓRD my rock; * be not / sílent to <u>me</u>:
Lest, if thou be sí- / lent to <u>me</u>, * I become like them that go down / into the <u>pit</u>.
2 Hear the voice of my supplications, when I crý / unto <u>thee</u>, * when I lift up my hands toward / thy hóly óracle.
3 Draw me not away / with the wícked, * and with the work- / ers óf iníquity,
Which speak péace / to their néighbours, * but / míschief is ín their hearts.
4 Give them ac- / córding tó their deeds, * and according to the wickedness / of théir endéavours:
Give them after the wórk / of their <u>hands</u>; * ren- / der tó them théir desert.
5 Because they regard not the wórks / of the <u>LORD</u>, * nor the op- / erátion óf his hands,
He / sháll destróy them, * and / nót build them <u>up</u>.
6 —/ Bléss-ed bé the LORD, * because he hath heard the voice of / my súpplicátions.
7 The LORD is my stréngth / and my shíeld-; * my heart trusted / in hím, and Í am helped:
Therefore my heart gréat- / ly rejóiceth; * and with my / sóng will I práise him.
8 The LÓRD / is their <u>strength</u>, * and he is the saving strength / of hís anóinted.

9 Save thy people, and bléss / thine inhéritance: * feed them also, and lift / them úp for éver.

Glory be to the Fá- / ther and tó the Son * - / and tó the Hóly Ghost.

As it was in the beginning, is now, and / éver sháll be, * - / wórld without énd. Amen.

Psalm-prayer. O God, the strength of all, preserve Thy people from going down into the pit; and so knit us together with one heart in Thy holy temple, that the peace which we profess with our mouth we may hold in our heart; through Jesus Christ our Lord, who liveth and reigneth with Thee and the Holy Ghost, ever one God, world without end. Amen.

[123]
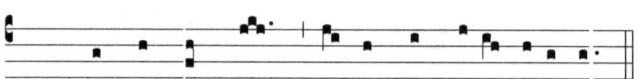

Ant. Wórship the LORD: * in the béauty of hóliness.

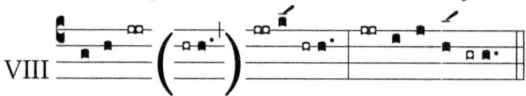

VIII

Psalm 29 *Afferte Domino*

1 Give unto the LORD, Ó ye / míghty, * give unto the LORD gló- / ry and strength.

2 Give unto the LORD the glory due únto his / name; * worship the LORD in the béau- / ty of hóliness.

3 The voice of the LORD is upon the waters: † the God of glóry / thúndereth: * the LORD is upon / mány wáters.

4 The voice of the LÓRD is / pówerful; * the voice of the LORD is / fúll of májesty.

5 The voice of the LORD bréaketh the / cédars; * yea, the LORD breaketh the cé- / dars of Lébanon.

6 He maketh them also to skíp like a / calf; * Lebanon and Sirion líke / a young únicorn.

7 The voice of the LORD divideth the flames of fire-. † 8 The voice of the LORD sháketh the / wílderness; * the LORD shaketh the wíl- / derness óf Kadesh.

9 The voice of the LORD maketh the hinds to calve, and discóvereth the / fórests: * and in his temple doth every one spéak / of his glóry.

10 The LORD sítteth up- / ón the flood; * yea, the LORD sitteth / Kíng for éver.

11 The LORD will give strength únto his / péople; * the LORD will bless his péo- / ple with peace.

Glory be to the Fáther and / tó the Son * and / tó the Hóly Ghost.
As it was in the beginning, is now, and éver / shàll be, * wórld / without énd. Amen.

Psalm-prayer. Grant, O Lord, strength to Thy people against the ills of all adversity; enrich us with the blessing of Thy peace, that in the abundance of our quiet we may all give glory to Thee in Thy holy Temple, and forgetting the misfortunes of this life, may ever render to Thee honour and praise; through our Lord Jesus Christ, who liveth and reigneth with Thee and the Holy Ghost, ever one God, world without end. Amen.

[124]

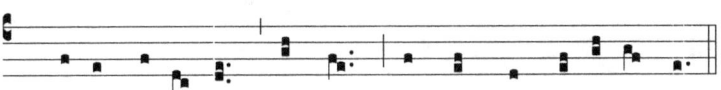

Ant. I will extól thee, * O LORD: for thou hast lífted me up.
(Do not repeat in verse 1.)

IV

Psalm 30 *Exaltabo te, Domine*
1 [I will extol thee, O LORD; for thou hast líft- / ed me up,] * and hast not made my foes / tó rejoice óver me.
2 O LORD my God, I críed / unto thee, * - / and thóu hast héaled me.
3 O LORD, thou hast brought up my sóul / from the grave: * thou hast kept me alive, that I should not go / dówn to the pit.
4 Sing unto the LORD, / Ó ye sáints of his, * and give thanks at the remem- / brance óf his hóliness.
5 For his anger endureth / bút a móment; * in his / fávour is life:
Weeping may endúre / for a night, * but joy com- / eth ín the mórning.
6 And in my pros- / péritý I said, * I shall / néver be moved.
7 LORD, by thy favour thou hast made my móun- / tain to stánd strong: * thou didst hide thy face, / and Í was tróubled.
8 I / críed to thée, O LORD; * and unto the LORD I / made súpplicátion.
9 What profit is there in my blood, when I go dówn / to the pit? * Shall the dust praise thee? / shall ít decláre thy truth?
10 Hear, O LORD, and have mér- / cy upón me: * LORD, / be thóu my hélper.
11 Thou hast turned for me my mourning / ínto dáncing: * thou hast put off my sackcloth, and gird- / ed mé with gládness;
12 To the end that my glory may sing praise to thee, and / nót be sílent. * O LORD my God, I will give thanks un- / to thée for éver.

Glory be to the Fá- / ther and tó the Son * - / and tó the Hóly Ghost.
As it was in the beginning, is now, and / éver shálll be, * - / wórld without énd. Amen.

Psalm-prayer. O most mighty God, who liftest us up, suffer not our enemies to triumph over us; but do Thou so strengthen us by Thy might, that, our mourning being turned into joy, we may ever give thanks at the remembrance of Thy holiness; through Jesus Christ our Lord, who liveth and reigneth with Thee and the Holy Ghost, ever one God, world without end. Amen.

Ant. Delíver mé, O Lord: ín Thy ríghteousness.

Psalm 31i *In te, Domine*
1 In thee, O LORD, do I pût my trust; † let me / néver bé ashamed: * deliver me / ín thy ríghteousness.
2 Bow down thine ear to me; de- / líver me spéedily: * be thou my strong rock, for an house of de- / fénce to sáve me.
3 For thou art my / róck and my fórtress; * therefore for thy name's sake léad / me, and guíde me.
4 Pull me out of the net that they have laid / prívily fór me: * - for / thóu art my <u>strength</u>.
5 Into thine hand I com- / mít my spírit: * thou hast redeemed me, / Ó LORD Gód of truth.
6 I have hated them that regard / lýing vánities: * but I / trúst in the <u>LORD</u>.
7 I will be glad and rejoice in thy mercy: † for thou hast con- / sídered my tróuble; * thou hast known my soul / ín advérsities;
8 And hast not shut me up into the / hánd of the énemy: * thou hast set my feet / ín a lárge room.
Glory be to the / Fáther and tó the Son * - and / tó the Hóly Ghost.
As it was in the beginning, is now, and / éver shálll be, * - wórld / without énd. Amen.

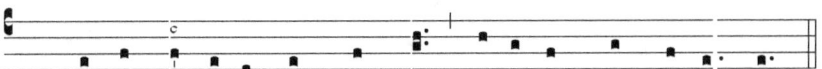

Ant. Let me nót be ashámed, O LORD: for I have cálled upon thee.

Psalm 31ii *Miserere mei, Domine*
9 Have mercy upon me, O LORD, for Í / am in tróuble: * mine eye is consumed with grief, yea, my / sóul and my bélly.
10 For my life is spent with grief, and my / yéars with síghing: * my strength faileth because of mine iniquity, and my / bónes are con<u>sumed</u>.
11 I was a reproach among all mine ênemies, † but especially among my neighbours, and a fear to / míne acquáintance: * they that did see / mé without fléd from me.
12 I am forgotten as a / déad man óut of mind: * I am like / a bróken véssel.
13 For I have heard the slán- / der of mány: * - / féar was on évery side:
While they took counsel togé- / ther agáinst me, * they devised / to táke awáy my life.
14 But I trúst- / ed in thée, O LORD: * I said, / Thóu art my <u>God</u>.
15 My times are în thy hand: † deliver me from the hánd / of mine énemies, * and from them that / pérsecute <u>me</u>.
16 Make thy face to shine up- / ón thy sérvant: * save / me fór thy mércies' sake.
17 Let me nót / be ashámed, O LORD; * for I have / cálled upon <u>thee</u>:
Let the / wícked bé ashamed, * and let them / be sílent ín the grave.
18 Let the lying lips be / pút to sílence; * which speak grievous things proudly and contemptuously / agáinst the ríghteous.
Glory be to the Fá- / **ther and tó the Son *** **-** / **and tó the Hóly Ghost.**
As it was in the beginning, is now, and / **éver sháll be, *** **-** / **wórld without énd. Amen.**

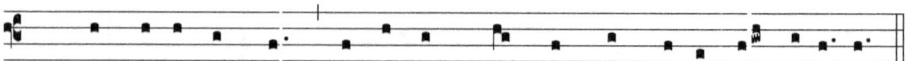

Ant. Bléss-ed bé the Lord: * for he hath heard the voice of my súpplicátions.

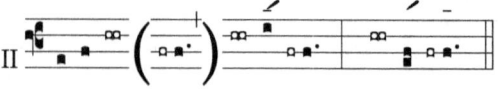

Psalm 31iii *Quam magna*

19 Oh how gréat is thy / góodness, * which thou hast laid up for thém that / féar thee;
Which thou hast wrought for thém that / trúst in thee * befóre the / sóns of men!
20 Thou shalt hide them in the secret of thy presence fróm the / príde of man: * thou shalt keep them secretly in a pavilion fróm the / strífe of tongues.
21 Bléss-ed / bé the LORD: * for he hath shewed me his marvellous kindness ín a strong / cíty.
22 For I said in my haste, I am cut off fróm be- / fóre thine eyes: * nevertheless thou heardest the voice of my supplications when I crίed un- / to <u>thee</u>.
23 O love the LORD, all yê his saints: † for the LORD presérveth the / fáithful, * and plentifully rewardeth thé proud / dóer.
24 Be of good courage, and he shall stréngthen your / <u>heart</u>, * all ye that hópe in / the <u>LORD</u>.
Glory be to the Fáther and / tó the Son * and tó the / Hóly Ghost.
As it was in the beginning, is now, and éver / shάll be, * wórld without / énd. Amen.

Psalm-prayer. We beseech Thee, O Lord, to bestow upon us the ineffable bounty of Thy sweetness; to the end that, while we seek for Thy truth, we may overcome all the temptations of pride; through Jesus Christ our Lord, who liveth and reigneth with Thee and the Holy Ghost, ever one God, world without end. Amen.

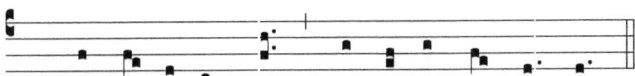

Ant. Be glád in the Lord: * and rejóice, ye ríghteous.

Psalm 32 *Beati quorum*
1 Bless-ed is he whose transgression / ís forgíven, * - whose / sín is cóvered.
2 Bless-ed is the man unto whom the LORD imputeth / nót iníquity, * and in whose spír- / it there ís no guile.
3 When / Í kept sílence, * my bones waxed old through my roaring / áll the day long.
4 For day and night thy hand was / héavy upón me: * my moisture is turned into the / dróught of súmmer.
5 I acknowledged my / sín unto thee, * and mine iniqui- / tý have Í not hid.
I said, I will confess my transgressions / únto the LORD; * and thou forgavest the iní- / quity óf my sin.
6 For this shall every one that is godly pray unto thee in a time when thou / máyest be found: * surely in the floods of great waters they shall not come / nígh unto him.
7 Thou art my hîding place; † thou shalt preserve / mé from tróuble; * thou shalt compass me about with sóngs / of delíverance.
8 I will instruct thee and teach thee in the / wáy which thóu shalt go: * I will / guíde thee wíth mine eye.
9 Be ye not as the horse, or as the mule, which have no / únderstánding: * whose mouth must be held in with bit and bridle, lest they come / néar unto thee.
10 Many sorrows shall / bé to the wícked: * but he that trusteth in the LORD, mercy shall / cómpass hím about.
11 Be glad in the LORD, and re- / jóice, ye ríghteous: * and shout for joy, all ye that are / úpright in heart.
Glory be to the / Fáther and tó the Son * - and / tó the Hóly Ghost.
As it was in the beginning, is now, and / éver sháll be, * - wórld / without énd. Amen.

Psalm-prayer. O Holy Lord, who forgiving sins, dost give blessedness to them that confess Thee, hear the prayer of Thy present family, and having destroyed the sting of sin, bedew us with spiritual exultation; through Jesus Christ our Lord, who liveth and reigneth with Thee and the Holy Ghost, ever one God, world without end. Amen.

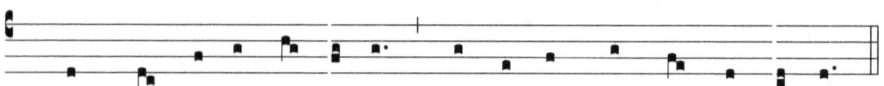

Ant. The Wórd of the Lórd is right: * and all His wórks are dóne in truth.

Psalm 33i *Exsultate, justi*
1 Rejoice in the LORD, / Ó ye ríghteous: * for praise is comely / fór the úpright.
2 —/ Práise the LÓRD with harp: * sing unto him with the psaltery and an instru- / mént of tén strings.
3 Sing unto / hím a néw song; * play skilfully / wíth a lóud noise.
4 For the / wórd of the LÓRD is right; * and all his / wórks are dóne in truth.
5 He loveth righteous- / néss and júdgment: * the earth is full of the / góodness óf the LORD.
6 By the word of the LORD / wére the héavens made; * and all the host of them by the / bréath of his <u>mouth</u>.
7 He gathereth the waters of the sea to- / géther ás an heap: * he layeth up the / dépth in stórehouses.
8 Let / áll the earth féar the LORD: * let all the inhabitants of the world / stánd in áwe of him.
9 For he / spáke, and ít was done; * he commanded, / ánd it stóod fast.
10 The LORD bringeth the counsel of the / héathen to <u>nought</u>: * he maketh the devices of the péo- / ple of nóne effect.
11 The counsel of the LORD / stándeth for éver, * the thoughts of his heart to all / generátions.
12 Bless-ed is the nation whose / Gód is the <u>LORD</u>; * and the people whom he hath chosen for his / ówn inhéritance.
Glory be to the / Fáther and tó the Son * - and / tó the Hóly Ghost.
As it was in the beginning, is now, and / éver sháll be, * - wórld / without énd. Amen.

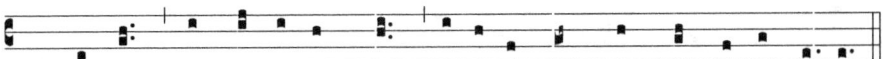

Ant. Behold, * the éye of the LORD: is upon them that hópe in his mércy.

Psalm 33ii *De caelo respexit*
13 The LORD / lóoketh from héaven; * he beholdeth / áll the sóns of men.
14 From the place of his / hábitátion * he looketh upon all the in- / hábitants óf the earth.
15 He fashion- / éth their héarts alike; * he con- / sídereth áll their works.
16 There is no king saved by the / múltitude óf an host: * a mighty man is not de- / lívered bý much strength.
17 An horse is a vain / thíng for sáfety: * neither shall he deliver / ány by hís great strength.
18 Behold, the eye of the LORD is upon / thém that féar him, * upon them that / hópe in his mércy;
19 To de- / líver their sóul from death, * and to keep them a- / líve in fámine.
20 Our soul / wáiteth fór the LORD: * he is our / hélp and our shield.
21 For our heart / sháll rejóice in him, * because we have trusted / ín his hóly name.
22 Let thy mercy, O LORD, / bé upón us, * according / ás we hópe in thee.
Glory be to the / Fáther and tó the Son * and / tó the Hóly Ghost.
As it was in the beginning, is now, and / éver sháll be, * - / wórld without énd. Amen.

Psalm-prayer. Feed, O Lord, Thy people, in the time of famine, with Thy Word, and deliver our souls from the death of sin; that, being filled with Thy mercy, we may, through Thy gift, be admitted to the joys of the righteous; through Jesus Christ our Lord, who liveth and reigneth with Thee and the Holy Ghost, ever one God, world without end. Amen.

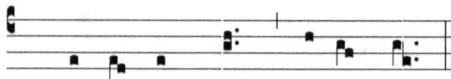

Ant. O fear the LORD, * ye his saints.

IV

Psalm 34i *Benedicam Dominum*
1 I will bless the / LÓRD at áll times: * his praise shall contin- / uallý be ín my mouth.
2 My soul shall make her bóast / in the LORD: * the humble shall / héar thereof, ánd be glad.
3 O magni- / fý the LÓRD with me, * and let us exalt / his náme together.
4 I sought the LORD, / ánd he héard me, * and deli- / vered mé from áll my fears.
5 They looked unto him, / ánd were líghtened: * and their / fáces were nót ashamed.
6 This poor man cried, ánd / the LORD héard him, * and saved him out / of áll his tróubles.
7 The angel of the LORD encampeth round about / thém that féar him, * and de- / lívereth them.
8 O taste and sée / that the LÓRD is good: * bless-ed is the man that / trústeth in him.
9 O féar / the LORD, yé his saints: * for there is no want / to thém that féar him.
10 The young lions do lack, and / súffer húnger: * but they that seek the LORD shall not / want ány góod thing.
Glory be to the Fá-/ ther and tó the Son * - / and tó the Hóly Ghost.
As it was in the beginning, is now, and / éver shálls be, * - / wórld without énd. Amen.

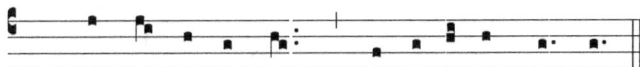

Ant. The éyes of the <u>LORD</u>: * are upón the ríghteous.

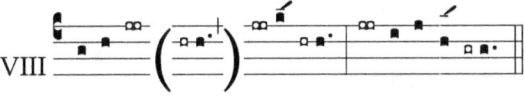
VIII

Psalm 34ii *Venite, filii*
11 Come, ye children, héarken / únto me: * I will teach you the féar / of the <u>LORD</u>.
12 What man is he thát de- / síreth life, * and loveth many days, that / hé may sée good?
13 Keep thy tóngue from / évil, * and thy lips from / spéaking guíle-.
14 Depart from évil, / ánd do good; * seek peace, / ánd pursúe it.
15 The eyes of the LORD are upón the / ríghteous, * and his ears are open ún- / to their <u>cry</u>.
16 The face of the LORD is against thém that do / évil, * to cut off the remembrance of thém / from the <u>earth</u>.
17 The righteous cry, ánd the LORD / héareth, * and delivereth them out of / áll their tróubles.
18 The LORD is nigh unto them that are óf a / bróken heart; * and saveth such as be of a / cóntrite spírit.
19 Many are the afflictions óf the / ríghteous: * but the LORD delivereth him óut / of them <u>all</u>.
20 He kéepeth / áll his bones: * not one of / thém is bróken.
21 Evil shall sláy the / wícked: * and they that hate the righteous / sháll be désolate.
22 The LORD redeemeth the sóul of his / sérvants: * and none of them that trust in him / sháll be désolate.
Glory be to the Fáther and / tó the Son * and / tó the Hóly Ghost.
As it was in the beginning, is now, and éver / sháll be, * wórld / without énd. Amen.

Psalm-prayer. O God, Ruler of the angels and of all creatures, send forth Thine Angel to encamp round about us, that we, being guarded by His protection, may be delivered from the most evil death of sin; through the same, our Lord Jesus Christ, who liveth and reigneth with Thee and the Holy Ghost, ever one God, world without end. Amen.

[130]

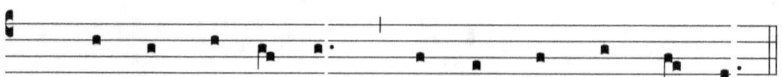

Ant. Plead my cause, O LORD, * with thém that strive with me.
(Do not repeat in verse 1.)

Psalm 35i *Judica, Domine*

1 [Plead my cause, O LORD, with / thém that strive with me:] * fight against them that / fíght agáinst me.
2 Take hold of / shíeld and búckler, * and stand / úp for mine <u>help</u>.
3 Draw out also the spear, and stop the way against them that / pérsecute <u>me</u>: * say unto my soul, I am / thý salvátion.
4 Let them be confounded and put to shame that seek / áfter my <u>soul</u>: * let them be turned back and brought to confusion / thát devíse my hurt.
5 Let them be as / cháff befóre the wind: * and let the angel óf / the LORD cháse them.
6 Let their way be / dárk and slíppery: * and let the angel of the LORD / pérsecute <u>them</u>.
7 For without cause have they hid for me their / nét in a <u>pit</u>, * which without cause they have / dígged for my <u>soul</u>.
8 Let destruction come upon him at ûnawares; † and let his net that / hé hath hid cátch himself: * into that very des- / trúction lét him fall.
9 And my soul shall be / jóyful ín the LORD: * it shall rejoice in / hís salvátion.
10 All my bones shall say, LORD, who is like ûnto thee, † which deliverest the poor from him that / ís too stróng for him, * yea, the poor and the needy from / hím that spóileth him?

Glory be to the / Fáther and tó the Son * - and / tó the Hóly Ghost.
As it was in the beginning, is now, and / éver sháll be, * - wórld / without énd. Amen.

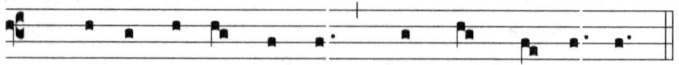

Ant. Réscue my sóul, O Lord: * from théir destrúctions.

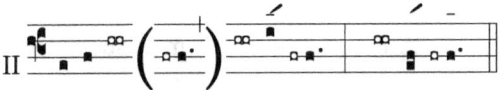

Psalm 35ii *Surgentes testes*

11 False wítnesses / díd rise up; * they laid to my charge thíngs that I / knéw not.

12 They rewarded me évil for / good * to the spóiling / óf my soul.

13 But as for me, when they were sick, my clothing was sackcloth: † I humbled my sóul with / fásting; * and my prayer returned into míne own / bósom.

14 I behaved myself as though he had been my fríend or / bróther: * I bowed down heavily, as one that mourneth fór his / móther. [131]

15 But in mine advérsity / théy rejoiced, * and gathered themsélves to- / géther:

Yea, the abjects gathered themselves together against me, ánd I / knéw it not; * they did téar me, and / céased not:

16 With hypocritical móckers in / feasts, * they gnashed upón me / wíth their teeth.

17 Lord, how long wilt thou look on? † rescue my soul from théir des- / trúctions, * my darling fróm the / líons.

Glory be to the Fáther and / tó the Son * and tó the / Hóly Ghost.

As it was in the beginning, is now, and éver / shálll be, * wórld without / énd. Amen.

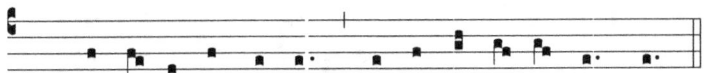

Ant. Stir úp thysélf, O God: * and awáke to my júdgment.

Psalm 35iii *Confitebor tibi*

18 I will give thee thanks in the great / cóngregátion: * I will praise thee / amóng much péople.

19 Let not them that are mine enemies wrongfully rejóice / over me: * neither let them wink with the eye that / háte me withóut a cause.

20 —/ Fór they spéak not peace: * but they devise deceitful matters against them that / are quíet ín the land.

21 Yea, they opened their mouth wide agáinst / me, and said, * Aha, aha, / our éye hath séen it.

22 This thou hast seen, O LORD: / kéep not sílence: * O / Lord, bé not fár

from me.

23 Stir up thyself, and awáke / to my júdgment, * even unto my cause, my / Gód and my Lord.
24 Judge me, O LORD my God, according / tó thy ríghteousness; * and let them not re- / jóice over me.
25 Let them not say in their hearts, Ah, só / would we háve it: * let them not say, We have / swállowed him up.
26 Let them be ashamed and brought to confusion together that rejóice / at mine hurt: * let them be clothed with shame and dishonour that magnify / themsélves agáinst me.
27 Let them shout for joy, and be glad, that favour my rîghteous cause: † yea, let them say continually, Let the / LÓRD be mágnified, * which hath pleasure in the prosperi- / ty óf his sérvant.
28 And my tongue shall spéak / of thy ríghteousness * and of thy praise / áll the day long.
Glory be to the Fá- / ther and tó the Son * - / and tó the Hóly Ghost.
As it was in the beginning, is now, and / éver sháll be, * - / wórld without énd. Amen.

Psalm-prayer. O God, our salvation and protection, arm us with the Helmet of Hope, and with the Shield of Thy glorious Defense, that we, being helped by Thee in all time of our necessity, may enter into the joy of them that love Thee; through the same our Lord Jesus Christ, who liveth and reigneth with Thee and the Holy Ghost, ever one God, world without end. Amen.

[132]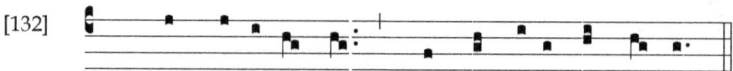

Ant. Thy mércy, O Lord: * reacheth únto the héavens.

VIII

Psalm 36 *Dixit injustus*
1 The transgression of the wicked sáith with- / ín my heart, * that there is no fear of / Gód befóre his eyes.
2 For he flattereth himself ín his / ówn eyes, * until his iniquity be fóund / to be háteful.
3 The words of his mouth are iníquity / ánd deceit: * he hath left off to be wise, ánd / to do good.
4 He deviseth mischief upôn his bed; † he setteth himself in a wáy that / ís not good; * he abhór- / reth not évil.

5 Thy mercy, O LORD, is ín the / héavens; * and thy faithfulness reacheth ún- / to the <u>clouds</u>.
6 Thy righteousness is like the great mountains; † thy judgments áre a great / <u>deep</u>: * O LORD, thou pre- / sérvest mán and beast.
7 How excellent is thy lovingkíndness, O / <u>God</u>! * therefore the children of men put their trust under the / shádow óf thy wings.
8 They shall be abundantly satisfied with the fátness / óf thy house; * and thou shalt make them drink of the river / óf thy pléasures.
9 For with thee is the fóuntain of / <u>life</u>: * in thy / líght shall wé see light.
10 O continue thy lovingkindness unto thém that / knów thee; * and thy righteousness to the úp- / right in <u>heart</u>.
11 Let not the foot of pride cóme a- / gáinst me, * and let not the hand of the wíck- / ed remóve me.
12 There are the workers of iníquity / fállen: * they are cast down, and shall not be á- / ble to <u>rise</u>.

Glory be to the Fáther and / tó the Son * and / tó the Hóly Ghost.
As it was in the beginning, is now, and éver / sháll be, * wórld / without énd. Amen.

Psalm-prayer. O God, who art the fountain and source of everlasting life, glorify us with Thy heavenly mercy; that we, being satisfied with the fatness of Thy house, may evermore shun all deceit and excess of iniquity; through Jesus Christ, Thy Son, our Lord, who liveth and reigneth with Thee and the Holy Ghost, ever one God, world without end. Amen.

[133]

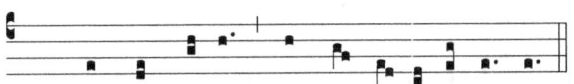

Ant. Fret not thyself * because of e-vil-do-ers. *(Do not repeat in verse 1.)*

IV

Psalm 37i *Noli aemulare*
1 [Fret not thyself because of / évildóers,] * neither be thou envious against the work- / ers óf iníquity.
2 For they shall soon be cut dówn / like the <u>grass</u>, * and with- / er ás the gréen herb.
3 Trust in the LÓRD, / and do <u>good</u>; * so shalt thou dwell in the land, and ve- / rilý thou shált be fed.
4 Delight thyself / álso ín the LORD; * and he shall give thee the de- / síres of thine <u>heart</u>.

5 Commit thy way ún- / to the LORD; * trust also in him; and he shall / bríng it to pass.
6 And he shall bring forth thy rígh- / teousness ás the light, * and thy judg- / ment ás the nóonday.
7 Rest in the LORD, and wait patiently for him: † fret not thyself because of him who prós- / pereth ín his way, * because of the man who bringeth wicked de- / víces to pass.
8 Cease from anger, ánd / forsake wrath: * fret not thyself in any / wíse to do évil.
9 For evildoers / shåll be cút off: * but those that wait upon the LORD, they shall in- / hérit the earth.
10 For yet a little while, and the / wícked sháll not be: * yea, thou shalt diligently consider his / place, ánd it sháll not be.
11 But the meek shall inhér- / it the earth; * and shall delight themselves in the a- / búndance of peace.
12 The wicked plót- / teth agáinst the just, * and gnasheth / upón him with his teeth.
13 The / Lórd shall láugh at him: * for he seeth that / his dáy is cóming.
14 The wicked have drawn out the sword, / ánd have bént their bow, * to cast down the poor and needy, and to slay such as be of up- / right cónversátion.
15 Their sword shall enter ín- / to their ówn heart, * and their / bóws shall be bróken.
Glory be to the Fá- / ther and tó the Son * - / and tó the Hóly Ghost.
As it was in the beginning, is now, and / éver sháll be, * - / wórld without énd. Amen.

[134]

Ant. The arms of the wicked sháll be bróken: * but the LORD up-hóldeth the

ríghteous.

Psalm 37ii *Melius est*

16 A little that a ríghteous man / hath * is better than the riches of / mány wícked.
17 For the arms of the wicked sháll be / bróken: * but the LORD uphóld- / eth the ríghteous.

186

18 The LORD knoweth the dáys of the / úpright: * and their inheritance shall / bé for éver.
19 They shall not be ashamed ín the / évil time: * and in the days of famine they / sháll be sátisfied.
20 But the wícked shall / pérish, * and the enemies of the LORD shall bé / as the fát of lambs:
Théy shall con- / sume; * into smoke shall / théy consúme away.
21 The wicked borroweth, and páyeth / nót again: * but the righteous sheweth mér-/ cy, and gíveth.
22 For such as be blessed of him shall inhérit the / earth; * and they that be cursed of him / shálll be cút off.
23 The steps of a good man are órdered / bý the LORD: * and he de- / líghteth ín his way.
24 Though he fall, he shall not be útterly / cást down: * for the LORD uphóld- / eth him wíth his hand.
25 I have been yóung, and / nów am old; * yet have I not seen the righteous forsaken, nór / his seed bégging bread.
26 He is ever mercifúl, and / léndeth; * - / ánd his séed is blessed.
27 Depart from évil, / ánd do good; * and / dwéll for évermore.
28 For the LORD lóveth / júdgment, * and for- / sáketh nót his saints;
They are presérved for / éver: * but the seed of the wicked shálll / be cut off.
29 The righteous shall inhérit the / land, * and dwell there- / ín for éver.
Glory be to the Fáther and / tó the Son * and / tó the Hóly Ghost.
As it was in the beginning, is now, and éver / shálll be, * wórld / without énd. Amen.

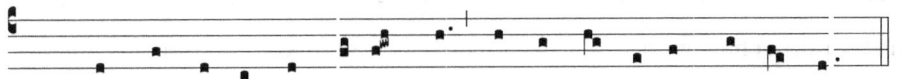

Ant. Mark the pérfect and úpright man: for the énd of that mán is peace.

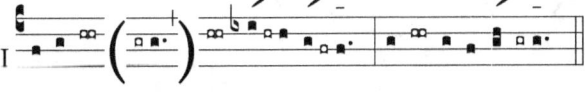

Psalm 37iii *Os justi*
30 The mouth of the righteous / spéaketh wísdom, * and his tongue tálk- / eth of júdgment.
31 The law of his / Gód is ín his heart; * - nóne / of his stéps shall slide.
32 The wicked / wátcheth the ríghteous, * and séek- / eth to sláy him.
33 The LORD will not / léave him ín his hand, * nor condemn / hím when hé is judged.
34 Wait on the LORD, and kêep his way, † and he shall exalt thee to in- /

hérit the land: * when the wicked are cut off, / thóu shalt sée it.
35 I have seen the wicked / ín great pówer, * and spreading himself líke / a green báy tree.
36 Yet he passed away, and, / ló, he was not: * yea, I sought him, but / hé could nót be found.
37 Mark the perfect man, and be- / hóld the úpright: * for the énd / of that mán is peace.
38 But the transgressors shall be des- / tróyed togéther: * the end of the wicked / sháll be cut off.
39 But the salvation of the / ríghteous is óf the LORD: * he is their strength in the / tíme of tróuble.
40 And the LORD shall help them, / ánd delíver them: * he shall deliver them from the wicked, and save them, be- / cáuse they trúst in him.
Glory be to the / Fáther and tó the Son * - and / tó the Hóly Ghost.
As it was in the beginning, is now, and / éver sháll be, * - wórld / without énd. Amen.

Psalm-prayer. O God, the blessedness of all who put their trust in Thee, who art both the witness and the judge of them that contend in the race of righteousness; we pray Thee that Thou wouldest so keep us from falling in this life, that Thou mayest crown us in the life to come; through our Lord Jesus Christ, who liveth and reigneth with Thee and the Holy Ghost, ever one God, world without end. Amen.

[136]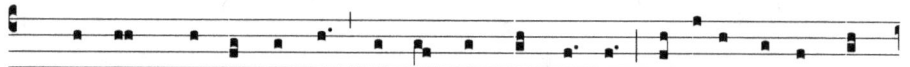

Ant. O Lord, chasten me not * in Thy hót displéasure: for I am feeble ánd

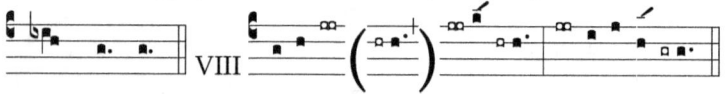

sore bróken.

Psalm 38i *Domine, ne in furore*
1 O LORD, rebuke me nót in thy / wrath: * neither chasten me in thy / hót displéasure.
2 For thine árrows stick / fást in me, * and thy hand prés- / seth me sore.
3 There is no soundness in my flesh becáuse of thine / ánger; * neither is there any rest in my bones becáuse / of my sin.
4 For mine iniquities are gone óver mine / head: * as an heavy burden they are too héav- / y for me.

5 My wounds stínk and / áre corrupt * becáuse / of my fóolishness.
6 I am troubled; I am bówed down / gréatly; * I go mourning áll / the day long.
7 For my loins are filled with a lóathsome di- / <u>sease</u>: * and there is no / sóundness ín my flesh.
8 I am feeble ánd sore / bróken: * I have roared by reason of the disquí- / etness óf my heart.
9 Lord, all my desíre is be- / fóre thee; * and my groaning / ís not híd from thee.
10 My heart panteth, mý strength / fáileth me: * as for the light of mine eyes, it ál- / so is góne from me.
11 My lovers and my friends stand alóof from my / <u>sore</u>; * and my kinsmen / stánd afár off.
12 They also that seek after my life lay snáres for me: † and they that seek my hurt speak míschievous / <u>things</u>, * and imagine deceits áll / the day <u>long</u>.
Glory be to the Fáther and / tó the Son * and / tó the Hóly Ghost.
As it was in the beginning, is now, and éver / shall be, * wórld / without énd. Amen.

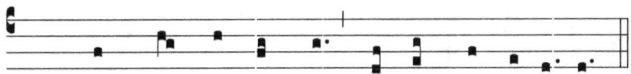

Ant. Make háste to hélp me: * O Lord mý salvátion.

Psalm 38ii *Ego autem, tanquam surdus*
13 But I, as a / déaf man, héard not; * and I was as a dumb man that ó- / peneth nót his mouth.
14 Thus I was as a / mán that héareth not, * and in whose / móuth are nó reproofs.
15 For in thee, O / LÓRD, do I <u>hope</u>: * thou wilt / héar, O Lórd my God.
16 For I said, Hear me, lest otherwise they should re- / jóice over <u>me</u>: * when my foot slippeth, they magnify them- / sélves agáinst me.
17 For I am / réady to <u>halt</u>, * and my sorrow is continual- / lý befóre me.
18 For I will declare / míne iníquity; * I will be / sórry fór my sin.
19 But mine enemies are / lívely, and théy are strong: * and they that hate me wrongful- / lý are múltiplied.
20 They also that render evil for good are mine / ádversáries; * because I follow the / thíng that góod is.
21 Forsake me nôt, O LORD: † O my God, / bé not fár from me. * 22 Make

haste to help me, O Lord / mý salvátion.
**Glory be to the / Fáther and tó the Son * - and / tó the Hóly Ghost.
As it was in the beginning, is now, and / éver sháll be, * - wórld / without énd. Amen.**

Psalm-prayer. O Thou that art the healer both of soul and body, send forth Thy Salvation and make us whole: that while we deplore all our sickness and all our infirmity, we may by Thy strength overcome the temptations of the enemy; through the same our Lord Jesus Christ, who liveth and reigneth with Thee and the Holy Ghost, ever one God, world without end. Amen.

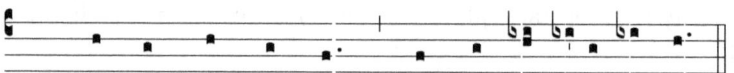

Ant. Héar my práyer, O LORD: * and give ear únto my <u>cry</u>.

Irr.

Psalm 39 *Dixi: Custodiam*
1 I said, I will take heed to my ways, that I sin nót with / my <u>tongue</u>: * I will keep my mouth with a bridle, while the wicked / ís befóre me.
2 I was dumb with silence, † I held my peace, éven / from <u>good</u>; * and my / sórrow was <u>stirred</u>.
3 My heart was hot within me, † while I was músing the / fíre- burned: * then spake / Í with my <u>tongue</u>,
4 LORD, make me to knôw mine end, † and the measure óf my days, / whát it is; * that I may / knów how fráil I am.
5 Behold, thou hast made my days as an handbreadth; † and mine age is as nóthing be- / fóre thee: * verily every man at his best state is alto- / géther vánity.
6 Surely every man walketh in a vain shew: † surely they are disquíet- / éd in vain: * he heapeth up riches, and knoweth not / whó shall gáther them.
7 And now, Lórd, what / wáit I for? * my / hópe is in <u>thee</u>.
8 Deliver me from all mý trans- / gréssions: * make me not the re- / próach of the fóolish.
9 I was dumb, I ópened / nót my mouth; * be- / cáuse thou dídst it.
10 Remove thy stróke a- / wáy from me: * I am consumed by the / blów of thine <u>hand</u>.
11 When thou with rebukes dost correct man for iníquity, † thou makest his beauty to consume awáy like / a <u>moth</u>: * surely every / mán is vánity.
12 Hear my prayer, O LORD, and give ear únto / my <u>cry</u>; * hold not thy /

péace at my tears:
For I am a stránger / with thee, * and a sojourner, as / áll my fáthers were. [138]
13 O spare me, that I máy re- / cóver strength, * before I go / hénce, and bé
no more.
Glory be to the Fáther and / tó the Son * and / tó the Hóly Ghost.
**As it was in the beginning, is now, and éver / sháll be, * - / wórld without
énd. Amen.**

Psalm-prayer. O Christ, Son of the Living God, who for our sakes wast made the Bread of the universe, grant that we may never be led away by the temptation of our enemy, but may follow Thee in the true government of our tongue; who livest and reignest with the Father and the Holy Ghost, ever one God, world without end. Amen.

Ant. The Lord * inclíned unto Me: and héard My voice.

Psalm 40 *Expectans expectavi*
1 I waited / pátiently fór the LORD; * and he inclined unto / mé, and héard
my cry.
2 He brought me up also out of an horrible pit, / óut of the míry clay, * and
set my feet upon a rock, and estáb- / lished my góings.
3 And he hath put a new song in my mouth, even praise / únto our God: *
many shall see it, and fear, and shall / trúst in the LORD.
4 Bless-ed is that man that / máketh the LÓRD his trust, * and respecteth not
the proud, nor such as / túrn asíde to lies.
5 Many, O LORD my God, are thy wonderful / wórks which thóu hast done,
* and thy thoughts which / áre to ús-ward:
They cannot be reckoned up in / órder únto thee: * if I would declare and
speak of them, they are more than / cán be númbered.
6 Sacrifice and offering thou didst nôt desire; † mine ears / hást thou
ópened: * burnt offering and sin offering hast thou / nót requíred.
7 Then / sáid I, Ló, I come: * in the volume of the book it is / wrítten of me,
8 I delight to do thy / wíll, O my God: * yea, thy láw / is withín my heart.
9 I have preached righteousness in the great / cóngregátion: * lo, I have not
refrained my lips, O / LÓRD, thou knówest.
10 I have not hid thy righteousness withîn my heart; † I have declared thy

faithfulness and / thý salvátion: * I have not concealed thy lovingkindness and thy truth from the great / cóngregátion.

11 Withhold not thou thy tender / mércies from mé, O LORD: * let thy lovingkindness and thy truth continual- / lý presérve me.

12 For innumerable evils have / cómpassed mé about: * mine iniquities have taken hold upon me, so that I am not á- / ble to lóok up;

They are more than the / háirs of mine head: * therefore / mý heart fáileth me.

[139] 13 Be pleased, O LORD, / tó delíver me: * O LORD, make / háste to hélp me.

14 Let them be ashamed and con- / fóunded togéther * that seek after my soul / tó destróy it;

Let them be driven / báckward and pút to shame * - that / wísh me évil.

15 Let them be desolate for a re- / wárd of their shame * that say unto / mé, Ahá, aha.

16 Let all those that seek thee rejoice / ánd be glád in thee: * let such as love thy salvation say continually, The / LÓRD be mágnified.

17 But I am / póor and néedy; * yet the Lord thínk- / eth upón me:

Thou art my help and / mý delíverer; * make no tár- / rying, Ó my God.

Glory be to the / Fáther and tó the Son * - and / tó the Hóly Ghost.

As it was in the beginning, is now, and / éver sháll be, * - wórld / without énd. Amen.

Psalm-prayer. God, which art the only expectation of Thy saints, whose advent into this world is set forth in the volume of the Book, graft, we pray Thee, Thy law in our hearts; to the end that we, declaring Thy righteousness, may be saved from every peril; who livest and reignest with the Father and the Holy Ghost, ever one God, world without end. Amen.

Ant. Lord, be mérciful únto me— : * heal my soul; for I have sínned a-

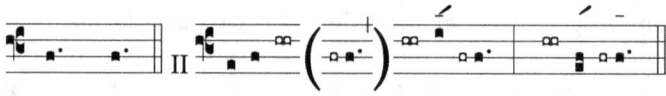

gáinst thee.

Psalm 41 *Beatus qui*

1 Bless-ed is he that consídereth the / poor: * the LORD will deliver him in tíme of / tróuble.

2 The LORD will preserve him, and keep him alive; † and he shall be bléss-

ed up- / ón the earth: * and thou wilt not deliver him unto the wíll of his / énemies.
3 The LORD will strengthen him upon the béd of / lánguishing: * thou wilt make all his bed ín his / síckness.
4 I said, LORD, be mérciful / únto me: * heal my soul; for I have sínned a- / gáinst thee.
5 Mine enemies speak évil of / <u>me</u>, * When shall he die, ánd his name / pérish?
6 And if he come to see me, he speaketh vânity: † his heart gathereth iníquity / tó itself; * when he goeth abróad, he / télleth it.
7 All that hate me whisper togéther a- / gáinst me: * against me do théy de- / víse my hurt.
8 An evil disease, say they, cleaveth fást unto / <u>him</u>: * and now that he lieth hé shall rise / úp no more.
9 Yea, mine own familiar friend, in whom I trusted, † which did éat of my / <u>bread</u>, * hath lifted up his héel a- / gáinst me.
10 But thou, O LORD, be mérciful / únto me, * and raise me up, that I máy re- / quíte them.
11 By this I know that thou fávourest / <u>me</u>, * because mine enemy doth not tríumph / óver me.
12 And as for me, thou upholdest me in míne in- / tégrity, * and settest me before thy fáce for / éver. [140]
13 Bless-ed be the LORD Gód of / Ísrael * from everlasting, and to everlasting. Amén, and / A<u>men</u>.
Glory be to the Fáther and / tó the Son * and tó the / Hóly Ghost.
As it was in the beginning, is now, and éver / shall be, * wórld without / énd. Amen.

Psalm-prayer. O everlasting God, who dost forgive and pass by our sins, and in whose promise to show mercy to the needy we put all our hope of escaping the evil day, have compassion, we pray Thee, on our sorrows; so that while Thou gently concealest our casual faults, Thou mayest graciously give us the pardon of our souls; through our Lord Jesus Christ, who liveth and reigneth with Thee and the Holy Ghost, ever one God, world without end. Amen.

Ant. My soul * thírsteth for <u>God</u>: fór the líving God.

I

Psalm 42i *Quemadmodum*

1 As the hart panteth / áfter the wáter brooks, * so panteth my soul / áfter thée, O God.

2 My soul thirsteth for God, / fór the líving God: * when shall I come and ap- / péar before <u>God</u>?

3 My tears have / béen my meat dáy and night, * while they continually say unto me, / Whére is thy <u>God</u>?

4 When I re- / mémber these <u>things</u>, * I pour / óut my sóul in me:
For I had gone / wíth the múltitude, * I went with them / tó the hóuse of God,
With the / vóice of jóy and praise, * with a multitude / thát kept hólyday.

5 Why art thou cast / dówn, O my <u>soul</u>? * and why art thou disquí- / eted ín me?
Hope thou in God: for / Í shall yet práise him * for the hélp / of his cóuntenance.

Glory be to the / Fáther and tó the Son * - and / tó the Hóly Ghost.
As it was in the beginning, is now, and / éver sháll be, * - wórld / without énd. Amen.

[141]

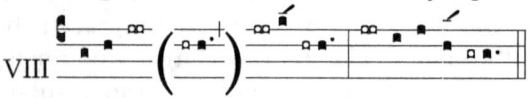

Ant. Hópe thou in <u>God</u>: * for Í shall yet práise Him.

VIII

Psalm 42ii *Ad meipsum*

6 O my God, my soul is cast down within me: † therefore will I remember thee from the lánd of / Jórdan, * and of the Hermonites, / fróm the híll Mizar.

7 Deep calleth unto deep at the nóise of thy / wáterspouts: * all thy waves and thy billows / áre gone óver me.

8 Yet the LORD will command his lovingkindness in the daytime, † and in the night his song sháll be / wíth me, * and my prayer unto the Gód / of

my <u>life</u>.
9 I will say unto God my rock, Why hast thóu for- / gótten me? * why go I mourning because of the oppression / óf the énemy?
10 As with a sword in my bones, mine enemíes re- / próach me; * while they say daily unto me, Whére / is thy <u>God</u>?
11 Why art thou cast dówn, O my / <u>soul</u>? * and why art thou disquiet- / éd withín me?
Hope thou in God: for Í shall yet / práise him, * who is the health of my cóun- / tenance, ánd my God.
Glory be to the Fáther and / tó the Son * and / tó the Hóly Ghost.
As it was in the beginning, is now, and éver / sháll be, * wórld / without énd. Amen.

Psalm-prayer. O God, who in the daytime commandest Thy mercy, and in the night manifestest Thyself, we pray Thee that Thou wouldst both in the day defend us for our salvation, and in the night protect us for our rest; through Jesus Christ our Lord, who liveth and reigneth with Thee and the Holy Ghost, ever one God, world without end. Amen.

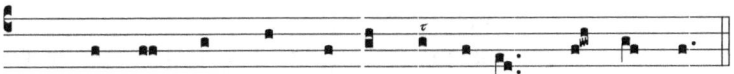

Ant. Thou art * the Health of my countenance, and my God.

Psalm 43 *Judica me*
1 Judge me, O God, and plead my cause against an un- / gódly nátion: * O deliver me from the decéit- / ful and únjust man.
2 For thou art the God of my strength: / whý dost thou cást me off? * why go I mourning because of the oppression / óf the énemy?
3 O send out thy light and thy truth: / lét them léad me; * let them bring me unto thy holy hill, and to thy / tábernácles.
4 Then will I go unto the altar of God, † unto / Gód my excéeding joy: * yea, upon the harp will I práise / thee, O Gód my God.
5 Why art thou cast / dówn, O my <u>soul</u>? * and why art thou disquiet- / éd withín me?
Hope in God: for / Í shall yet práise him, * who is the health of my cóun- / tenance, ánd my God.
Glory be to the / Fáther and tó the Son * - and / tó the Hóly Ghost.
As it was in the beginning, is now, and / éver sháll be, * - wórld / without

énd. Amen.

Psalm-prayer. Almighty God, fountain of perpetual light, we pray Thee that, sending out Thy truth into our hearts, Thou wouldst lighten us with the new brightness of Thine eternal light; through Jesus Christ our Lord, who liveth and reigneth with Thee and the Holy Ghost, ever one God, world without end. Amen.

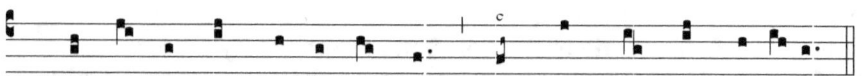

Ant. In God we boast áll the day <u>long</u>: * and praise thy náme for éver.

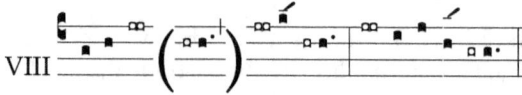

VIII

Psalm 44i *Deus, auribus*
1 We have heard with our ears, O God, our fáthers have / tóld us, * what work thou didst in their days, / ín the tímes of old.
2 How thou didst drive out the heathen with thy hánd, and / plánt-edst them; * how thou didst afflict the péo- / ple, and cást them out.
3 For they got not the land in possession bý their / ówn sword, * neither did their / ówn arm sáve them:
But thy right hand, and thine arm, and the líght of thy / cóuntenance, * because thou hadst a / fávour únto them.
4 Thóu art my / Kíng, O God: * command deliveran- / cés for Jácob.
5 Through thee will we push dówn our / énemies: * through thy name will we tread them under that rise / úp agáinst us.
6 For I will not trúst in my / <u>bow</u>, * neither shall / mý sword sáve me.
7 But thou hast saved us fróm our / énemies, * and hast put them to / sháme that háted us.
8 In God we boast áll the day / <u>long</u>, * and praise thy / náme for éver.
Glory be to the Fáther and / tó the Son * and / tó the Hóly Ghost.
As it was in the beginning, is now, and éver / sháll be, * wórld / without énd. Amen.

Ant. My confusion * is continuallý befóre me: and the shame of my fáce hath

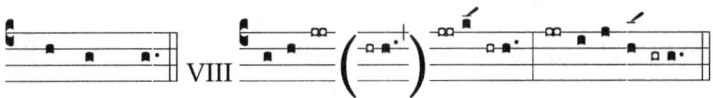

cóvered me.

Psalm 44ii *Nunc autem*
9 But thou hast cast off, and pút us to / shame; * and goest not forth / wíth our ármies.
10 Thou makest us to turn báck from the / énemy: * and they which hate us spóil / for themselves.
11 Thou hast given us like sheep appóinted for / meat; * and hast scattered us a- / móng the héathen.
12 Thou sellest thy péople for / nought, * and dost not incréase / thy wealth bý their price.
13 Thou makest us a repróach to our / néighbours, * a scorn and a derision to them that are / róund abóut us.
14 Thou makest us a byword amóng the / héathen, * a shaking of the head a- / móng the péople.
15 My confusion is continuallý be- / fóre me, * and the shame of my / fáce hath cóvered me,
16 For the voice of him that reproacheth ánd blas- / phémeth; * by reason of the enemy / ánd avénger.
Glory be to the Fáther and / tó the Son * and / tó the Hóly Ghost.
As it was in the beginning, is now, and éver / sháll be, * wórld / without énd. Amen.

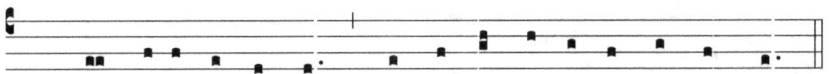

Ant. Lord, aríse for our help: * and redeem us fór thy mércies' sake.

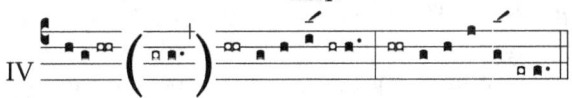

Psalm 44iii *Haec omnia*
17 All this is come upon us; yet have we / nót forgótten thee, * neither have we dealt false- / ly ín thy cóvenant.
18 Our / héart is nót turned back, * neither have our steps de- / clíned from thy way;
19 Though thou hast sore broken us in the / pláce of drágons, * and covered us with the / shádow of death.
20 If we have forgotten the náme / of our God, * or stretched out our /

hánds to a stránge god;
21 Sháll / not God seárch this out? * for he knoweth / the sécrets óf the heart.
22 Yea, for thy sake are we killed áll / the day long; * we are counted as / shéep for the sláughter.
23 Awake, why / sléepest thóu, O Lord? * arise, cast us / not óff for éver.

[144] 24 Wherefore / hídest thóu thy face, * and forgettest our affliction / and óur oppréssion?
25 For our soul is bowed dówn / to the dust: * our belly cleaveth / únto the earth.
26 Aríse / for our help, * and redeem / us fór thy mércies' sake.
Glory be to the Fá-/ ther and tó the Son * -/ and tó the Hóly Ghost.
As it was in the beginning, is now, and / éver sháll be, * -/ wórld without énd. Amen.

Psalm-prayer. Arise, O Lord, and help us, and deliver us from all temptations of Satan; and do Thou, who in the days of our fathers didst overthrow the plotting of Thine enemies, deliver us by the light of Thy countenance from the snares of the devil; through Jesus Christ our Lord, who liveth and reigneth with Thee and the Holy Ghost, ever one God, world without end. Amen.

Ant. Thóu art fáirer: * than the children of mén, O Lord Christ.

Psalm 45 *Eructavit*
1 My heart is inditing a good matter: † I speak of the things which I have made tóuch- / ing the king: * my tongue is the pen of / a réady wríter.
2 Thou art fairer than the children of men: † grace is poured ín- / to thy lips: * therefore God hath / bléssed thee for éver.
3 Gird thy sword upon thy thigh, / Ó most míghty, * with thy glo- / ry ánd thy májesty.
4 And in thy majesty ride prosperously because of truth and méek- / ness and ríghteousness; * and thy right hand shall teach thee / térrible things.
5 Thine arrows are sharp in the heart óf / the king's énemies; * whereby the / péople fall únder thee.
6 Thy throne, O God, is for év- / er and éver: * the sceptre of thy kingdom /

ís a right scéptre.
7 Thou lovest righteousness, and / hátest wíckedness: * therefore God, thy God, hath anointed thee with the oil of gladness / abóve thy féllows.
8 All thy garments smell of myrrh, and ál- / oes, and cássia, * out of the ivory palaces, where- / bý they have máde thee glad.
9 Kings' daughters were among thy hónour- / able wómen: * upon thy right hand did stand the queen / in góld of Óphir.
10 Hearken, O daughter, and consider, / ánd inclíne thine ear; * forget also thine own peo- / ple, ánd thy fáther's house;
11 So shall the king greatly de- / síre thy béauty: * for he is thy Lord; and / wórship thou <u>him</u>.
12 And the daughter of Tyre shall be thére / with a <u>gift</u>; * even the rich among the people shall / intréat thy fávour.
13 The king's daughter is all gló- / rious with<u>in</u>: * her cloth- / ing ís of wróught gold.
14 She shall be brought unto the king in rái- / ment of néedlework: * the virgins her companions that follow her shall be / bróught unto <u>thee</u>. [145]
15 With gladness and rejói- / cing shall théy be brought: * they shall enter in- / tó the king's pálace.
16 Instead of thy fathers shall / bé thy chíldren, * whom thou mayest make / prínces in áll the earth.
17 I will make thy name to be remembered in áll / generátions: * therefore shall the people praise thee for / éver and éver.
Glory be to the Fá-/ ther and tó the Son * - / and tó the Hóly Ghost.
As it was in the beginning, is now, and / éver sháll be, * - / wórld without énd. Amen.

Psalm-prayer. O Christ, the Word of the Father, by whom all things were created; keep, we beseech Thee, Thy Church gathered together from the various nations of the Gentiles; that loving Thee with a pure heart, we may inherit participation of Thine eternal kingdom; where with the Father and the Holy Ghost, Thou livest and reignest, ever one God, world without end. Amen.

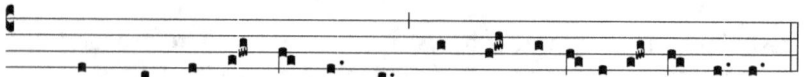

Ant. The Lord of hósts is wíth us: * the God of Jacob ís our réfuge.

Psalm 46 *Deus noster*

1 God is our / réfuge and <u>strength</u>, * a very present / hélp in tróuble.
2 Therefore will not we fear, though the / eárth be re<u>moved</u>, * and though the mountains be carried into the / mídst of the <u>sea</u>;
3 Though the waters thereof / róar and be tróubled, * though the mountains shake with the / swélling there<u>of</u>.
4 There is a river, the streams whereof shall make glad the / cíty of <u>God</u>, * the holy place of the tabernacles / óf the móst High.
5 God is in the midst of her; / shé shall nót be moved: * God shall help her, and / thát right éarly.
6 The heathen raged, the / kíngdoms were <u>moved</u>: * he uttered his vóice, / the earth mélted.
7 The LORD of / hósts is wíth us; * the God of Jacob / ís our réfuge.
8 Come, behold the / wórks of the <u>LORD</u>, * what desolations he hath / máde in the <u>earth</u>.
9 He maketh wars to cease unto the end of the earth; † he breaketh the bow, and cutteth the / spéar in súnder; * he burneth the / cháriot ín the fire.
10 Be still, and / knów that Í am God: * I will be exalted among the heathen, I will be ex- / álted ín the earth.
11 The LORD of / hósts is wíth us; * the God of Jacob / ís our réfuge.
  Glory be to the / Fáther and tó the Son * - and / tó the Hóly Ghost.
[146] **As it was in the beginning, is now, and / éver sháll be, * - wórld / without énd. Amen.**

Psalm-prayer. O most merciful Lord, our consolation and refuge, sanctify with the river of Thy grace the tabernacles of our hearts, that Thou, the God of Jacob, helping us, every earthly enemy may be overthrown; through Jesus Christ our Lord, who liveth and reigneth with Thee and the Holy Ghost, ever one God, world without end. Amen.

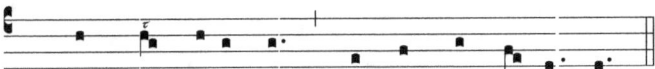

Ant. Oh, shóut unto God: * with the vóice of trí-umph.

Psalm 47 *Omnes gentes*
1 O clap your hands, / áll ye péople; * shout unto God with the / vóice of tríumph.
2 For the LORD most / hígh is térrible; * he is a great King / óver áll the earth.
3 He shall subdue the / péople únder us, * and the nations / únder our feet.
4 He shall choose our in- / héritance fór us, * the excellency of / Jácob whóm he loved.
5 God is gone / úp with a shout, * the LORD with the sóund / of a trúmpet.
6 Sing praises to / Gód, sing práises: * sing praises unto our / Kíng, sing práises.
7 For God is the / Kíng of áll the earth: * sing ye praises with / únderstánding.
8 God reigneth / óver the héathen: * God sitteth upon the thróne / of his hóliness.
9 The princes of the people are / gáthered togéther, * even the people of the / Gód of Ábraham:
For the shields of the earth be- / lóng unto God: * he is gréat- / ly exálted.
Glory be to the / Fáther and tó the Son * - and / tó the Hóly Ghost.
As it was in the beginning, is now, and / éver sháll be, * - wórld / without énd. Amen.

Psalm-prayer. Christ Jesus our Lord and terrible God, in whose nativity the angels offered praises together with the shepherds; to whom, after the author of death had been conquered, all the people clapped their hands together, and lifted up their hearts; Thou whom, when Thou didst carry back to heaven the victorious trophies of Thy triumphs, the faith of the Apostles also followed; grant that we may both celebrate the mysteries of our redemption, and the glories of Thine Ascension, with the jubilations of faith, and may, together with the princes of the people, be well-pleasing to Thee, the God of Abraham; who livest and reignest with the Father and the Holy Ghost, ever one God, world without end. Amen.

[147]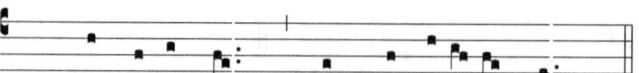

Ant. Great is the LORD, * and greatly to be praised. *(Do not repeat in verse 1.)*

Psalm 48 *Magnus Dominus*
1 [Great is the LORD, and / gréatly tó be praised] * in the city of our God, in the mountain / óf his hóliness.
2 Beautiful for situation, the / jóy of the whóle earth, * is mount Zion, on the sides of the north, the city / óf the gréat King.
3 God is known in her palaces / fór a réfuge. * 4 For, lo, the kings were assembled, they passed / bý togéther.
5 They saw it, and / só they márvelled; * they were troubled, and / hásted a<u>way</u>.
6 Fear took / hóld upón them there, * and pain, as of a / wóman ín travail.
7 Thou breakest the / shíps of Társhish * - / wíth an éast wind.
8 As we have heard, so have we seen † in the city of the LORD of hosts, in the / cíty óf our God: * God will establish / ít for éver.
9 We have thought of thy loving- / kíndness, O <u>God</u>, * in the mídst / of thy témple.
10 According to thy name, O God, so is thy praise unto the / énds of the <u>earth</u>: * thy right hand is / fúll of ríghteousness.
11 Let mount Zion rejoice, let the daughters of / Júdah be <u>glad</u>, * becáuse / of thy júdgments.
12 Walk about Zion, and go / róund abóut her: * tell the / tówers there<u>of</u>.
13 Mark ye well her bulwarks, con- / síder her pálaces; * that ye may tell it to the gener- / átion fóllowing.
14 For this God is our God for / éver and éver: * he will be our guide / éven únto death.
 Glory be to the / Fáther and tó the Son * - and / tó the Hóly Ghost.
As it was in the beginning, is now, and / éver sháll be, * - wórld / without énd. Amen.

Psalm-prayer. O God, Thou that art great and terrible, who art adorned as the glorious prince in the heavenly Jerusalem, expand our souls with spiritual knowledge, that Thy mercy tabernacling within our breasts, we may be deemed worthy to tell forth Thy Holy Name; through Jesus Christ our Lord, who liveth and reigneth with Thee and the Holy Ghost, ever one God, world without end. Amen.

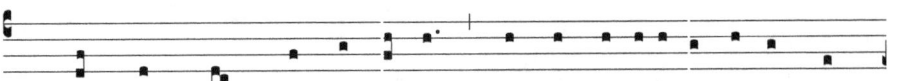

Ant. My mouth shall spéak of wísdom: * and the meditation of my heart

shall be of únderstánding.

Psalm 49i *Audite haec*
1 Hear this, all ye people; † give ear, all ye in- / hábitants óf the world: * 2 Both low and high, rich and / póor, togéther.
3 My mouth shall / spéak of wísdom; * and the meditation of my heart shall be of / únderstánding.
4 I will incline mine / éar to a párable: * I will open my dark sáy- / ing upón the harp.
5 Wherefore should I fear in the / dáys of évil, * when the iniquity of my heels shall / cómpass mé about?
6 They that / trúst in their <u>wealth</u>, * and boast themselves in the multitude / óf their ríches;
7 None of them can by any means re- / déem his bróther, * nor give to God a / ránsom for <u>him</u>:
8 For the redemption of their / sóul is précious, * and it céas- / eth for éver:
9 That he should still / líve for éver, * and not / sée corrúption.
10 For he seeth that wise men die, † likewise the fool and the brutish / pérson pérish, * and leave their / wéalth to óthers.
11 Their inward thought is, that their houses shall continue for ever, † and their dwelling places to all / génerátions; * they call their lands áf- / ter their ówn names.
12 Nevertheless man being in / hónour abídeth not: * he is like the / béasts that pérish.
Glory be to the / Fáther and tó the Son * - and / tó the Hóly Ghost.
As it was in the beginning, is now, and / éver sháll be, * - wórld / without énd. Amen.

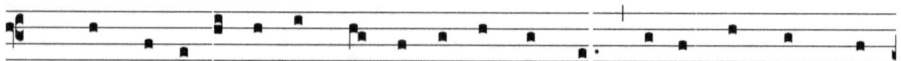

Ant. Man that is in honour, and únderstándeth not: * is like the béasts that

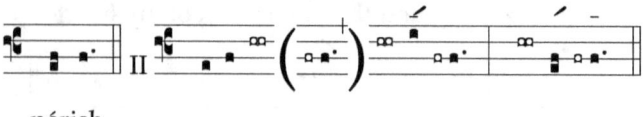

pérish.

Psalm 49ii *Haec via*
13 This their wáy is their / fólly: * yet their posterity appróve their / sáyings.
14 Like sheep they are láid in the / grave; * déath shall / féed on them;
And the upright shall have dominion over them ín the / mórning; * and their beauty shall consume in the grave fróm their / dwélling.
15 But God will redeem my soul from the pówer / óf the grave: * for hé shall re- / céive me.
16 Be not thou afraid when óne is made / rich, * when the glory of his hóuse is / increased;
17 For when he dieth he shall carry nóthing a- / way: * his glory shall nót descend / áfter him.
18 Though while he líved he / bléssed his soul: * and men will praise thee, when thou doest wéll to / thyself.
19 He shall go to the generation óf his / fáthers; * they shall néver / see light.
20 Man that is in honour, and únder- / stándeth not, * is like the béasts that / pérish.
**Glory be to the Fáther and / tó the Son * and tó the / Hóly Ghost.
As it was in the beginning, is now, and éver / sháll be, * wórld without / énd. Amen.**

Psalm-prayer. Fill, O Lord, our mouths with Thy wisdom; that we, being always mindful that Thou didst become man, and didst redeem us from the power of the grave, may be filled with the light of Thy countenance; who livest and reignest with the Father and the Holy Ghost, ever one God, world without end. Amen.

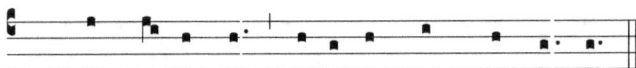

Ant. The mighty God, * even the Lord, hath spoken.
(Do not repeat in verse 1.)

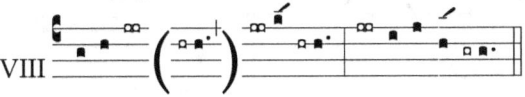

Psalm 50i *Deus deorum*
1 [The mighty God, even the LÓRD, hath / spóken,] * and called the earth from the rising of the sun unto the / góing dówn thereof.
2 Out of Zion, the perfection of béauty, / Gód hath shined. * 3 Our God shall come, and shall / nót keep sílence:
A fire shall devóur be- / fóre him, * and it shall be very tempestuous / róund abóut him.
4 He shall call to the héavens / fróm above, * and to the earth, that he may / júdge his péople.
5 Gather my saints togéther / únto me; * those that have made a covenant with / mé by sácrifice.
6 And the heavens shall decláre his / ríghteousness: * for / Gód is júdge himself.
7 Hear, O my people, and I will speak; † O Israel, and I will testifý a- / gáinst thee: * I am God, / éven thý God.
8 I will not reprove thee for thy sacrifices or thý burnt / ófferings, * to have been continual- / lý befóre me.
9 I will take no bullock óut of thy / house, * nor he goats óut / of thy folds.
10 For every beast of the fórest is / mine, * and the cattle up- / ón a thóusand hills.
11 I know all the fowls óf the / móuntains: * and the wild beasts / óf the field are mine.
12 If I were hungry, I wóuld not / téll thee: * for the world is mine, and the fúl- / ness thereof.
13 Will I éat the / flésh of bulls, * or / drínk the blóod of goats?
14 Offer unto Gód thanks- / gíving; * and pay thy vows ún- / to the móst High:
15 And call upon me in the dáy of / tróuble: * I will deliver thee, and thou shalt gló- / rify me.
Glory be to the Fáther and / tó the Son * and / tó the Hóly Ghost. [150]
As it was in the beginning, is now, and éver / sháll be, * wórld / without énd. Amen.

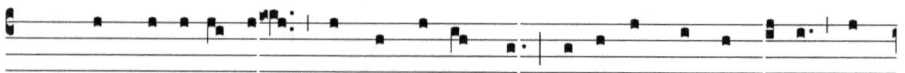

Ant. Now consi-der this, * yé that forgét God: lest I tear you in pieces, and

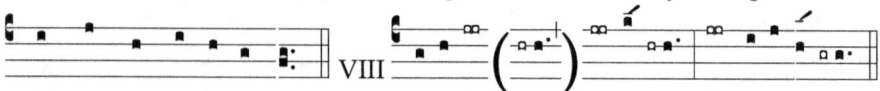

there be nóne to de-lí-ver.

Psalm 50ii *Peccatori*

16 But unto the wicked God saith, † What hast thou to do to decláre my / státutes, * or that thou shouldest take my có- / venant ín thy mouth?

17 Seeing thou hátest in- / strúction, * and castest my / wórds behínd thee.

18 When thou sawest a thief, then thou consént-eds*t* / wíth him, * and hast been partaker / wíth adúlterers.

19 Thou givest thy móuth to / évil, * and thy tongue frá- / meth de<u>ceit</u>.

20 Thou sittest and speakest agáinst thy / bróther; * thou slanderest / thíne own móther's son.

21 These things hast thou done, and Í kept / sílence; * thou thoughtest that I was altogether such a*n* óne / as thy<u>self</u>:

But I wíll re- / próve thee, * and set them in ór- / der befóre thine eyes.

22 Now consider this, yé that for- / gét God, * lest I tear you in pieces, and there be nóne / to delíver.

23 Whoso offereth praise glóri- / fíeth me: * and to him that ordereth his conversation aright will I shew the salvá- / tion of <u>God</u>.

Glory be to the Fáther and / tó the Son * and / tó the Hóly Ghost.

As it was in the beginning, is now, and éver / sháll be, * wórld / without énd. Amen.

Psalm-prayer. O Lord, the mighty God, we beseech Thee, that Thou wouldest receive from us the sacrifice of praise; so that we, being set free from the burden of our sins, may patiently run the race that is set before us; through Jesus Christ our Lord, who liveth and reigneth with Thee and the Holy Ghost, ever one God, world without end. Amen.

[151]

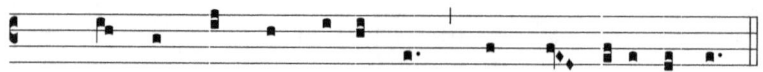

Ant. Wash me thór-ough-lý, O Lord: * from míne in-í-qui-ty.

Psalm 51 *Miserere mei*

1 Have mercy upon me, O God, according to thy / lóvingkíndness: * according unto the multitude of thy tender mercies blot out / mý transgréssions.
2 Wash me thoroughly from / míne iníquity, * and / cléanse me fróm my sin.
3 For I acknowledge / mý transgréssions: * and my sin is / éver befóre me.
4 Against thee, thee only, have I sinned, and done this / évil ín thy sight: * that thou mightest be justified when thou speakest, and be clear / whén thou júdgest.
5 Behold, I was shapen / ín iníquity; * and in sin did my / móther concéive me.
6 Behold, thou desirest truth / ín the ínward parts: * and in the hidden part thou shalt make / mé to know wísdom.
7 Purge me with hyssop, and / Í shall be <u>clean</u>: * wash me, and I shall be / whíter than <u>snow</u>.
8 Make me to hear / jóy and gládness; * that the bones which thou hast / bróken máy rejoice.
9 Hide thy / fáce from my <u>sins</u>, * and blot out / áll mine iníquities.
10 Create in / mé a clean héart, O God; * and renew a right / spírit withín me.
11 Cast me not a- / wáy from thy présence; * and take not thy holy / spírit fróm me.
12 Restore unto me the joy of / thý salvátion; * and uphold me with / thý free spírit.
13 Then will I teach trans- / gréssors thy <u>ways</u>; * and sinners shall be con- / vérted únto thee.
14 Deliver me from bloodguiltiness, O God, thou God of / mý salvátion: * and my tongue shall sing a- / lóud of thy ríghteousness.
15 O Lord, / ópen thóu my lips; * and my mouth / sháll shew fórth thy praise.
16 For thou desirest not sacrifice; / élse would I gíve it: * thou delightest / nót in burnt óffering.
17 The sacrifices of God are a / bróken spírit: * a broken and a contrite heart, O God, / thóu wilt nót despise.
18 Do good in thy good pleasure / únto Zíon: * build thou the / wálls of Jerúsalem.
19 Then shalt thou be pleased with the sacrifices of rîghteousness, † with

burnt offering and / whóle burnt óffering: * then shall they offer bullocks up- / ón thine áltar.
Glory be to the / Fáther and tó the Son * and / tó the Hóly Ghost.
As it was in the beginning, is now, and / éver sháll be, * - / wórld without énd. Amen.

Psalm-prayer. O Lord Jesus Christ, God of our salvation, who by Thy salutary Passion dost extinguish all our evil passions; give to us Thy servants forgiveness of our sins and remission of our guilt, to the end that from Thee, O Lord, we may one day receive eternal life; who livest and reignest with the Father and the Holy Ghost, ever one God, world without end. Amen.

[152]
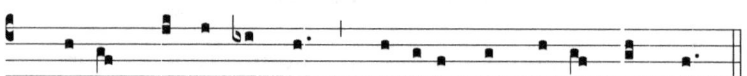

Ant. I will wáit on thy <u>name</u>: * for it is góod befóre thy saints.

Psalm 52 *Quid gloriaris*
1 Why boastest thou thyself in míschief, O / míghty man? * the goodness of God en- / dúreth contínually.
2 Thy tongue devíseth / míschiefs; * like a sharp razor, / wórking decéitfully.
3 Thou lovest évil / móre than good; * and lying rather / thán to speak ríghteousness.
4 Thou lovest áll de- / vóuring words, * O / thóu decéitful tongue.
5 God shall likewise destroy thée for / éver, * he shall / táke thee a<u>way</u>,
And pluck thee óut of thy / dwélling place, * and root thee out of the / lánd of the líving.
6 The righteous álso shall / sée, and fear, * - / ánd shall láugh at him:
7 Lo, this is the man that made not Gôd his strength; † but trusted in the abundance óf his / ríches, * and strengthened himself / ín his wíckedness.
8 But I am like a green olive tree ín the / hóuse of God: * I trust in the mercy of God for / éver and éver.
9 I will praise thee for ever, because thóu hast / dóne it: * and I will wait on thy name; for it is / góod befóre thy saints.
Glory be to the Fáther and / tó the Son * and / tó the Hóly Ghost.
As it was in the beginning, is now, and éver / sháll be, * - / wórld without énd. Amen.

Psalm-prayer. Only-begotten Word of the Father, Thou who art long-suffering towards the people that rise up against Thee, and of Thine infinite love dost endure the mighty man who boasteth in mischief; grant of Thine infinite goodness that we may follow Thine example of pardon; and may also have our portion among those that have been forgiven; who livest and reignest with the Father and the Holy Ghost, ever one God, world without end. Amen.

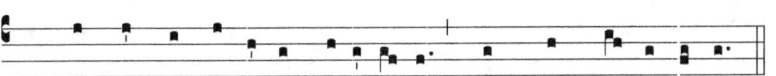

[153]

Ant. Oh that the salvátion of Ís-ra-el: * were come óut of Zí-on!

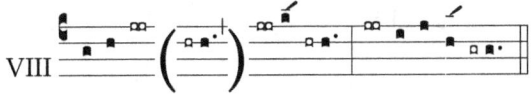

VIII

Psalm 53 *Dixit insipiens*
1 The fool hath said in his heart, There is no God. † Corrupt are they, and have done abominablé in- / íquity: * there is / nóne that dóeth good.
2 God looked down from heaven upon the chíldren of / <u>men</u>, * to see if there were any that did under- / stánd, that díd seek God.
3 Every one of them is gone back: † they are altogether bécome / fílthy; * there is none that dó- / eth good, nó, not one.
4 Have the workers of iniquity no knowledge? † who eat up my people ás they eat / <u>bread</u>: * they have not cálled / upon <u>God</u>.
5 There were they in great féar, where / nó fear was: * for God hath scattered the bones of him that encám- / peth agáinst thee:
Thou hast pút them to / <u>shame</u>, * because Gód / hath despísed them.
6 Oh that the salvation of Israel were come out of Zion! † When God bringeth back the captivity óf his / péople, * Jacob shall rejoice, and Ís- / ra-el sháll be glad.
Glory be to the Fáther and / tó the Son * and / tó the Hóly Ghost.
As it was in the beginning, is now, and éver / sháll be, * wórld / without énd. Amen.

Psalm-prayer. We beseech Thee, O Lord Jesus Christ, that we by Thy help being saved from our enemies, may both in will and deed follow Thee, our head who art in heaven; who livest and reignest with the Father and the Holy Ghost, ever one God, world without end. Amen.

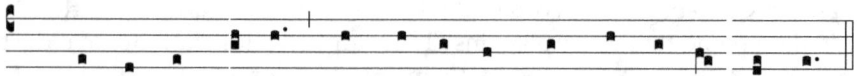

Ant. Gód is mine Hélper: * the Lord is with thém that uphóld my soul.

Psalm 54 *Deus, in nomine*
1 Save me, O God, by thy name, and / júdge me bý thy strength. * 2 Hear my prayer, O God; give ear to the / wórds of my <u>mouth</u>.
3 For strangers are risen up against me, † and oppressors seek áf- / ter my <u>soul</u>: * they have not / set Gód befóre them.
4 Behold, Gód / is mine hélper: * the Lord is with / them thát uphóld my soul.
5 He shall reward evil ún- / to mine énemies: * cut them / óff in thy <u>truth</u>.
6 I will freely sá- / crifice únto thee: * I will praise thy name, / O LÓRD; for ít is good.

[154] 7 For he hath delivered me óut / of all tróuble: * and mine eye hath seen his desire / upón mine énemies.
Glory be to the Fá-/ ther and tó the Son * -/ and tó the Hóly Ghost.
As it was in the beginning, is now, and / éver sháll be, * -/ wórld without énd. Amen.

Psalm-prayer. Save us, O Lord, by Thy Name, and avenge us by Thy strength; bring us out of trouble, and fill us with gladness, to the end that while Thy salvation is fully bestowed on us, we may joyfully chant Thy glory; who livest and reignest with the Father and the Holy Ghost, ever one God, world without end. Amen.

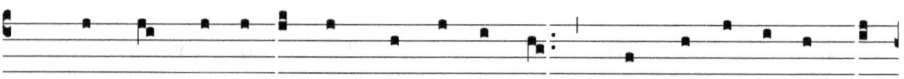

Ant. The Lord hath de-lí-vered my sóul in peace: * from the battle that wás

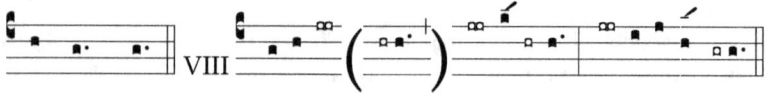

a-gáinst me.

Psalm 55 *Exaudi, Deus*
1 Give éar to my / práyer, O God; * and hide not thyself from my / súpplicátion.

210

2 Attend unto mé, and / héar me: * I mourn in my com- / pláint, and máke a noise;
3 Because of the vóice of the / énemy, * because of the oppression / óf the wícked:
For they cast iniquitý up- / ón me, * and in / wráth they háte me.
4 My heart is sore páined with- / ín me: * and the terrors of death are fál- / len upón me.
5 Fearfulness and trembling are cóme up- / ón me, * and horror hath / óverwhélmed me.
6 And I said, Oh that I had wíngs like a / <u>dove</u>! * for then would I fly a- / wáy, and bé at rest.
7 Lo, then would I wander far off, † and remáin in the / wílderness. * 8 I would hasten my escape from the windy / stórm and témpest.
9 Destroy, O Lord, ánd di- / víde their tongues: * for I have seen violence and strífe / in the cíty.
10 Day and night they go about it upón the / wálls thereof: * mischief also and sorrow are / ín the mídst of it.
11 Wickedness is ín the / mídst thereof: * deceit and guile depart nót / from her <u>streets</u>.
12 For it was not an enemy thát re- / próached me; * then I / cóuld have bórne it:
Neither was it he that hated me that did magnify himsélf a- / gáinst me; * then I would have híd / myself fróm him:
13 But it was thou, a mán mine / équal, * my guide, and / míne acquáintance.
14 We took sweet cóunsel to- / géther, * and walked unto the house of / Gód in cómpany.
15 Let death seize upon them, † and let them go down quíck into / <u>hell</u>: * for wickedness is in their dwellings, / ánd amóng them.
16 As for me, I will cáll upon / <u>God</u>; * and the / LÓRD shall sáve me.
17 Evening, and morning, and at noon, will I práy, and / crý aloud: * and / hé shall héar my voice.
18 He hath delivered my soul in peace from the battle that wás a- / gáinst me: * for there were / mány with me.
19 God shall hear, ánd af- /flíct them, * even he that abíd- / eth of <u>old</u>. [155]
Because they háve no / chánges, * thére- / fore they féar not God.
20 He hath put forth his hands against such as bé at / péace with him: * he hath bró- / ken his cóvenant.
21 The words of his mouth were smoother than butter, but wár was / ín his heart: * his words were softer than oil, yét / were they dráwn swords.
22 Cast thy burden upon the LORD, and he sháll su- / stáin thee: * he shall

never suffer the / ríghteous tó be moved.
23 But thou, O God, shalt bring them down into the pit of destruction: †
  bloody and deceitful men shall not líve out / hálf their days; * but / Í will
  trúst in thee.
Glory be to the Fáther and / tó the Son * and / tó the Hóly Ghost.
**As it was in the beginning, is now, and éver / sháll be, * wórld / without
  énd. Amen.**

Psalm-prayer. Lord Jesus, who wast before all ages with the Father and the Holy Ghost, and yet didst in the latter days take upon Thyself the nature of man, and wast betrayed by Thy companion and own familiar friend; grant, we beseech Thee, that we, praising Thee at morning, and evening, and noonday, may hear Thy Voice, because Thou art pleased to hear ours; who livest and reignest with the Father and the Holy Ghost, ever one God, world without end. Amen.

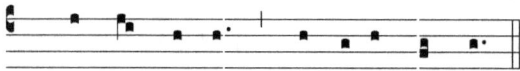

Ant. In Thee, O God, * have I put my trust.

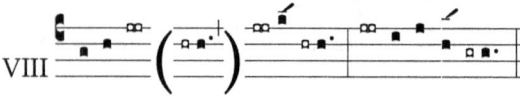

VIII

Psalm 56 *Miserere mei*
1 Be merciful unto me, O God: † for man would swállow me / up; * he fighting dáil- / y opprésseth me.
2 Mine enemies would daily swállow me / up: * for they be many that fight against / mé, O thóu most High.
3 What time Í am a- / fraid, * - / Í will trúst in thee.
4 In God I will praise his word, † in God Í have / pút my trust; * I will not fear what flésh / can do únto me.
5 Every dáy they / wrést my words: * all their thoughts are agáinst / me for évil.
6 They gather themselves together, they / híde themselves, * they mark my steps, when they wáit / for my soul.
7 Shall they escape bý in- / íquity? * in thine anger cast down the péo- / ple, O God.
8 Thou tellest my wânderings: † put thou my tears ínto thy / bóttle: * are they nót / in thy book?
9 When I cry unto thee, then shall mine énemies / túrn back: * this I know; for / Gód is fór me.

10 In Gód will I / práise his word: * in the LÓRD / will I práise his word.
11 In Gód have I / pút my trust: * I will not be afraid what mán / can do únto me.
12 Thy vows áre upon / mé, O God: * I will render / práises únto thee.
13 For thou hast delivered my soûl from death: † wilt not thou deliver my féet from / fálling, * that I may walk before God in the líght / of the líving?
Glory be to the Fáther and / tó the Son * and / tó the Hóly Ghost.   [156]
As it was in the beginning, is now, and éver / sháll be, * wórld / without énd. Amen.

Psalm-prayer. O God, we set forth to Thee, our Life, that Life which by death destroyed death; so that Thou, regarding not our merits, but His love, may both put our tears into Thy bottle in this life, and may everlastingly wipe them away in the Land of the Living; through the same Jesus Christ our Lord, who liveth and reigneth with Thee and the Holy Ghost, ever one God, world without end. Amen.

Ant. Be merciful unto me, O God, * be merci-ful un-to me: for my soul trust-

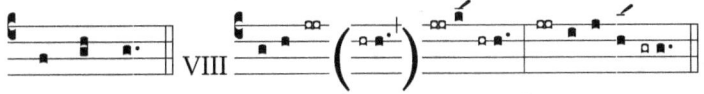

eth in thee. *(Do not repeat in verse 1.)*

Psalm 57 *Miserere mei*
1 [Be merciful unto me, O God, be mérciful / únto me: * for my soul trúst- / eth in <u>thee</u>:]
Yea, in the shadow of thy wings will I máke my / réfuge, * until these calami- / tíes be óverpast.
2 I will crý unto / Gód most high; * unto God that performeth / áll things fór me.
3 He shall send from heaven, † and save me from the reproach of him that would swállow me / <u>up</u>. * God shall send forth his / mércy ánd his truth.
4 My soul ís among / líons: * and I lie even among thém / that are sét on fire,
Even the sons of men, whose teeth are spéars and / árrows, * and their / tóngue a shárp sword.
5 Be thou exalted, O God, abóve the / héavens; * let thy glory bé / above áll the earth.
6 They have prepared a nét for my / <u>steps</u>; * my / sóul is bówed down:

213

They have digged a pít be- / fóre me, * into the midst whereof they are fál- / len them<u>selves</u>.

7 My heart is fixed, O Gód, my / héart is fixed: * I will síng / and give <u>praise</u>.

8 Awake up, my glory; † awake, psáltery and / <u>harp</u>: * I myself wíll / awake éarly.

9 I will praise thee, O Lord, amóng the / péople: * I will sing unto thee a- / móng the nátions.

10 For thy mercy is great únto the / héavens, * and thy truth ún- / to the <u>clouds</u>.

11 Be thou exalted, O God, abóve the / héavens: * let thy glory bé / above áll the earth.

Glory be to the Fáther and / tó the Son * and / tó the Hóly Ghost.

As it was in the beginning, is now, and éver / sháll be, * wórld / without énd. Amen.

Psalm-prayer. Take away, we beseech Thee, O Lord, the iniquity of this Thy family, which putteth its trust under the shadow of Thy wings; to the end that, Thy mercy being sent down from heaven, we may be preserved from the snares of our enemies, and from the nets of them that do evil; through Jesus Christ our Lord, who liveth and reigneth with Thee and the Holy Ghost, ever one God, world without end. Amen.

[157]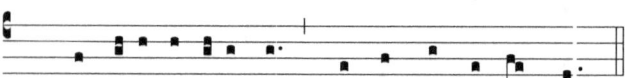

Ant. Ver-i-ly hé is a <u>God</u>: * that júdgeth ín the earth.

Psalm 58 *Si vere*

1 Do ye indeed speak righteousness, O / cóngregátion? * do ye judge uprightly, / Ó ye sóns of men?

2 Yea, in / héart ye work wíckedness; * ye weigh the violence of your / hánds in the <u>earth</u>.

3 The wicked are es- / tránged from the <u>womb</u>: * they go astray as soon as théy / be born, spéaking lies.

4 Their poison is like the poison / óf a sérpent: * they are like the deaf adder that / stóppeth her <u>ear</u>;

5 Which will not hearken to the / vóice of chármers, * charming név- / er so wísely.

6 Break their teeth, O / Gód, in their <u>mouth</u>: * break out the great teeth of the

young / líons, O LORD.
7 Let them melt away as waters which run contînually: † when he bendeth his bow to / shóot his árrows, * let them be as / cút in píeces.
8 As a snail which melteth, let every / óne of them páss away: * like the untimely birth of a woman, that they / máy not sée the sun.
9 Before your pots can fêel the thorns, † he shall take them away as / wíth a whírlwind, * both lív- / ing, and ín his wrath.
10 The righteous shall rejoice when he / séeth the véngeance: * he shall wash his feet in the blóod / of the wícked.
11 So that a man shall say, Verily there is a re- / wárd for the ríghteous: * verily he is a God that / júdgeth ín the earth.
Glory be to the / Fáther and tó the Son * - and / tó the Hóly Ghost.
As it was in the beginning, is now, and / éver sháll be, * - wórld / without énd. Amen.

Psalm-prayer. God, whose words are pure and whose judgments are right; stretch forth Thy Right Arm for our defense; smite the jawbones of the lions, O Lord, which would devour us; that in Thee the multitude of the redeemed may rejoice, seeing that Thou art the Crown of the righteous, and that to Thee we may sing the psalm of joy, when we arrive at the fruit of well-doing; through Jesus Christ our Lord, who liveth and reigneth with Thee and the Holy Ghost, ever one God, world without end. Amen.

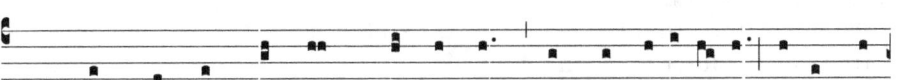

[158]

Ant. Thou therefore, O LORD, God of hosts* the Gód of Ís-ra-el: awake to

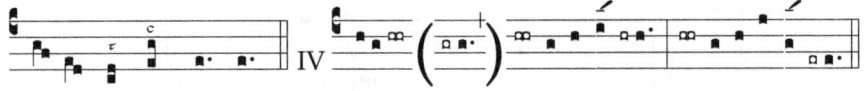

vis-it áll the héathen.

Psalm 59i *Eripe me*
1 Deliver me from mine én- / emies, Ó my God: * defend me from them that / rise úp agáinst me.
2 Deliver me from the workers / óf iníquity, * and / sáve me from blóody men.
3 For, lo, they lie in wait for my soul: † the mighty are gá- / thered agáinst me; * not for my transgression, / nór for my sín, O LORD.
4 They run and prepare them- / sélves withóut my fault: * awake / to hélp me, ánd behold.

5 Thou therefore, O LORD God of hosts, the God of Îsrael, † awake to visit / áll the héathen: * be not merciful to any / wícked transgréssors.
6 They return at evening: † they make a nóise / like a dog, * and go round / abóut the cíty.
7 Behold, they belch out with their mouth: / swórds are ín their lips: * for / whó, say they, dóth hear?
8 But thou, O / LÓRD, shalt láugh at them; * thou shalt have all the hea- / then ín derísion.
9 Because of his strength will I / wáit upón thee: * - / for Gód is mý defence.
Glory be to the Fá- / ther and tó the Son * - / and tó the Hóly Ghost.
As it was in the beginning, is now, and / éver sháll be, * - / wórld without énd. Amen.

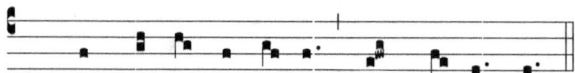

Ant. The God of my mercy * shall prevent me. *(Do not repeat in verse 10.)*

Psalm 59ii *Deus meus*
10 [The God of my mercy / sháll prevént me:] * God shall let me see my desire up- / ón mine énemies.
11 Slay them not, lest my people forget: † scatter them / bý thy pówer; * and bring them / dówn, O Lórd our shield.
12 For the sin of their mouth and the words of their lips † let them even be / táken ín their pride: * and for cursing and / lýing whích they speak.
13 Consume them in wrath, consume them, / thát they máy not be: * and let them know that God ruleth in Jacob unto the / énds of the earth.
14 And at evening let them return; † and let them make a / nóise like a dog, * and go round a- / bóut the cíty.
15 Let them wander / úp and dówn for meat, * and grudge if they / bé not sátisfied.
[159] 16 But I will / síng of thy pówer; * yea, I will sing aloud of thy mercy / ín the mórning:
For thou hast been my de- / fénce and réfuge * in the dáy / of my tróuble.
17 Unto thee, O my / stréngth, will I sing: * for God is my defence, and the Gód / of my mércy.
Glory be to the / Fáther and tó the Son * - and / tó the Hóly Ghost.
As it was in the beginning, is now, and / éver sháll be, * - wórld / without énd. Amen.

Psalm-prayer. O Christ, Son of God, who, without cause of sin, wast even delivered unto death, and caught in the snare of the fowlers; grant that, through Thine unmerited death, the death which we merit may be overcome, that Thou, who, though innocent, wast given up for us, mayest through the gift of innocency make us come at length in blessedness to Thee; who livest and reignest with the Father and the Holy Ghost, ever one God, world without end. Amen.

Ant. Give us help from tróuble, O Lord: * for váin is the hélp of man.

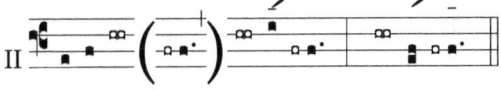

Psalm 60 *Deus, reppulisti*
1 O God, thou hast cast us off, thóu hast / scáttered us, * thou hast been displeased; O turn thysélf to / ús again.
2 Thou hast made the earth to tremble; thóu hast / bróken it: * heal the breaches thereof; fór it / sháketh.
3 Thou hast shewed thy péople / hárd things: * thou hast made us to drink the wíne of a- / stónishment.
4 Thou hast given a banner to thém that / féar thee, * that it may be displayed becáuse of / the truth.
5 That thy belov-ed may bé de- / lívered; * save with thy right hánd, and / héar me.
6 God hath spoken ín his / hóliness; * I will rejoice, I will divide Shechem, and mete out the válley of / Súccoth.
7 Gilead is mine, and Manasseh is mine; † Ephraim also is the stréngth of mine / head; * Judah ís my law- / gíver;
8 Moab is my washpot; † over Edom will Í cast / óut my shoe: * Philistia, triumph thóu be- / cáuse of me.
9 Who will bring me intó the strong / cíty? * who will lead me ínto / Édom?
10 Wilt not thou, O Gód, which hadst / cást us off? * and thou, O God, which didst not go óut with our / ármies?
11 Give us hélp from / tróuble: * for váin is the / hélp of man.
12 Through God wé shall do / váliantly: * for he it is that shall tread dówn our / énemies.
Glory be to the Fáther and / tó the Son * and tó the / Hóly Ghost.
As it was in the beginning, is now, and éver / sháll be, * wórld without /

énd. Amen.

[160] *Psalm-prayer.* Most merciful God, save Thy suppliant people with the help of Thy right hand: that while in tribulation it is roused to good works, it may ever be comforted by Thy grace; through Jesus Christ our Lord, who liveth and reigneth with Thee and the Holy Ghost, ever one God, world without end. Amen.

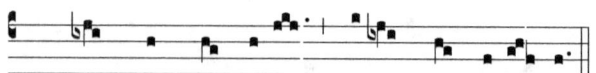

Ant. Our King shall abide * before God forev-er.

Psalm 61 *Exaudi, Deus*
1 — Héar my / crý, O God; * attend / únto my <u>prayer</u>.
2 From the end of the earth will I cry ûnto thee, † when my héart is / óverwhelmed: * lead me to the rock that is / hígher than <u>I</u>.
3 For thou hast been a shélter for / <u>me</u>, * and a strong tower / fróm the énemy.
4 I will abide in thy tabernácle for / éver: * I will trust in the / cóvert óf thy wings.
5 For thou, O Gód, hast / héard my vows: * thou hast given me the heritage of / thóse that féar thy name.
6 Thou wilt prolóng the / kíng's life: * and his years as many / generátions.
7 He shall abide before Gód for / éver: * O prepare mercy and truth, which / máy presérve him.
8 So will I sing praise unto thy náme for / éver, * that I may / dáily perfórm my vows.
Glory be to the Fáther and / tó the Son * and / tó the Hóly Ghost.
As it was in the beginning, is now, and éver / sháll be, * - / wórld without énd. Amen.

Psalm-prayer. O Lord, vouchsafe to grant us, that conformed to Thy glory, and delivered from the corruption of the second death, we may sing to Thy Name in the performance of our spiritual vows; through Jesus Christ our Lord, who liveth and reigneth with Thee and the Holy Ghost, ever one God, world without end. Amen.

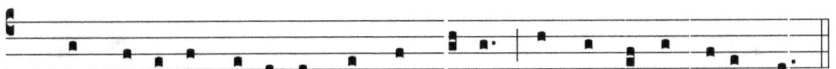

Ant. In God is my salvation ánd my glóry: * and my réfuge ís in God.

Psalm 62 *Nonne Deo*

1 Truly my soul / wáiteth upón God: * from him cometh / mý salvátion.
2 He only is my rock and / mý salvátion; * he is my defence; I shall / nót be gréatly moved.
3 How long will ye imagine mischief agâinst a man? † ye / sháll be slain áll of you: * as a bowing wall shall ye be, and / ás a tóttering fence.
4 They only consult to cast him down from his excellency: / théy delíght in lies: * they bless with their mouth, but / théy curse ínwardly.
5 My soul, wait thou / ónly upón God; * for my expec- / tátion ís from him.
6 He only is my rock and / mý salvátion: * he is my defence; / Í shall nót be moved.
7 In God is my salvation / ánd my glóry: * the rock of my strength, and my / réfuge, ís in God.
8 Trust in him at all times; † ye people, pour out your / héart befóre him: * God is a / réfuge fór us.
9 Surely men of low degree are vânity, † and men of / hígh degree áre a lie: * to be laid in the balance, they are altogether líght- / er than vánity.
10 Trust not in oppression, and become not / váin in róbbery: * if riches increase, set not your / héart upón them.
11 God hath spoken once; † twice / háve I héard this; * that power be- / lóngeth únto God.
12 Also unto thee, O Lord, be- / lóngeth mércy: * for thou renderest to every man ac- / córding tó his work.
Glory be to the / Fáther and tó the Son * - and / tó the Hóly Ghost.
As it was in the beginning, is now, and / éver sháll be, * - wórld / without énd. Amen.

Psalm-prayer. Subdue our souls unto Thee, O Lord; for Thou art our very expectation: that we, rejecting the uncertainty of riches, and despising all earthly vanity, may follow Thee only; through Jesus Christ our Lord, who liveth and reigneth with Thee and the Holy Ghost, ever one God, world without end. Amen.

Ant. Thus will I bléss thee whíle I live: * I will lift up my hánds in thy name.

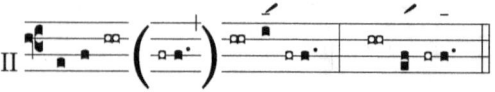

Psalm 63 *Deus, Deus meus*
1 O God, thou art my God; early wíll I / séek thee: * my soul thirsteth for thee, my flesh longeth for thee in a dry and thirsty land, whére no / wáter is;
2 To see thy power ánd thy / glóry, * so as I have seen thee in the sánctu- / áry.
3 Because thy lovingkindness is bétter than / life, * my líps shall / práise thee.
4 Thus will I bléss thee / whíle I live: * I will lift up my hánds in / thy name.
5 My soul shall be satisfied as with márrow and / fátness; * and my mouth shall práise thee with / jóyful lips:
6 When I remember thée up- / ón my bed, * and meditate on thee ín the night / wátches.
7 Because thóu hast / béen my help, * therefore in the shadow of thy wíngs will / Í rejoice.
8 My soul followeth hárd after / thee: * thy right hánd up- / hóldeth me.
9 But those that seek my sóul, to des- / tróy it, * shall go into the lower párts of / the earth.
10 They shall fáll by the / sword: * they shall be a pórtion for / fóxes.
11 But the king shall rejôice in God; † every one that sweareth by hím shall / glóry: * but the mouth of them that speak líes shall / be stopped.
**Glory be to the Fáther and / tó the Son * and tó the / Hóly Ghost.
As it was in the beginning, is now, and éver / sháll be, * wórld without / énd. Amen.**

[162]

Psalm-prayer. O God, our God, grant that we may watch unto Thee in prayer from the light of the Spirit, and thirst for Thee, that by the gift of Thy grace, our soul may be filled with the marrow and fatness of virtue, and clinging to Thee by faith, may be lifted up by Thy right hand into the heavenly places; through Jesus Christ our Lord, who liveth and reigneth with Thee and the same Holy Spirit, ever one God, world without end. Amen.

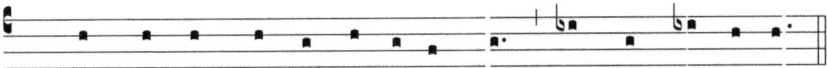

Ant. The righteous shall be glád in the Lord: * ánd shall trúst in him.

Irr.

Psalm 64 *Exaudi, Deus*
1 Hear my voice, O Gód, in / my prayer: * preserve my life from / féar of the énemy.
2 Hide me from the secret counsel óf the / wícked; * from the insurrection of the workers / óf iníquity:
3 Who whet their tóngue like / a sword, * and bend their bows to shoot their arrows, / éven bítter words:
4 That they may shoot in secret át the / pérfect: * suddenly do they shoot at / hím, and féar not.
5 They encourage themselves in an evil matter: † they commune of láying snares / prívily; * they say, / Whó shall sée them?
6 They search out inîquities; † they accomplish a díli- / gent search: * both the inward thought of every one of them, / ánd the héart, is deep.
7 But God shall shoot at them with an / árrow; * suddenly shall / théy be wóunded.
8 So they shall make their own tongue to fáll up- / ón themselves: * all that / sée them shall flée away.
9 And all men shall fear, and shall decláre the / wórk of God; * for they shall wisely consider / óf his dóing.
10 The righteous shall be glad in the LORD, ánd shall / trúst in him; * and all the upright in / héart shall glóry.
Glory be to the Fáther and / tó the Son * and / tó the Hóly Ghost.
As it was in the beginning, is now, and éver / shall be, * - / wórld without énd. Amen.

Psalm-prayer. O God, the Protection of all believers, keep Thy Church from the counsel of the wicked, who strive to assault it with secret arrows; that holding to Thee with a sound and right mind, it may always rejoice in Thy work and may wisely consider of Thy doing; through Jesus Christ our Lord, who liveth and reigneth with Thee and the Holy Ghost, ever one God, world without end. Amen.

[163]

Ant. Praise waiteth for thee, * O God, in Sion. *(Do not repeat in verse 1).*

VIII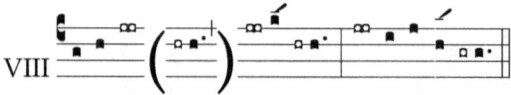

Psalm 65 *Te decet hymnus*

1 [Praise waiteth for thee, O Gód, in / Síon:] * and unto thee shall the vów / be per<u>form</u>ed.
2 O thóu that / héarest prayer, * unto / thée shall áll flesh come.
3 Iniquities preváil a- / gáinst me: * as for our transgressions, thou shalt púrge / them a<u>way</u>.
4 Bless-ed is the man whom thou choosest, † and causest to appróach unto / <u>thee</u>, * that he may dwéll / in thy <u>courts</u>:
We shall be satisfied with the góodness / óf thy house, * even of thy / hóly témple.
5 By terrible things in righteousness wílt thou / ánswer us, * O God of / óur salvátion;
Who art the confidence of all the énds of the / <u>earth</u>, * and of them that are afar / óff upón the sea:
6 Which by his strength setteth fást the / móuntains; * being gírd- / ed with pówer:
7 Which stilleth the noise of the seas, † the nóise of their / <u>waves</u>, * and the tumult / óf the péople.
8 They also that dwell in the uttermost parts are afráid at thy / tókens: * thou makest the outgoings of the morning and / év<u>en</u>ing tó rejoice.
9 Thou visitest the earth, and wáterest / <u>it</u>: * thou greatly enrichest it with the river of God, which is / fúll of wáter:
Thou prepárest them / <u>corn</u>, * when thou hast so pro- / víded fór it.
10 Thou waterest the ridges theréof a- / búndantly: * thou settlest the fúr- / rows there<u>of</u>:
Thou makest it sóft with / shówers: * thou blessest the spríng- / ing there<u>of</u>.
11 Thou crownest the yéar with thy / góodness; * and thy / páths drop fátness.
12 They drop upon the pastures óf the / wílderness: * and the little hills re- / jóice on év<u>er</u>y side.
13 The pastures are clôthed with flocks; † the valleys also are covered óver with / <u>corn</u>; * they shout for / jóy, they álso sing.
Glory be to the Fáther and / tó the Son * and / tó the Hóly Ghost.
As it was in the beginning, is now, and éver / sháll be, * wórld / without

énd. Amen.

Psalm-prayer. O God, the hope of all the ends of the earth, hearken to the humble prayer of Thy family, that while it praiseth Thee with tuneful harmony and the chanted hymn, it may, adorned by the gift of the Comforter, be enriched with abundant fruit; through the same our Lord Jesus Christ, who liveth and reigneth with Thee and the same Holy Ghost, ever one God, world without end. Amen.

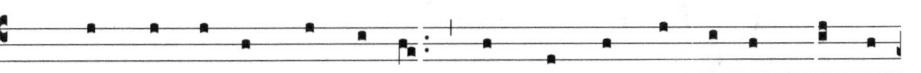

[164]

Ant. Come and sée the wórks of God: * and make the voice of His práise to

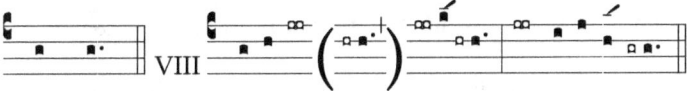

be <u>heard</u>.

Psalm 66i *Jubilate Deo*
1 Make a joyful noise unto Gód, all ye / <u>lands</u>: * 2 sing forth the honour of his name: máke / his praise glórious.
3 Say unto God, How terrible art thóu in thy / <u>works</u>! * through the greatness of thy power shall thine enemies submít / themselves únto thee.
4 All the earth shall wôrship thee, † and shall síng unto / <u>thee</u>; * they shall síng / to thy <u>name</u>.
5 Come and sée the / wórks of God: * he is terrible in his doing toward the chíl- / dren of <u>men</u>.
6 He turned the sea into dry land: † they went thróugh the / flóod on foot: * there did / wé rejóice in him.
7 He ruleth by his power for ever; † his eyes behóld the / nátions: * let not the rebél- / lious exált themselves.
8 O bless our Gód, ye / péople, * and make the voice of his práise / to be <u>heard</u>:
9 Which hóldeth our / sóul in life, * and suffereth not our féet / to be <u>moved</u>.
10 For thou, O Gód, hast / próved us: * thou hast tried us, as síl- / ver is <u>tried</u>.
11 Thou broughtest us ínto the / <u>net</u>; * thou laidst afflíc- / tion upón our loins.
12 Thou hast caused men to ride over our heads; † we went through fire ánd through / wáter: * but thou broughtest us out ín- / to a wéalthy place.
Glory be to the Fáther and / tó the Son * and / tó the Hóly Ghost.

As it was in the beginning, is now, and éver / sháll be, * wórld / without énd. Amen.

Ant. Come and hear, all ye: * that fear God.

IV

Psalm 66ii *Introibo*
13 I will go into thy hóuse / with burnt ófferings: * I will / páy thee my vows,
14 Which my / líps have úttered, * and my mouth hath spoken, when / Í was in tróuble.
15 I will offer unto thee burnt sacrifices of fatlings, with the ín- / cense of rams; * I will offer / búllocks with goats.
16 Come and hear, all yé / that fear God, * and I will declare what he hath / dóne for my soul.
17 I cried unto hím / with my mouth, * and he was ex- / tólled with my tongue.
18 If I regard iní- / quity ín my heart, * the / Lórd will not héar me:
19 But verily / Gód hath héard me; * he hath attended to the / vóice of my prayer.
20 Bless-ed be God, which hath not / túrned awáy my prayer, * nor his / mércy from me.
Glory be to the Fá- / ther and tó the Son * - / and tó the Hóly Ghost.
As it was in the beginning, is now, and / éver sháll be, * - / wórld without énd. Amen.

Psalm-prayer. Instil into our mind, O Lord, the glory of Thy praise, that while we shun the burnings of this world, we may, under Thy guidance, be carried into eternal refreshment; through Jesus Christ our Lord, who liveth and reigneth with Thee and the Holy Ghost, ever one God, world without end. Amen.

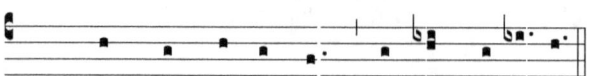

Ant. Cáuse Thy fáce to shine: * O Lórd, upón us.

Irr.

Psalm 67 *Deus misereatur*

1 God be merciful unto ús, and / bléss us; * and cause his face to / shíne upón us;
2 That thy way may be knówn up- / on earth, * thy saving health a- / móng all nátions.
3 Let the people práise thee, / O God; * let all the / péople práise thee.
4 O let the nations be glad and sîng for joy: † for thou shalt judge the péople / ríghteously, * and govern the / nátions upón earth.
5 Let the people práise thee, / O God; * let all the / péople práise thee.
6 Then shall the earth yíeld her / íncrease; * and God, even our own / Gód, shall bléss us.
7 Gód shall / bléss us; * and all the ends of the / éarth shall féar him.
Glory be to the Fáther and / tó the Son * and / tó the Hóly Ghost.
As it was in the beginning, is now, and éver / sháll be, * - / wórld without énd. Amen.

Psalm-prayer. Cause Thy face to shine upon us, O Lord, and pour Thy blessing abundantly into our breasts; that our hearts, bedewed with the gladness of Thy light, may know Thy way upon earth, and be glad in the full knowledge of the holy faith among all nations; through Jesus Christ our Lord, who liveth and reigneth with Thee and the Holy Ghost, ever one God, world without end. Amen.

[166]

Ant. Let God a-rise, * let his en-e-mies be scattered. *(Do not repeat in verse 1.)*

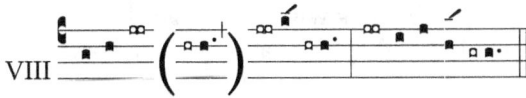
VIII

Psalm 68i *Exsurgat Deus*

1 [Let God arise, let his enemíes be / scáttered:] * let them also that hate him / flée befóre him.
2 As smoke is driven away, só drive / thém away: * as wax melteth before the fire, so let the wicked perish at the pré- / sence of God.
3 But let the righteous be glad; † let them rejóice before / God: * yea, let them ex- / céedinglý rejoice.
4 Sing unto God, sing práises / tó his name: * extol him that rideth upon the

225

heavens by his name JAH, and re- / jóice befóre him.
5 A father of the fatherless, and a júdge of the / wídows, * is God in his holy / hábitátion.
6 God setteth the solitary in famílies: † he bringeth out those whích are / bóund with chains: * but the rebellious dwéll / in a drý land.
7 O God, when thou wentest forth befóre thy / péople, * when thou didst march / thróugh the wílderness;
8 The earth shook, the heavens also dropped at the présence of / <u>God</u>: * even Sinai itself was moved at the presence of God, the / Gód of Ísrael.
9 Thou, O God, didst send a pléntiful / <u>rain</u>, * whereby thou didst confirm thine inheritance, when / ít was wéary.
10 Thy congregátion hath / dwélt therein: * thou, O God, hast prepared of thy / góodness fór the poor.
Glory be to the Fáther and / tó the Son * and / tó the Hóly Ghost.
As it was in the beginning, is now, and éver / shál be, * wórld / without énd. Amen.

Ant. Our God is the God: * of salvation.

VI

Psalm 68ii *Dominus dabit*
11 — The / Lórd gave the <u>word</u>: * great was the company of / thóse that públished it.
12 Kings of / ármies did flée apace: * and she that tarried at home diví- / ded the spóil-.
13 Though ye have lien amông the pots, † yet shall ye be as the / wíngs of a <u>dove</u> * covered with silver, and her féa- / thers with yéllow gold.
14 When the Almighty / scáttered kíngs in it, * it was white as / snów in Sálmon.
15 The hill of God is as the / híll of Báshan; * an high hill as the / híll of Báshan.
16 Why leap ye, ye high hills? † this is the hill which God de- / síreth to dwéll in; * yea, the LORD will dwell in / ít for éver.
17 The chariots of God are twenty thousand, even / thóusands of ángels: * the Lord is among them, as in Sinai, / ín the hóly place.
18 Thou hast a- / scénded on <u>high</u>, * thou hast led captí- / vity cáptive:
Thou hast received gífts for men; † yea, for the re- / béllious álso, * that the

LORD God might / dwéll amóng them.
19 Bless-ed be the Lord, who daily loadeth / ús with bénefits, * even the God of / óur salvátion.
20 He that is our God is the / Gód of salvátion; * and unto GOD the Lord belong the ís- / sues from <u>death</u>.
21 But God shall wound the / héad of his énemies, * and the hairy scalp of such an one as goeth on stíll / in his tréspasses.
22 The Lord said, I will bring a- / gáin from Báshan, * I will bring my people again from the dépths / of the <u>sea</u>:
23 That thy foot may be dipped in the / blóod of thine énemies, * and the tongue of thy dógs / in the <u>same</u>.
Glory be to the / Fáther and tó the Son * - and / tó the Hóly Ghost.
As it was in the beginning, is now, and / éver sháll be, * - wórld / without énd. Amen.

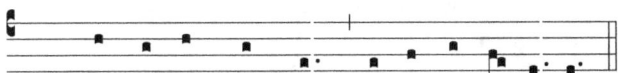

Ant. Bléss ye Gód, the Lord: * in the cóngregátions.

Psalm 68iii *Viderunt*
24 They have seen thy / góings, O <u>God</u>; * even the goings of my God, my King, in the / sánctuáry.
25 The singers went before, the players on instruments / fóllowed áfter; * among them were the damsels pláy- / ing with tímbrels.
26 Bless ye God in the / cóngregátions, * even the Lord, from the fóun- / tain of Ísrael.
27 There is little Benjamin with their ruler, † the princes of Judah / ánd their cóuncil, * the princes of Zebulun, and the prínc- / es of Náphtali.
28 Thy God hath com- / mánded thy <u>strength</u>: * strengthen, O God, that which / thóu hast wróught for us.
29 Because of thy temple / át Jerúsalem * shall kings bring / présents únto thee.
30 Rebuke the compa- / ný of spéarmen, * the multitude of the bulls, with the cálves / of the péople,
Till every one submit himself with / píeces of sílver: * scatter thou the people / thát delíght in war.
31 Princes shall come / óut of Égypt; * Ethiopia shall soon stretch out her / hánds unto <u>God</u>.

32 Sing unto God, ye / kíngdoms óf the earth; * O sing praises / únto the <u>Lord</u>;

33 To him that rideth upon the heavens of / héavens, which wére of old; * lo, he doth send out his voice, and / thát a míghty voice.

[168] 34 Ascribe ye / stréngth unto <u>God</u>: * his excellency is over Israel, and his / stréngth is ín the clouds.

35 O God, thou art terrible out of thy / hóly pláces: * the God of Israel is he that giveth strength and power unto his people. / Bléss-ed be <u>God</u>.

Glory be to the / Fáther and tó the Son * - and / tó the Hóly Ghost.

As it was in the beginning, is now, and / éver sháll be, * - wórld / without énd. Amen.

Psalm-prayer. O Lord our God, who, vouchsafing a spiritual banquet to the righteous, makest them joyful in gladness: grant that Thy flock may understand Thy death, and confess Thee, the Victor over death, sitting at the right hand of the Father; who livest and reignest with the same Father and the Holy Ghost, ever one God, world without end. Amen.

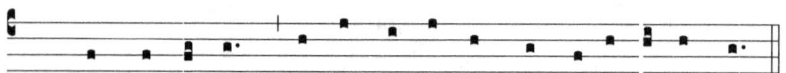

Ant. Save me, O God; * for the waters are come in unto my soul.
(*Do not repeat in verse 1.*)

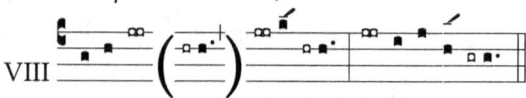

Psalm 69i *Salvum me fac*

1 [Save me, O God; for the waters are come in únto my / <u>soul</u>.] * 2 I sink in deep mire, where there / ís no stánding:

I am come ínto deep / wáters, * where the flóods / overflów me.

3 I am weary of my crýing, my / thróat is dried: * mine eyes fail while I wáit / for my <u>God</u>.

4 They that háte me with- / óut a cause * are more than the háirs / of mine <u>head</u>:

They that would destroy me, being mine enemies wrongfullý, are / míghty: * then I restored that which / Í took nót away.

5 O God, thou knówest my / fóolishness; * and my síns / are not híd from thee.

6 Let not them that wait on thee, O Lord GOD of hosts, be ashámed for / mý sake: * let not those that seek thee be confounded for my sake, O / Gód of Ísrael.

7 Because for thy sake Í have / bórne reproach; * shame hath cóv- / ered my face.
8 I am become a stranger únto my / bréthren, * and an alien unto my / móther's chíldren.
9 For the zeal of thine house hath éaten me / up; * and the reproaches of them that reproached thee are fál- / len upón me.
10 When I wept, and chastened my sóul with / fásting, * thát / was to mý reproach.
11 I made sackcloth álso my / gárment; * and I became a pró- / verb to them.
12 They that sit in the gate spéak a- / gáinst me; * and I was the sóng / of the drúnkards.
Glory be to the Fáther and / tó the Son * and / tó the Hóly Ghost.
As it was in the beginning, is now, and éver / sháll be, * wórld / without énd. Amen.

[169]

Ant. Draw nigh * únto my sóul, O Lord: ánd redéem it.

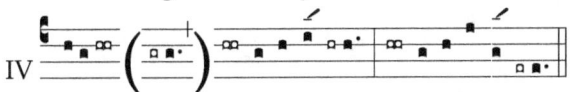

IV

Psalm 69ii *Ego vero orationem*
13 But as for me, my prayer is unto thee, O LORD, in an accép- / table time: * O God, in the multitude of thy mercy hear me, in the truth / of thý salvátion.
14 Deliver me out of the mire, and lét / me not sink: * let me be delivered from them that hate me, and out / óf the deep wáters.
15 Let not the waterflood overflow me, † neither let the deep swál- / low me up, * and let not the pit shut / her móuth upón me.
16 Hear me, O LORD; for thy lovingkínd- / ness is good: * turn unto me according to the multitude of / thy ténder mércies.
17 And hide not thy face / fróm thy sérvant; * for I am in trou- / ble: héar me spéedily.
18 Draw nigh unto my soul, / ánd redéem it: * deliver me be- / cáuse of mine énemies.
19 Thou hast known my reproach, and my shame, and / mý dishónour: * mine adversaries / are áll befóre thee.
20 Reproach hath broken my heart; and I am full of hêaviness: † and I looked for some to take pí- / ty, but thére was none; * and for comforters, / bút I found none.

21 They gave me also gáll / for my meat; * and in my thirst they gave / me vínegár to drink.
22 Let their table become a / snáre befóre them: * and that which should have been for their welfare, / lét it becóme a trap.
23 Let their eyes be darkened, / thát they sée not; * and make their loins / contínuallý to shake.
24 Pour out thine indigná- / tion upón them, * and let thy wrathful / ánger take hóld of them.
25 Let their habitá- / tion be désolate; * and let none / dwéll in their tents.
26 For they persecute him whom / thóu hast smítten; * and they talk to the grief of those / whom thóu hast wóunded.
27 Add iniquity unto / théir iníquity: * and let them not come / ínto thy ríghteousness.
28 Let them be blotted out of the bóok / of the líving, * and not be writ- / ten wíth the ríghteous.
Glory be to the Fá- / ther and tó the Son * - / and tó the Hóly Ghost.
As it was in the beginning, is now, and / éver sháll be, * - / wórld without énd. Amen.

[170]
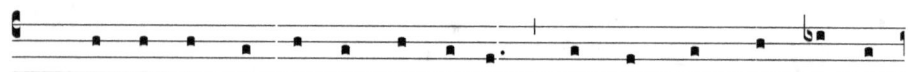

Ant. The humble shall sée this, ánd be glad: * and your heart shall líve that

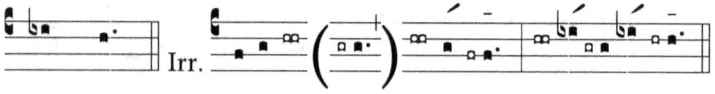

seek God.

Psalm 69iii *Ego sum pauper*
29 But I am póor and / sórrowful: * let thy salvation, O God, / sét me úp on high.
30 I will praise the name of Gód with / a song, * and will magnify him / with thanksgíving.
31 This álso shall / pléase the LORD * better than an ox or bullock / thát hath hórns and hoofs.
32 The humble shall sée this, / ánd be glad: * and your heart shall / líve that seek God.
33 For the LORD héareth / the poor, * and despiseth / nót his prísoners.
34 Let the héaven and earth / práise him, * the seas, and every thing that / móveth therein.
35 For God will save Zion, and will build the cíties of / Júdah: * that they

may dwell there, and have it / ín posséssion.

36 The seed also of his servants sháll in- / hérit it: * and they that love his / náme shall dwéll therein.

Glory be to the Fáther and / tó the Son * and / tó the Hóly Ghost.

As it was in the beginning, is now, and éver / sháll be, * - / wórld without énd. Amen.

Psalm-prayer. O most merciful Lord, hear us in the truth of Thy salvation, that, delivered from the filth of sin, we may be written in the Book of Life by Thy heavenly finger; through Jesus Christ our Lord, who liveth and reigneth with Thee and the Holy Ghost, ever one God, world without end. Amen.

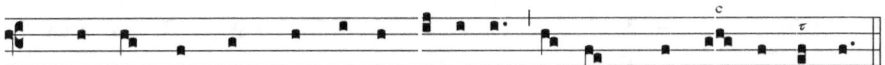

Ant. Be thou my Help and mý De-lív-er-er: * O Lord, máke no tár-ry-ing.

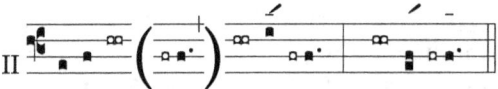

Psalm 70 *Deus, in adjutorium*
1 Make haste, O God, tó de- / líver me; * make haste to hélp me, / O <u>LORD</u>.
2 Let them be ashamed and confounded that seek áfter my / <u>soul</u>: * let them be turned backward, and put to confusion, thát de- / síre my hurt.
3 Let them be turned back for a rewárd of their / <u>shame</u> * that sáy, A- / há, aha.
4 Let all those that seek thee rejóice and be / glád in thee: * and let such as love thy salvation say continually, Let Gód be / mágnified.
5 But I am póor and / néedy: * make háste unto / mé, O God:
Thou art my help and mý de- / líverer; * O LORD, máke no / tárrying.
Glory be to the Fáther and / tó the Son * and tó the / Hóly Ghost. [171]
As it was in the beginning, is now, and éver / sháll be, * wórld without / énd. Amen.

Psalm-prayer. O Everlasting God, whose help is inexhaustible, make haste to help Thy humble servants, that overcoming the reproaches of the ungodly, we may ever be guarded by Thine aid; through Jesus Christ our Lord, who liveth and reigneth with Thee and the Holy Ghost, ever one God, world without end. Amen.

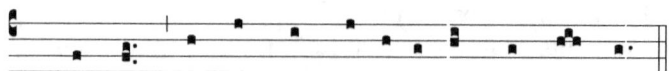

Ant. O Lord, * incline thine ear unto me, and save me.

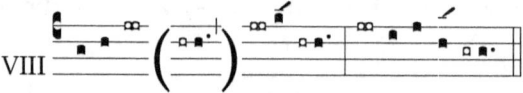

Psalm 71i *In te, Domine, speravi*
1 In thee, O LÓRD, do I / pút my trust: * let me never be pút / to confúsion.
2 Deliver me in thy righteousness, and cáuse me / tó escape: * incline thine ear unto / mé, and sáve me.
3 Be thou my strong habitation, whereunto I may contínu*a*l- / lý resort: * thou hast given commandment to save me; for thou art my róck / and my fórtress.
4 Deliver me, O my God, out of the hánd of the / wícked, * out of the hand of the unrígh- / teous and crúel man.
5 For thou art my hópe, O Lord / GOD: * thou art my trúst / from my youth.
6 By thee have I been holden up from the womb: † thou art he that took me out of my móther's / bówels: * my praise shall be con- / tínu*a*llý of thee.
7 I am as a wonder únto / mány; * but thou art / mý strong réfuge.
8 Let my mouth be fílled with thy / praise * and with thy / hónour áll the day.
9 Cast me not off in the tíme of / óld age; * forsake me not when / mý strength fáileth.
10 For mine enemies spéak a- / gáinst me; * and they that lay wait for my soul take cóun- / sel togéther,
11 Saying, Gód hath for- / sáken him: * persecute and take him; for there is nóne / to delíver him.
12 O God, bé not / fár from me: * O my God, make háste / for my help.
Glory be to the Fáther and / tó the Son * and / tó the Hóly Ghost.
As it was in the beginning, is now, and éver / sháll be, * wórld / without énd. Amen.

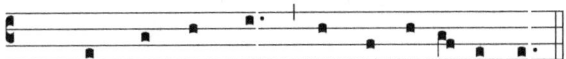

Ant. Thy righteousness: * O God, is ve-ry high.

VII

Psalm 71ii *Confundantur*

13 Let them be confounded and consumed that are adver- / sáries tó my soul; * let them be covered with reproach and dis- / hónour that séek my hurt.
14 But I will / hópe contínually, * and will yet / práise thee móre and more.
15 My mouth shall shew forth thy righteousness and thy sal- / vátion áll the day; * for I know not the / númbers there<u>of</u>.
16 I will go in the / stréngth of the Lórd GOD: * I will make mention of thy righteousness, even / óf thine ónly.
17 O God, thou hast / táught me fróm my youth: * and hitherto have I de- / cláred thy wóndrous works.
18 Now also when I am old and grayheaded, O God, forsâke me not; † until I have shewed thy strength unto this / génerátion, * and thy power to every / óne that ís to come.
19 Thy righteousness also, O God, is very high, / whó hast dóne great things: * O God, who is / líke unto <u>thee</u>!
20 Thou, which hast shewed me great and sore troubles, shalt / quícken mé again, * and shalt bring me up again from the / dépths of the <u>earth</u>.
21 Thou shalt in- / créase my gréatness, * and comfort / mé on évery side.
22 I will also praise thee with the psaltery, even thy / trúth, O my <u>God</u>: * unto thee will I sing with the harp, O thou Holy / Óne of Ísrael.
23 My lips shall greatly rejoice when I / síng unto <u>thee</u>; * and my soul, which / thóu hast re<u>deemed</u>.
24 My tongue also shall talk of thy righteousness / áll the day <u>long</u>: * for they are confounded, for they are brought unto / sháme, that séek my hurt.
Glory be to the / Fáther and tó the Son * and / tó the Hóly Ghost.
As it was in the beginning, is now, and / éver sháll be, * - / wórld without énd. Amen.

Psalm-prayer. Incomprehensible ruler of the throne on high, who sufferest not them that trust in Thee to be condemned to everlasting confusion, fill our lips, we beseech Thee, with Thy praise, and ever inspire us with thoughts of holy things; through Jesus Christ our Lord, who liveth and reigneth with

Thee and the Holy Ghost, ever one God, world without end. Amen.

[173]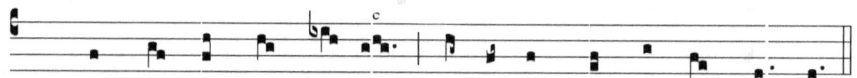

Ant. Mén shall be bléssed in Him: * all nations shall cáll Him bléss-ed.

Psalm 72 *Deus, judicium*

1 Give the king thy / júdgments, O God, * and thy righteousness ún- / to the kíng's son.
2 He shall judge thy / péople with ríghteousness, * and thy / póor with júdgment.
3 The mountains shall bring / péace to the péople, * and the little / hílls, by ríghteousness.
4 He shall judge the poor of the people, † he shall save the children / óf the néedy, * and shall break in pieces / thé oppréssor.
5 They shall fear thee as long as the / sún and móon endure, * throughout all / génerátions.
6 He shall come down like rain up- / ón the mówn grass: * as showers that / wáter the earth.
7 In his days shall the / ríghteous flóurish; * and abundance of peace so long as the / móon endúreth.
8 He shall have dominion / álso from séa to sea, * and from the river unto the / énds of the earth.
9 They that dwell in the wilderness shall / bów befóre him; * and his ene- / míes shall líck the dust.
10 The kings of Tarshish and of the isles / sháll bring présents: * the kings of Sheba and Sé- / ba shall óffer gifts.
11 Yea, all kings shall fall / dówn befóre him: * all ná- / tions shall sérve him.
12 For he shall deliver the needy / whén he críeth; * the poor also, and him that / háth no hélper.
13 He shall spare the / póor and néedy, * and shall save the sóuls / of the néedy.
14 He shall redeem their soul from de- / céit and víolence: * and precious shall their / blóod be ín his sight.
15 And he shall live, and to him shall be given of the gold of Sheba: † prayer also shall be made for / hím contínually; * and dái- / ly shall hé be praised.
16 There shall be an handful of corn in the earth upon the top of the

mountains; † the fruit thereof shall / sháke like Lébanon: * and they of the city shall flourish like / gráss of the <u>earth</u>.
17 His name shall en- / dúre for éver: * his name shall be continued as / lóng as the <u>sun</u>:
And men / sháll be bléssed in him: * all nations shall / cáll him bléss-ed.
18 Bless-ed be the LORD God, the / Gód of Ísrael, * who only / dóeth wóndrous things.
19 And bless-ed be his glorious / náme for éver: * and let the whole earth be filled with his glory; A- / mén, and A<u>men</u>.
Glory be to the / Fáther and tó the Son * - and / tó the Hóly Ghost.
As it was in the beginning, is now, and / éver sháll be, * - wórld / without énd. Amen.

Psalm-prayer. O Lord, to Whom the kings and the isles bring gifts, Who with Thine unconquered power, and through Thy heavenly pity, camest to save the poor from the mighty, and frail mankind from the sway of the ancient enemy; seeing that we are far from Thee, and in need of Thy mercies, that we are subject to his unrighteousness, tied and bound with the chains of our sins, let Thy lovingkindness deliver us now from his service, restore us to Thee, and keep us safely to abide with Thee, that we, who confess ourselves redeemed by Thy mercy, may hereafter glory in the gifts attained by Thy bounty; who livest and reignest with the Father and the Holy Ghost, ever one God, world without end. Amen. [174]

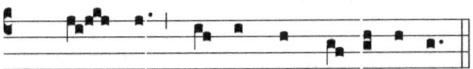

Ant. Tru- ly * God is good to Is-ra-el. *(Do not repeat in verse 1.)*

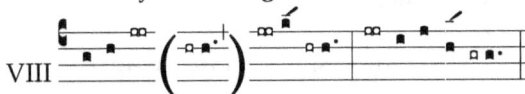
VIII

Psalm 73i *Quam bonus*
1 [Truly God is góod to / Ísrael,] * even to such as are / óf a cléan heart.
2 But as for me, my féet were / álmost gone; * my / stéps had wéll nigh slipped.
3 For I was envious át the / fóolish, * when I saw the prosperity / óf the wícked.
4 For there are no bánds in / théir death: * - / bút their stréngth is firm.
5 They are not in tróuble as / óther men; * neither are they / plágued like óther men.
6 Therefore pride compasseth them abóut as a / <u>chain</u>; * violence covereth

them / ás a gárment.
7 Their eyes stand óut with / fátness: * they have / móre than héart could wish.
8 They are corrupt, and speak wickedly concérning op- / préssion: * - / théy speak lóftily.
9 They set their mouth agáinst the / héavens, * and their tongue / wálketh thróugh the earth.
Glory be to the Fáther and / tó the Son * and / tó the Hóly Ghost.
As it was in the beginning, is now, and éver / sháll be, * wórld / without énd. Amen.

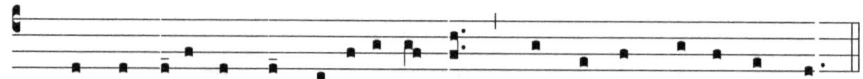

Ant. I went into the sanc-tu-á-ry of God: * then únderstood Í their end.

Psalm 73ii *Ideo convertetur*
10 Therefore his people / retúrn híther: * and waters of a full cup / áre wrung óut to them.
11 And they say, / Hów doth God know? * and is there knowledge / ín the móst High?
12 Behold, these are the ungodly, who / prósper ín the world; * they in- / créase in ríches.
13 Verily I have / cléansed my héart in vain, * and washed my hands in / ínnocency.
14 For all the day / lóng have Í been plagued, * and chastened / évery mórning.
15 If I say, / Í will spéak thus; * behold, I should offend against the generation / óf thy chíldren.
16 When I / thóught to knów this, * it was too / páinful for me;
17 Until I went into the sanctu- / áry of God; * then ún- / derstood Í their end.
Glory be to the / Fáther and tó the Son * - and / tó the Hóly Ghost.
As it was in the beginning, is now, and / éver sháll be, * - wórld / without énd. Amen.

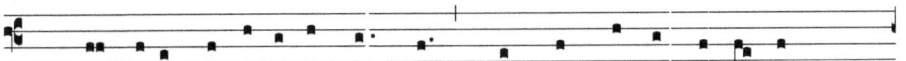

Ant. Lord, I am contínu*a*lly wíth thee: * thou hast holden me bý my

ríght hand.

Psalm 73iii *Verumtamen*
18 Surely thou didst set them in slíppery / pláces: * thou casteds*t* them down ínto des- / trúction.
19 How are they brought into desolation, as ín a / móment! * they are utterly consúmed with / térrors.
20 As a dream when óne a- / wáketh; * so, O Lord, when thou awakest, thou shalt despíse their / ímage.
21 Thús my / héart was grieved, * and I was prícked in / my <u>reins</u>.
22 So foolish was Í, and / ígnorant: * I was as a béast be- / fóre thee.
23 Nevertheless I am contínu*a*lly / wíth thee: * thou hast holden me bý my / ríght hand.
24 Thou shalt guide me wíth thy / cóunsel, * and afterward receive mé to / glóry.
25 Whom have I in héaven but / <u>thee</u>? * and there is none upon earth that I desíre be- / síde thee.
26 My flesh and mý heart / fáileth: * but God is the strength of my heart, and my pórtion for / éver.
27 For, lo, they that are far from thée shall / pérish: * thou hast destroyed all them that go a whóring / from <u>thee</u>.
28 But it is good for mé to draw / néar to God: * I have put my trust in the Lord GOD, that I may decláre all / thy <u>works</u>.
Glory be to the Fáther and / tó the Son * and tó the / Hóly Ghost.
As it was in the beginning, is now, and éver / sháll be, * wórld without / énd. Amen.

Psalm-prayer. O Lord, make us ever hold fast to Thee, and in Thee put all our trust, that we may tell of Thy praises in the everlasting gates; through Jesus Christ our Lord, who liveth and reigneth with Thee and the Holy Ghost, ever one God, world without end. Amen.

[176]

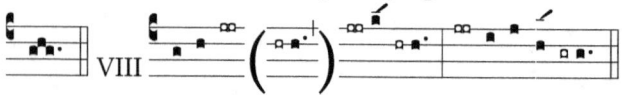

Ant. Remember, Lord, * thy cóngregátion: which thou hast púrchased of old.

Psalm 74i *Ut quid, Deus*
1 O God, why hast thou cast us óff for / éver? * why doth thine anger smoke against the shéep / of thy pásture?
2 Remember thy congregation, which thou hast purchased of old; † the rod of thine inheritance, which thóu hast re- / <u>deemed</u>; * this mount Zion, wherein / thou hast <u>dwelt</u>.
3 Lift up thy feet unto the perpetual déso- / látions; * even all that the enemy hath done wickedly in the / sánctuáry.
4 Thine enemies roar in the midst of thy cóngre- / gátions; * they set up their én- / signs for <u>signs</u>.
5 A man was famous according as he had lífted up / áxes * up- / ón the thíck trees.
6 But now they break down the carved wórk there- / óf at once * with áx- / es and hámmers.
7 They have cast fire into thy sánctu- / áry, * they have defiled by casting down the dwelling place of thy náme / to the <u>ground</u>.
8 They said in their hearts, Let us destróy them to- / géther: * they have burned up all the synagogues of Gód / in the <u>land</u>.
9 We see not our signs: † there is no more ány / próphet: * neither is there among us any that knów- / eth how <u>long</u>.
Glory be to the Fáther and / tó the Son * and / tó the Hóly Ghost.
As it was in the beginning, is now, and éver / sháll be, * wórld / without énd. Amen.

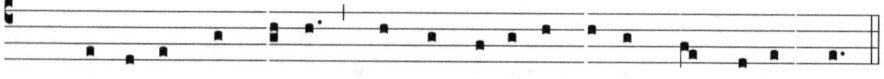

Ant. Gód is my Kíng of old: * working salvation in the mídst of the <u>earth</u>.

238

Psalm 74ii *Usquequo, Deus*
10 O God, how long shall the adversár- / y re<u>proach</u>? * shall the enemy blaspheme / thy náme for éver?
11 Why withdrawest thou thy hand, év- / en thy ríght hand? * pluck it / óut of thy bósom.
12 For Gód / is my Kíng of old, * working salvation in the / mídst of the <u>earth</u>.
13 Thou didst divide the séa / by thy <u>strength</u>: * thou brakest the heads of the dra- / gons ín the wáters.
14 Thou brakest the heads of levia- / thán in píeces, * and gavest him to be meat to the people inha- / bitíng the wílderness.
15 Thou didst cleave the / fóuntain ánd the flood: * thou dri-edst / up míghty rívers.
16 The day is thine, the night ál- / so is <u>thine</u>: * thou hast prepared the / líght and the <u>sun</u>.
17 Thou hast set all the / bórders óf the earth: * thou hast made / súmmer and wínter.
Glory be to the Fá- / ther and tó the Son * - / and tó the Hóly Ghost.
As it was in the beginning, is now, and / éver sháll be, * - / wórld without énd. Amen.

[177]

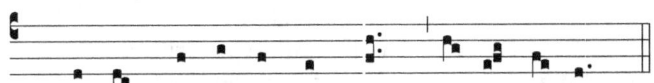

Ant. O Lord, let not the oppressed * return ashamed.

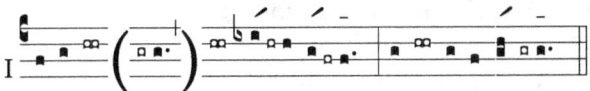

Psalm 74iii *Memor esto*
18 Remember this, that the enemy / háth repróached, O LORD, * and that the foolish people have / blásphemed thy <u>name</u>.
19 O deliver not the soul of thy turtledove unto the multitude / óf the wícked: * forget not the congregation of thy / póor for éver.
20 Have respect / únto the cóvenant: * for the dark places of the earth are full of the habitá- / tions of crúelty.
21 O let not the op- / préssed retúrn ashamed: * let the poor and / néedy práise thy name.
22 Arise, O God, / pléad thine own <u>cause</u>: * remember how the foolish man

repróach- / eth thee dáily.

23 Forget not the / vóice of thine énemies: * the tumult of those that rise up against thee incréas- / eth contínually.

Glory be to the / Fáther and tó the Son * - and / tó the Hóly Ghost.

As it was in the beginning, is now, and / éver sháll be, * - wórld / without énd. Amen.

Psalm-prayer. O God, creator of all the elements, King everlasting before the worlds, remember Thy flock which Thou hast redeemed by the shedding of Thine own Blood, and graciously hear the voices of all them that seek Thee, O Saviour of the world; who livest and reignest with the Father and the Holy Ghost, ever one God, world without end. Amen.

[178]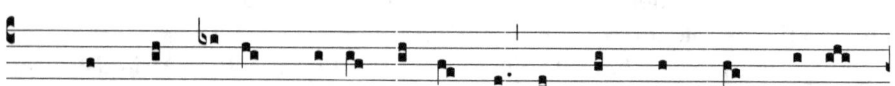

Ant. Thy name, O God, * is néar to sáve us: thy wondrous wórks decláre

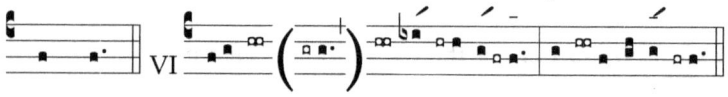

the same.

Psalm 75 *Confitebimur*

1 Unto thee, O God, do wê give thanks, † unto / thée do wé give thanks: * for that thy name is near thy / wóndrous wórks declare.
2 When I shall receive the / cóngregátion * I will / júdge upríghtly.
3 The earth and all the inhabitants there- / óf are dis<u>solved</u>: * I bear up the / píllars óf it.
4 I said unto the fools, / Déal not fóolishly: * and to the wicked, / Líft not úp the horn:
5 Lift not / úp your hórn on high: * speak not / wíth a stíff neck.
6 For promotion cometh / néither fróm the east, * nor from the west, nór / from the <u>south</u>.
7 But / Gód is the <u>judge</u>: * he putteth down one, and setteth / úp anóther.
8 For in the hand of the LORD there is a cup, / ánd the wíne is red; * it is full of mixture; and he poureth óut / of the <u>same</u>:
But the dregs thereof, all the / wícked óf the earth * shall wring them / óut, and drínk them.
9 But I will de- / cláre for éver; * I will sing praises to the / Gód of Jácob.
10 All the horns of the wicked also / wíll I cut <u>off</u>; * but the horns of the righteous shall / bé exálted.

Glory be to the / Fáther and tó the Son * - and / tó the Hóly Ghost.
As it was in the beginning, is nów, and / éver sháll be, * - wórld / without énd. Amen.

Psalm-prayer. O Good Shepherd, who, for the ransom of Thy mortal sheep, hast drunk the cup of the Passion; we humbly call upon Thy Name, that, establishing us upon the pillars of wisdom, Thou wouldst strengthen us with the hallowing of Thy sevenfold Spirit; who livest and reignest with the Father and the same Spirit, ever one God, world without end. Amen.

Ant. In Judah is God known: * his name is great in Is-ra-el.
(Do not repeat in verse 1).

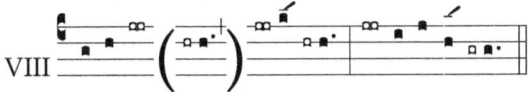

VIII

Psalm 76 *Notus in Judaea*
1 [In Júdah is / Gód known: * his name is / gréat in Ísrael.]
2 In Salem also is his táber- / nácle, * and his dwelling / pláce in Zíon.
3 There brake he the árrows / óf the bow, * the shield, and the sword, / ánd the báttle.
4 Thou art more glórious and / éxcellent * than the móun- / tains of <u>prey</u>.
5 The stouthearted are spoiled, théy have / slépt their sleep: * and none of the men of / míght have fóund their hands.
6 At thy rebuke, O Gód of / Jácob, * both the chariot and horse are cast ín- / to a déad sleep.
7 Thou, even thou, árt to be / <u>feared</u>: * and who may stand in thy sight when once / thóu art ángry?
8 Thou didst cause judgment to be héard from / héaven; * the earth féared, / and was <u>still</u>,
9 When God aróse to / júdgment, * to save all the méek / of the <u>earth</u>.
10 Surely the wrath of mán shall / práise thee: * the remainder of / wráth shalt thóu restrain.
11 Vow, and pay únto the / LÓRD your God: * let all that be round about him bring presents unto him that óught / to be <u>feared</u>.
12 He shall cut off the spírit of / prínces: * he is terrible to the kíngs / of the <u>earth</u>.
Glory be to the Fáther and / tó the Son * and / tó the Hóly Ghost.
As it was in the beginning, is now, and éver / sháll be, * wórld / without

[179]

énd. Amen.

Psalm-prayer. Grant, O fearsome God, effectual working to the thoughts which confess Thee, that we, enlightened from the everlasting hills, may, while we look for the glory of Thy resurrection, be free from shame in the judgment to come; who livest and reignest with the Father and the Holy Ghost, ever one God, world without end. Amen.

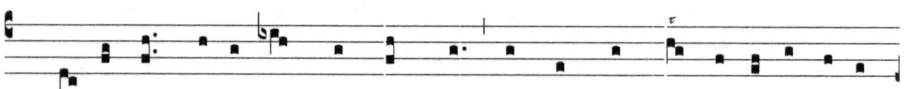

Ant. I will cry * unto Gód with my voice: for God hath not forgotten tó be

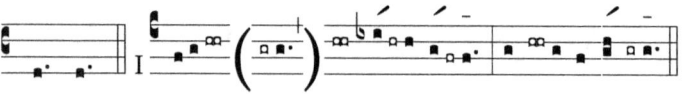

grácious.

Psalm 77i *Voce mea*
1 I cried unto / Gód with my voice, * even unto God with my voice; and he / gáve ear únto me.
2 In the day of my trouble I sôught the Lord: † my sore ran in the / níght, and céased not: * my soul refúsed / to be cómforted.
3 I remembered God, / ánd was tróubled: * I complained, and my spír- / it was óverwhelmed.
4 Thou holdest / míne eyes wáking: * I am so troubled that / Í cannot speak.
5 I have con- / sídered the dáys of old, * - the / yéars of áncient times.
6 I call to remembrance my song in the night: † I com- / múne with míne own heart: * and my spirit made / díligent search.
7 Will the Lord cast / óff for éver? * and will he be fáv- / rable nó more?
8 Is his mercy clean / góne for éver? * doth his promise / fáil for évermore?
9 Hath God forgotten / tó be grácious? * hath he in anger shut up his / ténder mércies?
10 And I said, This is / mý infírmity: * but I will remember the years of the right hand / óf the móst High.
11 I will remember the / wórks of the LORD: * surely I will remember thy / wónders of old.
12 I will meditate / álso of áll thy work, * and tálk / of thy dóings.
Glory be to the / Fáther and tó the Son * - and / tó the Hóly Ghost.
As it was in the beginning, is now, and / éver sháll be, * - wórld / without énd. Amen.

Ant. Thou art the God that dóest wónders: * thou hast declared thy strength

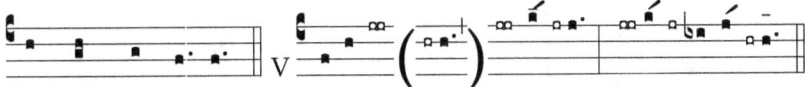

a-móng the péople.

Psalm 77ii *Deus, in sancto*

13 Thy way, O God, is in the sánctu- / áry: * who is so great a / Gód as óur God?
14 Thou art the God that dóest / wónders: * thou hast declared thy strength a- / móng the péople.
15 Thou hast with thine arm redéemed thy / péople, * the sons of / Jácob and Jóseph.
16 The waters saw thee, O God, the wáters / sáw thee; * they were afraid: the depths / álso were tróubled.
17 The clouds poured out water: † the skíes sent / óut a sound: * thine arrows / álso wént abroad.
18 The voice of thy thunder was in the heaven: † the lightnings líghtened the / world: * the earth / trémbled and shook.
19 Thy way is in the sea, and thy path ín the great / wáters, * and thy / fóotsteps are nót known.
20 Thou leddest thy péople / líke a flock * by the hand of / Móses and Áaron.
**Glory be to the Fáther and / tó the Son * and / tó the Hóly Ghost.
As it was in the beginning, is now, and éver / shálll be, * - / wórld without énd. Amen.**

Psalm-prayer. O God incomprehensible, who doest great wonders, who changedst the waters, which once stood still in Thy sight, at later time into wine, we humbly beseech Thee to hear the voice of our crying, to bestow on us such remembrance that we may never forget Thee; who livest and reignest with the Father and the Holy Ghost, ever one God, world without end. Amen.

[181]

Ant. The Lord est-ab-lished * a tes-ti-mó-ny in Jácob: and ap-pointed a láw

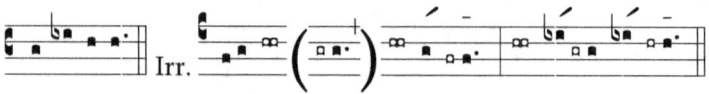

in Ísra-el.

Psalm 78i *Attendite*
1 Give ear, O my péople, / tó my law: * incline your ears to the / wórds of my <u>mouth</u>.
2 I will open my mouth ín a / párable: * I will utter dark / sáyings of <u>old</u>:
3 Which wé have / héard and known, * and our / fáthers have tóld us.
4 We will not hide them from their children, † shewing to the generation to come the práises / óf the LORD, * and his strength, and his wonderful / wórks that hé hath done.
5 For he established a testimóny in / Jácob, * and appointed a / láw in Ísrael,
Which he commánded our / fáthers, * that they should make them / knówn to their chíldren:
6 That the generation to come might know them, † even the chíldren which / shóuld be born; * who should arise and declare them / tó their chíldren:
7 That they might set their hôpe in God, † and not forgét the / wórks of God, * but / kéep his commándments:
8 And might not bé as their / fáthers, * a stubborn and rebellious / génerátion;
A generation that set nót their / héart aright, * and whose spirit was not / stédfast with <u>God</u>.
9 The children of Ephraim, being armed, and cárry- / ing <u>bows</u>, * turned back in the / dáy of báttle.
10 They kept not the cóve- / nánt of God, * and refused to / wálk in his <u>law</u>;
11 Ánd for- / gát his works, * and his wonders that / hé had shéwed them.
Glory be to the Fáther and / tó the Son * and / tó the Hóly Ghost.
As it was in the beginning, is now, and éver / sháll be, * - / wórld without énd. Amen.

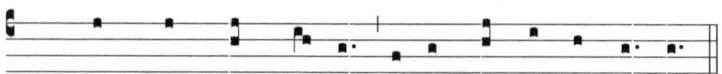

Ant. Marvellous things did he * in the sight of their fathers.
(Do not repeat in verse 12.)

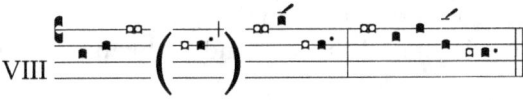

Psalm 78ii *Coram patribus*

12 [Marvellous things did he in the síght of their / fáthers,] * in the land of Egypt, in the / fíeld of Zó-an.
13 He divided the sea, and caused thém to / páss through; * and he made the waters to stánd / as an <u>heap</u>.
14 In the daytime also he léd them / wíth a cloud, * and all the night with a / líght of fíre-.
15 He clave the rócks in the / wílderness, * and gave them drink as óut / of the gréat depths.
16 He brought streams also óut of the / <u>rock</u>, * and caused waters to run / dówn like rívers.

[182]

Glory be to the Fáther and / tó the Son * and / tó the Hóly Ghost.
As it was in the beginning, is now, and éver / sháll be, * wórld / without énd. Amen.

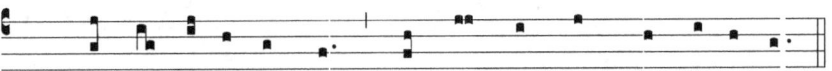

Ant. Mán did eat ángels' food: * The Lord sent them méat to the <u>full</u>.

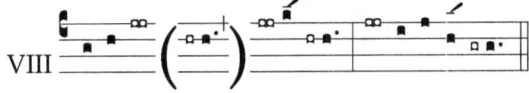

Psalm 78iii *Et apposuerunt*

17 And they sinned yet móre a- / gáinst him * by provoking the most High / ín the wílderness.
18 And they tempted Gód in their / <u>heart</u> * by asking méat / for their <u>lust</u>.
19 Yea, they spáke against / <u>God</u>; * they said, Can God furnish a table / ín the wílderness?
20 Behold, he smote the rock, that the waters gushed out, and the streams overflowed; † can he gíve bread / álso? * can he provide flésh / for his péople?
21 Therefore the LORD heard this, and was wroth: † so a fire was kindled ágainst / Jácob, * and anger also came úp / against Ísrael;
22 Because they belíeved not in / <u>God</u>, * and trusted not in / hís salvátion:
23 Though he had commanded the clóuds from a- / <u>bove</u>, * and opened the / dóors of héaven,
24 And had rained down manna upón them to / <u>eat</u>, * and had given them of the / córn of héaven.

25 Mán did eat / ángels' food: * he sent them méat / to the <u>full</u>.
26 He caused an east wind to blów in the / héaven: * and by his power he brought / ín the sóuth wind.
27 He rained flesh also upón them as / <u>dust</u>, * and feathered fowls like as the sánd / of the <u>sea</u>:
28 And he let it fall in the mídst of their / <u>camp</u>, * round about their / hábitátions.
29 So they did eat, ánd were / wéll filled: * for he gave them their / ówn desíre;-
30 They were not estránged from their / <u>lust</u>. * But while their meat was yét / in their <u>mouths</u>,
31 The wrath of God came upon them, † and slew the fáttest of / <u>them</u>, * and smote down the chosen / mén of Ísrael.
Glory be to the Fáther and / tó the Son * and / tó the Hóly Ghost.
As it was in the beginning, is now, and éver / sháll be, * wórld / without énd. Amen.

[183]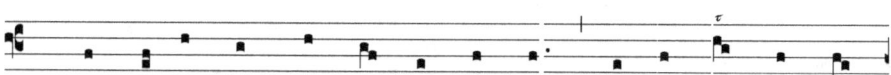

Ant. They remembered that Gód was their <u>rock</u>: * and the high God théir

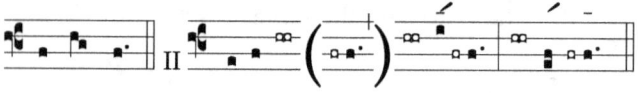

redéemer.

Psalm 78iv *In omnibus his*
32 For all thís they / sínned still, * and believed not fór his / wóndrous works.
33 Therefore their days did he consúme in / vánity, * and their yéars in / tróuble.
34 When he slew them, thén they / sóught him: * and they returned and enquired éarly / áfter God.
35 And they remembered that Gód was their / <u>rock</u>, * and the high God théir re- / déemer.
36 Nevertheless they did flátter him / wíth their mouth, * and they lied unto hím with / their <u>tongues</u>.
37 For their héart was not / ríght with him, * neither were they stedfast ín his / cóvenant.
38 But he, being full of compassion, forgáve their in- / íquity, * ánd des- / tróyed them not:

Yea, many a time turned he his ánger a- / way, * and did not stír up / áll his wrath.

39 For he remembered that théy were but / flesh; * a wind that passeth away, and cómeth / nót again.

Glory be to the Fáther and / tó the Son * and tó the / Hóly Ghost.

As it was in the beginning, is now, and éver / sháll be, * wórld without / énd. Amen.

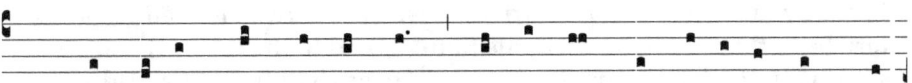

Ant. They remémbered nót his hand: * nor the day when he de-li-vered them

fróm the én-e-my.

Psalm 78v *Quoties*

40 How oft did they provoke him / ín the wílderness, * and grieve / him ín the désert!

41 Yea, they turned / báck and témpted God, * and limited the Ho- / ly Óne of Ísrael.

42 They re- / mémbered nót his hand, * nor the day when he delivered / them fróm the énemy.

43 How he had wrought his / sígns in Égypt, * and his wonders in / the fíeld of Zóan:

44 And had turned their / rívers ínto blood; * and their floods, that / théy could not drink.

45 He sent divers sorts of flies among them, / whích devóured them; * and / frogs, whích destróyed them.

46 He gave also their increase unto the / cáterpíller, * and their labour / únto the lócust.

47 He de- / stróyed their vínes with hail, * and their / sýcomore trées with frost.

48 He gave up their cattle / álso tó the hail, * and their / flócks to hot thúnderbolts.

49 He cast upon them the fierceness of his anger, † wrath, and indigná- / tion, and tróuble, * by sending evil / ángels amóng them.

50 He made a way to his anger; † he spared / nót their sóul from death, * but gave their life o- / ver tó the péstilence;

51 And smote all the fírst- / born in Égypt; * the chief of their strength in the

[184]

taber- / nácles of Ham:

52 But made his own people / tó go fórth like sheep, * and guided them in the / wílderness líke a flock.
53 And he led them on safely, so / thát they féared not: * but the sea o- / verwhélmed their énemies.
54 And he brought them to the border of his / sánctuáry, * even to this mountain, which his / right hánd had púrchased.
55 He cast out the heathen also before them, † and divided them an inhér- / itance bý line, * and made the tribes of Israel to / dwéll in their tents.

Glory be to the Fá- / ther and tó the Son * - / and tó the Hóly Ghost.
As it was in the beginning, is now, and / éver sháll be, * - / wórld without énd. Amen.

Ant. The Lord built his sánctu-á-ry: * líke high pálaces.

Psalm 78vi *Et tentaverunt*
56 Yet they tempted and pro- / vóked the móst high God, * and kept not his / téstimónies:
57 But turned back, and dealt unfaithfully / líke their fáthers: * they were turned aside líke / a decéitful bow.
58 For they provoked him to anger with / théir high pláces, * and moved him to jealousy with their / gráven ímages.
59 When God / héard this, hé was wroth, * and greatly / ábhorred Ísrael:
60 So that he forsook the taber- / nácle of Shíloh, * the tent which he / pláced amóng men;
61 And delivered his strength / ínto captívity, * and his glory into the / énemy's hand.
62 He gave his people over also / únto the sword; * and was wroth with / hís inhéritance.
63 The fire con- / súmed their yóung men; * and their maidens were not gív- / en to márriage.
64 Their priests / féll by the sword; * and their widows made no / lámentátion.
65 Then the Lord awaked as / óne out of sleep, * and like a mighty man that shouteth by / réason of wine.
66 And he smote his enemies / ín the hínder parts: * he put them to a per- /

pétual reproach.
67 Moreover he refused the taber- / nácle of Jóseph, * and chose not the / tríbe of Éphraim:
68 But chose the / tríbe of Júdah, * the mount / Zíon whích he loved.
69 And he built his sanctuary / líke high pálaces, * like the earth which he hath estáb- / lished óf éver.
70 He chose David / álso his sérvant, * and took him / fróm the shéepfolds: [185]
71 From following the ewes great with young † he brought him to feed / Jácob his péople, * and Israel / hís inhéritance.
72 So he fed them according to the in- / tégrity óf his heart; * and guided them by the skíl- / fulness óf his hands.
Glory be to the / Fáther and tó the Son * - and / tó the Hóly Ghost.
As it was in the beginning, is now, and / éver sháll be, * - wórld / without énd. Amen.

Psalm-prayer. Almighty God, most bountiful provider, refresh us with the food of spiritual manna, that, guided by the skilfulness of Thine hands, we may glory at Thy right hand in the mountain Thou hast purchased; through Jesus Christ our Lord, who liveth and reigneth with Thee and the Holy Ghost, ever one God, world without end. Amen.

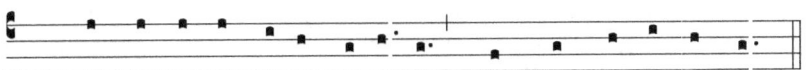

Ant. Help us, O God of óur salvátion: * and púrge awáy our sins.

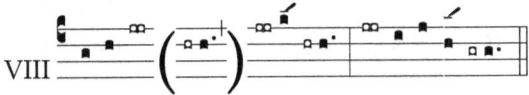
VIII

Psalm 79 *Deus, venerunt*
1 O God, the heathen are come into thine inhêritance; † thy holy temple have théy de- / fíled; * they have laid Je- / rúsalém on heaps.
2 The dead bodies of thy servants have they given to be meat unto the fówls of the / héaven, * the flesh of thy saints unto the béasts / of the earth.
3 Their blood have they shed like water round abóut Je- / rúsalem; * and there was / nóne to búry them.
4 We are become a repróach to our / néighbours, * a scorn and derision to them that are / róund abóut us.
5 How long, LORD? wilt thou be ángry for / éver? * shall thy jealousy / búrn like fíre-?
6 Pour out thy wrath upon the heathen that háve not / knówn thee, * and upon the kingdoms that have not / cálled upón thy name.

7 For they have devóured / Jácob, * and laid / wáste his dwélling place.
8 O remember not against us former inîquities: † let thy tender mercies speedilý pre- / vént us: * for wé / are brought véry low.
9 Help us, O God of our salvation, for the glóry / óf thy name: * and deliver us, and purge away our sins, / fór thy náme's sake.
10 Wherefore should the heathen say, Where is their God? † let him be known among the héathen / ín our sight * by the revenging of the blood of thy / sérvants whích is shed.
11 Let the sighing of the prisoner cóme be- / fóre thee; * according to the greatness of thy power preserve thou those that are appóin- / ted to <u>die</u>;
12 And render unto our neighbours sevenfold into their bósom / théir reproach, * wherewith they have repróached / thee, O <u>Lord</u>.
13 So we thy people and sheep of thy pasture will give thee thánks for / éver: * we will shew forth thy praise to all / génerátions.

[186] Glory be to the Fáther and / tó the Son * and / tó the Hóly Ghost.
As it was in the beginning, is now, and éver / sháll be, * wórld / without énd. Amen.

Psalm-prayer. O Lord, let Thy mercy speedily come before us, for there is neither comforting hope, nor trust in merit, nor helpful assistance to support us; but the guilt and trouble of our life, the consciousness of our sins, or the vengeance on our offences rebukes us in our unrest. Deliver us for the glory of Thy Name, and purge away our sins for Thy Name's sake, that when Thou hast done both for Thyself, and hast looked on Thy people with Thy wonted loving-kindness, we may give Thee glory for our deliverance, and obtain propitiation through Thy Name; through Jesus Christ our Lord, who liveth and reigneth with Thee and the Holy Ghost, ever one God, world without end. Amen.

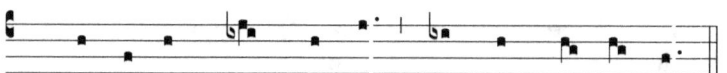

Ant. Stír up thy stréngth, O Lord: * and cóme and sáve us.

Psalm 80 *Qui regis Israel*
1 Give ear, O Shepherd of Îsrael, † thou that leadest Jóseph / líke a flock; * thou that dwellest between the / chérubims, shíne forth.
2 Before Ephraim and Benjamin ánd Ma- / násseh * stir up thy strength, and / cóme and sáve us.

3 Turn us again, O God, and cáuse thy / fáce to shine; * and / wé shall be <u>saved</u>.
4 Ó LORD / Gód of hosts, * how long wilt thou be angry against the / práyer of thy péople?
5 Thou feedest them wíth the / bréad of tears; * and givest them tears to / drínk in great méasure.
6 Thou makest us a strife únto our / néighbours: * and our enemies / láugh amóng themselves.
7 Turn us again, O God of hosts, and cáuse thy / fáce to shine; * and / wé shall be <u>saved</u>.
8 Thou hast brought a vine óut of / Égypt: * thou hast cast out the / héathen, and plánted it.
9 Thou prepar-edst room before it, and didst cáuse it to / táke deep root, * - / ánd it fílled the land.
10 The hills were covered with the shádow / óf it, * and the boughs thereof were like the / góodly cédars.
11 She sent out her boughs únto the / <u>sea</u>, * and her branches / únto the ríver.
12 Why hast thou then broken dówn her / hédges, * so that all they which pass by the / wáy do plúck her?
13 The boar out of the wóod doth / wáste it, * and the wild beast of the field / dóth devóur it.
14 Return, we beséech thee, O / Gód of hosts: * look down from heaven, and behold, and / vísit this <u>vine</u>; [187]
15 And the vineyard which thy right hánd hath / plánted, * and the branch that thou madest / stróng for thy<u>self</u>.
16 It is burned with fire, ít is / cút down: * they perish at the rebuke / óf thy cóuntenance.
17 Let thy hand be upon the mán of thy / ríght hand, * upon the son of man whom thou madest / stróng for thy<u>self</u>.
18 So will not wé go / báck from thee: * quicken us, and we will / cáll upón thy name.
19 Turn us again, Ó LORD / Gód of hosts, * cause thy face to shine; and / wé shall be <u>saved</u>.
Glory be to the Fáther and / tó the Son * and / tó the Hóly Ghost.
As it was in the beginning, is now, and éver / sháll be, * - / wórld without énd. Amen.

Psalm-prayer. Visit, O Lord, this vine, which Thou hast brought out of the Egypt of troubles with Thy strong Right Hand; that quickened by the light of Thy countenance, it may be glad with the plenteousness of good fruits in Thee; through the same, Jesus Christ our Lord, who liveth and reigneth with

Thee and the Holy Ghost, ever one God, world without end. Amen.

Ant. Ópen thý mouth wide: * and I, the LÓRD, will fíll it.

Psalm 81 *Exsultate Deo*

1 Sing aloud / únto Gód our strength: * make a joyful noise unto / the Gód of Jácob.
2 Take a psalm, and bring hí- / ther the tímbrel, * the pleasant / hárp with the psáltery.
3 Blow up the trumpet / ín the néw moon, * in the time appointed, on / our sólemn féast day.
4 For this was a stá- / tute for Ísrael, * and a law of / the Gód of Jácob.
5 This he ordained in Joseph for a testimony, † when he went out through the / lánd of Égypt: * where I heard a language that / I únderstóod not.
6 I removed his shoulder / fróm the búrden: * his hands were / delívered fróm the pots.
7 Thou calledst in trouble, and I delîvered thee; † I answered thee in the secret / pláce of thúnder: * I proved thee at the / wáters of Méribah.
8 Hear, O my people, and I will té- / stify únto thee: * O Israel, if thou / wilt héarken únto me;
9 There shall nó / strange god bé in thee; * neither shalt thou wor- / ship ány stránge god.
10 I am the LORD thy God, which brought thee out of the / lánd of Égypt: * open thy mouth wide, / and Í will fíll it.
11 But my people would not / héarken tó my voice; * and Is- / ra-él would nóne of me.
12 So I gave them up ún- / to their ówn hearts' lust: * and they walked / in théir own cóunsels.

[188] 13 Oh that my people had / héarkened únto me, * and Israel had / wálked in my <u>ways</u>!
14 I should soon have sub- / dúed their énemies, * and turned my hand against / their ádversáries.
15 The haters of the LORD should have submitted / thémselves únto him: * but their time should have / endúred for éver.
16 He should have fed them also with the / fínest óf the wheat: * and with honey out of the rock should I have / sátisfied <u>thee</u>.

Glory be to the Fá- / ther and tó the Son * - / and tó the Hóly Ghost.
As it was in the beginning, is now, and / éver shall be, * - / wórld without énd. Amen.

Psalm-prayer. Open, O Lord, the mouths of Thy humble servants to show forth Thy praise, that leaving the works of Egypt behind, we may rejoice in the confession of Thy Name; through Jesus Christ our Lord, who liveth and reigneth with Thee and the Holy Ghost, ever one God, world without end. Amen.

Ant. Aríse, O God, * júdge the earth: for Thou shalt in-hér-it all nátions.

Psalm 82 *Deus stetit*
1 God standeth in the congregation / óf the míghty; * he / júdgeth amóng the gods.
2 How long will ye / júdge unjústly, * and accept the per- / sons óf the wícked?
3 Defend the / póor and fátherless: * do justice to the af- / flícted and néedy.
4 Deliver the / póor and néedy: * rid them out of the / hánd of the wícked.
5 They know not, neither will they únderstand; † they walk / ón in dárkness: * all the foundations of / the éarth are óut of course.
6 I have sáid, / Ye are <u>gods</u>; * and all of you are chil- / dren óf the móst High.
7 But / yé shall díe like men, * and fall like / óne of the prínces.
8 Aríse, / O God, júdge the earth: * for thou shalt in- / hérit all nátions.
Glory be to the Fá- / ther and tó the Son * - / and tó the Hóly Ghost.
As it was in the beginning, is now, and / éver shall be, * - / wórld without énd. Amen.

Psalm-prayer. Arise, O Lord, who judgest the earth, and as Thou dwellest in loving ownership of the faith of all nations, suffer us not to abide in darkness, but cause us to see the light of Thy truth, that we may build the foundations of our faith not upon the sand, which the whirlwind may cast down, but on the rock, whose strength Thou art; who livest and reignest with the Father and the Holy Ghost, ever one God, world without end. Amen.

[189]

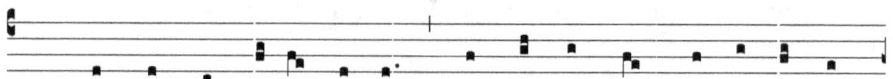

Ant. Keep not thou silence, O God: * hold not thy peace, and be not still,

O God. *(Do not repeat in verse 1.)*

Psalm 83 *Deus, quis*

1 [Keep not thou / sílence, O <u>God</u>: * hold not thy peace, and / bé not stíll, O God.]
2 For, lo, thine enemies / máke a túmult: * and they that hate thee have / lífted úp the head.
3 They have taken crafty counsel a- / gáinst thy péople, * and consulted a- / gáinst thy hídden ones.
4 They have said, Come, and let us cut them off from / béing a nátion; * that the name of Israel may be no more / ín remémbrance.
5 For they have consulted to- / géther with óne consent: * they are confeder- / áte agáinst thee:
6 The tabernacles of Edom, / ánd the Ísh-mael-ites; * of Moab, / ánd the Hágarenes;
7 Gebal, and / Ámmon, and Ámalek; * the Philistines with the inhabi- / tánts of Týre-;
8 Assur / álso is jóined with them: * they have holpen the / chíldren of <u>Lot</u>.
9 Do unto them as un- / tó the Mídianites; * as to Sisera, as to Jabin, at the / bróok of Kíson:
10 Which / pérished at Éndor: * they became as / dúng for the <u>earth</u>.
11 Make their nobles like / Óreb, ánd like Zeeb: * yea, all their princes as Zebah, and / ás Zalmúnna:
12 Who said, Let us / táke to our<u>selves</u> * the houses of God / ín posséssion.
13 O my God, / máke them líke a wheel; * as the stúb- / ble befóre the wind.
14 As the fire / búrneth a <u>wood</u>, * and as the flame setteth the móun- / tains on fíre-;
15 So persecute them / wíth thy témpest, * and make them a- / fráid with thy <u>storm</u>.
16 Fill their / fáces with <u>shame</u>; * that they may / séek thy náme, O LORD.
17 Let them be confounded and / tróubled for éver; * yea, let them be put to / sháme, and pérish:
18 That men may know that thou, whose name a- / lóne is JEHÓVAH, * art

the most high / óver áll the earth.
Glory be to the / Fáther and tó the Son * - and / tó the Hóly Ghost.
As it was in the beginning, is now, and / éver sháll be, * - wórld / without énd. Amen.

Psalm-prayer. Let the Gentiles, for whom Thou didst hang upon the rood of the Cross, know, O Christ, that Thy Name is the LORD, and let knowledge bring them back to their Maker, as ignorance gave them up to sloth, that they may be converted through knowledge of the faith, and rejoice in the hope of glory; who livest and reignest with the Father and the Holy Ghost, ever one God, world without end. Amen.

[190]

Ant. Bless-ed * are they that dwéll in Thy hóuse, O Lord: They will bé still

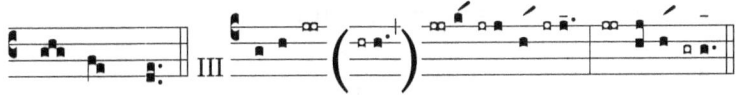

práising thee.

Psalm 84 *Quam dilecta*

1 How amiable are thy tabernacles, O LORD of hosts! † 2 My soul longeth, yea, even fainteth for the / cóurts of the <u>LORD</u>: * my heart and my flesh crieth out fór / the líving God.
3 Yea, the sparrow hath found an house, † and the swallow a nest for herself, where / shé may láy her young, * even thine altars, O LORD of hosts, my / Kíng, and my <u>God</u>.
4 Bless-ed are they that / dwéll in thy <u>house</u>: * they will bé / still práising thee.
5 Bless-ed is the man whose / stréngth is in <u>thee</u>; * in whose heart áre / the wáys of them.
6 Who passing through the valley of Baca / máke it a <u>well</u>; * the rain also / fílleth the <u>pools</u>.
7 They / gó from stréngth to strength, * every one of them in Zion appéareth / befóre God.
8 O LORD / Gód of hosts, héar my prayer: * give ear, O Gód / of Jácob.
9 Be- / hóld, O Gód our shield, * and look upon the face of thíne / anóinted.
10 For a day in thy courts is better / thán a thóusand. * I had rather be a doorkeeper in the house of my God, than to dwell in the ténts / of wíckedness.

11 For the LORD God is a sun and shield: † the LORD will give / gráce and glóry: * no good thing will he withhold from them that wálk / upríghtly.
12 O LORD of hosts, / bléss-ed ís the man * that / trústeth in <u>thee</u>.
Glory be to the / Fáther and tó the Son * and tó / the Hóly Ghost.
As it was in the beginning, is now, and / éver shállbe, * wórld with- / out énd. Amen.

Psalm-prayer. O God, the defender of them that trust in Thee, save us who abide in Thy service, that separated from the tents of the ungodly, we may be fitted to dwell in Thy holy house; through Jesus Christ our Lord, who liveth and reigneth with Thee and the Holy Ghost, ever one God, world without end. Amen.

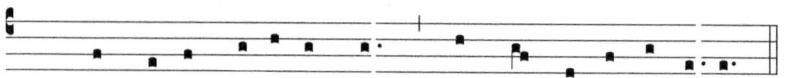

Ant. Shew us thy mércy, O <u>LORD</u>, * and grant us thý salvátion.

Psalm 85 *Benedixisti*
1 LORD, thou hast been favourable ún- / to thy <u>land</u>: * thou hast brought back the capti- / vitý of Jácob.
2 Thou hast forgiven the iniquity / óf thy péople, * thou / hast cóvered áll their sin.
3 Thou hast taken awáy / all thy <u>wrath</u>: * thou hast turned thyself from the fierce- / ness óf thine ánger.
[191] 4 Turn us, O God of / óur salvátion, * and cause thine / ánger toward ús to cease.
5 Wilt thou be angry with / ús for éver? * wilt thou draw out thine anger to / all génerátions?
6 Wilt thou not revíve / us a<u>gain</u>: * that thy peo- / ple máy rejóice in thee?
7 Shew us thy mér- / cy, O <u>LORD</u>, * and grant / us thý salvátion.
8 I will hear what God the LÔRD will speak: † for he will speak peace unto his people, ánd / to his <u>saints</u>: * but let them not turn / agáin to fólly.
9 Surely his salvation is nígh / them that féar him; * that glory may / dwéll in our <u>land</u>.
10 Mercy and truth are / mét togéther; * righteousness and peace / have kíssed óther.
11 Truth shall spring óut / of the <u>earth</u>; * and righteousness shall / look dówn from héaven.

12 Yea, the LORD shall give thát / which is good; * and our land / shall yíeld her íncrease.
13 Righteousness shall / gó befóre him; * and shall set us in the / wáy of his steps.
Glory be to the Fá- / ther and tó the Son * - / and tó the Hóly Ghost.
As it was in the beginning, is now, and / éver sháll be, * - / wórld without énd. Amen.

Psalm-prayer. Forgive, O Lord, the offences of Thy people, and show us Thy mercy, to lead us, with righteousness going before, in the way of peace; through Jesus Christ our Lord, who liveth and reigneth with Thee and the Holy Ghost, ever one God, world without end. Amen.

Ant. Lord, * give Thy strength únto Thy sérvant: and save the són of Thine

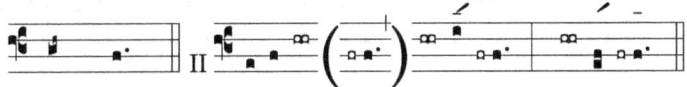

hándmaid.

Psalm 86 *Inclina, Domine*
1 Bow down thine éar, O LORD, / héar me: * for I am póor and / néedy.
2 Preserve my soul; for Í am / hóly: * O thou my God, save thy servant that trústeth / in thee.
3 Be merciful únto / mé, O Lord: * for I cry únto thee / dáily.
4 Rejoice the sóul of thy / sérvant: * for unto thee, O Lord, do Í lift / úp my soul.
5 For thou, Lord, art good, and ready / tó forgive; * and plenteous in mercy unto all them that cáll up- / on thee.
6 Give ear, O LORD, únto my / prayer; * and attend to the voice of my súppli- / cátions.
7 In the day of my trouble I will cáll upon / thee: * for thóu wilt / ánswer me.
8 Among the gods there is none líke unto / thée, O Lord; * neither are there any works líke unto / thý works.
9 All nations whom thou hast made shall come and worship befóre thee, O / Lord; * and shall glóri- / fý thy name.
10 For thou art great, and dóest / wóndrous things: * thóu art / Gód alone.
11 Teach me thy wây, O LORD; † I will wálk in thy / truth: * unite my héart

to / féar thy name.

12 I will praise thee, O Lord my Gód, with / áll my heart: * and I will glorify thy náme for / évermore.

13 For great is thy mércy toward / me: * and thou hast delivered my soul fróm the / lówest hell.

14 O God, the proud are risen against me, † and the assemblies of violent men have sought áfter my / soul; * and have not set thée be- / fóre them.

15 But thou, O Lord, art a God full of compássion, and / grácious, * longsuffering, and plenteous in mércy / and truth.

16 O turn unto me, and have mércy up- / ón me; * give thy strength unto thy servant, and save the són of thine / hándmaid.

17 Shew me a token for good; † that they which hate me may sée it, and / bé ashamed: * because thou, LORD, hast holpen me, and cómfort- / ed me.

Glory be to the Fáther and / tó the Son * and tó the / Hóly Ghost.

As it was in the beginning, is now, and éver / sháll be, * wórld without / énd. Amen.

Psalm-prayer. Rejoice, O Lord, the countenance of Thy servants; and deliver our souls from the lowest hell, that protected by Thy mercy, we may with spiritual strength tread fleshly desires under foot; through Jesus Christ our Lord, who liveth and reigneth with Thee and the Holy Ghost, ever one God, world without end. Amen.

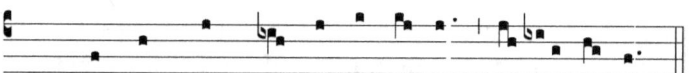

Ant. Glor*i*ous things are spóken of thee: * O cíty of God.

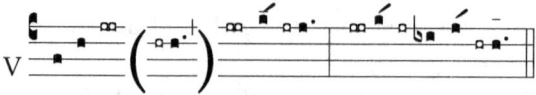

Psalm 87 *Fundamenta*

1 His foundation is in the hóly / móuntains. * 2 The LORD loveth the gates of Zion more than all the / dwéllings of Jácob.

3 Glorious things are spóken of / thee, * O / cíty of God.

4 I will make mention of Rahab and Babylon to thém that / knów me: * behold Philistia, and Tyre, with Ethiopia; / thís man was bórn there.

5 And of Zion it shâll be said, † This and thát man was / bórn in her: * and the highest himself / sháll estáblish her.

6 The LORD shall count, when he writeth úp the / péople, * that / thís man was bórn there.

7 As well the singers as the players on instruménts shall / bé there: * all my

/ spríngs are in thee.
**Glory be to the Fáther and / tó the Son * and / tó the Hóly Ghost.
As it was in the beginning, is now, and éver / shall be, * - / wórld without énd. Amen.**

Psalm-prayer. O God, the foundation of our faith, who settest up the gates of eternity with the strong wall of righteousness in holy minds as upon lofty mountains; grant that we may believe gloriously in Thee, and confess by preaching that Thou wast made Man for our redemption; who livest and reignest with the Father and the Holy Ghost, ever one God world without end. Amen. [193]

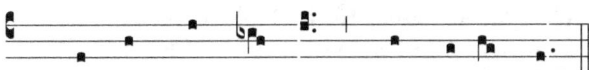

Ant. Lét my práyer, O Lord: * cóme befóre Thee.

Psalm 88 *Domine, Deus salutis*

1 O LORD God of mý sal- / vátion, * I have cried day and / níght befóre thee:
2 Let my prayer cóme be- / fóre thee: * incline thine ear / únto my cry:
3 For my soul is fúll of / tróubles: * and my life draweth nigh / únto the grave.
4 I am counted with them that go down ínto the / pit: * I am as a / mán that háth no strength:
5 Frée a- / móng the dead, * like the slain that / líe in the grave,
Whom thou remémberest / nó more: * and they are cut / óff from thy hand.
6 Thou hast laid me ín the / lówest pit, * in / dárkness, ín the deeps.
7 Thy wrath lieth hárd up- / ón me, * and thou hast afflicted / mé with áll thy waves.
8 Thou hast put away mine acquaintance fâr from me; † thou hast made me an abominátion / únto them: * I am shut up, and / Í cannót come forth.
9 Mine eye mourneth by reason of affliction: † LORD, I have called dáily up- / ón thee, * I have stretched out my / hánds unto thee.
10 Wilt thou shew wónders / tó the dead? * shall the dead a- / ríse and práise thee?
11 Shall thy lovingkindness be decláred in the / grave? * or thy faithfulness / ín destrúction?
12 Shall thy wonders be knówn in the / dark? * and thy righteousness in the

/ lánd of forgétfulness?

13 But unto thée have I / críed, O LORD; * and in the morning shall my / práyer prevént thee.

14 LORD, why cástest thou / óff my soul? * why hidest / thóu thy fáce from me?

15 I am afflicted and ready to die fróm my / yóuth up: * while I suffer thy terrors I / ám distrácted.

16 Thy fierce wrath góeth / óver me; * thy / térrors have cút me off.

17 They came round about me dáily like / wáter; * they compassed me a- / bóut togéther.

18 Lover and friend hast thóu put / fár from me, * and mine acquaintance / ínto dárkness.

Glory be to the Fáther and / tó the Son * and / tó the Hóly Ghost.

As it was in the beginning, is now, and éver / shall be, * - / wórld without énd. Amen.

Psalm-prayer. O God, Redeemer of all, and ineffable giver of our salvation, who passing into hell for us, wast free among the dead, hear the prayer of Thy servants, and deliver us from the grievous bondage of the crafty foe; who livest and reignest with the Father and the Holy Ghost, ever one God world without end. Amen.

[194]

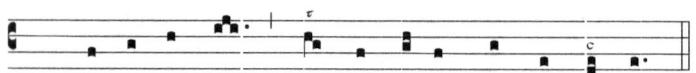

Ant. Mercy and truth * shall go before Thy face, O Lord.

Psalm 89i *Misericordias*

1 I will sing of the mercies of the / LÓRD for éver: * with my mouth will I make known thy faithfulness to all / génerátions.

2 For I have said, Mercy shall be built / úp for éver: * thy faithfulness shalt thou establish in the / véry héavens.

3 I have made a covenant / wíth my chósen, * I have sworn unto / Dávid my sérvant,

4 Thy seed will I e- / stáblish for éver, * and build up thy throne to all / génerátions.

5 And the heavens shall praise thy / wónders, O LORD: * thy faithfulness also in the congre- / gátion óf the saints.

6 For who in the heaven can be compared / únto the LORD? * who among

the sons of the mighty can be likened / únto the LORD?
7 God is greatly to be feared in the as- / sémbly óf the saints, * and to be had in reverence of all them that / áre abóut him.
8 O LORD God of hosts, who is a strong LORD / líke unto thee? * or to thy faithfulness / róund abóut thee?
9 Thou rulest the / ráging óf the sea: * when the waves thereof a- / ríse, thou stíllest them.
10 Thou hast broken Rahab in pieces, as / óne that is slain; * thou hast scattered thine enemies / wíth thy stróng arm.
11 The heavens are thine, the earth / álso is thine: * as for the world and the fulness thereof, / thóu hast fóunded them.
12 The north and the south thou / hást creáted them: * Tabor and Hermon shall re- / jóice in thy name.
13 Thou / hást a míghty arm: * strong is thy hand, and / hígh is thy ríght hand.
14 Justice and judgment are the habi- / tátion óf thy throne: * mercy and truth shall / gó befóre thy face.
15 Bless-ed is the people that / knów the jóyful sound: * they shall walk, O LORD, in the / líght of thy cóuntenance.
16 In thy name shall / théy rejoice áll the day: * and in thy righteousness shall they / bé exálted.
17 For thou art the / glóry óf their strength: * and in thy favour our horn shall / bé exálted.
18 For the / LÓRD is óur defence; * and the Holy One of / Ísrael ís our king.
Glory be to the / Fáther and tó the Son * and / tó the Hóly Ghost.
As it was in the beginning, is now, and / éver sháll be, * - / wórld without énd. Amen.

[195]

Ant. I will make hím my Fírstborn: * higher than the kíngs of the earth.

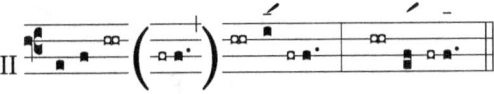

Psalm 89ii *Tunc locutus*

19 Then thou spakest in vision to thy holy one, and saidst, † I have laid help upon óne that is / míghty; * I have exalted one chosen óut of the / péople.
20 I have found Dávid my / sérvant; * with my holy oil have Í a- / nóinted him:
21 With whom my hand shall bé es- / táblished: * mine arm álso shall /

stréngthen him.
22 The enemy shall not exáct up- / ón him; * nor the son of wickednéss af- / flíct him.
23 And I will beat down his fóes be- / fóre his face, * and plágue them that / háte him.
24 But my faithfulness and my mercy sháll be / wíth him: * and in my name shall his horn bé ex- / álted.
25 I will set his hand álso / ín the sea, * and his right hand ín the / rívers.
26 He shall cry unto me, Thóu art my / fáther, * my God, and the rock of mý sal- / vátion.
27 Also I will máke him my / fírstborn, * higher than the kíngs of / the <u>earth</u>.
28 My mercy will I keep for hím for / évermore, * and my covenant sháll stand / fást with him.
29 His seed also will I make to endúre for / éver, * and his throne as the dáys of / héaven.
30 If his chíldren for- / sáke my law, * and walk nót in my / júdgments;
31 If they bréak my / státutes, * and keep not mý com- / mándments;
32 Then will I visit their transgréssion / wíth the rod, * and their iníquity / with <u>stripes</u>.
33 Nevertheless my lovingkindness will I not útterly / táke from him, * nor suffer my fáithfulness/ tó fail.
34 My covenant wíll I not / <u>break</u>, * nor alter the thing that is gone óut of / my <u>lips</u>.
35 Once have I swórn by my / hóliness * that I will not líe unto / Dávid.
36 His seed shall endúre for / éver, * and his throne as the sún be- / fóre me.
37 It shall be established for éver / ás the moon, * and as a faithful wítness in / héaven.
Glory be to the Fáther and / tó the Son * and tó the / Hóly Ghost.
As it was in the beginning, is now, and éver / sháll be, * wórld without / énd. Amen.

[196]

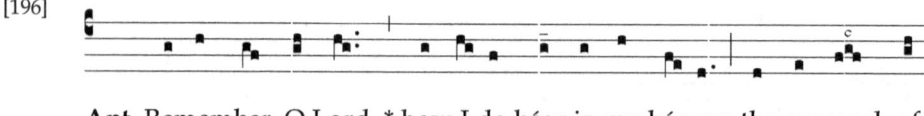

Ant. Remember, O Lord, * how I do béar in my bósom: the reproach of áll

the míghty people.

Psalm 89iii *Tu vero*

38 But thou hast cast óff and ab- / <u>horred</u>, * thou hast been wroth with / thíne anóinted.
39 Thou hast made void the covenant óf thy / sérvant: * thou hast profaned his crown by cást- / ing it tó the ground.
40 Thou hast broken down áll his / hédges; * thou hast brought his stróng / holds to rúin.
41 All that pass bý the way / spóil him: * he is a repróach / to his néighbours.
42 Thou hast set up the right hand of his ádver- / sáries; * thou hast made all his én- / emies tó rejoice.
43 Thou hast also turned the édge of his / <u>sword</u>, * and hast not made him to stánd / in the báttle.
44 Thou hast made his glóry to / <u>cease</u>, * and cast his throne dówn / to the <u>ground</u>.
45 The days of his youth hást thou / shórtened: * thou hast / cóvered hím with shame.
46 How long, LORD? wilt thou hide thysélf for / éver? * shall thy wrath / búrn like fíre-?
47 Remember how shórt my / tíme is: * wherefore hast thou / máde all mén in vain?
48 What man is he that liveth, ánd shall / nót see death? * shall he deliver his soul from the hánd / of the <u>grave</u>?
49 Lord, where are thy former lóving- / kíndnesses, * which thou swarest unto / Dávid ín thy truth?
50 Remember, Lord, the repróach of thy / sérvants; * how I do bear in my bosom the reproach of all the / míghty péople;
51 Wherewith thine enemies háve re- / próached, O LORD; * wherewith they have reproached the footsteps of / thíne anóinted.
52 Bless-ed be the LÓRD for / évermore. * Amén, / and A<u>men</u>.
Glory be to the Fáther and / tó the Son * and / tó the Hóly Ghost.
As it was in the beginning, is now, and éver / shálll be, * wórld / without énd. Amen.

Psalm-prayer. Deliver our souls, O Lord, from the hand of hell; who for us didst mightily break hell to pieces, that we, singing Thy mercies, may be delivered from the shame of our sins and from everlasting death; through Jesus Christ our Lord, who liveth and reigneth with Thee and the Holy Ghost, ever one God, world without end. Amen.

[197]

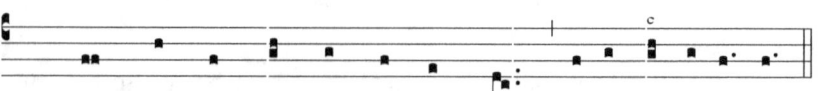

Ant. Lord, thou hast béen our dwélling place: * in all gén-er-á-tions.
(Do not repeat in verse 1.)

Psalm 90 *Domine, refugium*

1 [Lord, thou hast / béen our dwélling place * in all / génerátions.]
2 Before the mountains were brought forth, † or ever thou hadst formed the / éarth and the <u>world</u>, * even from everlasting to ever- / lásting, thóu art God.
3 Thou turnest / mán to destrúction; * and sayest, Return, ye chíl- / dren of <u>men</u>.
4 For a thousand years in thy sight are but as yesterday / whén it is <u>past</u>, * and as a wátch / in the <u>night</u>.
5 Thou carriest them away as with a flood; / théy are ás a sleep: * in the morning they are like / gráss which gróweth up.
6 In the morning it flourish- / éth, and gróweth up; * in the evening it is cut / dówn, and withereth.
7 For we are consumed / bý thine ánger, * and by thy wráth / are we tróubled.
8 Thou hast set our iniqui- / tíes befóre thee, * our secret sins in the líght / of thy cóuntenance.
9 For all our days are passed a- / wáy in thy <u>wrath</u>: * we spend our years as a tále / that is <u>told</u>.
10 The days of our years are threescore yêars and ten; † and if by reason of strength they be fourscore years, yet is their strength / lábour and sórrow; * for it is soon cut off, / ánd we flý away.
11 Who knoweth the power / óf thine ánger? * even according to thy fear, só / is thy <u>wrath</u>.
12 So teach us to / númber our <u>days</u>, * that we may apply our héarts / unto wísdom.
13 Re- / túrn, O LORD, hów long? * and let it repent thee concér- / ning thy sérvants.
14 O satisfy us early / with thy mércy; * that we may rejoice and be glád / all our <u>days</u>.
15 Make us glad according to the days wherein / thóu hast afflícted us, * and the years wherein wé / have seen évil.
16 Let thy work appear / únto thy sérvants, * and thy glory ún- / to their

chíldren.

17 And let the beauty of the LORD our God be upon us: † and establish thou the work of our / hánds upón us; * yea, the work of our hands estáb- / lish thou it.

Glory be to the / Fáther and tó the Son * - and / tó the Hóly Ghost.

As it was in the beginning, is now, and / éver sháll be, * - wórld / without énd. Amen.

Psalm-prayer. Keep us, O Lord, from one generation to another, and let not us, who have clung to Thy foundation, be carried away with this present world, but arise to be our Comforter in trouble, and by the bestowal of joy wipe away our sorrows; through Jesus Christ our Lord, who liveth and reigneth with Thee and the Holy Ghost, ever one God, world without end. Amen.

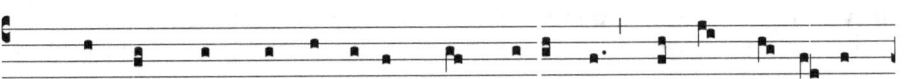

[198]

Ant. The Lord shall give his angels chárge over thee: * to kéep thee in áll

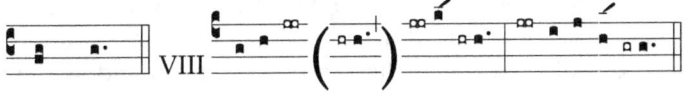

thy ways.

Psalm 91 *Qui habitat*

1 He that dwelleth in the secret place óf the / móst High * shall abide under the shadow óf / the Almíghty.
2 I will say of the LORD, He is my refuge ánd my / fórtress: * my God; in hím / will I trust.
3 Surely he shall deliver thee from the snáre of the / fówler, * and from the / nóisome péstilence.
4 He shall cover thee with his feathers, † and under his wíngs shalt thou / trust: * his truth shall be thy / shíeld and búckler.
5 Thou shalt not be afraid for the térror by / night; * nor for the arrow that flí- / eth by day;
6 Nor for the pestilence that wálketh in / dárkness; * nor for the destruction that wást- / eth at nóonday.
7 A thousand shall fall at thy side, † and ten thousand át thy / ríght hand; * but it shall / nót come nígh thee.
8 Only with thine éyes shalt / thóu behold * and see the rewárd / of the wícked.

9 Because thou hast made the LORD, which ís my / réfuge, * even the most High, thy / hábitátion;
10 There shall no évil be- / fáll thee, * neither shall any plague come / nígh thy dwélling.
11 For he shall give his angels chárge over / thee, * to kéep / thee in áll thy ways.
12 They shall bear thee úp in their / hands, * lest thou dash thy / fóot agáinst a stone.
13 Thou shalt tread upon the líon and / ádder: * the young lion and the dragon shalt thou / trámple únder feet.
14 Because he hath set his love upon me, therefore will Í de- / líver him: * I will set him on high, because / hé hath knówn my name.
15 He shall call upon me, and I will ânswer him: † I will be wíth him in / tróuble; * I will deliver / hím, and hónour him.
16 With long life will I sátisfy / him, * and shew him / mý salvátion.
Glory be to the Fáther and / tó the Son * and / tó the Hóly Ghost.
As it was in the beginning, is now, and éver / sháll be, * wórld / without énd. Amen.

Psalm-prayer. Grant us, O Lord, by invocation of Thy Name, to tread under foot the deadly poison of the adder and dragon, that Thou mayest show us Thy salvation, and we be protected under the shadow of Thy shield against the snares of the spiritual enemy; through Jesus Christ our Lord, who liveth and reigneth with Thee and the Holy Ghost, ever one God, world without end. Amen.

[199]

Ant. It is a good thing * to give thanks unto the LORD.
(Do not repeat in verse 1.)

Psalm 92 *Bonum est*
1 [It is a good thing to give thanks / únto the LORD,] * and to sing praises unto thy náme, / O most High:
2 To shew forth thy lovingkindness / ín the mórning, * and thy fáith- / fulness évery night,
3 Upon an instrument of ten strings, and up- / ón the psáltery; * upon the harp / with a sólemn sound.

266

4 For thou, LORD, hast made me / glád through thy <u>work</u>: * I will triumph in the wórks / of thy <u>hands</u>.

5 O LORD, how / gréat are thy <u>works</u>! * and thy / thóughts are véry deep.

6 A / brútish man knóweth not; * neither doth a fool / únderstánd this.

7 When the wicked / spríng as the <u>grass</u>, * and when all the workers of iniqui- / tý do flóurish;

It is that they shall be des- / tróyed for éver: * 8 But thou, LORD, art most / hígh for évermore.

9 For, lo, thine enemies, O LORD, † for, lo, thine ene- / míes shall pérish; * all the workers of iniquity / sháll be scáttered.

10 But my horn shalt thou exalt like the / hórn of an únicorn: * I shall be anointed / wíth fresh óil-.

11 Mine eye also shall see my desire / ón mine énemies, * and mine ears shall hear my desire of the wicked that rise / úp agáinst me.

12 The righteous shall flourish / líke the pálm tree: * he shall grow like a cé- / dar in Lébanon.

13 Those that be planted in the / hóuse of the <u>LORD</u> * shall flourish in the cóurts / of our <u>God</u>.

14 They shall still bring forth / frúit in old <u>age</u>; * they shall be / fát and flóurishing;

15 To shew that the / LÓRD is úpright: * he is my rock, and there is no unrígh- / teousness ín him.

Glory be to the / Fáther and tó the Son * - and / tó the Hóly Ghost.

As it was in the beginning, is now, and / éver sháll be, * - wórld / without énd. Amen.

Psalm-prayer. O God, the eternal rejoicing of the saints, who makest the righteous, strengthened with divers gifts of good things, to flourish unfadingly in the palm-bearing courts; we beseech Thee, that putting away the weight of our sins, Thou mayest bestow upon us fellowship with them; through Jesus Christ our Lord, who liveth and reigneth with Thee and the Holy Ghost, ever one God, world without end. Amen.

[200]

Ant. Thy testimónies * are véry sure: holiness becometh thine house, O

LÓRD, for éver.

Psalm 93 *Dominus regnavit*
1 The LORD reigneth, he is / clóthed with májesty; * the LORD is clothed with strength, wherewith he hath / gírded him<u>self</u>:
The world ál- / so is stáblished, * - / that ít cannót be moved.
2 Thy throne is estáb- / lished of <u>old</u>: * thou art / from éverlásting.
3 The floods have lifted up, O LORD, † the floods have / lífted úp their voice; * - / the flóods lift úp their waves.
4 The LORD on high is mightier than the noise of / mány wáters, * yea, than the mighty / wáves of the <u>sea</u>.
5 Thy testimó- / nies are véry sure: * holiness becometh thine house, / O LÓRD, for éver.
Glory be to the Fá- / ther and tó the Son * - / and tó the Hóly Ghost.
As it was in the beginning, is now, and / éver shall be, * - / wórld without énd. Amen.

Psalm-prayer. O Lord Almighty, Jesus Christ, who, clothed with the Father's strength, hast set heaven, sea, and earth in their places; hearken unto Thy humble servants: grant us faith in Thy testimonies, and clothe us with strength and beautiful holiness; who livest and reignest with the same Father and the Holy Ghost, ever one God, world without end. Amen.

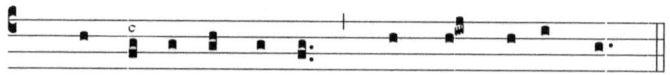

Ant. Lift úp thysélf, O Lord: * thou júdge of the <u>earth</u>.

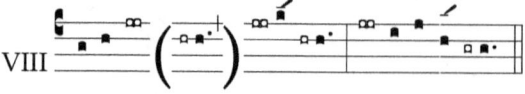

Psalm 94 *Deus ultionum*
1 O LORD God, to whom véngeance be- / lóngeth; * O God, to whom vengeance be- / lóngeth, shéw thyself.
2 Lift up thyself, thou júdge of the / <u>earth</u>: * render a rewárd / to the <u>proud</u>.

268

3 LORD, how lóng shall the / wícked, * how long shall the / wícked tríumph?
4 How long shall they útter and / spéak hard things? * and all the workers of iní- / quity bóast themselves?
5 They break in pieces thy péople, O / LORD, * and af- / flíct thine héritage.
6 They slay the widow ánd the / stránger, * and múr- / der the fátherless.
7 Yet they say, The LÓRD shall not / see, * neither shall the God of Já- / cob regárd it.
8 Understand, ye brutish amóng the / péople: * and ye fools, / whén will yé be wise?
9 He that planted the ear, sháll he not / hear? * he that formed the eye, sháll / he not see?
10 He that chastiseth the heathen, sháll not / hé correct? * he that teacheth man knowledge, sháll / not he know?
11 The LORD knóweth the / thóughts of man, * that / théy are vánity.
12 Bless-ed is the man whom thou chásten- / ést, O LORD, * and teachest him óut / of thy law;
13 That thou mayest give him rest from the dáys of ad- / vérsity, * until the pit be digged / fór the wícked.
14 For the LORD will not cast óff his / péople, * neither will he forsáke / his inhéritance.
15 But judgment shall retúrn unto / ríghteousness: * and all the upright in / héart shall fóllow it.
16 Who will rise up for me against the évil- / dóers? * or who will stand up for me against the workers / óf iníquity?
17 Unless the LÓRD had / béen my help, * my soul had almost / dwélt in sílence.
18 When I said, Mý foot / slíppeth; * thy mercy, O LÓRD, / held me up.
19 In the multitude of my thóughts with- / ín me * thy cóm- / forts delíght my soul.
20 Shall the throne of iniquity have féllowship / wíth thee, * which frameth / míschief bý a law?
21 They gather themselves together against the sóul of the / ríghteous, * and condemn the ín- / nocent blood.
22 But the LÓRD is / mý defence; * and my God is the róck / of my réfuge.
23 And he shall bring upon them their own iníquity, † and shall cut them off in théir own / wíckedness; * yea, the LORD our / Gód shall cút them off.
Glory be to the Fáther and / tó the Son * and / tó the Hóly Ghost.
As it was in the beginning, is now, and éver / shált be, * wórld / without énd. Amen.

Psalm-prayer. Teach us, O Lord, out of Thy law, and be our refuge in trouble,

[201]

who wisely teachest man knowledge and givest him rest; through Jesus Christ our Lord, who liveth and reigneth with Thee and the Holy Ghost, ever one God, world without end. Amen.

Ant. O come, * let us wórship and bów down: let us kneel before the LÓRD

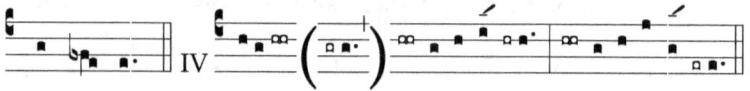

our máker.

Psalm 95 *Venite, exsultemus*
1 O come, let us sing ún- / to the LORD: * let us make a joyful noise to the rock / of óur salvátion.
2 Let us come before his presence / wíth thanksgíving, * and make a joyful / noise únto hím with psalms.
3 For the LÓRD / is a gréat God, * and a / great Kíng abóve all gods.
4 In his hand are the deep / pláces óf the earth: * the strength of the / hílls is his álso.
5 The sea is his, / ánd he máde it: * and his / hands fórmed the drý land.
6 O come, let us wór- / ship and bów down: * let us kneel before / the LÓRD our máker.
7 For he is our God; † and we are the people / óf his pásture, * and the / shéep of his hand.
8 To day if ye will hear his voice, harden not your heart, as in the / próvocátion, * and as in the day of tempta- / tion ín the wílderness:
9 When your / fáthers témpted me, * - / proved mé, and sáw my work.
10 Forty years long was I grieved with this generá- / tion, and said, * It is a people that do err in their heart, and they have / nót known my ways:
11 Unto whom I swáre / in my wrath * that they should not enter / ínto my rest.
Glory be to the Fá- / ther and tó the Son * - / and tó the Hóly Ghost.
As it was in the beginning, is now, and / éver sháll be, * - / wórld without énd. Amen.

Psalm-prayer. O God, the glorious salvation of all Thy people, graciously look upon the sheep of Thy pasture, and bestowing upon them the salt of prudence, vouchsafe to bring them unhurt into everlasting rest; who livest and reignest with the Father and the Holy Ghost, ever one God, world without end. Amen.

Ant. O sing unto the LORD * a new song. *(Do not repeat in verse 1.)*

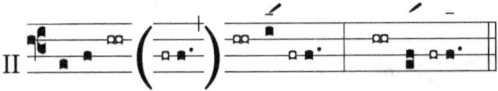

Psalm 96 *Cantate Domino*
1 [O sing unto the LÓRD a / néw song:] * sing unto the LÓRD, all / the earth.
2 Sing unto the LÓRD, bless his / name; * shew forth his salvátion from / dáy to day.
3 Declare his glory amóng the / héathen, * his wonders amóng all / péople.
4 For the LORD is great, and gréatly / tó be praised: * he is to be féared a- / bóve all gods.
5 For all the gods of the nátions are / ídols: * but the LÓRD made the / héavens.
6 Honour and majesty áre be- / fóre him: * strength and beauty are in his sánctu- / áry.
7 Give unto the LORD, O ye kindreds óf the / péople, * give unto the LORD glóry / and strength.
8 Give unto the LORD the glory due únto his / name: * bring an offering, and cóme in- / tó his courts.
9 O worship the LORD in the béauty of / hóliness: * fear befóre him, / áll the earth.
10 Say among the heathen that the LORD reigneth: † the world also shall be established that ít shall / nót be moved: * he shall judge the péople / ríghteously.
11 Let the heavens rejoice, and lét the / éarth be glad; * let the sea roar, and the fúlness / thereof.
12 Let the field be joyful, and áll that / ís therein: * then shall all the trées of the / wóod rejoice
13 Before the LORD: fór he / cómeth, * for he cómeth to / júdge the earth:
He shall judge the wórld with / ríghteousness, * and the péople / wíth his truth.
 Glory be to the Fáther and / tó the Son * and tó the / Hóly Ghost.
As it was in the beginning, is now, and éver / shall be, * wórld without / énd. Amen.

Psalm-prayer. O God, the Maker of heaven, Creator of earth, to whom all the earth payeth the melody of a new song, we beseech Thee, that as we humbly confess Thee reigning from the tree, so leaving behind us all Gentile error, we may with keen perception await the glory of Thy future coming; who livest and reignest with the Father and the Holy Ghost, ever one God, world without end. Amen.

[203]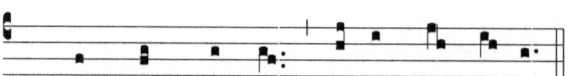

Ant. The LORD reigneth; * let the earth rejoice. *(Do not repeat in verse 1.)*

VIII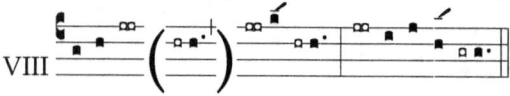

Psalm 97 *Dominus regnavit*
1 [The LORD reigneth; lét the / éarth rejoice;] * let the multitude of / ísles be gládthereof.
2 Clouds and darkness are róund a- / bóut him: * righteousness and judgment are the habi- / tátion óf his throne.
3 A fire góeth be- / fóre him, * and burneth up his én- / emies róund about.
4 His lightnings enlíghtened the / world: * the earth / sáw, and trémbled.
5 The hills melted like wax at the présence / óf the LORD, * at the presence of the Lórd / of the whóle earth.
6 The heavens decláre his / ríghteousness, * and all the people / sée his glóry.
7 Confounded be all they that serve graven îmages, † that boast themsélves of / ídols: * wór- / ship him, áll ye gods.
8 Zion héard, and was / glad; * and the daughters of Judah rejoiced because of thy júdg- / ments, O LORD.
9 For thou, LORD, art hígh above / áll the earth: * thou art exalted / fár abóve all gods.
10 Ye that love the LORD, hate evil: † he preserveth the sóuls of his / saints; * he delivereth them out of the hánd / of the wícked.
11 Light is sówn for the / ríghteous, * and gladness for the úp- / right in heart.
12 Rejoice in the LÓRD, ye / ríghteous; * and give thanks at the remembrance / óf his hóliness.
Glory be to the Fáther and / tó the Son * and / tó the Hóly Ghost.
As it was in the beginning, is now, and éver / sháll be, * wórld / without énd. Amen.

Psalm-prayer. O God, Preserver of holy souls, whose kingdom is the perfect lot of the righteous, grant that the lightnings of the prophets and evangelists may enter into our hearts, and if there be aught found therein covered with the ancient veil, let it be disclosed by the revelation of the Holy Ghost; through Jesus Christ our Lord, who liveth and reigneth with Thee and the same Holy Ghost, ever one God, world without end. Amen.

[204]

Ant. Oh, máke a jóyful noise: * befóre the Lórd, the King.

Psalm 98 *Cantate Domino*
1 O sing unto the LORD a new song; † for he hath done már- / vellous <u>things</u>: * his right hand, and his holy arm, hath got- / ten hím the víctory.
2 The LORD hath made known / hís salvátion: * his righteousness hath he openly shewed in the / síght of the héathen.
3 He hath remembered his mercy and his truth toward the / hóuse of Ísrael: * all the ends of the earth have seen the / salvátion óf our God.
4 Make a joyful noise unto the LÓRD, / all the <u>earth</u>: * make a loud noise, and re- / jóice, and sing <u>praise</u>.
5 Sing unto the LÓRD / with the <u>harp</u>; * with the harp, and the / vóice of a <u>psalm</u>.
6 With trumpets and / sóund of córnet * make a joyful noise / befóre the LÓRD, the King.
7 Let the sea roar, and the fúl- / ness there<u>of</u>; * the world, / and théy that dwéll therein.
8 Lét / the floods cláp their hands: * let the hills be joyful to- / géther befóre the LORD;
9 For he cóm- / eth to júdge the earth: * with righteou<u>sn</u>ess shall he judge the world, and the / péople with équity.
Glory be to the Fá- / ther and tó the Son * - / and tó the Hóly Ghost.
As it was in the beginning, is now, and / éver sháll be, * - / wórld without énd. Amen.

Psalm-prayer. O Lord, who hast openly shewed Thy righteousness in the sight of the heathen, and hast made known Thy salvation, grant that as Thou didst once come to be judged on behalf of the lost, Thou mayest bestow mercy when Thou comest to judge, on them for whom Thou wast judged;

who livest and reignest with the Father and the Holy Ghost, ever one God, world without end. Amen.

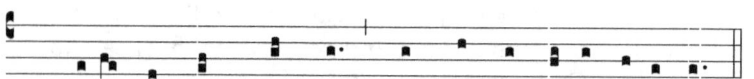

Ant. Exált the LÓRD our God: * and worship át his hóly hill.

IV

Psalm 99 *Dominus regnavit*
1 The LORD reigneth; let the / péople trémble: * he sitteth between the cheru- / bims; lét the éarth be moved.
2 The LORD is / gréat in Zíon; * and he is high a- / bove áll the péople.
3 Let them praise thy great and tér- / rible <u>name</u>; * - / for ít is hóly.
4 The king's strength also loveth judgment; † thou dost es- / táblish équity, * thou executest judgment and righ- / teousnéss in Jácob.
5 Exalt ye the LORD our God, and worship / át his fóotstool; * - / for hé is hóly.
6 Moses and Aaron amông his priests, † and Samuel among them that / cáll upón his name; * they called upon the / LÓRD, and he ánswered them.
7 He spake unto them in the / clóudy píllar: * they kept his testimonies, and the ordi- / nance thát he gáve them.
8 Thou answer-eds*t* them, O LÔRD our God: † thou wast a God / thát forgávest them, * though thou tookest vengeance / of théir invéntions.
9 Exalt the LORD our God, and worship / át his hóly hill; * for the LORD / our Gód is hóly.
Glory be to the Fá- / ther and tó the Son * - / and tó the Hóly Ghost.
As it was in the beginning, is now, and / éver sháll be, * - / wórld without énd. Amen.

Psalm-prayer. O Lord our Redeemer, who art acknowledged to be high above the people, and great in Zion, increase and perfect the belief of Thy Church in Thee, and make the nations to unite in the sincerity thereof, that as we are confessing Thy Name, which is great, and with faithful service paying honor to Thy kingly glory, Thou mayest graciously look upon us from on high, and bring us from this low place of earth to the dwellings of heaven; who livest and reignest with the Father and the Holy Ghost, ever One God, world without end. Amen.

Ant. Make a joyful noise * unto the LORD, all ye lands.
(Do not repeat in verse 1.)

Psalm 100 *Jubilate Deo*
1 [Make a joyful noise unto the LORD, all ye lands.] † 2 Serve the / LÓRD with gládness: * come before his / présence with sínging.
3 Know ye that the LORD he is God: † it is he that hath made us, and nót / we our<u>selves</u>; * we are his people, and the / shéep of his pásture.
4 Enter into his gates with thanksgiving, and ín- / to his cóurts with praise: * be thankful un- / to hím, and bléss his name.
5 For the LORD is good; his mercy is / éverlásting; * and his truth endureth to / áll generátions.
Glory be to the Fá- / ther and tó the Son * - / and tó the Hóly Ghost.
As it was in the beginning, is now, and / éver sháll be, * - / wórld without énd. Amen.

Psalm-prayer. We rejoice in thee, O Lord everlasting, with gladness and exultation, beseeching Thee, that while the gates of our hearts are thrown open in Thy praise, they may also be flung wide to receive Thy mercy and truth; through Jesus Christ our Lord, who liveth and reigneth with Thee and the Holy Ghost, ever one God, world without end. Amen.

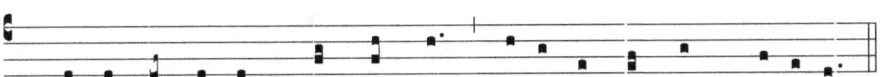

[206]

Ant. I will sing of mercy and judgment: * unto thee, O LORD, will I sing.
(Do not repeat in verse 1.)

Psalm 101 *Misericordiam*
1 [I will sing of / mércy and júdgment: * unto thee, O / LÓRD, will I <u>sing</u>.]
2 I will behave myself wisely in a pêrfect way. † O when wilt thou / cóme unto <u>me</u>? * I will walk within my house / wíth a pérfect heart.
3 I will set no wicked thing befôre mine eyes: † I hate the work of / thém that túrn aside; * - it / sháll not cléave to me.

275

4 A froward heart / sháll depárt from me: * I will not know a / wícked pérson.

5 Whoso privily slandereth his neighbour, / hím will I cút off: * him that hath an high look and a proud heart will / nót I súffer.

6 Mine eyes shall be upon the faithful of the land, that / théy may dwéll with me: * he that walketh in a perfect way, / hé shall sérve me.

7 He that worketh deceit shall not / dwéll withín my house: * he that telleth lies shall not / tárry ín my sight.

8 I will early destroy all the / wícked óf the land; * that I may cut off all wicked doers from the / cíty óf the LORD.

Glory be to the / Fáther and tó the Son * - and / tó the Hóly Ghost.

As it was in the beginning, is now, and / éver sháll be, * - wórld / without énd. Amen.

Psalm-prayer. We sing of mercy and judgment unto Thee, O Lord, our Savior and Judge; help us with the one, warn us with the other; on that side is the light of pity, on this the rule of inquiry. Grant us, Thy humble servants, O Lord, that a froward heart may depart from us, and that wicked things before our eyes may not allure us, but that walking in the simplicity of innocence, Thou mayest lead us on in Thy pity and love, and absolve us as a truthful Judge; who livest and reignest with the Father and the Holy Ghost, ever one God, world without end. Amen.

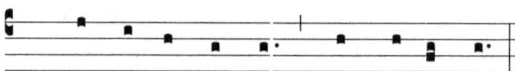

Ant. Let my cry, O Lord * come unto Thee.

VIII

Psalm 102i *Domine, exaudi*

1 Hear my prayer, O LORD, and let my crý come / únto thee. * 2 Hide not thy face from me in the day when Í / am in tróuble;

Incline thine éar unto / <u>me</u>: * in the day when I call án- / swer me spéedily.

3 For my dáys are con- / súmed like smoke, * and my bones are búrned / as an <u>hearth</u>.

4 My heart is smitten, and wíthered like / <u>grass</u>; * so that I for- / gét to éat my bread.

5 By reason of the vóice of my / <u>groaning</u> * my bones cléave / to my <u>skin</u>.

6 I am like a pelican of the wilderness: † I am like an ówl of the / désert. * 7 I watch, and am as a sparrow alone up- / ón the hóuse top.

8 Mine enemies repróach me / áll the day; * and they that are mad against me are / swórn agáinst me.
9 For I have eaten áshes like / <u>bread</u>, * and mingled my / drínk with wéeping,
10 Because of thine indignátion / ánd thy wrath: * for thou hast lifted me / úp, and cást me down.
11 My days are like a shadow thát de- / clíneth; * and I am wí- / thered like <u>grass</u>.
Glory be to the Fáther and / tó the Son * and / tó the Hóly Ghost.
As it was in the beginning, is now, and éver / sháll be, * wórld / without énd. Amen.

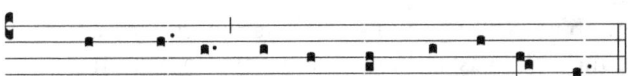

Ant. From heaven * did the LORD behold the earth.

Psalm 102ii *Tu resurgens*
12 But thou, O LORD, shalt en- / dúre for éver; * and thy remembrance unto all / generátions.
13 Thou shalt arise, and have mercy / úpon Zíon: * for the time to favour her, yea, the / sét time, is <u>come</u>.
14 For thy servants take / pléasure ín her stones, * and fá- / vour the dúst thereof.
15 So the heathen shall fear the / náme of the <u>LORD</u>, * and all the kings of the / éarth thy glóry.
16 When the LORD shall / búild up Zíon, * he shall appéar / in his glóry.
17 He will regard the / práyer of the déstitute, * - and / nót despíse their prayer.
18 This shall be written for the gene- / rátion to <u>come</u>: * and the people which shall be creá- / ted shall práise the LORD.
19 For he hath looked down from the height of his / sánctuáry; * from heaven did the / LÓRD behóld the earth;
20 To hear the groaning / óf the prísoner; * to loose those that are ap- / póinted to <u>death</u>;
21 To declare the name of the / LÓRD in Zíon, * and his práise / in Jerúsalem;
22 When the people are / gáthered togéther, * and the kíng- / doms, to sérve the LORD.

Glory be to the / Fáther and tó the Son * - and / tó the Hóly Ghost.
As it was in the beginning, is now, and / éver sháll be, * - wórld / without énd. Amen.

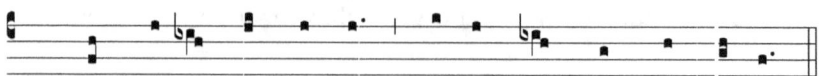

Ant. Thou árt the sáme, O Lord: * and thy yéars shall háve no end.

Psalm 102iii *Respondit ei*
23 He weakened my stréngth in the / <u>way</u>; * he / shórtened my <u>days</u>.
24 I said, O my God, take me not away in the mídst of my / <u>days</u>: * thy years are throughout all / génerátions.
25 Of old hast thou laid the foundátion / óf the earth: * and the heavens are the / wórk of thy <u>hands</u>.
26 They shall perish, but thóu shalt en- / <u>dure</u>: * yea, all of them shall wax old / líke a gárment;
As a vesture shált thou / chánge them, * and / théy shall be <u>changed</u>:
27 But thóu art the / <u>same</u>, * and thy / yéars shall háve no end.
28 The children of thy servants sháll con- / tínue, * and their seed shall be es- / táblished befóre thee.
Glory be to the Fáther and / tó the Son * and / tó the Hóly Ghost.
As it was in the beginning, is now, and éver / sháll be, * - / wórld without énd. Amen.

Psalm-prayer. Thine enemies reviled Thee unjustly all the day long, when they not only failed to know Thee the Lord of the world, but the men of peace swore against Thee. Grant us, therefore, that as we truly believe in Thy Passion, we may also live without end together with Thee in the everlasting Resurrection; who livest and reignest with the Father and the Holy Ghost, ever one God, world without end. Amen.

Ant. Bless the Lord, * O my soul. *(Do not repeat in verse 1.)*
Psalm 103i *Benedic, anima*
1 [Bless the LÓRD, O my / <u>soul</u>:] * and all that is within me, / bléss his hóly name.

2 Bless the LÓRD, O my / soul, * and forget not / áll his bénefits:
3 Who forgiveth áll thine in- / íquities; * who healeth áll / thy diséases;
4 Who redeemeth thy life from des- / trúction; * who crowneth thee with lovingkindness and / ténder mércies;
5 Who satisfieth thy móuth with / góod things; * so that thy youth is renewed / líke the éagle's.
6 The LORD executeth righteousnéss and / júdgment * for / áll that áre oppressed.
7 He made known his wáys unto / Móses, * his acts unto the chíl- / dren of Ísrael.
8 The LORD is mercifúl and / grácious, * slow to anger, and plén- / teous in mércy.
9 He will nót always / chide: * neither will he keep his án- / ger for éver.
10 He hath not dealt with us áfter our / sins; * nor rewarded us according to / óur iníquities.
11 For as the heaven is hígh a- / bóve the earth, * so great is his mercy toward / thém that féar him.
12 As far as the éast is / fróm the west, * so far hath he removed our trans- / gréssions fróm us.
Glory be to the Fáther and / tó the Son * and / tó the Hóly Ghost.
As it was in the beginning, is now, and éver / sháll be, * wórld / without énd. Amen.

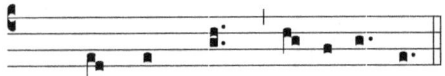

Ant. Bless the LORD * ye his angels.

IV

Psalm 103ii *Quomodo miseretur*
13 Like as a father pí- / tieth his chíldren, * so the LORD pi- / tieth thém that féar him.
14 For he knów- / eth our frame; * he re- / mémbereth that wé are dust.
15 As for man, his dáys / are as grass: * as a flower of the / field, só he flóurisheth.
16 For the wind passeth over / ít, and ít is gone; * and the place thereof shall / knów it no more.
17 But the mercy of the LORD is from everlasting to everlasting upon / thém that féar him, * and his righteousness un- / to chíldren's chíldren;
18 To such as / kéep his cóvenant, * and to those that remember his com- /

mándments to dó them.
19 The LORD hath prepared his thróne / in the héavens; * and his king- / dom rúleth óver all.
20 Bless the LORD, ye his angels, / thát excél in strength, * that do his commandments, hearkening unto the / vóice of his word.
21 Bless ye the / LÓRD, all yé his hosts; * ye ministers of his, / that dó his pléasure.
22 Bless the LORD, all his works in all places of / hís domínion: * bless the / LÓRD, O my soul.
Glory be to the Fá- / ther and tó the Son * - / and tó the Hóly Ghost.
As it was in the beginning, is now, and / éver sháll be, * - / wórld without énd. Amen.

Psalm-prayer. O Lord, heal the infirmities of Thy people, who dost always pity sinners as a father his children; that delivered from the destruction of everlasting death, our soul may praise Thee, and our life glorify Thee; through Jesus Christ our Lord, who liveth and reigneth with Thee and the Holy Ghost, ever one God, world without end. Amen.

[210]

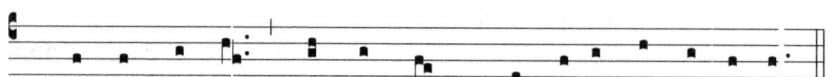

Ant. O Lórd my God * Thóu art clothed: with hónor and má-jes-ty.

Psalm 104i *Benedic anima mea*
1 Bless the LORD, O my soul. † O LORD my God, / thóu art véry great; * thou art clothed with hó- / nour and májesty.
2 Who coverest thyself with light / ás with a gárment: * who stretchest out the heavens / líke a cúrtain:
3 Who layeth the beams of his chambers in the waters: † who maketh the / clóuds his cháriot: * who walketh upon the wíngs / of the wind:
4 Who maketh his / ángels spírits; * his ministers a / fláming fíre-:
5 Who laid the foun- / dátions óf the earth, * that it should not be re- / móved for éver.
6 Thou cover-edst it with the deep as / wíth a gárment: * the waters stood a- / bóve the móuntains.
7 At / thý rebúke they fled; * at the voice of thy thunder they hást- / ed away.
8 They go up / bý the móuntains; * they go down by the valleys unto the

place which thou hast / fóunded fór them.
9 Thou hast set a bound that they may / nót pass óver; * that they turn not again to cóv- / er the <u>earth</u>.
10 He sendeth the springs / ínto the válleys, * - which / rún amóng the hills.
11 They give drink to every / béast of the <u>field</u>: * the wild / ásses quénch their thirst.
12 By them shall the fowls of the heaven have their / hábitátion, * which sing a- / móng the bránches.
Glory be to the / Fáther and tó the Son * - and / tó the Hóly Ghost.
As it was in the beginning, is now, and / éver shálll be, * - wórld / without énd. Amen.

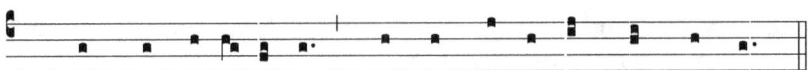

Ant. The éarth is sát-is-fied: * with the frúit of thy wórks, O Lord.

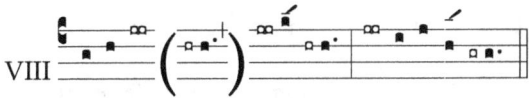
VIII

Psalm 104ii *Rigans montes*
13 He watereth the hílls from his / chámbers: * the earth is satisfied with the frúit / of thy <u>works</u>.
14 He causeth the grass to grow for the cattle, † and herb for the sérvice of / <u>man</u>: * that he may bring forth food óut / of the <u>earth</u>;
15 And wine that maketh glad the hêart of man, † and oil to máke his / fáce to shine, * and bread which stréng- / theneth mán's heart.
16 The trees of the LÓRD are / fúll of sap; * the cedars of Lebanon, which / hé hath plánted;
17 Where the bírds make their / <u>nests</u>: * as for the stork, the / fír trees áre her house.
18 The high hills are a refuge fór the / wíld goats; * and the rócks / for the cónies.
19 He appointed the móon for / séasons: * the sun knów- / eth his góing down.
20 Thou makest dárkness, and / ít is night: * wherein all the beasts of the / fórest dó creep forth.
21 The young lions roar áfter their / <u>prey</u>, * and / séek their méat from God.
22 The sun ariseth, they gather themsélves to- / géther, * and lay them dówn / in their <u>dens</u>.
23 Man goeth forth únto his / <u>work</u> * and to his labour un- / tíl the évening.
Glory be to the Fáther and / tó the Son * and / tó the Hóly Ghost.

[211]

As it was in the beginning, is now, and éver / sháll be, * wórld / without énd. Amen.

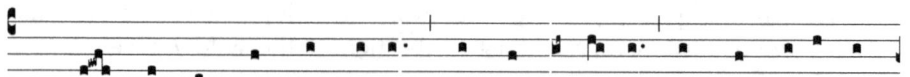

Ant. Thou sendest forth thy Spirit, * they áre cre-át-ed: and thou renewest

the fáce of the earth.

Psalm 104iii *Quam magnificata*

24 O LORD, how manifold are thy works! † in wisdom / hást thou máde them all: * the earth is fúll / of thy ríches.
25 So is this great and wide sea, wherein are things / créeping innúmerable, * - both / smáll and gréat beasts.
26 There go the ships: there is / thát levíathan, * whom thou hast / máde to pláy therein.
27 These wait / áll upón thee; * that thou mayest give them their méat / in due séason.
28 That thou givest / thém they gáther: * thou openest thine hand, / théy are fílled with good.
29 Thou hidest thy face, / théy are tróubled: * thou takest away their breath, they die, and re- / túrn to their dust.
30 Thou sendest forth thy spirit, they / áre creáted: * and thou renewest the / fáce of the earth.
31 The glory of the LORD shall en-/ dúre for éver: * the LORD shall re- / jóice in his works.
32 He looketh on the earth, / ánd it trémbleth: * he toucheth the / hílls, and they smoke.
33 I will sing unto the LORD as / lóng as I live: * I will sing praise to my God / whíle I háve my being.
34 My meditation of / hím shall be sweet: * I will be / glád in the LORD.
35 Let the sinners be consumed / óut of the earth, * and let the / wícked bé no more.
Bless thou the / LÓRD, O my soul. * - / Práise ye the LORD.
Glory be to the / Fáther and tó the Son * - and / tó the Hóly Ghost.
As it was in the beginning, is now, and / éver sháll be, * - wórld / without énd. Amen.

[212] *Psalm-prayer.* O Lord God Almighty, who hast commanded the evening and

the morning, and the noontide to be called one day, and hast bidden the sun to know his going down: pierce, we beseech Thee, the darkness of our hearts, that as Thou sheddest Thy rays, we may acknowledge Thee to be Very God and Light everlasting; through Jesus Christ our Lord, who liveth and reigneth with Thee and the Holy Ghost, ever one God, world without end. Amen.

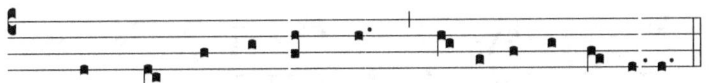

Ant. The Lord háth remémbered: * his covenánt for éver.

Psalm 105i *Confitemini Domino*
1 O give thanks unto the LORD; / cáll upón his name: * make known his deeds a- / móng the péople.
2 Sing unto him, sing / psálms unto him: * talk ye of / áll his wóndrous works.
3 Glory ye / ín his hóly name: * let the heart of them re- / jóice that séek the LORD.
4 Seek the / LÓRD, and his strength: * - séek / his face évermore.
5 Remember his marvellous / wórks that hé hath done; * his wonders, and the / júdgments óf his mouth;
6 O ye seed of Abra- / hám his sérvant, * ye children of Já- / cob his chósen.
7 — / Hé is the LÓRD our God: * his judgments / áre in áll the earth.
8 He hath remembered his cove- / nánt for éver, * the word which he commanded to a thousand / génerátions.
9 Which covenant he / máde with Ábraham, * and his oath / únto Ísaac;
10 And confirmed the same unto / Jácob fór a law, * and to Israel for an ever- / lásting cóvenant:
11 Saying, Unto thee will I give the / lánd of Cánaan, * the lot of / yóur inhéritance:
12 When they were but a few / mén in númber; * yea, very few, and / strángers ín it.
13 When they went from one nation / tó anóther, * from one kingdom to an- / óther péople;
14 He suffered / nó man to dó them wrong: * yea, he reproved / kíngs for their sakes;
15 Saying, Touch not / míne anóinted, * and do my / próphets no harm.
Glory be to the / Fáther and tó the Son * - and / tó the Hóly Ghost.

As it was in the beginning, is now, and / éver shálll be, * - wórld / without énd. Amen.

[213]
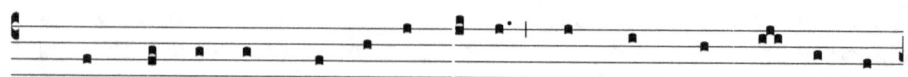

Ant. The Lord increased his péople gréatly: * and made them stronger thán

their énemies.

Psalm 105ii *Et vocavit*

16 Moreover he called for a fámine up- / ón the land: * he bráke / the whole stáff of bread.
17 He sent a mán be- / fóre them, * even Joseph, who was sóld / for a sérvant:
18 Whose feet they húrt with / fétters: * he was / láid in íron:
19 Until the tíme that his / wórd came: * the word óf / the LORD tríed him.
20 The king sént and / lóosed him; * even the ruler of the people, and lét / him go <u>free</u>.
21 He made him lórd of his / <u>house</u>, * and ruler of / áll his súbstance:
22 To bind his princes át his / pléasure; * and teach his sén- / ators wísdom.
23 Israel also came ínto / Égypt; * and Jacob sojourned / ín the lánd of Ham.
24 And he increased his péople / gréatly; * and made them stronger / thán their énemies.
25 He turned their heart to háte his / péople, * to deal subtilly / wíth his sérvants.
26 He sent Móses his / sérvant; * and Aaron whom / hé had chósen.
27 They shewed his sígns a- / móng them, * and wonders / ín the lánd of Ham.

Glory be to the Fáther and / tó the Son * and / tó the Hóly Ghost.

As it was in the beginning, is now, and éver / shálll be, * wórld / without énd. Amen.

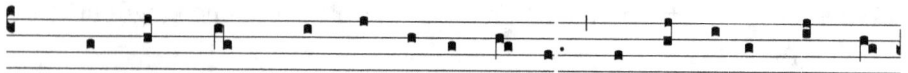

Ant. The Lord brought forth his péople with jóy:* and his chósen with glád-

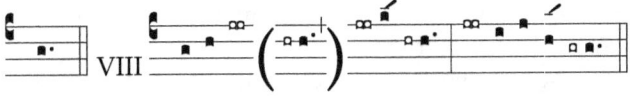

ness.

Psalm 105iii *Misit tenebras*

28 He sent dárkness, and / máde it dark; * and they rebelled / nót agáinst his word.
29 He turned their waters into blood, and slêw their fish. † 30 Their land brought forth frógs in a- / búndance, * in the / chámbers óf their kings.
31 He spake, and there came divérs sorts of / <u>flies</u>, * and / líce in áll their coasts.
32 He gáve them / háil for rain, * and flaming / fíre- ín their land.
33 He smote their vines also ánd their / fíg trees; * and brake the trées / of their <u>coasts</u>.
34 He spáke, and the / lócusts came, * and caterpillers, and thát / without númber,
35 And did eat up all the hérbs in their / <u>land</u>, * and devoured the frúit / of their <u>ground</u>.
36 He smote also all the fírstborn / ín their land, * the / chíef of áll their strength.
37 He brought them forth also with sílver and / <u>gold</u>: * and there was not one feeble pér- / son amóng their tribes.
38 Egypt was glad when théy de- / párted: * for the fear of them / féll upón them.
39 He spread a clóud for a / cóvering; * and fire to give líght / in the <u>night</u>.
40 The people asked, and hé brought / quáils-, * and satisfied them with the / bréad of héaven.
41 He opened the rock, and the wáters / gúshed out; * they ran in the dry places / líke a ríver.
42 For he remembered his hóly / prómise, * and Abra- / hám his sérvant.
43 And he brought forth his péople with / <u>joy</u>, * and his chó- / sen with gládness:
44 And gave them the lánds of the / héathen: * and they inherited the labour / óf the péople;
45 That they might obsérve his / státutes, * and keep his laws. Práise / ye the <u>LORD</u>.
Glory be to the Fáther and / tó the Son * and / tó the Hóly Ghost.
As it was in the beginning, is now, and éver / sháll be, * wórld / without énd. Amen.

Psalm-prayer. O Lord, we beseech Thee, as we call upon Thy Name, that as Thou didst feed our fathers with angels' food when the power of Thy Name went before them, so Thou wouldst cherish and renew us also with mystical delicacies; through Jesus Christ our Lord, who liveth and reigneth with Thee and the Holy Ghost, ever one God, world without end. Amen.

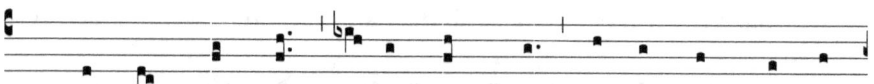

Ant. The Lord saved them * fór his náme's sake: that he might make his

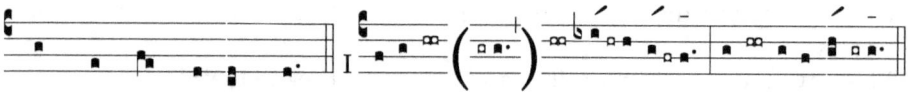

mighty pówer to be known.

Psalm 106i *Confitemini Domino*

1 Praise ye the LORD. O give thanks unto the / LÓRD; for hé is good: * for his mercy endúr- / eth for éver.
2 Who can utter the mighty / ácts of the LORD? * who can / shéw forth áll his praise?
3 Bless-ed are / théy that keep júdgment, * and he that doeth rígh- / teousness át all times.
4 Remember me, O LORD, with the favour that thou bearest / únto thy péople: * O visit me with / thý salvátion;
5 That I may see the good of thy chosen, † that I may rejoice in the gladness / óf thy nátion, * that I may glory with / thíne inhéritance.
6 We have sinned with our fathers, † we have com- / mítted iníquity, * - wé / have done wíckedly.
7 Our fathers understood not thy wonders in Egypt; † they remembered not the multitude / óf thy mércies; * but provoked him at the sea, even / át the Réd sea.
8 Nevertheless he saved them / fór his náme's sake, * that he might make his mighty / pówer tó be known.
9 He rebuked the Red sea also, and / ít was dríed up: * so he led them through the depths, as / thróugh the wílderness.
10 And he saved them from the hand of / hím that háted them, * and redeemed them from the hánd / of the énemy.
11 And the waters / cóvered their énemies: * there was not / óne of them left.
12 Then believed they his / wórds; they sáng his praise. * 13 They soon forgat his works; they waited nót / for his cóunsel:

14 But lusted exceedingly / ín the wílderness, * and tempted Gód / in the désert.
15 And he / gáve them théir request; * but sent leanness / ínto their soul.
Glory be to the / Fáther and tó the Son * - and / tó the Hóly Ghost.
As it was in the beginning, is now, and / éver shall be, * - wórld / without énd. Amen.

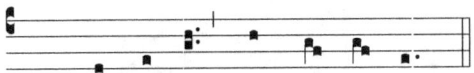

Ant. They forgat * God their saviour.

IV

Psalm 106ii *Et irritaverunt*
16 They envied Moses / álso ín the camp, * and Aaron the / sáint of the LORD.
17 The earth opened and swál- / lowed up Dáthan, * and covered the compan- / y óf Abíram.
18 And a fire was kindled / ín their cómpany; * the flame / burned úp the wícked.
19 They made a / cálf in Hóreb, * and worshipped / the mólten ímage.
20 Thus they / chánged their glóry * into the similitude of / an óx that éateth grass.
21 They forgat / Gód their sáviour, * which had done / great thíngs in Égypt;
22 Wondrous wórks / in the lánd of Ham, * and terrible / thíngs by the Réd sea.
23 Therefore he said that he would destroy them, † had not Moses his chosen stood before him in the breach, to / túrn awáy his wrath, * lest / he shóuld destróy them.
24 Yea, they de- / spísed the pléasant land, * they be- / lieved not his word:
25 But / múrmured ín their tents, * and hearkened not unto the / vóice of the LORD.
26 Therefore he lifted up his / hánd agáinst them, * to overthrow / them ín the wílderness:
27 To overthrow their seed also a- / móng the nátions, * and to / scátter them ín the lands.
28 They joined themselves also unto / Báalpéor, * and ate the sac- / rifíces óf the dead.
29 Thus they provoked him to anger with / théir invéntions: * and the

plague / brake ín upón them.

30 Then stood up Phinehas, and exe- / cúted júdgment: * - / and só the plágue was stayed.

31 And that was counted unto / hím for ríghteousness * unto all gene- / rátions for évermore.

Glory be to the Fá- / ther and tó the Son * - / and tó the Hóly Ghost.

As it was in the beginning, is now, and / éver sháll be, * - / wórld without énd. Amen.

[216]

Ant. The Lord regarded théir afflíction: * whén he héard their cry.

IV

Psalm 106iii *Et irritaverunt*

32 They angered him also at the wá- / ters of <u>strife</u>, * so that it went ill / with Móses fór their sakes:

33 Because they pro- / vóked his spírit, * so that he spake unad- / vísedly wíth his lips.

34 They did not de- / stróy the nátions, * concerning whom / the LÓRD commánded them:

35 But were mingled among the héa- / then, and léarned their works. * 36 And they served their idols, which / wére a snare únto them.

37 Yea, they sacrificed their sons and their daughters / únto dévils, * 38 And shed / ínnocent <u>blood,</u>

Even the blood of their sons and of their daughters, † whom they sacrificed unto the í- / dols of Cánaan: * and the land was pol- / lúted with <u>blood</u>.

39 Thus were they defíl- / ed with théir own works, * and went a whoring with / their ówn invéntions.

40 Therefore was the wrath of the LORD kindled a- / gáinst his péople, * insomuch that he abhorred / his ówn inhéritance.

41 And he gave them into the hánd / of the héathen; * and they that hat- / ed thém ruled óver them.

42 Their enemies ál- / so oppréssed them, * and they were brought into subjection / únder their <u>hand</u>.

43 Many times did he delîver them; † but they provoked him / with their cóunsel, * and were brought low / for théir iníquity.

44 Nevertheless he regarded their affliction, when he hêard their cry: † 45 And he remembered for / thém his cóvenant, * and repented according to

the multi- / tude óf his mércies.
46 He made them also / tó be pítied * of all those that / cárried them cáptives.
47 Save us, O LORD our God, and gather us from a- / móng the héathen, * to give thanks unto thy holy name, and / to tríumph ín thy praise.
48 Bless-ed be the LORD God of Israel from everlasting to / éverlásting: * and let all the people say, Amen. / Práise ye the <u>LORD</u>.
 Glory be to the Fá-/ther and tó the Son * -/ and tó the Hóly Ghost.
As it was in the beginning, is now, and / éver shall be, * -/ wórld without énd. Amen.

Psalm-prayer. Remember us, O Lord, according to the favour Thou bearest unto Thy people; and setting us free from the bondage of sin, save us by the visiting of Thy salvation; through the same Jesus Christ our Lord, who liveth and reigneth with Thee and the Holy Ghost, ever one God, world without end. Amen.

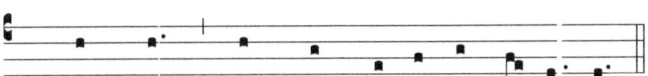

[217]

Ant. The LORD * saved them out of their distresses.

Psalm 107i *Confitemini Domino*
1 O give thanks unto the / LÓRD, for hé is good: * for his mercy endúr- / eth for éver.
2 Let the redeemed / óf the LORD sáy so, * whom he hath redeemed from the hánd / of the énemy;
3 And gathered them / óut of the <u>lands</u>, * from the east, and from the west, from the / nórth, and fróm the south.
4 They wandered in the wilderness in a / sólitáry way; * they found no cí- / ty to dwéll in.
5 —/ Húngry and thírsty, * their soul / fáinted ín them.
6 Then they cried unto the LORD / ín their tróuble, * and he delivered them out of / théir distrésses.
7 And he led them forth / bý the ríght way, * that they might go to a city of / hábitátion.
8 Oh that men would praise the LORD / fór his góodness, * and for his wonderful works to the / chíldren of <u>men</u>!
9 For he satis- / fíeth the lónging soul, * and filleth the hungry / sóul with

góodness.

10 Such as sit in darkness and in the / shádow of <u>death</u>, * being bound in afflíc- / tion and íron;

11 Because they rebelled a- / gáinst the wórds of God, * and contemned the counsel / óf the móst High:

12 Therefore he brought down their / héart with lábour; * they fell down, and / thére was nóne to help.

13 Then they cried unto the LORD / ín their tróuble, * and he saved them out of / théir distrésses.

14 He brought them out of darkness and the / shádow of <u>death</u>, * and brake their / bánds in súnder.

15 Oh that men would praise the LORD / fór his góodness, * and for his wonderful works to the / chíldren of <u>men</u>!

16 For he hath / bróken the gátes of brass, * and cut the bars of í- / ron in súnder.

Glory be to the / Fáther and tó the Son * - and / tó the Hóly Ghost.

As it was in the beginning, is now, and / éver sháll be, * - wórld / without énd. Amen.

[218]

Ant. These see the wórks of the <u>Lord</u>: * and his wónders ín the deep.

VII

Psalm 107ii *Suscepit eos*

17 Fools because of / théir transgréssion, * and because of their iniquities, / áre afflícted.

18 Their soul abhorreth all / mánner of <u>meat</u>; * and they draw near / únto the gátes of death.

19 Then they cry unto the LORD / ín their tróuble, * and he saveth them out of / théir distrésses.

20 He sent his / wórd, and héaled them, * and delivered them from / théir destrúctions.

21 Oh that men would praise the LORD / fór his góodness, * and for his wonderful works to the / chíldren of <u>men</u>!

22 And let them sacrifice the sacrifices / óf thanksgíving, * and declare his works / with rejóicing.

23 They that go down / tó the séa in ships, * that do business / ín great wáters;

24 These see the / wórks of the <u>LORD</u>, * and his / wónders ín the deep.
25 For he commandeth, and / ráiseth the stórmy wind, * which lifteth / úp the wáves thereof.
26 They mount up to the heaven, † they go down a- / gáin to the <u>depths</u>: * their soul is melted be- / cáuse of tróuble.
27 They reel to and fro, and stagger / líke a drúnken man, * and are / át their wíts' end.
28 Then they cry unto the LORD / ín their tróuble, * and he bringeth them out of / théir distrésses.
29 He / máketh the stórm a calm, * so that the / wáves theréof are still.
30 Then are they glad because / théy be quíet; * so he bringeth them unto their de- / síred háven.
31 Oh that men would praise the LORD / fór his góodness, * and for his wonderful works to the / chíldren of <u>men</u>!
32 Let them exalt him also in the congregation / óf the péople, * and praise him in the assembly / óf the élders.
Glory be to the / Fáther and tó the Son * and / tó the Hóly Ghost.
As it was in the beginning, is now, and / éver sháll be, * - / wórld without énd. Amen.

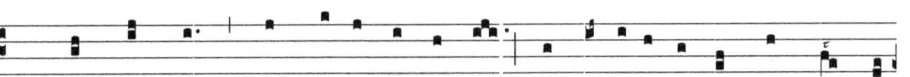

[219]

Ant. The righteous * shall sée it, ánd rejoice: and all in-i-qui-tý shall stóp her

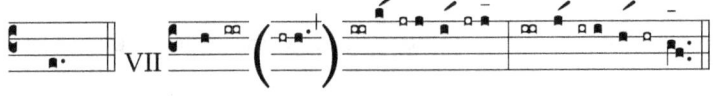

mouth.

Psalm 107iii *Posuit flumina*

33 He turneth rivers / ínto a wílderness, * and the watersprings / ínto drý ground;
34 A fruitful land / ínto bárrenness, * for the wickedness of / thém that dwéll therein.
35 He turneth the wilderness into a / stánding wáter, * and dry ground / ínto wátersprings.
36 And there he maketh the / húngry to <u>dwell</u>, * that they may prepare a city for / hábitátion;
37 And sow the fields, / ánd plant víneyards, * which may yield / frúits of íncrease.
38 He blesseth them also, so that they are / múltiplied gréatly; * and

suffereth not their / cáttle tó decrease.
39 Again, they are / mínished ánd brought low * through oppression, af- / flíction, and sórrow.
40 He poureth con- / témpt upon prínces, * and causeth them to wander in the wilderness, / whére there ís no way.
41 Yet setteth he the poor on high / fróm afflíction, * and maketh him / fámilies líke a flock.
42 The righteous shall / sée it, ánd rejoice: * and all iniqui- / tý shall stóp her mouth.
43 Whoso is wise, and / wíll obsérve these things, * even they shall understand the loving- / kíndness óf the LORD.
Glory be to the / Fáther and tó the Son * and / tó the Hóly Ghost.
As it was in the beginning, is now, and / éver shálll be, * - / wórld without énd. Amen.

Psalm-prayer. We confess Thy mercies, O Lord, which Thou constantly diplayest towards our need, beseeching Thee, that Thou, who art exalted in the churches, and sittest at the right hand of the Father on His throne, mayest grant us to understand and ponder the secret of such great lovingkindness; who livest and reignest with the Father and the Holy Ghost, ever one God, world without end. Amen.

[220]

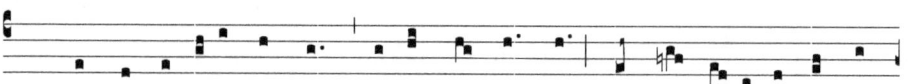

Ant. Be thou exalted, O God, * abóve the héavens: and thy glory ábove áll

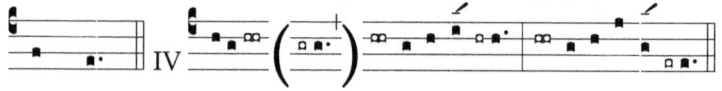

the earth.

Psalm 108 *Paratum cor meum*
1 - O / Gód, my héart is fixed; * I will sing and give praise, ev- / en wíth my glóry.
2 Awake, psál- / tery and <u>harp</u>: * I myself / wíll awake éarly.
3 I will praise thee, O LORD, a- / móng the péople: * and I will sing praises unto thee / amóng the nátions.
4 For thy mercy is great a- / bóve the héavens: * and thy truth reacheth / únto the <u>clouds</u>.
5 Be thou exalted, O God, a- / bóve the héavens: * and thy glory a- / bóve all the <u>earth</u>;

6 That thy belov-ed may / bé delívered: * save with thy / right hánd, and ánswer me.
7 God hath spoken / ín his hóliness; * I will rejoice, I will divide Shechem, and mete out the / válley of Súccoth.
8 Gilead is mine; Manasseh is mine; † Ephraim also is the stréngth / of mine head; * Judah / is mý lawgíver;
9 Moab is my washpot; † over Edom wíll / I cast óut my shoe; * over Philisti- / a wíll I tríumph.
10 Who will bring me intó / the strong cíty? * who will lead / me ínto Édom?
11 Wilt not thou, O God, / whó hast cást us off? * and wilt not thou, O God, go / fórth with our hosts?
12 Give us / hélp from tróuble: * for / váin is the hélp of man.
13 Through God wé / shall do váliantly: * for he it is that shall / tread dówn our énemies.
Glory be to the Fá- / ther and tó the Son * - / and tó the Hóly Ghost.
As it was in the beginning, is now, and / éver shálll be, * - / wórld without énd. Amen.

Psalm-prayer. Fill our ready heart, O Lord, with that gift whereby Thou mayest be pleased, that we may praise Thee with knowledge of the truth, and formed anew for the better, may rejoice in Thine honour; through Jesus Christ our Lord, who liveth and reigneth with Thee and the Holy Ghost, ever one God, world without end. Amen.

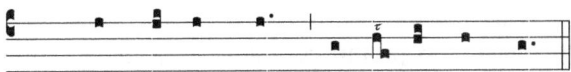

Ant. Hold not thy peace, * O God of my praise. *(Do not repeat in verse 1).*

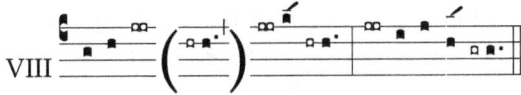
VIII

Psalm 109i *Deus, laudem*
1 [Hold not thy peace, O God of my praise;] † 2 for the mouth of the wicked and the mouth of the deceitful are ópened a- / gáinst me: * they have spoken against me / wíth a lýing tongue.
3 They compassed me about also with wórds of / hátred; * and fought against / mé withóut a cause.
4 For my love they are my ádver- / sáries: * but I give mysélf / unto prayer.   [221]
5 And they have rewarded me évil for / good, * and / hátred fór my love.
6 Set thou a wícked man / óver him: * and let Satan stánd / at his right hand.

293

7 When he shall be judged, lét him / bé condemned: * and let his práyer / become <u>sin</u>.
8 Lét his / dáys be few; * and let another / táke his óffice.
9 Let his chíldren be / fátherless, * and his / wífe a wídow.
10 Let his children be continually vága- / bónds, and beg: * let them seek their bread also out of their dé- / solate pláces.
Glory be to the Fáther and / tó the Son * and / tó the Hóly Ghost.
As it was in the beginning, is now, and éver / sháll be, * wórld / without énd. Amen.

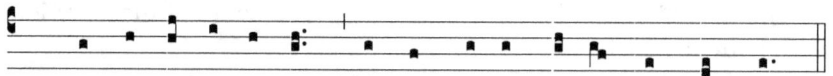

Ant. Let this bé the <u>reward</u>: * of mine ad-ver-sár-ies fróm the LORD.

Psalm 109ii *Scrutetur*
11 Let the extortioner catch / áll that he <u>hath</u>; * and let the strangers spóil / his lábour.
12 Let there be none to extend / mércy únto him: * neither let there be any to favour his fáther- / less chíldren.
13 Let his pos- / térity bé cut off; * and in the generation following let their náme / be blótted out.
14 Let the iniquity of his fathers be re- / mémbered wíth the LORD; * and let not the sin of his móther / be blótted out.
15 Let them be before the / LÓRD contínu*a*lly, * that he may cut off the memory of / thém from the <u>earth</u>.
16 Because that he remembered not to shew mercy, † but persecuted the / póor and néedy man, * that he might even slay the / bróken in <u>heart</u>.
17 As he loved cursing, so / lét it come únto him: * as he delighted not in blessing, so lét it / be fár from him.
18 As he clothed himself with cursing like as / wíth his gárment, * so let it come into his bowels like water, and like oil / ínto his <u>bones</u>.
19 Let it be unto him as the / gárment which cóvereth him, * and for a girdle wherewith he is gírded / contínu*a*lly.
20 Let this be the reward of mine adver- / sáries fróm the LORD, * and of them that speak évil / agáinst my soul.
Glory be to the / Fáther and tó the Son * and tó / the Hóly Ghost.
As it was in the beginning, is now, and / éver sháll be, * wórld with- / out énd. Amen.

Ant. Hélp me, O Lórd my God: * O save me according tó thy mércy.

Psalm 109iii *Et tu, Domine*

21 But do thou for me, O GOD the Lord, fór thy / náme's sake: * because thy mercy is good, de- / líver thou <u>me</u>.
22 For I am póor and / néedy, * and my heart is / wóunded withín me.
23 I am gone like the shadow when ít de- / clíneth: * I am tossed up and / dówn as the lócust.
24 My knees are wéak through / fásting; * and my flesh / fáileth of fátness.
25 I became also a repróach unto / <u>them</u>: * when they looked upon / mé they sháked their heads.
26 Hélp me, O / LÓRD my God: * O save me according / tó thy mércy:
27 That they may know that thís is thy / <u>hand</u>; * that / thóu, LORD, hast dóne it.
28 Let them curse, but bless thou: † when they arise, lét them / bé ashamed; * but let thy / sérvant re<u>joice</u>.
29 Let mine adversaries be clóth-ed with / <u>shame</u>, * and let them cover themselves with their own confusion, as / wíth a mántle.
30 I will greatly praise the LÓRD with my / <u>mouth</u>; * yea, I will praise him a- / móng the múltitude.
31 For he shall stand at the ríght hand / óf the poor, * to save him from / thóse that condémn his soul.
Glory be to the Fáther and / tó the Son * and / tó the Hóly Ghost.
As it was in the beginning, is now, and éver / sháll be, * - / wórld without énd. Amen.

Psalm-prayer. O God of unequaled mercy, who didst vouchsafe to undergo a curse, that Thou mightest save us from the curse of the Law, we beseech Thee that, dealing with us in mercy for Thy Name's sake, Thou wouldst deliver us from the sins which pursue us and the ungodly which molest us; who livest and reignest with the Father and the Holy Ghost, ever one God, world without end. Amen.

[223]

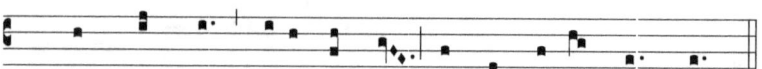

Ant. The Lord said * unto my Lord: Sit thou at my right hand.
(Do not repeat in verse 1.)

VII

Psalm 110 *Dixit Dominus*

1 [The LORD said unto my Lord, † Sit thou / át my ríght hand,] * until I make thine ene- / míes thy fóotstool.
2 The LORD shall send the rod of thy strength / óut of Zíon: * rule thou in the / mídst of thine énemies.
3 Thy people shall be willing in the day of thy power, † in the beauties of holiness from the / wómb of the mórning: * thou hast the / déw of thy <u>youth</u>.
4 The LORD hath / swórn, and will nót repent, * Thou art a priest for ever after the order / óf Melchízedek.
5 The Lord / át thy ríght hand * shall strike through kings in the / dáy of his <u>wrath</u>.
6 He shall judge among the heathen, † he shall fill the places / wíth the dead bódies; * he shall wound the heads over / mány cóuntries.
7 He shall drink of the / bróok in the <u>way</u>: * therefore shall he / líft up the <u>head</u>.
Glory be to the / Fáther and tó the Son * and / tó the Hóly Ghost.
As it was in the beginning, is now, and / éver sháll be, * - / wórld without énd. Amen.

Psalm-prayer. O God, begotten before the morning star, who wast before the beginning of every creature, we pray and beseech Thee that as Thou, sitting at the right hand of the Father, hast put Thine enemies under Thy feet, so Thou mayest make us meet for Thy service, doing away with the dominion of sin; who livest and reignest with the same Father and the Holy Ghost, ever one God, world without end. Amen.

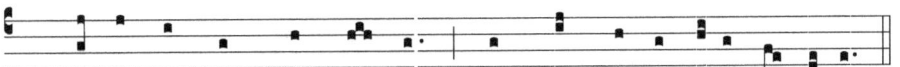

Ant. All his commándments are sure: * they stand fast for éver and éver.

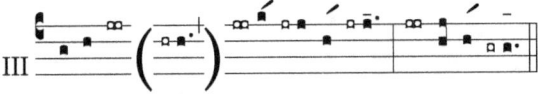

Psalm 111 *Confitebor tibi*

1 Praise ye the LORD. I will praise the / LÓRD with mý whole heart, * in the assembly of the upright, and in the cón- / gregátion.
2 The / wórks of the LÓRD are great, * sought out of all them that have / pléasure there<u>in</u>.
3 His work is honoura- / blé and glórious: * and his righteousness endúreth / for éver.
4 He hath made his wonderful works to / bé remémbered: * the LORD is gracious and fúll of / compássion.
5 He hath given meat unto / thém that féar him: * he will ever be mindful óf / his cóvenant.
6 He hath shewed his people the / pówer óf his works, * that he may give them the heritage óf / the héathen. [224]
7 The works of his hands are veri- / tý and júdgment; * all his com- / mándments are <u>sure</u>.
8 They stand fast for / éver and éver, * and are done in trúth / and úprightness.
9 He sent redemption unto his people: † he hath commanded his cove- / nánt for éver: * holy and réve- / rend ís his name.
10 The fear of the LORD is the beginning of wisdom: † a good understanding have all they that do / hís commándments: * his praise endúreth / for éver.
**Glory be to the / Fáther and tó the Son * and tó / the Hóly Ghost.
As it was in the beginning, is now, and / éver sháll be, * wórld with- / out énd. Amen.**

Psalm-prayer. O God, glorious confession of all saints, grant us the fear of Thy Name, which Thou hast declared to be the beginning of wisdom, that joined to the councils of Thy servants, we may be filled with the banquet of Thy mercy; through Jesus Christ our Lord, who liveth and reigneth with Thee and the Holy Ghost, ever one God, world without end. Amen.

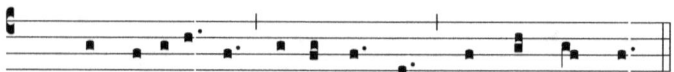

Ant. The generation * óf the úpright: sháll be bléss-ed.

VI

Psalm 112 *Beatus vir*
1 Praise ye the LORD. Bless-ed is the man that / féareth the <u>LORD</u>, * that delighteth greatly in / hís commándments.
2 His seed shall be / míghty upón earth: * the generation of the upright / sháll be bléss-ed.
3 Wealth and riches shall / bé in his <u>house</u>: * and his righteousness endúr- / eth for éver.
4 Unto the upright there ariseth / líght in the dárkness: * he is gracious, and full of compás- / sion, and ríghteous.
5 A good man sheweth / fávour, and léndeth: * he will guide his affáirs / with discrétion.
6 Surely he shall not be / móved for éver: * the righteous shall be in everlást- / ing remémbrance.
7 He shall not be afraid of / évil tídings: * his heart is fixed, / trústing ín the LORD.
8 His heart is established, † he shall / nót be <u>afraid</u>, * until he see his desire up- / ón his énemies.
9 — / Hé hath dis<u>persed</u>, * he hath / gíven tó the poor;
His righteousness en- / dúreth for éver; * his horn shall be exált- / ed with hónour.
10 The wicked shall see it, and be grieved; † he shall gnash with his / téeth, and mélt away: * the desire of the wíck- / ed shall pérish.
Glory be to the / Fáther and tó the Son * - and / tó the Hóly Ghost.
As it was in the beginning, is now, and / éver sháll be, * - wórld / without énd. Amen.

[225[*Psalm-prayer.* O God, everlasting light of the upright in heart, grant that we may love Thee; and make us glad with Thy glory, and so disperse abroad in this world, that we may hear no evil tidings in that which is to come; through Jesus Christ our Lord, who liveth and reigneth with Thee and the Holy Ghost, ever one God, world without end. Amen.

298

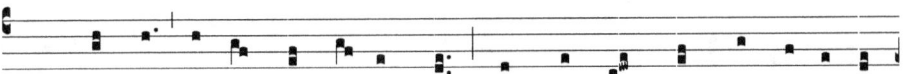

Ant. Bless-ed * be the náme of the Lord: from this time fórth and for-év-er-

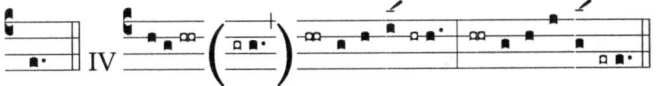

more.

Psalm 113 *Laudate, pueri*
1 Praise ye the LORD. Praise, O ye / sérvants óf the LORD, * praise the / náme of the LORD.
2 Bless-ed be the náme / of the LORD * from this time / fórth and for évermore.
3 From the rising of the sun unto the going dówn / of the same * the LORD'S name / ís to be praised.
4 The LORD is high a- / bóve all nátions, * and his glory / abóve the héavens.
5 Who is like ún- / to the LÓRD our God, * who / dwélleth on high,
6 Who húm- / bleth himself * to behold the things that are in heaven, / ánd in the earth!
7 He raiseth up the poor óut / of the dust, * and lifteth the needy / óut of the dúnghill;
8 That he may sét / him with prínces, * even with the prin- / ces óf his péople.
9 He maketh the barren wó- / man to kéep house, * and to be a joyful mother of children. / Práise ye the LORD.
Glory be to the Fá- / ther and tó the Son * - / and tó the Hóly Ghost.
As it was in the beginning, is now, and / éver sháll be, * - / wórld without énd. Amen.

Psalm-prayer. Almighty God, we who praise Thy holy Name beseech Thee that as Thou hast placed us in the bosom of our Mother, the Church, so Thou wouldst unite us in steadfastness of love; through Jesus Christ our Lord, who liveth and reigneth with Thee and the Holy Ghost, ever one God, world without end. Amen.

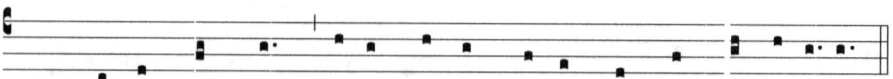

Ant. Tremble, thou earth, * át the présence: of the Lord, the Gód of Jácob.

Psalm 114 *In exitu Israel*

1 When Israel / went óut of Égypt, * the house of Jacob from a people óf / strange lánguage;
2 Judah was / his sánctuáry, * and Israel hís / domínion.
3 The / sea sáw it, and <u>fled</u>: * Jórdan / was dríven back.
4 — / The móuntains skípped like rams, * and the lít- / tle hílls like lambs.
5 What ailed thee, O thou / sea, thát thou fléddest? * thou Jordan, that thóu / wast dríven back?
6 Ye moun- / tains, thát ye skípped like rams; * and ye lít- / tle hílls, like lambs?
7 Tremble, thou earth, at / the présence óf the Lord, * at the presence of the Gód / of Jácob;
8 Which turned the rock into / a stánding wáter, * the flint into a fóuntain / of wáters.
Glory be to / the Fáther and tó the Son * and tó / the Hóly Ghost.
As it was in the beginning, is now, / and éver sháll be, * wórld with- / out énd. Amen.

Psalm-prayer. O God, mightiest of all beings, who turnest the rock into a standing water, let the earth of our bodies be moved to repentance at Thy presence, that there may thence be glory to Thy Name for mercifully granting us salvation in everlasting blessedness; through Jesus Christ our Lord, who liveth and reigneth with Thee and the Holy Ghost, ever one God, world without end. Amen.

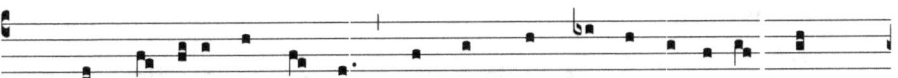

Ant. Our God is ín the héavens: * He hath done whatso-év-er Hé hath

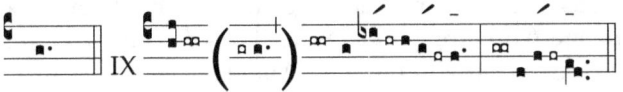

pleased.

Psalm 115 *Non nobis*
1 Not unto us, O LORD, not unto us, † but unto / thy náme give glóry, * for thy mercy, and fór / thy trúth's sake.
2 Where- / fore shóuld the héathen say, * Whére / is nów their God?
3 But our God / is ín the héavens: * he hath done whatsoév- / er hé hath pleased.
4 Their idols / are sílver and gold, * the wórk / of mén's hands.
5 They have / mouths, bút they spéak not: * eyes have they, bút / they sée not:
6 They have / ears, bút they héar not: * noses have they, bút / they sméll not:
7 They have hands, but they hándle not: † feet have / they, bút they wálk not: * neither spéak / they thróugh their throat.
8 They that make them / are líke unto them; * so is every one that trúst- / eth ín them.
9 O Isra- / el, trúst thou ín the LORD: * he is their hélp / and their shield.
10 O house of Aa- / ron, trúst in the LORD: * he is their hélp / and their shield.
11 Ye that fear the / LORD, trúst in the LORD: * he is their hélp / and their shield.
12 The LORD hath / been míndful of us: * hé / will bléss us;
He will bless / the hóuse of Ísrael; * he will bless the hóuse / of Áaron.
13 He will / bless thém that féar the LORD, * - / both smáll and great.
14 The LORD shall / incréase you móre and more, * yóu and / your chíldren.
15 Ye / are bléss-ed óf the LORD * which made héa- / ven and earth.
16 The heaven, even / the héavens, áre the LORD'S: * but the earth hath he given to the chíl- / dren of men.
17 The dead praise nôt the LORD, † neither any that go / down ínto sílence. * 18 But we will bless the LORD from this time forth and for éver- / more. Práise the LORD.
Glory be to / the Fáther and tó the Son * and tó / the Hóly Ghost.
As it was in the beginning, is now, / and éver sháll be, * wórld with- / out

[227]

énd. Amen.

Psalm-prayer. O God, unspeakable Name of Trinity, who didst awe the streams of Jordan with the aspect of Thy light, grant that Thou mayest never suffer those whom Thou hast washed and renewed in Holy Baptism to be defiled with the idols of image-worship; who livest and reignest, Father, Son, and Holy Ghost, ever one God, world without end. Amen.

Ant. Gracious is the LÓRD, and ríghteous: * yea, our Gód is mérci-ful.

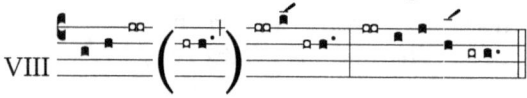
VIII

Psalm 116 *Dilexi, quoniam*

1 I love the LORD, because hé hath / héard my voice * and my / súpplicátions.
2 Because he hath inclíned his ear / únto me, * therefore will I call upon him as lóng / as I <u>live</u>.
3 The sorrows of death cômpassed me, † and the pains of hell gat hóld up- / ón me: * I found tróu- / ble and sórrow.
4 Then called I upon the náme of the / <u>LORD</u>; * O LORD, I beseech thee, delí- / ver my <u>soul</u>.
5 Gracious is the LÓRD, and / ríghteous; * yea, our / Gód is mérciful.
6 The LORD presérveth the / símple: * I was brought lów, / and he hélped me.
7 Return unto thy rést, O my / <u>soul</u>; * for the LORD hath dealt bóun- / tif*u*lly with thee.
8 For thou hast delívered my / sóul from death, * mine eyes from tears, and my / féet from fálling.
9 I will wálk be- / fóre the LORD * in the lánd / of the líving.
10 I believed, therefore have I spoken: † I was gréatly af- / flícted: * 11 I said in my haste, All / mén are líars.
12 What shall I render únto the / <u>LORD</u> * for all his bé- / nefits tóward me?
13 I will take the cúp of sal- / vátion, * and call upon the náme / of the <u>LORD</u>.
14 I will pay my vows únto the / <u>LORD</u> * now in the presence of / áll his péople.
15 Precious in the síght of the / <u>LORD</u> * is the déath / of his <u>saints</u>.
16 O LORD, truly I am thy servant; † I am thy servant, and the són of thine /

hándmaid: * - / thóu hast lóosed my bonds.
17 I will offer to thee the sacrifice óf thanks- / gíving, * and will call upon the náme / of the LORD.
18 I will pay my vows únto the / LORD * now in the presence of / áll his péople,
19 In the cóurts of the / LÓRD'S house, * in the midst of thee, O Jerusalem. Práise / ye the LORD.
Glory be to the Fáther and / tó the Son * and / tó the Hóly Ghost.
As it was in the beginning, is now, and éver / sháll be, * wórld / without énd. Amen.

Psalm-prayer. O Lord, washer away of sins, who quickly comfortest the soul that faithfully calleth on Thee, we beseech Thee that Thou wouldst deliver us from the peril of hell, and doing away with the death of sin, restore us to the land of the living; through Jesus Christ our Lord, who liveth and reigneth with Thee and the Holy Ghost, ever one God, world without end. Amen.

Ant. O praise the LORD, * all ye nations. *(Do not repeat in verse 1.)*

Psalm 117 *Laudate Dominum*
1 [O praise the / LÓRD, all ye nátions:] * praise him, / áll ye péople.
2 For his merciful / kíndness is gréat toward us: * and the truth of the LORD endureth for ever. Práise / ye the LORD.
Glory be to the / Fáther and tó the Son * - and / tó the Hóly Ghost.
As it was in the beginning, is now, and / éver sháll be, * - wórld / without énd. Amen.

Psalm-prayer. O most Almighty Lord God, who art praised by the mouth of all nations, we beseech Thee to enlarge our soul with Thy truth, and to confirm Thy merciful kindness upon us; through Jesus Christ our Lord, who liveth and reigneth with Thee and the Holy Ghost, ever one God, world without end. Amen.

[229]

Ant. O give thanks unto the Lord; * for he is good: because his mercy endur-

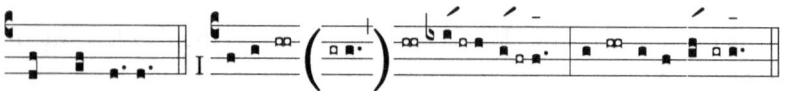

eth for ever. *(Do not repeat in verse 1.)*

Psalm 118i *Confitemini Domino*
1 [O give thanks unto the / LÓRD; for hé is good: * because his mercy endúr- / eth for éver.]
2 Let / Ísrael nów say, * that his mercy endúr- / eth for éver.
3 Let the house of / Áaron nów say, * that his mercy endúr- / eth for éver.
4 Let them now that / féar the LÓRD say, * that his mercy endúr- / eth for éver.
5 I called upon the / LÓRD in dis<u>tress</u>: * the LORD answered me, and set me / ín a lárge place.
6 The LORD is on my / síde; I wíll not fear: * what can / mán do únto me?
7 The LORD taketh my part with / thém that hélp me: * therefore shall I see my desire upon / thém that háte me.
8 It is better to trust in the LORD than to put / cónfidénce in man. * 9 It is better to trust in the LORD than to put confi- / dénce in prínces.
Glory be to the / Fáther and tó the Son * - and / tó the Hóly Ghost.
As it was in the beginning, is now, and / éver sháll be, * - wórld / without énd. Amen.

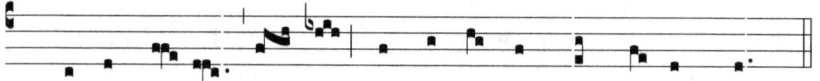

Ant. I sháll not díe, * but live: and declare the wórks of the <u>LORD</u>.

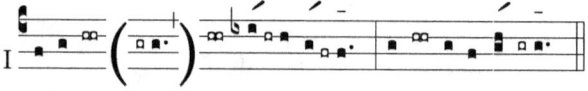

Psalm 118ii *Omnes gentes*
10 All nations / cómpassed mé about: * but in the name of the LORD will / Í destróy them.
11 They compassed me about; † yea, they / cómpassed mé about: * but in the name of the LORD I / wíll destróy them.
12 They compassed me about like bees; † they are quenched as the / fíre- of <u>thorns</u>: * for in the name of the LORD I / wíll destróy them.

304

13 Thou hast thrust sore at / mé that Í might fall: * - bút / the LORD hélped me.
14 The / LÓRD is my stréngth and song, * and is become / mý salvátion.
15 The voice of rejoicing and salvation is in the tabernacles / óf the ríghteous: * the right hand of the LORD / dóeth váliantly.
16 The right hand of the / LÓRD is exálted: * the right hand of the LORD / dóeth váliantly.
17 I / sháll not díe, but live, * and declare the / wórks of the LORD.
18 The LORD hath / chástened me sore: * but he hath not given me / óver únto death.
Glory be to the / Fáther and tó the Son * - and / tó the Hóly Ghost.
As it was in the beginning, is now, and / éver sháll be, * - wórld / without énd. Amen.

[230]

Ant. This is the gáte of the Lord: * in- to which the ríghteous shall énter.

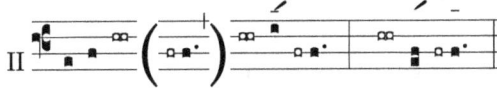

Psalm 118iii *Aperite mihi*
19 Open to me the gátes of / ríghteousness: * I will go into them, and Í will / práise the LORD:
20 This gáte of the / LORD, * into which the ríghteous shall / énter.
21 I will praise thee: for thóu hast / héard me, * and art become mý sal- / vátion.
22 The stone which the búilders re- / fused * is become the head stone óf the / córner.
23 This ís the LORD'S / dóing; * it is márvellous / ín our eyes.
24 This is the dáy which the / LÓRD hath made; * we will rejóice and be / glád in it.
25 Save now, I beséech thee, O / LORD: * O LORD, I beseech thee, send nów pros- / périty.
26 Bless-ed be he that cometh in the náme of the / LORD: * we have blessed you out of the hóuse of / the LORD.
27 God is the LORD, whích hath / shéwed us light: * bind the sacrifice with cords, even unto the hórns of the / áltar.
28 Thou art my God, and Í will / práise thee: * thou art my God, Í will ex- / ált thee.
29 O give thanks unto the LÓRD; for / hé is good: * for his mercy endúreth

for / éver.
Glory be to the Fáther and / tó the Son * and tó the / Hóly Ghost.
As it was in the beginning, is now, and éver / sháll be, * wórld without / énd. Amen.

Psalm-prayer. O most merciful God, consolation of our troubles, who bedewest the tabernacles of the righteous with joy and gladness, exalt Thy Church with the power of Thy mighty right hand, that it may become the gate of righteousness, and so bind itself together with the steadfast cornerstone as to shine with glory in Thy resurrection; who livest and reignest with the Father and the Holy Ghost, ever one God, world without end. Amen.

Ant. Deal bountifully * wíth thy sérvant: that I may líve, and kéep thy word.

Psalm 119i-vi *Beati immaculati*
i. 1 Bless-ed are the undefíled / ín the way, * who walk in the / láw of the LORD.
2 Bless-ed are they that keep his tésti- / mónies, * and that seek him / wíth the whóle heart.
[231] 3 They also do nó in- / íquity: * they / wálk in his <u>ways</u>.
4 Thou hást com- / mánded us * to keep thy precepts / díligent<u>ly</u>.
5 O that my ways wére di- / récted * to / kéep thy státutes!
6 Then shall I nót be a- / <u>shamed</u>, * when I have respect unto / áll thy commándments.
7 I will praise thee with upríghtness of / <u>heart</u>, * when I shall have learned thy / ríghteous júdgments.
8 I will kéep thy / státutes: * O for- / sáke me not útterly.
ii. 9 Wherewithal shall a yóung man / cléanse his way? * by taking heed thereto ac- / córding tó thy word.
10 With my whole heart háve I / sóught thee: * O let me not wander from / thý commándments.
11 Thy word have I híd in mine / <u>heart</u>, * that I might not / sín agáinst thee.
12 Bléss-ed art / thóu, O LORD: * - / téach me thy státutes.
13 With my líps have / Í declared * all the / júdgments óf thy mouth.
14 I have rejoiced in the way of thy tésti- / mónies, * as much as / ín all ríches.

15 I will meditate ín thy / précepts, * and have respect / únto thy <u>ways</u>.
16 I will delight myself ín thy / státutes: * I will / nót forgét thy word.
iii. 17 Deal bountifully wíth thy / sérvant, * that I may / líve, and kéep thy word.
18 Ópen / thóu mine eyes, * that I may behold wondrous things / óut of thy <u>law</u>.
19 I am a stránger / ín the earth: * hide not thy com- / mándments fróm me.
20 My soul breaketh for the lónging / thát it hath * unto thy / júdgments at áll times.
21 Thou hast rebuked the próud that are / <u>cursed</u>, * which do err from / thý commándments.
22 Remove from me repróach and con- / <u>tempt</u>; * for I have kept thy / téstimónies.
23 Princes also did sit and spéak a- / gáinst me: * but thy servant did meditate / ín thy státutes.
24 Thy testimonies also áre my de- / <u>light</u> * - / ánd my cóunsellors.
iv. 25 My soul cleaveth únto the / <u>dust</u>: * quicken thou me ac- / córding tó thy word.
26 I have declared my ways, ánd thou / héardest me: * - / téach me thy státutes.
27 Make me to understand the wáy of thy / précepts: * so shall I / tálk of thy wóndrous works.
28 My soul mélteth for / héaviness: * strengthen thou me according / únto thy <u>word</u>.
29 Remove from me the wáy of / lýing: * and grant me / thý law gráciously.
30 I have chósen the / wáy of truth: * thy judgments have I / láid befóre me.
31 I have stuck unto thy tésti- / mónies: * O LORD, / pút me nót to shame.
32 I will run the way of thý com- / mándments, * when / thóu shalt enlárge my heart.
v. 33 Teach me, O LORD, the wáy of thy / státutes; * and I shall keep it / únto the <u>end</u>.
34 Give me understanding, and Í shall / kéep thy law; * yea, I shall observe it / wíth my whóle heart.
35 Make me to go in the path of thý com- / mándments; * for there- / ín do Í delight.
36 Incline my heart unto thy tésti- / mónies, * and not to / cóvetous<u>ness</u>.
37 Turn away mine eyes from behólding / vánity; * and quicken thou / mé in thy <u>way</u>.
38 Stablish thy word únto thy / sérvant, * who is de- / vóted tó thy fear.
39 Turn away my repróach which I / <u>fear</u>: * for thy / júdgments are <u>good</u>.
40 Behold, I have longed áfter thy / précepts: * quicken me / ín thy

[232] vi. 41 Let thy mercies come also únto / mé, O LORD, * even thy salvation, ac- / córding tó thy word.
42 So shall I have wherewith to answer hím that re- / próacheth me: * for I / trúst in thy <u>word</u>.
43 And take not the word of truth utterly óut of my / <u>mouth</u>; * for I have / hóped in thy júdgments.
44 So shall I / kéep thy law * continually for / éver and éver.
45 And I will wálk at / líberty: * for I / séek thy précepts.
46 I will speak of thy testimonies álso be- / fóre kings, * and will / nót be a-<u>shamed</u>.
47 And Í will de- / líght myself * in thy com- / mándments, which Í have loved.
48 My hands also will I lift up unto thy commándments, which / Í have loved; * and I will meditate / ín thy státutes.
Glory be to the Fáther and / tó the Son * and / tó the Hóly Ghost.
As it was in the beginning, is now, and éver / shall be, * - / wórld without énd. Amen.

Part i. *Psalm-prayer*. Forsake us not utterly, O Lord; and as Thou teachest us by trial, so, we beseech Thee, confirm us with Thine unconquerable might; through Jesus Christ our Lord, who liveth and reigneth with Thee and the Holy Ghost, ever one God, world without end. Amen.
Part ii. *Psalm-prayer*. Let us delight, O Lord, in the way of Thy testimonies, as in all manner of riches; lest we should lack anything when we know Thee to be with us; through Jesus Christ our Lord, who liveth and reigneth with Thee and the Holy Ghost, ever one God, world without end. Amen.
Part iii. *Psalm-prayer*. O God, who removest the darkness of sin, and makest us behold the wondrous things out of Thy law, take away from us the shame of our sins, and grant us the keeping of Thy commandments; through Jesus Christ our Lord, who liveth and reigneth with Thee and the Holy Ghost, ever one God, world without end. Amen.
Part iv. *Psalm-prayer*. Remove from us, O Lord, the way of unrighteousness, and with Thy Word have mercy on us, that Thou mayest take away the habit of sin, and, enlarging our heart, grant us perseverance in running the way of Thy commandments; through Jesus Christ our Lord, who liveth and reigneth with Thee and the Holy Ghost, ever one God, world without end. Amen.
Part v. *Psalm-prayer*. Quicken us, O Lord, in Thy righteousness, incline our heart unto Thy testimonies, and not to covetousness, give us also understanding that we may know Thy law, and keep it with our whole heart; through Jesus Christ our Lord, who liveth and reigneth with Thee and the Holy Ghost, ever one God, world without end. Amen.

Part vi. *Psalm-prayer.* Let Thy mercies come unto us, O Lord, that wrath be not fierce against us; and let us have for our healing the Saviour whom we behold as our propitiation and Judge; through the same, Jesus Christ our Lord, who liveth and reigneth with Thee and the Holy Ghost, ever one God, world without end. Amen.

[233]

Ant. Ó Lord, quícken me: * according tó Thy mércy.

IV

Psalm 119vii-xii *Memor esto*

vii. 49 Remember the word ún- / to thy sérvant, * upon which thou hast / cáused me to hope.
50 This is my comfort in / mý afflíction: * for / thy wórd hath quíckened me.
51 The proud have had me greatly / ín derísion: * yet have I not de- / clíned from thy law.
52 I remembered thy júdg- / ments of óld, O LORD; * and / have cómfortéd myself.
53 Horror hath taken / hóld upón me * because of the wick- / ed thát forsáke thy law.
54 Thy stá- / tutes have béen my songs * in the / hóuse of my pílgrimage.
55 I have remembered thy name, O LORD, in the night, / ánd have képt thy law. * 56 This I had, because / I képt thy précepts.
viii. 57 Thou art my pór- / tion, O LORD: * I have said / that Í would kéep thy words.
58 I intreated thy fá- / vour with mý whole heart: * be merciful unto me / accórding tó thy word.
59 I thóught / on my ways, * and turned my feet unto / thy téstimónies.
60 I made haste, / ánd deláyed not * to / keep thý commándments.
61 The bands of the wick- / ed have róbbed me: * but I have not for- / gótten thy law.
62 At midnight I will rise to give thánks / unto thee * because of / thy ríghteous júdgments.
63 I am a companion of all / thém that féar thee, * and of them / that kéep thy précepts.
64 The earth, O LORD, is fúll / of thy mércy: * - / téach me thy státutes.
ix. 65 Thou hast dealt well with thy sér- / vant, O LORD, * according / únto thy word.

66 Teach me good júdg- / ment and knówledge: * for I have be- / lieved thý commándments.
67 Before I was afflíct- / ed I wént astray: * but / nów have I képt thy word.
68 Thou art / góod, and dóest good; * - / téach me thy státutes.
69 The proud have forged a / líe agáinst me: * but I will keep thy pre- / cepts wíth my whóle heart.
70 Their héart / is as fát as grease; * but I de- / líght in thy <u>law</u>.
71 It is good for me that I have / béen afflícted; * that I / might léarn thy státutes.
72 The law of thy mouth is / bétter únto me * than thousands / of góld and sílver.

x. 73 Thy hands have máde / me and fáshioned me: * give me understanding, that I may / léarn thy commándments.
74 They that fear thee will be glád / when they sée me; * because I have / hóped in thy <u>word</u>.
75 I know, O LORD, that thy júdg- / ments are <u>right</u>, * and that thou in faithful- / ness hást afflícted me.
76 Let, I pray thee, thy merciful kindness bé / for my cómfort, * according to thy word / únto thy sérvant.

[234] 77 Let thy tender mercies come unto / mé, that Í may live: * for / thy láw is mý delight.
78 Let the proud be ashamed; † for they dealt perversely with / mé withóut a cause: * but I will medi- / tate ín thy précepts.
79 Let those that féar / thee turn únto me, * and those that have known / thy téstimónies.
80 Let my heart be sóund / in thy státutes; * - / that Í be nót ashamed.

xi. 81 My soul fainteth for / thý salvátion: * but I / hópe in thy <u>word</u>.
82 Mine eyes fail fór / thy word, sáying, * - / When wílt thou cómfort me?
83 For I am become like a / bóttle ín the smoke; * yet do I not / forgét thy státutes.
84 How many are the dáys / of thy sérvant? * when wilt thou execute judgment on them that / pérsecute <u>me</u>?
85 The próud / have digged píts for me, * which are not / áfter thy <u>law</u>.
86 All thy commánd- / ments are fáithful: * they persecute me / wróngfully; hélp thou me.
87 They had almost consumed mé / upon <u>earth</u>; * but I for- / sook nót thy précepts.
88 Quicken me after thy / lóvingkíndness; * so shall I keep the tes- / timóny óf thy mouth.

xii. 89 For év- / er, O <u>LORD</u>, * thy word is / séttled in héaven.
90 Thy faithfulness is unto all / generátions: * thou hast established the

earth, / and it abídeth.
91 They continue this day according / tó thine órdinances: * for / áll are thy sérvants.
92 Unless thy law had béen / my de<u>light</u>s, * I should then have perished / in míne afflíction.
93 I will never for- / gét thy précepts: * for with / them thóu hast quíckened me.
94 Í / am thine, sáve me; * for I / have sóught thy précepts.
95 The wicked have waited for me / tó destróy me: * but I will consider / thy téstimónies.
96 I have seen an end of / áll perféction: * but thy command- / ment ís excéeding broad.
Glory be to the Fá- / ther and tó the Son * - / and tó the Hóly Ghost.
As it was in the beginning, is now, and / éver sháll be, * - / wórld without énd. Amen.

Part vii. *Psalm-prayer.* O God, who during this time of waiting comfortest us in lowliness with the hope of everlasting life, grant us always to serve Thee in the house of our pilgrimage, and grant that we may enjoy the blessedness of our eternal country; through Jesus Christ our Lord, who liveth and reigneth with Thee and the Holy Ghost, ever one God, world without end. Amen.

Part viii. *Psalm-prayer.* Be Thou our portion, O Lord: grant that we may keep Thy law, to the end that Thou mayest be our heritage, and Thyself possess us without end; through Jesus Christ our Lord, who liveth and reigneth with Thee and the Holy Ghost, ever one God, world without end. Amen.

Part ix. *Psalm-prayer.* O Christ our God, who didst bear the suffering of Thy Passion for us all, when Thou wast found peaceful among them that hated peace; and innocent wast crucified by the guilty, and so by Thy death dost transfix the death of mankind; Grant that the multiplied unrighteousness of the proud may not prevail against us, and that the meditation of Thy law may not depart from the affections of our heart; that as Thou only hast endured death and the grave for us, Thou mayest bestow the light and reward of eternal life upon them that believe in Thee; who livest and reignest with the Father and the Holy Ghost, ever one God, world without end. Amen.

Part x. *Psalm-prayer.* We know, O Lord, that Thy judgment is just; but we beseech Thy mercy, that Thy compassions may come upon us, that we be not confounded with the proud nor condemned with the ungodly; through Jesus Christ our Lord, who liveth and reigneth with Thee and the Holy Ghost, ever one God, world without end. Amen.

Part xi. *Psalm-prayer.* O God, whose Word the eyes of the soul desire, and for whose salvation they faint, help us in our days, that we fall not by the persecution of unrighteousness; through Jesus Christ our Lord, who liveth and reigneth with Thee and the Holy Ghost, ever one God, world without end. Amen.

Part xii. *Psalm-prayer.* O God, whose truth and Word abide in heaven; whose light and day continue, make us to abide steadfastly in Thy service, that we may be the children of light; through Jesus Christ our Lord, who liveth and reigneth with Thee and the Holy Ghost, ever one God, world without end. Amen.

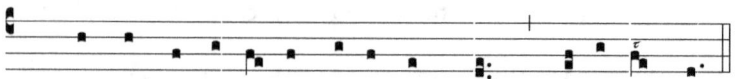

Ant. Uphold me according únto Thy <u>Word</u>: * thát I may <u>live</u>.

Psalm 119xiii-xvii *Quomodo dilexi*

xiii. 97 — O how / lóve I thy <u>law</u>! * it is my medi- / tátion áll the day.

98 Thou through thy commandments hast made me wiser / thán mine énemies: * for they are / éver wíth me.

99 I have more understanding than / áll my téachers: * for thy testimonies are my / méditátion.

100 I understand / móre than the áncients, * because I / kéep thy précepts.

101 I have refrained my feet from / évery évil way, * - that / Í might kéep thy word.

102 I have not departed / fróm thy júdgments: * - for / thóu hast táught me.

103 How sweet are thy words / únto my <u>taste</u>! * yea, sweeter than / hóney tó my mouth!

104 Through thy precepts I get / únderstánding: * therefore I hate / évery fálse way.

xiv. 105 Thy word is a lamp / únto my <u>feet</u>, * and a light / únto my <u>path</u>.

106 I have sworn, and I / wíll perfórm it, * that I will keep thy / ríghteous júdgments.

107 I am af- / flícted véry much: * quicken me, O LORD, according / únto thy <u>word</u>.

108 Accept, I beseech thee, the freewill offerings / óf my móuth, O LORD, * and téach / me thy júdgments.

109 My soul is con- / tínually ín my hand: * yet do I / nót forgét thy law.

110 The wicked have / láid a snáre for me: * yet I erred not / fróm thy précepts.

111 Thy testimonies have I taken as an heri- / táge for éver: * for they are the re- / jóicing óf my heart.
112 I have inclined mine heart to perform thy / státutes álway, * even / únto the <u>end</u>.
xv. 113 I hate vain thoughts: but thy / láw do I <u>love</u>. * 114 Thou art my hiding place and my shield: I / hópe in thy <u>word</u>.
115 Depart from me, ye / évildóers: * for I will keep the com- / mándments óf my God.
116 Uphold me according unto thy / wórd, that Í may live: * and let me not be a- / shámed of my <u>hope</u>.   [236]
117 Hold thou me up, and / Í shall be <u>safe</u>: * and I will have respect unto thy stá- / tutes contínually.
118 Thou hast trodden down all them that / érr from thy státutes: * for their de- / céit is fálsehood.
119 Thou puttest away all the wicked / óf the éarth like dross: * therefore I love thy / téstimónies.
120 My flesh / trémbleth for féar of thee; * and I am afráid / of thy júdgments.
xvi. 121 I have done / júdgment and jústice: * leave me not to / míne oppréssors.
122 Be surety for thy / sérvant for <u>good</u>: * let not the / próud oppréss me.
123 Mine eyes fail for / thý salvátion, * and for the wórd / of thy ríghteousness.
124 Deal with thy servant according / únto thy mércy, * and téach / me thy státutes.
125 I / ám thy sérvant; * give me understanding, that I may know thy / téstimónies.
126 It is time for / thée, LORD, to <u>work</u>: * for théy / have made vóid thy law.
127 Therefore I love thy com- / mándments abóve gold; * - yéa, / above fíne gold.
128 Therefore I esteem all thy precepts concerning all / thíngs to be <u>right</u>; * and I hate / évery fálse way.
xvii. 129 Thy testi- / mónies are wónderful: * therefore dóth / my soul kéep them.
130 The entrance of thy / wórds giveth <u>light</u>; * it giveth understanding ún- / to the símple.
131 I opened my / móuth, and pánted: * for I longed for / thý commándments.
132 Look thou upon me, and be / mérciful únto me, * as thou usest to do unto / thóse that lóve thy name.
133 Order my / stéps in thy <u>word</u>: * and let not any iniquity have do- /

mínion óver me.

134 Deliver me from the op- / préssion of <u>man</u>: * so will I / kéep thy précepts.

135 Make thy face to shine up- / ón thy sérvant; * and téach / me thy státutes.

136 Rivers of / wáters run dówn mine eyes, * because they / kéep not thy <u>law</u>.

Glory be to the / Fáther and tó the Son * - and / tó the Hóly Ghost.

As it was in the beginning, is now, and / éver sháll be, * - wórld / without énd. Amen.

Part xiii. *Psalm-prayer.* Vouchsafe, O Lord, that we may so love Thy law, as to meditate on it always in our heart, and ever to go onward in works that are acceptable unto Thee; through Jesus Christ our Lord, who liveth and reigneth with Thee and the Holy Ghost, ever one God, world without end. Amen.

Part xiv. *Psalm-prayer.* Let Thy Word, O Lord, be a lamp unto our feet, and a light to our paths, that it may teach us to understand, and show us whither we are hastening; through Jesus Christ our Lord, who liveth and reigneth with Thee and the Holy Ghost, ever one God, world without end. Amen.

Part xv. *Psalm-prayer.* O God, who commandest us always to love our enemies, and to keep Thy law, enlighten the eyes of our heart, that by Thy constant help we may begin to obey Thee, and be delivered from evil works; through Jesus Christ our Lord, who liveth and reigneth with Thee and the Holy Ghost, ever one God, world without end. Amen.

Part xvi. *Psalm-prayer.* Teach us, O Lord, to do judgment and justice, that we be not left to our oppressors, nor be put under unrighteous slanderers, but loving Thy words with steadfast minds, may be delivered from all evil snares; through Jesus Christ our Lord, who liveth and reigneth with Thee and the Holy Ghost, ever one God, world without end. Amen.

Part xvii. *Psalm-prayer.* Show the light of Thy countenance upon us, O Lord, that the declaration of Thy words may enlighten our hearts and understanding, and nourish the breasts of the simple, that as we desire Thy commandments, we may with open heart take in the Spirit of wisdom and understanding; through Jesus Christ our Lord, who liveth and reigneth with Thee and the same Holy Ghost, ever one God, world without end. Amen.

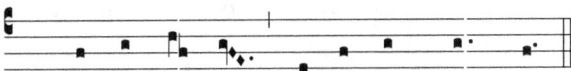

Ant. Lét my soul <u>live</u>: * and ít shall práise thee.

VI

Psalm 119xviii-xxii *Justus es*

xviii. 137 — / Ríghteous art thóu, O LORD, * and upright / áre thy júdgments.
138 Thy testimonies that / thóu hast commánded * are righteous and / véry fáithful.
139 My zeal / háth consúmed me, * because mine enemies have forgót- / ten thy <u>words</u>.
140 Thy / wórd is véry pure: * therefore thy / sérvant lóveth it.
141 I am / smáll and des<u>pised</u>: * yet do not I for- / gét thy précepts.
142 Thy righteousness is an ever- / lásting ríghteousness, * and thy láw / is the <u>truth</u>.
143 Trouble and anguish have / táken hóld on me: * yet thy commánd- / ments are mý delights.
144 The righteousness of thy testimonies is / éverlásting: * give me understán- / ding, and Í shall live.
xix. 145 I cried with my whole heart; / héar me, O <u>LORD</u>: * I will / kéep thy státutes.
146 I / críed unto <u>thee</u>; * save me, and I shall keep thy / téstimónies.
147 I prevented the dawning of the / mórning, and <u>cried</u>: * I hóped / in thy <u>word</u>.
148 Mine eyes pre- / vént the night wátches, * that I might méd- / itate ín thy word.
149 Hear my voice according unto thy / lóvingkíndness: * O LORD, quicken me according / tó thy júdgment.
150 They draw nigh that follow / áfter míschief: * they are fár / from thy <u>law</u>.
151 — / Thóu art néar, O LORD; * and all thy commánd- / ments are <u>truth</u>.
152 Concerning thy testimonies, / Í have knówn of old * that thou hast founded / thém for éver.
xx. 153 Consider mine affliction, / ánd delíver me: * for I do / nót forgét thy law.
154 Plead my cause, / ánd delíver me: * quicken me ac- / córding tó thy word.
155 Salvation is / fár from the wícked: * for they seek / nót thy státutes.

156 Great are thy tender / mércies, O LORD: * quicken me according / tó thy júdgments.

157 Many are my persecutors / ánd mine énemies; * yet do I not decline from thy / téstimónies.

158 I beheld the trans- / gréssors, ánd was grieved; * because / théy kept nót thy word.

159 Consider how I / lóve thy précepts: * quicken me, O LORD, according to thy / lóvingkíndness.

[238] 160 Thy word is true / fróm the begínning: * and every one of thy righteous judgments endúr- / eth for éver.

xxi. 161 Princes have persecuted / mé withóut a cause: * but my heart standeth in áwe / of thy word.

162 I re- / jóice at thy word, * as one that fínd- / eth great spóil-.

163 I hate / ánd abhor lýing: * but thy láw / do I love.

164 Seven times a day / dó I práise thee * because of thy / ríghteous júdgments.

165 Great peace have / théy which lóve thy law: * and nothing / sháll offénd them.

166 LORD, I have hoped for / thý salvátion, * and done / thý commándments.

167 My soul hath kept thy / téstimónies; * and I lóve / them excéedingly.

168 I have kept thy precepts and thy / téstimónies: * for all my ways / áre befóre thee.

xxii. 169 Let my cry come / néar before thée, O LORD: * give me understanding ac- / córding tó thy word.

170 Let my supplication / cóme befóre thee: * deliver me ac- / córding tó thy word.

171 My / líps shall útter praise, * when thou hast táught / me thy státutes.

172 My tongue shall / spéak of thy word: * for all thy commánd- / ments are ríghteousness.

173 – / Lét thine hand hélp me; * for I have chó- / sen thy précepts.

174 I have longed for thy sal- / vátion, O LORD; * and thy / láw is mý delight.

175 Let my soul live, and / ít shall práise thee; * and let thy / júdgments hélp me.

176 I have gone astray / líke a lóst sheep; * seek thy servant; for I do not forget / thý commándments.

Glory be to the / Fáther and tó the Son * - and / tó the Hóly Ghost.

As it was in the beginning, is now, and / éver sháll be, * - wórld / without énd. Amen.

Part xviii. *Psalm-prayer.* Make us, Thy servants, O Lord, to love Thy fiery

316

word, to drive out the filth of our sins with its heat, and to kindle in us the light of knowledge; through Jesus Christ our Lord, who liveth and reigneth with Thee and the Holy Ghost, ever one God, world without end. Amen.

Part xix. *Psalm-prayer.* Hear our voice, O Lord, according to Thy plenteous mercy, and condemn us not as the guilty, but in Thy love and mercifulness reward us as the blessed; through Jesus Christ our Lord, who liveth and reigneth with Thee and the Holy Ghost, ever one God, world without end. Amen.

Part xx. *Psalm-prayer.* O God, who hast put the salvation of the faithful far from the wicked, be mindful of Thy mercies, and protect our lowliness from the assaults of the ungodly; through Jesus Christ our Lord, who liveth and reigneth with Thee and the Holy Ghost, ever one God, world without end. Amen.

Part xxi. *Psalm-prayer.* Great peace have they which love Thy law, O Lord, and nothing shall make them stumble. Grant that we, who do not prefer anything in this world to Thy love, may never be troubled in our thoughts; through Jesus Christ our Lord, who liveth and reigneth with Thee and the Holy Ghost, ever one God, world without end. Amen.

Part xxii. *Psalm-prayer.* Let our prayer, O Lord, enter into the presence of Thy majesty, and as Thou hast recalled us like lost sheep from our former errors, so grant that, taught by the preaching of Thy judgments, we may attain to the full grace of Thy loving-kindness; through Jesus Christ our Lord, who liveth and reigneth with Thee and the Holy Ghost, ever one God, world without end. Amen.

[239]

Ant. I cried únto the LORD: * ánd he héard me.

VII

Psalm 120 *Ad Dominum*

1 In my distress I cried / únto the LORD, * - / ánd he héard me.
2 Deliver my soul, O / LÓRD, from lýing lips, * and / fróm a decéitful tongue.
3 What shall be / gíven únto thee? * or what shall be done unto / thée, thou fálse tongue?
4 Sharp arrows / óf the míghty, * with / cóals of júniper.
5 Woe is me, that I / sójourn in Mésech, * that I dwell in the / ténts of Kédar!
6 My soul hath long dwelt with / hím that háteth peace. * 7 I am for peace:

but when I speak, / théy are for <u>war</u>.
**Glory be to the / Fáther and tó the Son * and / tó the Hóly Ghost.
As it was in the beginning, is now, and / éver sháll be, * - / wórld without énd. Amen.**

Psalm-prayer. O God, merciful softener of our trouble, deliver the souls of the faithful far from the lips of the ungodly slanderers, that defended by spiritual aids, they may not be overthrown by any attacks; through Jesus Christ our Lord, who liveth and reigneth with Thee and the Holy Ghost, ever one God, world without end. Amen.

Ant. My help cómeth fróm the Lord: * which made héaven and éarth.

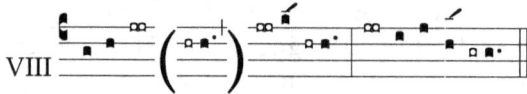

Psalm 121 *Levavi oculos*
1 I will lift up mine eyes únto the / <u>hills</u>, * from whence cóm- / eth my <u>help</u>.
2 My help cómeth / fróm the LORD, * which made héa- / ven and <u>earth</u>.
3 He will not suffer thy fóot to be / <u>moved</u>: * he that keepeth thee / wíll not slúmber.
4 Behold, he that kéepeth / Ísrael * shall neither slúm- / ber nor <u>sleep</u>.
5 The LÓRD is thy / kéeper: * the LORD is thy shade up- / ón thy ríght hand.
6 The sun shall not smíte thee by / <u>day</u>, * - / nór the móon by night.
7 The LORD shall preserve thee fróm all / évil: * he / sháll presérve thy soul.
8 The LORD shall preserve thy going oút and thy / cóming in * from this time forth, and év- / en for évermore.
**Glory be to the Fáther and / tó the Son * and / tó the Hóly Ghost.
As it was in the beginning, is now, and éver / sháll be, * wórld / without énd. Amen.**

Psalm-prayer. O Lord God, keeper of Israel, who neither slumberest nor sleepest, keep Thy people, and that we be not burned by day, defend us from the scandals of this world; through Jesus Christ our Lord, who liveth and reigneth with Thee and the Holy Ghost, ever one God, world without end. Amen.

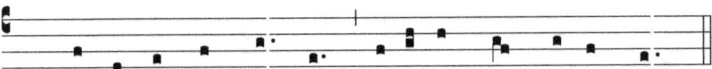

Ant. Let us gó with gládness: * into the hóuse of the <u>Lord</u>.

IV

Psalm 122 *Laetatus sum*
1 I was glad when they sáid / unto <u>me</u>, * Let us go into the / hóuse of the <u>LORD</u>.
2 Our feet shall stand within thy gates, / Ó Jerúsalem. * 3 Jerusalem is builded as a city that is / cómpact togéther:
4 Whither the tribes go up, the tríbes / of the <u>LORD</u>, * unto the testimony of Israel, to give thanks unto the / náme of the <u>LORD</u>.
5 For there are set / thrónes of júdgment, * the thrones of / the hóuse of Dávid.
6 Pray for the péace / of Jerúsalem: * they shall / prósper that lóve thee.
7 Péace / be withín thy walls, * and prosperity / withín thy pálaces.
8 For my brethren and companions' sakes, I will now say, Peace / bé withín thee. * 9 Because of the house of the LORD our / God Í will séek thy good.
Glory be to the Fá- / ther and tó the Son * - / and tó the Hóly Ghost.
As it was in the beginning, is now, and / éver shálll be, * - / wórld without énd. Amen.

Psalm-prayer. Almighty God, vouchsafe to bestow plenteousness of peace on them that walk in the courts of Thine house, that while we give thanks unto Thee with all the eagerness of our hearts, we may attain Thy good things in heavenly places; through Jesus Christ our Lord, who liveth and reigneth with Thee and the Holy Ghost, ever one God, world without end. Amen.

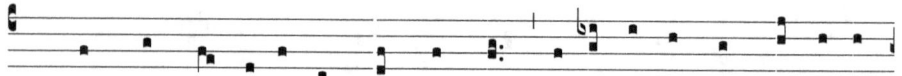

Ant. Our eyes wait upón the Lórd our God: * until that he have mércy up-

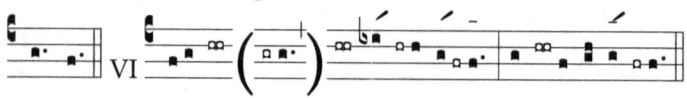

ón us.

Psalm 123 *Ad te levavi*

1 Unto thee / líft I úp mine eyes, * O thou that dwellest / ín the héavens.
2 Behold, as the eyes of servants look unto the / hánd of their másters, * and as the eyes of a maiden unto the hánd / of her místress;
[241] So our eyes wait up- / ón the LÓRD our God, * until that he have mér- / cy upón us.
3 Have mercy upon us, O LORD, have / mércy upón us: * for we are exceedingly fílled / with con<u>tempt</u>.
4 Our soul is exceedingly filled with the scorning of / thóse that áre at ease, * and with the contémpt / of the <u>proud</u>.

Glory be to the / Fáther and tó the Son * - and / tó the Hóly Ghost.
As it was in the beginning, is now, and / éver sháll be, * - wórld / without énd. Amen.

Psalm-prayer. O God, dweller in the heavens, unto Thee do we lift up our eyes in prayer, that Thou mayest put to silence the scorning of the proud, and graciously bestow on us Thy wonted mercy; through Jesus Christ our Lord, who liveth and reigneth with Thee and the Holy Ghost, ever one God, world without end. Amen.

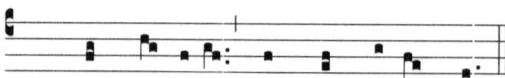

Ant. Our help is in * the name of the Lord.

Psalm 124 *Nisi quia Dominus*

1 If it had not been the / LÓRD who was ón our side, * now may / Ís-ra-el <u>say</u>;
2 If it had not been the / LÓRD who was ón our side, * when men rose / úp agáinst us:

3 Then they had / swállowed us úp quick, * when their wrath was kín- / dled agáinst us:
4 Then the waters had overwhelmed us, † the stream had gone / óver our soul: * 5 then the proud waters had gone / óver our soul.
6 — / Bléss-ed bé the LORD, * who hath not given us as a / préy to their teeth.
7 Our soul is escaped as a bird out of the / snáre of the fówlers: * the snare is broken, and / wé are escaped.
8 Our help is in the / náme of the LORD, * who made / héaven and earth.
Glory be to the / Fáther and tó the Son * - and / tó the Hóly Ghost.
As it was in the beginning, is now, and / éver shall be, * - wórld / without énd. Amen.

Psalm-prayer. Shut, O Lord, the gaping mouths of the wicked, who attempt to devour us with the cruel teeth of slander, that we, who trust not in our own strength, may be defended by the help of Thy Name; through Jesus Christ our Lord, who liveth and reigneth with Thee and the Holy Ghost, ever one God, world without end. Amen.

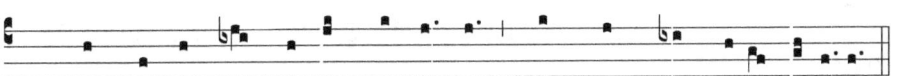

[242]

Ant. The Lord is round abóut His péople: * from henceforth éven foréver.

Psalm 125 *Qui confidunt*
1 They that trust in the LORD shall bé as mount / Zíon, * which cannot be removed, but a- / bídeth for éver.
2 As the mountains are round abóut Jer- / úsalem, * so the LORD is round about his people from henceforth / éven for éver.
3 For the rod of the wicked shall not rest upon the lót of the / ríghteous; * lest the righteous put forth their hands / únto iníquity.
4 Do good, O LORD, unto thóse that be / good, * and to them that are / úpright ín their hearts.
5 As for such as turn aside unto their cróoked ways, † the LORD shall lead them forth with the workers óf in- / íquity: * but peace shall / bé upon Ísrael.
Glory be to the Fáther and / tó the Son * and / tó the Hóly Ghost.
As it was in the beginning, is now, and éver / shall be, * - / wórld without énd. Amen.

Psalm-prayer. Drive away, O Lord, from the lot of the righteous, the wickedness of the evil who arise against it, that they who trust in Thee may not be shaken with any temptations; through Jesus Christ our Lord, who liveth and reigneth with Thee and the Holy Ghost, ever one God, world without end. Amen.

Ant. The Lord hath dóne great thíngs for us: * whereóf we are glad.

VII

Psalm 126 *In convertendo*
1 When the LORD turned again the captivi- / tý of Zíon, * - / wé were like thém that dream.
2 Then was our mouth / fílled with láughter, * and our / tóngue with sínging:
Then said they a- / móng the héathen, * The LORD hath / dóne great thíngs for them.
3 The LORD hath / dóne great thíngs for us; * where- / óf we are glad.
4 Turn again our captivity, O LORD, as the / stréams in the south. * 5 They that sow in / téars shall réap in joy.
6 He that goeth forth and weepeth, / beáring précious seed, * shall doubtless come again with rejoicing, / brínging his shéaves with him.
**Glory be to the / Fáther and tó the Son * and / tó the Hóly Ghost.
As it was in the beginning, is now, and / éver sháll be, * - / wórld without énd. Amen.**

[243] *Psalm-prayer.* Comfort Thy people, O Lord, and deliver us from the evil captivity of sin, that what we sow here in tears, we may reap in joy through Thy bounty; through Jesus Christ our Lord, who liveth and reigneth with Thee and the Holy Ghost, ever one God, world without end. Amen.

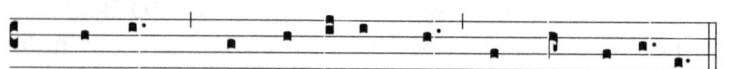

Ant. O LORD, * búild for ús the house: and kéep the cí-ty.

Psalm 127 *Nisi Dominus*

1 Except the LORD build the house, they labour in / váin that buíld it: *
except the LORD keep the city, the watchman / wáketh bút in vain.
2 It is vain for you to rise up early, to sît up late, † to eat the / bréad of
sórrows: * for so he giveth / hís belóv-ed sleep.
3 Lo, children are an / héritage óf the LORD: * and the fruit of the / wómb is
hís reward.
4 As arrows are in the / hánd of a míghty man; * so are / chíldren óf the
youth.
5 Happy is the man that hath his / quíver fúll of them: * they shall not be
ashamed, but they shall speak with the / énemies ín the gate.
Glory be to the / Fáther and tó the Son * and / tó the Hóly Ghost.
**As it was in the beginning, is now, and / éver sháll be, * - / wórld without
énd. Amen.**

Psalm-prayer. O God, the builder of spiritual houses, we beseech Thee to keep
us, and uniting us unto Thine elect, fill our desire and will with Thy love;
through Jesus Christ our Lord, who liveth and reigneth with Thee and the
Holy Ghost, ever one God, world without end. Amen.

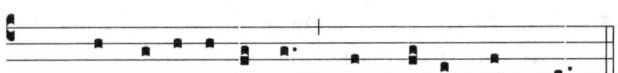

Ant. Bless-ed is every one * that feareth the LORD. *(Do not repeat in verse 1.)*

Psalm 128 *Beati omnes*

1 [Bless-ed is every one that / féareth the LORD;] * - that / wálketh ín his
ways.
2 For thou shalt eat the / lábour óf thine hands: * happy shalt thou be, and it
/ shálл be wéll with thee.
3 Thy wife shall be as a fruitful vine by the / sídes of thine house: * thy
children like olive plants round a- / bóut thy táble.
4 Behold, that / thús shall the mán be blessed * - that / féareth the LORD. [244]
5 The LORD shall bless thee / óut of Zíon: * and thou shalt see the good of
Jerusalem all the / dáys of thy life.
6 Yea, thou shalt see thy / chíldren's chíldren, * and péace / upon Ísrael.

Glory be to the / Fáther and tó the Son * - and / tó the Hóly Ghost.
As it was in the beginning, is now, and / éver sháll be, * - wórld / without énd. Amen.

Psalm-prayer. Bless us, O Lord, who fear Thee, and make us to walk continually in Thy ways; bless us with Thy holy benediction, that we may see the everlasting good of Jerusalem; through Jesus Christ our Lord, who liveth and reigneth with Thee and the Holy Ghost, ever one God, world without end. Amen.

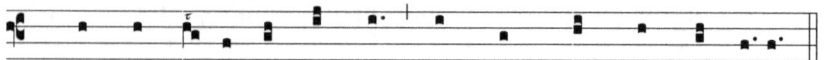

Ant. Let them áll be confóunded: * and turned báck that hate Zíon.

Psalm 129 *Saepe expugnaverunt*
1 Many a time have they afflícted me / fróm my youth, * may Ísrael / nów say:
2 Many a time have they afflícted me / fróm my youth: * yet they have not preváiled a- / gáinst me.
3 The plowers plówed up- / ón my back: * they made lóng their / fúrrows.
4 The LÓRD is / ríghteous: * he hath cut asunder the córds of the / wícked.
5 Let them áll be con- / fóunded * and turned báck that hate / Zíon.
6 Let them be as the grass upón the / hóusetops, * which withereth afóre it / gróweth up:
7 Wherewith the mower fílleth / nót his hand; * nor he that bindeth shéaves his / bósom.
8 Neither do they which go by say, † The blessing of the LORD bé up- / ón you: * we bless you in the náme of / the <u>LORD</u>.
Glory be to the Fáther and / tó the Son * and tó the / Hóly Ghost.
As it was in the beginning, is now, and éver / sháll be, * wórld without / énd. Amen.

Psalm-prayer. Defend Thy Church, O Lord, with the protection of Thy right hand, from all wickedness of them that war against her, that when her enemies are turned back, she may be filled by Thee with holy benediction; through Jesus Christ our Lord, who liveth and reigneth with Thee and the Holy Ghost, ever one God, world without end. Amen.

Ant. Out of the depths * have I cried unto thee, O LORD.
(Do not repeat in verse 1.)

VIII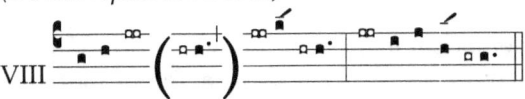

Psalm 130 *De profundis*
1 [Out of the depths have I cried únto / thée, O LORD.] * 2 Lord, hear my voice: let thine ears be attentive to the voice of my / súpplicátions.
3 If thou, LORD, shouldest márk in- / íquities, * - / Ó Lord, whó shall stand?
4 But there is forgíveness with / <u>thee</u>, * that thou máy- / est be <u>feared</u>.
5 I wait for the LÓRD, my / sóul doth wait, * and in his wórd / do I <u>hope</u>.
6 My soul waiteth for the Lord more than they that wátch for the / mórning: * I say, more than they that wátch / for the mórning.
7 Let Israel hope in the LORD: † for with the LÓRD there is / mércy, * and with him is plén- / teous redémption.
8 And he sháll redeem / Ísrael * from áll / his iníquities.
**Glory be to the Fáther and / tó the Son * and / tó the Hóly Ghost.
As it was in the beginning, is now, and éver / sháll be, * wórld / without énd. Amen.**

Psalm-prayer. O Lord, we beseech Thee: let Thy merciful ears attend to the prayer of Thy humble servants, because with Thee there is forgiveness of sins; that Thou mayest not mark our iniquities, but vouchsafe to us Thy mercies; through Jesus Christ our Lord, who liveth and reigneth with Thee and the Holy Ghost, ever one God, world without end. Amen.

Ant. Lord, my heart is not haughty * nor mine eyes lof-ty.
(Do not repeat in verse 1.)

Irr.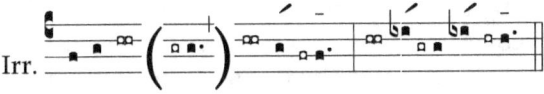

Psalm 131 *Domine, non est*
1 [LORD, my heart is not haughty, nor míne eyes / lófty:] * neither do I exercise myself in great matters, or in / thíngs too hígh for me.
2 Surely I have behaved and quieted myself, as a child that is weaned óf his

/ móther: * my soul is even / ás a weaned child.
3 Let Israel hópe in / the LORD * from henceforth / ánd for éver.
Glory be to the Fáther and / tó the Son * and / tó the Hóly Ghost.
As it was in the beginning, is now, and éver / shall be, * - / wórld without énd. Amen.

Psalm-prayer. Almighty Lord, suffer us not to be lifted up with worldly pride; but Thou who art meek and lowly of heart, teach us to agree in that holy conduct which is pleasing unto Thee; who livest and reignest with the Father and the Holy Ghost, ever one God, world without end. Amen.

[246]
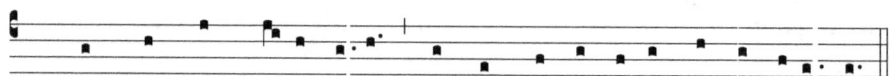

Ant. The Lord hath chósen Zíon: * He hath desired it for His háb-i-tá-tion.

Psalm 132 *Memento, Domine*
1 LORD, remember David, and / áll his afflíctions: * 2 How he sware unto the LORD, and vowed unto the mighty Gód / of Jácob;
3 Surely I will not come into the taber- / nácle óf my house, * nor go up / ínto my bed;
4 I will not give / sléep to mine eyes, * or slumber tó / mine éyelids,
5 Until I find out a / pláce for the LORD, * an habitation for the mighty Gód / of Jácob.
6 Lo, we heard of / ít at Éphratah: * we found it in the fí- / elds óf the wood.
7 We will go into his / tábernácles: * we will worship át / his fóotstool.
8 Arise, O LORD, / ínto thy rest; * thou, and the / árk of thy strength.
9 Let thy priests be / clóthed with ríghteousness; * and let thy / sáints shout for joy.
10 For thy / sérvant Dávid's sake * turn not away the face of thíne / anóinted.
11 The LORD hath sworn in truth unto David; † he / wíll not túrn from it; * Of the fruit of thy body will I sét / upón thy throne.
12 If thy children will keep my côvenant † and my testimony that / Í shall téach them, * their children shall also sit upon thy thróne / for évermore.
13 For the LORD hath / chósen Zíon; * he hath desired it for his háb- / itátion.
14 This is my / rést for éver: * here will I dwell; for I háve / desíred it.
15 I will abundantly / bléss her provísion: * I will satisfý / her póor with

bread.

16 I will also clothe her priests / wíth salvátion: * and her saints shall shóut / alóud for joy.
17 There will I make the horn of / Dávid to <u>bud</u>: * I have ordained a lamp for míne / anóinted.
18 His enemies / wíll I clóthe with shame: * but upon himself sháll his / crown flóurish.
Glory be to the / Fáther and tó the Son * and tó / the Hóly Ghost.
As it was in the beginning, is now, and / éver sháll be, * wórld with- / out énd. Amen.

Psalm-prayer. Remember us, Almighty God, in all our afflictions, and clothe us with priestly righteousness, that we may be fit to be brought into Thine everlasting tabernacles; through Jesus Christ our Lord, who liveth and reigneth with Thee and the Holy Ghost, ever one God, world without end. Amen.

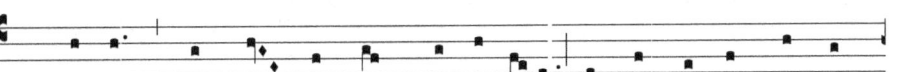

[247]

Ant. Behold, * how good and how pleasant it is: for brethren to dwell to-

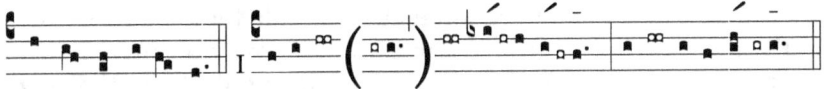

gether in u-ni-ty! *(Do not repeat in verse 1.)*

Psalm 133 *Ecce, quam*
1 [Behold, how good and how / pléasant it <u>is</u> * for brethren to dwell togé- / ther in únity!]
2 It is like the precious ointment upôn the head, † that ran down upon the beard, / éven Áaron's beard: * that went down to the skírts / of his gárments;
3 As the / déw of Hérmon, * and as the dew that descended upon the móun- / tains of Zíon:
For there the LORD com- / mánded the bléssing, * even / lífe for évermore.
Glory be to the / Fáther and tó the Son * - and / tó the Hóly Ghost.
As it was in the beginning, is now, and / éver sháll be, * - wórld / without énd. Amen.

Psalm-prayer. Pour, O Lord, upon Thy Church the charity of brotherly love and peace amongst us, that sprinkled with the dew of spiritual anointing, we may rejoice in the grace of Thy blessing; through Jesus Christ our Lord, who liveth and reigneth with Thee and the Holy Ghost, ever one God, world without end. Amen.

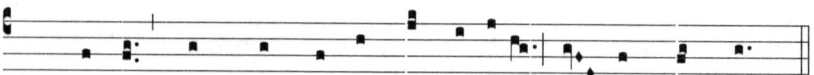

Ant. Lift úp * your hands: in the sanc-tu-á-ry and bléss the LORD.

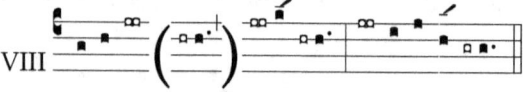
VIII

Psalm 134 *Ecce, nunc*
1 Behold, bless ye the LORD, all ye sérvants / óf the LORD, * which by night stand in the hóuse / of the <u>LORD</u>.
2 Lift / úp your hands * in the sanctuá- / ry, and bléss the LORD.
3 The LORD that made héaven and / <u>earth</u> * bless thee / óut of Zíon.
**Glory be to the Fáther and / tó the Son * and / tó the Hóly Ghost.
As it was in the beginning, is now, and éver / sháll be, * wórld / without énd. Amen.**

Psalm-prayer. All we Thy servants, O Lord, blessing Thee, make our prayer, that Thou wouldest vouchsafe to enlighten us, shrouded in the night of this world, that while we lift up our hands in prayer, we may obtain abundant blessing from Thee; through Jesus Christ our Lord, who liveth and reigneth with Thee and the Holy Ghost, ever one God, world without end. Amen.

[248]

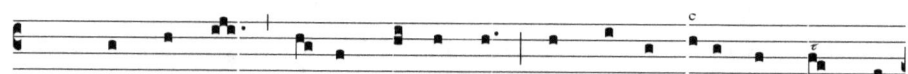

Ant. Praise the Lord, * fór the Lórd is good: sing praises unto his name, for

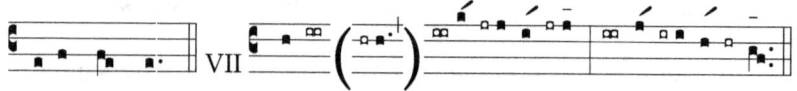
VII

ít is pléasant.

Psalm 135 *Laudate nomen*
1 Praise ye the LORD. Praise ye the / náme of the <u>LORD</u>; * praise him, O ye / sérvants óf the LORD.
2 Ye that stand in the / hóuse of the <u>LORD</u>, * in the courts of the / hóuse of our <u>God</u>,
3 Praise the LORD; / fór the LÓRD is good: * sing praises unto his name; for

/ ít is pléasant.
4 For the LORD hath chosen Jacob / únto him<u>self</u>, * and Israel for his pe- / cúliar tréasure.
5 For I know / thát the LÓRD is great, * and that our / Lórd is abóve all gods.
6 Whatsoever the LORD pleased, that did / hé in héaven, * and in earth, in the seas, and / áll deep pláces.
7 He causeth the vapours to ascend from the ends of the earth; † he maketh / líghtnings fór the rain; * he bringeth the wind / óut of his tréasuries.
8 Who smote the / fírstborn of Égypt, * - / bóth of mán and beast.
9 Who sent tokens and wonders into the midst of / thée, O Égypt, * upon Pharaoh, and upon / áll his sérvants.
10 Who / smóte great nátions, * - / ánd slew míghty kíngs;
11 Sihon king of the Âmorites, † and Og / kíng of Báshan, * and all the / kíngdoms of Cánaan:
12 And gave their / lánd for an héritage, * an heritage unto Isra- / él his péople.
13 Thy name, O LORD, en- / dúreth for éver; * and thy memorial, O LORD, throughout all / génerátions.
14 For the LORD will / júdge his péople, * and he will repent himself con- / cérning his sérvants.
15 The idols of the heathen are / sílver and <u>gold</u>, * the / wórk of mén's hands.
16 They have mouths, / bút they spéak not; * eyes have they, / bút they sée not;
17 They have ears, / bút they héar not; * neither is there any / bréath in their <u>mouths</u>.
18 They that make them / áre like únto them: * so is every one that / trústeth in <u>them</u>.
19 Bless the LORD, O / hóuse of Ísrael: * bless the LORD, O / hóuse of Áaron:
20 Bless the LORD, O / hóuse of Lévi: * ye that / féar the LORD, bléss the LORD.
21 Bless-ed be the LORD / óut of Zíon, * which dwelleth at Jerusalem. / Práise ye the <u>LORD</u>.
Glory be to the / Fáther and tó the Son * and / tó the Hóly Ghost.
As it was in the beginning, is now, and / éver sháll be, * - / wórld without énd. Amen.

Psalm-prayer. O God of surpassing sweetness, whom the whole earth praiseth because of Thy merciful pleasantness, we beseech Thee to take away from us the error of vain superstition, that we may be joined unto Thy will; through

Jesus Christ our Lord, who liveth and reigneth with Thee and the Holy Ghost, ever one God, world without end. Amen.

[249]
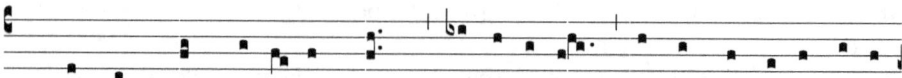

Ant. O give thanks unto the LORD; * for he is good: for his mercy endureth

for ever. *(Do not repeat in verse 1.)*

Psalm 136i *Confitemini Domino*
1 [O give thanks unto the / LÓRD; for hé is good: * for his mercy endúr- / eth for éver.]
2 O give thanks / únto the Gód of gods: * for his mercy endúr- / eth for éver.
3 O give / thánks to the Lórd of lords: * for his mercy endúr- / eth for éver.
4 To him who alone / dóeth great wónders: * for his mercy endúr- / eth for éver.
5 To him that by wisdom / máde the héavens: * for his mercy endúr- / eth for éver.
6 To him that stretched out the earth a- / bóve the wáters: * for his mercy endúr- / eth for éver.
7 To / hím that máde great lights: * for his mercy endúr- / eth for éver:
8 The / sún to rúle by day: * for his mercy endúr- / eth for éver:
9 The moon and / stárs to rúle by night: * for his mercy endúr- / eth for éver.
Glory be to the / Fáther and tó the Son * - and / tó the Hóly Ghost.
As it was in the beginning, is now, and / éver sháll be, * - wórld / without énd. Amen.

Ant. The Lord remembered us * ín our lów estate: for his mercy endúreth

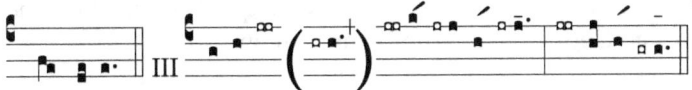

for éver.

Psalm 136ii *Qui percussit*
10 To him that smote Egypt / ín their fírstborn: * for his mercy endúreth / for éver:
11 And brought out Israel / fróm amóng them: * for his mercy endúreth / for éver:
12 With a strong hand, and / wíth a strétched out arm: * for his mercy endúreth / for éver.
13 To him which divided the / Réd sea ínto parts: * for his mercy endúreth / for éver:
14 And made Israel to pass / thróugh the mídst of it: * for his mercy endúreth / for éver:
15 But overthrew Pharaoh and his host / ín the Réd sea: * for his mercy endúreth / for éver.
16 To him which led his people / thróugh the wílderness: * for his mercy endúreth / for éver.
17 To / hím which smóte great kings: * for his mercy endúreth / for éver:
18 — / Ánd slew fámous kings: * for his mercy endúreth / for éver:
19 Sihon / kíng of the Ámorites: * for his mercy endúreth / for éver:
20 And Og the / kíng of Báshan: * for his mercy endúreth / for éver: [250]
21 And gave their land / fór an héritage: * for his mercy endúreth / for éver:
22 Even an heritage unto Isra- / él his sérvant: * for his mercy endúreth / for éver.
23 Who remembered us / ín our lów estate: * for his mercy endúreth / for éver:
24 And hath redeemed us / fróm our énemies: * for his mercy endúreth / for éver.
25 Who giveth / fóod to all <u>flesh</u>: * for his mercy endúreth / for éver.
26 O give thanks unto the / Gód of héaven: * for his mercy endúreth / for éver.
Glory be to the / Fáther and tó the Son * and tó / the Hóly Ghost.
As it was in the beginning, is now, and / éver sháll be, * wórld with- / out énd. Amen.

Psalm-prayer. Almighty God, remember our low estate, and have mercy upon us, and as Thou didst in time of old give our fathers their enemies' land for an heritage, so set us free from sin, and bestow Thine heritage upon us; through Jesus Christ our Lord, who liveth and reigneth with Thee and the Holy Ghost, ever one God, world without end. Amen.

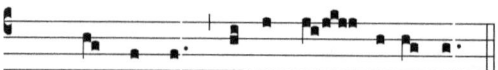

Ant. Sing us one * of the songs of Zi-on.

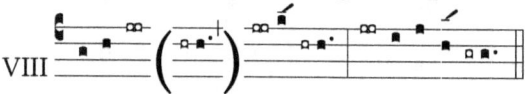

Psalm 137 *Super flumina Babylonis*

1 By the rivers of Babylon, thére we sat / <u>down</u>, * yea, we wept, when we re- / mémbered Zíon.
2 We hanged our harps upón the / wíllows * - / ín the mídst thereof.
3 For there they that carried us away captive requíred of us a song; † and they that wasted us requíred of us / <u>mirth</u>, * saying, Sing us one of the / sóngs of Zíon.
4 How shall we sing the LORD'S sóng in a / stránge land? * 5 If I forget thee, O Jerusalem, let my right hand for- / gét her cúnning.
6 If I do not remember thee, let my tongue cleave to the róof of my / <u>mouth</u>; * if I prefer not Jerusalem a- / bóve my chíef joy.
7 Remember, O LORD, the children of Edom in the dáy of Jer- / úsalem; * who said, Rase it, rase it, even to the foundá- / tion there<u>of</u>.
8 O daughter of Babylon, who árt to / bé destroyed; * happy shall he be, that rewardeth thee as / thóu hast sérved us.
9 Happy shall he be, that táketh and / dásheth * thy little / ónes agáinst the stones.
Glory be to the Fáther and / tó the Son * and / tó the Hóly Ghost.
As it was in the beginning, is now, and éver / shálll be, * wórld / without énd. Amen.

Psalm-prayer. O God, Almighty Looser of our captivity, grant that we may sing Thy praise with spiritual harmony, so that the lifting up of Thy right hand may restore to heavenly citizenship those whom the load of sin exiles from Thee; through Jesus Christ our Lord, who liveth and reigneth with Thee and the Holy Ghost, ever one God, world without end. Amen.

Ant. I will práise Thy náme, O Lord: * for Thy loving-kíndness and fór Thy

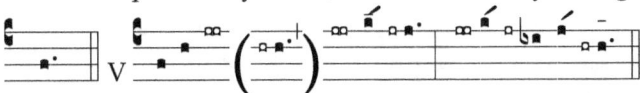

truth.

Psalm 138 *Confitebor tibi*
1 I will praise thee wíth my / whóle heart: * before the gods will I sing / práise unto <u>thee</u>.
2 I will worship toward thy holy temple, † and praise thy name for thy lovingkíndness and / fór thy truth: * for thou hast magnified thy / wórd above áll thy name.
3 In the day when I cried thou ánswer-eds*t* / <u>me</u>, * and strengthen-eds*t* me with / stréngth in my <u>soul</u>.
4 All the kings of the earth shall práise thee, O / <u>LORD</u>, * when they hear the / wórds of thy <u>mouth</u>.
5 Yea, they shall sing in the wáys of the / <u>LORD</u>: * for great is the / glóry óf the LORD.
6 Though the LORD be high, yet hath he respect únto the / lówly: * but the proud he / knóweth afár off.
7 Though I walk in the midst of trouble, thou wilt revive me: † thou shalt stretch forth thine hand against the wráth of mine / énemies, * and thy right / hánd shall sáve me.
8 The LORD will perfect that which concêrneth me: † thy mercy, O LORD, endúreth for / éver: * forsake not the / wórks of thíne own hands.
Glory be to the Fáther and / tó the Son * and / tó the Hóly Ghost.
As it was in the beginning, is now, and éver / sháll be, * - / wórld without énd. Amen.

Psalm-prayer. Multiply Thy strength, O Lord, in the souls of Thy humble servants, that while we ever worship Thee in Thy holy temple, we may, together with Thy holy angels, rejoice in beholding Thee; through Jesus Christ our Lord, who liveth and reigneth with Thee and the Holy Ghost, ever one God, world without end. Amen.

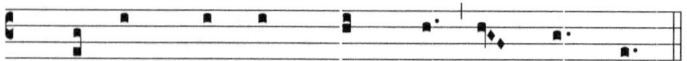

Ant. O LORD, thou hast searched me * and known me.
(Do not repeat in verse 1.)

Psalm 139i *Domine, probasti me*
1 [O LORD, thou hast searched me, and known me.] † 2 Thou knowest my downsitting and / míne uprísing, * thou understandest my / thóught afár off.
3 Thou compassest my / páth and my lýing down, * and art ac- / quáinted with áll my ways.
4 For there is not a / wórd in my tongue, * but, lo, O LORD, thou knowest it / áltogéther.
5 Thou hast beset me be- / hínd and before, * and laid thine / hánd upón me.
6 Such knowledge is too / wónderful fór me; * it is high, I can- / nót attain únto it.
7 Whither shall I / gó from thy spírit? * or whither shall I / flée from thy présence?
8 If I ascend up into / héaven, thóu art there: * if I make my bed in hell, be- / hóld, thou art there.
9 If I take the / wíngs of the mórning, * and dwell in the uttermost / párts of the sea;
10 Even there shall / thý hand léad me, * and thy right / hánd shall hóld me.
11 If I say, Surely the / dárkness shall cóver me; * even the night shall be / líght abóut me.
12 Yea, the darkness hideth nôt from thee; † but the night / shíneth ás the day: * the darkness and the light are / bóth alíke to thee.
Glory be to the / Fáther and tó the Son * and / tó the Hóly Ghost.
As it was in the beginning, is now, and / éver sháll be, * - / wórld without énd. Amen.

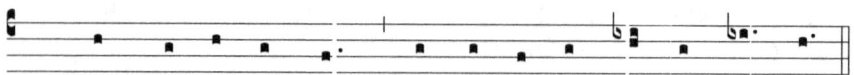

Ant. Márvellous áre thy works: * and that my soul knóweth ríght well.

Psalm 139ii *Quia tu*

13 For thóu hast pos- / séssed my reins: * thou hast covered me / ín my móther's womb.

14 I will praise thee; for I am fearfully and wónder- / fu*l*ly <u>made</u>: * marvellous are thy works; and that my soul / knóweth ríght well.

15 My substance was not hid from thee, when I was máde in / sécret, * and curiously wrought in the lowest / párts of the <u>earth</u>.

16 Thine eyes did see my substance, yet bé*i*ng un- / pérfect; * and in thy book all my / mémbers were wrítten,

Which in continuánce were / fáshioned, * when as yet / thére was nóne of them.

17 How precious also are thy thóughts unto / mé, O God! * how / gréat is the súm of them!

18 If I should count them, they are more in númber / thán the sand: * when I awake, / Í am still wíth thee.

19 Surely thou wilt slay the wícked, / O <u>God</u>: * depart from me / thérefore, ye blóody men.

20 For they speak agáinst thee / wíckedly, * and thine enemies / táke thy náme in vain.

21 Do not I hate them, O LÓRD, that / háte thee? * and am not I grieved with those that rise / úp agáinst thee?

22 I hate them with pérfect / hátred: * I / cóunt them mine énemies.

23 Search me, O Gód, and / knów my heart: * - / trý me, and knów my thoughts:

24 And see if there be any wícked / wáy in me, * and lead me in the way / éverlásting.

Glory be to the Fáther and / tó the Son * and / tó the Hóly Ghost.

As it was in the beginning, is now, and éver / sháll be, * - / wórld without énd. Amen.

Psalm-prayer. O God, protector of heaven and earth, in whose death hell was harrowed, by whose rising again the multitude of saints was gladdened; at whose ascension the host of angels exulted; we make our prayer to the exceeding might of so much glory, that led in the way everlasting, we may be protected by that arm wherein Thine honoured friends rejoice with Thee in heaven; who livest and reignest with the Father and the Holy Ghost, ever one God, world without end. Amen.

[253]

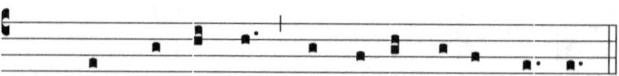

Ant. Grant not, O Lord * the desires of the wicked.

Psalm 140 *Eripe me, Domine*
1 Deliver me, O LORD, / fróm the évil man: * preserve / me fróm the víolent man;
2 Which imagine / míschiefs ín their heart; * continually are they gathered to- / géther for <u>war</u>.
3 They have sharpened their tongues / líke a sérpent; * adders' poison is / únder their <u>lips</u>.
4 Keep me, O LORD, from the hands of the wicked; † preserve me / fróm the víolent man; * who have purposed to o- / ver thrów my góings.
5 The proud have hid a snare for me, and cords; † they have spread a net / bý the wáyside; * - / théy have set gíns for me.
6 I said unto the LORD, Thóu / art my <u>God</u>: * hear the voice of my suppli- / cátions, O <u>LORD</u>.
7 O GOD the Lord, the strength of / mý salvátion, * thou hast covered my head in / the dáy of báttle.
8 Grant not, O LORD, the desires / óf the wícked: * further not his wicked device; / lest théy exált themselves.
9 As for the head of those that / cómpass mé about, * let the mischief of / their ówn lips cóver them.
10 Let burning coals fall upon them: † let them be cast ín- / to the fíre-; * into deep pits, that / they ríse not úp again.
11 Let not an evil speaker be es- / táblished ín the earth: * evil shall hunt the violent man / to óverthrów him.
12 I know that the LORD will maintain the cause óf / the afflícted, * and the / ríght of the <u>poor</u>.
13 Surely the righteous shall give thanks ún- / to thy <u>name</u>: * the upright shall / dwéll in thy présence.
Glory be to the Fá-/ ther and tó the Son * -/ and tó the Hóly Ghost.
As it was in the beginning, is now, and / éver shánl be, * - / wórld without énd. Amen.

Psalm-prayer. O God, strength of our salvation, defend Thy Church from the deadly poison of sectarians, that overshadowed by Thee, we may never be entangled by the cords of the enemy; through Jesus Christ our Lord, who liveth and reigneth with Thee and the Holy Ghost, ever one God, world without end. Amen.

[254]

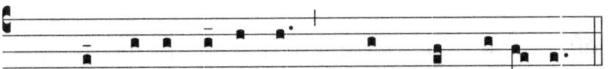

Ant. Lord, I cry unto thee, * make haste unto me. *(Do not repeat in verse 1.)*

Psalm 141 *Domine, clamavi*
1 [LORD, I cry unto thee: make háste / unto me;] * give ear unto my voice, when I / crý unto thee.
2 Let my prayer be set forth befóre / thee as íncense; * and the lifting up of my hands as / the évening sácrifice.
3 Set a watch, O / LÓRD, befóre my mouth; * keep the / dóor of my lips.
4 Incline not my heart to any êvil thing, † to practise wicked works with men that / wórk iníquity: * and let me not / éat of their dáinties.
5 Let the righteous smite me; it shall / bé a kíndness: * and let him reprove me; it shall be an / éxcellent óil-,
Which / sháll not bréak my head: * for yet my prayer also shall be / in théir calámities.
6 When their judges are overthrown in / stóny pláces, * they shall hear / my wórds; for théy are sweet.
7 Our bones are scattered / át the gráve's mouth, * as when one cutteth and cleav- / eth wóod upón the earth.
8 But mine eyes are unto / thée, O GÓD the Lord: * in thee is my trust; leave / nót my soul déstitute.
9 Keep me from the snares which / théy have láid for me, * and the gins of the work- / ers óf iníquity.
10 Let the wicked fall ín- / to their ówn nets, * whilst / that Í withál escape.
**Glory be to the Fá- / ther and tó the Son * - / and tó the Hóly Ghost.
As it was in the beginning, is now, and / éver sháll be, * - / wórld without énd. Amen.**

Psalm-prayer. Hearken to our voice, O Lord, as we cry unto Thee; reprove us, not in anger, but in mercy when we sin; set a watch before our mouth, and suffer not our heart to incline to words of sin and wickedness, but cause our tongue to rejoice evermore in Thy glorious praise; through Jesus Christ our Lord, who liveth and reigneth with Thee and the Holy Ghost, ever one God, world without end. Amen.

[255]

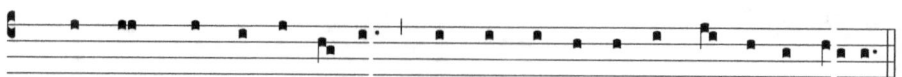

Ant. O Lord, thou árt my réfuge: * and my portion in the lánd of the líving.

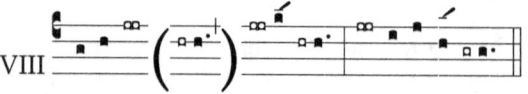

VIII

Psalm 142 *Voce mea*

1 I cried unto the LÓRD with my / voice; * with my voice unto the LORD did I make my / súpplicátion.
2 I poured out my compláint be- / fóre him; * I shewed before / hím my tróuble.
3 When my spirit was overwhélmed with- / ín me, * then thou knéw- / est my path.
In the wáy where- / ín I walked * have they privily / láid a snáre for me.
4 I looked on myríght hand, / ánd beheld, * but there was no man / thát would knów me:
Réfuge / fáiled me; * no man cáred / for my soul.
5 I críed unto / thée, O LORD: * I said, Thou art my refuge and my portion in the lánd / of the líving.
6 Attend unto my cry; for Í am brought / véry low: * deliver me from my persecutors; for they are strón- / ger than I.
7 Bring my soul out of prison, that Í may / práise thy name: * the righteous shall compass me about; for thou shalt deal bóun- / tifully wíth me.
Glory be to the Fáther and / tó the Son * and / tó the Hóly Ghost.
As it was in the beginning, is now, and éver / shall be, * wórld / without énd. Amen.

Psalm-prayer. O Lord, we make our prayer unto Thee with a lowly voice, beseeching Thy lovingkindness, that by Thy help, who art our hope, we may obtain with Thine elect a portion in the land of the living; through Jesus Christ our Lord, who liveth and reigneth with Thee and the Holy Ghost, ever one God, world without end. Amen.

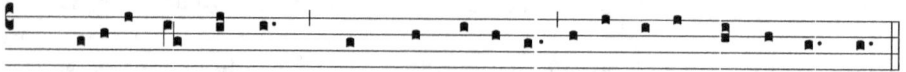

Ant. Deliver me, O Lord, * fróm mine énemies: I flee unto Thée to híde me.

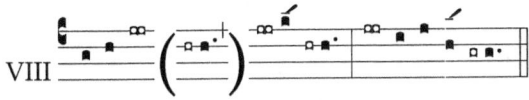

Psalm 143 *Domine, exaudi*

1 Hear my prayer, O LORD, give ear to my súppli- / cátions: * in thy faithfulness answer me, and / ín thy ríghteousness.
2 And enter not into judgment wíth thy / sérvant: * for in thy sight shall no man lív- / ing be jústified.
3 For the enemy hath persecúted my / soul; * he hath smitten my life dówn / to the ground;
He hath made me to dwéll in / dárkness, * as those that / háve been lóng dead.
4 Therefore is my spirit overwhélmed with- / ín me; * my heart withín / me is désolate. [256]
5 I remember the dâys of old; † I meditáte on / áll thy works; * I muse on the wórk / of thy hands.
6 I stretch forth my hánds unto / thee: * my soul thirsteth after thee, / ás a thírsty land.
7 Hear me speedily, O LORD: my spírit / fáileth: * hide not thy face from me, lest I be like unto them that go down ín- / to the pit.
8 Cause me to hear thy lovingkindness ín the / mórning; * for in thée / do I trust:
Cause me to know the way whereín I should / walk; * for I lift up my sóul / unto thee.
9 Deliver me, O LORD, fróm mine / énemies: * I flee unto / thée to híde me.
10 Teach me to do thy will; for thóu art my / God: * thy spirit is good; lead me into the / lánd of úprightness.
11 Quicken me, O LORD, fór thy / náme's sake: * for thy righteousness' sake bring my sóul / out of tróuble.
12 And of thy mercy cut off mine ênemies, † and destroy all them thát af- / flíct my soul: * for Í / am thy sérvant.
Glory be to the Fáther and / tó the Son * and / tó the Hóly Ghost.
As it was in the beginning, is now, and éver / sháll be, * wórld / without énd. Amen.

Psalm-prayer. O God, who madest joy to be heard in the morning of Thy holy resurrection, when, returning from the grave, Thou filledst the earth with gladness, after leaving it in darkness, we beseech the unspeakable majesty of Thy power, that as Thou madest the apostolic band rejoice then in Thy holy arising, so Thou wouldst enlighten with the brightness of heavenly radiance Thy Church, which with outstretched hands implores Thy mercy; who livest and reignest with the Father and the Holy Ghost, ever one God, world without end. Amen.

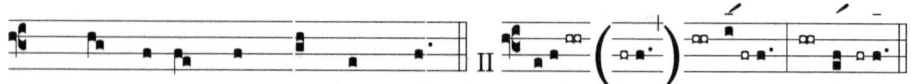

Ant. Bless-ed be * the Lord my strength. *(Do not repeat in verse 1.)*
Psalm 144i *Benedictus Dominus*
1 [Bless-ed be the LORD my strength,] † which téacheth my / hánds to war, * and my fíngers / to <u>fight</u>:
2 My goodness, ánd my / fórtress; * my high tower, and mý de- / líverer;
My shield, and hé in / whóm I trust; * who subdueth my péople / únder me.
3 LORD, what is man, that thou takest knówledge of / <u>him</u>! * or the son of man, that thou mákest ac- / cóunt of him!
4 Man is líke to / vánity: * his days are as a shadow that pásseth / a<u>way</u>.
5 Bow thy heavens, O LÓRD, and come / <u>down</u>: * touch the móuntains, and / théy shall smoke.
6 Cast forth líghtning, and / scátter them: * shoot out thine arrows, ánd des- / tróy them.
7 Send thine hand from above; † rid me, and deliver me óut of great / wáters, * from the hánd of strange / chíldren;
8 Whose mouth spéaketh / vánity, * and their right hand is a right hánd of / fálsehood.
Glory be to the Fáther and / tó the Son * and tó the / Hóly Ghost.
[257] **As it was in the beginning, is now, and éver / sháll be, * wórld without / énd. Amen.**

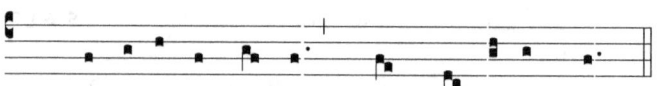

Ant. Happy ís that péople: * whose Gód is the <u>LORD</u>.

Psalm 144ii *Deus, canticum*
9 I will sing a new song / únto thée, O God: * upon a psaltery and an instrument of ten strings will I sing / práises únto thee.
10 It is he that giveth sal- / vátion únto kings: * who delivereth David his servant / fróm the húrtful sword.
11 Rid me, and deliver me from the hand of strange children, † whose mouth / spéaketh vánity, * and their right hand is a right / hánd of fálsehood:

12 That our sons may be as plants grown / úp in their youth; * that our daughters may be as corner stones, polished after the similitude / óf a pálace:
13 That our garners may be full, affording all / mánner of store: * that our sheep may bring forth thousands and ten / thóusands ín our streets:
14 That our oxen may be strong to labour; † that there be no breaking / ín, nor góing out; * that there be no com- / pláining ín our streets.
15 Happy is that people, / thát is in súch a case: * yea, happy is that people, whose Gód / is the LORD.
Glory be to the / Fáther and tó the Son * - and / tó the Hóly Ghost.
As it was in the beginning, is now, and / éver shálll be, * - wórld / without énd. Amen.

Psalm-prayer. Teach us, O Lord, to resist our hurtful sins with spiritual weapons, lest, made subject to earthly vanity, we be drawn from the governance of Thy Word; through Jesus Christ our Lord, who liveth and reigneth with Thee and the Holy Ghost, ever one God, world without end. Amen.

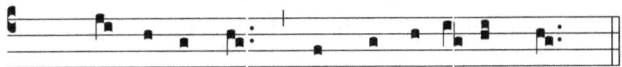

Ant. Gréat is the Lord: * and gréatly tó be praised.

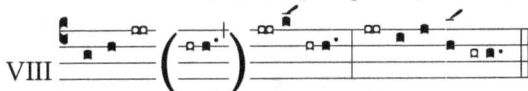

VIII

Psalm 145i *Exaltabo te, Deus*
1 I will extól thee, my / Gód, O king; * and I will bless thy name for év- / er and éver.
2 Every dáy will I / bléss thee; * and I will praise thy name for év- / er and éver.
3 Great is the LORD, and gréatly / tó be praised; * and his greatness / ís unséarchable.
4 One generation shall praise thy works tó an- / óther, * and shall de- / cláre thy míghty acts.
5 I will speak of the glorious honour óf thy / májesty, * and / óf thy wóndrous works.
6 And men shall speak of the might of thy térrible / acts: * and I will de- / cláre thy gréatness.
7 They shall abundantly utter the memory of thý great / góodness, * and shall síng / of thy ríghteousness.

Glory be to the Fáther and / tó the Son * and / tó the Hóly Ghost.
As it was in the beginning, is now, and éver / sháll be, * wórld / without énd. Amen.

Ant. The Lórd * is góod to all: and His tender mercies are óver áll His works.

Psalm 145ii *Miserator et misericors*

8 The LORD is gracious, and fúll / of compássion; * slow to anger, / ánd of great mércy.
9 The / LÓRD is góod to all: * and his tender mercies / are óver áll his works.
10 All thy works shall práise / thee, O LORD; * and / thy sáints shall bléss thee.
11 They shall speak of the glory / óf thy kíngdom, * and / tálk of thy pówer;
12 To make known to the sons of / mén his míghty acts, * and the glorious majes- / ty óf his kíngdom.
13 Thy kingdom is an ever- / lásting kíngdom, * and thy dominion endureth throughout / all génerátions.
14 The LORD up- / hóldeth áll that fall, * and raiseth up all / those thát be bówed down.
15 The eyes of all wáit / upon thee; * and thou givest them their / méat in due séason.
16 Thou óp- / enest thíne hand, * and satisfiest the desire / of évery líving thing.

Glory be to the Fá- / ther and tó the Son * - / and tó the Hóly Ghost.
As it was in the beginning, is now, and / éver sháll be, * - / wórld without énd. Amen.

Ant. The Lord * is righteous in all his ways: and holy in all his works.
(Do not repeat in verse 17.)

Psalm 145iii *Justus Dominus*

17 [The LORD is rígh- / teous in áll his ways, * and / hóly in áll his works.]
18 The LORD is nigh unto all them that cáll / upon him, * to all that / cáll upon hím in truth.
19 He will fulfil the desire of / thém that féar him: * he also will hear their / crý, and will sáve them.
20 The LORD preserveth all / thém that lóve him: * but all the / wícked will hé destroy. [259]
21 My mouth shall speak the práise / of the LORD: * and let all flesh bless his holy name for / éver and éver.
Glory be to the Fá- / ther and tó the Son * - / and tó the Hóly Ghost.
As it was in the beginning, is now, and / éver sháll be, * - / wórld without énd. Amen.

Psalm-prayer. O Lord, ruler of all ages, who ministerest spiritual food to our soul in due season; grant that we may evermore bless Thee, and faithfully speak of Thy majesty unto the sons of men; through Jesus Christ our Lord, who liveth and reigneth with Thee and the Holy Ghost, ever one God, world without end. Amen.

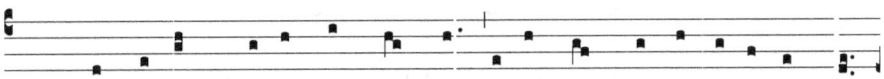

Ant. While I live, * wíll I práise the Lord: I will sing praises unto my God

while I have ány béing.

Psalm 146 *Lauda, anima mea*

1 Praise ye the LORD. Praise the LORD, O my soul. † 2 While I live / wíll I práise the LORD: * I will sing praises unto my God while I / have ány béing.
3 Put not your / trúst in prínces, * nor in the son of man, / in whóm there ís no help.
4 His breath goeth forth, he re- / túrneth tó his earth; * in that very / dáy his thoughts pérish.
5 Happy is he that hath the God of / Jácob fór his help, * whose hope / is ín the LÓRD his God:

6 Which made heaven, and earth, the sea, and áll / that thereín is: * which keep- / eth trúth for éver:
7 Which executeth judgment fór / the op<u>pressed</u>: * which giveth / fóod to the húngry.
The LORD lóos- / eth the prísoners: * 8 the LORD openeth the / éyes of the <u>blind</u>:
The LORD raiseth thém / that are bówed down: * the LORD / lóveth the ríghteous:
9 The LORD preserveth the strangers; † he relieveth the father- / léss and wídow: * but the way of the wicked / he túrneth úpside down.
10 The LORD shall / réign for éver, * even thy God, O Zion, unto all generations. / Práise ye the <u>LORD</u>.
Glory be to the Fá- / ther and tó the Son * - / and tó the Hóly Ghost.
As it was in the beginning, is now, and / éver sháll be, * - / wórld without énd. Amen.

Psalm-prayer. O glorious and almighty God, in whom the souls of the blessed place all the confidence of their hope, grant that we, enlightened by Thy help, may be able to love Thee always with a pure mind; through Jesus Christ our Lord, who liveth and reigneth with Thee and the Holy Ghost, ever one God, world without end. Amen.

[260]

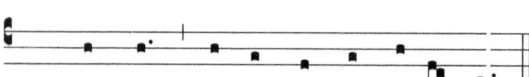

Ant. The Lord * healeth the broken in heart.

Psalm 147i *Laudate Dominum*

1 Praise ye the LORD: for it is good to sing praises / únto our <u>God</u>; * for it is pleasant; and / práise is cómely.
2 The LORD doth build / úp Jerúsalem: * he gathereth together the óut- / casts of Ísrael.
3 He healeth the / bróken in <u>heart</u>, * - and / bíndeth úp their wounds.
4 He telleth the / númber óf the stars; * he calleth them / áll by their <u>names</u>.
5 Great is our Lord, and / óf great pówer: * his understánd- / ing is ínfinite.
6 The LORD / lífteth úp the meek: * he casteth the wicked / dówn to the <u>ground</u>.
7 Sing unto the / LÓRD with thanksgíving; * sing praise upon the harp / únto our <u>God</u>:

8 Who covereth the heaven with clouds, † who prepareth / ráin for the earth, * who maketh grass to grow up- / ón the móuntains.
9 He giveth / tó the béast his food, * and to the young / rávens which cry.
10 He delighteth not in the / stréngth of the horse: * he taketh not pleasure in the / légs of a man.
11 The LORD taketh pleasure in / thém that féar him, * in those that hópe / in his mércy.
Glory be to the / Fáther and tó the Son * - and / tó the Hóly Ghost.
As it was in the beginning, is now, and / éver shálll be, * - wórld / without énd. Amen.

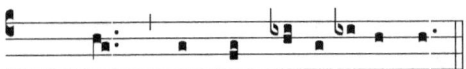

Ant. Praise * the Lord, O Jer-u-sa-lem. *(Do not repeat in verse 12.)*

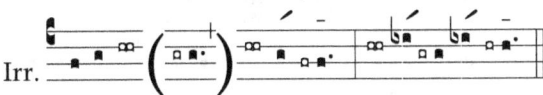
Irr.

Psalm 147ii *Lauda, Jerusalem*
12 [Praise the LORD, Ó Jer- / úsalem;] * praise thy / Gód, O Zíon.
13 For he hath strengthened the bárs of / thy gates; * he hath blessed thy / chíldren withín thee.
14 He maketh péace in thy / bórders, * and filleth thee with the / fínest óf the wheat.
15 He sendeth forth his commándment up- / ón earth: * his word runneth / véry swíftly.
16 He gíveth / snów like wool: * he scattereth the / hóarfrost like áshes.
17 He casteth forth his íce like / mórsels: * who can / stánd befóre his cold?
18 He sendeth out his wórd, and / mélteth them: * he causeth his wind to blow, / ánd the wáters flow.
19 He sheweth his word únto / Jácob, * his statutes and his judgments / únto Ísrael.
20 He hath not dealt so with ány / nátion: * and as for his judgments, they have not known them. / Práise ye the LORD.
Glory be to the Fáther and / tó the Son * and / tó the Hóly Ghost.
As it was in the beginning, is now, and éver / shálll be, * - / wórld without énd. Amen.

Psalm-prayer. O God, builder of the heavenly Jerusalem, who both numberest the multitude of the stars, and callest them all by their names; heal, we pray Thee, them that are broken of heart, gather together the outcasts, and enrich us with Thine infinite wisdom; through Jesus Christ our Lord, who liveth and reigneth with Thee and the Holy Ghost, ever one God, world without end. Amen.

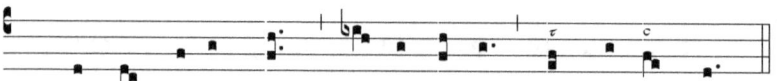

Ant. Ye kings of the earth, * ánd all péople: práise ye the LORD.

Psalm 148 *Laudate Dominum*
1 Praise ye the LORD. Praise ye the LORD / fróm the héavens: * - / práise him ín the heights.
2 Praise ye him, / áll his ángels: * - práise / ye him, áll his hosts.
3 - / Práise ye him, sún and moon: * praise him, / áll ye stárs of light.
4 Praise him, ye / héavens of héavens, * and ye waters that be a- / bóve the héavens.
5 Let them praise the / náme of the LORD: * for he commanded, and they / wére creáted.
6 He hath also stablished them for / éver and éver: * he hath made a de- / crée which sháll not pass.
7 Praise the / LÓRD from the earth, * - ye / drágons, ánd all deeps:
8 Fire, and hail; / snów, and vápour; * stormy wind ful- / fílling his word:
9 — / Móuntains, ánd all hills; * fruitful trees, / ánd all cédars:
10 Beasts, / ánd all cáttle; * creeping / thíngs, and flýing fowl:
11 Kings of the earth, / ánd all péople; * princes, and all / júdges óf the earth:
12 Both young / mén, and máidens; * - old / mén, and chíldren:
13 Let them praise the name of the LORD: † for his name a- / lóne is éxcellent; * his glory is above the / éarth and héaven.
14 He also exalteth the / hórn of his péople, * - the / práise of áll his saints;
Even of the / chíldren of Ísrael, * a people near unto him. / Práise ye the LORD.
Glory be to the / Fáther and tó the Son * - and / tó the Hóly Ghost.
As it was in the beginning, is now, and / éver sháll be, * - wórld / without énd. Amen.

Psalm-prayer. O God, supreme and most high power of the heavenly dwellings, grant unto Thy servants that as all things which we behold were created by Thy command, so what Thou commandest may be observed under Thy keeping; through Jesus Christ our Lord, who liveth and reigneth with Thee and the Holy Ghost, ever one God, world without end. Amen.

[262]

Ant. The Lord taketh pleasure * ín his péople: he will beau-ti-fy the méek

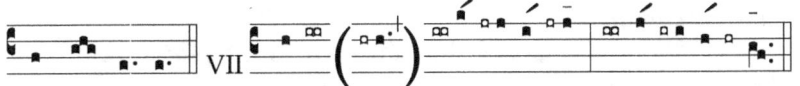

with salvátion.

Psalm 149 *Cantate Domino*
1 Praise ye the LORD. Sing unto the / LÓRD a néw song, * and his praise in the congre- / gátion of <u>saints</u>.
2 Let Israel rejoice in / hím that máde him: * let the children of Zion be / jóyful ín their King.
3 Let them praise his / náme in the <u>dance</u>: * let them sing praises unto him with the / tímbrel and <u>harp</u>.
4 For the LORD taketh pleasure / ín his péople: * he will beautify the / méek with salvátion.
5 Let the saints be / jóyful in glóry: * let them sing a- / lóud upón their beds.
6 Let the high praises of / Gód be ín their mouth, * and a twoedged / swórd in their <u>hand</u>;
7 To execute vengeance up- / ón the héathen, * and punishments up- / ón the péople;
8 To / bínd their kíngs with chains, * and their nobles with / fétters of íron;
9 To execute upon them the / júdgment wrítten: * this honour have all his saints. / Práise ye the <u>LORD</u>.
**Glory be to the / Fáther and tó the Son * and / tó the Hóly Ghost.
As it was in the beginning, is now, and / éver shǎll be, * - / wórld without énd. Amen.**

Psalm-prayer. O God, author of all goodness, who beautifiest all meekness that humbly confesseth Thee, grant that as Thou makest the saints to be joyful in glory, so Thou wouldst vouchsafe to keep the present Church undefiled by the pleasures of this world; through Jesus Christ our Lord, who liveth and reigneth with Thee and the Holy Ghost, ever one God, world without end. Amen.

Ant. Let ev*e*rything * that háth the bréath of life: práise the Lórd of life.

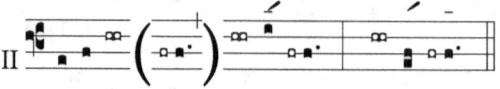

Psalm 150 *Laudate Dominum*
1 Praise ye the LORD. Praise God in his sánctu- / áry: * praise him in the firmament óf his / pówer.
2 Praise him fór his / míghty acts: * praise him according to his éxcellent / gréatness.
3 Praise him with the sóund of the / trúmpet: * praise him with the psáltery / and <u>harp</u>.
[263] 4 Praise him with the tímbrel and / <u>dance</u>: * praise him with stringed instruménts and / órgans.
5 Praise him upon the loud cymbals: † praise him upon the high sóunding / cýmbals. * 6 Let every thing that hath breath praise the LORD. Práise ye / the <u>LORD</u>.
Glory be to the Fáther and / tó the Son * and tó the / Hóly Ghost.
As it was in the beginning, is now, and éver / shǻll be, * wórld without / énd. Amen.

Psalm-prayer. O God, who art the object of praise from the zeal of the angels, and takest pleasure also in the worship of men, not as needing us for anything, but to find room in us for displaying Thy goodness, who willest that the habit of Thy praise should be the fruit of praising; hearken to our prayers, and grant that the clear confession of our faith may be Thy trumpet; our lips, and the well-attuned service of our inward and outward being, Thy cymbals; our souls, Thine harps; and altogether sweetly sing in clear strains the praise of Thy mercy; through Jesus Christ our Lord, who liveth and reigneth with Thee and the Holy Ghost, ever one God, world without end. Amen.

Weekday Propers

Appropriate for use in ordinary time (green seasons) or when no seasonal propers are given. In ordinary time, the seasonal propers are appropriate for Sunday. The Sunday antiphons for Benedictus *and* Magnificat *from the weekday propers can be used* ad libitum.

Sunday: Morning Prayer

Responsory

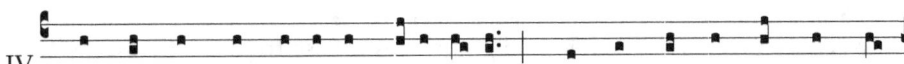

℟. Incline my heart unto thy téstimónies, ‡ that my way be stáblished ín thy word. ℟. Incline my... ℣. Turn away mine eyes from beholding van-i-

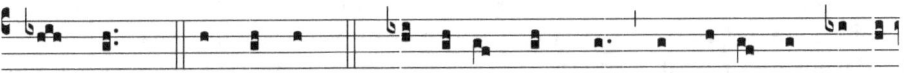

ty; and quicken thou mé in thy way. ‡ That my way... ℣. Glory be to the

Fáther and tó the Son : and tó the Hóly Ghost. ℟. Incline my...

Hymn. **Nocte surgentes.** *6th cent., trans. by P. Dearmer*

1. Father, we praise Thee, now the night is over, / Active and watchful, stand we all before Thee; / Singing we offer prayer and meditation: / Thus we adore Thee.
2. Monarch of all things, fit us for Thy mansions; / Banish our weakness, health and wholeness sending; / Bring us to heaven, where Thy Saints united / Joy without ending.
3. All-holy Father, Son and equal Spirit, / Trinity bless-ed, send us Thy salvation; / Thine is the glory, gleaming and resounding / Through all creation. Amen.

Or: **En dies est dominica.** *Thomas à Kempis, † 1471, trans. by J. M. Neale, alt.*

1. Again the Lord's own day is here, / The day to Christian people dear, / As, week by week, it bids them tell / How Jesus rose from death and hell.
2. For by His flock their Lord declared / His resurrection should be shared; / And we who trust in Him to save / With Him are risen from the grave.
3. We, one and all, of His possessed, / Are with exceeding treasures blessed; / For all He did, and all He bare, / He gives us as our own to share.
4. Eternal glory, rest on high, / A blessed immortality, / True peace and gladness, and a throne, / Are all His gifts, and all our own.
5. And therefore unto Thee we sing, / O Lord of peace, eternal King; / Thy love we praise, Thy name adore, / Both on this day and evermore.
6. All laud to God the Father be; / All praise, eternal Son, to Thee; / All glory, as is ever meet, / To God the Holy Paraclete. Amen.

Versicle
℣. The LORD reigneth, he is clothed with majesty.
℟. The LORD is clothed with strength, wherewith he hath girded himself.

Antiphon for Benedictus: from the Propers (pp. 389-569), or: [265]

Through the tender mércy * óf our God : the dayspring from on high hath

vís-i-ted us.

Luke 1:68-79 *Benedictus*
☩ |Bless-| ed be the Lord / Gód of Ísrael; * for he hath visited and re- / déemed his péople,
|And| hath raised up an horn of sal- / vátion fór us * in the house of his / sérvant Dávid;
|As| he spake by the mouth of his / hóly próphets, * which have been / sínce the wórld began:
|That| we should be saved / fróm our énemies, * and from the hand of / áll that háte us;
|To| perform the mercy promised / tó our fáthers, * and to remember his / hóly cóvenant;
|The| oath which he sware to our / fáther Ábraham, * that he would / gránt unto us,
|That| we being delivered out of the / hánd of our énemies * might serve / hím without fear,
|In| holiness and righteous- / néss befóre him, * all the / dáys of our life.
|And| thou, child, shalt be called the prophet / óf the Híghest: * for thou shalt go before the face of the / Lórd to prepáre his ways;
|To| give knowledge of salvation / únto his péople * by the re- / míssion óf their sins,
|Through| the tender / mércy óf our God; * whereby the dayspring from on high hath / vísited us,
|To| give light to them that sit in darkness and in the / shádow of death, * to guide our feet / ínto the wáy of peace.
|Glo-| ry be to the / Fáther and tó the Son * and / tó the Hóly Ghost.
|As| it was in the beginning, is now, and / éver shálll be, * - / wórld without énd. Amen.
Antiphon repeated.

Service continues on p. 41.

[266]

Sunday: Daytime Prayer

Responsory

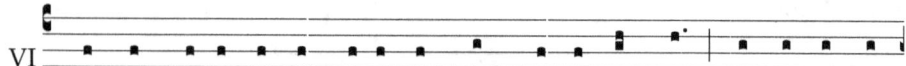

℟. Uphold me according unto thy wórd, that Í may live:‡ and let me not

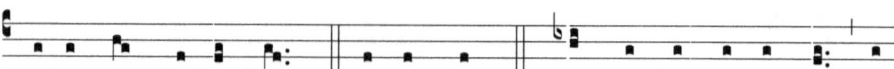

be ashámed of my <u>hope</u>. ℟. Uphold me... ℣. Hold thou me up, O Lord, and

Í shall be <u>safe</u>.‡ And let... ℣. Glory be to the Fáther and tó the Son : and tó

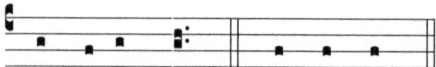

the Hóly Ghost. ℟. Uphold me...

Kyrie and Lord's Prayer (p. 52)

Versicle
℣. The LORD is my shepherd; I shâll not want.
℟. He maketh me to lie down in green pastures.
Service continues on p. 53.

Sunday: Evening Prayer

Responsory

℟. Redeem me, O LORD, and be mérciful ún- to me, ‡ for my foot standeth

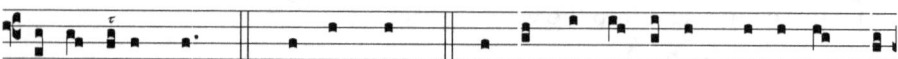

ín an éven place. ℟. Redeem me... ℣. In the congregations wíll I bléss the

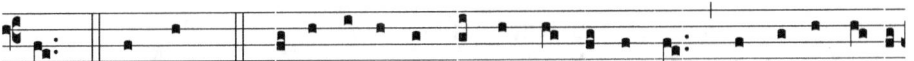

LORD. ‡ For my... ℣. Glory be to the Fáther and tó the Son : and tó the Hóly

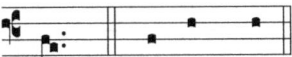

Ghost. ℟. Redeem me...

Hymn. **Lucis Creator optime.** *6ᵗʰ cent., trans. by J. M. Neale* [267]

1. O blest Creator of the light, / Who mak'st the day with radiance bright, / And o'er the forming world didst call / The light from chaos first of all;
2. Whose wisdom joined in meet array / The morn and eve, and named them day: / Night comes with all its darkling fears; / Regard Thy people's prayers and tears,
3. Lest, sunk in sin, and whelmed with strife, / They lose the gift of endless life; / While thinking but the thoughts of time, / They weave new chains of woe and crime.
4. But grant them grace that they may strain / The heavenly gate and prize to gain: / Each harmful lure aside to cast, / And purge away each error past.
5. O Father, that we ask be done, / Through Jesus Christ, Thine only Son; / Who, with the Holy Ghost and Thee, / Doth live and reign eternally. / Amen.

Versicle

℣. Let my prayers be set forth before Thee as incense:
℟. And the lifting up of my hands as the evening sacrifice.

Antiphon for Magnificat: From the Propers (389-569), or:

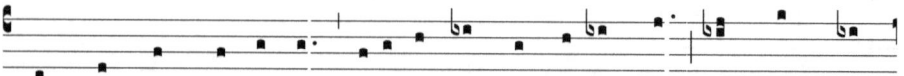

Christ our Lord and Savior, * eternal Gód and Máry's Son : we práise Thee

foréver.

Luke 1:46-55 *Magnificat*

✠ |My| soul / doth mágnifý the Lord, * |and| my spirit hath rejoiced in Gód / my Sáviour.

For / he háth regárded * |the| low estate of hís / handmáiden:

For, / behóld, from hénceforth * |all| generations shall cáll / me bléss-ed.

|For| he that is mighty / hath dóne to mé great things; * |and| hó- / ly ís his name.

|And| his mercy is / on thém that féar him * |from| generation to gén- / erátion.

|He| hath / shewed stréngth with his arm; * |he| hath scattered the proud in the imaginá- / tion óf their hearts.

|He| hath put down / the míghty fróm their seats, * |and| exalted thém / of lów degree.

|He| hath filled / the húngry with góod things; * |and| the rich he hath sent émp- / ty away.

|He| hath holpen / his sérvant Ísrael, * |in| remembrance óf / his mércy;
|As| he / spake tó our fáthers, * |to| Abraham, and to his séed / for éver.

**|Glo-| ry be to / the Fáther and tó the Son * |and| tó / the Hóly Ghost.
|As| it was in the beginning, is now, / and éver sháll be, * |wórld| with- / out énd. Amen.**

[268]   *Antiphon repeated.*
Service continues on p. 59.

Monday: Morning Prayer

Responsory

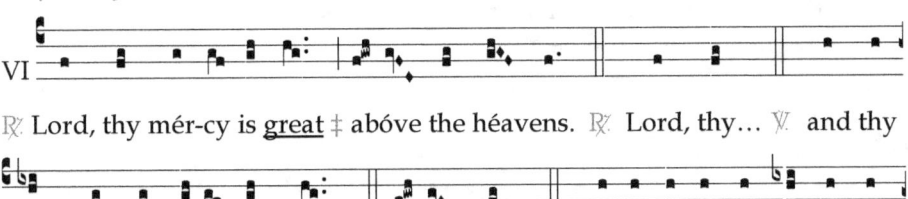

℟ Lord, thy mér-cy is <u>great</u> ‡ abóve the héavens. ℟ Lord, thy... ℣ and thy

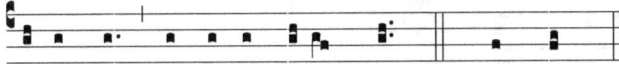

truth reacheth únto the <u>clouds</u>. ‡ Above the... ℣ Glory be to the Fáther and

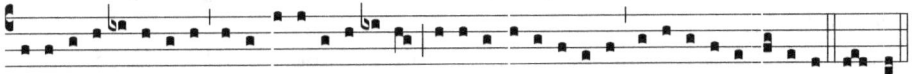

tó the Son : and tó the Hóly Ghost. ℟ Lord, thy...

Hymn. **Splendor paternae gloriae.** *St. Ambrose, † 397, composite trans.*

1. O Splendor of God's glory bright, / Who bringest forth the light from Light; / O Light of Light, light's Fountain-spring; / O Day, our days enlightening:
2. Come, very Sun of truth and love, / Come in Thy radiance from above / And shed the Holy Spirit's ray / On all we think or do today.
3. Likewise to Thee our prayers ascend, / Father of glory without end, / Father of saving grace, for power / to conquer in temptation's hour.
4. Teach us to work with all our might; / Beat back the devil's threatening spite; / Turn all to good that seems most ill; / Help us our calling to fulfill.
5. Direct and govern heart and mind, / With body chaste and disciplined; / Let faith her eager fires renew / And hate the false and love the true.
6. On Christ, the true Bread, let us feed, / Let Him to us be drink indeed, / And let us taste with joyfulness / The Holy Spirit's plenteousness.
7. Oh, joyful be the livelong day, / Our thoughts as pure as morning ray, / Our faith like noonday's glowing height, / Our souls undimmed by shades of night.
8. The dawn begins to speed her way, / Let the true Dawn Himself display, / The Son with God the Father One, / And God the Father in the Son.
9. All praise to God the Father be, / All praise, eternal Son, to Thee, / Whom with the Spirit we adore / Forever and forevermore. Amen.

Versicle

℣. O satisfy us early with thy mercy:

℟. That we may rejoice and be glad.

[269] *Antiphon for Benedictus*

☩ Bless-ed be * the LORD God of Is-ra-el. *(Do not repeat in the Canticle.)*

VI

Luke 1:68-79 *Benedictus*

[☩ Bless-ed be the Lord Gód of Ísrael;] * for he hath visited and re- / déemed his péople,

| And hath | raised up an horn of sal- / vátion fór us * in the house of his / sérvant Dávid;

| As he | spake by the mouth of his / hóly próphets, * which have been / sínce the wórld began:

| That we | should be saved / fróm our énemies, * and from the hand of / áll that háte us;

| To per- | form the mercy promised / tó our fáthers, * and to remember his / hóly cóvenant;

| The oath | which he sware to our / fáther Ábraham, * that he would gránt / unto us,

| That we | being delivered out of the / hánd of our énemies * might serve hím / without fear,

| In ho- | liness and righteous- / néss befóre him, * all the dáys / of our life.

| And thou, | child, shalt be called the prophet / óf the Híghest: * for thou shalt go before the face of the Lórd / to prepáre his ways;

| To give | knowledge of salvation / únto his péople * by the re- / míssion óf their sins,

| Through the | tender / mércy óf our God; * whereby the dayspring from on high hath vís- / ited us,

| To give | light to them that sit in darkness and in the / shádow of death, * to guide our feet ín- / to the wáy of peace.

| Glory | be to the / Fáther and tó the Son * - and / tó the Hóly Ghost.

| As it | was in the beginning, is now, and / éver shálll be, * - wórld / without énd. Amen.

Antiphon repeated.

Service continues on p. 41.

Monday: Daytime Prayer

Responsory

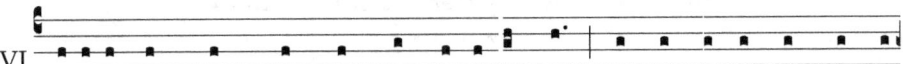

℟ Deliver me, LORD, and have mércy upón me, ‡ for thy lovingkindness ís

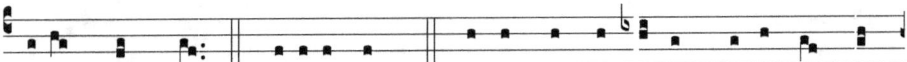

befóre mine eyes. ℟ Deliver me... ℣ In the congregations wíll I bléss the

LORD. ‡ For thy... ℣ Glory be to the Fáther and tó the Son : and tó the Hóly

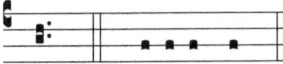

Ghost. ℟ Deliver me...

Kyrie and Lord's Prayer (p. 52)

Versicle
℣ O LORD thou art my help, forsâke me not.
℟ Take not thy hand from me, O God, my salvation.

Collects: **Collect of the week**

Da Pacem

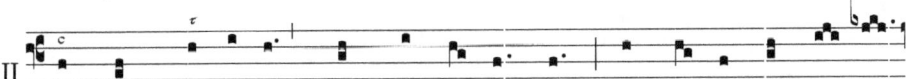

Grant peace graciously, * Lord God, in our times: For there is none oth- er

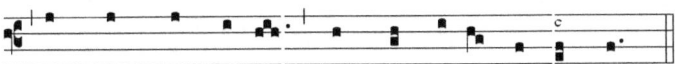

that could fight for us, but Thou alone, O our God.

℣. Peace be withîn thy walls:
℟. And prosperity within thy pâlaces.
℣. Let us pray. O Lord, we beseech Thee mercifully to hear the prayers of Thy church that we, being delivered from all adversities and serving Thee with a quiet mind, may enjoy Thy peace all the days of our life; through Jesus Christ, Thy Son, our Lord. ℟. Amen.

[271] *For the Church*

VIII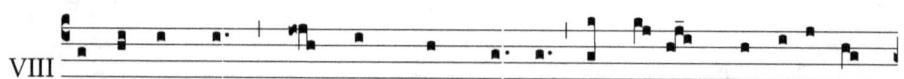

O God of hosts, * look down from heaven, and behold, and visit this

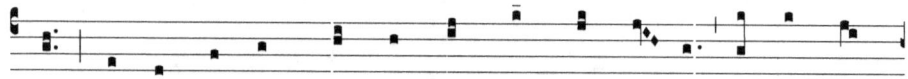

vine: And the vineyard which thy right hand hath planted, and the branch

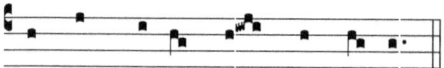

that thou madest strong for thyself.

℣. Do good in thy good pleasure unto Zion:
℟. Build thou the walls of Jerûsalem.
℣. Let us pray. O God, our Protector, behold, and look upon the face of Thine Anointed, who hath given Himself for the redemption of all, and grant that from the rising of the sun to the going down thereof Thy name may be great among the Gentiles and that in every place sacrifice and a pure offering may be made unto Thy name; through the same Jesus Christ, Thy Son, our Lord, who liveth and reigneth with Thee and the Holy Ghost, ever one God, world without end. ℟. Amen.
Service continues on p. 53.

MONDAY: EVENING PRAYER

Responsory

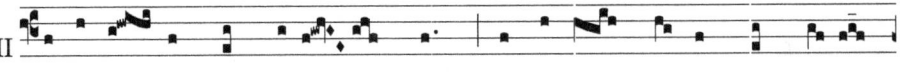

℟. I will pay my vows ún-to the LORD ‡ in the courts of the hóuse of the

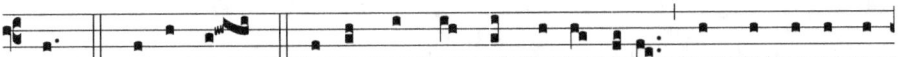

LORD. ℟. I will pay... ℣. I will take the cup of salvation, and call upon the

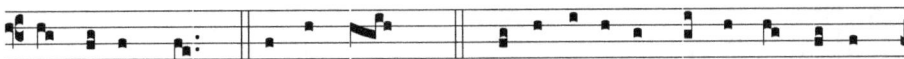

náme of the LORD. ‡ In the courts... ℣. Glory be to the Fáther and tó the

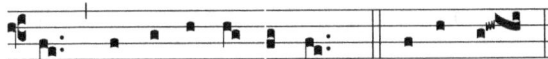

Son : and tó the Hóly Ghost. ℟. I will pay...

Hymn. **Immense caeli Conditor.** *6th cent., trans. by G. Gillett* [272]

1. O boundless Wisdom, God most high, / O Maker of the earth and sky, / Who bid'st the parted waters flow / In heaven above, on earth below:
2. The streams on earth, the clouds in heaven, / By Thee their ordered bounds were given, / Lest 'neath the untempered fires of day / The parch-ed soil should waste away.
3. E'en so on us who seek Thy face / Pour forth the waters of Thy grace; / Renew the fount of life within, / And quench the wasting fires of sin.
4. Let faith discern the eternal Light / Beyond the darkness of the night, / And through the mists of falsehood see / The path of truth revealed by Thee.
5. O Father, that we ask be done, / Through Jesus Christ, Thine only Son; / Who, with the Holy Ghost and Thee, / Doth live and reign eternally./ Amen.

Versicle

℣. Let my prayer be set forth before thee as incense:
℟. And the lifting up of my hands as the evening sacrifice.

Antiphon for Magnificat

My spirit * hath rejoiced in Gód my Sá-viour : For he hath regarded the low

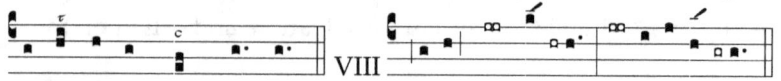

estate of hís handmáiden.

Luke 1:46-55 *Magnificat*

☩ |My soul| doth mágni- / fý the Lord, * and my spirit hath rejoiced in / Gód my Sáviour.
|For he| háth re- / gárded * the low estate of / hís handmáiden:
|For, be-| hóld, from / hénceforth * all generations shall / cáll me bléss-ed.
|For he| that is mighty hath dóne to / mé great things; * and / hóly ís his name.
|And his| mercy is on thém that / féar him * from generation to / génerátion.
|He hath| shewed stréngth with his / <u>arm</u>; * he hath scattered the proud in the imagin- / átion óf their hearts.
|He hath| put down the míghty / fróm their seats, * and exalted / thém of lów degree.
|He hath| filled the húngry with / góod things; * and the rich he hath sent émp- / ty a<u>way</u>.
|He hath| holpen his sérvant / Ísrael, * in remembrance / óf his mércy;
|As he| spake tó our / fáthers, * to Abraham, and to his / séed for éver.
|Glory| be to the Fáther and / tó the Son * and / tó the Hóly Ghost.
|As it| was in the beginning, is now, and éver / sháll be, * wórld / without énd. Amen.

[273] *Antiphon repeated.*
Service continues on p. 59.

Tuesday: Morning Prayer

Responsory

℟. Be merciful unto me, O God, be mérci-ful únto me ‡ for my soul trústeth

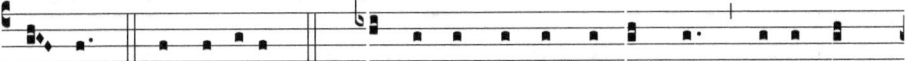

in <u>thee</u>: ℟. Be merciful… ℣. Yea, in the shadow of thy wings will I máke

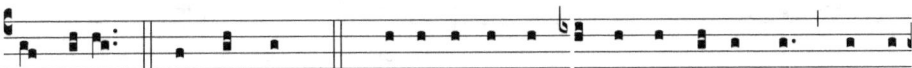

my réfuge. ‡ For my soul… ℣. Glory be to the Fáther and tó the Son : and tó

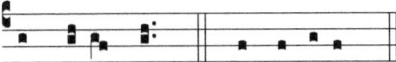

the Hóly Ghost. ℟. Be merciful…

Hymn. **Ales diei nuntius.** *Prudentius, 4th cent., trans. by J. M. Neale*

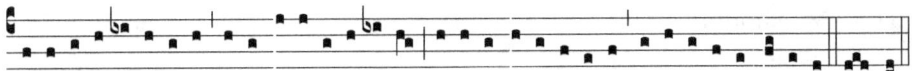

1. The wing-ed herald of the day / Proclaims the morn's approaching ray: / And Christ the Lord our souls excites, / And so to endless life invites.
2. Take up thy bed, to each He cries, / Who sick or wrapt in slumber lies; / and chaste and just and sober stand, / And watch: My coming is at hand.
3. With earnest cry, with tearful care, / Call we the Lord to hear our prayer; / While supplication, pure and deep, / Forbids each chastened heart to sleep.
4. Do Thou, O Christ, our slumbers wake; / Do Thou the chains of darkness break; / Purge Thou our former sins away, / And in our souls new light display.
5. All laud to God the Father be, / All praise, eternal Son, to Thee; / All glory, as is ever meet, / To God the holy Paraclete. Amen.

Versicle
℣. O satisfy us early with thy mercy:
℟. That we may rejoice and be glad.

Antiphon for Benedictus

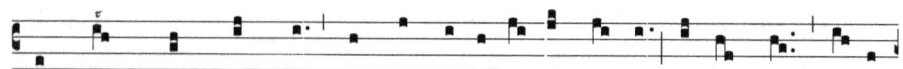

The LORD hath raised up * an horn of salvátion fór us : in the house of his

sérvant Dávid.

Luke 1:68-79 *Benedictus*
☩ |Bless-| ed be the Lord / Gód of Ísrael; * for he hath visited and re- / déemed his péople,
|And| hath raised up an horn of sal- / vátion fór us * in the house of his / sérvant Dávid;
|As| he spake by the mouth of his / hóly próphets, * which have been / sínce the wórld began:
|That| we should be saved / fróm our énemies, * and from the hand of / áll that háte us;
|To| perform the mercy promised / tó our fáthers, * and to remember his / hóly cóvenant;
|The| oath which he sware to our / fáther Ábraham, * that he would / gránt unto <u>us</u>,
|That| we being delivered out of the / hánd of our énemies * might serve / hím without <u>fear</u>,
|In| holiness and righteous- / néss befóre him, * all the / dáys of our <u>life</u>.
|And| thou, child, shalt be called the prophet / óf the Híghest: * for thou shalt go before the face of the / Lórd to prepáre his ways;
|To| give knowledge of salvation / únto his péople * by the re- / míssion óf their sins,
|Through| the tender / mércy óf our God; * whereby the dayspring from on high hath / vísited <u>us</u>,
|To| give light to them that sit in darkness and in the / shádow of <u>death</u>, * to guide our feet / ínto the wáy of peace.
|Glo- | ry be to the / Fáther and tó the Son * and / tó the Hóly Ghost.
|As| it was in the beginning, is now, and / éver sháll be, * - / wórld without énd. Amen.

Antiphon repeated.
Service continues on p. 41.

Tuesday: Daytime Prayer

Responsory

℟. I will bless the LORD at áll times: ‡ His praise shall continuállý be ín my

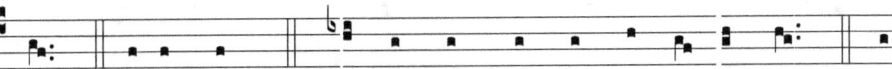

mouth. ℟. I will bless... ℣. My soul shall make her bóast in the LORD. ‡ His

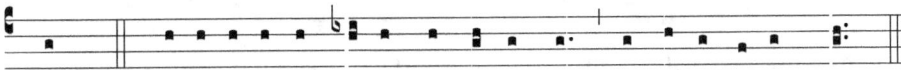

praise... ℣. Glory be to the Fáther and tó the Son : and tó the Hóly Ghost.

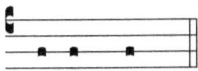

℟. I will bless...

Kyrie and Lord's Prayer (p. 52)

Versicle
℣. O LORD thou art my help, forsâke me not.
℟. Take not thy hand from me, O God, my salvation.

Collects: **Collect of the week**

Da Pacem

Grant peace graciously, * Lord God, in our times: For there is none oth- er

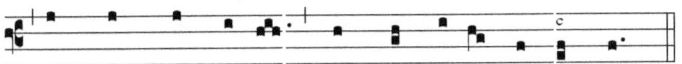

that could fight for us, but Thou alone, O our God.

℣. Peace be withîn thy walls:
℞. And prosperity within thy pâlaces.
℣. Let us pray. O Lord, we beseech Thee mercifully to hear the prayers of Thy church that we, being delivered from all adversities and serving Thee with a quiet mind, may enjoy Thy peace all the days of our life; through Jesus Christ, Thy Son, our Lord. ℞. Amen.

[276] *For pastors and theologians*

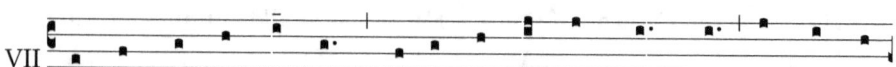
VII

O Lord give us shepherds * according to thine own heart and teachers

of righteousness: Take not from their mouths the word of truth, so that they

would feed us with doctrine and wisdom.

℣. Rejoice the soul of thy servants:
℞. And strengthen them with thy power.
℣. Let us pray. Almighty and gracious God, the Father of our Lord Jesus Christ, who hast commanded us to pray that Thou wouldest send forth laborers into Thy harvest, of Thine infinite mercy give us true teachers and ministers of Thy Word and put Thy saving Gospel in their hearts and on their lips that they may truly fulfill Thy command and preach nothing contrary to Thy holy Word, that we, being warned, instructed, nurtured, comforted, and strengthened by Thy heavenly Word, may do those things which are well-pleasing to Thee and profitable to us; through the same Jesus Christ, Thy Son, our Lord, who liveth and reigneth with Thee and the Holy Ghost, ever one God, world without end. ℞. Amen.
Service continues on p. 53.

TUESDAY: EVENING PRAYER

Responsory

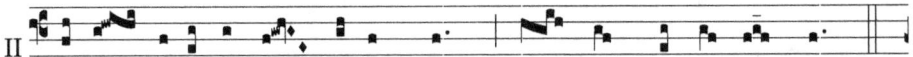

℟. Our help is in the náme of the LORD, ‡ who made héaven and earth.

℟. Our help... ℣. The LORD is round about his people from henceforth éven

for éver. ‡ Who made... ℣. Glory be to the Fáther and tó the Son : and tó

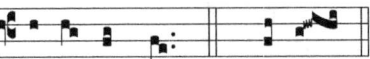

the Hóly Ghost. ℟. Our help...

Hymn. **Telluris ingens Conditor.** *7th cent., trans. anonymous 1854*

1. Earth's mighty Maker, whose command / Raised from the sea the solid land, / And drove each billowy heap away, / And bade the earth stand firm for aye:
2. That so, with flowers of golden hue, / The seeds of each it might renew; / And fruit-trees bearing fruit might yield, / And pleasant pasture of the field;
3. Our spirit's rankling wounds efface / With dewy freshness of Thy grace: / That grief may cleanse each deed of ill, / And o'er each lust may triumph still.
4. Let every soul Thy law obey, / And keep from every evil way; / Rejoice each promised good to win / And flee from every mortal sin.
5. O Father, that we ask be done, / Through Jesus Christ, Thine only Son; / Who, with the Holy Ghost and Thee, / Doth live and reign eternally. Amen.

Versicle
℣. Let my prayer be set forth before thee as incense:
℟. And the lifting up of my hands as the evening sacrifice.

Antiphon for Magnificat

He that is mighty * hath dóne to mé great things : and hóly ís his name.

Luke 1:46-55 *Magnificat*
✠ |My soul| doth / mágnifý the Lord, * and my spirit hath rejoiced in / Gód my Sáviour.
For he / háth regárded * the low estate of / hís handmáiden:
For, be- / hóld, from hénceforth * all generations shall / cáll me bléss-ed.
|For he| that is mighty hath / dóne to mé great things; * - and / hóly ís his name.
|And his| mercy is on / thém that féar him * from generation to / géneratión.
|He hath| shewed / stréngth with his <u>arm</u>; * he hath scattered the proud in the imagi- / nátion óf their hearts.
|He hath| put down the / míghty fróm their seats, * and exalted / thém of lów degree.
|He hath| filled the / húngry with góod things; * and the rich he hath sent / émpty a<u>way</u>.
|He hath| holpen his / sérvant Ísrael, * in remembrance / óf his mércy;
|As he| spake / tó our fáthers, * to Abraham, and to his / séed for éver.
[278] |Glory| be to the / Fáther and tó the Son * - and / tó the Hóly Ghost.
|As it| was in the beginning, is now, and / éver sháll be, * - wórld / without énd. Amen.
Antiphon repeated.
Service continues on p. 59.

366

WEDNESDAY: MORNING PRAYER

Responsory

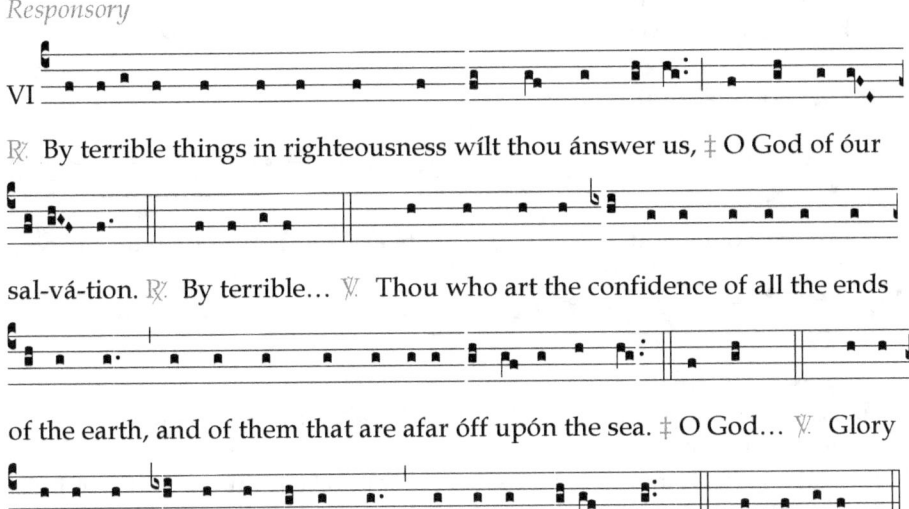

℟ By terrible things in righteousness wílt thou ánswer us, ‡ O God of óur sal-vá-tion. ℟ By terrible... ℣ Thou who art the confidence of all the ends of the earth, and of them that are afar óff upón the sea. ‡ O God... ℣ Glory be to the Fáther and tó the Son : and tó the Hóly Ghost. ℟ By terrible...

Hymn. **Nox et tenebrae et nubila.** *Prudentius, 4th cent., trans. by R. M. Pope*

1. Ye clouds and darkness, hosts of night, / That breed confusion and affright, / Begone! O'erhead the dawn shines clear, / The light breaks in and Christ is here.
2. Earth's gloom flees broken and dispersed, / By the sun's piercing shafts coerced: / The day-star's eyes rain influence bright, / And colours glimmer back to sight.
3. Thee, Christ, alone we know; to Thee / We bend in pure simplicity; / Our songs with tears to Thee arise; / Prove Thou our hearts with Thy clear eyes.
4. Though we be stained with blots within, / Thy quickening rays shall purge our sin; / Light of the Morning Star, Thy grace / Shed on us from Thy cloudless face.
5. All laud to God the Father be, / All praise, eternal Son, to Thee; / All glory, as is ever meet, / To God the holy Paraclete. Amen.

Versicle
℣. O satisfy us early with thy mercy:
℟. That we may rejoice and be glad.

Antiphon for Benedictus

[279]

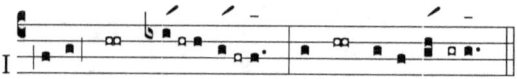

The Lord hath delivered us * fróm our énemies : and hath shówn us mércy.

Luke 1:68-79 *Benedictus*
☩ |Bless-ed| be the Lord / Gód of Ísrael; * for he hath visited and re- / déemed his péople,
|And hath| raised up an horn of sal- / vátion fór us * in the house of his / sérvant Dávid;
|As he| spake by the mouth of his / hóly próphets, * which have been / sínce the wórld began:
|That we| should be saved / fróm our énemies, * and from the hand of / áll that háte us;
|To per-| form the mercy promised / tó our fáthers, * and to remember his / hóly cóvenant;
|The oath| which he sware to our / fáther Ábraham, * that he would / gránt unto <u>us</u>,
|That we| being delivered out of the / hánd of our énemies * might serve / hím without <u>fear</u>,
|In ho-| liness and righteous- / néss befóre him, * all the / dáys of our <u>life</u>.
|And thou,| child, shalt be called the prophet / óf the Híghest: * for thou shalt go before the face of the Lórd / to prepáre his ways;
|To give| knowledge of salvation / únto his péople * by the re- / míssion óf their sins,
|Through the| tender / mércy óf our God; * whereby the dayspring from on high hath / vísited <u>us</u>,
|To give| light to them that sit in darkness and in the / shádow of <u>death</u>, * to guide our feet ín- / to the wáy of peace.
|Glory| be to the / **Fáther and tó the Son** * - and / **tó the Hóly Ghost.**
|As it| was in the beginning, is now, and / éver sháll be, * - wórld / **without énd. Amen.**

Antiphon repeated.
Service continues on p. 41.

WEDNESDAY: DAYTIME PRAYER

Responsory

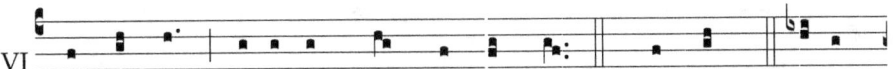

℟. Héal my soul, ‡ for I have sínned agáinst thee. ℟. Heal my... ℣. I said,

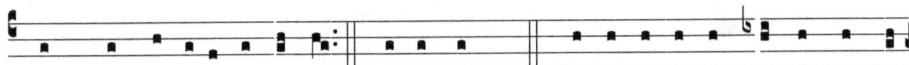

LORD, be mérciful únto me. ‡ For I have... ℣. Glory be to the Fáther and tó

the Son : and tó the Hóly Ghost. ℟. Heal my...

Kyrie and Lord's Prayer (p. 52) [280]

Versicle
℣. O LORD thou art my help, forsâke me not.
℟. Take not thy hand from me, O God, my salvation.

Collects: **Collect of the week**

Da Pacem

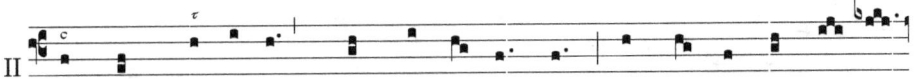

Grant peace graciously, * Lord God, in our times: For there is none oth- er

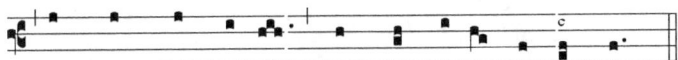

that could fight for us, but Thou alone, O our God.

℣. Peace be withîn thy walls:
℟. And prosperity within thy pâlaces.
℣. Let us pray. O Lord, we beseech Thee mercifully to hear the prayers of Thy church that we, being delivered from all adversities and serving Thee with a quiet mind, may enjoy Thy peace all the days of our life; through Jesus Christ, Thy Son, our Lord. ℟. Amen.

For Rulers

O Lord, give the rulers * peace and good dealings: that we may live

orderly under their reign in se-cu-ri-ty and ho-ne-sty.

℣. O Lord, hear us and be gracious únto us.
℟. O Lord, be thou our Salvation.
℣. Let us pray. Almighty and everlasting God, we humbly implore thee graciously to regard [the President of the United States], his counselors, and all others in authority over us; that they may be high in purpose, wise in counsel, and unwavering in duty; and in the administration of their solemn charge may wholly serve thy will, uphold the honor of our Nation, secure the protection of our people, and set forward every righteous cause; through Jesus Christ, Thy Son, our Lord, who liveth and reigneth with Thee and the Holy Ghost, ever one God, world without end. ℟. Amen.

[281] *Service continues on p. 53.*

Wednesday: Evening Prayer

Responsory

℟. I will praise thee, O Lord my Gód, with áll my heart: ‡ be-fore the gods will I sing práise unto <u>thee</u>. ℟. I will praise… ℣. I will worship toward thy holy témple, and práise thy name. ‡ Be-fore the gods… ℣. Glory

be to the Fáther and tó the Son : and tó the Hóly Ghost. ℟. I will praise…

Hymn. **Caeli Deus sanctissime.** *4th or 5th cent., trans. by M. F. Bell*

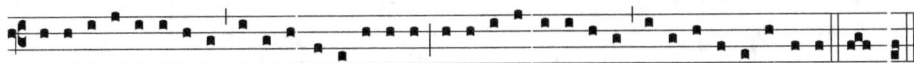

1. Most holy Lord and God of heaven, / Who to the glowing sky hast given / The fires that in the east are born / With gradual splendours of the morn;
2. Who, on the fourth day, didst reveal / The sun's enkindled flaming wheel, / Didst set the moon her ordered ways, / And stars their ever-winding maze;
3. That each in its appointed way / Might separate the night from day, / And of the seasons through the year / The well-remembered signs declare:
4. Illuminate our hearts within, / And cleanse our minds from stain of sin; / Unburdened of our guilty load / May we unfettered serve our God.
5. O Father, that we ask be done, / Through Jesus Christ, Thine only Son; / Who, with the Holy Ghost and Thee, / Doth live and reign eternally. Amen.

Versicle

℣. Let my prayer be set forth before thee as incense:
℟. And the lifting up of my hands as the evening sacrifice.

Antiphon for Magnificat [282]

The mercy of the LORD * is on thém that féar him : from gen-er-a-tion to

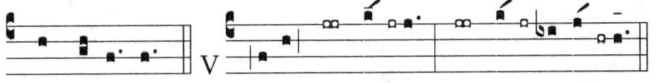

gén-er-á-tion.

Luke 1:46-55 *Magnificat*

☩ |My soul| doth mágni- / fý the Lord, * and my spirit hath rejoiced in / Gód my Sáviour.
|For he| háth re- / gárded * the low estate of / hís handmáiden:
|For, be-| hóld, from / hénceforth * all generations shall / cáll me bléss-ed.

|For he| that is mighty hath dóne to / mé great things; * and / hóly ís his name.
|And his| mercy is on thém that / féar him * from generation to / génerátion.
|He hath| shewed stréngth with his / arm; * he hath scattered the proud in the imagi- / nátion óf their hearts.
|He hath| put down the míghty / fróm their seats, * and exalted / thém of lów degree.
|He hath| filled the húngry with / góod things; * and the rich he hath sent / émpty a<u>way</u>.
|He hath| holpen his sérvant / Ísrael, * in remembrance / óf his mércy;
|As he| spake tó our / fáthers, * to Abraham, and to his / séed for éver.
|Glory| be to the Fáther and / tó the Son * and / tó the Hóly Ghost.
|As it| was in the beginning, is now, and éver / sháll be, * - / wórld without énd. Amen.

Antiphon repeated.
Service continues on p. 59.

Thursday: Morning Prayer

Responsory

℟. Lord, thou hast been our dwelling place in all gén-er-á-tions, ‡ thou art

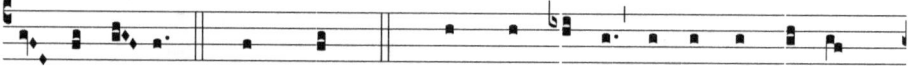

Gód for-év- er. ℟. Lord, thou… ℣. Thou who sayest: Return, ye children

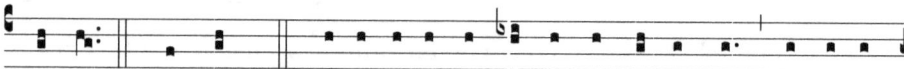

of <u>men</u>. ‡ Thou art… ℣. Glory be to the Fáther and tó the Son : and tó the

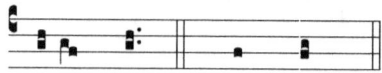

Hóly Ghost. ℟. Lord, thou…

Hymn. Lux ecce surgit aurea. *Prudentius, 4th cent., trans. by R. M. Pope*

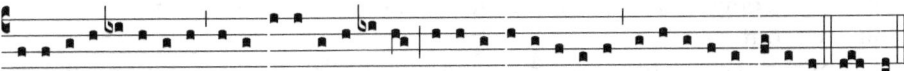

1. Lo! Golden light rekindles day: / Let paling darkness steal away, / Which all too long o'erwhelmed our gaze / And led our steps by winding ways.
2. We pray Thee, rising Light serene, / E'en as Thyself our hearts make clean; / Let no deceit our lips defile, / Nor let our souls be vexed by guile.
3. O keep us, as the hours proceed, / From lying word and evil deed; / Our roving eyes from sin set free, / Our body from impurity.
4. For Thou dost from above survey / The converse of each fleeting day; / Thou dost foresee from morning light / Our every deed, until the night.
5. All laud to God the Father be, / All praise, eternal Son, to Thee; / All glory, as is ever meet, / To God the holy Paraclete. Amen.

Versicle
℣. O satisfy us early with thy mercy:
℟. That we may rejoice and be glad.

Antiphon for Benedictus

In holiness and righteousnéss * be-fóre him : let us serve the Lord without

fear all the dáys of our life.

Luke 1:68-79 *Benedictus*

☩ |Bless-| ed be the Lord / Gód of Ísrael; * for he hath visited and re- / déemed his péople,
|And| hath raised up an horn of sal- / vátion fór us * in the house of his / sérvant Dávid;
|As| he spake by the mouth of his / hóly próphets, * which have been / sínce the wórld began:
|That| we should be saved / fróm our énemies, * and from the hand of / áll that háte us;
|To| perform the mercy promised / tó our fáthers, * and to remember his / hóly cóvenant;
|The| oath which he sware to our / fáther Ábraham, * that he would / gránt

unto <u>us</u>,

|That| we being delivered out of the / hánd of our énemies * might serve / hím without <u>fear</u>,

|In| holiness and righteous- / néss befóre him, * all the / dáys of our <u>life</u>.

|And| thou, child, shalt be called the prophet / óf the Híghest: * for thou shalt go before the face of the / Lórd to prepáre his ways;

|To| give knowledge of salvation / únto his péople * by the re- / míssion óf their sins,

[284] |Through| the tender / mércy óf our God; * whereby the dayspring from on high hath / vísited <u>us</u>,

|To| give light to them that sit in darkness and in the / shádow of <u>death</u>, * to guide our feet / ínto the wáy of peace.

|Glo- | ry be to the / Fáther and tó the Son * and / tó the Hóly Ghost.

|As| it was in the beginning, is now, and / éver sháll be, * - / wórld without énd. Amen.

Antiphon repeated.
Service continues on p. 41.

Thursday: Daytime Prayer

Responsory

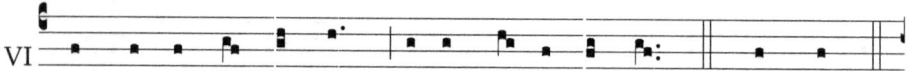

℟. Téach me thy wáy, O LORD; ‡ I will wálk in thy <u>truth</u>: ℟. Téach me...

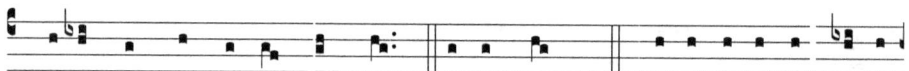

℣. Unite my héart to féar thy name. ‡ I will wálk... ℣. Glory be to the Fáther

and tó the Son : and tó the Hóly Ghost. ℟. Téach me...

Kyrie and Lord's Prayer (p. 52)

Versicle
℣. O LORD thou art my help, forsâke me not.
℟. Take not thy hand from me, O God, my salvation.

Collects: **Collect of the week**

Da Pacem

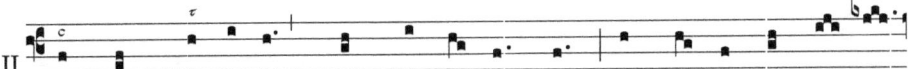

Grant peace graciously, * Lord God, in our times: For there is none oth- er

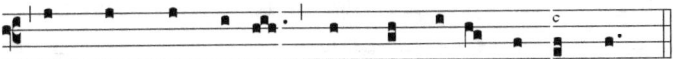

that could fight for us, but Thou alone, O our God.

℣. Peace be withîn thy walls:
℟. And prosperity within thy pâlaces.
℣. Let us pray. O Lord, we beseech Thee mercifully to hear the prayers of Thy church that we, being delivered from all adversities and serving Thee with a quiet mind, may enjoy Thy peace all the days of our life; through Jesus Christ, Thy Son, our Lord. ℟. Amen.

For our Enemies [285]

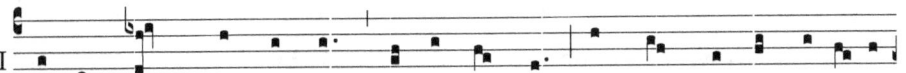

For thy name's sake, O Lord, * remember now and break not thy covenant

with us: Thou art the Lord, our God, we will wait on thee.

℣. Fashion our heârts alike.
℟. We trust in thy hôly name.
℣. Let us pray. O almighty, everlasting God, who through Thine only Son, our blessed Lord, hast commanded us to love our enemies, to do good to them that hate us, and to pray for them that persecute us, we earnestly beseech Thee that by Thy gracious visitation they may be led to true repentance and may have the same love and be of one accord and of one mind and heart with us and with Thy whole Church; through the same, Jesus Christ, Thy Son, our Lord, who liveth and reigneth with Thee and the Holy Ghost, ever one God, world without end. ℟. Amen.

Service continues on p. 53.

Thursday: Evening Prayer

Responsory

℟. I cry unto thee: ‡ make háste unto me. ℟. I cry... ℣. Give ear unto my voice, when I crý unto thee. ‡ Make háste... ℣. Glory be to the Fáther and tó the Son : and tó the Hóly Ghost. ℟. I- cry...

Hymn. **Magnae Deus potentiae.** *6th or 7th cent., trans. by J. M. Neale*

[286]

1. Almighty God, who from the flood / Didst bring to light a twofold brood; / Part in the firmament to fly, / And part in ocean's depths to lie;
2. Appointing fishes in the sea, / And fowls in open air to be, / That each, by origin the same, / Its separate dwelling-place might claim:
3. Grant that Thy servants, by the tide / Of blood and water purified, / No guilty fall from Thee may know, / Nor death eternal undergo.
4. Be none submerged in sin's distress, / None lifted up in boastfulness; / That contrite hearts be not dismayed, / Nor haughty souls in ruin laid.
5. O Father, that we ask be done, / Through Jesus Christ, Thine only Son; / Who, with the Holy Ghost and Thee, / Doth live and reign eternally. Amen.

Versicle

℣. Let my prayer be set forth before thee as incense:
℟. And the lifting up of my hands as the evening sacrifice.

Antiphon for Magnificat

The LORD * hath shewed stréngth with his arm: He hath scattered the proud

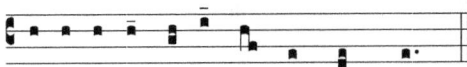

in the i-ma-gi-ná-tion óf their hearts.

VII

Luke 1:46-55 *Magnificat*

☩ |My| soul doth / mágnifý the Lord, * and my spirit hath rejoiced in / Gód my Sáviour.
|For| he / háth regárded * the low estate of / hís handmáiden:
|For,| be- / hóld, from hénceforth * all generations shall / cáll me bléss-ed.
|For| he that is mighty hath / dóne to mé great things; * and / hóly ís his name.
|And| his mercy is on / thém that féar him * from generation to / génerátion.
|He| hath shewed / stréngth with his <u>arm</u>; * he hath scattered the proud in the imagi- / nátion óf their hearts.
|He| hath put down the / míghty fróm their seats, * and exalted / thém of lów degree.
|He| hath filled the / húngry with góod things; * and the rich he hath sent / émpty a<u>way</u>.
|He| hath holpen his / sérvant Ísrael, * in remembrance / óf his mércy;
|As| he spake / tó our fáthers, * to Abraham, and to his / séed for éver.
|Glo-| ry be to the / Fáther and tó the Son * and / tó the Hóly Ghost.
|As| it was in the beginning, is now, and / éver sháll be, * - / wórld without énd. Amen.
Antiphon repeated.
Service continues on p. 59.

Responsory

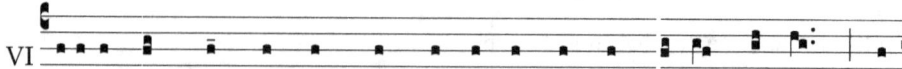

℟. It is a good thing to shew forth thy lovingkindness ín the mórning, ‡ and

thy fáithfulness évery night: ℟. It is a good... ℣. And to sing praises unto thy

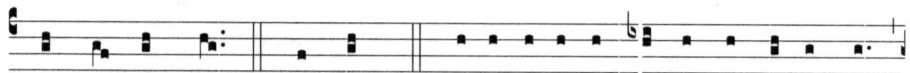

náme, O most High: ‡ And thy... ℣. Glory be to the Fáther and tó the Son :

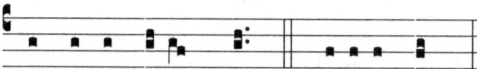

and tó the Hóly Ghost. ℟. It is a good...

Hymn. **Aeterna caeli gloria.** *6th cent., trans. by J. M. Neale*

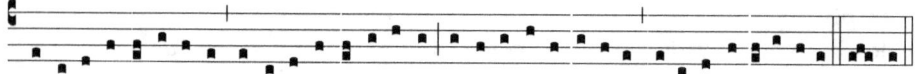

1. Eternal Glory of the sky, / Blest hope of frail humanity, / The Father's sole-begotten One, / Yet born a spotless Virgin's Son!
2. Uplift us with Thine arm of might, / And let our hearts rise pure and bright, / And, ardent in God's praises, pay / The thanks we owe Him every day.
3. The day-star's rays are glittering clear, / And tell that day itself is near: / The shadows of the night depart; / Thou, holy Light, illume the heart!
4. Within our senses ever dwell, / And worldly darkness thence expel; / Long as the days of life endure, / Preserve our souls devout and pure.
5. The faith that first must be possessed, / Root deep within our inmost breast; / And joyous hope in second place, / Then charity, Thy greatest grace.
6. All laud to God the Father be, / All praise, eternal Son, to Thee; / All glory, as is ever meet, / To God the holy Paraclete. Amen.

Versicle
℣. O satisfy us early with thy mercy:
℟. That we may rejoice and be glad.

Antiphon for Benedictus
[288]

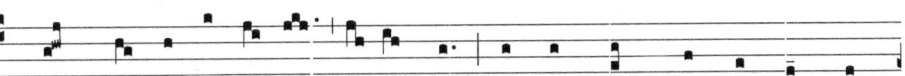

Through the tender mér-cy * óf our God : the dayspring from on high hath

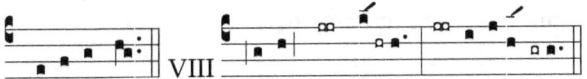

vísited us.

Luke 1:68-79 *Benedictus*
✠ |Bless-ed| be the Lord Gód of / Ísrael; * for he hath visited and re- / déemed his péople,
|And hath| raised up an horn of salvátion / fór us * in the house of his / sérvant Dávid;
|As he| spake by the mouth of his hóly / próphets, * which have been / sínce the wórld began:
|That we| should be saved fróm our / énemies, * and from the hand of / áll that háte us;
|To per-| form the mercy promised tó our / fáthers, * and to remember his / hóly cóvenant;
|The oath| which he sware to our fáther / Ábraham, * that he would gránt / unto us,
|That we| being delivered out of the hánd of our / énemies * might serve hím / without fear,
|In ho-| liness and righteousnéss be- / fóre him, * all the dáys / of our life.
|And thou,| child, shalt be called the prophet óf the / Híghest: * for thou shalt go before the face of the Lórd / to prepáre his ways;
|To give| knowledge of salvation únto his / péople * by the re- / míssion óf their sins,
|Through the| tender mércy / óf our God; * whereby the dayspring from on high hath vís- / ited us,
|To give| light to them that sit in darkness and in the shádow of / death, * to guide our feet ín- / to the wáy of peace.
|Glory| be to the Fáther and / tó the Son * and / tó the Hóly Ghost.
|As it| was in the beginning, is now, and éver / sháll be, * wórld / without énd. Amen.

Antiphon repeated.
Service continues on p. 41.

Friday: Daytime Prayer

Responsory

℟. Foréver, O <u>LORD</u>, ‡ thy word is séttled in héaven. ℟. Foréver, O…

℣. Thy faithfulness is unto all gén-er-á-tions. ‡ Thy word… ℣. Glory be to the

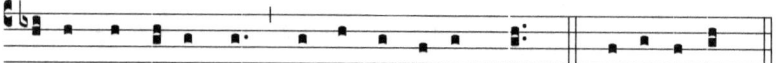

Fáther and tó the Son : and tó the Hóly Ghost. ℟. Forever, O…

[289] *Kyrie and Lord's Prayer (p. 52)*

Versicle
℣. O LORD thou art my help, forsâke me not.
℟. Take not thy hand from me, O God, my salvation.

Collects: **Collect of the week**

Da Pacem

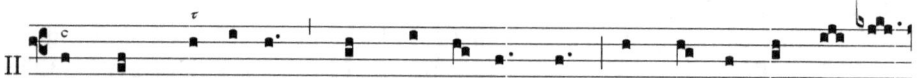

Grant peace graciously, * Lord God, in our times: For there is none oth- er

that could fight for us, but Thou alone, O our God.

℣. Peace be withîn thy walls:
℟. And prosperity within thy pâlaces.
℣. Let us pray. O Lord, we beseech Thee mercifully to hear the prayers of

Thy church that we, being delivered from all adversities and serving Thee with a quiet mind, may enjoy Thy peace all the days of our life; through Jesus Christ, Thy Son, our Lord. ℟. Amen.

For Prisoners

O Lord, let the groaning * of prisoners come before thee: for thou art the

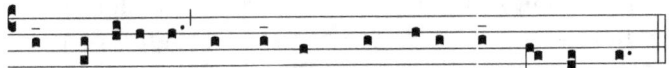

hope of Is-ra-el, the saviour thereof in time of trouble.

℣. Be their help from the sanctuary:
℟. And strengthen them out of Zion.
℣. Let us pray. Almighty God, who didst bring the Apostle Peter forth out of prison, have mercy upon all who are suffering unjust imprisonment and set them free from their bonds, that we may rejoice in their deliverance and continually give praise to Thee; through Jesus Christ, Thy Son, our Lord, who liveth and reigneth with Thee and the Holy Ghost, ever one God, world without end. ℟. Amen.
Service continues on p. 53.

Friday: Evening Prayer

Responsory

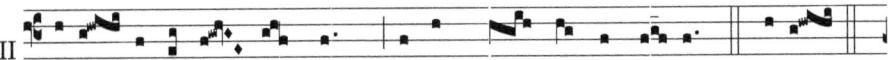

℟. I crίed unto thée, O LORD: ‡ I said, Thóu art my réfuge. ℟. I crίed...

℣. And my portion in the lánd of the líving. ‡ I said... ℣. Glory be to the

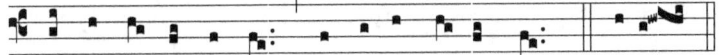

Fáther and tó the Son : and tó the Hóly Ghost. ℟. I crίed...

Hymn. **Plasmator hominis, Deus.** *7th cent., trans. by J. D. Chambers*

1. Maker of man, who from Thy throne / Dost order all things, God alone; / By whose decree the teeming earth / To reptile and to beast gave birth:
2. The mighty forms that fill the land, / Instinct with life at Thy command, / Are given subdued to humankind / For service in their rank assigned.
3. From all Thy servants drive away / Whate'er of thought impure today / Hath been with open action blent, / Or mingled with the heart's intent.
4. In heaven Thine endless joys bestow, / And grant Thy gifts of grace below; / From chains of strife our souls release, / Bind fast the gentle bands of peace.
5. O Father, that we ask be done, / Through Jesus Christ, Thine only Son; / Who, with the Holy Ghost and Thee, / Doth live and reign eternally. Amen.

Versicle

℣. Let my prayer be set forth before thee as incense:
℟. And the lifting up of my hands as the evening sacrifice.

[291] *Antiphon for Magnificat*

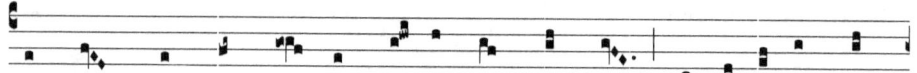

The Lord * hath put down the míghty fróm their seats : and ex-al-ted thém

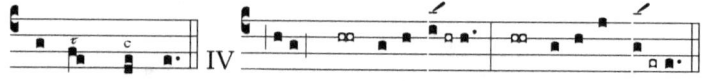 IV

of lów degree.

Luke 1:46-55 *Magnificat*

✠ |My soul| doth / mágnifý the Lord, * and my spirit hath rejoiced / in Gód my Sáviour.
For he / háth regárded * the low estate / of hís handmáiden:
For, be- / hóld, from hénceforth * all generations / shall cáll me bléss-ed.
|For he| that is mighty hath / dóne to mé great things; * - / and hóly ís his name.
|And his| mercy is on / thém that féar him * from generation / to génerátion.
|He hath| shewed stréngth / with his <u>arm</u>; * he hath scattered the proud in the ima- / ginátion óf their hearts.

382

| He hath | put down the / míghty fróm their seats, * and exal- / ted thém of lów degree.
| He hath | filled the hún- / gry with góod things; * and the rich he hath sent / émpty a<u>way</u>.
| He hath | holpen his / sérvant Ísrael, * in remem- / brance óf his mércy;
| As he | spake / tó our fáthers, * to Abraham, and to / his séed for éver.
| Glory | be to the Fá- / ther and tó the Son * - / and tó the Hóly Ghost.
| As it | was in the beginning, is now, and / éver sháll be, * - / wórld without énd. Amen.

Antiphon repeated.
Service continues on p. 59.

Saturday: Morning Prayer

Responsory

℟. Cause me to hear thy lovingkindness ín the mórning ‡ fór in thée I trust:

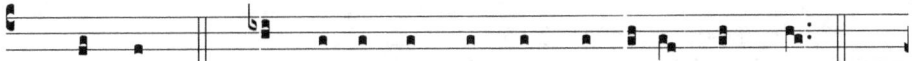

℟. Cause me... ℣. Cause me to know the way whereín I should <u>walk</u>. ‡

Fór in thée... ℣. Glory be to the Fáther and tó the Son : and tó the Hóly

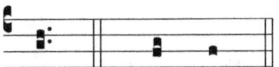

Ghost. ℟. Cause me...

[292] *Hymn.* **Aurora jam spargit polum.** *Before 8th cent., trans. by E. Caswall*

1. The dawn is sprinkling in the east / Its golden shower, as day flows in; / Fast mount the pointed shafts of light: / Farewell to darkness and to sin!
2. Away, ye midnight phantoms all! / Away, despondence and despair! / Whatever guilt the night has brought / Now let it vanish into air.
3. So, Lord, when that last morning breaks, / Looking to which we sigh and pray, / O may it to Thy minstrels prove / The dawning of a better day.
4. To God the Father glory be, / And to His sole-begotten Son; / Glory, O Holy Ghost, to Thee / While everlasting ages run. Amen.

Versicle
℣. O satisfy us early with thy mercy:
℟. That we may rejoice and be glad.

Antiphon for Benedictus

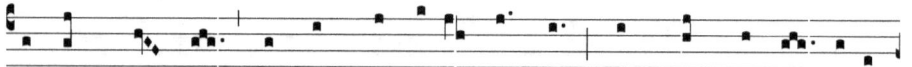

O LORD, give light * to them that sít in dárkness : and guide our feet into

the way of peace, Gód of Ís- ra-el.

Luke 1:68-79 *Benedictus*

✠ |Bless-ed| be the Lord Gód of / Ísrael; * for he hath visited and re- / déemed his péople,

|And hath| raised up an horn of salvátion / fór us * in the house of his / sérvant Dávid;

|As he| spake by the mouth of his hóly / próphets, * which have been / sínce the wórld began:

|That we| should be saved fróm our / énemies, * and from the hand of / áll that háte us;

|To per-| form the mercy promised tó our / fáthers, * and to remember his / hóly cóvenant;

|The oath| which he sware to our fáther / Ábraham, * that he would gránt / unto us,

|That we| being delivered out of the hánd of our / énemies * might serve

him / without <u>fear,</u>
|In ho-| liness and righteousnéss be- / fóre him, * all the dáys / of our <u>life.</u>
|And thou,| child, shalt be called the prophet óf the / Híghest: * for thou shalt go before the face of the Lórd / to prepáre his ways;
|To give| knowledge of salvation únto his / péople * by the re- / míssion óf their sins,
|Through the| tender mércy / óf our God; * whereby the dayspring from on high hath vís- / ited <u>us,</u>
|To give| light to them that sit in darkness and in the shádow of / <u>death,</u> * [293] to guide our feet ín- / to the wáy of peace.
|Glory| be to the Fáther and / tó the Son * and / tó the Hóly Ghost.
|As it| was in the beginning, is now, and éver / sháll be, * wórld / without énd. Amen.

Antiphon repeated.
Service continues on p. 41.

Saturday: Daytime Prayer

Responsory

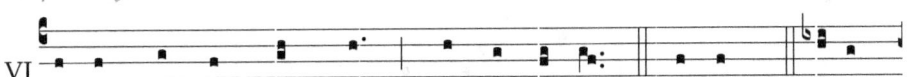

℟. I cried wíth my whóle heart: ‡ Héar me, O <u>Lord.</u> ℟. I cried… ℣. I will

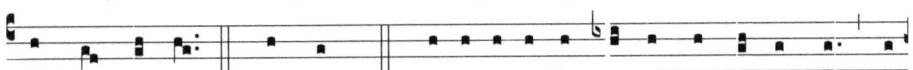

kéep thy státutes. ‡ Héar me… ℣. Glory be to the Fáther and tó the Son : and

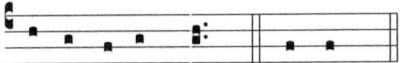

tó the Hóly Ghost. ℟. I cried…

Kyrie and Lord's Prayer (p. 52)

Versicle
℣. O LORD thou art my help, forsâke me not.
℟. Take not thy hand from me, O God, my salvation.

Collects: **Collect of the week**

Da Pacem

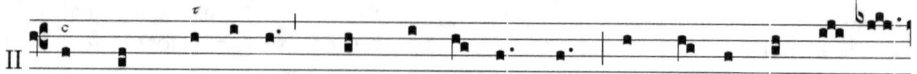

Grant peace graciously, * Lord God, in our times: For there is none oth- er

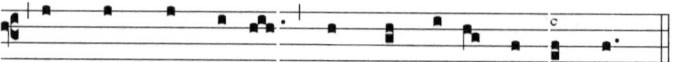

that could fight for us, but Thou alone, O our God.

℣. Peace be withîn thy walls:
℟. And prosperity within thy pâlaces.
℣. Let us pray. O Lord, we beseech Thee mercifully to hear the prayers of Thy church that we, being delivered from all adversities and serving Thee with a quiet mind, may enjoy Thy peace all the days of our life; through Jesus Christ, Thy Son, our Lord. ℟. Amen.

[294] *For the Word and Faith*

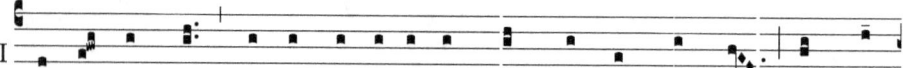

Uphold us, Lord, * according unto thy word that we might live: Thy word

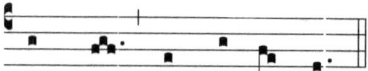

helps those that trust in Thee.

℣. O Lord, our eyes fail for thy salvation.
℟. And for the word of thy rîghteousness.
℣. Let us pray. Blessed Lord, who hast caused all Holy Scriptures to be written for our learning, grant that we may in such wise hear them, read, mark, learn, and inwardly digest them that by patience and comfort of Thy holy Word we may embrace, and ever hold fast, the blessed hope of everlasting life which Thou hast given us in our Savior Jesus Christ, who liveth and reigneth with Thee and the Holy Ghost, ever one God, world without end. ℟. Amen.

Service continues on p. 53.

Saturday: Evening Prayer

Responsory

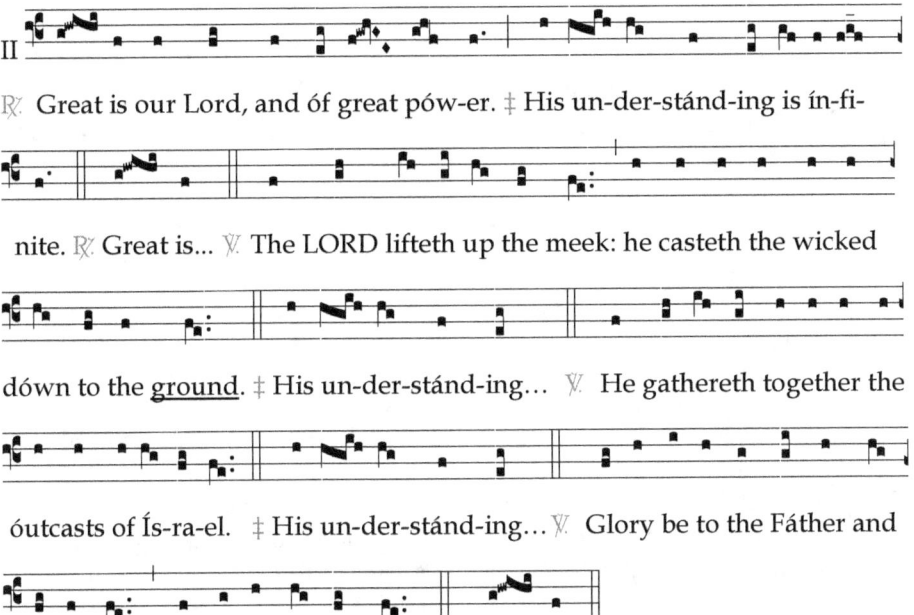

℟. Great is our Lord, and óf great pów-er. ‡ His un-der-stánd-ing is ín-fi-nite. ℟. Great is... ℣. The LORD lifteth up the meek: he casteth the wicked dówn to the ground. ‡ His un-der-stánd-ing... ℣. He gathereth together the óutcasts of Ís-ra-el. ‡ His un-der-stánd-ing... ℣. Glory be to the Fáther and tó the Son : and tó the Hóly Ghost. ℟. Great is...

Hymn. O Lux beata Trinitas. *St. Ambrose, 4th cent., trans. by J. M. Neale* [295]

1. O Trinity of bless-ed light, / O Unity of sovereign might, / As now the fiery sun departs, / Shed Thou Thy beams within our hearts.
2. To Thee our morning song of praise, / To Thee our evening prayer we raise; / Thee may our glory evermore / In lowly reverence adore.
3. All praise to God the Father be, / All praise, eternal Son, to Thee, / Whom with the Spirit we adore / Forever and forevermore. Amen.

Versicle
℣. Let our evening prayer come up before thee, O Lord:
℟. And let thy mercy come down upon us.

Antiphon for Magnificat

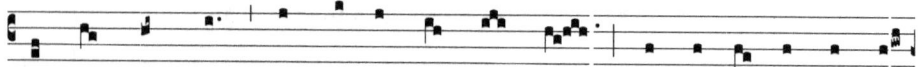

The Lord hath filled * the húngry with góod things : and the rich he hath sent

émpty a-<u>way</u>.

Luke 1:46-55 Magnificat
✠ |My| soul doth / mágnifý the Lord, * and my spirit hath rejoiced in / Gód my Sáviour.
|For| he / háth regárded * the low estate of / hís handmáiden:
|For,| be- / hóld, from hénceforth * all generations shall / cáll me bléss-ed.
|For| he that is mighty hath / dóne to mé great things; * and / hóly ís his name.
|And| his mercy is on / thém that féar him * from generation to / géneratión.
|He| hath shewed / stréngth with his <u>arm</u>; * he hath scattered the proud in the imagi- / nátion óf their hearts.
|He| hath put down the / míghty fróm their seats, * and exalted / thém of lów degree.
|He| hath filled the / húngry with góod things; * and the rich he hath sent / émpty a<u>way</u>.
|He| hath holpen his / sérvant Ísrael, * in remembrance / óf his mércy;
|As| he spake / tó our fáthers, * to Abraham, and to his / séed for éver.
|Glo-| ry be to the / Fáther and tó the Son * and / tó the Hóly Ghost.
|As| it was in the beginning, is now, and / éver shall be, * - / wórld without énd. Amen.
Antiphon repeated.
Service continues on p. 59.

Seasonal Propers
The Season of Advent

From the 1st Sunday in Advent until Compline of December 23. Each Sunday has proper antiphons for the Benedictus and the Magnificat. These antiphons may be used for the Gospel Canticles throughout the week. The days from Dec. 17 through Dec. 23 have special antiphons for the Magnificat which replace the antiphons of the weekday propers.

Invitatory for the Venite (Ps. 95 at Vigils).

Be-hóld, the King cóm-eth : O cóme, let us wórship Him.

Antiphons for Psalms (appropriate for use on Sundays)
1. Behold, the name of the Lord cómeth from <u>far</u> : and let the whole earth be fílled with His glóry.
2. Come, O Lord, and máke no tárrying : loosen the bonds of Thy péople Ísrael.
3. Rejoice greatly, Ó Jerúsalem : behóld, thy King cómeth.
4. Behold, the Lord shall come and áll His saints with Him : and in that day the light shall be great, állelúia.
5. Out of Zion, the perfection of béauty, Gód hath shined : Our God shall come, állelúia. *(Ps. 50i)*
6. Prepare ye the way of the Lord, állelúia : Make His paths straight, állelúia.
7. Drop down, ye heavens, from above, and let the skies póur down ríghteousness : Let the earth open and bring fórth salvátion.

Responsory for Advent.

℟. Behold, the days come, saith the Lord, that I will raise unto David a rîghteous Branch, † and a King shall reign and prosper and shall execute judgment and jústice ín the earth. ‡ And this is His name whereby He shall be called, The Lórd Our Ríghteousness. ℟. Behold, the days... ℣. In His days shall Judah be saved, and Israel sháll dwell sáfely. ‡ And this is... ℣. Glory be to the Fáther and tó the Son: and tó the Hóly Ghost. ℟. Behold, the days...

First Sunday in Advent
1st Week of the Four-Week Psalm Schedule
Psalms. **25, 85, 145, 93, 24, 122, 110, 6**
Gospel (at Morning Prayer). **Matthew 21:1-9**

Hymn (at Morning Prayer). [297]
Verbum supernum prodiens. *10ᵗʰ cent., trans. by Charles Bigg*

1. High Word of God, who once didst come, / Leaving Thy Father and Thy home, / To succor by Thy birth our kind, / When, towards Thine advent, time declined,
2. Pour light upon us from above, / And fire our hearts with Thy strong love, / That, as we hear Thy Gospel read, / All fond desires may flee in dread;
3. That when Thou comest from the skies, / Great Judge, to open Thine assize, / To give each hidden sin its smart, / And crown as kings the pure in heart,
4. We be not set at Thy left hand, / Where sentence due would bid us stand, / But with the saints Thy face may see, / Forever wholly loving Thee.
5. Praise to the Father and the Son, / Through all the ages as they run; / And to the holy Paraclete / Be praise with Them and worship meet. Amen.

℣. Show me Thy ways, O Lord. ℟. Teach me Thy paths.
Antiphon for Benedictus. **Tell ye the daughter of Sion, Behold, thy King cómeth únto thee : meek, and sitting upon an ass, and a colt the foal of an ass, állelúia.**

Epistle (at Evening Prayer). **Romans 13:11-14**

Hymn (at Evening Prayer). **Conditor alme siderum.** *7ᵗʰ cent., trans. by J. M. Neale*

1. Creator of the stars of night, / Thy people's everlasting light, / Jesus, Redeemer, save us all, / Hear Thou Thy servants when they call.
2. Thou, sorrowing at the helpless cry / Of all creation doomed to die, / Didst save our lost and guilty race / By healing gifts of heavenly grace.
3. Thou cam'st, the Bridegroom of the bride, / As drew the world to eventide; / Proceeding from a virgin shrine, / The spotless Victim all divine.
4. At Thy great Name, exalted now, / All knees in lowly homage bow; / All things in heaven and earth adore, / And own Thee King for evermore.
5. To Thee, O Holy One, we pray, / Our Judge in that tremendous day, / Ward off, while yet we dwell below, / The weapons of our crafty foe.
6. To God the Father, God the Son, / And God the Spirit, Three in One, / Laud, honor, might and glory be / From age to age eternally. Amen.

℣. Show me Thy ways, O Lord. ℟. Teach me Thy paths.

Antiphon for Magnificat.

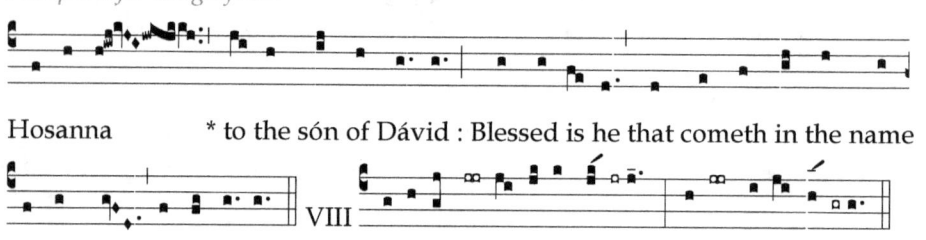

Hosanna　　　* to the són of Dávid : Blessed is he that cometh in the name of the Lord; ál-le-lú-ia.

Collect Stir up, we beseech Thee, Thy power, O Lòrd and come : that by Thy protection we may be rescued from the threatening perils of our sìns; and saved by Thy mighty deliverance; who livest and reignest with the Father and the Hòly Ghost : ever one God, world without end. Amen.

Second Sunday in Advent
Psalms. **80, 50, 85, 1, 75, 96, 126, 38**
Gospel (at Morning Prayer). **Luke 21:25-36**
Epistle (at Evening Prayer). **Romans 15:4-13**
Hymns. As for 1ˢᵗ S. in Advent

℣. Out of Zion, the perfection of beauty. ℞. God hath shined.
Antiphon for Benedictus. Upon the throne of David, and óver his kíngdom : shall he reign from henceforth even forever, állelúia.

Antiphon for Magnificat.

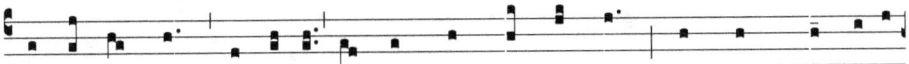

Blessed art thou, * O Mary, for thát thou hást believed : and there shall be a

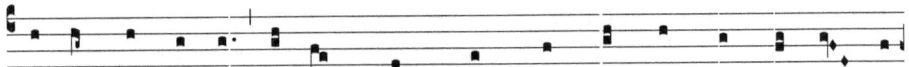

performance in thee of those things which were told thee from the Lord, ál-

le-lú-ia.

Collect. Stir up our heàrts, O Lord : to make ready the way of Thine only-begottèn Son; so that by His coming we may be enabled to serve Thee with pure minds; through the same Jesus Christ, Thy Son, oùr Lord; who liveth and reigneth with Thee and the Hòly Ghost : ever one God, world without end. Amen.

Third Sunday in Advent
Psalms. **85, 90, 111, 81, 4, 106, 9, 102**
Gospel (at Morning Prayer). **Matthew 11:2-10**
Epistle (at Evening Prayer). **1 Corinthians 4:1-5**
Hymns. As for 1ˢᵗ S. in Advent

℣. Remember us, O Lord, with the favor that Thou bearest unto Thy people.
℞. Oh, visit us with Thy salvation.
Antiphon for Benedictus. Now when John had heard in the prison the works of Christ, he sent two of his disciples, and sáid unto <u>Him</u> : Art Thou He that should come or do we lóok for anóther?

Antiphon for Magnificat.

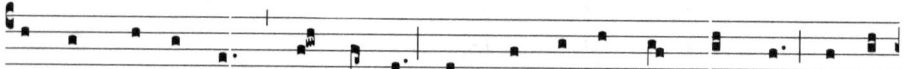

Go your way to Jóhn, * and sáy ye : The blind do see, and deaf hear; the le-

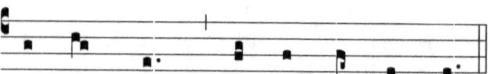

pers are cleansed, ánd the láme do walk.

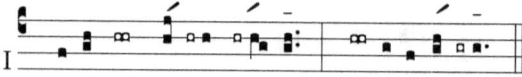

Collect. Lord, wè beseech Thee : give ear to our pràyers, and lighten the darkness of our hearts by Thy gracious visitation; who livest and reignest with the Father and the Hòly Ghost: ever one God, world without end. Amen.

Ember Days in Advent

Ember days are ancient days of repentance which occur four times per year: on the Wednesday, Friday, and Saturday after Advent 3, Lent 1, Pentecost, and Holy Cross Day (September 14—usually the third week of September). It is appropriate to fast on Ember days. Hymns dealing with the holy ministry are appropriate on Ember days. Propers for the Ember days in Advent are:

EMBER WEDNESDAY
Gospel (at Morning Prayer). **Luke 1:26-38**
Epistle (at Evening Prayer). **Isaiah 7:10-15**

℣. Remember us, O Lord, with the favor that Thou bearest unto Thy people.
℟. Oh, visit us with Thy salvation.
Antiphon for Benedictus. The Angel Gabriel was sént to Máry : a virgin espóused to Jóseph.

Antiphon for Magnificat (if before Dec. 17).

Behold the hándmaid óf the Lord : be it unto me accórding tó thy word.

VIII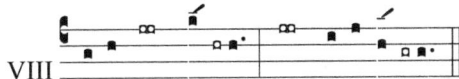

Collect. Grant, we beseech Thee, Almìghty God : that the coming festival of our redemption may obtain for us the comfort of thy help in this lìfe, and in the life to come the reward of eternal joy; through Jesus Christ, Thy Son, oùr Lord; who liveth and reigneth with Thee and the Hòly Ghost : ever one God, world without end. Amen.

EMBER FRIDAY
Gospel (at Morning Prayer). **Luke 1:39-47**
Epistle (at Evening Prayer). **Isaiah 11:1-5**

℣. Remember us, O Lord, with the favor that Thou bearest unto Thy people.
℟. Oh, visit us with Thy salvation.
Antiphon for Benedictus. As soon as the voice of thy salutation sóunded ín mine ears : the babe leaped in my womb for joy, álleúia.

Antiphon for Magnificat (if before Dec. 17).

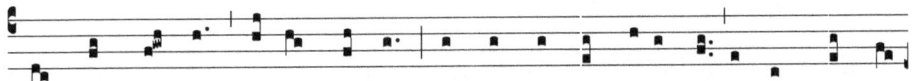

John bare witness * óf him, sáying : He that cometh after me is preférred be-

fóre me.

Collect. Stir up, we beseech thee, O Lord, thy power, and còme among us : that we, who put our trust and confidence in thy mercý, may speedily be delivered from all our adversities; who livest and reignest with the Father and the Hòly Ghost : ever one God, world without end. Amen.

EMBER SATURDAY
Gospel (at Morning Prayer). **Luke 3:1-6**
Epistle (at Evening Prayer). **2 Thessalonians 2:1-8**

℣. Remember us, O Lord, with the favor that Thou bearest unto Thy people.
℟. Oh, visit us with Thy salvation.
Antiphon for Benedictus. How shall this be, O angel of God, seeing Í know nót a man? : Hearken, O virgin Mary; the Holy Ghost shall come upon thee, and the power of the Highest shall óvershádow thee.
Antiphon for Magnificat: Great O Antiphon.

Collect. O God, who seest us to be sore afflicted by reason of the frailty of our mòrtal nature : grant, we beseech thèe, that we may be relieved by thy gracious visitation; who livest and reignest with the Father and the Hòly Ghost : ever one God, world without end. Amen.

Fourth Sunday in Advent
Psalms. **19, 145, 9, 27, 8, 5, 21, 143**
Gospel (at Morning Prayer). **John 1:19-28**
Epistle (at Evening Prayer). **Philippians 4:4-7**
Hymns. As for 1ˢᵗ S. in Advent

℣. Fear not, ye that are of a fearful heart. ℟. Our God will come and save us.
Antiphon for Benedictus. The angel said, Hail Mary, full of grace, the Lórd is with thee : Blessed art thou among women, álleIúia.
Antiphon for Magnificat. (The appropriate O Antiphon is sung today. See below.)

Collect. Stir up, O Lord, we beseech Thee, Thy pòwer and come : and with great might succòr us; that by the help of Thy grace whatsoever is hindered by our sins my be speedily accomplished through Thy mercy and satisfaction; who livest and reignest with the Father and Hòly Ghost : ever one God, world without end. Amen.

THE GREAT O ANTIPHONS FOR THE MAGNIFICAT

December 17, Antiphon for Magnificat.

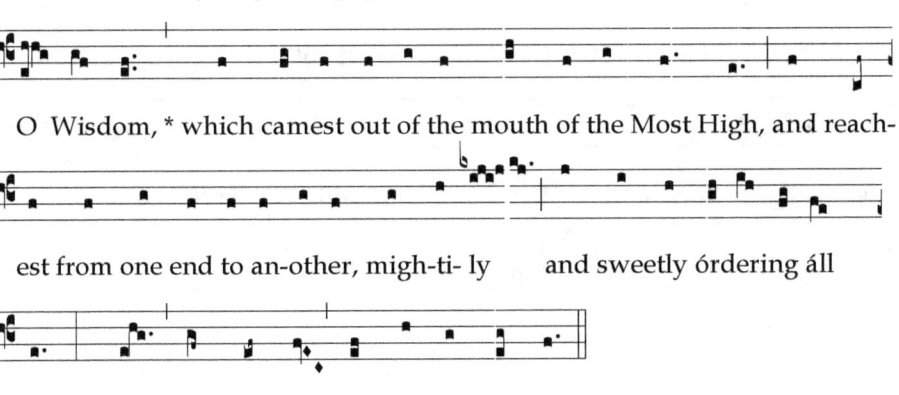

O Wisdom, * which camest out of the mouth of the Most High, and reach-est from one end to an-other, migh-ti- ly and sweetly órdering áll things : Come and teach us the wáy of prúdence.

December 18, Antiphon for Magnificat.

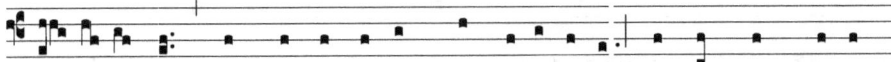

O A-do-nai, * and Leader of the house of Is-ra-el, who ap-pear-edst in the bush to Moses in a flame of fire-, and gavest him the Láw in Sínai :

Come and redeem us wíth an óutstretched arm.

December 19, Antiphon for Magnificat.

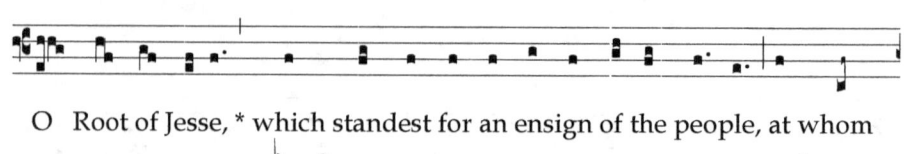

O Root of Jesse, * which standest for an ensign of the people, at whom

kings shall shut their mouths, to whom the Géntiles shall <u>seek</u> : Come and

de-li-ver ús, and tár-ry not.

December 20, Antiphon for Magnificat.

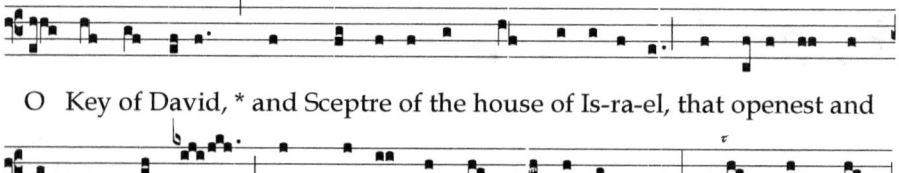

O Key of David, * and Sceptre of the house of Is-ra-el, that openest and

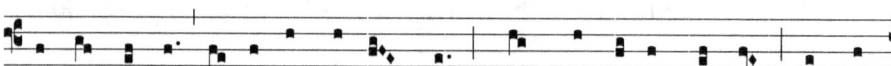

no man shutteth, and shuttest and nó man ó-pen-eth : Come and bring

the pris-o-ners out of the prison-house, them that sit in darkness and the

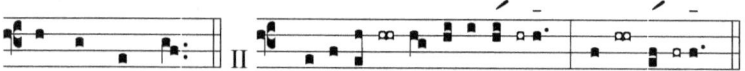

shádow of <u>death</u>.

December 21, Antiphon for Magnificat.

O Day-spring, * Brightness of Light Everlasting, and Sún of Ríghteous-

ness : Come and en-lighten them that sit in darkness and the shádow of

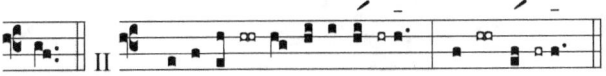

death.

December 22, Antiphon for Magnificat.

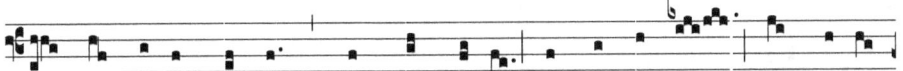

O King of the Nations, * and their Desire, the Cornerstone who mákest

both one : Come and save mankind, whom thou fórm-edst of clay.

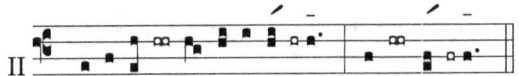

December 23, Antiphon for Magnificat.

O Em-man-u-el, * our King and Lawgiv-er, the De-sire of all na-tions

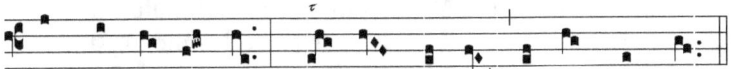

and théir Sal-vá-tion : come and sáve us, O Lórd our God.

CHRISTMASTIDE
From Christmas Eve until Jan. 5.

Invitatory.

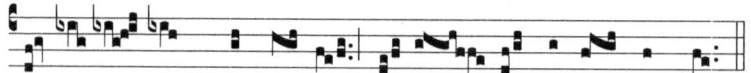

Un- to ús the Chríst is born : O cóme, let us wórship Him.

Antiphons for Psalms (appropriate for use on Feasts and Sundays)
1. The Lord hath sáid unto <u>Me</u> : Thou art My Son; this day have Í begótten Thee. *(Ps. 2)*
2. The Lord hath sent redemption únto His péople : He hath commanded His covenánt foréver. *(Ps. 111)*
3. Of the frúit of thy bódy : will I sét upón thy throne. *(Ps. 132)*
4. Christ the Lord, our Savior, everlasting Gód and Máry's Son : We práise Thee évermore.
5. At even ye shall know thát the Lórd will come : And in the morning, then shall ye see the glóry óf the Lord.
6. As the bridegroom fróm his chámber : Cometh forth the Lórd to rún His race. *(Ps. 19)*
7. The Word was made flesh, állelúia : And dwelt among us, állelúia.
8. Blessed is He that cometh in the náme of the <u>Lord</u> : God is the Lord, whích hath shówed us light. *(Ps. 118)*
9. Unto us a Child is born, állelúia : Unto us a Son is given, állelúia.
10. Unto you is born this day a Savior, állelúia : Which is Christ the Lord, állelúia.

Responsory for Christmastide.

VI

℟. The Word was made flesh and dwélt a-móng us; ‡ And we beheld His glory, the glory as of the Only-begotten of the Father, fúll of gráce and truth.

℟. The Word was... ℣. In the beginning was the Word, and the Word was with God, and the Word was God. ‡ And we beheld... ℣. Glory be to the Fá-ther and tó the Son: and tó the Hóly Ghost. ℟. The Word was...

[301] The Eve of the Nativity of Our Lord (First Vespers)
Psalms. 2, 8, 19, 45, 72, 85, 96, 98, 132, 145, 95, 80, 24, 93
Epistle. Isaiah 9:2-7

Hymn. Christe, Redemptor omnium. *6th c., trans. by J. M. Neale*

1. Jesus, the Father's only Son, / Whose death for all redemption won; / Before the worlds, of God most high / Begotten all ineffably.
2. The Father's light and splendor Thou, / Their endless hope to Thee that bow; / Accept the prayers and praise today / That through the world Thy servants pay.
3. Salvation's Author, call to mind / How, taking form of humankind, / Born of a Virgin undefiled, / Thou in man's flesh becam'st a child.
4. Thus testifies the present day, / Through every year in long array, / That Thou, salvation's source alone, / Proceedest from the Father's throne.
5. Whence sky, and stars, and sea's abyss, / And earth, and all that therein is, / Shall still, with laud and carol meet, / The Author of Thine advent greet.
6. And we who, by Thy precious blood / From sin redeemed, are marked for God, / On this the day that saw Thy birth, / Sing the new song of ransomed earth:
7. For that Thine advent glory be, / O Jesus, Virgin-born, to Thee; / with Father, and with Holy Ghost, / From men and from the heavenly host. Amen.

℣. Unto us a Child is born. ℟. Unto us a Son is given.

Antiphon for Magnificat.

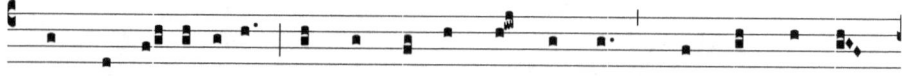

When the sun is risen, * ye shall sée the Kíng of kings : who pro-ceed-eth

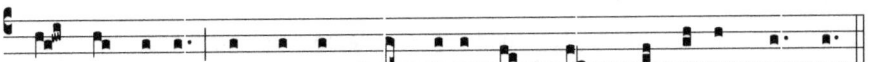

from the Father, and cometh forth as a bridegroom óut of his chámber.

VIII

Collect. O God, who hast made this most holy night to shine with the brightness of thè true Light : grant, we beseech Thee, that, as we have known on earth the mysteries of that Lìght; we may also come to the fullness of its joys in heaven; through the same Jesus Christ, Thy Son, oùr Lord; who liveth and reigneth with Thee and the Hòly Ghost : ever one God, world without end. Amen.

The Nativity of Our Lord (Dec. 25)
Psalms. 2, 8, 19, 45, 72, 85, 96, 98, 132, 145, 95, 80, 24, 93
Gospel (at Morning Prayer). Luke 2:(1-14)15-20

Hymn. **Veni, Redemptor gentium.** *St. Ambrose (340-397), trans. by J. M. Neale* [302]

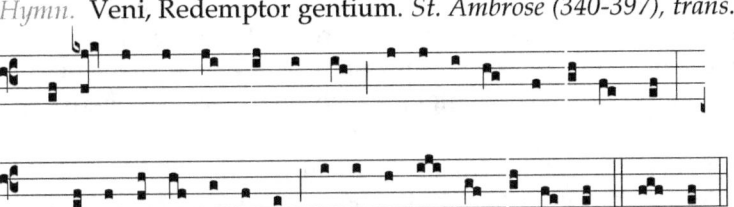

1. Come, Thou Redeemer of the earth, / And manifest Thy virgin birth: / Let every age adoring fall; / Such birth befits the God of all.
2. Begotten of no human will, / But of the Spirit, Thou art still / The Word of God in flesh arrayed, / The promised fruit to man displayed.
3. The virgin womb that burden gained / With virgin honor all unstained; / The banners there of virtue glow; / God in His temple dwells below.
4. Forth from His chamber goeth He, / That royal home of purity, / A giant in twofold substance one, / Rejoicing now His course to run.
5. From God the Father He proceeds, / To God the Father back He speeds; / His course He runs to death and hell, / Returning on God's throne to dwell.
6. O equal to Thy Father, Thou! / Gird on Thy fleshly mantle now; / The weakness of our mortal state / With deathless might invigorate.
7. Thy cradle here shall glitter bright, / And darkness breathe a newer light, / Where endless faith shall shine serene, / And twilight never

intervene.
8. All laud to God the Father be, / All praise, eternal Son, to Thee; / All glory, as is ever meet, / To God the Holy Paraclete. Amen.

Or: A solis ortus cardine. *Coelius Sedulius, c. 450, trans. by John Ellerton*

1. From east to west, from shore to shore, / Let every heart awake and sing / The holy child whom Mary bore, / The Christ, the everlasting King.
2. Behold, the world's Creator wears / The form and fashion of a slave; / Our very flesh our Maker shares, / His fallen creature, man, to save.
3. For this how wondrously he wrought! / A maiden, in her lowly place, / Became, in ways beyond all thought, / The chosen vessel of His grace.
4. She bowed her to the angel's word / Declaring what the Father willed, / And suddenly the promised Lord / That pure and hallowed temple filled.
5. He shrank not from the oxen's stall, / He lay within the manger-bed, / And he, whose bounty feedeth all, / At Mary's breast Himself was fed.
6. And while the angels in the sky / Sang praise above the silent field, / To shepherds poor the Lord Most High, / The one great Shepherd, was revealed.
7. All glory for this blessed morn / To God the Father ever be; / All praise to Thee, O Virgin-born, / All praise, O Holy Ghost, to Thee. Amen.

[303]

℣. The Word was máde flesh, al-le-lu-ia.
℟. And dwelt amóng us, al-le-lu-ia.
Antiphon for Benedictus. Glory to Gód in the híghest : and on earth peace, good will to men, alleluia, álleluía.

Collect. Grant, we beseech Thee, Almìghty God : that the new birth of Thine only-begotten Son in the flesh may set us frèe; who are held in the old bondage under the yoke of sin; through the same Jesus Christ, Thy Son, oùr Lord; who liveth and reigneth with Thee and the Hòly Ghost : ever one God, world without end. Amen.

Epistle (at Evening Prayer). **Titus 2:11-14**
Hymn. As for Christmas Eve.

Versicle (Music as at Morning Prayer)
℣. The Word was máde flesh, alleluia. ℟. And dwelt amóng us, alleluia.

Antiphon for Magnificat.

This is the time * whén the Chríst was born : this is the time when a Sáviour

ap-<u>peared</u>. This is the time when on earth Ángels were sínging : Archángels

re-jóicing. This is the time when the righteous shóuld exúlt and say : Glo-

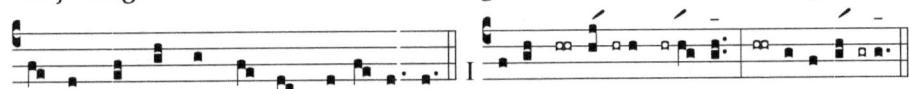

ry to God in the highest, ál-le-lú-ia.

St. Stephen, the First Martyr (Dec. 26)
All from Common of Martyrs (p. 541) except the following:
Psalms. **119iii, xi, i; 12, 26, 52, 56, 59, 116**
Gospel (at Morning Prayer). **Matthew 23:34-39**
Epistle (at Evening Prayer). **Acts 6:8-15; 7:54-60**

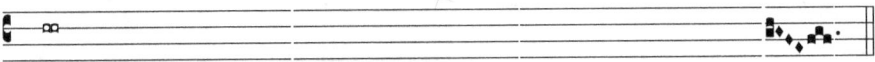

Versicle tone
℣. They gather themselves together against the soul of the righ-teous.
℟. And condemn the innocent ....blood.
Antiphon for Benedictus. O Jerusalem, Jerusalem, thou that killest the prophets, and stonest them which are sént unto <u>thee</u>: how often would I have gathered thy children together, even as a hen gathereth her chickens under her wíngs, and yé would not!

Antiphon for Magnificat.

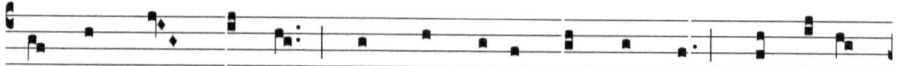

And they stoned Stephen, * who cálled upon Gód, and said : Lord Jesus,

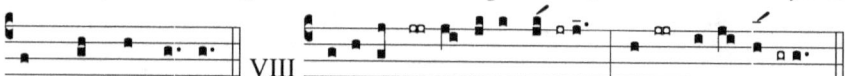

re-céive my spírit.

Collect. Grant, O Lord, that in all our sufferings here upon earth for the testimony of Thy truth we may steadfastly look up to heaven and by faith behold the glory that shall bè revealed : and, being filled with the Holy Ghost, may learn to love and bless our persecutors by the example of Thy first martyr, Saint Stephèn; who prayed for his murderers to Thee, O blessed Jesus, who standest at the right hand of God to succor all those that suffer for Thee, our only Mediator and Advocate; who livest and reignest with the Father and the Hòly Ghost : ever one God, world without end. Amen.

St. John, Apostle and Evangelist (Dec. 27)
All from Common of Apostles and Evangelists (p. 538), except the following:
Psalms. 92, 11, 119xii, 125, 145, 91, 56
Gospel (at Morning Prayer). **John 21:19-24**
Epistle (at Evening Prayer). **1 John 1:1-10**

℣. The Lord fed him with the bread of life and of understanding.
℟. And gave him to drink of the water of salutary wisdom.
Antiphon for Benedictus. This is the same John who leaned on the Lord's bosom át the Last Súpper : the blessed Apostle, unto whom were revealed the sécrets of héaven.

Antiphon for Magnificat.

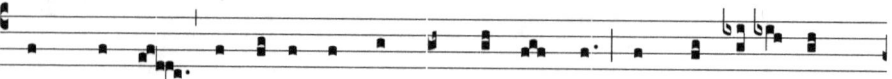

Then went this * saying abroad among the brethren that that di-scí-ple

should nót die : yet Jesus said not unto him, he shall not die, but, if I will

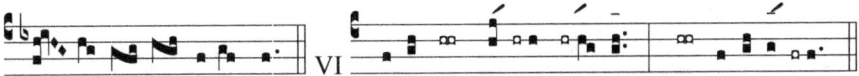

that he tár-ry tíll I come.

Collect. Merciful Lord, we beseech Thee to cast the bright beams of Thy light upòn Thy church : that it, being instructed by the doctrines of Thy blessed Apostle and Evangelist Saint Jòhn, may attain to the light of everlasting life; through the same Jesus Christ, Thy Son, oùr Lord, who liveth and reigneth with Thee and the Hòly Ghost : ever one God, world without end. Amen.

The Holy Innocents, Martyrs (Dec. 28)
All from Common of Martyrs (p. 541), except the following:
Psalms. **9, 124, 113, 37, 72, 79, 94, 23**
Gospel (at Morning Prayer). **Matthew 2:13-18**
Epistle (at Evening Prayer). **Revelation 14:1-5**

Hymn. **Salvete, flores martyrum.**
Aurelius C. Prudentius, d. 413, cento, trans. by H. W. Baker, alt.

1. Sweet flowerets of the martyr band, / Plucked by the tyrant's ruthless hand / Upon the threshold of the morn, / Like rosebuds by a tempest torn;
2. First victims for the incarnate Lord, / A tender flock to feel the sword; / Beside the very altar, gay, / With palm and crown, ye seemed to play.
3. Ah, what availed King Herod's wrath? / He could not stop the Savior's path. / Alone, while others murdered lay, / In safety Christ is borne away.
4. O Lord, the Virgin-born, to Thee / Eternal praise and glory be, / Whom with the Father we adore / And Holy Ghost forevermore. Amen.

℣. The souls of the righteous are in the hand of God.
℟. And there shall no torment touch them.
Antiphon for Benedictus. These are they which were not defiled with women, for théy are vírgins : and they follow the Lamb whithersoéver he góeth.

Antiphon for Magnificat.

Many in-no-cent children * were sláin in Chríst's behalf : the very sucklings

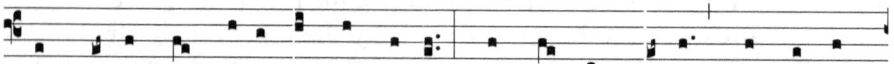

were put to death by a rúthless týrant; Pure and un-spotted, they fóllow

the Lámb himself : and say without ceasing, Glory bé to thée, O Lord.

Collect. O God, whose martyred innocents showed forth Thy praise not by speaking bùt by dying : mortify all vices within ùs, that our lives may in deed confess Thy faith which our tongue uttereth; through Jesus Christ, Thy Son, oùr Lord, who liveth and reigneth with Thee and the Hòly Ghost : ever one God, world without end. Amen.

Non-Feast Days Before the Sunday After Christmas

These days follow the order for Christmas Day but use the following Collect.

Collect. **Almighty God,** who hast given Thine only-begotten Son to take our nature upon Him and to be born òf a virgin : grant that we, being regenerate and made Thy children by adoptiòn, may daily be renewed by Thy Holy Spirit; through the same Jesus Christ, Thy Son, oùr Lord; who liveth and reigneth with Thee and the Hòly Ghost : ever one God, world without end. Amen.

Sunday after Christmas

Psalms. **93, 45, 91, 26, 110, 111, 84**
Gospel (at Morning Prayer). **Luke 2:33-40**
Epistle (at Evening Prayer). **Galatians 4:1-7**
Hymn. As for Christmas.

Versicle tone

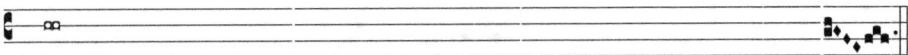

℣. The Lord reigneth, He is clothed with majes- ty.
℟. The Lord is clothed with strength, wherewith He hath girded Him-self.

Antiphon for Benedictus. Behold, this child is set for the fall and rising again of mány in Ísrael : and for a sign which shall be spoken against, állelúia.

Antiphon for Magnificat.

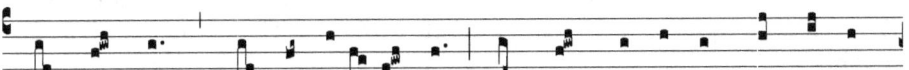

When all things * were in quiet si-lence, and night was in the mídst of hér

swift course: Thine Almighty Word, O Lord, leaped down from heaven out

of the royal throne, ál-le-lú-ia.

Collect. **Almighty and everlàsting God** : direct our actions according to Thy good pleasùre; that in the name of Thy beloved Son we may be made to abound in good works; through the same Jesus Christ, Thy Son, oùr Lord; who liveth and reigneth with Thee and the Hòly Ghost : ever one God, world without end. Amen.

[306] The Circumcision and the Name of Jesus (Jan. 1)
Psalms. **98, 8, 40, 92, 85, 117, 67**
Gospel (at Morning Prayer). **Luke 2:21**
Hymn. As for Christmas.

Or: (at Morning Prayer).
Jesu, dulcis memoria. *Bernard of Clairvaux, 12th c., trans. by J. M. Neale*

1. Jesus! the very thought is sweet; / In that dear name all heart-joys meet; / But O, than honey sweeter far / The glimpses of His presence are.
2. No word is sung more sweet than this, / No sound is heard more full of bliss, / No thought brings sweeter comfort nigh, / Than Jesus, Son of God most high.
3. Jesus, the hope of souls forlorn, / How good to them for sin that mourn! / To them that seek thee, O how kind! / But what art thou to them that find?
4. No tongue of mortal can express, / No pen can write, the blessedness: / He only who hath proved it knows / What bliss from love of Jesus flows.
5. O Jesus, King of wondrous might! / O Victor, glorious from the fight! / Sweetness that may not be expressed, / And altogether loveliest!
6. Abide with us, O Lord, today, / Fulfill us with Thy grace, we pray; / And with Thine own true sweetness feed / Our souls from sin and darkness freed.
7. All honor, laud, and glory be, / O Jesus, Virgin-Born, to Thee; / Whom with the Father we adore, / And Holy Ghost, for evermore. Amen.

℣. The Word was made flesh, alleluia. ℟. And dwelt among us, alleluia.
Antiphon for Benedictus.
A great and wondrous mystery is made knówn to ús this day : in a new manner are natures united, for God is becóme incárnate.
What He was, He still abode, and what He was not, He took únto Him<u>self</u> : suffering in His Person neither confusion nór divísion.

Epistle (at Evening Prayer). **Galatians 3:23-29**
Hymn. As for Christmas.

Or: (at Evening Prayer). **Exultet cor praecordiis.** *15th c., trans. by P. Dearmer*

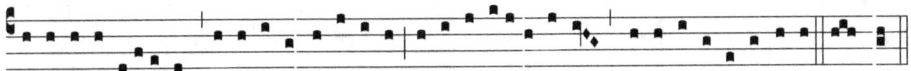

1. O let the heart beat high with bliss, / Yea, let it triumph at the sound / Of Jesus' Name, so sweet it is, / For every joy therein is found.
2. The Name that comforteth in woe, / The Name of Jesus healing sin, / The Name that curbs the powers below / And drives away the death within.
3. The Name that soundeth ever sweet / In speech or verse or holy song, / And bids us run with willing feet, / Consoled and comforted and strong.
4. Then let the Name of Jesus ring / With lofty praise in every place; / Let heart and voice together sing, / That Name shall every ill efface.
5. Ah! Jesus, health of sinful men, / Give ear unto our loving prayer; / Guide Thou our wandering feet again, / And hold our doings in Thy care.
6. Lord, may Thy Name supply our needs, / And keep us all from danger free, / And make us perfect in good deeds, / That we may lose our sins by Thee.
7. O Jesus, of the Virgin born, / Immortal honor be to Thee; / Praise to the Father infinite, / And Holy Ghost eternally. Amen.

℣. The Word was made flesh, alleluia. ℟. And dwelt among us, alleluia.

Antiphon for Magnificat.

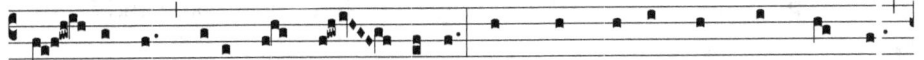

Heirs are we * óf a great mýs- ter-y : the womb of her that knew not man

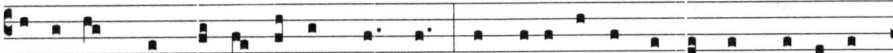

is become the temple óf the Gódhead. He, of a Virgin incarnate, suffereth

nó defílement : all the nations shall gather, saying, Glory bé to Thée,

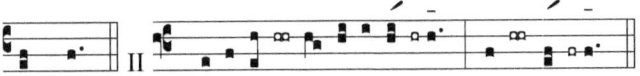

O Lord.

Collect. O Lord God, who for our sakes hast made Thy blessed Son, our Savior, subject to the Law and caused Him to endure the circumcision òf the flesh : grant us the true circumcision of the Spirìt; that our hearts may be pure from all sinful desires and lusts; through the same Jesus Christ, Thy Son, oùr Lord; who liveth and reigneth with Thee and the Hòly Ghost : ever one God, world without end. Amen.

Non-Feast Days January 2-5.
Antiphons from January 1. Everything else from the Sunday after Christmas.

Sunday after New Year
Psalms. **8, 106, 145, 138, 16, 72, 97**
Gospel (at Morning Prayer). **Matthew 2:13-23**
Epistle (at Evening Prayer). **1 Peter 4:12-19**

℣. The Word was made flesh, alleluia. ℟. And dwelt among us, alleluia.
Antiphon for Benedictus. When Israel was a child, thén I lóved him : and out of Egypt háve I cálled My Son.

Antiphon for Magnificat.

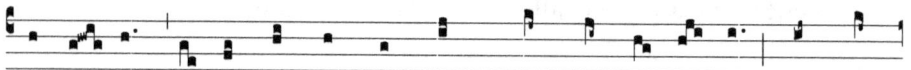

And Jo-seph * a-rose and took the young Child ánd His móther : and came

in-to the lánd of Ís-ra-el.

Collect. Almighty and everlàsting God : direct our actions according to Thy good pleasùre; that in the name of Thy beloved Son we may be made to abound in good works; through the same Jesus Christ, Thy Son, oùr Lord; who liveth and reigneth with Thee and the Hòly Ghost : ever one God, world without end. Amen.

EPIPHANYTIDE

From Epiphany until the Saturday before Septuagesima. The variable number of Sundays in Epiphanytide is due to the variable date of Easter. The propers for the 6th Sunday after Epiphany (Transfiguration) are used on the last Sunday after Epiphany. In the week after Transfiguration, however, the Collect of the actual Sunday (2nd, 3rd, 4th, 5th, or 6th Sunday after Epiphany as the case may be) is used, not the propers from Transfiguration.

Invitatory.

Christ hath ap- péared un-to us : O cóme,   let us wórship Him.

Antiphons for Psalms (appropriate for use on Feasts and Sundays) [308]

1. Give unto the Lord glóry and strength : Worship the Lord in the béauty of hóliness. *(Ps. 29)*
2. The Lord hath made known His word, állelúia : The Word of His salvation, állelúia.
3. A Light to líghten the Géntiles : And the Glory of Thy péople Ísrael.
4. We have seen His stár in the East : And are cóme to wórship Him.
5. The kings of Tarshish and of the isles shall bring presents, állelúia : The kings of Sheba and Seba shall offer gifts, állelúia. *(Ps. 72)*
6. And they from Sheba shall come, állelúia : They shall bring gold and incense, állelúia.
7. Oh, praise the Lord, all ye nations, állelúia : Praise Him, all ye people, állelúia. *(Ps. 117)*

Responsory for Epiphanytide.

℟. Arise, shine, fór thy Líght is come, ‡ And the Glory of the Lord is rís-en upón thee. ℟. Arise, shine, for... ℣. And the Gentiles shall come to thy Light and kings to the brightness óf thy rísing. ‡ And the Glory... ℣. Glory be to the Fáther and tó the Son: and tó the Hóly Ghost. ℟. Arise, shine, for...

The Epiphany of our Lord (Jan. 6)
Psalms. 72, 19, 45, 47, 48, 67, 87, 96, 100
Gospel (at Morning Prayer). **Matthew 2:1-12**
Epistle (at Evening Prayer). **Isaiah 60:1-6**

Hymn. **Hostis Herodes impie.** *Coelius Sedulius, c. 450, trans. by J. M. Neale, alt.*

1. The star proclaims the King is here; / But, Herod, why this senseless fear? / He takes no realms of earth away / Who gives the realms of heavenly day.
2. The wiser Magi see from far / And follow on His guiding star; / And led by light, to light they press / And by their gifts their God confess.
3. Within the Jordan's crystal flood / In meakness stands the Lamb of God / And, sinless, sanctifies the wave, / Mankind from sin to cleanse and save.
4. At Cana first His power is shown; / His might the blushing waters own / And, changing as He speaks the word, / Flow wine, obedient to their Lord.
5. All glory, Jesus, be to Thee / For this Thy glad epiphany; /

Whom with the Father we adore / And Holy Ghost forevermore. Amen.

℣. Three gifts did the Magi offer. ℟. Gold, frankincense, and myrrh.
Antiphon for Benedictus.
On this day is the church espoused to her héavenly Brídegroom : forasmuch
as in Jordan Christ hath cleansed hér iníquities.
Therefore do the Wise Men hasten with their offerings to the róyal núptials :
where the guests are gladdened with water made wine, álleluía.

Antiphon for Magnificat.

The Wise Men * be-holding the star, said óne to anóther : This is the sign of

a mighty King; Forth fare wé to séek Him. And let us óf-fer Him gifts : gold

and in-cense and myrrh, ál-le-lú-ia.

VIII

Collect. O God, who by the leading of a star didst manifest Thine only-
begotten Son tò the Gentiles : mercifully grant that we, who know Thee now
by fàith, may after this life have the fruition of Thy glorious Godhead;
through the same Jesus Christ, Thy Son, oùr Lord, who liveth and reigneth
with Thee and the Hòly Ghost : ever one God, world without end. Amen.

Non-Feast Days from Jan. 7-13.
On these days, the order for Epiphany is followed, except for the first Sunday after Epiphany, which has its own propers.

First Sunday After the Epiphany (Baptism of Our Lord)
Psalms. 45, 145, 100, 72, 50, 51, 119i, ii, v; 128, 27, 40, 122
Gospel (at Morning Prayer). Matthew 3:13-17
Epistle (at Evening Prayer). Isaiah 42:1-7

℣. The Lord hath made known His salvation.
℟. His righteousness hath He openly shewed in the sight of the heathen.
Antiphon for Benedictus.
And Jesus, when he was baptized, went up straightway óut of the wáter :
 and, lo, the heavens were ópened únto him,
And he saw the Spirit of God descénding líke a dove : and lighting upon
 him, állelúia.

Antiphon for Magnificat.

John said unto Jesus, * I have need to be baptized of Thee, and cómest Thóu

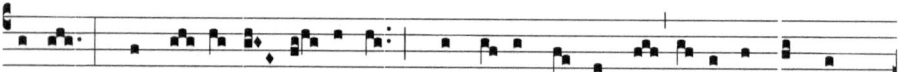

to me? : And Jesus said unto him, Thus it be-cometh us to fulfil all right-

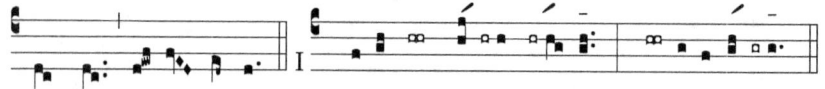

eousness, ál- le- lú-ia.

Collect. O God, our heavenly Father, whose voice was heard at the Baptism of Thine only-begotten Son, declaring Him to be the One with whom Thou àrt well-pleased : pour down Thy Holy Ghost upon Thy faithful peoplè, that we may rejoice in this same sonship that we have received from Thee through our Baptism into Christ; who liveth and reigneth with Thee and the same Hòly Ghost : ever one God, world without end. Amen.

Non-Feast Days Jan. 14 until the 2nd Sunday After Epiphany (Historic 1st Sunday After the Epiphany)
Psalms. 145, 100, 72, 50, 51, 119i, ii, v; 128, 27, 40, 122
Gospel (at Morning Prayer). Luke 2:41-52
Epistle (at Evening Prayer). Romans 12:1-5

℣. The Lord hath made known His salvation.
℟. His righteousness hath He openly shewed in the sight of the heathen.
Antiphon for Benedictus. The Child Jesus tarried behind in Jerusalem, and Joseph and his mother knéw not óf it : But they, supposing Him to have been in the company, sought Him among their kinsfolk ánd acquáintance.

Antiphon for Magnificat.

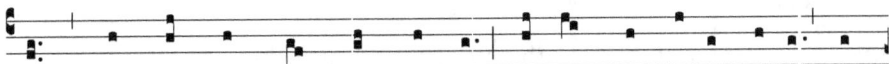

Son, * why hast Thóu thus déalt with us? : behold, Thy father and I have

sóught Thee sórrowing. How is it thát ye sóught Me? : Knew ye not that I [310]

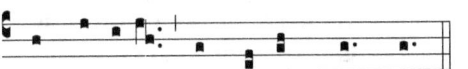

must be about My Fáther's búsiness?

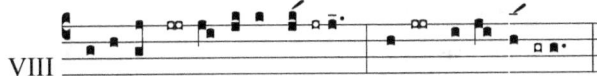
VIII

Collect. O Lord, wè beseech Thee : mercifully to receive the prayers of Thy people who call upon Theè; and grant that they may both perceìve and know what things they ought to do and also may have grace and power faithfully to fulfill the same; through Jesus Christ, Thy Son, oùr Lord; who liveth and reigneth with Thee and the Hòly Ghost : ever one God, world without end. Amen.

Second Sunday After the Epiphany
Psalms. **66, 107, 15, 145, 36, 115, 127, 128, 23**
Gospel (at Morning Prayer). **John 2:1-11**
Epistle (at Evening Prayer). **Romans 12:6-16**

℣. Let all the earth worship Thee, O God.
℟. And sing praise to Thy name, O Thou most High.
Antiphon for Benedictus. Now there was a marriage in Cána of Gálilee : and Jesus Himself was there, with Máry His Móther.

417

Antiphon for Magnificat.

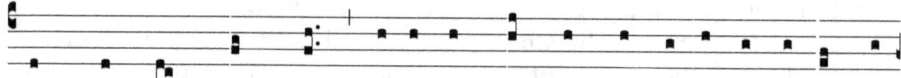

And when they lacked wine, * Jesus commanded them to fill the water-póts

with wáter : and straitway was the water máde into <u>wine</u>.

Collect. Almighty and everlasting God, who dost govern all things in heavèn and earth : mercifully hear the supplications of Thy peoplè; and grant us Thy peace all the days of our life; through Jesus Christ, Thy Son, oùr Lord; who liveth and reigneth with Thee and the Hòly Ghost : ever one God, world without end. Amen.

Third Sunday After the Epiphany
Psalms. 97, 102, 118, 101, 144, 56, 103, 116, 117
Gospel (at Morning Prayer). **Matthew 8:1-13**
Epistle (at Evening Prayer). **Romans 12:16-21**

℣. The Lord reigneth, let the earth rejoice.
℟. Let the multitude of isles be glad thereof.
Antiphon for Benedictus.
When Jesus was come down from the mountain, behold, there came a leprous man, and gave Him wórship and <u>said</u> : Lord, if Thou wilt, Thóu canst máke me clean;
And He put forth His hand and tóuched him, sáying : I wíll; be thou <u>clean</u>.

Antiphon for Magnificat.

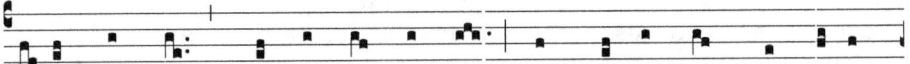

Many shall come * fróm the eást and west : and shall sit down with Abra-

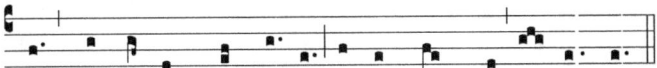

ham, and I-saac, and Jacob, in the kíngdom of héaven.

IV

Collect. Almighty and everlàsting God : mercifully look upon our infirmìties; and in all our dangers and necessities stretch forth the right hand of Thy majesty to help and defend us; through Jesus Christ, Thy Son, oùr Lord; who liveth and reigneth with Thee and the Hòly Ghost : ever one God, world without end. Amen.

Fourth Sunday After the Epiphany

[311]

Psalms. 7, 119xii, xiii; 29, 65, 77, 20, 107
Gospel (at Morning Prayer). Matthew 8:23-27
Epistle (at Evening Prayer). Romans 13:8-10

℣. Worship the Lord, alleluia. ℟. In His holy temple, alleluia.
Antiphon for Benedictus. And when Jesus entered into a ship, behold, there arose a great témpest ín the sea : and His disciples came and awoke Him, saying, Lord, sáve us; we pérish.

Antiphon for Magnificat.

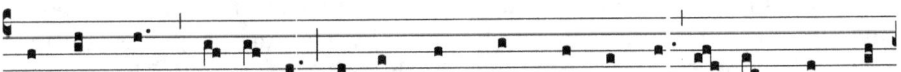

Save us, Lórd, * we pérish : rebuke the winds and the sea, O God, and máke

I

a great <u>calm</u>.

Collect. Almighty God, who knowest us to be set in the midst of so many and great dangers that by reason of the frailty of our nature we cannot alwàys stand upright : grant to us such strength and protection as may support us in all dangèrs; and carry us through all temptations; through Jesus Christ, Thy Son, oùr Lord; who liveth and reigneth with Thee and the Hòly Ghost : ever one God, world without end. Amen.

Fifth Sunday After the Epiphany
Psalms. **32, 92, 105, 28, 36, 78:1-24**
Gospel (at Morning Prayer). **Matthew 13:24-30**
Epistle (at Evening Prayer). **Colossians 3:12-17**

℣. Worship the Lord, alleluia. ℟. In His holy temple, alleluia.
Antiphon for Benedictus. Sir, didst not Thou sow good seed in Thy field? † From whénce then háth it tares? : And the house-holder made answer, An enemý hath dóne this.

Antiphon for Magnificat.

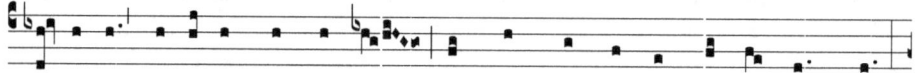

Gather ye * together first the tares, and bind them in búndles to búrn them :

but gather the wheat in-to my bárn, saith the Lord.

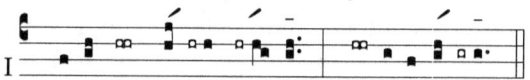

Collect. O Lord, wè beseech Thee : to keep Thy Church and household continually in Thy true religiòn, that they who do lean upon the hope of Thy heavenly grace may evermore be defended by Thy mighty power; through Jesus Christ, Thy Son, oùr Lord, who liveth and reigneth with Thee and the Hòly Ghost : ever one God, world without end. Amen.

Sixth Sunday After the Epiphany (Transfiguration)

Psalms. 77, 84, 112, 45, 110, 61, 97, 104, 16, 63
Epistle (at Evening Prayer). 2 Peter 1:16-21

Hymn (at Evening Prayer). **Caelestis formam gloriae.** *15th cent., trans. by R. E. Roberts* [312]

1. An image of that heavenly light, / The goal the Church keeps ay in sight, / Christ on the holy mount displays / Where He outshines the sun's bright rays.
2. Let every age proclaimer be / How, on this day, the chosen three / With Moses and Elias heard / The Lord speak many a gracious word.
3. As witnesses to grace are nigh / Those twain, the Law and Prophecy; / And to the Son, from out the cloud, / The Father's record thunders loud.
4. With garments whiter than the snows, / And shining face, Lord Jesus shows / What glory for those saints shall be / Who joy in God with piety.
5. The vision and the mystery / Make faithful hearts beat quick and high, / So on this solemn day of days / The cry goes up of prayer and praise.
6. O God the Father, God the Son, / And Holy Spirit, Three in One, / Vouchsafe to bring us, by Thy grace, / To see Thy glory face to face. Amen.

℣. Thou hast appeared glorious in the sight of the Lord.
℞. Therefore the Lord hath clothed Thee with strength.

1st Vespers, Antiphon for Magnificat.

Christ Jesus, * the brightness of the Father and the express image of his Per-

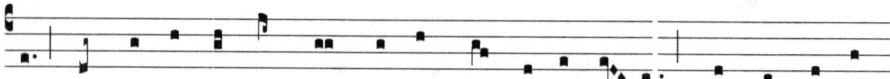

son, who upholdeth all things by the word of his power, while he was by

himself púrging awáy our sins : vouchsafed on this day to shew himself in

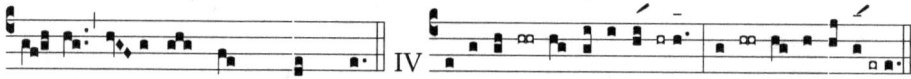

glo-ry upón an high móuntain.

Gospel (at Morning Prayer). **Matthew 17:1-9**
Hymn (at Morning Prayer).
O nata Lux de lumine. *10ᵗʰ cent., trans. by L. Housman, alt.*

1. O Light of Light, by love inclined, / Jesus, Redeemer of mankind, / With loving-kindness deign to hear / From suppliant voices praise and prayer.
2. Thou who to raise our souls from hell / Didst deign in fleshly form to dwell, / Vouchsafe us, when our race is run, / In Thy fair body to be one.
3. More bright than day Thy face did show, / Thy raiment whiter than the snow, / When on the mount to mortals blest / Man's maker Thou wast manifest.
4. Two prophets, that had faith to see, / With thine elect found company, / Where unto each, divinely shown, / The Godhead veiled in form was

known.
5. The heavens above His glory named, / The Father's voice His Son proclaimed; / To whom, the King of glory now, / All faithful hearts adoring bow.
6. May all who seek Thy praise aright / Through purer lives show forth Thy light; / So to the brightness of the skies / By faith and love our hearts shall rise.
7. Eternal God, to Thee we raise, / The King of kings, our hymn of praise, / Who Three in One and One in Three / Dost live and reign eternally. Amen.

℣. Thou hast appeared glorious in the sight of the Lord. [313]
℟. Therefore the Lord hath clothed Thee with strength.
Antiphon for Benedictus. And behold, there was a voice óut of the clóud, which said : This is my beloved Son, in whom I am well pleased; hear ye him, álleluia.

Collect. O God, who in the glorious transfiguration of Thine only begotten Son confirmed the mysteries of the faith by the testimony of the fathers and who, in the voice that came from the bright cloud, didst in a wonderful manner foreshow the adoptiòn of sons : mercifully make and keep us co-heirs with the King of His glorý, and bring us to the enjoyment of the same; through the same Jesus Christ, Thy Son, oùr Lord, who liveth and reigneth with Thee and the Hòly Ghost : ever one God, world without end. Amen.

2nd Vespers: All as at 1st Vespers, except:
℣. Thou hast appeared glorious in the sight of the Lord.
℟. Therefore the Lord hath clothed Thee with strength.

Antiphon for Magnificat.

And when the disciples * heard the Voice, they fell on their face, ánd were

sóre afraid : and Jesus came and touched them and said, A-rise and be not

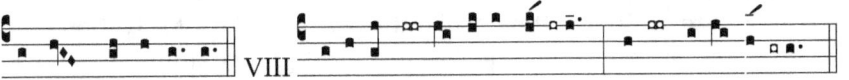

a-fraid, ál-le-lú-ia.

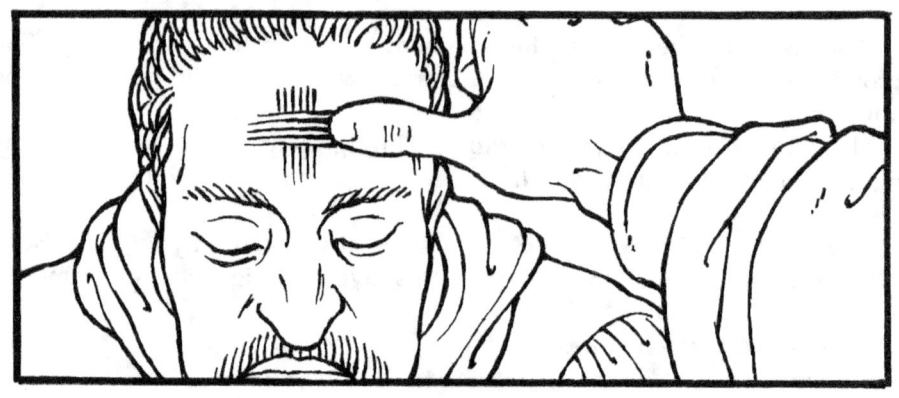

LENTENTIDE

Lententide is divided into three parts:
1. *Pre-Lent (Septuagesimatide)*   *From Septuagesima Sunday till Tuesday after Quinquagesima.*
2. *Lent (Quadragesimatide)*   *From Ash Wednesday until Saturday before Judica.*
3. *Passiontide*   *From Judica until Wednesday of Holy Week.*

In all three parts of Lententide, the **Alleluia** *is not said anywhere in the Office. In the opening versicles of the Office,* **Alleluia** *is replaced by* **Praise to Thee, O Christ, King of eternal glory**.

Invitatory.

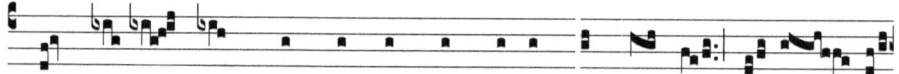

Christ, for our sakes, hath endured temptátion and súffering : O cóme, let

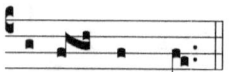

us wórship Him.

Antiphons for Psalms (appropriate for use on Feasts and Sundays)
1. Man shall not líve by bréad alone : But by every word that proceedeth óut of the móuth of God.
2. Behold, now is thé accépted time : Behold, now is the dáy of salvátion.
3. The kings of the earth set themselves, and the rulers take cóunsel togéther : Against the Lord and against Hís annóinted. *(Ps. 2)*
4. He was oppressed, and He was afflicted, yet He ópened nót His mouth :

And the Lord hath laid on Him the iníquity óf us all.
5. Save me from the líon's móuth, O Lord : And deliver me from the hórns of the únicorns. *(Ps. 22)*
6. Christ became obédient únto death : Even the déath of the cross.
7. Christ was wounded for óur transgréssions : He was bruised for óur iníquities.

Responsory for Pre-Lent. [314]

IV

℟. The Lord will be a Refuge for the oppressed, a Refuge in tímes of tróuble. ‡ And they that know Thy name will pút their trúst in Thee. ℟. The Lord will... ℣. For Thou, Lord, hast not forsaken thém that séek Thee. ‡ And they that... ℣. Glory be to the Fáther and tó the Son : and tó the Hó-ly Ghost.

℟. The Lord will...

Septuagesima

Psalms. 18, 9, 130, 92, 31, 86, 102, 42
Gospel (at Morning Prayer). Matthew 20:1-16
Epistle (at Evening Prayer). 1 Corinthians 9:24-10:5

℣. I will love Thee, O Lord my strength.
℞. The Lord is my rock, and my fortress, and my deliverer.

Antiphon for Benedictus. The kingdom of heaven is like unto a man that ís an hóuseholder : which went out early in the morning to hire labourers into his víneyard, sáith the Lord.

Antiphon for Magnificat.

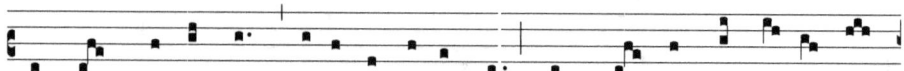

The householder saith * unto the labourers, Why stand ye here áll the day

ídle? : They say unto him, Because nó man hath híred us. Go ye al- so ín-

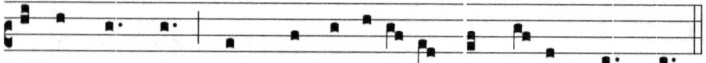

to the víneyard : and whatso-ever is right, Í will gíve you.

VII

Collect. O Lord, wè beseech Thee : favorably to hear the prayers of Thy peoplè, that we, who are justly punished for our offenses, may be mercifully delivered by Thy goodness, for the glory of Thy name; through Jesus Christ, Thy Son, oùr Lord, who liveth and reigneth with Thee and the Hòly Ghost : ever one God, world without end. Amen.

Sexagesima

Psalms. 44, 83, 60, 17, 43, 143, 25, 83
Gospel (at Morning Prayer). Luke 8:4-15
Epistle (at Evening Prayer). 2 Corinthians 11:19-12:9

℣. Arise, O Lord, help us. ℞. And redeem us because of Thy holy name.

Antiphon for Benedictus. When much people were gathered together unto Jesus, and were come to Him out of every city, He spáke by a párable : A sower went óut to sów His seed.

Antiphon for Magnificat.

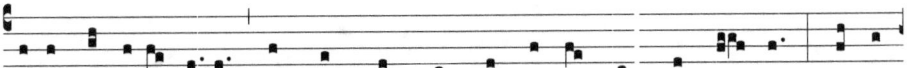

Unto you it is given * to know the mystéries of the kíngdom of God : but to

others in par-a-bles, said Jesus unto Hís di-scí-ples.

VI

Collect. O God, who seest that we put not our trust in anything thàt we do : mercifully grant that by Thy powèr, we may be defended against all adversity; through Jesus Christ, Thy Son, oùr Lord, who liveth and reigneth with Thee and the Hòly Ghost : ever one God, world without end. Amen.

Quinquagesima
Psalms. 31, 77, 100, 119i, ii, iii; 15, 78, 146, 33
Gospel (at Morning Prayer). Luke 18:31-43
Epistle (at Evening Prayer). 1 Corinthians 13:1-3

℣. In Thee, O Lord, do I put my trust, let me never be ashamed.
℟. Deliver me in Thy righteousness.
Antiphon for Benedictus. [315]

Behold, we go up to Jerusalem, and all things that are written by the Prophets concerning the Son of Man shall bé accómplished : for He shall be delivered unto the Gentiles, and shall be mócked, and spítted on;
And they shall scourge Him, and pút Him to death : and the third day Hé shall ríse again.

Antiphon for Magnificat.

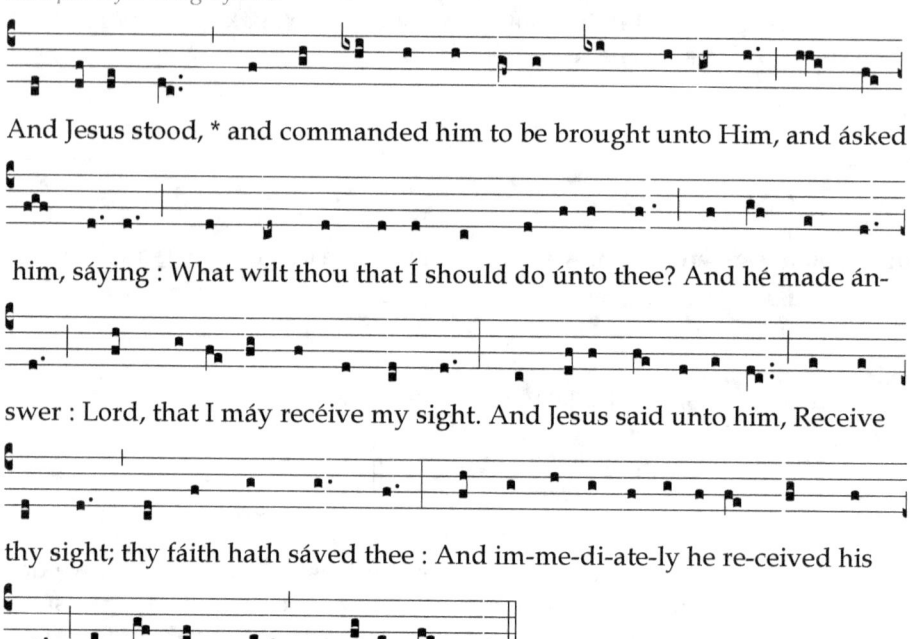

And Jesus stood, * and commanded him to be brought unto Him, and ásked him, sáying : What wilt thou that Í should do únto thee? And hé made ánswer : Lord, that I máy recéive my sight. And Jesus said unto him, Receive thy sight; thy fáith hath sáved thee : And im-me-di-ate-ly he re-ceived his sight and followed Him, gló-ri-fý-ing God.

Collect. O Lord, wè beseech Thee : mercifully hear oùr prayers, and, having set us free from the bonds of sin, defend us from all evil; through Jesus Christ, Thy Son, oùr Lord, who liveth and reigneth with Thee and the Hòly Ghost : ever one God, world without end. Amen.

Lent

From Ash Wednesday until Saturday before Judica. From Ash Wednesday until Easter it is appropriate to fast. The Suffrages are prayed at Morning Prayer (Lauds) and Evening Prayer (Vespers) on Weekdays.

Responsory for Lent.

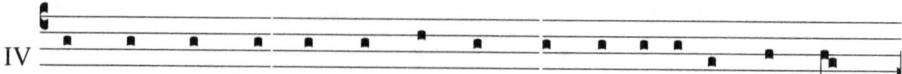

℟. Rend your heart, and not your garments, and turn únto the Lórd your

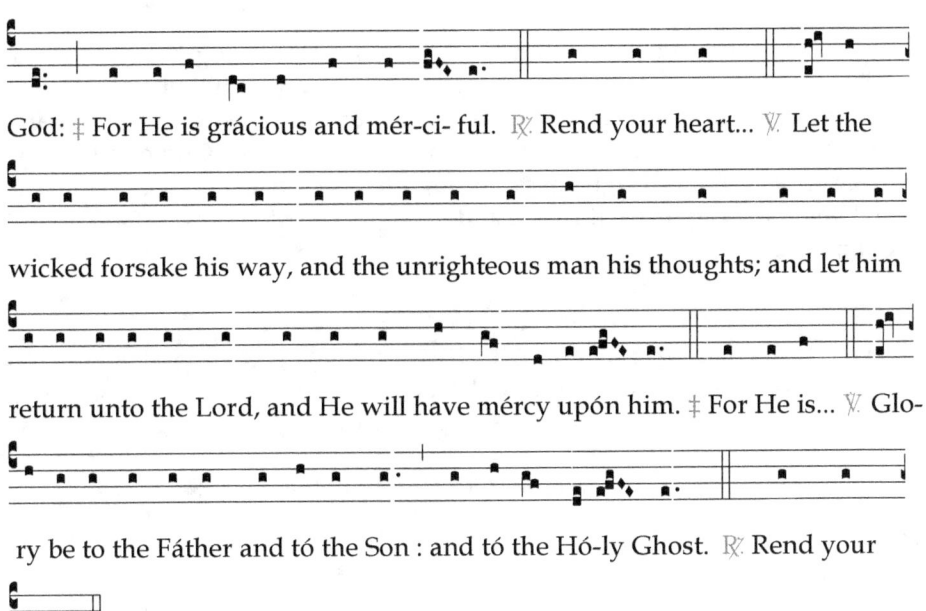

God: ‡ For He is grácious and mér-ci- ful. ℟. Rend your heart... ℣. Let the wicked forsake his way, and the unrighteous man his thoughts; and let him return unto the Lord, and He will have mércy upón him. ‡ For He is... ℣. Glory be to the Fáther and tó the Son : and tó the Hó-ly Ghost. ℟. Rend your heart...

Ash Wednesday
Psalms. 6, 32, 38, 51, 102, 130, 143, 69, 57, 79
Gospel (at Morning Prayer). **Matthew 6:16-21**
Epistle (at Evening Prayer). **Joel 2:12-19**

℣. In Thee, O Lord, do I put my trust, let me never be ashamed.
℟. Deliver me in Thy righteousness.
Antiphon for Benedictus. When ye fast, be not ás the hýpocrites : óf a sad cóuntenance.

Antiphon for Magnificat.

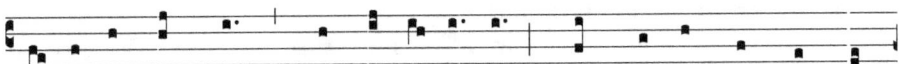

Lay up for yourselves * tréasures in héaven : where neither moth nor rúst

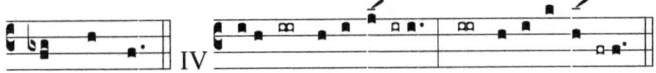

doth corrupt.

Collect. **Almighty and everlasting God, who hatest nothing that Thou hast made and dost forgive the sins of all those who are pènitent : create and make in us new and contrite heàrts, that we, worthily lamenting our sins and acknowledging our wretchedness, may obtain of Thee, the God of all mercy, perfect remission and forgiveness; through Jesus Christ, Thy Son, oùr Lord, who liveth and reigneth with Thee and the Hòly Ghost : ever one God, world without end. Amen.**

[316] Invocavit, the First Sunday in Lent
Psalms. 91, 31, 1, 42, 32, 34, 121, 55, 27, 73
Gospel (at Morning Prayer). **Matthew 4:1-11**

Hymn (at Morning Prayer).
Audi benigne Conditor. *Gregory the Great, 6th cent., trans. by T. A. Lacey*

1. O kind Creator, bow Thine ear / To mark the cry, to know the tear / Before Thy throne of mercy spent / In this thy holy fast of Lent.
2. Our hearts are open, Lord, to Thee: / Thou knowest our infirmity; / Pour out on all who seek Thy face / Abundance of Thy pardoning grace.
3. Our sins are many, this we know; / Spare us, good Lord, Thy mercy show; / And for the honor of Thy name / Our fainting souls to life reclaim.
4. Give us the self-control that springs / From discipline of outward things, / That fasting inward secretly / The soul may purely dwell with Thee.
5. We pray Thee, Holy Trinity, / One God, unchanging Unity, / That we from this our abstinence / May reap the fruits of penitence. Amen.

℣. He shall call upon me, and I will answer him.
℟. I will deliver him and honor him.
Antiphon for Benedictus. **Then was Jesus led up of the Spirit into the wilderness, to be tempted óf the dévil : and when He had fasted forty days and forty nights, He was afterwárd an húngered.**

Epistle (at Evening Prayer). **2** Corinthians 6:1-10

Hymn (at Evening Prayer). Ex more docti mystico. *6ᵗʰ cent., trans. by J. M. Neale*

1. The fast, as taught by holy lore, / We keep in solemn course once more; / The fast to all men known, and bound / In forty days of yearly round.
2. The law and seers that were of old / In diverse ways this Lent foretold, / Which Christ, all seasons' King and Guide, / In after ages sanctified.
3. More sparing therefore let us make / The words we speak, the food we take, / Our sleep and mirth,— and closer barred / Be every sense in holy guard.
4. In prayer together let us fall, / And cry for mercy, one and all, / And weep before the Judge's feet, / And His avenging wrath entreat.
5. Thy grace have we offended sore, / By sins, O God, which we deplore; / But pour upon us from on high, / O pardoning One, Thy clemency.
6. Remember Thou, though frail we be, / That yet Thine handiwork are we; / Nor let the honor of Thy name / Be by another put to shame.
7. Forgive the sin that we have wrought; / Increase the good that we have sought; / That we at length, our wanderings o'er, / May please Thee here and evermore.
8. We pray Thee, Holy Trinity, / One God, unchanging Unity, / That we from this our abstinence / May reap the fruits of penitence. Amen.

[317] ℣. He shall call upon me, and I will answer him.
℟. I will deliver him and honor him.

Antiphon for Magnificat.

Behold * now is the accepted time; behold now is the dáy of salvátion: let us

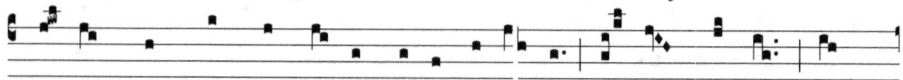

therefore show ourselves as the ministers of God, in much patience, in

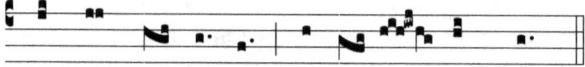

watchings, in fastings, ánd by lóve un-feigned.

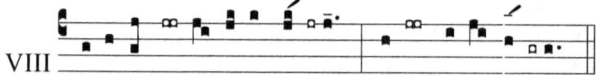

VIII

Collect. O Lord, mercifully hèar our prayer : and stretch forth the right hand of Thy majèsty, to defend us from them that rise up against us; through Jesus Christ, Thy Son, oùr Lord, who liveth and reigneth with Thee and the Hòly Ghost : ever one God, world without end. Amen.

Ember Days in Lent
EMBER WEDNESDAY
Gospel (at Morning Prayer). **Matthew 12:38-50**
Epistle (at Evening Prayer). **1 Kings 19:3-8**

℣. God shall give his angels charge over thee.
℟. To keep thee in all thy ways.
Antiphon for Benedictus. **An** evil and adulterous generation seeketh áfter a <u>sign</u> : and there shall no sign be given to it, but the sign of the próphet Jónas.

Antiphon for Magnificat.

For as Jonas * was three days and three nights in the whále's bél-ly : so shall

the Son of Man be in the héart of the earth.

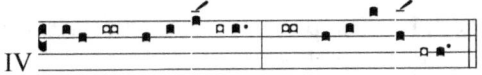

IV

Collect. We beseech Theè O Lord : that Thou wouldst graciously hear our pràyers, and stretch forth the right hand of Thy majesty to be our defence against all adversities; through Jesus Christ, Thy Son, oùr Lord, who liveth and reigneth with Thee and the Hòly Ghost : ever one God, world without end. Amen.

EMBER FRIDAY
Gospel (at Morning Prayer). **John 5:1-15**
Epistle (at Evening Prayer). **Ezekiel 18:20-28**

℣. God shall give his angels charge over thee.
℟. To keep thee in all thy ways.
Antiphon for Benedictus. An angel of the Lord went down from heaven, and tróubled the wáters : and whosoever first did step thereín was made whole.

Antiphon for Magnificat.

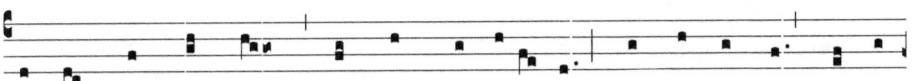

He that made me whole, * the same sáid unto me : Take up thy béd, and gó

in peace.

Collect. We beseech Thèe O Lord : mercifully to have compassion on Thy peoplè, that they, which by Thee are enabled to serve Thee, may ever be comforted by Thy gracious and ready help; through Jesus Christ, Thy Son, oùr Lord, who liveth and reigneth with Thee and the Hòly Ghost : ever one God, world without end. Amen.

EMBER SATURDAY
Gospel (at Morning Prayer). **Matthew 17:1-9**
Epistle (at Evening Prayer). **1 Thessalonians 5:14-23**

℣. God shall give his angels charge over thee.
℞. To keep thee in all thy ways.
Antiphon for Benedictus. And Jesus taketh his disciples, and bringeth them up into an high móuntain apart : and was transfígured befóre them.

Antiphon for Magnificat.

Tell the vision * which ye have séen to nó man : until the Son of Man be ris-

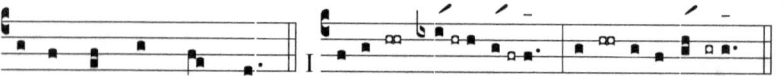

en agáin from the dead.

Collect. We beseech Thèe O Lord : graciously to hear the prayers of Thy peoplè, and of Thy great goodness turn aside from them the scourges of Thine anger; through Jesus Christ, Thy Son, oùr Lord, who liveth and reigneth with Thee and the Hòly Ghost : ever one God, world without end. Amen.

Reminiscere, the Second Sunday in Lent
Psalms. 25, 119x; 5, 15, 38, 39, 141, 60
Gospel (at Morning Prayer). **Matthew 15:21-28**
Epistle (at Evening Prayer). **1 Thessalonians 4:1-7**
Hymn. As for 1st S. in Lent

[318] ℣. Unto Thee, O Lord, do I lift up my soul.
℞. O my God, I trust in Thee, let me not be ashamed.
Antiphon for Benedictus. And Jesus went thence, and departed into the borders of Tyre and Sidon; † and behold, a woman of Canaan came out of the same borders, ánd cried, sáying : Have mercy on me, O Lord, Thou Són of Dávid.

Antiphon for Magnificat.

Jesus * said unto the wóman of Cánaan : it is not meet to take the children's bread, and to cást it únto dogs. And the wóman said, Trúth, Lord : yet the dogs do eat of the crumbs which fall from their máster's táble. And Jesus made answer, O woman, gréat is thy <u>faith</u> : be it unto thee éven ás thou wilt.

IV

Collect. O God, who seest that of ourselves we hàve no strength : keep us both outwardly and inwàrdly, that we may be defended from all adversities which may happen to the body and from all evil thoughts which may assault and hurt the soul; through Jesus Christ, Thy Son, oùr Lord, who liveth and reigneth with Thee and the Hòly Ghost : ever one God, world without end. Amen.

Oculi, the Third Sunday in Lent

Psalms. 25, 9, 19, 84, 123, 12, 40, 6
Gospel (at Morning Prayer). Luke 11:14-28

Hymn (at Morning Prayer).
Clarum decus jejunii. *Gregory the Great, 6th cent., trans. by M. F. Bell*

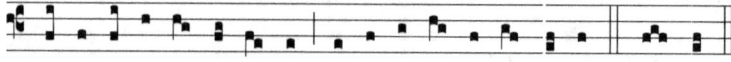

1. The glory of these forty days / We celebrate with songs of praise; / For Christ, through whom all things were made, / Himself has fasted and has prayed.
2. Alone and fasting Moses saw / The loving God who gave the law; / And to Elijah, fasting, came / The steeds and chariots of flame.
3. So Daniel trained his mystic sight, / Delivered from the lions' might; / And John, the Bridegroom's friend, became / The herald of Messiah's name.
4. Then grant us, Lord, like them to be / Full oft in fast and prayer with Thee; / Our spirits strengthen with Thy grace, / And give us joy to see Thy face.
5. O Father, Son, and Spirit blest, / To Thee be every prayer addressed, / Who art in three-fold Name adored, / From age to age, the only Lord. Amen.

℣. Unto Thee lift I up mine eyes. ℟. O Thou that dwellest in the heavens.
Antiphon for Benedictus. When a strong man armed kéepeth his pálace : his goods and possessions are in péace and sáfety.

Epistle (at Evening Prayer). **Ephesians 5:1-9**
Hymn (at Evening Prayer). **Ecce tempus idoneum.** *Before 12th c., trans. by T. A. Lacey*

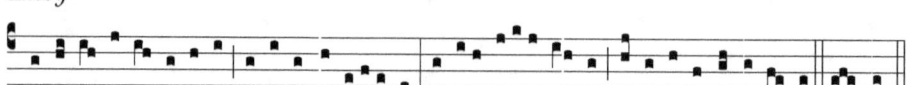

1. Now is the healing time decreed / For sins of heart, of word or deed, / When we in humble fear record / The wrong that we have done the Lord;
2. Who, always merciful and good, / Has borne so long our wayward mood, / Nor cut us off unsparingly / In our so great iniquity.
3. Therefore with fasting and with prayer, / Our secret sorrow we declare; /

With all good striving seek his face, / And lowly-hearted plead for grace.
4. Cleanse us, O Lord, from every stain, / Help us the meed of praise to gain, / Till with the angels linked in love / Joyful we tread Thy courts above.
5. Father and Son and Spirit blest, / To Thee be every prayer addressed, / Who art in threefold Name adored, / From age to age, the only Lord. Amen.

℣. Unto Thee lift I up mine eyes. ℟. O Thou that dwellest in the heavens.

Antiphon for Magnificat.

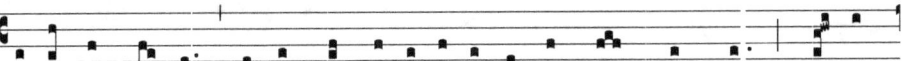

A certain woman * of the company lifted úp her vóice, and cried : Blessed

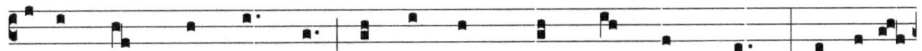

is the womb that bare thee, and the páps which thóu hast sucked. But Jesus

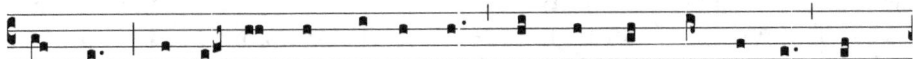

answered, Yea rather, bléss-ed are they : that hear the word of Gód, and

kéep it.

Collect. We beseech Thee, Almìghty God : look upon the hearty desires of Thy humble servànts, and stretch forth the right hand of Thy majesty to be our Defense against all our enemies; through Jesus Christ, Thy Son, oùr Lord, who liveth and reigneth with Thee and the Hòly Ghost : ever one God, world without end. Amen.

Laetare, the Fourth Sunday in Lent
Psalms. **122, 125, 135, 5, 37, 33, 105, 51**
Gospel (at Morning Prayer). **John 6:1-15**
Epistle (at Evening Prayer). **Galatians 4:21-31**
Hymn. As for the 3rd S. in Lent.

℣. Cleanse Thou me from secret faults, O Lord.
℟. Keep back Thy servant also from presumptuous sins.

Antiphon for Benedictus.
When Jesus lifted up His eyes, and saw a great company come unto Him, He saith únto Phílip : Whence shall we buy bréad that thése may eat?
And this He sáid to próve him : for He Himself knéw what Hé would do.

Antiphon for Magnificat.

And Jesus * went up ínto a móuntain : and there He sat with Hís di-scí-ples.

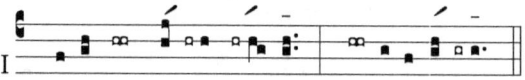

Collect. Grant, we beseech Thee, Almìghty God : that we, who for our evil deeds do worthily deserve to be punìshed, by the comfort of Thy grace may mercifully be relieved; through Jesus Christ, Thy Son, oùr Lord, who liveth and reigneth with Thee and the Hòly Ghost : ever one God, world without end. Amen.

[320] PASSIONTIDE

From Judica until Wednesday in Holy Week. During Passiontide, **Glory be...** *is said in the Opening Versicles, Psalmody, and Canticles, but is omitted from the Responsories.*

Responsory for Passiontide.

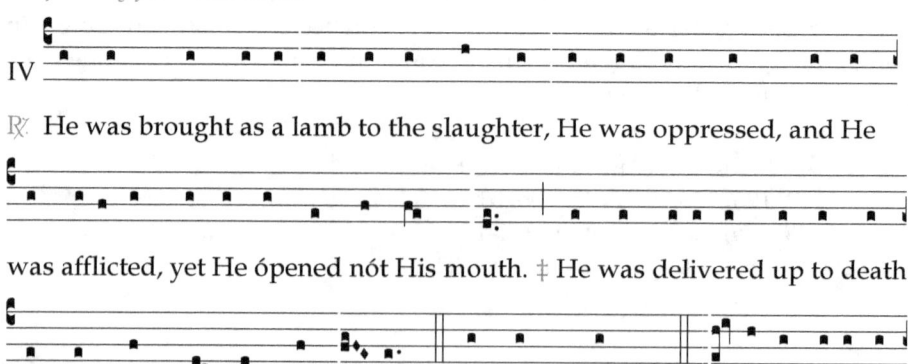

℟. He was brought as a lamb to the slaughter, He was oppressed, and He was afflicted, yet He ópened nót His mouth. ‡ He was delivered up to death that He might quícken His péople. ℟. He was brought... ℣. In Salem also is

His tabernacle and His dwelling pláce in Zíon. ✠ He was delivered... ℟ He

was brought...

Judica, the Fifth Sunday in Lent
Psalms. 43, 143, 129, 119i, iv; 120, 69, 109
Gospel (at Morning Prayer). John 8:46-59

Hymn (at Morning Prayer).
Pange lingua gloriosi praelium. V. *Fortunatus, 6th cent., trans. by J. M. Neale*

1. Sing, my tongue, the glorious battle, / Sing the last, the dread affray; / O'er the cross, the victor's trophy, / Sound the high triumphal lay, / How, the pains of death enduring, / Earth's Redeemer won the day.
2. When at length the appointed fulness / Of the sacred time was come, / He was sent, the world's Creator, / From the Father's heavenly home, / And was found in human fashion, / Offspring of the virgin's womb.
3. Now the thirty years are ended / Which on earth He willed to see, / Willingly He meets his passion, / Born to set His people free; / On the cross the Lamb is lifted, / There the sacrifice to be.
4. There the nails and spear He suffers, / Vinegar and gall and reed; / From His sacred body pierc-ed / Blood and water both proceed: / Precious flood, which all creation / From the stain of sin hath freed.
[5. Faithful cross, above all other, / One and only noble tree, / None in foliage, none in blossom, / None in fruit thy peer may be; / Sweet the wood, and sweet the iron, / And thy load, most sweet is He.
6. Bend, O lofty tree, thy branches, / Thy too rigid sinews bend; / And awhile the stubborn hardness, / Which thy birth bestowed, suspend; / And the limbs of heaven's high Monarch / Gently on thine arms extend.
7. Thou alone wast counted worthy / This world's Ransom to sustain, / That

a shipwrecked race for ever / Might a port of refuge gain, / With the sacred blood anointed / Of the Lamb for sinners slain.]

May be sung at end of either part:

8. Praise and honor to the Father, / Praise and honor to the Son, / Praise and honor to the Spirit, / Ever Three and ever One: / One in might, and One in glory, / While eternal ages run. Amen.

[321]   Or: **Lustra sex qui jam peracta.** *V. Fortunatus, 569, trans. by J. M. Neale*

1. Thirty years among us dwelling, / His appointed time fulfilled, / Born for this, He meets His passion, / For that this He freely willed: / On the Cross the Lamb is lifted, / Where His life-blood shall be spilled.
2. He endured the nails, the spitting, / Vinegar and spear and reed; / From that holy body pier-ced / Blood and water forth proceed; / Earth and stars and sky and ocean / By that flood from stain are freed.
3. Faithful cross, above all other, / One and only noble tree! / None in foliage, none in blossom, / None in fruit thy peer may be; / Sweetest wood and sweetest iron! / Sweetest weight is hung on thee.
4. Bend thy boughs, O tree of glory! / Thy too rigid sinews bend; / For awhile the ancient rigor / That thy birth bestowed, suspend; / And the King of heavenly beauty / On thy bosom gently tend!
5. Thou alone wast counted worthy / This world's Ransom to uphold; / For a shipwrecked race preparing / Harbor, like the ark of old; / With the sacred blood anointed / From the smitten Lamb that rolled.
6. To the Trinity be glory / Everlasting, as is meet: / Equal to the Father, equal / To the Son and Paraclete: / Trinal Unity, whose praises / All created things repeat. Amen.

℣. The heavens declare the glory of God.
℟. And the firmament sheweth His handywork.

Antiphon for Benedictus. **Jesus said unto the multitude of the Jews, and to the chief priests; † He that is of God héareth Gód's words : ye therefore hear them not, because yé are nót of God.**

Epistle (at Evening Prayer). **Hebrews 9:11-15**
Hymn (at Evening Prayer).
Vexilla Regis prodeunt. V. *Fortunatus, 569, cento.* Tr. *J. M. Neale, alt.*

1. The royal banners forward go; / The cross shines forth in mystic glow / Where He in flesh, our flesh who made, / Our sentence bore, our ransom paid;
2. Where deep for us the spear was dyed, / Life's torrent rushing from His side, / To wash us in that precious flood / Where mingled water flowed and blood.
3. Fulfilled is all that David told / In true prophetic song of old; / Amidst the nations, God, saith he, / Hath reigned and triumphed from the tree.
4. O tree of beauty, tree of light, / O tree with royal purple dight; / Elect, on whose triumphal breast / Those holy limbs should find their rest;
5. On whose hard arms, so widely flung, / The weight of this world's Ransom hung / The price of humankind to pay / And spoil the spoiler of his prey.
6. O Christ, our one reliance, hail! / So may Thy power with us avail / To give new virtue to the saint / And pardon to the penitent.
7. To Thee, eternal Three in One, / Let homage meet by all be done / Whom by the cross Thou dost restore, / Preserve, and govern evermore. Amen.

℣. The heavens declare the glory of God.
℟. And the firmament sheweth His handywork.

Antiphon for Magnificat.

Your father * A-bra-ham re-jóiced to sée my day : and he sáw it, ánd was

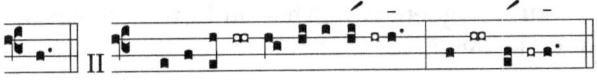

glad.

Collect. We beseech Thee, Almìghty God : mercifully to look upon Thy peoplè; that by Thy great goodness they may be governed and preserved evermore, both in body and soul; through Jesus Christ, Thy Son, oùr Lord, who liveth and reigneth with Thee and the Hòly Ghost : ever one God, world without end. Amen.

Palmarum, the Sixth Sunday in Lent
Psalms. 22, 73, 69, 7, 57, 24, 92, 41, 35
Gospel (at Morning Prayer). **Matthew 21:1-9**
Epistle (at Evening Prayer). **Philippians 2:5-11**

℣. Be not Thou far from me, O Lord.
℟. O my strength, haste Thee to help me.
Antiphon for Benedictus. Much people that were come to the Feast cried únto the <u>Lord</u> : Blessed is He that cometh in the Name of the Lord, Hosanna ín the híghest.

Antiphon for Magnificat.

For it is written, * I will smite the shepherd, and the sheep shall be scattered;

† But after I am risen a-gain, I will go before you ínto Gál-i-lee : there shall

VIII

ye sée Me, sáith the Lord.

Collect. Almighty and everlasting God, who hast sent Thy Son, our Savior Jesus Christ, to take upon Him our flesh and to suffer death upon the cross that all mankind should follow the example of His great humìlity : mercifully grant that we may both follow the example of His patiènce, and also be made partakers of His resurrection; through the same, Jesus Christ, Thy Son, oùr Lord, who liveth and reigneth with Thee and the Hòly Ghost : ever one God, world without end. Amen.

Monday of Holy Week
[323]

Psalms. 6, 7, 35, 63, 70, 79, 102
Gospel (at Morning Prayer). John 12:1-36 (37-43)
Epistle (at Evening Prayer). Isaiah 50:5-10

℣. Plead my cause, O Lord, with them that strive with me.
℟. Fight against them that fight against me.
Antiphon for Benedictus. O Father glorify Thou Mé with Thíne own self : with the glory which I had with Thee befóre the wórld began.

Antiphon for Magnificat.

Thou couldest * have no power at áll a-gáinst me : except it were gíven thee

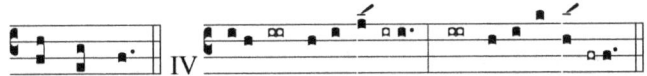

fróm a-bove.

Collect. Grant, we beseech Thee, Almìghty God : that we, who amid so many adversities do fail through our own infirmìties; may be restored through the Passion and intercession of Thine only-begotten Son; who liveth and reigneth with Thee and the Hòly Ghost : ever one God, world without end. Amen.

Tuesday of Holy Week
Psalms. 12, 38, 39, 55, 59, 74, 83
Gospel (at Morning Prayer). Mark 14:1-15:46
Epistle (at Evening Prayer). Jeremiah 11:18-20

℣. Deliver me, O Lord, from mine enemies. ℟. I flee unto Thee to hide me.
Antiphon for Benedictus. Now before the Feast of the Passover, when Jesus knéw that His hóur was come : having loved His own, He loved them únto the end.

Antiphon for Magnificat.

I have power * to láy down my life : and I have power to táke it a-gain.

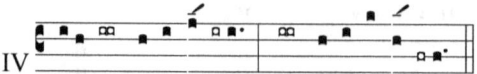

Collect. Almighty and Everlàsting God : grant us grace so to pass through this holy time of our Lord's Passiòn, that we may obtain the pardon of our sins; through the same Jesus Christ, Thy Son, oùr Lord, who liveth and reigneth with Thee and the Hòly Ghost : ever one God, world without end. Amen.

Wednesday of Holy Week
Psalms. 51, 88, 120, 130, 142, 143
Gospel (at Morning Prayer). **Luke 22:1-23:56**
Epistle (at Evening Prayer). **Isaiah 62:11-63:7**

℣. Be not Thou far from me, O Lord.
℟. O my strength, haste Thee to help me.
Antiphon for Benedictus. Símon, sléepest thou? : Couldest thou not watch with me éven fór one hour?

Antiphon for Magnificat.

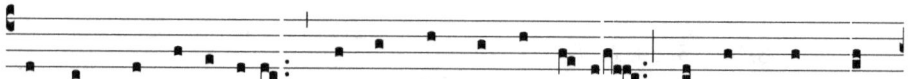

A maid said unto Peter, * Surely thóu art óne of them : for thy spéech be-

tráyeth thee.

[324] *Collect.* Grant, we beseech thee, Almìghty God : that we, who for our evil deeds are continually afflictèd, may mercifully be relieved by the Passion of Thine only-begotten Son; who liveth and reigneth with Thee and Hòly Ghost : ever one God, world without end. Amen.

Sacred Triduum

The Sacred Triduum—from Vigils (Matins) of Maundy Thursday through Afternoon Prayer (None) of Holy Saturday—reverts to an ancient custom of reciting the Office. **Glory be...** *is omitted wherever it occurs in the Office. The Opening Versicles, the Invitatory with Venite, the Hymns, the Salutation,* **Let us pray,** *the Benedicamus, and the Blessing are omitted from all Offices. In addition, the Responsory, the Da Pacem, and the Weekday Collects with their preceding Antiphons and Versicles are omitted from Midday Prayer. The Responsories are omitted from Morning Prayer and Evening Prayer. At Morning Prayer, Evening Prayer, and Compline, Psalm 51 is sung quietly after the Canticle. At Midday Prayer it is sung after the Versicle.*

<u>*Morning Prayer and Evening Prayer:*</u>
Psalmody, with Antiphons,
       without **Glory be...**
Reading
Versicle
Canticle, with Antiphon
Antiphon: **Christ for our sakes...**
Psalm 51 on one tone, quietly
Kyrie
Our Father
Collect of the Day, without Salutation,
       without **Let us pray**.

<u>*Midday Prayer*</u>
Psalmody as at Morning Prayer

Reading
Versicle

Antiphon: **Christ for our sakes...**
Psalm 51 on one tone, quietly
Kyrie
Our Father
Collect, as at Morn. Prayer

Vigils
Nocturnes:
Psalmody, with Antiphons, without **Glory be**...
Reading
Responsory, without **Glory be**...

Compline
Confiteor
Psalmody, as at Morn. Prayer
Canticle, as at Morn. Prayer
Antiphon: **Christ for our sakes**...
Psalm 51 on one tone, quietly
Kyrie
Our Father
Collect, as at Morn. Prayer

Maundy Thursday
Psalms. 86, 67, 23, 111, 114, 78:1-29; 105, 81, 116, 41, 55, 140
Gospel (at Morning Prayer). **John 13:1-15**
Epistle (at Evening Prayer). **1 Corinthians 11:23-32**

℣. My flesh is meat indeed. ℟. And My blood is drink indeed.
Antiphon for Benedictus. Now he that betrayed Him gave hím a sign, sáying : Whom I shall kiss, that sáme is He; Hóld Him fast.

Antiphon for Magnificat.

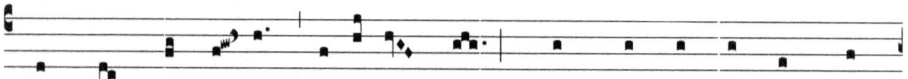

While they were eating, * Jesus took bread, which sáme He did <u>bless</u> : and

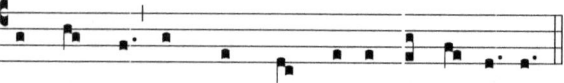

He brake it, and gave there-of to Hís di-scíples.

Antiphon before Psalm 51.

Christ * for our sakes be- came o-be- di-ent un- to death.

Collect. O Lord God, who hast left unto us in a wonderful Sacrament a memorial òf Thy Passion : grant, we beseech Thee, that we may so use this Sacrament of Thy body and blòod; that the fruits of Thy redemption may continually be manifest in us; Thou who livest and reignest with the Father and the Hòly Ghost : ever one God, world without end. Amen.

Good Friday

Psalms. **22, 56, 57, 69, 40, 3, 43, 49, 119xi, xvi; 142, 143**
Gospel (at Morning Prayer). **John 18:1-19:42**
Epistle (at Evening Prayer). **Isaiah 52:13-53:12**

℣. God spared not His own Son. ℟. But delivered Him up for us all.
Antiphon for Benedictus. And they set up over His head His accusátion wrítten : Jesus of Nazareth, the Kíng of the Jews.

Antiphon for Magnificat.

When He had received the vin-e-gar, * He said, Ít is fín-ished : and He

bowed His head, and gáve up the ghost.

Antiphon before Psalm 51.

Christ * for our sakes be- came o-be- di-ent un- to death, ev-en the

death of the Cross.

Collect. Almighty and Everlasting God, who hast willed that Thy Son should bear for us the pains of the cross that Thou mightest remove from us the power of the Àdversary : help us so to remember and give thanks for our Lord's Passiòn, that we may obtain remission of sins and redemption from everlasting death; through the same Jesus Christ, Thy Son, oùr Lord, who liveth and reigneth with Thee and the Hòly Ghost : ever one God, world without end. Amen.

Holy Saturday

Psalms: From Good Friday
Gospel (at Morning Prayer). **Matthew 27:57-66**
Epistle (at Evening Prayer). **1 Peter 3:17-22**

℣. The Lord breaketh the battles. ℟. The Lord is His name.
Antiphon for Benedictus. The women, sitting over against the sepulcher, made lámentátion : wéeping fór the Lord.

Antiphon before Psalm 51.

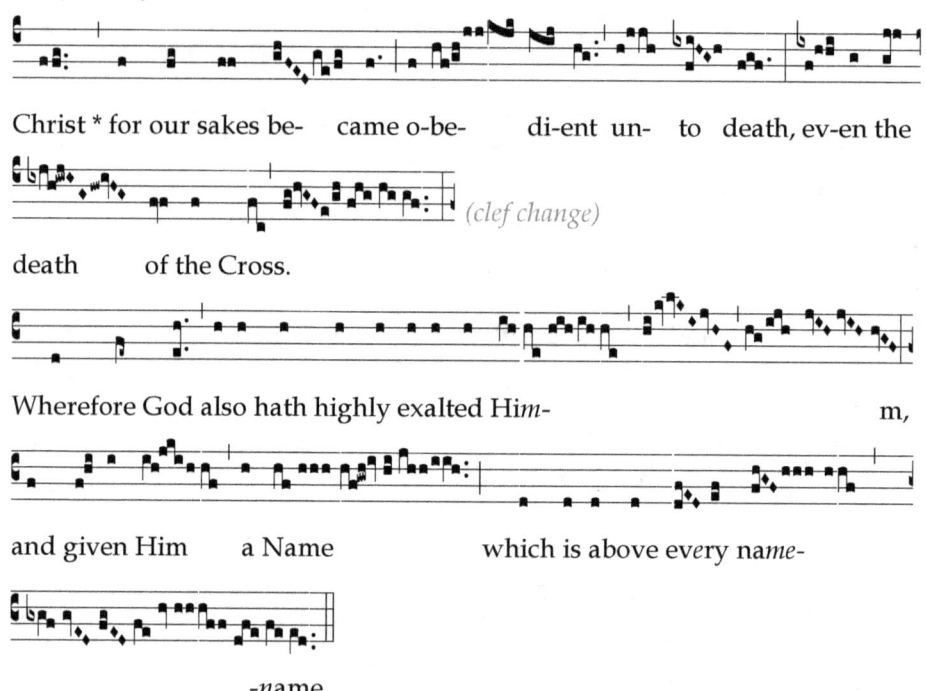

Christ * for our sakes be- came o-be- di-ent un- to death, ev-en the death of the Cross. *(clef change)*

Wherefore God also hath highly exalted Him- m, and given Him a Name which is above every name- -name.

Collect. Almighty God, we beseech Thee graciously to behold this Thy family, for which our Lord Jesus Christ was contented to be betrayed and given up unto the hands of wicked men and to suffer death upon the cross. (*Silently:* Through the same Jesus Christ, Thy Son, our Lord, who liveth and reigneth with Thee and the holy Ghost : ever one God, world without end. Amen.)

[326] *If the Easter Vigil take place early Sunday morning, Evening Prayer on Holy Saturday follows the order for Offices in the Sacred Triduum and uses the propers of Morning Prayer for this day.*

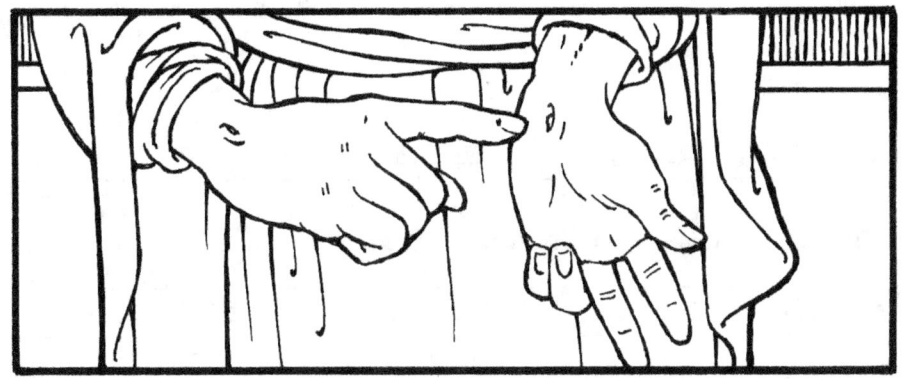

Eastertide

From Easter Sunday to Saturday after Pentecost. In Eastertide, the Opening Versicles are now again used, **Alleluia** *and* **Glory be...** *are sung now again. The Preces are not used. Throughout Eastertide, including the week after Pentecost, one does not kneel for the Prayers.*

Easter Week reverts to an ancient manner of praying the Office. The hymns are omitted in all Offices. The Responsories are omitted in all Offices except Vigils. "Alleluia" antiphons may be used for the Psalmody. The Te Deum is prayed every day at Vigils, or it may be used instead of the Hymn at Morning Prayer.

Invitatory.

The Lord is ris- en indeed, ál-le-lú- ia : O cóme, let us wórship Him.

Antiphons for Psalms (appropriate for use on Feasts and Sundays)
1. *The Alleluia antiphons (p. 114):* **Alleluia : alleluia, alleluia.**
2. I láid me dówn and slept : I awaked, for the Lord sustained me, állelúia. *(Ps. 3)*
3. Alleluia, the Lord is risen, állelúia : As He said unto you, alleluia, állelúia.
4. Alleluia, abide with us, for ít is toward évening : And the day is far spent, alleluia, állelúia.
5. The Lord is risen from the grave, állelúia : Who hung for us upon the tree, állelúia.
6. Then were the disciples glad, állelúia : When they saw the Lord, állelúia.
7. This is the day which the Lord hath made, állelúia : We will rejoice and be glad in it, állelúia. *(Ps. 118iii)*

8. The Lord is risen indeed, állelúia : And hath appeared unto Simon, állelúia.

Responsory for Eastertide.

℟. Christ, being raised from the dead, dieth no more; death hath no more do-

mínion ó- ver Him. ‡ In that He liveth, He liveth unto God, allelu-ia, ál-

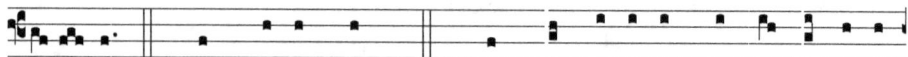

le-lú- ia. ℟. Christ, being raised... ℣. Christ was delivered for our of-fenses

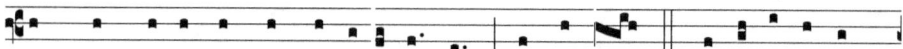

and raised again for our júst-i-fi-cá-tion. ‡ In that He... ℣. Glory be to the

Fáther and tó the Son: and tó the Hóly Ghost. ℟. Christ, being raised...

Benedicamus for Sundays and Feasts in Eastertide.

Lucas Lossius

℣. Bless we the Lord, al-le-lu-ia, al-le-lu-ia, al-le- lu- ia.
℟. Thanks be to God, al-le-lu-ia, al-le-lu-ia, al-le- lu- ia.

Another.

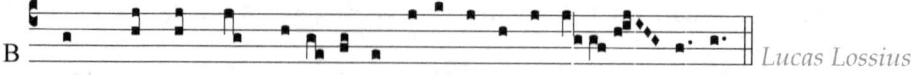
Lucas Lossius

℣. Bless we the Lord, al-le-lu-ia, al-le-lu-ia, al-le- lu- ia.
℟. Thanks be to God, al-le-lu-ia, al-le-lu-ia, al-le- lu- ia.

Weekdays in Eastertide.

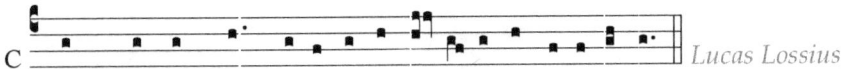 Lucas Lossius

℣. Bless we the Lord, al-le-lu-ia, al-le-lu-ia, al-le-lu-ia.
℟. Thanks be to God, al-le-lu-ia, al-le-lu-ia, al-le-lu-ia.

Easter Eve
If the Easter Vigil take place on Holy Saturday, Evening Prayer may be prayed after the Easter Vigil using the following Antiphon and Collect.

℣. The Lord is risen indeed, alleluia.
℟. And hath appeared to Simon, alleluia.

Antiphon for Magnificat.

In the end of the Sabbath, * as it began to dawn toward the first day óf the

week : came Ma-ry Mag-da-lene, and the other Mary, to see the sepulcher,

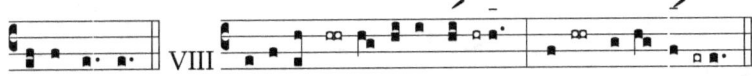

ál-le-lú-ia.

Collect. O God, who didst enlighten this most holy night with the glory of the Lord's rèsurrection : preserve in all Thy people the spirit of adoption which Thou hast givèn, so that, renewed in body and soul, they may perform unto Thee a pure service; through the same Jesus Christ, Thy Son, oùr Lord, who liveth and reigneth with Thee and the Hòly Ghost : ever one God, world without end. Amen.

Easter Day, the Feast of the Resurrection of our Lord
1st Week of the Four-Week Psalm Schedule
Psalms. **139, 118, 76, 2, 8, 16, 34, 61, 81, 100, 105, 110, 114, 116, 124, 132, 135, 138, 1, 23, 30, 66, 113**
Gospel (at Morning Prayer). **Mark 16:1-8**

[327]

Epistle (at Evening Prayer). **1 Corinthians 5:6-8**

Instead of the Hymn, the following chant is sung:

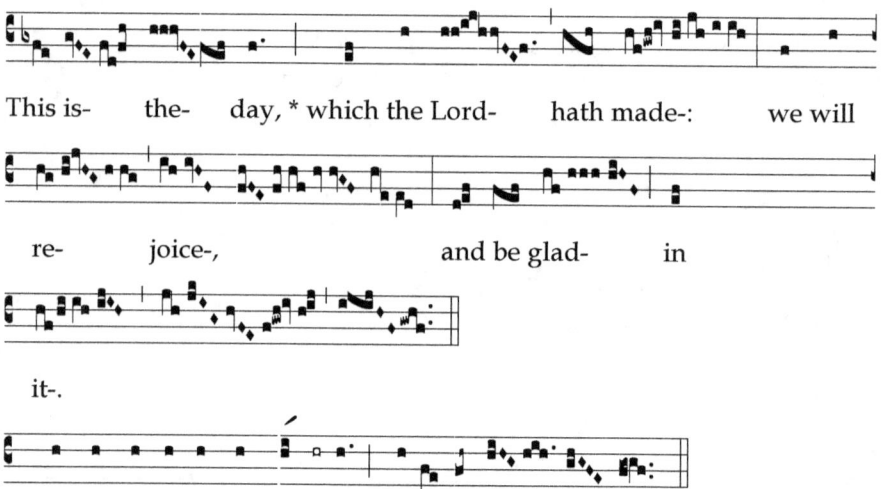

This is- the- day, * which the Lord- hath made-: we will re-joice-, and be glad- in it-.

℣. In Thy resurrection, Ó Christ, al-le-lu-ia.
℟. Let heaven and eárth rejoice, al-le-lu-ia.

Antiphon for Benedictus. And very early in the morning, on the Fírst Day óf the week : they came unto the sepulcher at the rising of the sun, állelúia.

Antiphon for Magnificat.

And when they looked, * they saw that the stóne was rólled away : for it was

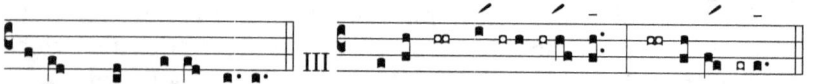

ve-ry great, ál-le-lú-ia.

Collect. Almighty God, who through Thine only-begotten Son Jesus Christ, hast overcome death and opened unto us the gate of everlàsting life : we humbly beseech Thee that, as Thou dost put into our minds good desìres, so by Thy continual help we may bring the same to good effect; through the same Jesus Christ, Thy Son, oùr Lord, who liveth and reigneth with Thee and the Hòly Ghost : ever one God, world without end. Amen.

Easter Monday

Gospel (at Morning Prayer). **Luke 24:13-35**
Epistle (at Evening Prayer). **Acts 10:34-41**

Versicle (music from Easter)
℣. The Lord hath risen fróm the tomb, alleluia.
℟. Who hath hung for us ón the tree, alleluia.
Antiphon for Benedictus. Jesus Himself drew near to His disciples in the way, and went with them, but their eyes were holden that they shóuld not knów Him : and He rebuked them saying, O fools and slow of heart to believe all that the Prophets have spoken, állelúia.

Antiphon for Magnificat.

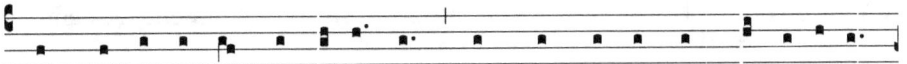

What manner of com-mu-ni-ca-tions * are these that ye have óne to an-ó-

ther : as ye walk, and are sad? Ál-le-lú-ia.

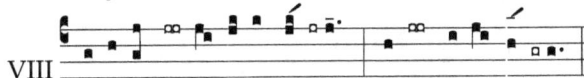

VIII

Collect. O God, who in the Paschal Feast hast bestowed restoration upòn the world : continue unto Thy people Thy heavenly gìft, that they may both attain unto perfect freedom and advance unto life eternal; through Jesus Christ, Thy Son, oùr Lord, who liveth and reigneth with Thee and the Hòly Ghost : ever one God, world without end. Amen.

Easter Tuesday

Gospel (at Morning Prayer). **Luke 24:36-48**
Epistle (at Evening Prayer). **Acts 13:26-33**

Versicle (music from Easter)
℣. The Lord is risen índeed, alleluia.
℟. And hath appeared to Símon, alleluia.
Antiphon for Benedictus. Jesus stood in the midst of His disciples, and sáid unto them : Peace be unto you, alleluia, állelúia.

Antiphon for Magnificat.

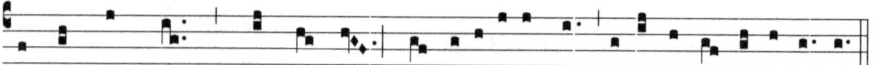

Behold my hánds * and my <u>feet</u> : that it is I myself, al-le-lu-ia, ál-le-lú-ia.

VIII

Collect. **Almighty God, who through the resurrection of Thy Son didst secure peace for our troùbled conscience : grant unto us evermore this peàce, that in the merit of Thy Son, we at length come unto the perfect peace of heaven; through the same, Jesus Christ, Thy Son, oùr Lord, who liveth and reigneth with Thee and the Hòly Ghost : ever one God, world without end. Amen.**

The Rest of the Octave of Easter

The Office is prayed with the propers from Easter Day. Alleluia antiphons may be used for the Psalmody.

Quasimodogeniti, the First Sunday After Easter

From today on, the Office takes its normal form.
Psalms. **81, 91, 19, 9, 92, 134, 101, 145**
Gospel (at Morning Prayer). **John 20:19-31**

[329] *Hymn (at Morning Prayer).* **Aurora lucis rutilat.** *4th/5th c., trans. by T. A. Lacey*

1. The day draws on with golden light, / Glad songs go echoing through the height, / The broad earth lifts an answering cheer, / The deep makes moan with wailing fear.
2. For lo, He comes, the mighty King, / To take from death his power and sting, / To trample down his gloomy reign / And break the weary prisoner's chain.
3. Enclosed He lay in rocky cell, / With guard of arm-ed sentinel; / But thence returning, strong and free, / He comes with pomp of jubilee.
4. The sad apostles mourn him slain, / Nor hope to see their Lord again; /

Their Lord, whom rebel thralls defy, / Arraign, accuse and doom to die.
5. But now they put their grief away, / The pains of hell are loosed today; / For by the grave, with flashing eyes, / "Your Lord is risen," the Angel cries.
6. Maker of all, to Thee we pray, / Fulfill in us Thy joy today; / When death assaults, grant, Lord, that we / May share Thy paschal mystery.
7. To Thee, who, dead, again dost live, / All glory, Lord, Thy people give; / All glory, as is ever meet, / To Father and to Paraclete. Amen.

Or: **Sermone blando Angelus.** *4th/5th cent., trans. by T. A. Lacey*

1. His cheering message from the grave / An angel to the women gave: / "Full soon your Master ye shall see; / He goes before to Galilee."
2. But while with flying steps they press / To bear the news, all eagerness, / Their Lord, the living Lord, they meet, / And prostrate fall to kiss His feet.
3. So when His mourning followers heard / The tidings of that faithful word, / Quick went they forth to Galilee, / Their loved and lost once more to see.
4. On that fair day of paschal joy, / The sunshine was without alloy, / When to their very eyes restored / They looked upon the risen Lord.
5. The wounds before their eyes displayed. / They see in living light arrayed, / And that they see they testify / In open witness fearlessly.
6. O Christ, the King of gentleness, / Our several hearts do Thou possess, / That we may render all our days / Thy meed of thankfulness and praise.
7. Maker of all, to Thee we pray, / Fulfill in us Thy joy today; / When death assails, grant, Lord, that we / May share Thy paschal victory.
8. To Thee who, dead, again dost live, / All glory, Lord, Thy people give; / All glory, as is ever meet, / To Father and to Paraclete. Amen.

Versicle
(On Sunday, music from Easter; thereafter music from Misericordias Domini, p. 458.)
℣. Christ our passover is sacrifíced for us, alleluia. ℟. Therefore let us keep the feast with the unleavened bread of sincerity ánd truth, alleluia.
Antiphon for Benedictus. The same day at evening, being the First Day of the week, when the doors were shut where the disciples wére assémbled : came Jesus and stood in the midst of them and said, Peace be unto you, állelúia.

Epistle (at Evening Prayer). **1 John 5:4-10** [330]

Hymn (at Evening Prayer). **Ad cenam Agni providi.** *7th cent., trans. by J. M. Neale*

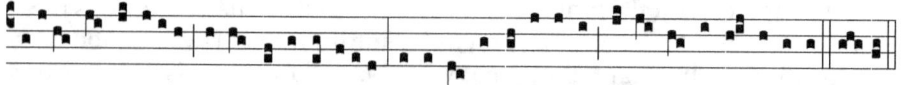

1. The Lamb's high banquet we await / In snow-white robes of royal state; / And now, the Red Sea's channel passed, / To Christ, our Prince, we sing at last.
2. Upon the altar of the cross / His Body hath redeemed our loss; / And tasting of His roseate Blood, / Our life is hid with Him in God.
3. That paschal eve God's arm was bared; / The devastating angel spared: / By strength of hand our hosts went free / From Pharoah's ruthless tyranny.
4. Now Christ our Passover is slain, / The Lamb of God that knows no stain; / The true oblation offered here, / Our own unleavened Bread sincere.
5. O Thou from whom hell's monarch flies, / O great, O very Sacrifice, / Thy captive people are set free, / And endless life restored in Thee.
6. For Christ, arising from the dead, / From conquered hell victorious sped; / He thrusts the tyrant down to chains, / And paradise for man regains.
7. Maker of all, to Thee we pray, / Fulfill in us Thy joy today; / When death assails, grant, Lord, that we / May share Thy paschal victory.
8. To Thee who, dead, again dost live, / All glory, Lord, Thy people give; / All glory, as is ever meet, / To Father and to Paraclete. Amen.

Or: **Chorus novae Jerusalem.** *Fulbert of Chartre, 11th cent., trans. by J. M. Neale*

1. Ye choirs of new Jerusalem, / To sweet new strains attune your theme; / The while we keep, from care released, / With sober joy our Paschal feast:
2. When Christ, unconquered Lion, first / The dragon's chains by rising burst: / And while with living voice He cries, / The dead of other ages rise.
3. Engorged in former years, their prey / Must death and hell restore to-day: / And many a captive soul, set free, / With Jesus leaves captivity.
4. Right gloriously He triumphs now, / Worthy to whom should all things bow; / And joining heaven and earth again, / Links in one commonweal the twain.
5. And we, as these His deeds we sing, / His suppliant soldiers, pray our

King, / That in His palace, bright and vast, / We may keep watch and ward at last.
6. Long as unending ages run, / To God the Father, laud be done: / To God the Son, our equal praise, / And God the Holy Ghost, we raise. Amen.

℣. Christ our passover is sacrificed for us, alleluia. ℟. Therefore let us keep the feast with the unleavened bread of sincerity ánd truth, alleluia.

[331]

Antiphon for Magnificat.

After eight days, * when the doors were shút, the Lord én-tered : and said

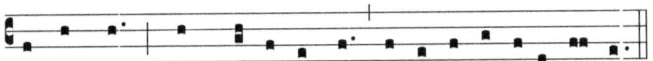

un-to them peace be unto you, al-le-lu-ia, ál-le-lú- ia.

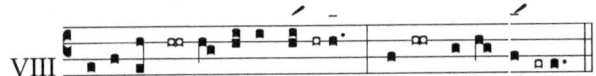

VIII

Collect. Grant, we beseech Thee, Almìghty God : that we who have celebrated the solemnities of the Lord's resurrectiòn, may, by the help of Thy grace bring forth the fruits thereof in our life and conversation; through the same, Jesus Christ, Thy Son, oùr Lord, who liveth and reigneth with Thee and the Hòly Ghost : ever one God, world without end. Amen.

Misericordias Domini, the Second Sunday After Easter

Psalms. 33, 63, 23, 80, 21, 121, 146, 95, 100
Gospel (at Morning Prayer). John 10:11-16
Epistle (at Evening Prayer). 1 Peter 2:21-25
Hymn. As on Quasimodogeniti

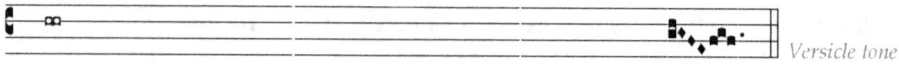 *Versicle tone*

℣. Oh, give thanks unto the Lord, for He is good, allelu-ia.
℟. For His mercy endureth forever, allelu-   ia.
Antiphon for Benedictus.
I am the Shépherd óf the sheep : I am the way and the trúth and the life;
I ám the Good Shépherd : and I know my sheep, and am known of mine, alleluia, állelúia.

Antiphon for Magnificat.

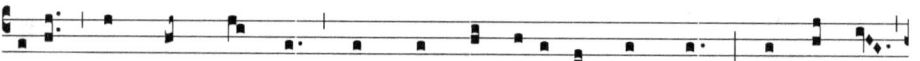

I am * the Good Shepherd, and therefore dó I féed my sheep : and for them

I lay down My life, ál-le-lú-ia.

Collect. God, who by the humiliation of Thy son didst raise up the fàllen world : grant unto Thy faithful ones perpetual gladnèss, and those whom Thou hast delivered from the dangers of everlasting death do Thou make partakers of eternal joys; through the same, Jesus Christ, Thy Son, oùr Lord, who liveth and reigneth with Thee and the Hòly Ghost : ever one God, world without end. Amen.

Jubilate, the Third Sunday After Easter

Psalms. 66, 146, 82, 101, 40, 30, 17, 124
Gospel (at Morning Prayer). John 16:16-23
Epistle (at Evening Prayer). 1 Peter 2:11-20
Hymn. As on Quasimodogeniti

℣. Make a joyful noise unto God, all ye lands, alleluia.
℟. Sing forth the honor of His name, alleluia.

Antiphon for Benedictus. A little while, and ye shall not see Me with your oútward eyes, sáith the Lord : and again, a little while, and ye shall see Me with the eyes of your soul, because I go to the Father, alleluia, álleluía.

Antiphon for Magnificat. [332]

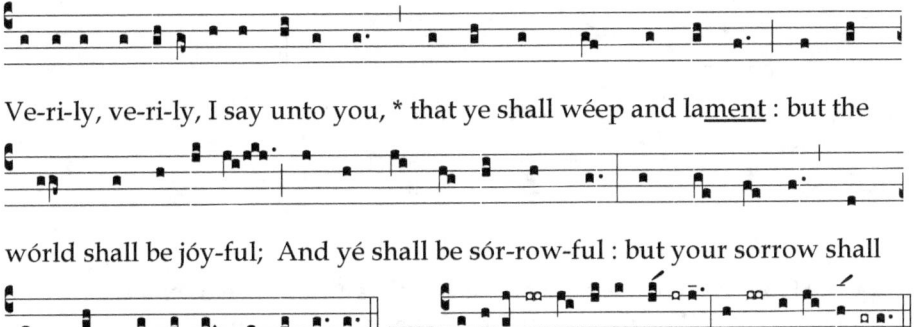

Ve-ri-ly, ve-ri-ly, I say unto you, * that ye shall wéep and la<u>ment</u> : but the world shall be jóy-ful; And yé shall be sór-row-ful : but your sorrow shall be turned in-to joy, ál-le-lú-ia.

Collect. Almighty God, who showest to them that be in error the light of Thy truth to the intent that they may return into the way of rìghteousness : grant unto all them that are admitted into the fellowship of Christ's religion that they may avoid those things that are contrary to their professiòn; and follow all such things as are agreeable to the same; through Jesus Christ, Thy Son, oùr Lord, who liveth and reigneth with Thee and the Hòly Ghost : ever one God, world without end. Amen.

Cantate, the Fourth Sunday After Easter
Psalms. **99, 66, 136, 145, 148, 104, 83, 117**
Gospel (at Morning Prayer). **John 16:5-15**
Epistle (at Evening Prayer). **James 1:16-21**
Hymn. As on Quasimodogeniti

℣. Oh, sing unto the Lord a new song, alleluia.
℟. For He hath done marvelous things, alleluia.
Antiphon for Benedictus. I go My way to Hím that sént Me : and none of you asketh Me, Whither goest Thou? Alleluia, álleluía.

Antiphon for Magnificat.

I go My way * to Hím that sént Me : but because I have said these things

unto you, sorrow hath filled your heart, ál-le-lú-ia.

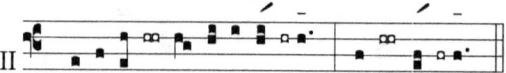

Collect. O God, who makest the minds of the faithful to be òf one will : grant unto Thy people that they may love what Thou commandest and desire what Thou dost promìse, that among the manifold changes of this world our hearts may there be fixed where true joys are to be found; through Jesus Christ, Thy Son, oùr Lord, who liveth and reigneth with Thee and the Hòly Ghost : ever one God, world without end. Amen.

Rogate, the Fifth Sunday After Easter
Psalms. 66, 54, 96, 1, 15, 26, 20, 64, 121
Gospel (at Morning Prayer). **John 16:23-30**
Epistle (at Evening Prayer). **James 1:22-27**
Hymn. As on Quasimodogeniti

℣. With the voice of singing declare ye and tell this, alleluia.
℟. The Lord hath redeemed His people, alleluia.
Antiphon for Benedictus. Hitherto have ye asked nóthing ín My Name : ask ye, and ye shall receive, állelúia.

Antiphon for Magnificat.

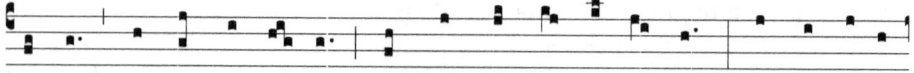

Ask ye, * and ye shall receive, that your joy may be fulfilled; † for the Father

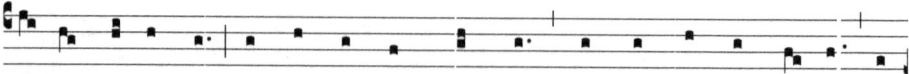

himself loveth you because yé have lóved Me : and have believed in Me and

in all my sayings, ál-le-lú-ia.

Collect. O God, from whom all good things do come : grant to us, Thy humble servànts, that by Thy holy inspiration we may think those things that be right and by Thy merciful guiding may perform the same; through Jesus Christ, Thy Son, oùr Lord, who liveth and reigneth with Thee and the Hòly Ghost : ever one God, world without end. Amen.

The Rogation Days

[333]

The three days before Ascension Thursday, known also as "The Lesser Litanies," are days of supplication and prayer. On these three days it is appropriate to pray the Great Litany (p. 570) after Morning Prayer. The Gospel, Epistle, and Collects are the same for all three days. Each day has its own proper antiphons.

Gospel (at Morning Prayer). **Luke 11:5-13**
Epistle (at Evening Prayer). **James 5:16-20**

Collect (at Morning Prayer). Grant, we beseech Thee, Almìghty God : that we who in all our troubles and adversities do put our trust and confidence in Thy mercý, may ever be defended by Thy mighty power; through Jesus Christ, Thy Son, oùr Lord, who liveth and reigneth with Thee and the Hòly Ghost : ever one God, world without end. Amen.
Collect (at Evening Prayer): from Sunday.

ROGATION MONDAY

Antiphon for Benedictus. Ask and it shall be given you; séek and yé shall find : knock and it shall be opened unto you, állelúia.

Antiphon for Magnificat.

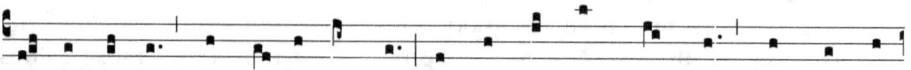

For the Father * himself loveth you because yé have lóved me : and have be-

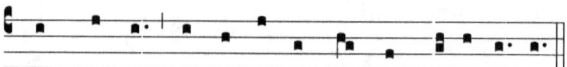

lieved in me, and in all my sayings, ál-le-lú-ia.

VIII

ROGATION TUESDAY

Antiphon for Benedictus. Thus it behoved Chríst to súffer : and to rise again from the dead, állelúia.

Antiphon for Magnificat.

I came forth from the Father, * and am come ínto the world : again, I leave

VIII

the world, and go to the Father, ál-le-lú-ia.

ROGATION WEDNESDAY

Antiphon for Benedictus. Fáther, the hóur is come : glorify Thy Son with the glory which I had with Thee before the world was, állelúia.

Ascensiontide

Invitatory.

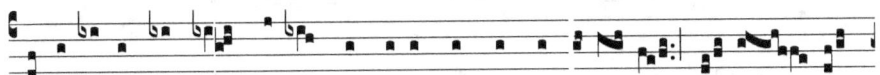

Al-le-lu-ia, the King ascendeth into heaven, ál-le-lú- ia : O cóme, let

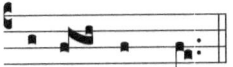

us wórship Him.

Antiphons for Psalms (appropriate for use on Feasts and Sundays)
1. If I go not away, the Comforter will nót come únto you : But if I depart, I will send Him unto you, állelúia.
2. Alleluia, Christ hath ascended up on high, állelúia : And hath led captivity captive, alleluia, állelúia. *(Ps. 68ii)*
3. I ascend unto My Father ánd your Fáther : And to My God and your God, állelúia.
4. I will not leave you comfortless, állelúia : I go away and come again unto you, állelúia.
5. God is gone up with a shout, állelúia : The Lord with the sound of a trumpet, állelúia. *(Ps. 47)*

[334]

Responsory for Ascension.

℟. Go ye into all the world and preach the Gos-pel, ál-le- lú- ia. ‡ He that be- lieveth and is baptized shall be saved, al-le-lu-ia, ál-le- lú-ia. ℟. Go ye into... ℣. In the name of the Father and of the Son and óf the Hóly Ghost. ‡ He that be- lieveth... ℣. Glory be to the Fáther and tó the Son: and tó the Hóly Ghost. ℟. Go ye into...

The Ascension of Our Lord (Thursday After Rogate)
Psalms. **47, 68, 21, 24, 67, 110, 99, 93, 96, 97**
Gospel (at Morning Prayer). **Mark 16:14-20**
Epistle (at Evening Prayer). **Acts 1:1-11**

Hymn (at 1ˢᵗ Vespers). **Aeterne Rex altissime.** *c. 5ᵗʰ c., trans. by J. M. Neale, alt.*

1. Eternal Monarch, King most high, / Whose blood hath brought redemption nigh, / By whom the death of death was wrought, / And conquering grace's battle fought.
2. Ascending to the throne of might, / And seated at the Father's right, / All power in heaven is Jesus' own, / That here His manhood had not shown.
3. That so, in nature's triple frame, / Each heavenly and each earthly name, /

And things in hell's abyss abhorred, / May bend the knee and own Him Lord.
4. Yea, angels tremble when they see / How changed is our humanity; / That flesh hath purged what flesh had stained, / And God, the flesh of God, hath reigned.
5. Be Thou our joy and strong defense, / Who art our future recompense: / So shall the light that springs from Thee / Be ours through all eternity.
6. O risen Christ, ascended Lord, / All praise to Thee let earth accord, / Who art, while endless ages run, / With Father and with Spirit one. Amen.

℣. Christ, ascending ón high, al-le-lu-ia.
℟. Hath led captivity captive and given gífts to men, alleluia.

Antiphon for Magnificat. (1st Vespers of Ascension)

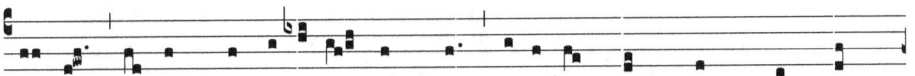

Fa-ther, * I have man-i-fested Thy Name unto the men whom Thóu hast

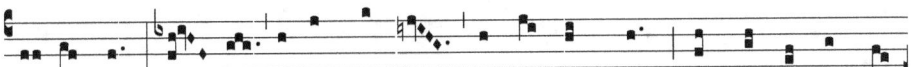

gí-ven me : and now I pray for them, not for the world, because I come to

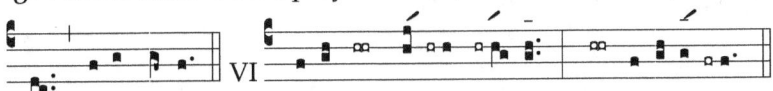

Thee, ál-le-lú-ia.

[335] *Hymn (at Morning Prayer).*
Tu Christe nostrum gaudium. *c. 5th cent., trans. by L. Housman*

1. O Christ, our joy, to whom is given / A throne o'er all the thrones of heaven, / In Thee, whose hand all things obey, / The world's vain pleasures pass away.
2. So, suppliants here, we seek to win / Thy pardon for Thy people's sin, / That, by Thine all-prevailing grace, / Uplifted, we may seek Thy face.
3. And when, all heaven beneath Thee bowed, / Thou com'st to judgment throned in cloud, / Then from our guilt wash out the stain / And give us our lost crowns again.
4. Be Thou our joy and strong defense, / Who art our future recompense: / So shall the light that springs from Thee / Be ours through all eternity.
5. O risen Christ, ascended Lord, / All praise to Thee let earth accord, / Who art, while endless ages run, / With Father and with Spirit One. Amen.

Versicle (Music from 1st Vespers)
℣. God is gone up with a shout, alleluia.
℟. The Lord with the sound of a trúmpet, alleluia.
Antiphon for Benedictus. I ascend to My Father ánd your Fáther : to My God and your God, álleluia.

Hymn (at 2nd Vespers).
Hymnum canamus gloriae. *The Venerable Bede, d. 735, trans. by B. Webb, alt.*

1. A hymn of glory let us sing; / New songs throughout the world shall ring: / Christ, by a road before untrod, / Ascendeth to the throne of God.
2. The holy apostolic band / Upon the Mount of Olives stand, / And with His followers they see / Jesus' resplendent majesty.
3. To whom the angels, drawing nigh, / "Why stand and gaze upon the sky? / This is the Savior," thus they say, / "This is His noble triumph day."
4. "Again shall ye behold Him so / As ye today have seen Him go, / In glorious pomp ascending high, / Up to the portals of the sky."
5. Oh, grant us thitherward to tend / And with unwearied hearts ascend /

Unto Thy kingdom's throne, where Thou, / As is our faith, art seated now.
6. Be Thou our Joy and strong Defense, / Who art our future Recompense: / So shall the light that springs from Thee / Be ours through all eternity.
7. O risen Christ, ascended Lord, / All praise to Thee let earth accord, / Who art, while endless ages run, / With Father and with Spirit One. Amen.

Versicle (Music from 1st Vespers)
℣. Christ, ascending ón high, alleluia.
℟. Hath led captivity captive and given gífts to men, alleluia.

Antiphon for Magnificat (at 2nd Vespers).

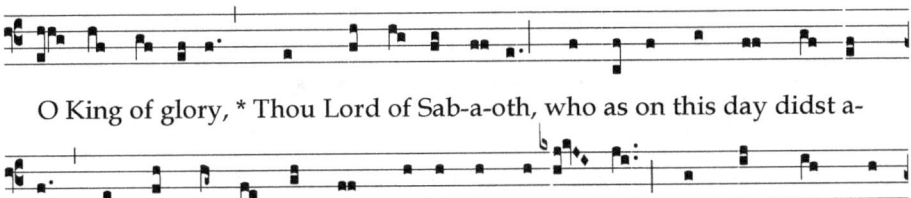

O King of glory, * Thou Lord of Sab-a-oth, who as on this day didst a-scend with ex-ceeding tri-umph far abóve all héa-vens : we pray Thee, leave us not comfortless, but send on us the Promise of the Father, even the Spirit of Truth, ál-le-lú-ia.

Collect. Grant, we beseech Thee, Almìghty God : that like as we do believe Thine only-begotten Son, our Lord Jesus Christ, to have ascended into the heavèns, so may we also in heart and mind thither ascend and with Him continually dwell; who liveth and reigneth with Thee and the Hòly Ghost : ever one God, world without end. Amen. [336]

Non-Feast Days After Ascension

From Friday after Ascension until Saturday before Pentecost, the "Alleluia" antiphons may be used for the Psalmody, and the Antiphons from Ascension may be used for the Canticles.

Exaudi, the Sunday After the Ascension

Psalms. **27, 47, 104, 146, 10, 119xi, xii; 51**
Gospel (at Morning Prayer). **John 15:26-16:4**
Epistle (at Evening Prayer). **1 Peter 4:7-11**

Versicle (Music from 1st Vespers of Ascension)
℣. God is gone up wíth a shout, alleluia.
℟. The Lord with the sound of a trúmpet, alleluia.

Antiphon for Benedictus. **When the Comforter is come, whom I will send unto you, even the Spirit of Truth which proceedeth fróm the Fáther : He shall testify of Me, állelúia.**

Antiphon for Magnificat.

These things have I told you, * that when the hóur cómeth: ye may re-

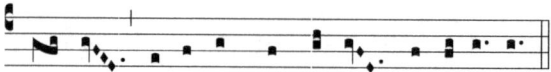

mem-ber that I told you of them, ál-le-lú-ia.

VIII

Collect. **Almighty, Everlàsting God : make us to have always a devout will towards Thèe, and to serve Thy majesty with a pure heart; through Jesus Christ, Thy Son, oùr Lord, who liveth and reigneth with Thee and the Hòly Ghost : ever one God, world without end. Amen.**

WHITSUNTIDE
The week of Pentecost.

Invitatory.

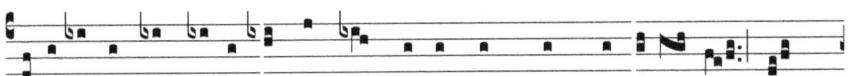

Al-le-lu-ia, the Spirit of the Lord filleth the world, ál-le-lú- ia : O

cóme, let us wórship Him.

Antiphons for Psalms (appropriate for use on Feasts and Sundays)
1. Come, Holy Ghost, and fill the hearts of Thy faithful people, † and kindle in them the fíre of Thy <u>love</u> : Thou, who through diverse tongues gatherest together the nations in the unity of the faith, alleluia, álleluia.
2. Thou sendest forth Thy Spirit, they áre creáted : And Thou renewest the face of the earth, alleluia, álleluia. *(Ps. 104iii)*
3. I will not leave you comfortless, álleluia : I come to you, and your heart shall rejoice, álleluia.
4. The Comforter, which is the Holy Ghost, álleluia : He shall teach you all things, álleluia.
5. And they were all filled with the Holy Ghost, álleluia : And they began to speak, álleluia.
6. Create in me a clean heart, O God, álleluia : And renew a right spirit within me, álleluia. *(Ps. 51)*

Responsory for Whitsuntide.

℟. And there appeared unto the Apostles cloven tongues like as of fire, ál-le-

lú- ia. ‡ And the Ho- ly Ghost sat upon each of them, al-le-lu-ia, ál-

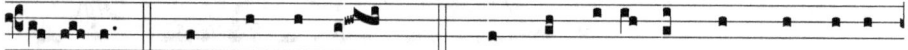

le- lú-ia. ℟. And there appeared... ℣. And they began to speak with other

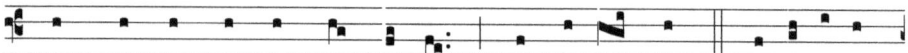

tongues the wón-der-ful wórks of God. ‡ And the Ho- ly... ℣. Glory be to

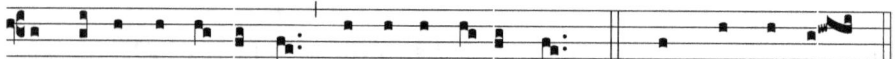

the Fáther and tó the Son: and tó the Hóly Ghost. ℟. And there appeared...

Whitsunday, the Feast of Pentecost
Psalms. **68; 104:24-35; 33, 145, 48, 87, 84, 81, 18, 67, 46, 80, 117, 100, 78, 99, 76, 9, 50, 101, 75**

Gospel (at Morning Prayer). **John 14:23-31**
Hymn. **Jam Christus astra ascenderunt.** *c. 4th cent., trans. by P. Dearmer*

1. When Christ our Lord had passed once more / Into the heaven he left before, / He sent a Comforter below / The Father's promise to bestow.
2. The solemn time was soon to fall / Which told the number mystical; / For since the resurrection day / A week of weeks has passed away.
3. At the third hour a rushing noise / Came like the tempest's sudden voice, / And mingled with the Apostles' prayer, / Proclaiming loud that

God was there.
4. From out the Father's light it came, / That beautiful and kindly flame, / To kindle every Christian heart, / And fervor of the Word impart.
5. As then, O Lord, Thou didst fulfill / Each holy heart to do Thy will, / So now do Thou our sins forgive / And make the world in peace to live.
6. To God the Father, God the Son, / And God the Spirit, praise be done; / May Christ the Lord upon us pour / The Spirit's gift for evermore. Amen.

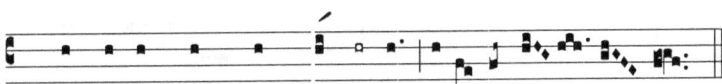

℣. The Holy Ghost, the Cómforter, al-le-lu-ia.
℟. He shall teach you áll things, alleluia.
Antiphon for Benedictus. Receive yé the Hóly Ghost : whosoever sins ye remit, they are remitted unto them, állelúia.

Epistle (at Evening Prayer). Acts 2:1-21
Hymn. Beata nobis gaudia. *c. 4th cent., trans. by R. E. Roberts* [338]

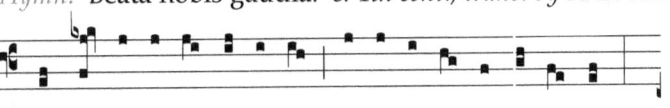

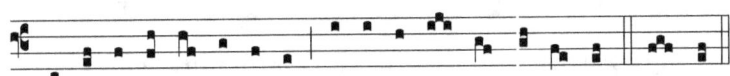

1. Rejoice! the year upon its way / Has brought again that bless-ed day, / When on the chosen of the Lord / The Holy Spirit was outpoured.
2. On each the fire, descending, stood, / In quivering tongues' similitude, / Tongues, that their words might ready prove, / And fire, to make them flame with love.
3. To all in every tongue they spoke; / Amazement in the crowd awoke, / Who mocked, as overcome with wine, / Those who were filled with power divine.
4. These things were done in type that day, / When Eastertide had passed away, / The number told which once set free / The captive at the jubilee.
5. And now, O holy God, this day / Regard us as we humbly pray, / And send us, from Thy heavenly seat, / The blessings of the Paraclete.
6. To God the Father, God the Son, / And God the Spirit, praise be done; / May Christ the Lord upon us pour / The Spirit's gift for evermore. Amen.

℣. Now, O God, thou givest a grácious rain, al-le-lu-ia.
℟. And thine inheritance, which is dry, thou dost máke alive, alleluia.

Antiphon for Magnificat.

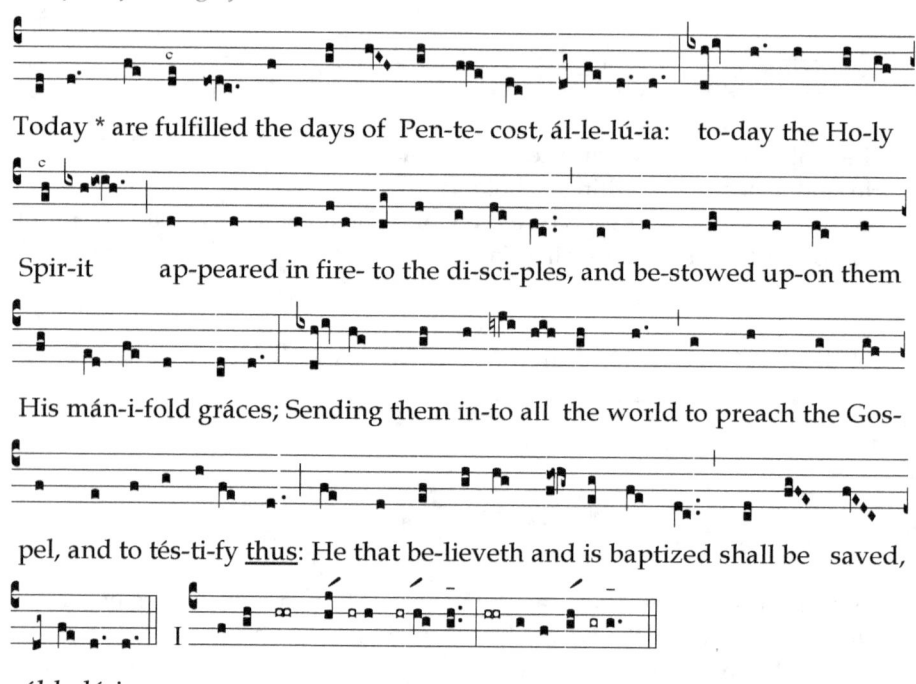

Today * are fulfilled the days of Pen-te-cost, ál-le-lú-ia: to-day the Ho-ly Spir-it ap-peared in fire- to the di-sci-ples, and be-stowed up-on them His mán-i-fold gráces; Sending them in-to all the world to preach the Gos-pel, and to tés-ti-fy <u>thus</u>: He that be-lieveth and is baptized shall be saved, ál-le-lú-ia.

Collect. O God, who didst teach the hearts of Thy faithful people by sending to them the light of Thy Hòly Spirit : grant us by the same Spirit to have a right judgment in all thìngs, and evermore to rejoice in His holy comfort; through Jesus Christ, Thy Son, oùr Lord, who liveth and reigneth with Thee in the unity of the same Hòly Spirit : ever one God, world without end. Amen.

COMPLINE

Hymn. **Veni, creator Spiritus, mentes.**
Rhabanus Maurus, † 856, trans. by E. Caswall

1. Come, Holy Ghost, Creator blest, / Vouchsafe within our souls to rest; / Come with Thy grace and heavenly aid / And fill the hearts which Thou hast made.
2. To Thee, the Comforter, we cry, / To Thee, the Gift of God Most High, / The Fount of life, the Fire of love, / The soul's Anointing from above.
3. The sevenfold gifts of grace are Thine, / O Finger of the Hand Divine; / True Promise of the Father Thou, / Who dost the tongue with speech endow.
4. Thy light to every thought impart / And shed Thy love in every heart; / The weakness of our mortal state / With deathless might invigorate. [339]
5. Drive far away our wily Foe / And Thine abiding peace bestow; / If Thou be our protecting Guide, / No evil can our steps betide.
6. Make Thou to us the Father known, / Teach us the eternal Son to own / And Thee, whose name we ever bless, / Of both the Spirit, to confess.
7. Praise we the Father and the Son / And Holy Spirit, with them One; / And may the Son on us bestow / The gifts that from the Spirit flow. Amen.

Antiphon for Nunc Dimittis

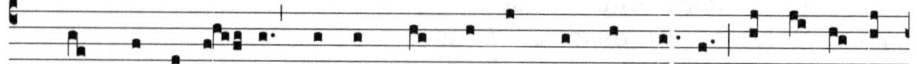

Come, Ho-ly Spir- it, * fill the hearts of Thy faithful people and kindle in

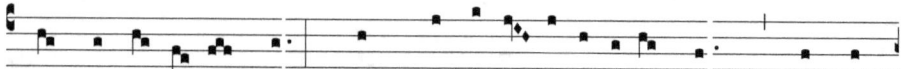

them the fíre of Thy <u>love</u>: through the di-ver-si-ty of all tongues Thou ga-

there*d*est to-ge-ther the na-tions in the u-ni-ty of the faith, Al-le-lu- ia,

ál-le-lú-ia.

Monday of Whitsun Week
Gospel (at Morning Prayer). **John 3:16-21**
Epistle (at Evening Prayer). **Acts 10:42-48**

Versicle (music from Pentecost)
℣. The apostles began to speak with óther tongues, alleluia.
℟. The wonderful wórks of God, alleluia.
Antiphon for Benedictus. God so loved the world, that He gave His ónly-begótten Son : to the end that all that believe in Him should not perish, but have everlasting life, álleluía.

Antiphon for Magnificat.

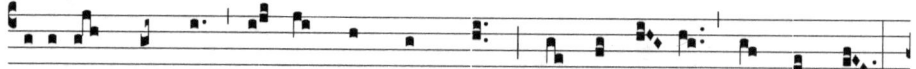

If a man love me, * he will keep My words; and My Fá-ther will lóve him :

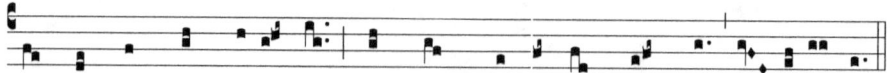

and We will come unto him, and make Our a-bode with him, ál- le-lú-ia.

III

Collect. O God, who didst give Thy Holy Spirit to Thìne Apostles : grant unto Thy people the performance of their petitiòns, so that on us, to whom Thou hast given faith, Thou mayest bestow also peace; through Jesus Christ, Thy Son, oùr Lord, who liveth and reigneth with Thee in the unity of the same Hòly Spirit : ever one God, world without end. Amen.

Tuesday of Whitsun Week
Gospel (at Morning Prayer). **John 10:1-10**
Epistle (at Evening Prayer). **Acts 8:14-17** [340]

Versicle (music from Pentecost)
℣. The Spirit of the Lord filléth the world, alleluia.
℟. And that which containeth all things hath knowledge óf the voice, alleluia.
Antiphon for Benedictus. I am the Dóor, saith the <u>Lord</u> : by me if any man enter in, he shall be saved, and shall find pasture, állelúia.

Antiphon for Magnificat.

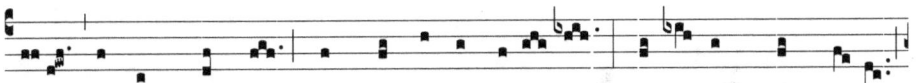

Peace * I leave with you, My péace I give únto you : not as the world giveth,

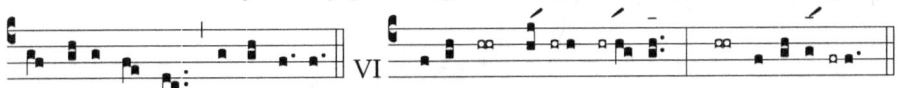
VI

give I un-to you, ál-le-lú-ia.

Collect. O God, who didst teach the hearts of Thy faithful people by sending to them the light of Thy Hòly Spirit : grant us by the same Spirit to have a right judgment in all thìngs, and evermore to rejoice in His holy comfort; through Jesus Christ, Thy Son, oùr Lord, who liveth and reigneth with Thee in the unity of the same Hòly Spirit : ever one God, world without end. Amen.

The Rest of Whitsun Week
The Office is prayed with the propers from Pentecost. Alleluia antiphons may be used for the Psalmody.

Ember Days in Pentecost
(Wednesday, Friday, and Saturday After Whitsunday)

EMBER WEDNESDAY
Gospel (at Morning Prayer). **John 6:44-51**
Epistle (at Evening Prayer). **Acts 5:12-16**

℣. The Apostles did speak in other tongues, alleluia.
℟. The wonderful works of God, alleluia.
Antiphon for Benedictus. I am the living bréad, saith the Lord : which came down from heaven, alleluia, álleluía.

Antiphon for Magnificat.

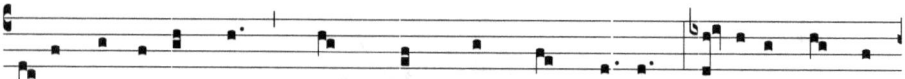

I am the living bread * which came down from heaven; † if a-ny man eat

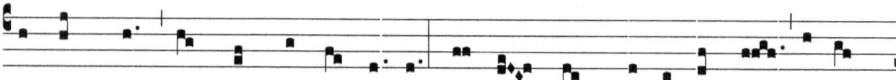

of this bread, he shall líve for év-er : and the bread that I will give is my

flesh, for the life of the world, ál-le-lú-ia.

Collect. We beseech Thèe, O Lord : that the Comforter which proceedeth from Thee may enlighten our mìnds, and lead us, as Thy Son hath promised, into all truth; through the same, Jesus Christ, Thy Son, oùr Lord, who liveth and reigneth with Thee in the unity of the same Hòly Spirit : ever one God, world without end. Amen.

EMBER FRIDAY
Gospel (at Morning Prayer). **Luke 5:17-26**
Epistle (at Evening Prayer). **Joel 2:23-24, 26-27**

℣. The Apostles did speak in other tongues, alleluia.
℟. The wonderful works of God, alleluia.

Antiphon for Benedictus. Jesus said, But that ye may know that the Son of Man hath power on earth tó forgive <u>sins</u> : I say unto thee, Arise, take up thy bed, and go thy way into thy house, állelúia.

Antiphon for Magnificat.

But the Comforter, * which is the Holy Ghost, whom the Father will sénd in

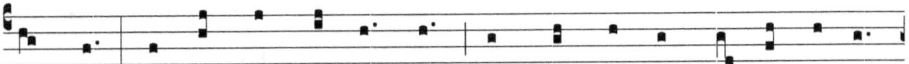

my <u>Name</u> : he will teach you all things, and bring all things to your remem-

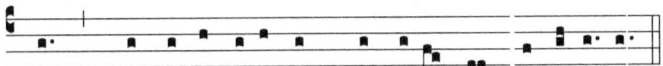

brance, whatso-ev-er I have said unto you, ál-le-lú-ia.

VIII

Collect. Most merciful God, wè beseech Thee : that Thy Church being joined together in the unity of the Holy Spirìt, may be preserved evermore from all the assaults of the enemy; through Jesus Christ, Thy Son, oùr Lord, who liveth and reigneth with Thee in the unity of the same Hòly Spirit : ever one God, world without end. Amen.

E<small>MBER</small> S<small>ATURDAY</small>
Gospel (at Morning Prayer). **Luke 4:38-44**
Epistle (at Evening Prayer). **Romans 5:1-5**

℣. The Apostles did speak in other tongues, alleluia.
℟. The wonderful works of God, alleluia.
Antiphon for Benedictus. The love of God is shed abróad in our <u>hearts</u> : by the Holy Ghost which is given unto us, állelúia.

Collect. O Lòrd, we pray Thee : that Thy Holy Spirit, who doth preserve us by His wisdom and govern us by His provìdence, may by Thy mercy be poured forth upon the hearts of us Thy servants; through Jesus Christ, Thy

Son, oùr Lord, who liveth and reigneth with Thee in the unity of the same Hòly Spirit : ever one God, world without end. Amen.

TRINITYTIDE

From Trinity Sunday until Saturday before Advent 1. Trinitytide consists of at least 23 and at most 27 Sundays, due to the variable date of Easter. The propers for the 27th Sunday after Trinity shall be used on the last Sunday of the Church Year, regardless of the actual enumeration of those Sundays.

For Holy Trinity and the week thereafter:
Invitatory.

The true God, One in Thrée and Thrée in One : O cóme, let us wórship Him.

Antiphons for Psalms (appropriate for use on Feasts and Sundays)
1. Unto Thee do we call, Thee do we praise, Thée do we wórship : O bléssed Trínity.
2. Glory be to Thee, coéqual Trínity : One God before all worlds began, and nów and forévermore.
3. Holy, holy, holy, Lord Gód Almíghty : Which was and ís and ís to come.
4. We bless the Father and the Son ánd the Hóly Ghost : Praise Him and magnify Hím foréver.

Responsory for Trinity and the week thereafter.

IV

℟. We bless the Father and the Son ánd the Hóly Ghost. ‡ Praise Him and mag-ni-fy Hím for-év-er. ℟. We bless the... ℣. Blessed art Thou, O Lord, in the firmament of heaven and above all to be praised and glo-ri-fíed for-év-er. ‡ Praise Him and... ℣. Glory be to the Fáther and tó the Son: and tó the Hó-ly Ghost. ℟. We bless the...

Responsory for the time after Trinity.

II

℟. For-ev-er, O Lord, Thy Word is settled in heaven; Thy Word is a lamp un-to my feet and a light ún-to my path. ‡ Lord, I have loved the habi-tation of Thy house and the place where Thine hónor dwélleth. ℟. For-ev-er, O Lord... ℣. Blessed are they that hear the Word of Gód and kéep it. ‡

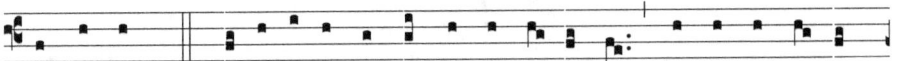

Lord, I have... ℣. Glory be to the Fáther and tó the Son: and tó the Hó-ly

Ghost. ℟. For-ev-er, O Lord...

The Feast of the Holy Trinity
Psalms. 8, 33, 48, 75, 86, 115, 135, 67

Gospel (at Morning Prayer). **John 3:1-15**
Hymn (at Morning Prayer). **O Pater sancte.** *c. 10th c., trans. by P. Dearmer* [342]

1. Father most holy, merciful and tender, / Jesus, our Savior, with the Father reigning, / Spirit of comfort, advocate, defender, / Light never waning;
2. Trinity blessed, unity unshaken, / Goodness unbounded, very God of heaven, / Light of the angels, joy of those forsaken, / Hope of all living;
3. Maker of all things, all Thy creatures praise Thee; / All for Thy worship were and are created; / Now as we also worship Thee devoutly, / Hear Thou our voices.
4. Lord God Almighty, unto Thee be glory, / One in three persons, over all exalted. / Glory we offer, praise Thee and adore Thee, / Now and forever. Amen.

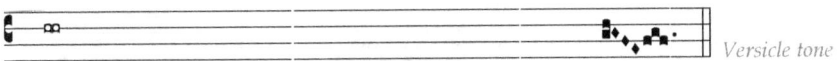
Versicle tone

℣. We bless the Father and the Son and the Holy Ghost.
℟. Praise Him and magnify Him forev-   er.

Antiphon for Benedictus. Blessed be the Creator and Governór of áll things : God the holy and undivided Trinity, both now and ever, through éndless áges.

Epistle (at Evening Prayer). **Romans 11:33-36**
Hymn (at Evening Prayer). **Adesto, sancta Trinitas.** *c. 10th cent., trans. by J. M. Neale*

1. Be present, holy Trinity, / Like splendor, and one Deity; / Of things above, and things below, / Beginning, that no end shall know.
2. Thee all the armies of the sky / Adore, and laud, and magnify; / And nature, in her triple frame, / For ever sanctifies Thy Name.
3. And we, too, thanks and homage pay, / Thine own adoring flock today; / O join to that celestial song / The praises of our suppliant throng!
4. Light, sole and one, we Thee confess, / With triple praise we rightly bless; / Alpha and Omega we own, / With every spirit round Thy throne.
5. To Thee, O unbegotten One, / And Thee, O sole-begotten Son, / And Thee, O Holy Ghost, we raise / Our equal and eternal praise. Amen.

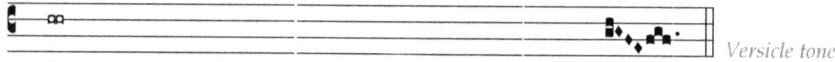 *Versicle tone*

℣. We bless the Father and the Son and the Holy Ghost.
℟. Praise Him and magnify Him forever.

[343] *Antiphon for Magnificat.*

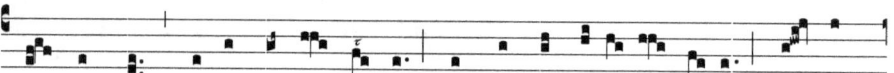

Thee, O God * Father un-be-gotten; Thee, O Son only-be-gotten; Thee O

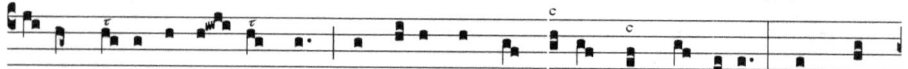

Ho-ly Spírit the Pá- ra-clete : O Holy and un-di-ví-ded Trín-i-ty; With our

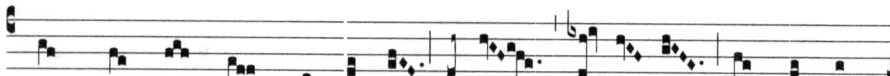

whole heart and mouth we confess, we práise, and we <u>bless</u> : to Thee be

gló-ry for-év-er.

Collect. Almighty and Everlasting God, who hast given unto us, Thy servants, grace, by the confession of a true faith, to acknowledge the glory of the eternal Trinity and in the power of the Divine Majesty to worship the Ùnity : we beseech Thee that Thou wouldst keep us steadfast in this fàith, and evermore defend us from all adversities; who livest and reignest, èver one God : world without end. Amen.

First Sunday After Trinity
Psalms. **13, 41, 5, 9, 58, 39, 14, 119i, ii**
Gospel (at Morning Prayer). **Luke 16:19-31**
Epistle (at Evening Prayer). **1 John 4:16b-21**

℣. I have trusted in Thy mercy. ℟. My heart shall rejoice in Thy salvation.
Antiphon for Benedictus. **Abraham saith unto him, They have Moses ánd the próphets : lét them hear <u>them</u>.**

Antiphon for Magnificat.

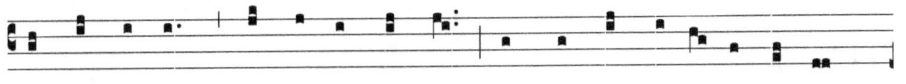

It came to páss, * that the béggar died : and was carried by the angels

in-to Á- braham's bósom.

Collect. O God, the Strength of all them that put their trùst in Thee : mercifully accept our prayers; and because through the weakness of our mortal nature we can do no good thing without Thee, grant us the help of Thy gràce, that in keeping Thy commandments we may please Thee both in will and deed; through Jesus Christ, Thy Son, oùr Lord, who liveth and reigneth with Thee and the Hòly Ghost : ever one God, world without end. Amen.

Second Sunday After Trinity
Psalms. 18, 120, 7, 6, 64, 26, 49, 119iii, iv
Gospel (at Morning Prayer). Luke 14:16-24
Epistle (at Evening Prayer). 1 John 3:13-18

℣. I will love Thee, O Lord, my strength.
℟. The Lord is my rock, and my fortress, and my deliverer.
Antiphon for Benedictus. A certain man made a great feast of good things; †
and bade many, and sent his servant at supper-time to tell them thát were
bídden : Come ye unto me, for all things are now ready, állelúia.

Antiphon for Magnificat.

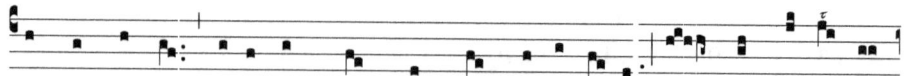

Go out quickly * in-to the streets and lánes of the cí-ty: and bring in hither

the poor and the maimed, the halt and the blind, that my house may be

filled, ál-le-lú-ia.

Collect. O Lord, who never failest to help and govern those whom Thou dost
bring up in Thy steadfast feàr and love : make us to have a perpetual fear
and love of Thy holy name; through Jesus Christ, Thy Son, oùr Lord, who
liveth and reigneth with Thee and the Hòly Ghost : ever one God, world
without end. Amen.

Third Sunday After Trinity
Psalms. 25, 55, 9, 17, 107, 32, 103, 119v, vi
Gospel (at Morning Prayer). Luke 15:1-10
Epistle (at Evening Prayer). 1 Peter 5:6-11

℣. Turn Thee unto me, and have mercy upon me.
℟. For I am desolate and afflicted.
Antiphon for Benedictus. What man of you, having an hundred sheep, if he
lose but one of them, doth not leave the ninety and nine ín the wílderness :

and go after that which is lost, until he find it? álleluia.

Antiphon for Magnificat.

What woman, * having ten pieces of silver, íf she lóse one piece : doth not

light a candle, and sweep the house, and seek di-li-gent-ly un-tíl she fínd it?

VI

Collect. O God, the Protector of all that trust in Thee, without whom nothing is strong, nothìng is holy : increase and multiply upon us Thy mercý, that, Thou being our Ruler and Guide, we may so pass through things temporal that we finally lose not the things eternal; through Jesus Christ, Thy Son, oùr Lord, who liveth and reigneth with Thee and the Hòly Ghost : ever one God, world without end. Amen.

Fourth Sunday After Trinity
Psalms. 27, 79, 13, 15, 52, 107, 119vii, viii
Gospel (at Morning Prayer). Luke 6:36-42
Epistle (at Evening Prayer). Romans 8:18-23

℣. Help us, O God of our salvation.
℟. For the glory of Thy name, and deliver us.
Antiphon for Benedictus. Be ye thérefore mérciful : as your Father also is mérciful, sáith the Lord.

Antiphon for Magnificat.

Judge not, * thát ye bé not judged : for with what judgment ye judge, ye

 VIII

shall be júdged, saith the <u>Lord</u>.

Collect. **Grant, O Lord, wè beseech Thee** : that the course of this world may be so peaceably ordered by Thy govèrnance, that Thy Church may joyfully serve Thee in all godly quietness; through Jesus Christ, Thy Son, oùr Lord, who liveth and reigneth with Thee and the Hòly Ghost : ever one God, world without end. Amen.

Fifth Sunday After Trinity
Psalms. 27, 84, 71, 16, 112, 119ix, x
Gospel (at Morning Prayer). **Luke 5:1-11**
Epistle (at Evening Prayer). **1 Peter 3:8-15**

℣. Behold, O God our shield. ℟. And look upon the face of Thine Anointed.
Antiphon for Benedictus. **And Jesus entered into a ship, ánd sat dówn therein :** and taught the people, álleluía.

Antiphon for Magnificat.

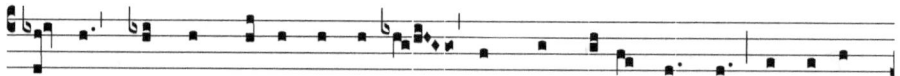

Master, * we have toiled all the night, and have táken nóthing: neverthe-

less at thy word I will lét down the <u>net</u>.

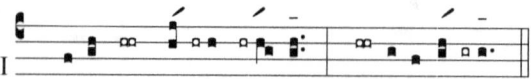
I

Collect. **O God, who hast prepared for them that love Thee such good things** as pass man's ùnderstanding : pour into our hearts such love toward Thèe, that we, loving Thee above all things, may obtain Thy promises, which exceed all that we can desire; through Jesus Christ, Thy Son, oùr Lord, who liveth and reigneth with Thee and the Hòly Ghost : ever one God, world without end. Amen.

Sixth Sunday After Trinity
Psalms. 28, 90, 17, 36, 53, 129, 119xi, xii
Gospel (at Morning Prayer). Matthew 5:20-26
Epistle (at Evening Prayer). Romans 6:3-11

℣. The Lord is the strength of His people.
℟. And He is the saving strength of His anointed.
Antiphon for Benedictus. It was said by them of old time, Thou shalt not kill; † and whosoever shall kill, shall be in danger óf the júdgement : but I say unto yóu much móre than this.

Antiphon for Magnificat.

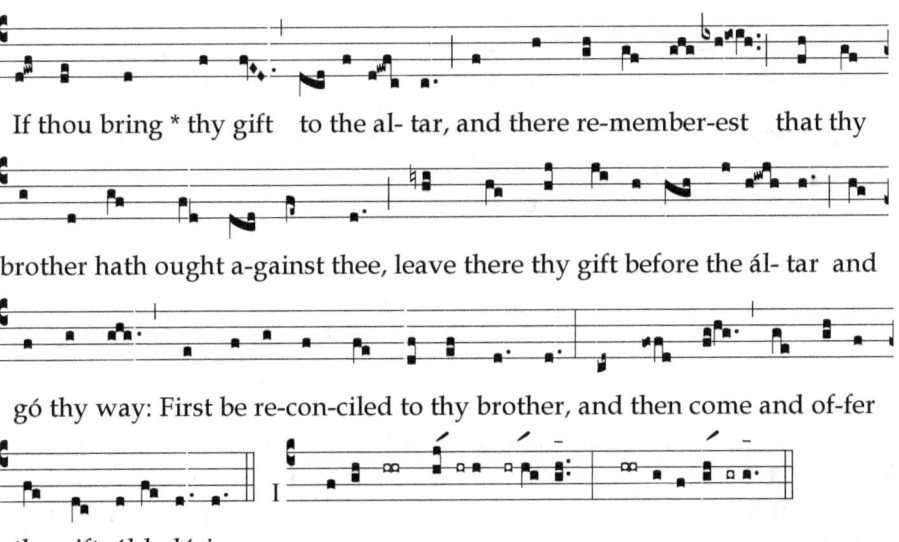

If thou bring * thy gift to the al- tar, and there re-member-est that thy brother hath ought a-gainst thee, leave there thy gift before the ál- tar and gó thy way: First be re-con-ciled to thy brother, and then come and of-fer thy gift, ál-le-lú-ia.

Collect. Lord of all Power and might, who art the Author and Giver of àll good things : graft in our hearts the love of Thy nàme, increase in us true religion, nourish us with all goodness, and of Thy great mercy keep us in the same; through Jesus Christ, Thy Son, oùr Lord, who liveth and reigneth with Thee and the Hòly Ghost : ever one God, world without end. Amen.

Seventh Sunday After Trinity

Psalms. 47, 34, 65, 107, 145, 146, 119xiii, xiv
Gospel (at Morning Prayer). **Mark 8:1-9**
Epistle (at Evening Prayer). **Romans 6:19-23**

℣. O clap your hands, all ye people.
℟. Shout unto God with the voice of triumph.
Antiphon for Benedictus. **The multitude being very great, and having nothing to eat, Jesus called His disciples unto Him, and sáith unto <u>them</u> : I have compassion on the multitude, because they have now been with me three days, and have nothing to eat, álleluía.**

Antiphon for Magnificat.

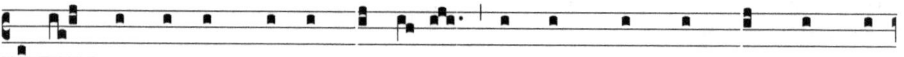

I have compassion * on the mul-ti-tude, be-cause they have now been with

me three days, and have nóthing to <u>eat</u>: and if I send them away fasting,

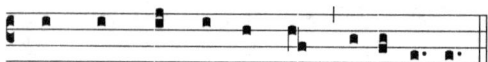

they will faint by the way, ál-le-lú-ia.

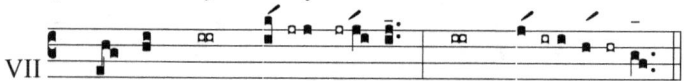

VII

Collect. O God, whose never-failing providence ordereth all things both in heaven ànd on earth : we humbly beseech Thee to put away from us all hurtfùl things, and to give us those things which be profitable for us; through Jesus Christ, Thy Son, oùr Lord, who liveth and reigneth with Thee and the Hòly Ghost : ever one God, world without end. Amen.

Eighth Sunday After Trinity

Psalms. 48, 31, 34, 70, 75, 1, 140, 119xv, xvi
Gospel (at Morning Prayer). **Matthew 7:15-23**
Epistle (at Evening Prayer). **Romans 8:12-17**

℣. We have thought of Thy lovingkindness, O God.
℟. In the midst of Thy temple.
Antiphon for Benedictus. Beware of false prophets, which come to you in sheep's clothing, but inwardly they are ravening <u>wolves</u> : Ye shall know them by their fruits, állelúia.

Antiphon for Magnificat.

A good tree * cannot bring forth e-vil fruit, neither can a corrupt tree bríng

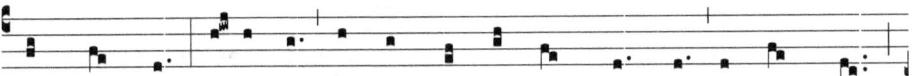

forth good fruit: ev'ry tree that bringeth not forth good fruit is hewn down,

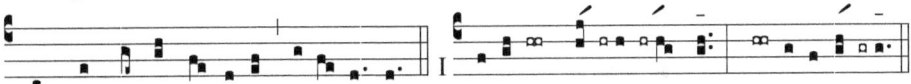

and cast in-to the fire, ál-le-lú-ia.

Collect. Grant to us, Lord, wè beseech Thee : the Spirit to think and do always such things as are rìght, that we, who cannot do anything that is good without Thee, may by Thee be enabled to live according to Thy will; through Jesus Christ, Thy Son, oùr Lord, who liveth and reigneth with Thee and the Hòly Ghost : ever one God, world without end. Amen.

Ninth Sunday After Trinity
Psalms. **54, 8, 81, 19, 62, 12, 119xvii, xviii**
Gospel (at Morning Prayer). **Luke 16:1-9**
Epistle (at Evening Prayer). **1 Corinthians 10:6-13**

℣. Behold, God is mine helper.
℟. The Lord is with them that uphold my soul.
Antiphon for Benedictus. And the lord said unto his steward, What is this thát I héar of thee? : Give an account of thy stewardship, állelúia.

Antiphon for Magnificat.

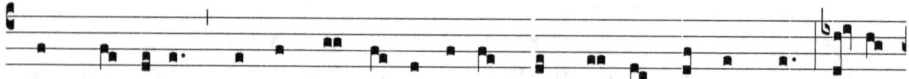

What shall I do? * for my lord taketh away from mé the stéwardship: I can-

not dig; to bég I ám ashamed. I am resolved what to do, that, when I am

put out of the stewardship, they may receive me ín-to their hóuses.

IV

Collect. Let Thy merciful ears, O Lord, be open to the prayers of Thy hùmble servants : and that they may obtain their petitiòns, make them to ask such things as shall please Thee; through Jesus Christ, Thy Son, oùr Lord, who liveth and reigneth with Thee and the Hòly Ghost : ever one God, world without end. Amen.

Tenth Sunday After Trinity
Psalms. 55, 17, 88, 74, 81, 5, 58, 119xix, xx
Gospel (at Morning Prayer). Luke 19:41-48
Epistle (at Evening Prayer). 1 Corinthians 12:1-11

℣. When I cried unto the Lord. ℟. He heard the voice of my supplications.
Antiphon for Benedictus.
When the Lord was come near tó Jerúsalem : He beheld the city, and wept óver it, sáying,
If thou hadst known, even thou, for the days shall cóme upón thee : that thine enemies shall cast a trench about thee, and compass thee round, and keep thee ín on évery side,
And shall lay thee éven wíth the ground : because thou knewest not the time of thy visitation, állelúia.

Antiphon for Magnificat.

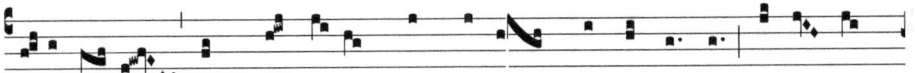

It is written, * My house is the house of práyer for all péople: but ye have

made it a den of thieves; And He taught daily ín the témple.

VIII

Collect. O God, who declarest Thine almighty power chiefly in showing mercý and pity : mercifully grant unto us such a measure of Thy gràce, that we, running the way of Thy Commandments, may obtain Thy gracious promises and be made partakers of Thy heavenly treasure; through Jesus Christ, Thy Son, oùr Lord, who liveth and reigneth with Thee and the Hòly Ghost : ever one God, world without end. Amen.

Eleventh Sunday After Trinity
Psalms. 68, 27, 90, 30, 51, 32, 131, 119xxi, xxii
Gospel (at Morning Prayer). Luke 18:9-14
Epistle (at Evening Prayer). 1 Corinthians 15:1-10

℣. Unto Thee will I cry, O Lord my rock, be not silent to me.
℟. O Lord, be not far from me.
Antiphon for Benedictus. And the Publican, standing afar off, would not lift up so much as his eyes únto héaven : but smote upon his breast, saying, God be merciful to mé a sínner.

Antiphon for Magnificat.

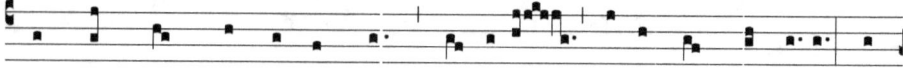

This man went down to his house * just-i-fied rather thán the óther: for

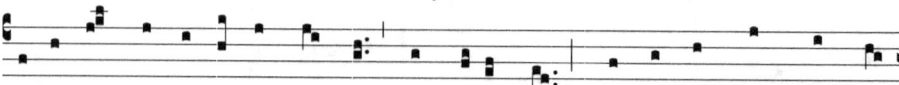

every one that ex-al-teth himself shall be a-based; and he that humbleth him-

self shall bé ex-ál-ted.

Collect. Almighty and everlasting God, who art always more ready to hear than we to pray and art wont to give more than either we desire òr deserve : pour down upon us the abundance of Thy mercy, forgiving us those things whereof our conscience is afràid, and giving us those good things which we are not worthy to ask, but through the merits and mediation of Jesus Christ, Thy Son, oùr Lord, who liveth and reigneth with Thee and the Hòly Ghost : ever one God, world without end. Amen.

Twelfth Sunday After Trinity
Psalms. 70, 34, 95, 104, 115, 143, 147
Gospel (at Morning Prayer). Mark 7:31-37
Epistle (at Evening Prayer). 2 Corinthians 3:4-11

℣. I will bless the Lord at all times.
℟. His praise shall continually be in my mouth.
Antiphon for Benedictus. When the Lord had passed through the cóasts of Týre : He made the deaf to hear ánd the dúmb to speak.

Antiphon for Magnificat.

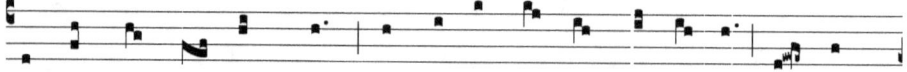

Hé hath done áll things well: * He maketh both the deaf to hear, ánd the

dúmb to speak.

Collect. Almighty and merciful God, of whose only gift it cometh that Thy faithful people do unto Thee true and laudàble service : grant, we beseech Thee, that we may so faithfully serve Thee in this life, that we fail not finally to attain Thy heavenly promises; through Jesus Christ, Thy Son, oùr Lord, who liveth and reigneth with Thee and the Hòly Ghost : ever one God, world without end. Amen.

Thirteenth Sunday After Trinity

Psalms. 74, 31, 15, 89, 149, 62, 112
Gospel (at Morning Prayer). **Luke 10:23-37**
Epistle (at Evening Prayer). **Galatians 3:15-22**

℣. O Lord God of my salvation.   ℟. I have cried day and night before Thee.
Antiphon for Benedictus.
Blessed are the eyes which see the thíngs that yé see : For I tell you, that
   many prophets and kings have desired to see those things which ye see,
   and háve not séen them;
And to hear those thíngs which ye <u>hear</u> : and have not heard them, álleluía.

Antiphon for Magnificat.

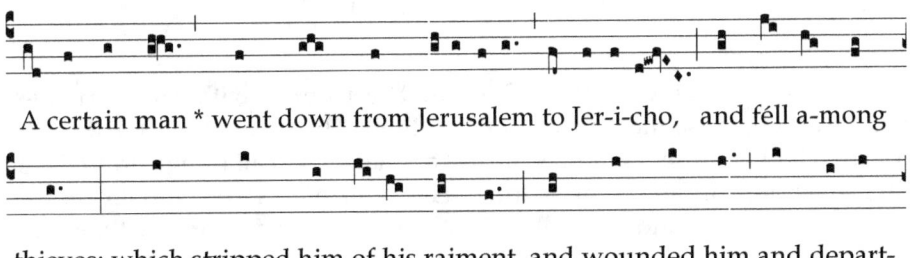

A certain man * went down from Jerusalem to Jer-i-cho,   and féll a-mong thieves: which stripped him of his raiment, and wounded him and depart-

ed, léaving him hálf dead.

Collect. Almighty and everlàsting God : give unto us the increase of faith, hope, and charìty; and that we may obtain that which Thou dost promise, make us to love that which Thou dost command; through Jesus Christ, Thy Son, oùr Lord, who liveth and reigneth with Thee and the Hòly Ghost : ever one God, world without end. Amen.

Fourteenth Sunday After Trinity
Psalms. **84, 92, 34, 38, 30, 36, 41, 39, 146**
Gospel (at Morning Prayer). **Luke 17:11-19**
Epistle (at Evening Prayer). **Galatians 5:16-24**

℣. Lord, Thou hast been our dwelling place. ℟. In all generations.
Antiphon for Benedictus. As Jesus passed through a certain village, there met him ten men thát were lépers : which stood afar off, and they lifted up their voices, and said, Jesus, Master, have mércy on us.

Antiphon for Magnificat.

And one of them, * when he saw   that hé was héaled, turned back: and with

a loud voice glor-i-fied God, ál-le-lú-ia.

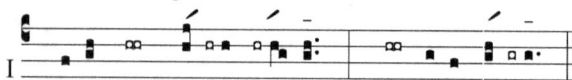

Collect. Keep, we beseech thee, O Lord, Thy Church with Thy perpetù-al mercy : and because the frailty of man without Thee cannot bùt fall, keep us ever by Thy help from all things hurtful and lead us to all things profitable to our salvation; through Jesus Christ, Thy Son, oùr Lord, who liveth and reigneth with Thee and the Hòly Ghost : ever one God, world without end. Amen.

Fifteenth Sunday After Trinity
Psalms. **86, 118, 108, 40, 28, 107, 133**
Gospel (at Morning Prayer). **Matthew 6:24-34**
Epistle (at Evening Prayer). **Galatians 5:25-6:10**

℣. It is a good thing to give thanks unto the Lord.
℞. And to sing praises unto Thy name, O most High.

Antiphon for Benedictus. Be ye not therefore anxious, saying, what shall we eat? † Or, whát shall we <u>drink</u>? : For your heavenly Father knoweth that ye have need of all these things, álleluía.

Antiphon for Magnificat.

Seek ye first * the kingdom of God, ánd his ríghteousness: and all these

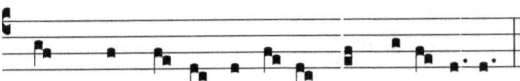

things shall be added unto you, ál-le-lú-ia.

Collect. O Lord, we beseech Thee, let Thy continual pity cleanse and defènd Thy Church : and because it cannot continue in safety without Thy succòr, preserve it evermore by Thy help and goodness; through Jesus Christ, Thy Son, oùr Lord, who liveth and reigneth with Thee and the Hòly Ghost : ever one God, world without end. Amen.

Sixteenth Sunday After Trinity

Psalms. 86, 102, 40, 71, 23, 84, 91, 39
Gospel (at Morning Prayer). Luke 7:11-17
Epistle (at Evening Prayer). Ephesians 3:13-21

℣. O Lord, make haste to help me.
℞. Let them be confounded that seek after my soul.

Antiphon for Benedictus. Jesus went into a cíty called <u>Nain</u> : and behold, there was a dead man carried out, the only són of his móther.

Antiphon for Magnificat.

A great Prophet * is risen úp amóng us: and God hath vis-i-téd His péople.

Collect. Lord, we pray Thee that Thy grace may always go before and follow àfter us : and make us continually to be given to all good works; through Jesus Christ, Thy Son, oùr Lord, who liveth and reigneth with Thee and the Hòly Ghost : ever one God, world without end. Amen.

Seventeenth Sunday After Trinity
Psalms. **119xviii, 33, 76, 26, 48, 92, 37**
Gospel (at Morning Prayer). **Luke 14:1-11**
Epistle (at Evening Prayer). **Ephesians 4:1-6**

℣. Righteous art Thou, O Lord. ℟. And upright are Thy judgments.
Antiphon for Benedictus. As Jesus went into the house of one of the chief Pharisees to eat bread on the Sabbath Day; † behold there was a certain man before him which hád the drópsy : and he took him, and héaled him, and lét him go.

Antiphon for Magnificat.

When thou art bidden * tó a wédding : sit down ín the lówest place; That he

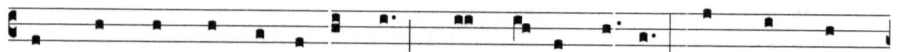

that bade thee may say unto thee, Friend, gó up hígher : then shalt thou

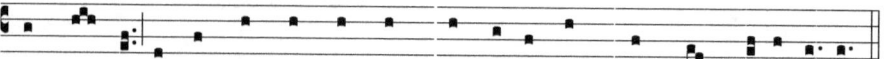

have glo-ry in the presence of them that sit at meat with thee, ál-le-lú-ia.

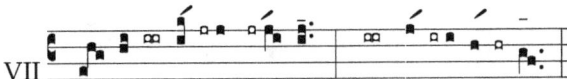
VII

Collect. Lord, we beseech Thee, grant Thy people grace to withstand the temptations òf the devil : and with pure hearts and minds to follow Thee, the only God; through Jesus Christ, Thy Son, oùr Lord, who liveth and reigneth with Thee and the Hòly Ghost : ever one God, world without end. Amen.

Eighteenth Sunday After Trinity

Psalms. 122, 96, 100, 81, 42, 110, 82, 149
Gospel (at Morning Prayer). Matthew 22:34-46
Epistle (at Evening Prayer). 1 Corinthians 1:4-9

℣. Let my prayer be set forth. ℟. Before Thee as incense.
Antiphon for Benedictus. Master, which is the great commándment ín the Law? : Jesus said unto him, Thou shalt love the Lord thy God with all thy heart, álleluía.

Antiphon for Magnificat.

What * think ye of Chríst? Whose Són is He? : They say un-to Him, The Són

of Dá-vid. Je-sus saith unto them, How then doth David in spírit cáll him

Lord : saying, The Lord said unto my Lord, Sit thou ón my ríght hand?

IV

Collect. O God, forasmuch as without Thee we are not ablè to please Thee : mercifully grant that Thy Holy Spirit may in all things direct and rule our hearts; through Jesus Christ, Thy Son, oùr Lord, who liveth and reigneth with Thee and the Hòly Ghost : ever one God, world without end. Amen.

Nineteenth Sunday After Trinity
Psalms. 35, 48, 141, 119iv, v; 138, 52, 71, 32
Gospel (at Morning Prayer). **Matthew 9:1-8**
Epistle (at Evening Prayer). **Ephesians 4:22-28**

℣. Yea, though I walk through the valley of the shadow of death.
℟. I will fear no evil.
Antiphon for Benedictus. The Lord said unto the sick of the palsy, Son, bé of Good cheer : thy síns be forgíven thee.

Antiphon for Magnificat.

The sick of the palsy * therefore took up his bed whereon he lay, gló-ri-fý-

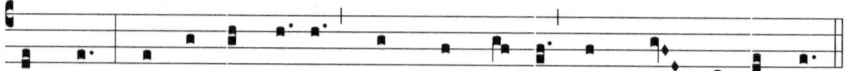
ing God : and all the people, when they saw it, gave práise un-to God.

IV

Collect. O Almighty and most merciful God : of Thy bountiful goodness keep us, we beseech Thee, from all things that may hurt ùs, that we, being ready, both in body and soul, may cheerfully accomplish those things that Thou wouldst have done; through Jesus Christ, Thy Son, oùr Lord, who liveth and reigneth with Thee and the Hòly Ghost : ever one God, world without end. Amen.

Twentieth Sunday After Trinity
Psalms. 48, 145, 130, 137, 43, 75, 111
Gospel (at Morning Prayer). **Matthew 22:1-14**
Epistle (at Evening Prayer). **Ephesians 5:15-21**

℣. The eyes of all wait upon Thee, O Lord.
℟. And Thou givest them their meat in due season.
Antiphon for Benedictus. Tell them which are bidden, Behold, I have prepáred my dínner : come unto the marriage, állelúia.

Antiphon for Magnificat.

And when the king came in * to see the guests, he saw there a man which

had not on a wédding gárment : and he said unto him, Friend, how camest

thou in hither not having a wédding gárment?

III

Collect. Grant, we beseech Thee, merciful Lord, to Thy faithful people pardòn and peace : that they may be cleansed from all their sìns, and serve Thee with a quiet mind; through Jesus Christ, Thy Son, oùr Lord, who liveth and reigneth with Thee and the Hòly Ghost : ever one God, world without end. Amen.

Twenty-First Sunday After Trinity

Psalms. **119i, 90, 146, 27, 91, 136, 119xiv, 42**
Gospel (at Morning Prayer). **John 4:46b-54**
Epistle (at Evening Prayer). **Ephesians 6:10-17**

℣. My heart shall rejoice in Thy salvation. ℟. And I have hoped in Thy Word.
Antiphon for Benedictus. There was a certain nobleman whose son was sick át Capérnaum : when he heard that Jesus was come out of Judaea into Galilee, he besought Him that Hé would héal his son.

Antiphon for Magnificat.

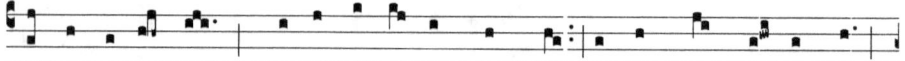

So the father knew * that it was at the same hour in the which Je-sus said,

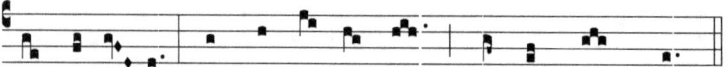

Thý son líveth : and himself be-lieved, ánd his whole house.

III

Collect. Lord, we beseech Thee to keep Thy household, the church, in continù-al godliness : that through Thy protection it may be free from all adversìties, and devoutly given to serve Thee in good works, to the glory of Thy name; through Jesus Christ, Thy Son, oùr Lord, who liveth and reigneth with Thee and the Hòly Ghost : ever one God, world without end. Amen.

Twenty-Second Sunday After Trinity
Psalms. **130, 133, 32, 36, 63, 82, 72**
Gospel (at Morning Prayer). **Matthew 18:23-35**
Epistle (at Evening Prayer). **Philippians 1:3-11**

℣. Show us Thy mercy, O Lord. ℟. And grant us Thy salvation.
Antiphon for Benedictus. Then said the lord unto the servant, Pay me whát thou ówest : The servant therefore fell down and worshipped him, saying, Lord, have patience with me, and Í will páy thee all.

Antiphon for Magnificat.

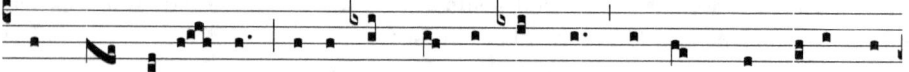

Thou wick-ed servant, * I forgave thee all that debt, because thóu desír-edst

me : shouldest not thou also have had compassion on thy fellow-servant,

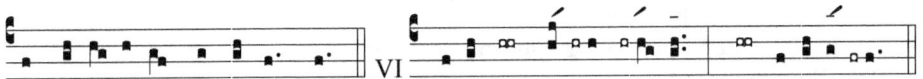

ev-en as I had pí-ty on <u>thee</u>?

Collect. O God, our Refuge and Strength, who art the Author òf all godliness : be ready, we beseech thee, to hear the devout prayers of Thy Chùrch, and grant that those things which we ask faithfully we may obtain effectually; through Jesus Christ, Thy Son, oùr Lord, who liveth and reigneth with Thee and the Hòly Ghost : ever one God, world without end. Amen.

Twenty-Third Sunday After Trinity

[352]

Psalms. 85, 44, 147, 17, 140, 116, 99
Gospel (at Morning Prayer). **Matthew 22:15-22**
Epistle (at Evening Prayer). **Philippians 3:17-21**

℣. If Thou, Lord, shouldest mark iniquities. ℟. O Lord, who shall stand?
Antiphon for Benedictus. **Master, we knów that thóu art true : and teachest the way of God in truth, álleluía.**

Antiphon for Magnificat.

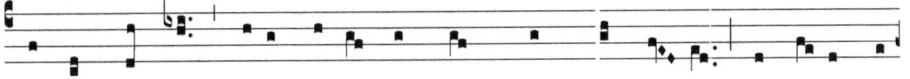

Render therefore * unto Caesar the thíngs which are Caésar's: and unto God

the things that are God's, ál-le- lú-ia.

Collect. **Absolve, we beseech Thee, O Lord, Thy people from thèir offenses : that from the bonds of our sins, which by reason of our frailty we have brought upon ùs, we may be delivered by Thy bountiful goodness; through Jesus Christ, Thy Son, oùr Lord, who liveth and reigneth with Thee and the Hòly Ghost : ever one God, world without end. Amen.**

Twenty-Fourth Sunday After Trinity

Psalms. 100, 116, 36, 71, 119ix, 38, 14, 56
Gospel (at Morning Prayer). **Matthew 9:18-21**
Epistle (at Evening Prayer). **Colossians 1:9-14**

℣. Lord, Thou hast been favorable unto Thy land.
℟. Thou hast brought back the captivity of Jacob.
Antiphon for Benedictus. For she sáid withín herself : if I may but touch the hem of His garment, Í shall be whole.

Antiphon for Magnificat.

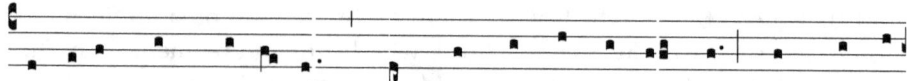

But Jesus turned him a-bout, * and when He saw her, He said, Daughter, bé

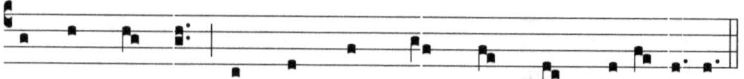

of good cómfort : thy faith hath made thee whole, ál-le-lú-ia.

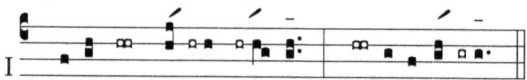

Collect. Stir up, we beseech Thee, O Lord, the wills of Thy fàithful people : that they, plenteously bringing forth the fruit of good wòrks, may of Thee be plenteously rewarded; through Jesus Christ, Thy Son, oùr Lord, who liveth and reigneth with Thee and the Hòly Ghost : ever one God, world without end. Amen.

Twenty-Fifth Sunday After Trinity
(Third-Last Sunday of Church Year)
Psalms. **31**, **74**, **46**, **102**, **29**, **94**, **10**
Gospel (at Morning Prayer). **Matthew 24:15-28**
Epistle (at Evening Prayer). **1 Thessalonians 4:13-18**

℣. Thou hast forgiven the iniquity of Thy people, O Lord.
℟. Thou hast covered all their sin.
Antiphon for Benedictus. Behold, I have told you before; † For then shall be great tribulation, such as was not since the beginning of the wórld to this time : no, nor ever shall be, állelúia.

Antiphon for Magnificat.

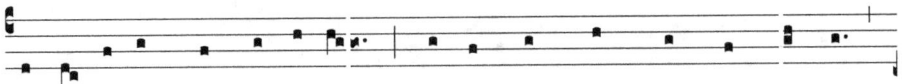

Behold, I have told you before; * † Except those days should be shortened,

there should nó flesh be saved : but for the e-lect's sake those days shall

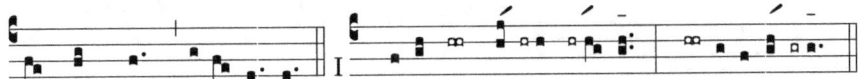

be shortened, ál-le-lú-ia.

Collect. **Almighty God, wè beseech Thee : show Thy mercy unto Thy humble servànts, that we who put no trust in our own merits may not be dealt with after the severity of Thy judgment, but according to Thy mercy; through Jesus Christ, Thy Son, oùr Lord, who liveth and reigneth with Thee and the Hòly Ghost : ever one God, world without end. Amen.**

Twenty-Sixth Sunday After Trinity
(Second-Last Sunday of Church Year)
Psalms. 54, 50, 15, 20, 21, 126, 9, 96
Gospel (at Morning Prayer). **Matthew 25:31-46**
Epistle (at Evening Prayer). **2 Peter 3:3-14**

℣. Thou hast taken away all Thy wrath, O Lord.
℟. Thou hast turned Thyself from the fierceness of Thine anger.
Antiphon for Benedictus. When the Son of man shall come in his glory, and all the holy ángels wíth him : then shall he sit upon the throne of his glory, állelúia.

Antiphon for Magnificat.

Come, ye blessed * óf my Fáther : inherit the kingdom prepared for you from

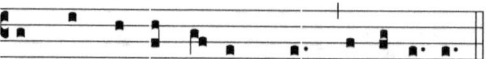

the foundation of the world, ál-le-lú-ia.

VII

Collect. O God, so rule and govern our hearts and minds by Thy Hòly Spirit : that, being ever mindful of the end of all things and the day of Thy just Judgmènt, we may be stirred up to holiness of living here and dwell with Thee forever hereafter; through Jesus Christ, Thy Son, oùr Lord, who liveth and reigneth with Thee and the Hòly Ghost : ever one God, world without end. Amen.

Twenty-Seventh Sunday After Trinity (Last Sunday of Church Year)

Psalms. 45, 73, 3, 17, 75, 110, 124, 87
Gospel (at Morning Prayer). **Matthew 25:1-13**
Epistle (at Evening Prayer). **1 Thessalonians 5:1-11**

Hymn.
O quanta qualia sunt illa sabbata. *Peter Abelard, 12ᵗʰ c., trans. by J. M. Neale*

1. O what their joy and their glory must be, / Those endless Sabbaths the bless-ed ones see; / Crown for the valiant, to weary ones rest: / God shall be All, and in all ever blest.
2. What are the Monarch, his court and his throne? / What are the peace and the joy that they own? / O that the blest ones, who in it have share, / All that they feel could as fully declare!
3. Truly, "Jerusalem" name we that shore, / City of peace that brings joy evermore; / Wish and fulfillment are not severed there, / Nor do things prayed for come short of the prayer.

4. There, where no troubles distraction can bring, / We the sweet anthems of Zion shall sing; / While for Thy grace, Lord, their voices of praise / Thy bless-ed people eternally raise.

5. Now, in the meantime, with hearts raised on high, / We for that country must yearn and must sigh, / Seeking Jerusalem, dear native land, / Through our long exile on Babylon's strand.

6. Low before him with our praises we fall, / Of whom and in whom and through whom are all; / Of whom, the Father; and in whom, the Son; / Through whom, the Spirit, with them ever One. Amen.

℣. If Thou, Lord, shouldest mark iniquities. ℟. O Lord, who shall stand?

Antiphon for Benedictus. **Watch therefore, for ye know neither the dáy nor the hóur- : wherein the Són of man cómeth.**

Antiphon for Magnificat.

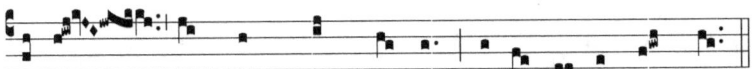

Be-hold, * the Brídegroom cómeth : go ye óut to méet him.

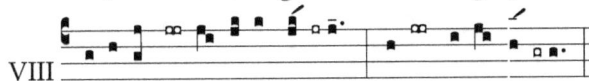

VIII

Collect. **Absolve, we beseech Thee, O Lord, Thy people from thèir offenses : that from the bonds of our sins which by reason of our frailty we have brought upon ùs, we may be delivered by Thy bountiful goodness; through Jesus Christ, Thy Son, oùr Lord, who liveth and reigneth with Thee and the Hòly Ghost : ever one God, world without end. Amen.**

Saint's Day Propers

Saint Andrew the Apostle's Day (Nov. 30)
All from Common of Apostles (p. 538) except the following:
Psalms. **139, 19, 44, 45, 26, 122, 3**
Gospel (at Morning Prayer). **Matthew 4:18-22**
Epistle (at Evening Prayer). **Romans 10:8-18**

℣. Their line is gone out through all the earth.
℟. And their words to the end of the world.
Antiphon for Benedictus. For with the heart man believeth únto ríghteousness : and with the mouth confession is made únto salvátion.

Antiphon for Magnificat.

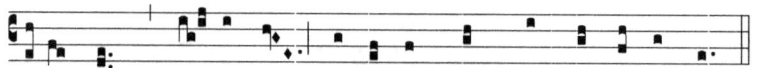

Jésus saith, * Fól-low me : and I will make you físhers of men.

VIII

Collect. **Almighty God, by whose grace Thine Apostle Saint Andrew obeyed the call of Thy Son Jèsus Christ : grant unto us also grace to follow Him in heart and life; through the same, Jesus Christ, Thy Son, oùr Lord, who liveth and reigneth with Thee and the Hòly Ghost : ever one God, world without end. Amen.**

Saint Thomas the Apostle (Dec. 21)
All from Common of Apostles (p. 538) except the following:
Psalms. **9, 120, 101, 2, 139, 136, 11**
Gospel (at Morning Prayer). **John 20:24-31**
Epistle (at Evening Prayer). **Ephesians 1:3-6**

℣. Their line is gone out through all the earth.
℟. And their words to the end of the world.
Antiphon for Benedictus. And after eight days again His disciples were within, and Thómas with them : then came Jesus, the doors being shut, and stood in the midst, and said, Péace be únto you.

Antiphon for Magnificat.

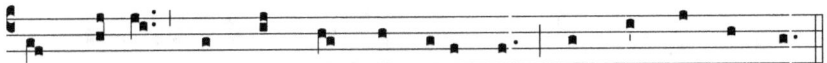

And Thomas * answered and sáid unto Him : My Lórd and my God.

VIII

Collect. Almighty and everliving God, who through the Word of Thy Son didst mightily strengthen the faith of Thine Apostlè Saint Thomas : by the same Word keep us ever steadfast in the faith unto our end; through the same, Jesus Christ, Thy Son, oùr Lord, who liveth and reigneth with Thee and the Hòly Ghost : ever one God, world without end. Amen.

St. Stephen, the First Martyr (Dec. 26)
St. John, Apostle and Evangelist (Dec. 27)
The Holy Innocents, Martyrs (Dec. 28)
See p. 405 ff.

The Conversion of Saint Paul (Jan. 25)
All from Common of Apostles (p. 538) except the following:
Psalms. 21, 45, 46, 48, 44, 113, 117   [355]
Gospel (at Morning Prayer). **Matthew 19:27-30**
Epistle (at Evening Prayer). **Acts 9:1-22**

℣. He is a chosen vessel unto Me.
℟. To bear My name before the Gentiles, and kings, and the children of Israel.
Antiphon for Benedictus. And every one that hath forsaken houses, or brethren, or sisters, or father, or mother, or wife, or children, or lands, fór My Náme's sake : shall receive an hundredfold, and shall inherit éverlásting life.

Antiphon for Magnificat.

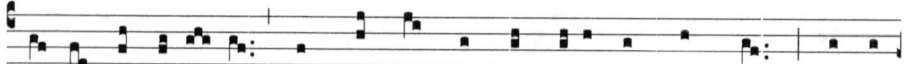

And im-me-di-ate-ly * there fell from his eyes ás it hád been scales : and he

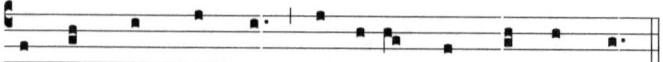

received sight forthwith, and arose, ánd was bap<u>tized</u>.

VIII

Collect. O God, who through the preaching of the blessed Apostle Saint Paul hast caused the light of Thy Gospel to shine to the Gèntile world : give us grace ever to joy in the saving light of Thy Gospèl, and to spread it to the uttermost parts of the earth; through the same, Jesus Christ, Thy Son, oùr Lord, who liveth and reigneth with Thee and the Hòly Ghost : ever one God, world without end. Amen.

The Presentation of Our Lord & the Purification of Mary (Feb. 2)
All from Common of the B.V.M. (p. 534) except the following:
Psalms. **48, 134, 2, 26, 76, 36, 87**
Gospel (at Morning Prayer). **Luke 2:22-32**
Epistle (at Evening Prayer). **Malachi 3:1-4**

℣. Grace is poured into thy lips. ℟. Therefore God hath blessed thee forever.
Antiphon for Benedictus. The Lord, whom ye seek, shall suddenly come to his temple, even the messenger of the covenant, whom yé delíght in : behold, he shall come, sáith the LÓRD of hosts.

℣. It was revealed unto Simeon by the Holy Ghost.
℟. That he should not see death before he had seen the Lord's Christ.

Antiphon for Magnificat.

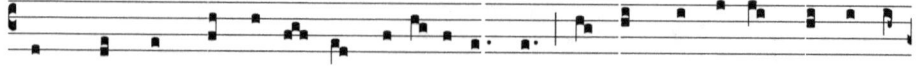

And when the days of Ma-ry's pu-ri-fi-ca-tion * ac-cor-ding to the law of Mo-

ses wére ac-cómplished : they brought Jesus to Je-ru-sa-lem, to pre-sént Him

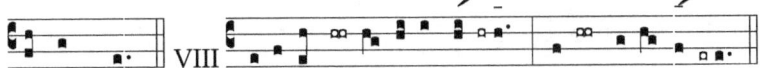

tó the Lord.

Collect. Almighty and everlasting God, wè beseech Thee : grant that we may know and praise Thy dear Sòn, even as Simeon of old, taking Him in his arms, spiritually knew and with his lips confessed Him, who liveth and reigneth with Thee and the Hòly Ghost : ever one God, world without end. Amen.

St. Matthias the Apostle's Day (Feb. 24)
All from Common of Apostles (p. 538) except the following:
Psalms. **68, 4, 140, 56, 87, 99, 32**
Gospel (at Morning Prayer). **Matthew 11:25-30**
Epistle (at Evening Prayer). **Acts 1:15-26**

℣. Their line is gone out through all the earth.
℟. And their words to the end of the world.
Antiphon for Benedictus. And they prayed, and said, Thou, Lord, which knowest the héarts of all <u>men</u> : shew whether of these two Thóu hast chósen.

Antiphon for Magnificat.

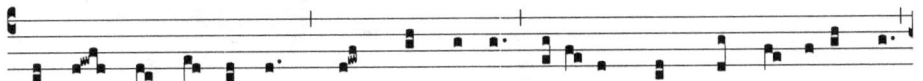

Take my yoke upon you, * and learn of me; for I am meek and lówly in <u>heart</u>:

and ye shall find rest ún-to your <u>souls</u>.

Collect. Almighty God, who into the place of the traitor Judas didst choose

Thy faithful servànt Matthias : grant that Thy church, ever being preserved from false apostlès, may continually abide in the doctrine of Thy true Apostles; through Jesus Christ, Thy Son, oùr Lord, who liveth and reigneth with Thee and the Hòly Ghost : ever one God, world without end. Amen.

The Annunciation to the Blessed Virgin Mary (March 25)
All from Common of the B.V.M. (p. 534) except the following:
Antiphons for Psalms
1. Behold, our Lord shall cóme with pówer : to enlighten the éyes of his sérvants.
2. Drop down, ye heavens, from above, and let the skies póur down ríghteousness : let the earth open and bring fórth a Sáviour.
3. The Angel Gabriel was sént to Máry : a virgin espóused to Jóseph.
4. The Lord shall give unto him the throne of his fáther Dávid : and he shall reign over the house of Jácob foréver.

Psalms. 45, 72, 85, 98, 110, 33, 76, 132, 149
Gospel (at Morning Prayer). Luke 1:26-38
Epistle (at Evening Prayer). Isaiah 7:10-16

℣. Behold, thou shalt conceive in thy womb, and bring forth a Son.
℟. And shalt call His name JESUS.
Antiphon for Benedictus. How shall this be, O Angel of God, seeing Í know nót a man? : The Holy Ghost shall come upon thee, and the power of the Highest shall óvershádow thee.

Antiphon for Magnificat.

And the angel * came in unto her, and said, Hail, thou that art highly fa-

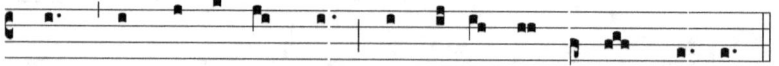

voured, the Lórd is wíth thee : blessed art thóu a-mong wómen.

Collect. Almighty God, who didst will that agreeably to the angel's message

Thy Son become incarnate of the Vìrgin Mary : mercifully grant that our sinful conception may be cleansed by His immaculate conception; through the same, Jesus Christ, Thy Son, oùr Lord, who liveth and reigneth with Thee and the Hòly Ghost : ever one God, world without end. Amen.

Saint Mark the Evangelist's Day (April 25)

April 25 is also known as the Greater Litany. Today it is appropriate to pray the Litany (p. 570) after Morning Prayer.

All from Common of Evangelists (p. 538) except the following:
Psalms. **45, 64, 37, 89, 52, 67, 46**   [357]
Gospel (at Morning Prayer). **Luke 10:1-9**
Epistle (at Evening Prayer). **Ephesians 4:7-16**

Out of Eastertide:
℣. Their line is gone out through all the earth.
℟. And their words to the end of the world.
In Eastertide:
℣. O ye holy and righteous, rejoice in the Lord, alleluia.
℟. For blessed is the people whom God hath chosen for His own inheritance, alleluia.

Antiphon for Benedictus.
He that descended is the same also that ascended up far abóve all héavens : that hé might fíll all things.
And He gave some, apostles; and some, prophets; and sóme, evángelists : and some, pástors and téachers.

Antiphon for Magnificat.

After these things * the Lord appointed other séventy álso : and sent them

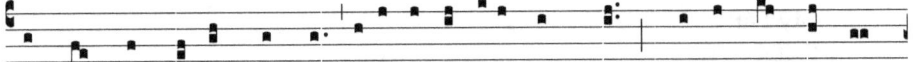

two and two before His face into every city and place, whither Hé himsélf

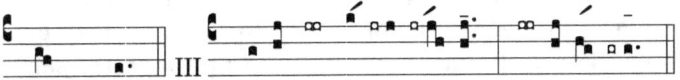

would come.

Collect. O Almighty God, who hast enriched Thy church with the precious Gospel written by Thine Evangelìst Saint Mark : give us grace that we may firmly believe Thy glad tidings of salvatiòn, and daily walk as it becometh the Gospel of Christ; through the same, Jesus Christ, Thy Son, oùr Lord, who liveth and reigneth with Thee and the Hòly Ghost : ever one God, world without end. Amen.

Saint Philip and Saint James the Apostle's Day (May 1)
All from Common of Apostles (p. 538) except the following:
Psalms. **19, 43, 4, 1, 81, 16, 84**
Gospel (at Morning Prayer). **John 14:1-14**
Epistle (at Evening Prayer). **Ephesians 2:19-22**

℣. Their line is gone out through all the earth.
℟. And their words to the end of the world.
Antiphon for Benedictus. Now therefore ye are no more strangers and foreigners, but fellow citizens with the saints, and of the hóusehold of <u>God</u> : and are built upon the foundation of the apostles and prophets, Jesus Christ himself béing the chief córner stone.

Antiphon for Magnificat.

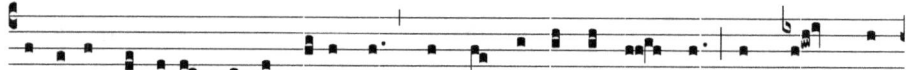
Ve-ri-ly, ve-ri-ly, * I say unto you, He that believeth on me, the works that

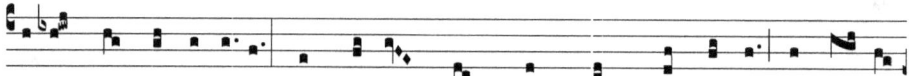
I do shall hé do álso : and greater works than these shall he do; because I

go únto My Fáther.

Collect. **Almighty God, whom to know is everlàsting life : grant unto us that, as Thy Son gave knowledge of life eternal to Thine Apostles Philip and James by revealing Himself to them as the only Way to Thèe, we may by a true and living faith ever know Him as our only Savior; through the same, Jesus Christ, Thy Son, oùr Lord, who liveth and reigneth with Thee and the Hòly Ghost : ever one God, world without end. Amen.**

The Nativity of Saint John the Baptist (June 24)

Antiphons for Psalms

1. He shall go before the Lord in the spirit and power óf Elías : to make ready a people prepáred for the <u>Lord</u>.
2. Thou shalt call his name John; † he shall drink neither wíne nor stróng drink : and many shall rejóice at his <u>birth</u>.
3. From the womb of one aged and bárren was bróught forth John : the Fórerunner óf the Lord.
4. This child shall be great in the síght of the <u>Lord</u> : for the hand of the Lórd is wíth him.
5. He shall be a Nâzarite; † therefore he shall drink neither wíne nor stróng drink : and he shall be filled with the Holy Ghost, even fróm his móther's womb.

Psalms. 92, 44, 105, 110, 136, 147, 116
Gospel (at Morning Prayer). Luke 1:57-80
Epistle (at Evening Prayer). Isaiah 40:1-5

Hymn. **Antra deserti.** *Paulus Diaconus, 8th c., trans. R. E. Roberts, alt.*
At Morning Prayer: stanzas 1-4, 8. At Evening Prayer: stanzas 5-8.

1. Let the example of Saint John remind us, / Ere we can meetly sing his deeds of wonder, / Hearts must be chastened, and the bonds that bind us / Broken asunder!
2. Lo! a swift angel, from the skies descending, / Tells to his father what shall be his naming; / All his life's greatness to its bitter ending / Duly proclaiming.
3. But when he doubted what the angel told him, / Came to him dumbness to confirm the story; / At John's appearing, healed again behold him, / Chanting John's glory!
4. Oh! what a splendour and a revelation / Came to each mother, at his joyful leaping, / Greeting his Monarch, King of ev'ry nation, / In the womb sleeping.

5. E'en in his childhood, 'mid the desert places, / He had a refuge from the city gain-ed, / Far from all slander and its bitter traces / Living unstain-ed.

6. Often had prophets in the distant ages / Sung to announce the Daystar and to name Him; / But as the Savior, last of all the sages, / John did proclaim Him.

7. Than John the Baptist, none of all Eve's daughters / E'er bore a greater, whether high or lowly: / He was thought worthy, washing in the waters / Jesus the holy.

8. Angels in orders everlasting praise Thee, / God, in Thy triune Majesty tremendous; / Hark to the prayers we, penitents, upraise Thee: / Save and defend us. Amen.

℣. This child shall be great in the sight of the Lord.
℟. For the hand of the Lord is with him.

Antiphon for Benedictus. And thou, child, shalt be called the prophet óf the Híghest : for thou shalt go before the face of the Lórd to prepáre His ways.

℣. There was a man sent from God whose name was John.
℟. The same came for a witness.

Antiphon for Magnificat.

The child which is born un-to us * is more than a prophet; for this is he of

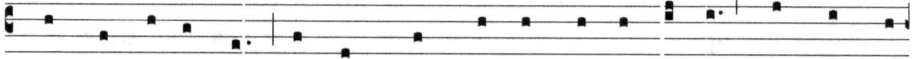

whóm the Sávior says: A-mong them that are born of women there hath not

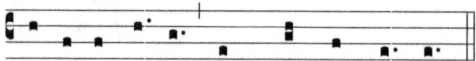

ris-en a greater than Jóhn the Báptist.

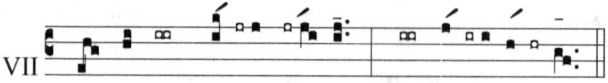

Collect. Almighty God, who through John the Baptist, the forerunner of Christ, didst proclàim salvation : grant that we may know this Thy salvatiòn, and serve Thee in holiness and righteousness all the days of our life; through the same, Jesus Christ, Thy Son, oùr Lord, who liveth and reigneth with Thee and the Hòly Ghost : ever one God, world without end. Amen.

The Presentation of the Augsburg Confession (June 25)
On this day, the propers for the Festival of the Reformation (p. 530) are used.

Saint Peter and Saint Paul the Apostles' Day (June 29)
All from Common of Apostles (p. 538) except the following:
Psalms. **21, 45, 46, 48, 44, 113, 117**
Gospel (at Morning Prayer). **Matthew 16:13-20**
Epistle (at Evening Prayer). **Acts 12:1-11**

℣. Their line is gone out through all the earth.
℟. And their words to the end of the world.

Antiphon for Magnificat at 1st Vespers.

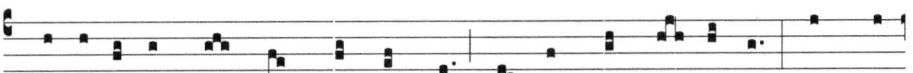

Whatso-ev-er * thou shalt bind on earth shall be boúnd in héaven: and what-

so-ev-er thou shalt loose on earth shall be loosed in heaven, said the Lord

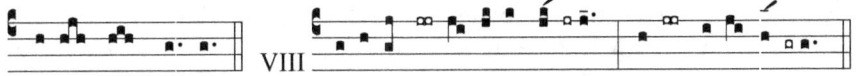

VIII

to Sí-mon Pé-ter.

Antiphon for Benedictus. **Simon Peter said, Thóu art the <u>Christ</u> : the Són of the lívíng God.**

Antiphon for Magnificat at 2nd Vespers.

Today * Simon Peter mounted the wood of the cross, ál-le-lú-ia : Today the

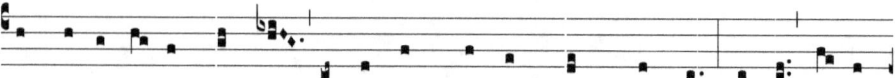

keybearer of the kingdom of heaven wént to Chríst with joy. Today the A-

postle Paul, the light of the world, bowed his head fór the Náme of Christ :

and re-ceived the crown of martyrdom, ál-le-lú-ia.

Collect. O God, who didst give Thine Apostles Peter and Paul grace to lay down their lives for the sake of Thý dear Son : endow us, we beseech Thee, with like constàncy, that we may at all times be ready to lay down our lives for Him who laid down His life for us; through the same, Jesus Christ, Thy Son, oùr Lord, who liveth and reigneth with Thee and the Hòly Ghost : ever one God, world without end. Amen.

The Visitation of the Blessed Virgin Mary to Elisabeth
(July 2; new calendar: May 31)

All from Common of the B.V.M. (p. 534) except the following:
Psalms. **45, 2, 110, 132, 138, 145, 149**
Gospel (at Morning Prayer). **Luke 1:39-56**
Epistle (at Evening Prayer). **Isaiah 11:1-5**

Hymn at Morning Prayer.
Mundi salus affutura. *15th cent., trans. by L. Housman*

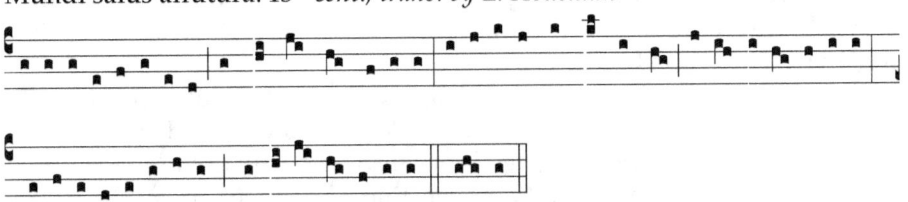

[360]

1. Portal of the world's salvation, / Lo, a virgin pure and mild, / Humble-hearted, high in station, / Form of beauty undefiled, / Crown of earth's anticipation, / Comes the mother-maid with child.
2. Here the serpent's power subduing, / See the bush unburned by fire, / Gideon's fleece of heaven's imbuing, / Aaron's rod of bright attire, / Fair, and pure, and peace-ensuing, / Spouse of Solomon's desire.
3. Jesse's branch received its flower, / Mother of Emmanuel, / Portal sealed and mystic bower / Promised by Ezekiel, / Rock of Daniel's dream, whose power / Smote, and lo, the image fell!
4. See in flesh so great a wonder / By the power of God ordained,— / Him, whose feet all worlds lay under, / In a virgin's womb contained;— / So on earth, her bonds to sunder, / Righteousness from heaven hath rained.
5. Virgin sweet, with love o'erflowing, / To the hills in haste she fares; / On a kindred heart bestowing / Blessing from the joy she bears; / Waiting while with mystic showing / Time the sacred birth prepares.
6. What fair joy o'ershone that dwelling, / Called so great a Guest to greet; / What her joy whose love compelling / Found a rest for Mary's feet, / When, the bliss of time foretelling, / Lo, the Voice and Word did meet!
7. God most high, the heaven's foundation, / Ruler of eternity; / Jesus, who for man's salvation / Came in flesh to make us free; / Spirit, moving all creation, / Evermore be praise to Thee! Amen.

Hymn at Evening Prayer.
Festum matris gloriosae. *15th cent., trans. by L. Housman*

1. Now in holy celebration / Sing we of that mother blest, / In whose flesh for men's salvation / God incarnate deigned to rest, / When a kindred salutation / Named in faith the mystic Guest.
2. Lo, the advent Word confessing, / Spake for joy the voice yet dumb, / Through his mother's lips addressing / Her, of motherhood the sum,— / Bow'r of beauty, blest and blessing, / Crowned with fruit of life to come.
3. "Whence," she cried, at that fair meeting, / "Comes to me this great reward? / For when I first heard the greeting / Of the mother of my Lord, / In my womb, the joy repeating, / Leapt my babe in sweet accord!"
4. Lo, at that glad commendation / Joy found voice, in Mary's breast / While in holy exultation / She her Maker's power confessed, / At whose word each generation / Now henceforward names her blest.
5. Triune Godhead, health supplying, / Ruler of eternity, / On the Fount of Grace relying, / We uplift our hearts to Thee, / Praying that in realms undying / We at one with Life may be.
6. Laud and honor to the Father, / Laud and honor to the Son, / Laud and honor to the Spirit, / Ever Three and ever One, / Consubstantial, co-eternal, / While unending ages run. Amen.

[361] ℣. Blessed art thou among women. ℟. And blessed is the Fruit of thy womb.
Antiphon for Benedictus. And there shall come forth a rod out of the stém of Jésse : and a branch shall grow óut of his <u>roots</u>.

Antiphon for Magnificat.

And E-lis-a-beth * spake out wíth a loud vóice, and said : Bless-ed art thou

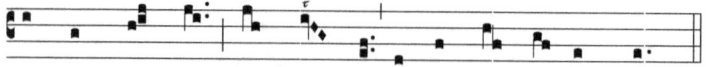

a-mong wo-men, and bless-ed is the Frúit of thy <u>womb</u>.

VII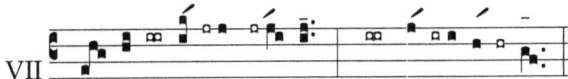

Collect. Almighty God, who hast dealt wonderfully with Thy handmaiden, the virgin Mary, and hast chosen her to be the mother of Thy Son and hast graciously made known that Thou regardest the poor and lowly and thè despised : grant us grace in all humility and meekness to receive Thy Word with hearty fàith, and so to be made one with Jesus Christ, Thy Son, oùr Lord, who liveth and reigneth with Thee and Hòly Ghost : ever one God, world without end. Amen.

Saint Mary Magdalene's Day (July 22)
All from Common of a Holy Woman (p. 554) except the following:
Psalms. **45**, **112**, **32**, **51**, **63**, **92**, **103**
Gospel (at Morning Prayer). **Luke 7:36-50**
Epistle (at Evening Prayer). **Proverbs 31:10-31**

℣. Praise the Lord, O my soul. ℟. Who healeth all thy diseases.
Antiphon for Benedictus. Wherefore I say unto thee, Her sins, which are many, are forgiven; fór she lóved much : but to whom little is forgiven, the same lóveth líttle.

Antiphon for Magníficat.
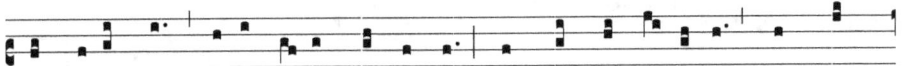
And Jesus said * unto Mary Magdalene, Thy síns are forgíven : Thy faith
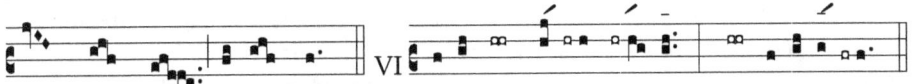
hath sáved thee; gó in peace.

Collect. O Almighty God, whose blessed Son did sanctify Mary Magdalene, and grant her to be a witness to His Rèsurrection : Mercifully grant that by Thy grace we may be healed of all our infirmìties, and serve Thee in the power of His endless life; who liveth and reigneth with Thee and the Hòly Ghost : ever one God, world without end. Amen.

Saint James the Elder the Apostle's Day (July 25)

All from Common of Apostles (p. 538) except the following:
Psalms. **139, 19, 1, 13, 26, 119viii, xxi**
Gospel (at Morning Prayer). **Matthew 20:20-28**
Epistle (at Evening Prayer). **Romans 8:28-39**

℣. Their line is gone out through all the earth.
℟. And their words to the end of the world.

Antiphon for Benedictus.
Whosoever will be great among you, let him bé your mínister : and whosoever will be chief among you, let him bé your sérvant;
Even as the Son of man came not to be ministered unto, bút to mínister : and to give His life a ránsom for mány.

Antiphon for Magnificat.

For whom * He did foreknow, He al-so did predestinate to be conformed to

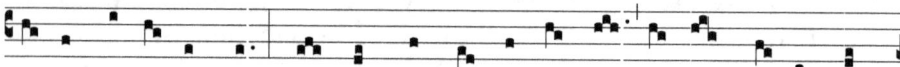

the ím-age óf His Son : that He might be the firstborn a-mong mány bréth-

ren.

[362] *Collect.* Grant, O Lord, that, as Thine Apostle Saint James readily obeyed the calling of Thy Son Jèsus Christ : we may by Thy grace be enabled to forsake all worldly and carnal affectiòns, and to follow Him alone; who liveth and reigneth with Thee and the Hòly Ghost : ever one God, world without end. Amen.

The Dormition of Saint Mary, the Mother of God (Aug. 15)

All from Common of the B.V.M. (p. 534) except the following:
Psalms. 45, 72, 85, 98, 110, 33, 76, 132, 149
Gospel (at Morning Prayer). Luke 1:46-55
Epistle (at Evening Prayer). Isaiah 61:7-11

℣. Blessed is the womb that bore Thee, Lord Jesus, and the breasts which nursed Thee.
℟. Yea, blessed are those who hear the Word of God and keep it.
Antiphon for Benedictus. He hath clothed me with the garments óf salvátion : as a bride adorneth herself wíth her jéwels.

Antiphon for Magnificat.

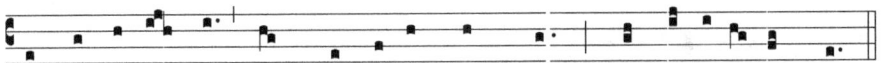

He that is mighty * hath dóne to mé great things : and hó-ly ís His name.

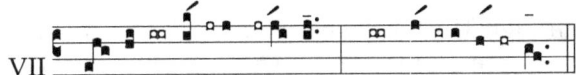
VII

Collect. O God, who hast taken to Thyself the blessed Mary, mother of Thine ònly Son : Grant that we who have been redeemed by His blòod, may share with her the glory of Thine eternal kingdom; through the same, Jesus Christ, Thy Son, oùr Lord, who liveth and reigneth with Thee and the Hòly Ghost : ever one God, world without end. Amen.

Saint Bartholomew the Apostle's Day (Aug. 24)

All from Common of Apostles (p. 538) except the following:
Psalms. 56, 9, 53, 54, 37, 129, 147
Gospel (at Morning Prayer). Luke 22:24-30
Epistle (at Evening Prayer). 2 Corinthians 4:7-10

℣. Their line is gone out through all the earth.
℟. And their words to the end of the world.
Antiphon for Benedictus. But we have this treasure in éarthen véssels : that the excellency of the power may be of Gód, and nót of us.

Antiphon for Magnificat.

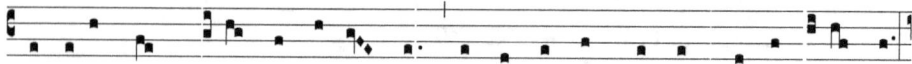

And I appoint * unto you a kingdom, as My Father hath appóinted únto me :

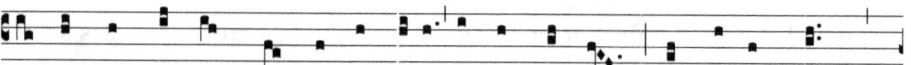

that ye may eat and drink at my table in My kingdom, and sit on thrones

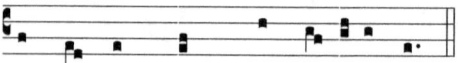

judging the twelve tríbes of Ís-ra-el.

VIII

Collect. **Almighty God, who through Thy Son Jesus Christ didst choose Saint Bartholomew to be an Apostle to preach the blèssed Gospel : give unto Thy church evermore faithful teachèrs, to proclaim the glory of Thy name; through the same, Jesus Christ, Thy Son, oùr Lord, who liveth and reigneth with Thee and the Hòly Ghost : ever one God, world without end. Amen.**

The Beheading of Saint John the Baptist (August 29)
All from Common of Martyrs (p. 541) except the following:
Gospel (at Morning Prayer). **Mark 6:17-29**
Epistle (at Evening Prayer). **Jeremiah 1:17-19**

℣. The righteous shall flourish like the palm tree.
℟. And shall grow like a cedar in Lebanon.
Antiphon for Benedictus. **The unbelieving King sent his hateful servants, and bade them slay a just man ánd a hóly : even John the Baptist the Lórd's Forerúnner.**

Antiphon for Magnificat.

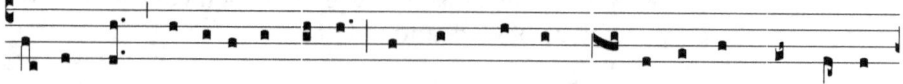

Herod sent * an ex-e-cu-tioner, and commanded him to behead Jóhn in the

príson : and when his di-sci-ples heard of it, they came and took up his bo-

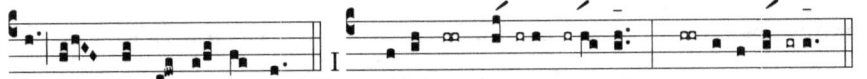

dy, and láid it ín a tomb.

Collect. O God, who didst send thy messenger, John the Baptist, to be the forerunner of the Lord, and to glorify thee bý his death : Grant that we, who have received the truth of thy most holy Gospel, may bear our witness thereùnto, and after his example constantly speak the truth, boldly rebuke vice, and patiently suffer for the truth's sake; through Jesus Christ, Thy Son, oùr Lord, who liveth and reigneth with Thee and the Hòly Ghost : ever one God, world without end. Amen.

Nativity of the Blessed Virgin Mary (Sep. 8)
All from Common of B.V.M. (p. 534) except the following: [363]
Gospel (at Morning Prayer). **Matthew 1:1-16**
Epistle (at Evening Prayer). **Sirach 24:22-31**
Collect. Grant, O Lord, we beseech Thee, unto Thy servants the gift of Thy heavènly grace : that as the child-bearing of the blessed virgin Mary was the beginning of salvatiòn, so the joyful festival of her nativity may bring us an increase of peace; through Jesus Christ, Thy Son, oùr Lord, who liveth and reigneth with Thee and Hòly Ghost : ever one God, world without end. Amen.

Holy Cross Day (Sep. 14)
Antiphons for Psalms
1. O mighty wórk of mércy! : Death then died when Life díed on the <u>tree</u>.
2. Save us, O Christ our Savior, by the pówer óf the cross : Thou who savedst Peter perishing in the sea, have mércy upón us.
3. Behold the days cóme, saith the <u>Lord</u> : that I will raise unto Dávid a ríghteous branch.
4. God forbíd that Í should boast : except in the cross of óur Lord Jésus Christ.
5. And being found in fashion as a Man, He húmbled Him<u>self</u> : and became obedient unto death, even the déath of the <u>cross</u>.

Psalm. 1, 2, 3, 4, 11, 21, 96, 97, 98
Gospel (at Morning Prayer). **John 12:20-33**
Epistle (at Evening Prayer). **1 Corinthians 1:18-24**

Hymn at Morning Prayer.
Crux mundi benedictio. *P. Damiani, † 1072, trans. by J. M. Neale, alt.*

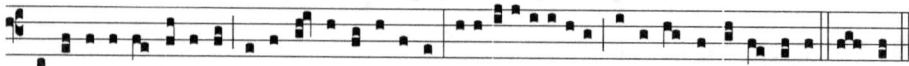

1. The cross, whereby the world is blessed, / Certain redemption, hope and rest, / Once as the tree of torture known, / Now the bright gate to Jesus' throne!
2. On it the Christ was lifted high, / Who to Himself drew all men nigh; / Whom this world's prince in malice sought, / And in His spotless soul found naught.
3. Thou, by Thy cross, O Christ, we pray, / To life's reward direct our way, / Who of old time upon the tree / Our ransom didst vouchsafe to be.
4. The unbegotten Father's praise, / And the begotten Son's we raise; / All equal laud and glory be, / Spirit of both, for aye to Thee. Amen.

Hymn at Evening Prayer.
Crux benedicta nitet. *Venantius Fortunatus, † 600, trans. by J. M. Neale, alt.*

1. Lo, the blest cross is displayed, / Where the Lord in the flesh was suspended, / And by His Blood from their sins / Cleansed and redeemed His elect;
2. Where by His hands trans- pierced / He redeem-ed the world from its ruin, / And by His lifegiving death / Closed up the path of the grave.
3. Strong in its fertile array, / The- tree of- sweetness and glory, / Bearing such newfound- fruit / 'Mid the green leaves of its boughs,
4. Stately it reareth its head / By the streams of the clear-running waters, / Shedding from flower-decked boughs / Leaves for the healing of men.
5. Come let us worship the King / From the cross in His majesty reigning, / Who by the pain of His death / Joy hath restored to the world. Amen.

℣. We adore Thee, O Christ, and we bless Thee.
℟. Because by Thy holy cross Thou hast redeemed the world.
Antiphon for Benedictus. God forbid that I should boast except in the cross of óur Lord Jésus Christ : By whom the world has been crucified to me, and Í to

the <u>world</u>.

Antiphon for Magnificat.

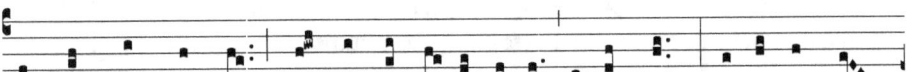

He humbled Himself * and became o-bé-di-ent únto death : Even the déath

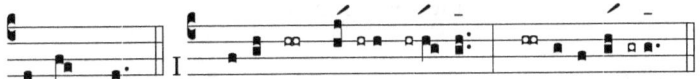

of the <u>cross</u>.

Collect. Merciful and everlasting God, who didst not spare Thine only Son but delivered Him up for us all that He might bear our sins òn the cross : Grant that our hearts may be so fixed with steadfast faith in Hìm, that we may not fear the power of any adversaries; through the same, Jesus Christ, Thy Son, oùr Lord, who liveth and reigneth with Thee and the Hòly Ghost : ever one God, world without end. Amen.

Ember Days after Holy Cross Day

EMBER WEDNESDAY (WEDNESDAY AFTER HOLY CROSS DAY)
Gospel (at Morning Prayer). **Mark 9:16-28**
Epistle (at Evening Prayer). **Ezra 8:1-10**
Collect. Vouchsafe, O Lord, we pray thee, to aid our infirmities with the healing of Thy lòving-kindness : that we, which are made weak by the frailty of our natùre, may be strengthened by the power of Thy mercy; through Jesus Christ, Thy Son, oùr Lord, who liveth and reigneth with Thee and the Hòly Ghost : ever one God, world without end. Amen.

EMBER FRIDAY
Gospel (at Morning Prayer). **Luke 7:36-50**
Epistle (at Evening Prayer). **Hosea 14:2-10**
Collect. Grant, we beseech Thee, Almìghty God : that we, who put our trust in Thèe, may serve Thee acceptably both in body and soul; through Jesus Christ, Thy Son, oùr Lord, who liveth and reigneth with Thee and the Hòly Ghost : ever one God, world without end. Amen.

EMBER SATURDAY
Gospel (at Morning Prayer). **Luke 13:6-17**
Epistle (at Evening Prayer). **Hebrew 9:2-12**
Collect. Almighty and everlasting God, who dost command bodily discipline and hast attached promisès thereto : grant that we may constantly serve Thee in soul and bodý, that no temptation may cause us to stumble; through Jesus Christ, Thy Son, oùr Lord, who liveth and reigneth with Thee and the Hòly Ghost : ever one God, world without end. Amen.

Saint Matthew the Apostle and Evangelist's Day (Sep. 21)
All from Common of Apostles (p. 538) except the following:
Psalms. **68, 62, 80, 132, 149, 137, 84**
Gospel (at Morning Prayer). **Matthew 9:9-13**
Epistle (at Evening Prayer). **Ephesians 4:7-14**

℣. Their line is gone out through all the earth.
℟. And their words to the end of the world.
Antiphon for Benedictus.
He that descended is the same also that ascended up far abóve all héavens : that hé might fíll all things.
And He gave some, apostles; and some, prophets; and sóme, evángelists : and some, pástors and téachers.

Antiphon for Magnificat.

He said unto them, * They that be whole need nót a phy-sí-cian : but théy

that are sick. But go ye and learn what that meaneth, I will have mercy, ánd

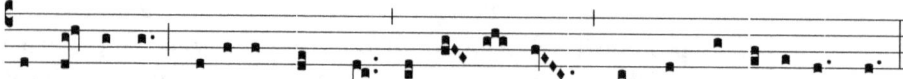

not sác-ri-fice : for I am not come to call righteous, but sinners tó repéntance.

Collect. O Almighty God, who by Thy blessed Son didst call Saint Matthew from the receipt of custom to be an Apostle ànd Evangelist : grant us grace to forsake all covetous desires and inordinate love of richès, and to follow the same, Jesus Christ, Thy Son, oùr Lord, who liveth and reigneth with Thee and the Hòly Ghost : ever one God, world without end. Amen.

Saint Michael and All Angels' Day (Sep. 29) [365]
All from Common of the Holy Angels (p. 560) except the following:
Psalms. **103, 91, 34, 8, 68, 104, 33**
Gospel (at Morning Prayer). **Matthew 18:1-11**
Epistle (at Evening Prayer). **Revelation 12:7-12**

Hymn (at Morning Prayer). **Tibi, Christe, splendor Patris.**
Rabanus Maurus, 9th c., trans. by J. M. Neale

1. Thee, O Christ, the Father's splendor, / Life and virtue of the heart, / In the presence of the angels / Sing we now with tuneful art, / Mostly in alternate chorus / Bearing our responsive part.
2. Thus we praise with due thanksgiving / All the armies of the sky; / Chiefly him, the warrior primate, / Of celestial chivalry, / Michael, who in princely virtue / Cast Abaddon from on high.
3. By whose watchful care repelling — / King of everlasting grace — / Every ghostly adversary, / All things evil, all things base, / Grant us of Thine only goodness / In Thy paradise a place.
4. Laud and honor to the Father, / Laud and honor to the Son, / Laud and honor to the Spirit, / Ever Three and ever One, / Consubstantial, co-eternal, / While unending ages run. Amen.

℣. An angel stood at the altar of the temple.
℟. Having a golden censer in his hand.
Antiphon for Benedictus. And I heard a loud voice saying in heaven, Now is come salvation, and strength, and the kingdom of our God, and the pówer of His <u>Christ</u> : for the accuser of our brethren is cast down, which accused them befóre our God dáy and night.

Antiphon for Magnificat.

Take heed that ye despise not óne * of these líttle ones : for I say unto you,

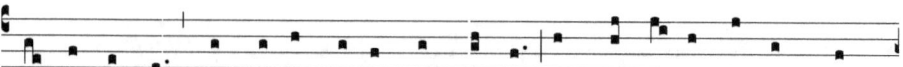

That in heaven their angels do always behold the face of my Father which

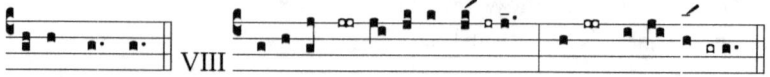

ís in héaven.

Collect. O Everlasting God, who hast ordained and constituted the services of angels and men in a wondèrful order : mercifully grant that, as Thy holy angels always do Thee service in heavèn, so by Thine appointment they may succor and defend us on earth; through Jesus Christ, Thy Son, oùr Lord, who liveth and reigneth with Thee and the Hòly Ghost : ever one God, world without end. Amen.

Saint Luke the Evangelist's Day (Oct. 18)
All from Common of Evangelists (p. 538) except the following:
Psalms. 45, 19, 34, 67, 84, 87, 117
Gospel (at Morning Prayer). **Luke 10:1-9**
Epistle (at Evening Prayer). **2 Timothy 4:5-15**

℣. Their line is gone out through all the earth.
℟. And their words to the end of the world.
Antiphon for Benedictus.
He that descended is the same also that ascended up far abóve all héavens : that hé might fíll all things.
And He gave some, apostles; and some, prophets; and sóme, evángelists : and some, pástors and téachers.

Antiphon for Magnificat.

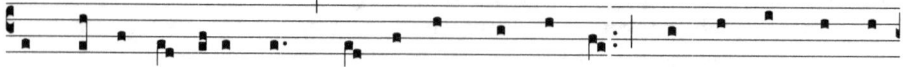

The harvest truly is great, * but the lábourers are <u>few</u> : pray ye therefore the

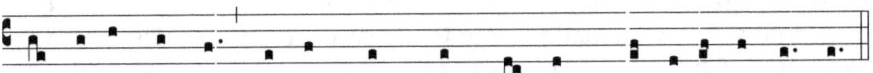
Lord of the harvest, that He would send forth labourers into His hárvest.

VIII

Collect. Almighty God, who calledst Saint Luke the physician to be an Evangelist and physician òf the soul : heal, we beseech Thee, all the diseases of our sòuls, by the wholesome medicine of Thy Word; through Jesus Christ, Thy Son, oùr Lord, who liveth and reigneth with Thee and the Hòly Ghost : ever one God, world without end. Amen.

Saint Simon and Saint Jude the Apostles' Day (Oct. 28)

All from Common of Apostles (p. 538) except the following:
Psalms. 1, 7, 20, 36, 80, 92, 138
Gospel (at Morning Prayer). John 15:17-21
Epistle (at Evening Prayer). 1 Peter 1:3-9

℣. Their line is gone out through all the earth.

[366]

℟. And their words to the end of the world.
Antiphon for Benedictus.
Remember the word that I sáid unto you : The servant is not gréater thán his lord.
If they have persecuted me, they will also pérsecute you : If they have kept my saying, they will kéep yours álso.

Antiphon for Magnificat.

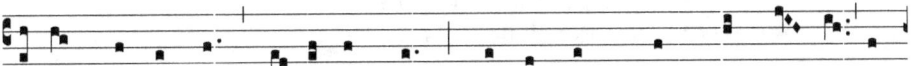
I have chosen you * óut of the world : and all these things they will do un-

VIII

to you fór My Náme's sake.

Collect. O Almighty God, who hast built Thy church upon the foundation of the Apostles and Prophets, Jesus Christ Himself being the head

Còrnerstone : grant us to be joined together in unity of spirit by their doctrìne, that we may be made a holy temple acceptable unto Thee; through the same, Jesus Christ, Thy Son, oùr Lord, who liveth and reigneth with Thee and the Hòly Ghost : ever one God, world without end. Amen.

The Festival of the Reformation (Oct. 31)
Invitatory.

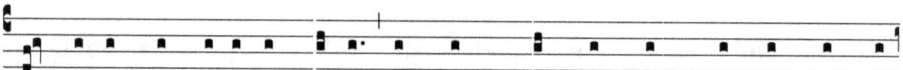

Now is the time of Reformation, in which Christ the High Priest of things to

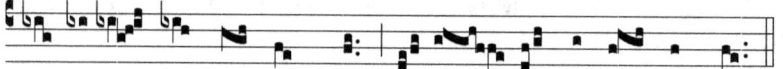

come is conféssed be-fore <u>kings</u> : O cóme, let us wórship Him.

Antiphons for Psalms
1. I will speak of Thy testimonies álso befóre kings : and will nót be a<u>shamed</u>. *(Ps. 119vi)*
2. Thy Word is a lamp unto my feet, álleluia : And a light unto my path, álleluia. *(Ps. 119xiv)*
3. The Lord, our God, be with us, álleluia : As He was with our fathers, álleluia.
4. Do good in Thy good pleasure unto Zion, álleluia : Build Thou the walls of Jerusalem, álleluia. *(Ps. 51)*
5. Stand fast therefore in the liberty, álleluia : Wherewith Christ hath made you free, álleluia.

Psalms. 46, 48, 62, 73, 78, 85, 97, 119vi, 124, 125
Gospel (at Morning Prayer). **Matthew 11:12-15**
Epistle (at Evening Prayer). **Revelation 14:6-7**

Responsory.

℟. I will speak of Thy testimonies álso befóre kings, ‡ And shall nót be a-shamed. ℟. I will speak... ℣. And I will delight myself in Thy commánd-ments, which Í have loved. ‡ And shall not... ℣. Glory be to the Fáther and tó the Son : and tó the Hóly Ghost. ℟. I will speak...

℣. Now is the time of Reformation. ℟. In which Christ the High Priest of things to come is confessed before kings.

Antiphon for Benedictus. The kingdom of heaven súffereth víolence : and the violent táke it by <u>force</u>.

Antiphon for Magnificat.

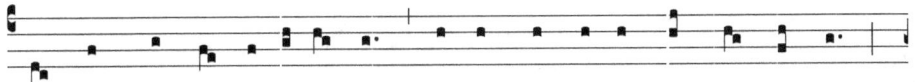

Fear God, and give glory to Him; * for the hour of His júdgment is <u>come</u> :

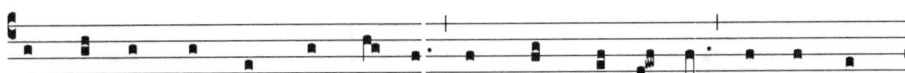

and worship Him that made heaven, and earth, and the sea, and the fóun-

tains of wáters.

Collect. O Lord God, heavènly Father : pour out, we beseech Thee, Thy Holy Spirit upon Thy faithful peoplè, keep them steadfast in Thy grace and truth, protect and comfort them in all temptations, defend them against all enemies

[367]

of Thy Word, and bestow upon Christ's church Militant Thy saving peace; through the same, Jesus Christ, Thy Son, oùr Lord, who liveth and reigneth with Thee and the Hòly Ghost : ever one God, world without end. Amen.

All Saints' Day (Nov. 1)
All from Common of a Holy Man (p. 556) except the following:

Antiphons for Psalms
1. I beheld a great multitude which nó man could númber : of all nations, stánding befóre the throne.
2. And they sang a new song to the Lamb, † Thou hast redeemed us to God by thy blood out of every kindred and tongue and péople and nátion : and hast made us unto óur God kíngs and priests.
3. Bless ye the Lord, all yé his e<u>lect</u> : keep days of joy, and give glóry únto him. *(Ps. 103ii, 134)*
4. All his saints shall praise him, even the chíldren of Ísrael : even the péople that sérveth him. *(Ps. 148)*
5. These are they which came out of great tribulátion : and have washed their robes, and made them white in the blóod of the Lámb.

Psalms. 1, 4, 8, 15, 24, 32, 34, 61, 97
Gospel (at Morning Prayer). **Matthew 5:1-12**
Epistle (at Evening Prayer). **Revelation 7:2-17**

Responsory.

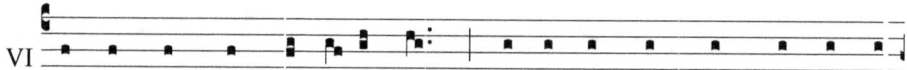

℟. At midnight there wás a crý made, ‡ Behold the Bridegroom cometh, go

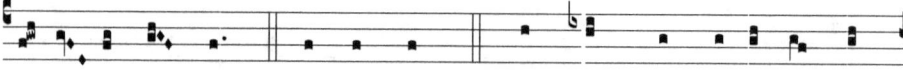

ye óut to méet Him. ℟. At midnight... ℣. Trim your lamps, Ó ye wise vír-

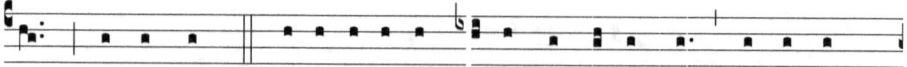

gins. ‡ Behold the... ℣. Glory be to the Fáther and tó the Son : and tó the

Hóly Ghost. ℟. At midnight...

℣. Let the saints be joyful in glory. ℟. Let them sing aloud upon their beds.
Antiphon for Benedictus. The glorious company of the Apostles praise Thee; the goodly fellowship of the Prophets praise Thee; the noble army of Mártyrs práise Thee : all Thy Saints and Elect with one voice do acknowledge Thee, O blessed Trínity, óne God.

Antiphon for Magnificat.

Rejoice, * and be exceeding glad, for great is your rewárd in héaven : for so

per-se-cu-ted they the prophets which wére befóre you.

VI

Collect. O Almighty God, who hast knit together Thine elect in one communion and fellowship in the mystical body of Thy Son Jesus Chrìst, our Lord : grant us grace so to follow Thy blessed saints in all virtuous and godly livìng, that we may come to the unspeakable joys which Thou hast prepared for those who unfeignedly love Thee; through the same, Jesus Christ, Thy Son, oùr Lord, who liveth and reigneth with Thee and the Hòly Ghost : ever one God, world without end. Amen.

COMMON OF SAINTS
Common of the Blessed Virgin Mary (B.V.M.)

Invitatory.

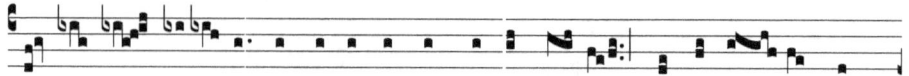

Let us keep hol-i-day in honor of the Vírgin Má- ry : Let us worship the

Vírgin's Son, Chríst the Lord.

Antiphons for Psalms

1. Quando venit ergo sacri plenitúdo tempóris : missus est ab arce Patris natus, orbis conditór in térris.
2. Stirps Jesae virgam produxit, virgaque florem, et super hunc florem requiescit Spíritus álmus : Virgo Dei genitrix virga est, flos Fílius éjus.
3. The stem of Jesse shall produce a rod, and the rod a flower, and the nourishing Spirit shall rést upón Him : The virgin mother of God is the rod, her Són the flówer.
4. O wondrous interchange! The Creator of mankind, taking upon Him a living body, vouchsafed to be born óf a pure vírgin : and by His Humanity, which was begotten in no earthly wise, hath made us partakers of Hís Divínity.
5. The Root of Jesse hath budded, the Star hath come out of Jacob, † the virgin hath bórne the Sávior : we práise Thee, Ó our God.
6. The Lord, whom ye seek, shall suddenly cóme to His témple : be glad then, ye children of Zion, and rejóice in the Lórd your God.

Psalms. 8, 19, 24, 45, 46, 87, 96, 97, 98, 110, 113, 122, 127, 147
Gospel (at Morning Prayer). **Luke 11:27-28**
Epistle (at Evening Prayer). **Isaiah 7:10-15**

Responsory.

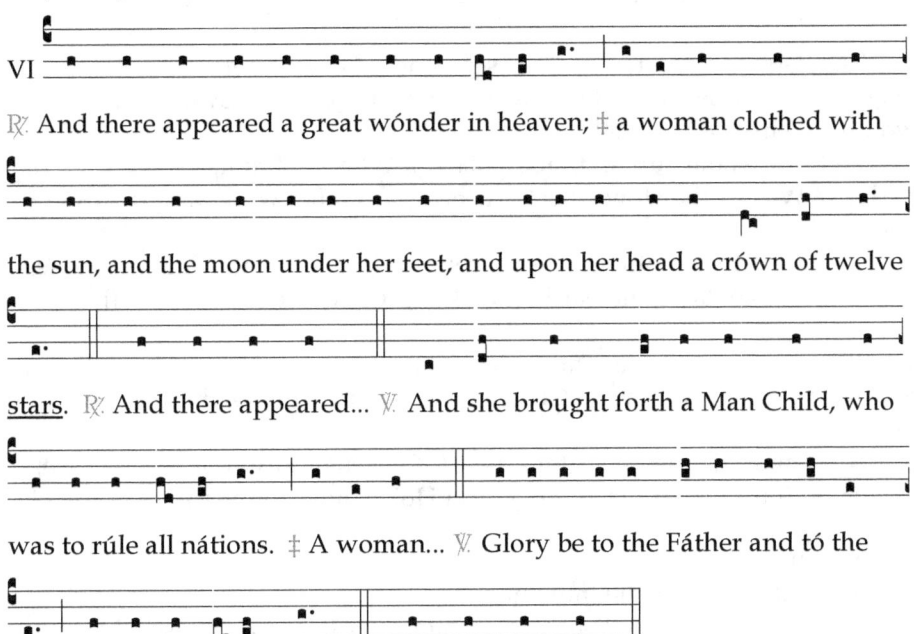

℟. And there appeared a great wónder in héaven; ‡ a woman clothed with the sun, and the moon under her feet, and upon her head a crówn of twelve stars. ℟. And there appeared... ℣. And she brought forth a Man Child, who was to rúle all nátions. ‡ A woman... ℣. Glory be to the Fáther and tó the Son : and tó the Hóly Ghost. ℟. And there appeared...

Hymn. Quem terra, pontus, sidera. *Fortunatus, 6th cent., trans. by J. M. Neale*

1. The God whom earth, and sea, and sky / Adore, and laud, and magnify, / Whose might they own, whose praise they swell, / In Mary's womb vouchsafed to dwell.
2. The Lord whom sun and moon obey, / Whom all things serve from day to day, / Was by the Holy Ghost conceived, / Of her who through His grace believed.
3. How blest that mother, in whose shrine / The great Artificer divine, / Whose hand contains the earth and sky, / Once deigned, as in His ark, to lie:—
4. Blest in the message Gabriel brought, / Blest by the work the Spirit wrought; / From whom the Great Desire of earth / Took human flesh and human birth.
5. All honor, laud, and glory be, / O Jesus, Virgin-born, to Thee, / Whom with the Father we adore, / And Holy Ghost, forevermore. Amen.

[369] ℣. A virgin shall conceive and bear a Son.
℟. And shall call His name Immanuel.

Antiphon for Benedictus. Today is a holiday in honor of blessed Mary, the virgin who sprang from the líneage of Dávid : through whom the world's Salvation appéared to the fáithful.

Antiphon for Magnificat.

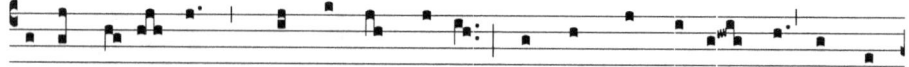

All ge-ner- a-tions * shall cáll me bléssed : for God hath re-gard-ed the low

estate of Hís handmáiden.

Collect. Almighty God, who didst exalt the lowly Virgin Mary bý grace : give us ever humble heàrts, that we may never fail of Thy grace; through Jesus Christ, Thy Son, oùr Lord, who liveth and reigneth with Thee and the

Hòly Ghost : ever one God, world without end. Amen.

Benedicamus.

 *Lucas Lossius*

℣ Bless   we the Lord.
℟ Thanks be   to God.

Common of Apostles and Evangelists

Invitatory.

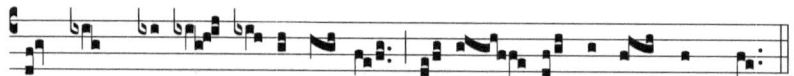

The Lord, the Kíng of A-pó- stles : O cóme, let us wórship Him.

Antiphons for Psalms
1. This is My commandment, that ye love óne anóther : as Í have loved <u>you</u>.
2. Greater love hath nó man than <u>this</u> : that a man lay down his lífe for his <u>friends</u>.
3. Ye are my fríends, saith the <u>Lord</u> : if ye do whatsoever Í commánd you.
4. Blessed are the children of God, even the peacemakers ánd the púre in heart : blessed indeed are they, for théy shall see <u>God</u>.
5. Be ye steadfast, and thereby in your patience posséss ye your <u>souls</u> : and preserve them unto lífe etérnal.

Psalms. 19, 34, 45, 47, 61, 64, 75, 97, 99, 110, 113, 116, 126, 139
Gospel (at Morning Prayer). **Mark 6:7-13**
Epistle (at Evening Prayer). **Isaiah 42:5-12**

Responsory.

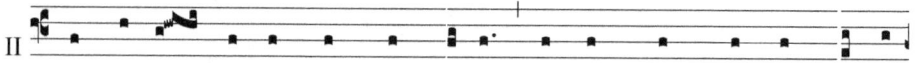

℟. When ye stand before kings and princes, take no thought how or whát ye

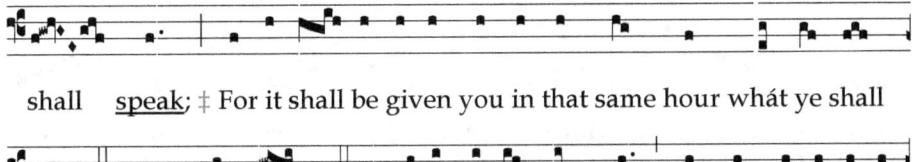

shall speak; ‡ For it shall be given you in that same hour whát ye shall speak. ℟. When ye stand... ℣. For it is not ye that speak, but the Spirit of your Father which spéaketh ín you. ‡ For it shall... ℣. Glory be to the Fáther and tó the Son : and tó the Hóly Ghost. ℟. When ye stand...

Hymn. **Aeterna Christi munera.** *Before 11th cent., trans. by J. M. Neale*

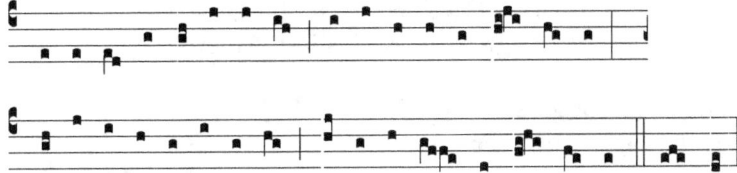

1. The eternal gifts of Christ the King, / The Apostles' glory, let us sing! / Let all with hearts of gladness raise / Due hymns of thankfulness and praise.
2. The princes of the Church are they, / Her chiefs triumphant in the fray, / The heavenly King's own warrior band, / His lights, still lightening every land.
3. Theirs was the steadfast faith of saints, / The hope that never yields nor faints, / The love of Christ in full degree, / Victorious o'er sin's tyranny.
4. The Father's glory they display; / In them the Spirit had His way; / The Son Himself exults in them; / Joy fills the new Jerusalem.
5. Redeemer, hear us of Thy love, / That, with this glorious band above / Hereafter, of Thine endless grace, / Thy servants also may have place.
6. All laud to God the Father be; / All praise, eternal Son, to Thee; / All glory, as is ever meet, / To God the Holy Paraclete. Amen.

[370]

Or: Exultet caelum laudibus. *c. 10th cent., trans. by Richard Mant, alt.*

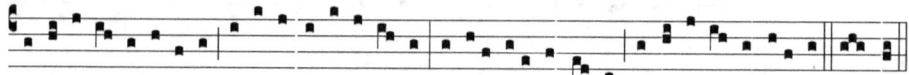

1. Let the round world with songs rejoice; / Let heav'n return the joyful voice; / All mindful of the A-postles' fame, / Let heaven and earth their praise proclaim.
2. These servants who once bore the light / Of Gospel truth o'er heathen night, / Still may their work that light impart, / To glad our eyes and cheer our heart.
3. O God, by whom to them was given / The key that shuts and opens heaven, / Our chains unbind, our loss repair, / And grant us grace to enter there;
4. For at Thy will they preached the Word / Which cured disease, which health conferred: / O may that healing power once more / Our souls to grace and health restore:
5. That when Thy Son again shall come, / And speak the world's unerring doom, / He may with them pronounce us blest, / And place us in Thine endless rest.
6. To Thee, O Father; Son, to Thee; / To Thee, blest Spirit, glory be! / So was it ay for ages past, / So shall through endless ages last. Amen.

℣. Their line is gone out through all the earth.
℟. And their words to the end of the world.

Antiphon for Benedictus. Ye which have forsaken all, and followed me, shall recéive an húndredfold : and shall inherit éverlásting life.

Antiphon for Magnificat.

They will de-liv-er you * up to the councils, and they will scourge you ín

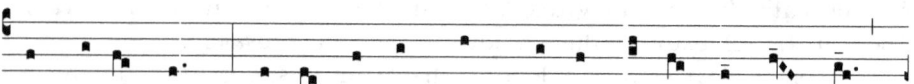

their sýn-a-gogues : and ye shall be brought before gov-er-nors and kings

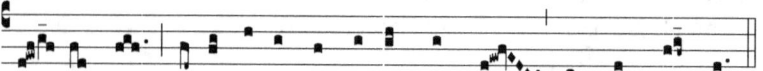

for my sake, for a tes-ti-mo-ny a-gainst them ánd the Géntiles.

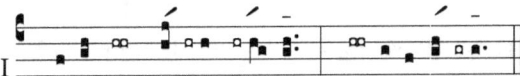

Collect. O Almighty God, who hast built Thy church upon the foundation of the Apostles and Prophets, Jesus Christ Himself being the head Còrnerstone : grant us to be joined together in unity of spirit by their doctrìne, that we may be made a holy temple acceptable unto Thee; through the same, Jesus Christ, Thy Son, oùr Lord, who liveth and reigneth with Thee and the Hòly Ghost : ever one God, world without end. Amen.

Benedicamus.

Lucas Lossius

℣. Bless we the Lord.
℟. Thanks be to God.

Benedicamus in Eastertide.

Lucas Lossius

℣. Bless we the Lord, al-le-lu-ia, al-le- lu-ia, al- le- lu- ia.
℟. Thanks be to God, al-le-lu-ia, al-le- lu-ia, al- le- lu- ia.

Common of Martyrs
Invitatory.

The Lord, the Kíng of mártyrs : O cóme, let us wórship Him.

Antiphons for Psalms
1. And the Lord said, Whosoever shall confess mé before <u>men</u> : him will I confess also befóre my Fáther.
2. He that followeth me shall not wálk in dárkness : but shall have the líght of life, sáith the Lord.
3. If any man serve me, lét him fóllow me : and where I am, there shall álso my sérvant be.
4. If ány man sérve me : him will my Father hónor, sáith the Lord.

Psalms. **1, 2, 3, 4, 5, 8, 11, 15, 16, 21, 24, 33, 34, 46, 79, 110, 111, 112, 113, 116**
Gospel (at Morning Prayer). **Luke 21:9-19**
Epistle (at Evening Prayer). **Romans 8:12-39**

[371] *Responsory.*

℟. Precious in the sight of the Lord is the déath of His <u>saints</u>. ‡ The Lord

keepeth all their bones, so that not one of thém is bróken. ℟. Precious in the...

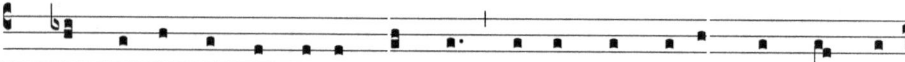

℣. Great are the troubles of the righteous, but the Lord de-live-reth them óut

of them <u>all</u>. ‡ The Lord keepeth... ℣. Glory be to the Fáther and tó the Son :

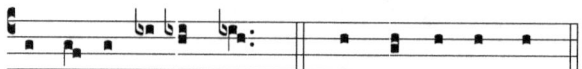

and tó the Hóly Ghost. ℟. Precious in the sight...

Hymn (for a male martyr). **Deus tuorum militum.** *6th cent., trans. by J. M. Neale*

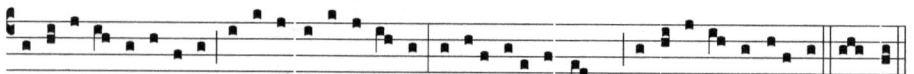

1. O God, Thy soldiers' crown and guard, / And their exceeding great reward; / From all transgressions set us free, / Who sing Thy martyr's victory.
2. The pleasures of the world he spurned, / From sin's pernicious lures he turned; / He knew their joys imbued with gall, / And thus he reached Thy heavenly hall.
3. For Thee through many a woe he ran, / In many a fight he played the man; / For Thee his blood he dared to pour, / And thence hath joy forevermore.

4. We therefore pray Thee, full of love, / Regard us from Thy throne above; / On this Thy martyr's triumph day, / Wash every stain of sin away.
5. O Christ, most loving King, to Thee, / With God the Father, glory be; / Like glory, as is ever meet, / To God the holy Paraclete. Amen.

Or: Rex gloriose Martyrum. *c. 6th cent., trans. by Richard F. Littledale and others*

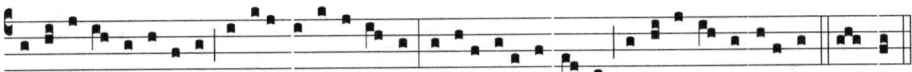

1. O glorious King of martyr hosts, / Thou Crown that each confessor boasts, / Who leadest to celestial day / The saints who cast earth's joys away;
2. Thine ear in mercy, Savior, lend, / While unto Thee our prayers ascend; / And as we count their triumphs won, / Forgive the sins that we have done.
3. Martyrs in Thee their triumphs gain, / Confessors grace from Thee obtain; / We sinners humbly seek to Thee, / From sin's offence to set us free.
4. All laud to God the Father be, / All praise, eternal Son, to Thee; / All glory, as is ever meet, / To God the holy Paraclete. Amen.

Or: Sanctorum meritis. *8th cent., trans. by J. M. Neale, alt.* [372]

1. The noble deeds of saints / Bless-ed for evermore, / Their love that never faints, / The toils they bravely bore: / For these the Church today / Pours forth her joyous lay: / These victors won the noblest bay.
2. They, whom this world of ill, / While it yet held, abhorred; / Its withering flowers that still / They spurned with one accord: / They knew them short-lived all, / And followed at Thy call, / King Jesus, to Thy heavenly hall.
3. Like sheep their blood they poured; / And without groan or tear, / They bent before the sword / For that their King most dear: / Their souls, serenely blest, / In patience they possessed, / And looked in hope to-wards their rest.
4. What tongue may here declare, / Fancy or thought descry, / The joys Thou dost prepare / For these Thy saints on high! / Empurpled in the flood / Of their victorious blood, / They won the laurel from their God.
5. To Thee, O Lord most high, / One in Three Persons still, / To pardon us as we cry, / And to preserve from ill: / Here give Thy servants peace, / Hereafter glad release, / And pleasures that shall never cease. Amen.

℣. Precious in the sight of the Lord. ℟. Is the death of His saints.

Antiphon for Benedictus. He that hateth his lífe in this <u>world</u> : shall keep it unto lífe etérnal.

Antiphon for Magnificat.

If any man will come after me, saith the Lord, * lét him dený himself : and

take up his cróss, and fóllow me.

Collect. Almighty God, who didst give Thy servant N. boldness to confess the Name of our Savior Jesus Christ before the rulers of this world, and courage to die fòr this faith : Grant that we likewise may ever be ready to give a reason for the hope that is in ùs, and to suffer gladly for His sake; through the same, Jesus Christ, Thy Son, oùr Lord, who liveth and reigneth with Thee and the Hòly Ghost : ever one God, world without end. Amen.

Common of Confessors

A confessor is one who has made the good confession under torture, though has not been killed for the Faith.

Invitatory.

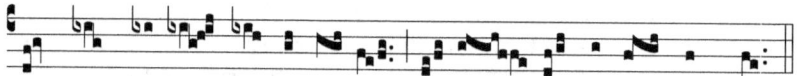

The Lord, the Kíng of confés-sors : O cóme, let us wórship Him.

Antiphons for Psalms
1. Lord, thou deliveredst unto mé five tálents : behold, I have gained beside them fíve talents <u>more</u>.
2. Well done, thou good servant, † in little thíngs found fáithful : enter thou into the jóy of thy <u>Lord</u>.
3. A wise and fáithful stéward : whom the Lord hath made ruler over áll his hóusehold.
4. Blessed is that servant whom his Lord, when he cometh and knócketh át the door : sháll find wátching.

Psalms. 1, 2, 3, 4, 5, 8, 15, 21, 24, 110, 111, 112, 113, 132 [373]
Gospel (at Morning Prayer). **Luke 12:35-44**
Epistle (at Evening Prayer). **Proverbs 2:1-22**

Responsory.

℟. And I will make thee unto this people as a fenced brasen wáll, saith the Lord. ‡ And they shall fight against thee, but they shall not prevail against thee, for Í am wíth thee. ℟. And I will... ℣. In the midst of your own selves shall men arise, speaking perverse things, to draw away di-scí-ples áfter them. ‡ And they shall... ℣. Glory be to the Fáther and tó the Son : and tó the Hóly Ghost. ℟. And I will...

Hymn. **Iste confessor.** *8th cent., trans. by L. Housman, alt.*

1. He, whose confession God of old accepted, / Whom through the ages all now hold in honor, / Gaining his wages this day came to enter / Heaven's high portal.
2. God-fearing, watchful, pure of mind and body, / Holy and humble, thus did all men find him; / While, through his members, to the life immortal / Mortal life called him.
3. Thus to the weary, from the Life enshrin-ed, / Potent in virtue, flowed humane compassion; / Sick and sore laden, howsoever burdened, / There they found healing.
4. So now in chorus, giving God the glory, / Raise we our anthem gladly to his honor, / That in fair kinship we may all be sharers / Here and hereafter.
5. Honor and glory, power and salvation, / Be in the highest unto Him who reigneth / Changeless in heaven over earthly changes, / Triune, eternal. Amen.

Or. **Rex gloriose Martyrum.** *c. 6th cent., trans. by R. F. Littledale and others*

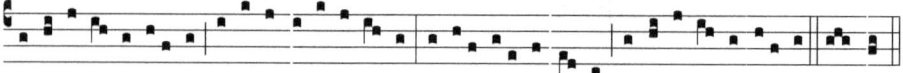

1. O glorious King of martyr hosts, / Thou Crown that each confessor boasts, / Who leadest to celestial day / The saints who cast earth's joys away;
2. Thine ear in mercy, Savior, lend, / While unto Thee our prayers ascend; / And as we count their triumphs won, / Forgive the sins that we have done.
3. Martyrs in Thee their triumphs gain, / Confessors grace from Thee obtain; / We sinners humbly seek to Thee, / From sin's offence to set us free.
4. All laud to God the Father be, / All praise, eternal Son, to Thee; / All glory, as is ever meet, / To God the holy Paraclete. Amen.

℣. The Lord led the righteous in right paths.
℟. And shewed him the kingdom of God.

Antiphon for Benedictus. Well done, good and faithful servant; † thou hast been faithful over a few things, I will make thee ruler óver mány things : Enter thou into the jóy of thy <u>Lord</u>.

Antiphon for Magnificat.

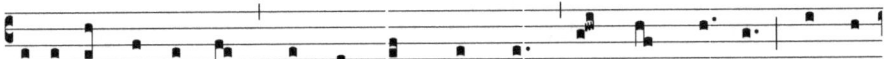

Lo, a servant of God * who esteemed as naught áll things éarthly : and by

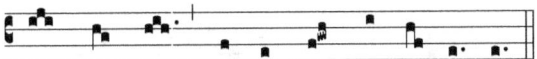

word and work laid up tréasures in héaven.

VIII

Collect. O God, who makest us glad with the yearly feast of Saint N., Thý confessor : mercifully grant, that, as we now observe his (her) heavenly birthdày, so we may follow him (her) in all virtuous and godly living; through Jesus Christ, Thy Son, oùr Lord, who liveth and reigneth with Thee and the Hòly Ghost : ever one God, world without end. Amen. [374]

Common of Doctors

Invitatory.

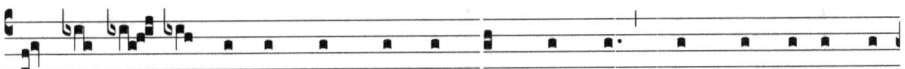

The Fountain of wisdom, the Word of God Most High, who hath given wis-

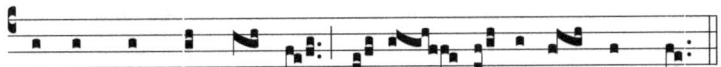

dom to thém that lóve him : O cóme, let us wórship Him.

Ants. for Psalmody

1. As saith the Prophet, The Lord God hath given me the tóngue of the léarned : that I should know how to speak a word in season to hím that is wéary.
2. As saith the Apostle, My speech and my preaching was not with enticing wórds of men's wísdom : but in the demonstration of the Spirit ánd of pówer.
3. Having therefore obtained help of God, I witness bóth to smáll and great : saying none other things than those which the Próphets did <u>say</u>.
4. For I determined not to know anything amóng you : save Jesus Christ and

him crúcified.

Psalms. 1, 2, 3, 4, 5, 8, 15, 21, 24, 110, 111, 112, 113, 117
Gospel (at Morning Prayer). **Matthew 5:13-19**
Epistle (at Evening Prayer). **Isaiah 50:4-11**

Responsory.

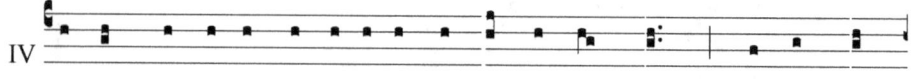

℞. In the midst of the congregation he ópened his <u>mouth</u>. ‡ And the Lord

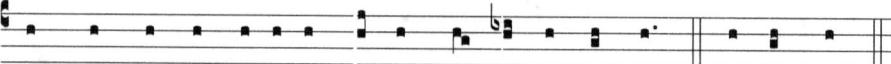

filled him with the Spirit of Wisdom and Únderstánding. ℞. In the midst...

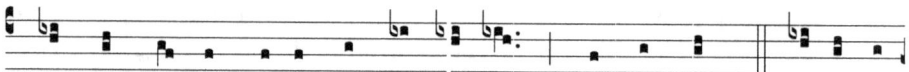

℣. He shall find joy, and a crówn of gládness. ‡ And the Lord... ℣. Glory be

to the Fáther and tó the Son : and tó the Hóly Ghost. ℞. In the midst...

Hymn. O qui perpetuus nos.

1. O Christ, the Father's Voice and His eternal Word, / What Thou wouldst still declare must needs on earth be heard; / And though we see Thee not, we yet may hear Thy speech, / For with Thy voice Thy doctors teach.
2. On Zion's towers they watch, lest heresy draw near / To breach its walls of faith and bring corruption drear; / With guardi-ans like these the Church abides secure, / For thus forewarned she can endure.
3. O Christ, eternal Truth, in Thee do we rejoice, / Though now our outward ears may not perceive Thy voice; / Still in Thy doctors' speech Thy teachings we discern, / And thus of Thee our spirits learn. Amen.

℣. With my lips have I declared all the judgments of Thy mouth.
℟. I have rejoiced in the way of Thy testimonies, as much as in all riches.
Antiphon for Benedictus. Blessed be the Name of God for ever and ever, for wisdom and might are his : I thank thee, O thou God of my fathers, who hast given us wisdom and might, in that thou hast revealed the deep and secret things.

Antiphon for Magnificat.

I will liken him   * únto a wíse man: which built his hóuse upón a rock.

Collect. O God, who hast endowed Thy servant N. with clarity of faith and holiness of life : Grant us to keep with steadfast minds the faith which he taught, and in his fellowship to be made partakers of eternal glory; through Jesus Christ, Thy Son, our Lord, who liveth and reigneth with Thee and the Holy Ghost : ever One God, world without end. Amen.

Common of Bishops, Pastors, and Missionaries
Invitatory.

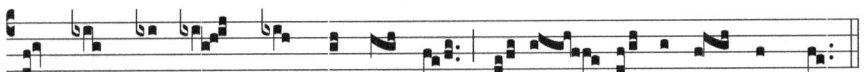

The Lord who doth shépherd His <u>flock</u> : O cóme, let us wórship Him.

Antiphons for Psalms
1. The law of his God is in his heart, and his góings shálll not slide : for the Lord maketh his way acceptable únto him<u>self</u>. *(Ps. 37iii)*
2. I have declared Thy righteousness and Thý salvátion : I have not kept back Thy loving mércy ánd Thy truth. *(Ps. 40)*
3. The priest's lips should keep knowledge; † and they should seek the láw at his <u>mouth</u> : for he is the messenger óf the LÓRD of hosts.
4. The Lord said, Good and fáithful sérvant : enter thou into the jóy of thy <u>Lord</u>.

Psalms. 34:11-22; 37:30-40; 1, 2, 3, 4, 5, 8, 15, 21, 24
Gospel (at Morning Prayer). **Matthew 25:14-30**
Epistle (at Evening Prayer). **Jeremiah 1:4-9**

Responsory.

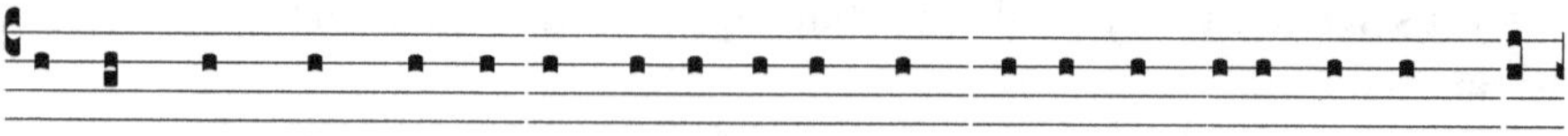

℟. Let the Lord, the God of the spirits of all flesh, set a man over the cóngregátion, ‡ which may go out before them, and which may go in before them, and which may lead them out, and whích may bríng them in. ℟. Let the Lord... ℣. That the con-gre-ga-tion of the Lord be not as sheep which háve no shépherd. ‡ Which may go... ℣. Glory be to the Fáther and tó the Son : and tó the Hóly Ghost. ℟. Let the Lord... *(Numbers 27:16-17)*

[376] *Hymn.* **Jesu, Redemptor omnium.** *8th cent., trans. by R. M. Benson*

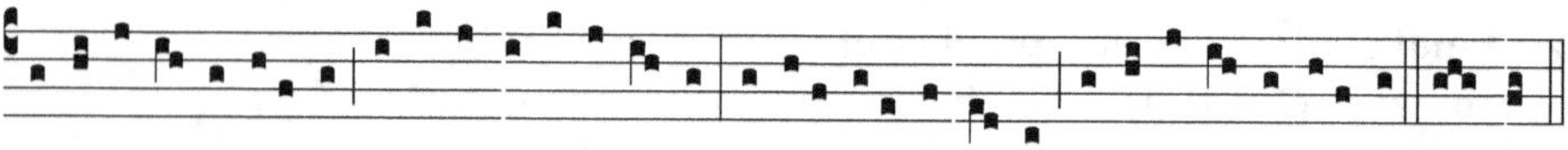

1. O Thou whose all-redeeming might / Crowns every chief in faith's true fight, / On this commemoration day / Hear us, good Jesus, while we pray.
2. In faithful strife for thy dear Name / Thy servant earned the saintly fame, / Which pious hearts with praise revere / In constant memory year by year.
3. Earth's fleeting joys he counted nought, / For higher, truer joys he

sought, / And now, with angels round Thy throne, / Unfading treasures are his own.

4. O grant that we, most gracious God, / May follow in the steps he trod; / And, freed from every stain of sin, / As he hath won may also win.

5. To Thee, O Christ, our loving King, / All glory, praise and thanks we bring; / Whom with the Father we adore / And Holy Ghost for evermore. Amen.

℣. The Lord led the righteous in right paths.
℟. And shewed him the kingdom of God.

Antiphon for Benedictus. **Never** was he moved bý respéct of men : but rather went ever gloriously on his way to the kíngdom of héaven.

Antiphon for Magnificat.

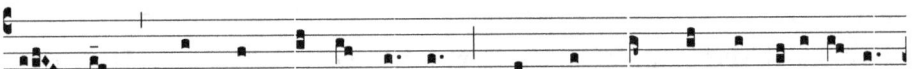
Well done, * good and faithful servant; † thou hast been faithful óver a féw
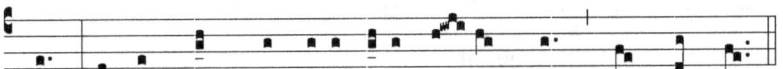
things : I will make thee ruler over má- ny things, sáith the Lord.

Collect. Accept, O Lord, our thanksgiving this day for Thy sèrvant N. : and grant that all ministers and stewards of Thy mysteries may afford to Thy faithful people, by word and examplè, the instruction which is of Thy grace; through Jesus Christ, Thy Son, oùr Lord, who liveth and reigneth with Thee and the Hòly Ghost : ever One God, world without end. Amen.

Common of Virgins
Invitatory.

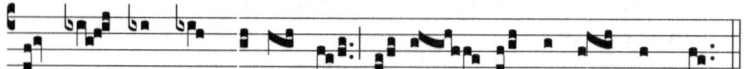

The Lord the Kíng of vír-gins : O cóme, let us wórship Him.

Psalms. 8, 19, 24, 45, 46, 48, 96, 97, 98
Gospel (at Morning Prayer). **Matthew 25:1-13**
Epistle (at Evening Prayer). **1 Corinthians 7:25-40**

Responsory.

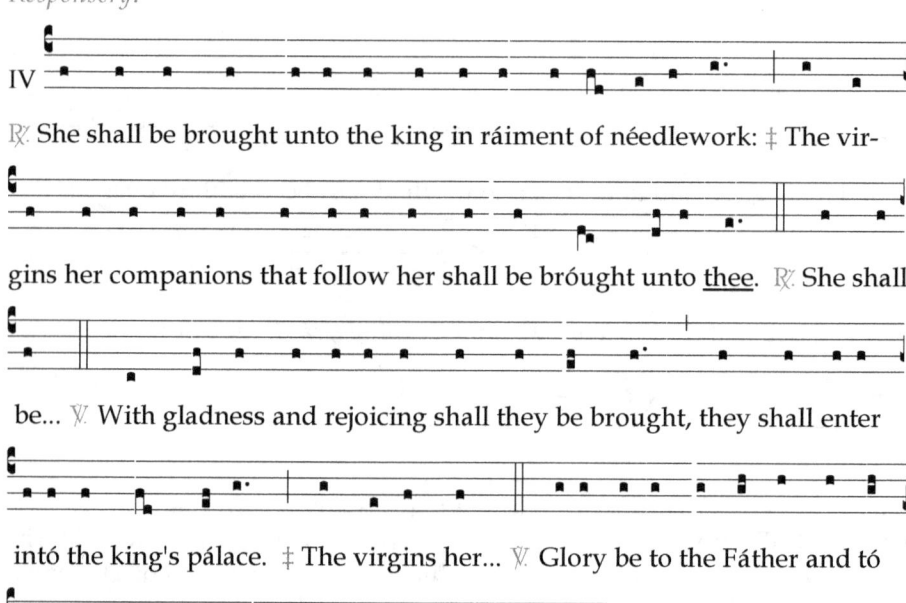

℟. She shall be brought unto the king in ráiment of néedlework: ‡ The virgins her companions that follow her shall be bróught unto <u>thee</u>. ℟. She shall be... ℣. With gladness and rejoicing shall they be brought, they shall enter intó the king's pálace. ‡ The virgins her... ℣. Glory be to the Fáther and tó the Son : and tó the Hóly Ghost. ℟. She shall be...

[377] *Hymn.* **Virginis Proles.** *8th cent., trans. by L. Housman, alt.*

repeat

1. Son of a virgin, Maker of Thy mother, / Thou, Rod and Blossom from a stem unstain-ed, / Now while a virgin fair of fame we honor, / Hear our

devotion!

2. Lo, on Thy handmaid fell a twofold blessing, / Who, in her body vanquishing the weakness, / In that same body, grace from heaven obtaining, / Bore the world witness.

3. Death, nor the rending pains of death appalled her; / Bondage and torment found her undefeated: / So by the shedding of her life attained she / Heavenly wages.

4. Fountain of mercy, hear the prayer we offer; / Purge our offenses, pardon our transgressions, / So that hereafter we to Thee may render / Praise with thanksgiving.

5. Thou, the All-Father, Thou the One-Begotten, / Thou Holy Spirit, Three in One co-equal, / Glory be henceforth thine through all the ages, / World without ending. Amen.

Or: Jesu, Corona virginum. *Ambrose of Milan, 4th cent., trans. by J. M. Neale*

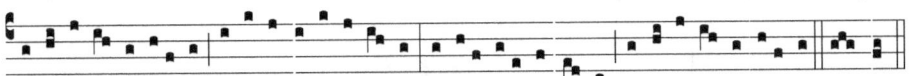

1. Jesus, the virgins' crown, do Thou / Accept us as in prayer we bow; / Born of that virgin whom alone / The mother and the maid we own.

2. Amongst the lilies Thou dost feed, / With virgin choirs accompanied— / With glory decked, the spotless brides / Whose bridal gifts Thy love provides.

3. They, wheresoe'er Thy footsteps bend, / With hymns and praises still attend; / In bless-ed troops they follow Thee, / With dance, and song, and melody.

4. We pray Thee therefore to bestow / Upon our senses here below / Thy grace, that so we may endure / From taint of all corruption pure.

5. All laud to God the Father be, / All praise, eternal Son, to Thee; / All glory, as is ever meet, / To God the holy Paraclete. Amen.

℣. With gladness and rejoicing shall they be brought.

℟. They shall enter into the King's palace.

Antiphon for Benedictus. The kingdom of heaven is like unto a merchantman seeking góodly péarls- : who when he had found one pearl of great price, went and sold all that he hád and bóught it.

Antiphon for Magnificat.

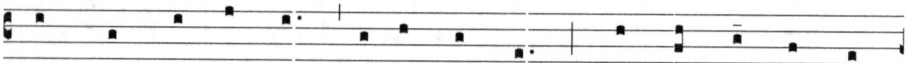

Come, thou bride of Chríst, * recéive the crown : which the Lord hath pre-

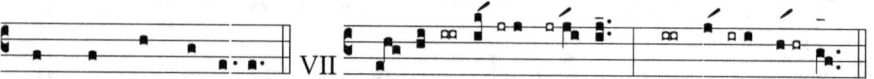

pared for thée for éver.

Collect. Graciously hear us, O God of oùr salvation : that, like as we do rejoice in the festival of blessed *N*. Thy holy virgìn, so we may learn to follow her in all godly and devout affections; through Jesus Christ, Thy Son, oùr Lord, who liveth and reigneth with Thee and the Hòly Ghost : ever One God, world without end. Amen.

[378] ## Common of a Holy Woman
Invitatory.

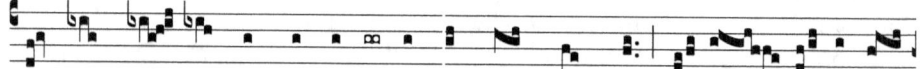

In thanks-giv-ing for blessed *N.* lét us práise our God : O cóme, let us wór-

ship Him.

Psalms. 8, 19, 24, 45, 46, 48, 96, 97, 98
Gospel (at Morning Prayer). **Matthew 13:44-46**
Epistle (at Evening Prayer). **Proverbs 31:10-31**

Responsory.

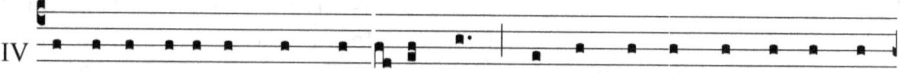

℟. Favour is deceitful, and béauty is <u>vain</u>. ‡ But the woman that feareth the

Lord, shé shall be <u>praised</u>. ℟. Favour is... ℣. Give her of the fruit of her

hands, and let her own works práise her ín the gates. ‡ But the woman...

℣. Glory be to the Fáther and tó the Son : and tó the Hóly Ghost.

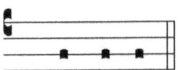

℞. Favour is...

Hymn. **Fortem, virili pectore.** *16ᵗʰ cent., trans. by A. Riley*

1. The praises of that saint we sing, / To whom all lands their tribute bring, / Who with indomitable heart, / Bore throughout life true woman's heart.
2. Restraining every froward sense / By gentle bonds of abstinence, / With prayer her hungry souls she fed, / And thus to heavenly joys hath sped.
3. King Christ, from whom all virtue springs, / Who only doest wondrous things, / As now to Thee she kneels in prayer, / In mercy our petitions hear.
4. All praise to God the Father be, / All praise, eternal Son, to Thee; / Whom with the Spirit we adore / Forever and forevermore. Amen.

Or: **Jesu, Redemptor omnium.** *8ᵗʰ cent., trans. by R. M. Benson*

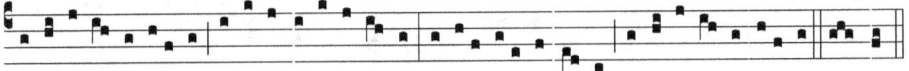

1. O Thou whose all-redeeming might / Crowns every chief in faith's true fight, / On this commemoration day / Hear us, good Jesus, while we pray.
2. In faithful strife for Thy dear Name / Thy servant earned the saintly fame, / Which pious hearts with praise revere / In constant memory year by year.
3. Earth's fleeting joys she counted nought, / For higher, truer joys she sought, / And now, with angels round Thy throne, / Unfading treasures are her own.
4. O grant that we, most gracious God, / May follow in the steps she trod; / And, freed from every stain of sin, / As she hath won may also win.

5. To Thee, O Christ, our loving King, / All glory, praise and thanks we bring; / Whom with the Father we adore / And Holy Ghost for evermore. Amen.

℣. God is in the midst of her, she shall not be moved.
℟. God shall help her, and that right early.

[379] *Antiphon for Benedictus.* Who can find a vírtu-ous wóman?: for her price is fár above rúbies.

Antiphon for Magnificat.

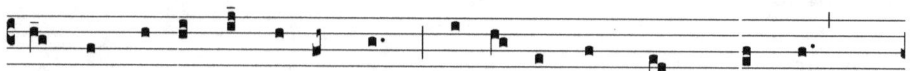

Give her * of the frúit of her <u>hands</u> : and let her own works práise her

ín the gates.

Collect. Graciously hear us, O God of oùr salvation : that, like as we do rejoice in the festival of blessed N. thy holy womàn, so we may learn to follow her in all godly and devout affections; through Jesus Christ, thy Son, oùr Lord, who liveth and reigneth with thee and the Hòly Ghost : ever One God, world without end. Amen.

Common of a Holy Man (Saints)
Invitatory.

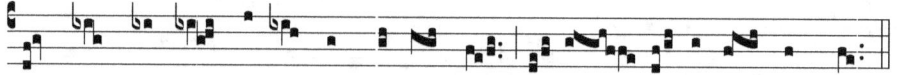

The Lord, the King of áll that conféss Him : O cóme, let us wórship Him.

Antiphons for Psalms
1. Lord, thou deliveredst unto mé five tálents : behold, I have gained beside them fíve talents <u>more</u>.
2. Well done, thou good servant, † in little thíngs found fáithful : enter thou into the jóy of thy <u>Lord</u>.
3. A wise and fáithful stéward : whom the Lord hath made ruler over áll his hóusehold.
4. Blessed is that servant whom his Lord, when he cometh and knócketh át the door : sháll find wátching.

Psalms. 1, 2, 3, 4, 5, 8, 15, 21, 24, 110, 111, 112, 113, 132
Gospel (at Morning Prayer). **Matthew 25:31-40**
Epistle (at Evening Prayer). **Hebrews 12:1-2**

Responsory.

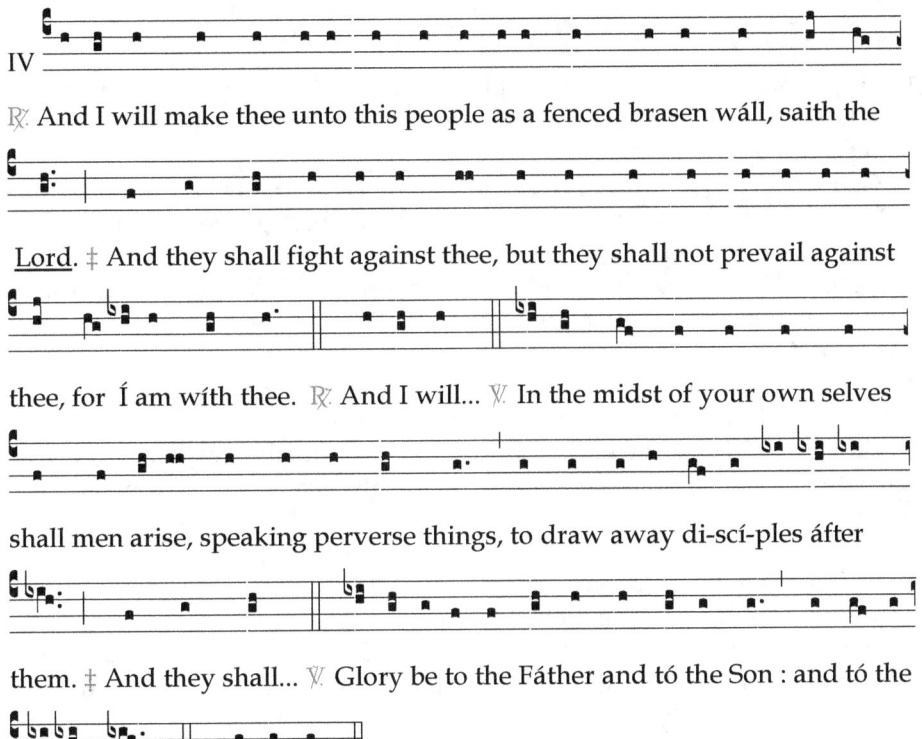

℟. And I will make thee unto this people as a fenced brasen wáll, saith the Lord. ‡ And they shall fight against thee, but they shall not prevail against thee, for Í am wíth thee. ℟. And I will... ℣. In the midst of your own selves shall men arise, speaking perverse things, to draw away di-scí-ples áfter them. ‡ And they shall... ℣. Glory be to the Fáther and tó the Son : and tó the Hóly Ghost. ℟. And I will...

Hymn. **Iste confessor.** *8th cent., trans. by L. Housman, alt.*
For several saints: "They," "their," and "them" instead of "he," "his," and "him."

1. He, whose confession God of old accepted, / Whom through the ages all now hold in honor, / Gaining his wages this day came to enter / Heaven's high portal.
2. God-fearing, watchful, pure of mind and body, / Holy and humble, thus did all men find him; / While, through his members, to the life immortal / Mortal life called him.
3. Thus to the weary, from the Life enshrin-ed, / Potent in virtue, flowed humane compassion; / Sick and sore laden, howsoever burdened, / There they found healing.
4. So now in chorus, giving God the glory, / Raise we our anthem gladly to his honor, / That in fair kinship we may all be sharers / Here and hereafter.
5. Honor and glory, power and salvation, / Be in the highest unto Him who reigneth / Changeless in heaven over earthly changes, / Triune, eternal. Amen.

[380] ℣. The Lord led the righteous in right paths.
℟. And shewed him the kingdom of God.
Antiphon for Benedictus. Well done, good and faithful servant; † thou hast been faithful over a few things, I will make thee ruler óver mány things : Enter thou into the jóy of thy <u>Lord</u>.

Antiphon for Magnificat.

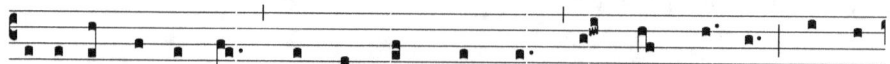

Lo, a servant of God * who esteemed as naught áll things éarthly : and by

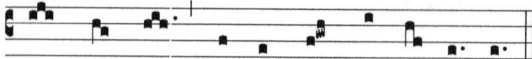

word and work laid up tréasures in héaven.

VIII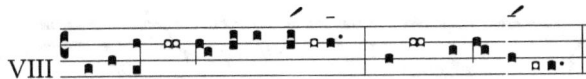

Collect. O almighty God, who has called us to faith in Thee, and hast compassed us about with so great a clòud of witnesses : Grant that we, encouraged by the good examples of Thy Saints, and especially of Thy servant(s) *N.*, may persevere in running the race that is set before ùs, until at length, through Thy mercy, we with them attain to Thine eternal joy; through Him who is the author and finisher of our faith, Thy Son Jesus Chrìst our Lord. Amen.

Common of the Holy Angels

Invitatory.

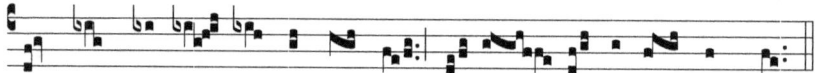

The Lord, the Kíng of Árch-an-gels : O cóme, let us wórship Him.

Antiphons for Psalms
1. An angel came and stóod at the áltar : having a gólden cénser.
2. While Michael the Archangel fought with the dragon, there was heard the vóice of thém which said : Salvátion tó our God.
3. The chariots of God are twenty thousand, even thóusands of ángels : The Lord is among them, as in Sinai, ín the hóly place. *(Ps. 68ii)*
4. He shall give His angels chárge over <u>thee</u> : to kéep thee in áll thy ways. *(Ps. 91)*
5. Bless the Lord, ye His angels, thát excél in strength : Bless ye the Lord, all ye His hosts, ye ministers of His, that dó His pléasure. *(Ps. 103ii)*

Psalms. 8, 10, 15, 19, 24, 34, 68, 78, 91, 96, 97, 103, 104, 148
Gospel (at Morning Prayer). **John 1:47-51**
Epistle (at Evening Prayer). **Revelation 5:11-14**

Responsory.

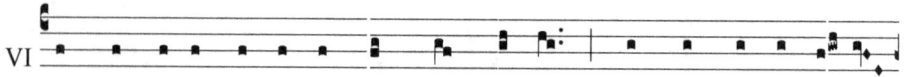

℟. The Lord Jesus shall be reveáled from heáven, ‡ with His mighty angels

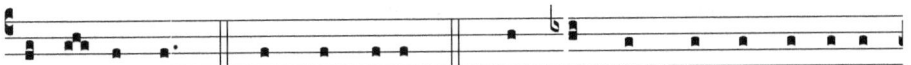

in fláming fíre-. ℟. The Lord Jesus... ℣. When He comes on that day to be

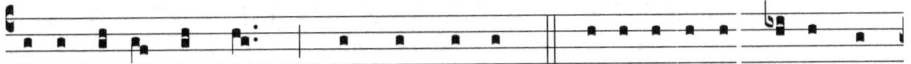

gló-ri-fied ín His saints. ‡ With His mighty... ℣. Glory be to the Fáther and

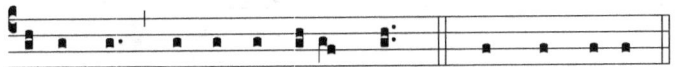

tó the Son : and tó the Hóly Ghost. ℟. The Lord Jesus...

Hymn. Christe, qui sedes Olympo. *Trans. by Neale, alt.*

1. Christ, in highest heaven enthron-ed, / Equal of the Father's might, / By pure spirits, trembling, own-ed, / God of God, and Light of light, / Thee 'mid angel hosts we sing, / Thee their maker and their King.
2. All who circling round adore Thee, / All who bow before Thy throne, / Burn with flaming zeal before Thee / Thy behests to carry down; / To and fro, 'twixt earth and heaven, / Speed they each on errands given.
3. First of all those legions glorious / Michael waves his sword of flame, / Who of old in war victorious / Did the dragon's fierceness tame; / Who with might invincible / Thrust the rebel down to hell.
4. Strong to aid the sick and dying, / Swift from heaven Thine angels fly, / Grace divine and strength supplying / In the hour of agony: / Souls released from bondage here / Safe to Paradise they bear.
5. To the Father praise be given / By the unfallen angel host / Who in His great war have striven / With the legions of the lost; / Equal praise in highest heaven / To the Son and Holy Ghost. Amen.

℣. An angel stood at the altar of the temple.
℟. Having a golden censer in his hand.
Antiphon for Benedictus. And there was war in heaven, Michael and his angels fought against the dragon, and the great drágon was cást out :

Therefore rejoice, ye heavens, and yé that dwéll in them.

Antiphon for Magnificat.

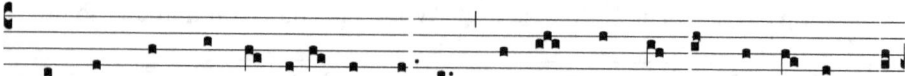

When the door was set open in heaven, * so that John beheld the sacred mys-

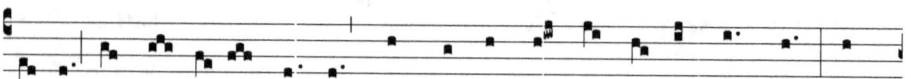

ter-ies, the Archangel Michael sounded his trumpet-cáll to júdgment : O

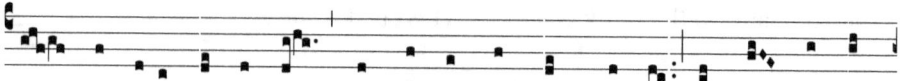

Thou that openest the book, and loosest the seals thereof, do Thou forgíve

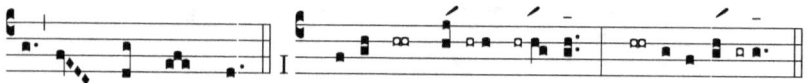

us, O Lórd our God.

[381] *Collect.* O everlasting God, who hast ordained and constituted the services of angels and men in a wondèrful order : mercifully grant that, as Thy holy angels always do Thee service in heavèn, so, by Thy appointment, they may succor and defend us on earth; through Jesus Christ, Thy Son, oùr Lord, who liveth and reigneth with thee and the Hòly Ghost : ever One God, world without end. Amen.

Benedicamus.

Lucas Lossius

℣. Bless we the Lord.
℞. Thanks be to God.

Day of Humiliation and Prayer
Invitatory.

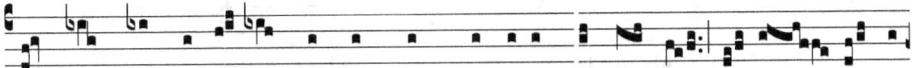

The Lord will be jealous for His land, and píty His péo-ple : O cóme,   let us

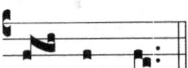

wórship Him.

Antiphons for Psalms
1. Be merciful unto me, O Lord, for I cry únto Thee dáily : Bow down Thine ear, O Lord, hear me, for I am póor and néedy. *(Ps. 86)*
2. Have mercy upon me, O God, according to Thy lóving-kíndness : According unto the multitude of Thy tender mercies blot out mý transgréssions. *(Ps. 51)*
3. Enter not into judgment with Thy sérvant, O <u>Lord</u> : For in Thy sight shall no man líving be jústified. *(Ps. 143)*
4. Lord, deal not with us áfter our <u>sins</u> : Nor reward us according to óur iníquities.
5. We have sínned with our fáthers : We have committed iniquity, wé have done wíckedly. *(Ps. 106i)*

Psalms. 6, 32, 38, 51, 102, 130, 143 (The Seven Penitential Psalms)
Gospel (at Morning Prayer). **Matthew 6:16-21**
Epistle (at Evening Prayer). **Joel 2:12-19**

Responsory.

℟. Seek ye the Lord whíle He máy be found: ‡ Call ye upon Hím while Hé

is near. ℟. Seek ye the Lord... ℣. Let the wicked forsake his way and the

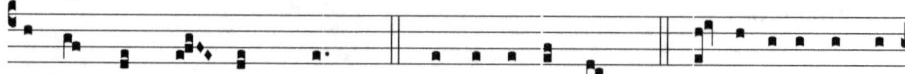

unríghteous mán his thoughts. ‡ Call ye upon Him... ℣. Glory be to the Fá-

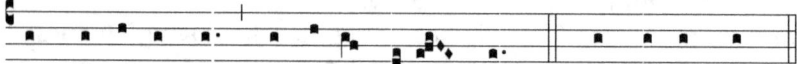

ther and tó the Son : and tó the Hó-ly Ghost. ℟. Seek ye the Lord...

℣. Create in us a clean heart, O God.
℟. And take not Thy Holy Spirit from us.
Antiphon for Benedictus. **Whére your tréasure is : there will your héart be álso.**

Antiphon for Magníficat.

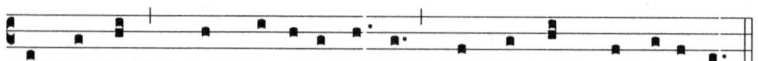

Thy Father, * which séeth in sécret : shall rewárd thee ópenly.

The Prayers: Include the Preces or the Litany (p. 577).

Collect (sung on one note). **Almighty and most merciful God, our heavenly Father, of whose compassion there is no end, who art long-suffering, gracious, and plenteous in goodness and truth, forgiving iniquity, transgression and sin, we have sinned and done perversely, we have forsaken and grievously offended Thee; against Thee, Thee only, have we sinned and done evil in Thy sight. But we beseech Thee, O Lord, remember not against us former iniquities; let Thy tender mercies speedily come to us, for we are brought very low; help us, O God of our salvation, and purge away our sins for the glory of Thy holy name and for the sake of Thy dear Son, Jesus Christ, our Savior, who liveth and reigneth with thee and the Holy Ghost : ever One God, world without end. Amen.

Anniversary of the Dedication of a Church

[382]

Invitatory.

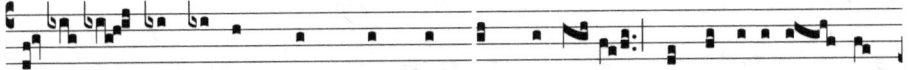

Ho-li- ness be-cometh thine house, O Lórd, for év-er : with a holy worship

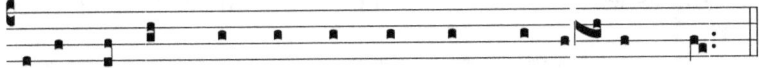

let us worship Christ the Lord, the Brídegroom óf the Church.

Antiphon for Psalms
1. The Lord is in His hóly témple : The Lord's thróne is in héaven.
2. Surely the Lórd is ín this place : This is none other but the house of God, and this is the gate of heaven, állelúia.
3. In all places where I record My name I will cóme unto <u>thee</u> : And bléss thee, sáith your God.
4. The sparrow hath found an house and the swallow a nest for herself, where shé may láy her young : Even Thine altars, O Lord of hosts, my King and my God, állelúia.

Psalms. **93, 138, 84, 46, 111, 99, 122, 132, 2, 21**
Gospel (at Morning Prayer). **Luke 19:1-10**
Epistle (at Evening Prayer). **Revelation 21:1-5**

Responsory.

℞ When the temple was ded-i-ca-ted the péople sang práises. ‡ And sweet

in their mouths wás the sóund thereof. ℞ When the temple... ℣ The

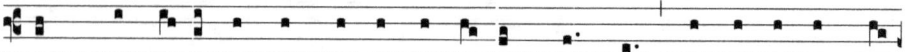

Lord's house is es-tablished in the top of the mountains, and all nations sháll

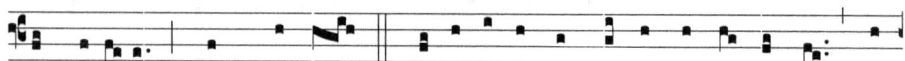

flow únto it. ‡ And sweet in... ℣ Glory be to the Fáther and tó the Son : and

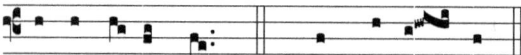

tó the Hóly Ghost. ℞ When the temple...

Hymn. **Urbs beata Jerusalem.** *c. 7th cent., trans. by J. M. Neale, alt.*

1. Blessed city, heavenly Salem, / Vision dear of peace and love, / Who of living stones art build-ed / In the height of heaven above, / And, with angel hosts encircled, / As a bride dost earthward move;
2. From celestial realms descending, / Bridal glory round thee shed, / Meet for Him whose love espoused thee, / To thy Lord shalt thou be led; / All thy streets and all thy bulwarks / Of pure gold are fashion-ed.
3. Bright thy gates of pearl are shining; / They are open evermore; / And by virtue of His merits / Thither faithful souls do soar, / Who for Christ's dear Name in this world / Pain and tribulation bore.
4. Many a blow and biting sculpture / Polished well those stones elect, / In their places now compacted / By the heavenly Architect, / Who therewith

hath willed for ever / That his palace should be decked.
5. Laud and honor to the Father, / Laud and honor to the Son, / Laud and honor to the Spirit, / Ever Three, and ever One, / Consubstantial, coeternal, / While unending ages run. Amen.

℣. Thy testimonies are very sure, (alleluia).
℟. Holiness becometh Thine house, O Lord, forever, (alleluia).

Antiphon for Benedictus.
Zacchaeus, make háste, and come <u>down</u> : for today I must abíde at thy <u>house</u>.
And he made haste, and came down, and received Him joyfully ínto his <u>house</u> : This day is salvation come to this hóuse from the <u>Lord</u>. [383]

Antiphon for Magnificat.

Sure-ly * the Lórd is ín this place : This is none other but the house of God,

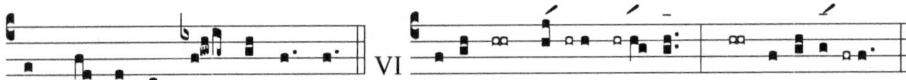

and this is the gáte of héaven.

Collect. Lord God, heavenly Father, the unfailing Giver òf good gifts : we thank Thee that Thou this day didst enter into this house with Thy Word; and we heartily beseech Thee continually to dwell among us with Thy Word and Thy Sacràments, so that by Thy grace we poor sinners may be converted unto Thee and saved eternally; through Jesus Christ, thy Son, oùr Lord, who liveth and reigneth with thee and the Hòly Ghost : ever One God, world without end. Amen.

Commemoration of the Dead

Invitatory.

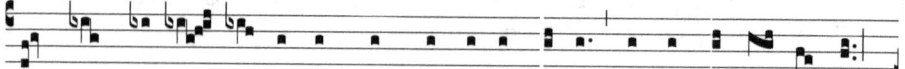

The Lord, the God not of the dead but of the living, for áll live ún- to Him :

O cóme, let us wórship Him.

Antiphons for Psalms

1. God shall wipe away all tears from their eyes; † and there shall be no more death, neither sorrow nor crying, neither shall there be ány more pain : for the former thíngs are pássed away.
2. If we believe that Jesus died and rose again, even so them also which sleep in Jesus will Gód bring wíth Him : Wherefore sorrow not even as óthers which háve no hope.
3. We have here no continuing city, álleluía : But we seek one to come, álleluía.
4. None of us liveth to himself, and no man díeth tó himself : Whether we live therefore or díe, we áre the Lord's.

Psalms. 130, 90, 23, 27, 34, 42, 73, 84, 91, 103, 116, 121, 126, 139, 146
Gospel (at Morning Prayer). John 14:1-6
Epistle (at Evening Prayer). 1 Peter 1:3-9

Responsory.

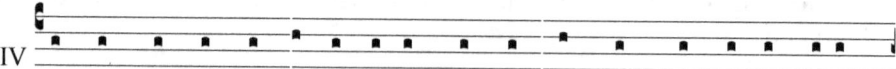
IV

℟. I know that my Redeemer liveth, and that He shall stand at the latter

dáy upón the earth: ‡ And in my flésh shall Í see God. ℟. I know that...

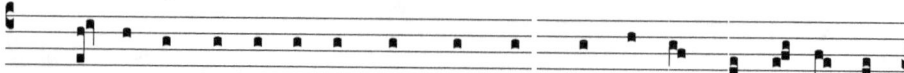

℣. Whom I shall see for myself, and mine eyes shall behold, and nót an-óth-

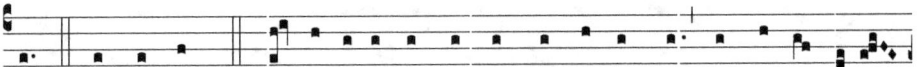

er. ‡ And in my... ℣. Glory be to the Father and to the Son and to the Holy

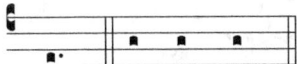

Ghost. ℟. I know that...

Hymn. From 27th Sunday after Trinity (p. 504).
℣. Blessed are the dead which die in the Lord, alleluia.
℟. They rest from their labors, and their works do follow them, alleluia.
Antiphon for Benedictus. He that goeth forth and weepeth, béaring précious seed : shall doubtless come again with rejoicing, brínging his shéaves with him.

Antiphon for Magnificat.

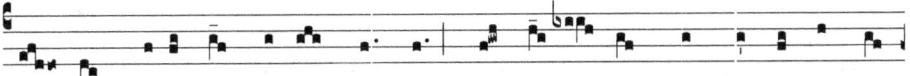

Oh, how glo-ri-ous * is that kingdom wherein all the saints dó rejóice with

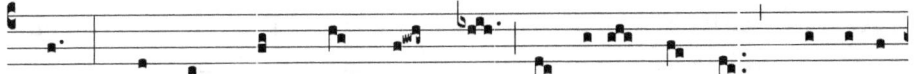

Christ! : They are clothed with white robes and follow the Lamb whitherso-

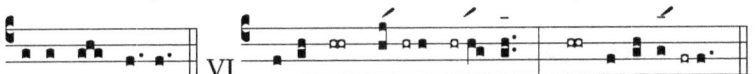

éver He góeth.

Collect. Almighty God, with whom do live the spirits of those who depart hence in the Lord, and with whom the souls of the faithful, after they are [384] delivered from the burden of the flesh, are in joy and felìcity : We give Thee hearty thanks for Thy grace bestowed upon Thy servants, who, having finished their course in faith, do now rest from their labòrs; and we beseech Thee that we, with all who have departed in the true faith of Thy holy Name, may have our perfect consummation and bliss, both in body and soul, in Thine eternal glory; through Jesus Christ, thy Son, oùr Lord, who liveth and reigneth with thee and the Hòly Ghost : ever One God, world without end. Amen.

The Seven Penitential Psalms with the Great Litany

Before this devotion is begun, it must be determined whether one Psalm, a selection, or all the Psalms are to be prayed. The antiphon is sung before the Psalmody and after each Psalm.

Antiphon for the Penitential Psalms

O Lord, * deal not with us after our sins, nor reward us according to our

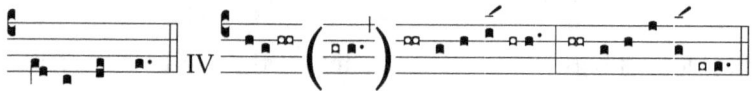

in-i-quities.

Psalm 6 *Domine, ne in furore*
1 O LORD, rebuke me not / ín thine ánger, * neither chasten me in / thy hót displéasure.
2 Have mercy upon me, O / LÓRD; for Í am weak: * O LORD, heal / me; fór my bónes are vexed.
3 My soul is ál- / so sore <u>vexed</u>: * - / but thóu, O LÓRD, how long?
4 Return, O LORD, delív- / er my <u>soul</u>: * oh save / me fór thy mércies' sake.
5 For in death there is no remém- / brance of <u>thee</u>: * in the / grave whó shall gíve thee thanks?
6 I am weary with my groaning; † all the night make / Í my béd to swim; * I water my / cóuch with my <u>tears</u>.
7 Mine eye is con- / súmed becáuse of grief; * it waxeth old because / of áll mine énemies.

570

8 Depart from me, all ye workers / óf iníquity; * for the LORD hath heard the / vóice of my wéeping.
9 The LORD hath heard my / súpplicátion; * the / LÓRD will recéive my prayer.
10 Let all mine enemies be ashámed / and sore <u>vexed</u>: * let them return and / bé ashamed súddenly.
Glory be to the Fá- / ther and tó the Son * - / and tó the Hóly Ghost.
As it was in the beginning, is now, and / éver sháll be, * - / wórld without énd. Amen.

Antiphon repeated

Psalm 32 *Beati quorum*
1 Bless-ed is he whose transgression / ís forgíven, * - / whose sín is cóvered.
2 Bless-ed is the man unto whom the LORD imputeth / nót iníquity, * and in whose / spírit there ís no guile.
3 When / Í kept sílence, * my bones waxed old through my roaring / áll the day <u>long</u>.
4 For day and night thy hand was héav- / y upón me: * my moisture is turned into / the dróught of súmmer.
5 I acknowledged my sín / unto <u>thee</u>, * and mine ini- / quitý have Í not hid.
I said, I will confess my transgressions ún- / to the <u>LORD</u>; * and thou forgavest the in- / íquity óf my sin.
6 For this shall every one that is godly pray unto thee in a time when thou máy- / est be <u>found</u>: * surely in the floods of great waters they shall not come / nígh unto <u>him</u>.
7 Thou art my híding place; † thou shalt preserve / mé from tróuble; * thou shalt compass me about with / sóngs of delíverance. [386]
8 I will instruct thee and teach thee in the / wáy which thóu shalt go: * I / will guíde thee wíth mine eye.
9 Be ye not as the horse, or as the mule, which have no / únderstánding: * whose mouth must be held in with bit and bridle, lest they come / néar unto <u>thee</u>.
10 Many sorrows shall bé / to the wícked: * but he that trusteth in the LORD, mercy / shall cómpass hím about.
11 Be glad in the LORD, and re- / jóice, ye ríghteous: * and shout for joy, all ye that are / úpright in <u>heart</u>.
Glory be to the Fá- / ther and tó the Son * - / and tó the Hóly Ghost.
As it was in the beginning, is now, and / éver sháll be, * - / wórld without énd. Amen.

Antiphon repeated

Psalm 38 *Domine, ne in furore*

1 O LORD, rebuke me nót / in thy <u>wrath</u>: * neither chasten me in / thy hót displéasure.
2 For thine ár- / rows stick fást in me, * and thy hand / présseth me <u>sore</u>.
3 There is no soundness in my flesh becáuse / of thine ánger; * neither is there any rest in my bones be- / cáuse of my <u>sin</u>.
4 For mine iniquities are gone óv- / er mine <u>head</u>: * as an heavy burden they are too / héavy for <u>me</u>.
5 My wounds / stínk and áre corrupt * be- / cáuse of my fóolishness.
6 I am troubled; I am / bówed down gréatly; * I go mourning / áll the day <u>long</u>.
7 For my loins are filled with a lóath- / some di<u>sease</u>: * and there is / no sóundness ín my flesh.
8 I am feeble / ánd sore bróken: * I have roared by reason of the dis- / quíetness óf my heart.
9 Lord, all my desíre / is befóre thee; * and my groan- / ing ís not híd from thee.
10 My heart panteth, / mý strength fáileth me: * as for the light of mine eyes, it / álso is góne from me.
11 My lovers and my friends stand alóof / from my <u>sore</u>; * and my kins- / men stánd afár off.
12 They also that seek after my life lay snáres for me: † and they that seek my hurt speak mís- / chievous <u>things</u>, * and imagine deceits / áll the day <u>long</u>.
13 But I, as a / déaf man, héard not; * and I was as a dumb man that / ópeneth nót his mouth.
14 Thus I was as a / mán that héareth not, * and in / whose móuth are nó reproofs.
15 For in thee, O LÓRD, / do I <u>hope</u>: * thou / wilt héar, O Lórd my God.
16 For I said, Hear me, lest otherwise they should rejóice / over <u>me</u>: * when my foot slippeth, they magnify / themsélves agáinst me.
17 For I am réad- / y to <u>halt</u>, * and my sorrow is contin- / u*all*ý befóre me.
18 For I will declare / míne iníquity; * I will / be sórry fór my sin.
19 But mine enemies are líve- / ly, and théy are strong: * and they that hate me wrong- / fullý are múltiplied.
20 They also that render evil for good are mine / ádversáries; * because I follow / the thíng that góod is.
21 Forsake me nôt, O LORD: † O my God, / bé not fár from me. * 22 Make haste to help me, O / Lord mý salvátion.

Glory be to the Fá- / ther and tó the Son * - / and tó the Hóly Ghost.
As it was in the beginning, is now, and / éver sháll be, * - / wórld without énd. Amen.

Antiphon repeated
Psalm 51 *Miserere mei*
1 Have mercy upon me, O God, according to thy / lóvingkíndness: * according unto the multitude of thy tender mercies blot / out mý transgréssions.
2 Wash me thoroughly from / míne iníquity, * - / and cléanse me fróm my sin.
3 For I acknowledge / mý transgréssions: * and my sin is / éver befóre me.
4 Against thee, thee only, have I sinned, and done this / évil ín thy sight: * that thou mightest be justified when thou speakest, and be / clear whén thou júdgest.
5 Behold, I was shapen / ín iníquity; * and in sin did my / móther concéive me.
6 Behold, thou desirest truth / ín the ínward parts: * and in the hidden part thou shalt make / mé to know wísdom.
7 Purge me with hyssop, and Í / shall be <u>clean</u>: * wash me, and I shall be / whíter than <u>snow</u>.
8 Make me to hear / jóy and gládness; * that the bones which thou / hast bróken máy rejoice.
9 Hide thy fáce / from my <u>sins</u>, * and blot out / áll mine iníquities.
10 Create in mé / a clean héart, O God; * and renew a right / spírit withín me.
11 Cast me not awáy / from thy présence; * and take not thy ho- / ly spírit fróm me.
12 Restore unto me the joy of / thý salvátion; * and uphold me / with thý free spírit.
13 Then will I teach transgrés- / sors thy <u>ways</u>; * and sinners shall be / convérted únto thee.
14 Deliver me from bloodguiltiness, O God, thou God of / mý salvátion: * and my tongue shall sing a- / lóud of thy ríghteousness.
15 O Lord, / ópen thóu my lips; * and my / mouth shall shew fórth thy praise.
16 For thou desirest not sacrifice; élse / would I gíve it: * thou delightest / nót in burnt óffering.
17 The sacrifices of God are a / bróken spírit: * a broken and a contrite heart, O / God, thóu wilt nót despise.
18 Do good in thy good pleasure / únto Zíon: * build thou the / wálls of Jerúsalem.
19 Then shalt thou be pleased with the sacrifices of ríghteousness, † with burnt offering and / whóle burnt óffering: * then shall they offer bullocks / upón thine áltar.

Glory be to the Fá-/ ther and tó the Son * -/ and tó the Hóly Ghost.
As it was in the beginning, is now, and / éver sháll be, * - / wórld without énd. Amen.

Antiphon repeated
Psalm 102 *Domine, exaudi*
1 Hear my prayer, O LORD, and let my / crý come únto thee. * 2 Hide not thy face from me in the day when / Í am in tróuble;
Incline thine éar / unto <u>me</u>: * in the day when I call / ánswer me spéedily.
3 For my dáys / are consúmed like smoke, * and my bones are / búrned as an <u>hearth</u>.
4 My heart is smitten, and with- / ered like <u>grass</u>; * so that I / forgét to éat my bread.
5 By reason of the vóice / of my gróaning * my bones / cléave to my <u>skin</u>.
6 I am like a pelican of the wílderness: † I am like an ówl / of the désert. * 7 I watch, and am as a sparrow alone / upón the hóuse top.
8 Mine enemies re- / próach me áll the day; * and they that are mad against me / are swórn agáinst me.
9 For I have eaten ásh- / es like <u>bread</u>, * and mingled / my drínk with wéeping,
10 Because of thine indig- / nátion ánd thy wrath: * for thou hast lifted / me úp, and cást me down.
11 My days are like a shadow / thát declíneth; * and I am / wíthered like <u>grass</u>.
12 But thou, O LORD, shalt en- / dúre for éver; * and thy remembrance unto / all generátions.
13 Thou shalt arise, and have mercy / upón Zíon: * for the time to favour her, yea, the / sét time, is <u>come</u>.
14 For thy servants take / pléasure ín her stones, * and / fávour the dúst thereof.
15 So the heathen shall fear the náme / of the <u>LORD</u>, * and all the kings of / the éarth thy glóry.
16 When the LORD shall / búild up Zíon, * he shall ap- / péar in his glóry.
17 He will regard the práyer / of the destítute, * - / and nót despíse their prayer.
18 This shall be written for the generá- / tion to <u>come</u>: * and the people which shall be cre- / áted shall práise the LORD.
19 For he hath looked down from the height of his / sánctuáry; * from heaven did / the LÓRD behóld the earth;
20 To hear the groaning / óf the prísoner; * to loose those that are ap- / póinted to <u>death</u>;
21 To declare the name of the / LÓRD in Zíon, * and his / práise in

Jerúsalem;
22 When the people are gáth- / ered togéther, * and the / kíngdoms, to sérve the LORD.
23 He weakened my stréngth / in the way; * he / shórtened my days.
24 I said, O my God, take me not away in the mídst / of my days: * thy years are throughout / all génerátions.
25 Of old hast thou laid the foun- / dátion óf the earth: * and the heavens are the / wórk of thy hands.
26 They shall perish, but thóu / shalt endure: * yea, all of them shall wax / old líke a gárment;
As a vesture / shált thou chánge them, * and / théy shall be changed:
27 But thóu / art the same, * and / thy yéars shall háve no end.
28 The children of thy servants / sháll contínue, * and their seed shall be es- / táblished befóre thee.
Glory be to the Fá- / ther and tó the Son * - / and tó the Hóly Ghost.
As it was in the beginning, is now, and / éver sháll be, * - / wórld without énd. Amen.

Antiphon repeated
Psalm 130 *De profundis*
1 Out of the depths have I cried / únto thée, O LORD. * 2 Lord, hear my voice: let thine ears be attentive to the voice of / my súpplicátions.
3 If thou, LORD, shouldest / márk iníquities, * - / - Ó Lord, whó shall stand? [389]
4 But there is forgíve- / ness with thee, * that thou / máy- / est be feared.
5 I wait for the / LÓRD, my sóul doth wait, * and in his / wórd do I hope.
6 My soul waiteth for the Lord more than they that wátch / for the mórning: * I say, more than they that / wátch for the mórning.
7 Let Israel hope in the LORD: † for with the LÓRD / there is mércy, * and with him is / plénteous redémption.
8 And he sháll / redeem Ísrael * from / áll his iníquities.
Glory be to the Fá- / ther and tó the Son * - / and tó the Hóly Ghost.
As it was in the beginning, is now, and / éver sháll be, * - / wórld without énd. Amen.

Antiphon repeated
Psalm 143 *Domine, exaudi*
1 Hear my prayer, O LORD, give ear to my / súpplicátions: * in thy faithfulness answer me, / and ín thy ríghteousness.
2 And enter not into judgment / wíth thy sérvant: * for in thy sight shall no man / líving be jústified.
3 For the enemy hath persecút- / ed my soul; * he hath smitten my life / dówn to the ground;

He hath made me to / dwéll in dárkness, * as those / that háve been lóng dead.

4 Therefore is my spirit over- / whélmed withín me; * my heart with- / ín me is désolate.

5 I remember the dâys of old; † I medi- / táte on áll thy works; * I muse on the / wórk of thy <u>hands</u>.

6 I stretch forth my hánds / unto <u>thee</u>: * my soul thirsteth after / thee, ás a thírsty land.

7 Hear me speedily, O LORD: my / spírit fáileth: * hide not thy face from me, lest I be like unto them that go down / ínto the <u>pit</u>.

8 Cause me to hear thy lovingkindness / ín the mórning; * for in / thée do I <u>trust</u>:

Cause me to know the way whereín / I should <u>walk</u>; * for I lift up my / sóul unto <u>thee</u>.

9 Deliver me, O LORD, / fróm mine énemies: * I flee un- / to thée to híde me.

10 Teach me to do thy will; for thóu / art my <u>God</u>: * thy spirit is good; lead me into / the lánd of úprightness.

11 Quicken me, O LORD, / fór thy náme's sake: * for thy righteousness' sake bring my / sóul out of tróuble.

12 And of thy mercy cut off mine ênemies, † and destroy all them / thát afflíct my soul: * for / Í am thy sérvant.

Glory be to the Fá-/ ther and tó the Son * -/ and tó the Hóly Ghost.

As it was in the beginning, is now, and / éver shálll be, * -/ wórld without énd. Amen.

Antiphon repeated

[390]

The Lection

Sit.

L: A reading from Hosea, the 14th chapter.

Thus saith the Lord: O Israel, return unto the LORD thy God; for thou hast fallen by thine iniquity. 2 Take with you words, and turn to the LORD: say unto him, Take away all iniquity, and receive us graciously / so will we render the calves of our lips. 3 Asshur shall not save us; we will not ride upon horses / neither will we say any more to the work of our hands, Ye are our gods: for in thee the fatherless findeth mercy. 4 I will heal their backsliding, I will love them freely: for mine anger is turned away from him. 5 I will be as the dew unto Israel: he shall grow as the lily, and cast forth his roots as Lebanon. 6 His branches shall spread, and his beauty shall be as the olive tree; and his smell as Lebanon. 7 They that dwell under his shadow shall return; they shall revive as the corn, and grow as the vine / the scent thereof shall be as the wine of Lebanon. 8 Ephraim shall say, What have I to do any more with idols? I have heard him, and observed him: I am like a green fir tree. From me is thy fruit found. 9 Who is wise, and he shall understand these things? prudent, and he shall know them? for the ways of the LORD are right; and the just shall walk in them / but the transgressors shall fall therein.

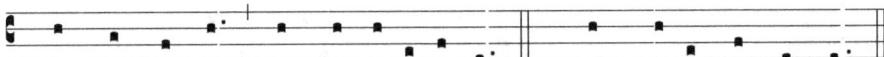

L: But Thou, O Lord, have mercy upon us. *A:* Thanks be to Thee, O Lord!

Responsory (C., S., A.)

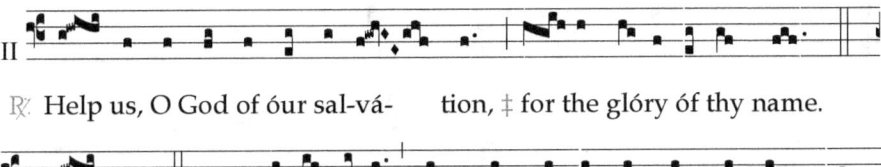

℟ Help us, O God of óur sal-vá- tion, ‡ for the glóry óf thy name.

℟ Help us... ℣ And de-liv-er us, and purge away our sins, fór thy náme's

sake. ‡ For the glory... ℣ Glory be to the Fáther and tó the Son : and tó the

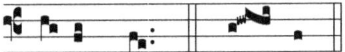

Hóly Ghost. ℟ Help us...

The Great Litany [391]

(O., A.) The responses (℟) may be repeated after each versicle (℣) or repeated only after each section as printed below. If the responses are repeated only after each section (as printed), then the officiant sings the versicles on one note, only singing the termination on the versicle directly preceding the response.

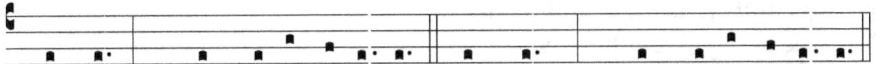

℣ O Lord, ℟ Have mercy upon us. ℣ O Christ, ℟ Have mercy upon us.

577

℣. O Lord, ℟. Have mercy upon us. ℣. O Christ, ℟. Hear Thou us.

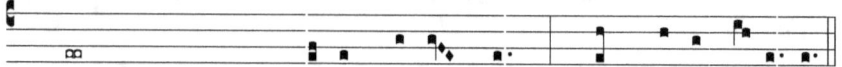

℣. O God the / Father in heav-en, ℟. Have mercy upon us.
℣. O God the Son, Re-/ deemer of the world, ℟. Have mercy upon us.
℣. O / God the Ho- ly Ghost, ℟. Have mercy upon us.

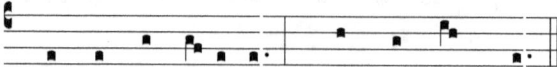

℣. Be gracious unto us. ℟. Spare us, good Lord.
℣. Be gracious unto us. ℟. Help us, good Lord.

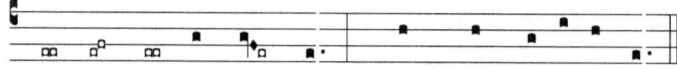

℣.   - / From all- sin; ℟. Good Lord, de-liv-er us.
℣.   From / all er- ror; ℟. Good Lord, de-liv-er us.
℣.   From / all e- vil: ℟. Good Lord, de-liv-er us.

℣. From the crafts and assáults of / the dev-il;
℣. From sudden / and evil death;
℣. From pestilence / and fam-ine;
℣. From war / and blood-shed;
℣. From sedition and / rebel-lion;
℣. From lightning / and tem-pest;
℣. From all calámity by fire / and wa-ter;
℣. And from ev- / erlasting death: ℟. Good Lord, deliver us.

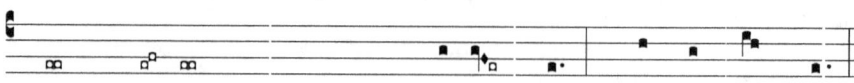

℣. By the mýstery of Thy holy in- / carna- tion; ℟. Help us, good Lord.
℣. By Thy holy / nativity;
℣. By Thy baptism, fasting, and / tempta-tion;
℣. By Thine agony / and bloody sweat;
℣. By Thy cross / and Pas-sion;
℣. By Thy precious death / and burial;
℣. By Thy glorious resurréction and / ascen-sion;

℣. And by the cóming of the Holy Ghost, / the Comforter:
℣. In all time of our trib- / ula-tion;
℣. In all time of our / prosperity;
℣. In / the hour of death;
℣. And in the day / of Judg-ment: ℟. Help us, good Lord.

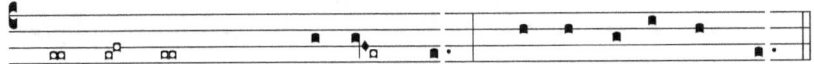

℣. We póor sinners do / beseech- Thee: ℟. To hear us, O Lord God,

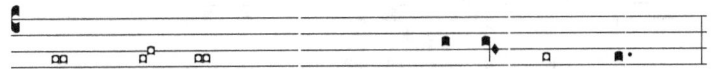

℣. And to rúle and govern Thy ho-/ly Christian Church;

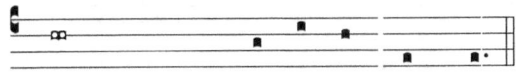

℟. We beseech Thee to hear us, good Lord.
℣. To presérve all pastors and ministers of Thy Church in the true knowledge and understanding of Thy Word and in ho- / liness of life;
℣. To put an énd to all schisms and caus- / es of offense;
℣. To bríng into the way of truth all such as have erred / and are deceived;
℣. To béat down Satan un- / der our- feet;
℣. To sénd faithful laborers into / Thy har-vest;
℣. To accómpany Thy Word with Thy Spir- / it and- grace;
℣. To ráise up them that fall and to strengthen such / as do- stand;
℣. And to cómfort and help the weakhearted and / the dis-tressed: ℟. We beseech Thee to hear us, good Lord.

℣. To gíve to all nations peace / and con-cord;
℣. To presérve our country from discord and / conten-tion;
℣. To gíve to our nation perpetual victory over all / its enemies;
℣. To direct and defénd our [President] and all in / authority;
℣. And to bless and kéep our magistrates and all / our peo-ple: ℟. We beseech Thee to hear us, good Lord.

℣. To behold and hélp all who are in danger, necessity, and trib- / ula-tion;
℣. To protect all / who trav-el;
℣. To presérve all women in the perils / of child-birth;
℣. To strengthen and kéep all sick persons and / young child-ren;
℣. To set frée all who are innocently / impris-oned;
℣. To defend and províde for all fatherless children / and wid-ows;

[393]

℣. And to have mércy / upon all men: ℟. We beseech Thee to hear us, good Lord.

℣. To forgíve our enemies, persecutors, and slanderers, and / to turn their hearts;
℣. To give and presérve to our use the fruits / of the- earth;
℣. And graciously / to hear our prayers: ℟. We beseech Thee to hear us, good Lord.

℣. O Lord Jésus Christ, / Son of- God, ℟. We beseech Thee to hear us.

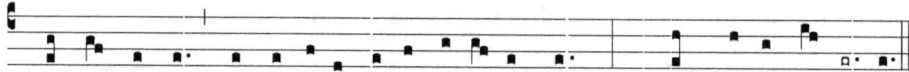

℣. O Lamb of God, that takest away the sin of the world, ℟. Have mercy up-on us.
℣. O Lamb of God, that takest away the sin of the world, ℟. Have mercy up-on us.
℣. O Lamb of God, that takest away the sin of the world, ℟. Grant us- Thy peace.

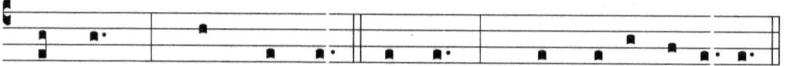

℣. O Christ, ℟. Hear Thou us. ℣. O Lord, ℟. Have mercy upon us.

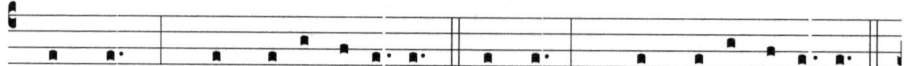

℣. O Christ, ℟. Have mercy upon us. ℣. O Lord, ℟. Have mercy upon us.

A. A- men.

(Then shall the officiant, and the congregation with him, say the Lord's Prayer, after which may be said one or more of the Litany Collects here following.)

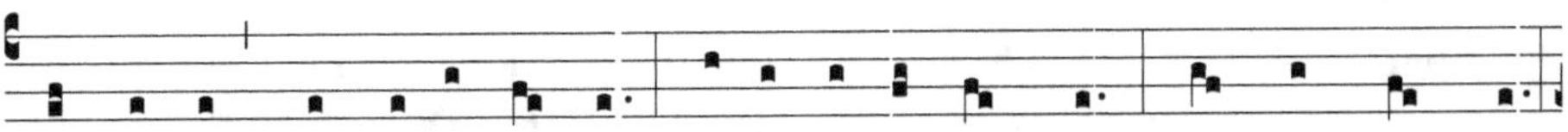

Our Father * who art in heaven, Hallowed be Thy name, Thy kingdom come,

Thy will be done on earth as it is in heaven, Give us this day our daily bread,

And forgive us our trespasses as we forgive those who trespass against us,

[394]

And lead us not into temptation, But de-liv-er us ✠ from e-vil. For thine is

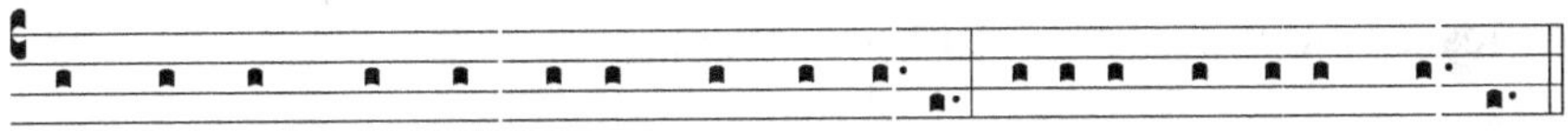

the kingdom, and the power, and the glory, forever and ever. Amen.

Litany Collects
1

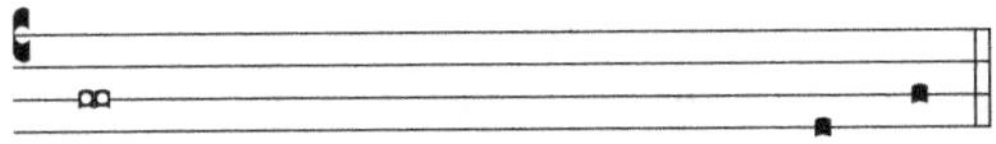

℣. O Lord, deal not with us after our <u>sins</u>.

℟ **Neither reward us according to our inîquities.**
O: Let us pray. Almighty God, our heavenly Father, who desirest not the death of a sinner, but rather that he should turn from his evil wày and live : we beseech Thee graciously to turn from us those punishments which we by our sins have desèrved, and to grant us grace ever hereafter to serve Thee in holiness and pureness of living; through Jesus Christ, Thy Son, oùr Lord, who liveth and reigneth with Thee and the Hòly Ghost : ever one God, world without end. **Amen.**

2

℣. Help us, O God of our salvation, for the glory ôf Thy name.
℟. **Deliver us and purge away our sins for Thy name's sake.**
O: Let us pray. Almighty and everlasting God, who by Thy Holy Spirit dost govern and sanctify the whole Chrìstian Church : hear our prayers for all members of the sàme, and mercifully grant that by Thy grace they may serve Thee in true faith; through Jesus Christ, Thy Sòn, our Lord. **Amen.**

3

℣. O Lord, deal not with us after our <u>sins</u>.
℟. **Neither reward us according to our inîquities.**
O: Let us pray. O God, merciful Father, who despisest not the sighing of a contrite heart nor the desire of such às are sorrowful : mercifully assist our prayers which we make before Thee in all our troubles and adversities, whensoever they oppress us, and graciously hear ùs, that those evils which the craft and subtlety of the devil or man worketh against us may by Thy good providence be brought to naught, that we, Thy servants, being hurt by no persecutions, may evermore give thanks unto Thee in Thy holy Church; through Jesus Christ, Thy Sòn, our Lord: **Amen.**

4

℣. O Lord, enter not into judgment with Thy servant.
℟. **For in Thy sight shall no man living be jûstified.**
O: Let us pray. Almighty God, who knowest us to be set in the midst of so many and great dangers that by reason of the frailty of our nature we cannot always stand upright : grant us such strength and protections as may support us in all dangèrs, and carry us through all temptations; through Jesus Christ, Thy Sòn, our Lord. **Amen.**

℣. Call upon Me in the day of trouble.
℟. **I will deliver thee, and thou shalt glorify <u>Me</u>.**

O: Let us pray. Spare us, O Lord, and mercifully forgive ùs our sins : and though by our continual transgressions we have merited Thy punìshments, be gracious unto us and grant that all those evils which we have deserved may be turned from us and overruled to our everlasting good; through Jesus Christ, Thy Son, oùr Lord, who liveth and reigneth with Thee and the Hòly Ghost : ever one God, world without end.

Amen.

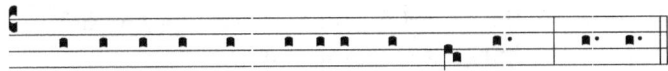

O: The almighty and merciful Lord hear us. *A:* Amen.

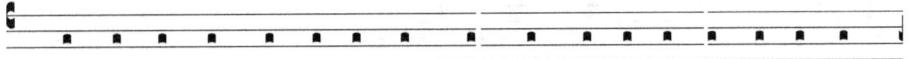

O: The God of grace and forgiveness bless and protect us: the Father, the ✠

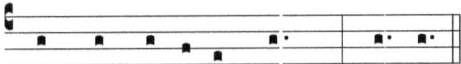

Son, and the Holy Ghost. *O:* Amen.

Litany of the Holy Sacrament of the Altar

Appropriate for use as The Prayers at Saturday or Sunday Vespers in non-festival seasons.

℣. Kyr- i- e ℟. **e-le-i-son.**
℣. - Christ-e ℟. **e-le-i-son.**
℣. Kyr- i- e ℟. **e-le-i-son.**   ℣. O Christ ℟. **hear us.**

℣. God the / Fa- ther in heaven: ℟. **have mercy up-/on us.**
℣. God the Son, Re- / deemer of the world: ℟. **have mercy up-/on us.**
℣. God the / Ho- ly Spir- it: ℟. **have mercy up-/on us.**
℣. / Ho-ly Triune God: ℟. **have mercy up-/on us.**

℣. Christ, thou bread of life, Thou God and Man, Thou Hidden One, who / art in our midst:
℣. Thou Passover Lamb, Thou Sacrifice for the world, Thou Source of Grace, Thou our Food, / Thou- our Joy:
℣. Thou Healing of the sick, Thou Comfort of the mourning, Thou / Strength of the dying:
℣. Thou our Hope, / Thou Bread from heaven:
℣. Through Thy Body, sacrificed for us; through Thy Blood, shed for us; through this sign of Thy love / and fidelity:
℣. Through Thy resurrection and ascension, through Thy presence, / at Thy return:

℟. **help us, good Lord.**

℣. We poor sinners do be-seech thee: ℟. **to hear us, O Lord.**

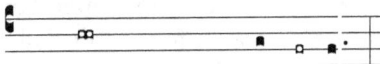

℣. That we become strong in faith, that we proclaim Thy death, that we

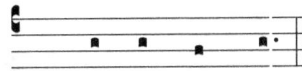

praise Thy re- / surrection:
℣. That we long for Thy Supper, that we be united at Thy Table, that none of us / betray thee:
℣. That we recognize Thy Way, that we go the Way in the power of Thy Food, that Thou lead us to the Marriage Feast of ev- / erlasting life:

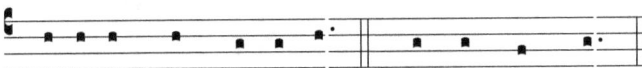

℟. **hear us, good Lord.**

℣. O Jesus Christ, Son of God: ℟. **hear us, good Lord.**

℣. O Lamb of God, that takest away the sin of the world, ℟. **have mercy up-on us.**
℣. O Lamb of God, that takest away the sin of the world, ℟. **have mercy up-on us.**
℣. O Lamb of God, that takest away the sin of the world, ℟. **grant us Thy peace.**

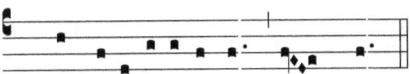

℣. O Christ ℟. **hear us.**   ℣. Kyr- i- e ℟. **e-le-i-son.**
                    ℣. - Christ-e ℟. **e-le-i-son.**

A. **Kyr-i-e e-le-i-son. A- men.**

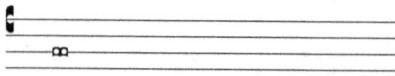

Our Father * who art in heaven...

℣. He has granted us a remembrance of His wonders.
℟. **The Lord is gracious and full of compassion.**
℣. Let us pray. O Lord Jesus Christ, who hast left to us the Mystery of Thy Sacrament and hast commanded, as often as we celebrate it, to remembèr Thy suffering : help us to receive Thy Body and Blood with fàith, and daily to live from the power of Thy redemption; who livest and reignest with the Father and the Hòly Ghost : ever one God, world without end.
℟. **Amen.**

Vespers continues with The Collect for the Day, other Collects, and the Collect for Peace (p. 61).

The Itinerarium
(Prayer Before Travel)

Antiphon

In the way of peace * ánd prospér-i-ty : the al-mighty and mer-ci-ful Lórd

diréct us. His holy angel accompany ús on the way : that in peace, in safe-

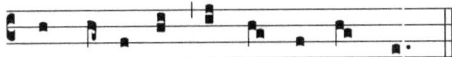

ty, and in joy we máy return home.

VII

Luke 1:68-79 *Benedictus*

☩ |Bless|-ed be the Lord / Gód of Ísrael; * for he hath visited and re- / déemed his péople,

|And| hath raised up an horn of sal- / vátion fór us * in the house of his / sérvant Dávid;

|As| he spake by the mouth of his / hóly próphets, * which have been / sínce the wórld began:

|That| we should be saved / fróm our énemies, * and from the hand of / áll that háte us;

|To| perform the mercy promised / tó our fáthers, * and to remember his / hóly cóvenant;

|The| oath which he sware to our / fáther Ábraham, * that he would / gránt unto us,

|That| we being delivered out of the / hánd of our énemies * might serve / hím without fear,

|In| holiness and righteous- / néss befóre him, * all the / dáys of our life.

|And| thou, child, shalt be called the prophet / óf the Híghest: * for thou shalt go before the face of the / Lórd to prepáre his ways;

|To| give knowledge of salvation / únto his péople * by the re- / míssion óf their sins,

|Through| the tender / mércy óf our God; * whereby the dayspring from on high hath / vísited us,

|To| give light to them that sit in darkness and in the / shádow of <u>death</u>, *
  to guide our feet / ínto the wáy of peace.
|Glo-|ry be to the / Fáther and tó the Son * and / tó the Hóly Ghost.
|As| it was in the beginning, is now, and / éver sháll be, * - / wórld
  without énd. Amen.
Antiphon repeated.

[399]

The Prayers

(O., A.) Then shall be said or chanted the prayers here following. It is appropriate to kneel for the prayers. On Sundays, Feasts, and in Eastertide all may stand. The officiant intones up to the asterisk (*).

The Kyrie

Kyri-e ele-ison!   *   Christ-e ele-ison! Kyri-e ele-ison!

The Lord's Prayer

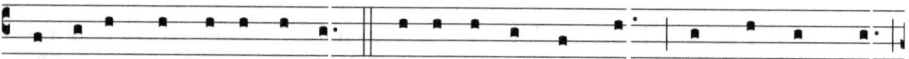

Our Father who art in heaven, * Hallowed be Thy name; Thy kingdom come;

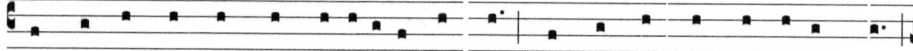

Thy will be done on earth as it is in heaven; Give us this day our daily bread;

And forgive us our trespasses, as we forgive those who trespass against us;

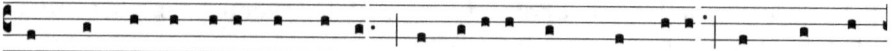

And lead us not into temptation; But deliver us ✠ from evil; For Thine is

the kingdom and the power and the glory forever and ever. Amen.

℣. O God, save thy ser-..vants:
℟. That trûst ....in ....thee.
℣. O Lord, send us help from the sanctua-.................................ry,
℟. And strengthen us out of Zi-...on;
℣. Be unto us, O Lord, a strong tow-..er,
℟. From the ên-..e-..........my.
℣. Let the enemy not exact upon ....us;
℟. Nor the son of wickedness afflict ....us.
℣. Bless-ed be the Lord dai-...ly,
℟. The God of our salvation grant us a safe jour-................ney.
℣. Show us Thy wâys, ...O....... Lord;
℟. Teach us ....Thy ......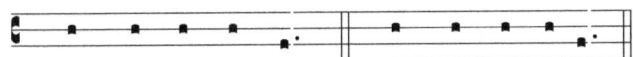paths.
℣. O that my ways were direct-..ed,
℟. To keep Thy sta-...tutes!
℣. The crooked shall be made ....straight,
℟. And the rough plâ-...ces ......plain.
℣. For he shall give his angels charge ô-.....................ver ......thee,
℟. To keep thee in âll ....thy .....ways.
℣. Hear my prâyer, ...O.......Lord.
℟. And let my cry come ûn-...to ....thee.

If the officiant is an ordained pastor, the Salutation shall be used. If a layman is serving as officiant, the Salutation shall be omitted.

[℣. The Lord be with you. ℟. And with thy spirit.]

℣. Let us pray. O God, who didst cause the Children of Israel to pass dry-shod through the midst of the sea and who by the leading of a star didst open to the Wise Men the way unto Thyself, grant to us, we beseech Thee, a prosperous journey and fair weather that, attended by Thy holy angel, we may happily arrive at that place whither we are going and finally attain to the haven of eternal salvation; where Thou livest and reignest with the Father and the Holy Ghost, ever one God world without end. ℟. Amen.

O God, who didst bring Abraham, Thy servant, from Ur of the Chaldees and didst keep him in safety through all the days of his pilgrimage, we beseech Thee that Thou wouldst protect Thy servants; be to us, O Lord, in setting forth our support, in the way a consolation, in heat a shadow, in rain and cold a covering, in weariness a chariot, in adversity a support, in slippery places a staff, in shipwreck a port that, Thou being our Leader, we may prosperously reach the place whither we go and at length return in safety to our home; through Jesus Christ our Lord. ℟ Amen.

[401] Assist us mercifully, O Lord, in these our supplications and prayer, and dispose the way of Thy servants towards the attainment of everlasting salvation that among all the changes and chances of this mortal life we may ever be defended by Thy most gracious and ready help; through Jesus Christ our Lord. ℟ Amen.

Grant, we beseech Thee, almighty God, that Thy family may walk in the way of salvation and, following the counsels of blessed John, the forerunner, may safely come to Him whom he foretold, Thy Son Jesus Christ, our Lord, who liveth and reigneth with Thee and the Holy Ghost, ever one God, world without end. ℟ Amen.

℣ Let us go fôrth in peace.
℟ In the name ✠ of the <u>Lord</u>.
 Amen.

Collects for All Occasions

General

Grant us, we beseech Thee, Almighty God, a steadfast faith in Jesus Christ, a cheerful hope in Thy mercy, and a sincere love to Thee and to all of our fellow men; through Jesus Christ, Thy Son, our Lord.

O Lord God, heavenly Father, we give Thee thanks that of Thy great goodness and mercy Thou didst allow Thine only-begotten Son to become incarnate and to redeem us from sin and everlasting death; and we beseech Thee to enlighten our hearts by Thy Holy Spirit that we may evermore give to Thee unending thanks for Thy grace and may comfort ourselves with the same in all time of tribulation and temptation; through the same Jesus Christ, Thy Son, our Lord.

Almighty God, who hast given us the commandment to pray for the gift of the Holy Ghost, most heartily we beseech Thee through Jesus Christ, our Advocate, to grant us Thy Holy Spirit that He may quicken our hearts by Thy saving Word and lead us into all truth, that He may guide, instruct, enlighten, govern, comfort, and sanctify us unto everlasting life; through the same Jesus Christ, Thy Son, our Lord.

Send, we beseech Thee, Almighty God, Thy Holy Spirit into our hearts that He may rule and direct us according to Thy will, comfort us in all our temptations and afflictions, defend us from all error, and lead us into all truth, that we, being steadfast in the faith, may increase in love and in all good works and in the end obtain everlasting life; through Jesus Christ, Thy

Son, our Lord.

Almighty God, our heavenly Father, who of Thy tender love toward us sinners hast given us Thy Son that, believing on Him, we might have everlasting life, grant us, we beseech Thee, Thy Holy Spirit that we may continue steadfast in this faith to the end and may come to everlasting life; through Jesus Christ, Thy Son, our Lord.

Almighty and everlasting God, who by Thy Son hast promised us forgiveness of sins and everlasting life, we beseech Thee so to rule and govern our hearts by Thy Holy Spirit that in our daily need, and especially in all time of temptation, we may seek help from Him and by a true and lively faith in Thy Word obtain the same; through Jesus Christ Thy Son, our Lord.

O Lord God, heavenly Father, we beseech Thee, let Thy Holy Spirit dwell in us that He may enlighten and lead us into all truth and evermore defend us from all adversities; through Jesus Christ, Thy Son, our Lord.

O Lord God, heavenly Father, who hast given Thine only Son to die for our sins and to rise again for our justification, quicken us, we beseech Thee, by Thy Holy Spirit, unto newness of life that through the power of His resurrection we may dwell with Christ forever; through the same Jesus Christ, Thy Son, our Lord.

[403] Almighty and ever-living God, who makest us both to will and to do those things which are good and acceptable unto Thy divine Majesty, let Thy fatherly hand, we beseech Thee, ever be over us; let Thy Holy Spirit ever be with us; and so lead us in the knowledge and obedience of Thy Word that in the end we may obtain everlasting life; through Jesus Christ, Thy Son, our Lord.

For the Church

Grant, we beseech Thee, Almighty God, unto Thy Church Thy Holy Spirit and the wisdom which cometh down from above that Thy Word may not be bound, but have free course and be preached to the joy and edifying of Christ's holy people, that in steadfast faith we may serve Thee and in the confession of Thy name abide unto the end; through Jesus Christ, Thy Son, our Lord.

Merciful God, we beseech Thee to cast the bright beams of Thy light upon Thy Church that, being instructed by the doctrine of the blessed Apostles, it may so walk in the light of Thy truth that it may at length attain to the light of everlasting life; through Jesus Christ, Thy Son, our Lord.

O God, our Protector, behold and look upon the face of Thine Anointed, who hath given Himself for the redemption of all, and grant that from the rising of the sun to the going down thereof Thy name may be great among the Gentiles and that in every place sacrifice and a pure offering may be made unto Thy name; through Jesus Christ, Thy Son, our Lord.

O Lord, favorably receive the prayers of Thy Church, that, being delivered from all adversity and error, it may serve Thee in safety and freedom; and grant us Thy peace in our time; through Jesus Christ, Thy Son, our Lord.

FOR THE CHILDREN OF THE CHURCH
Almighty and everlasting God, who wantest none of these little ones to perish and hast sent Thine only Son to seek and to save that which was lost and through Him hast said, Let the little children come to Me and do not forbid them, for of such is the kingdom of God; most heartily we beseech Thee so to bless and govern the children of Thy Church by Thy Holy Spirit that they may grow in grace and in knowledge of Thy Word; protect and defend them against all danger and harm, giving Thy holy angels charge over them; through Jesus Christ, Thy Son, our Lord.

FOR THE MINISTERS OF THE WORD
Almighty and everlasting God, who alone doest great wonders, send down upon Thy ministers and upon the congregations committed to their charge the healthful Spirit of Thy grace; and that they may truly please Thee, pour upon them the continual dew of Thy blessing through Jesus Christ, Thy Son, our Lord.

Almighty and gracious God, the Father of our Lord Jesus Christ, who hast commanded us to pray that Thou wouldest send forth laborers into Thy harvest, of Thine infinite mercy give us true teachers and ministers of Thy Word, and put Thy saving Gospel in their hearts and on their lips that they may truly fulfill Thy command and preach nothing contrary to Thy holy Word, that we, being warned, instructed, nurtured, comforted, and strengthened by Thy heavenly Word, may do those things which are well-pleasing to Thee and profitable to us; through Jesus Christ, Thy Son, our Lord. [404]

O almighty God, who by Thy Son, Jesus Christ, didst give to Thy holy Apostles many excellent gifts and commanded them earnestly to feed Thy flock, make, we beseech Thee, all pastors diligently to preach Thy holy Word and the people obediently to follow the same that they may receive the crown of everlasting glory; through Jesus Christ, Thy Son, our Lord.

For the Church in its Conflicts

Almighty and everlasting God, who wilt have all men to be saved and to come to the knowledge of the truth, we beseech Thy glorious majesty, through Jesus Christ, our Lord and Savior, impart the grace and help of Thy Holy Spirit to all ministers of Thy Word that they may purely teach it to the saving of men. Bring to naught by Thine almighty power and unsearchable wisdom all the counsels of those who hate Thy Word and who, by corrupt teaching or with violent hands, would destroy it, and enlighten them with the knowledge of Thy glory, that we, leading a quiet and peaceable life, may by a pure faith learn the riches of Thy heavenly grace and in holiness and righteousness serve Thee, the only true God; through Jesus Christ, Thy Son, our Lord.

Most gracious Father, we humbly beseech thee for thy holy catholic Church. Fill it with all truth, in all peace. Where it is corrupt, purify it; where it is in error, direct it; where anything is amiss, reform it; where it is right, strengthen and confirm it; where it is in want, provide for it; where it is divided and rent asunder, heal the breaches thereof, O thou Holy One of Israel; through Jesus Christ our Lord.

For Those Who Have Erred

Almighty God, our heavenly Father, whose attribute it is always to have mercy, we most earnestly beseech Thee to visit with Thy fatherly correction all such as have erred and gone astray from the truth of Thy holy Word and to bring them to a due sense of their error that they may again with a faithful heart receive and hold fast Thine unchangeable truth; through Jesus Christ, Thy Son, our Lord.

Almighty, merciful, and gracious God and Father, with our whole heart we beseech Thee for all who have forsaken the Christian faith, all who have wandered from any portion thereof or are in doubt or temptation through those who corrupt Thy Word, that Thou wouldest visit them as a Father, reveal unto them their error, and bring them back from their wanderings, that they, in singleness of heart, taking pleasure alone in the pure truth of

Thy Word, may be made wise thereby unto everlasting life through faith in Jesus Christ, Thy Son, our Lord.

FOR UNITY [405]

O God, who restorest to the right way them that err, who gatherest them that are scattered, and preservest them that are gathered, of Thy tender mercy we beseech Thee, pour upon Thy Christian people the grace of unity, that, all schisms being healed, Thy flock, united to the true Shepherd of Thy church, may worthily serve Thee; through Jesus Christ, Thy Son, our Lord.

FOR THE REMOVAL OF SCHISM

Bring to naught, O Christ, the schisms of heresy which seek to subvert Thy truth, that, as Thou art acknowledged in heaven and in earth as one and the same Lord, so Thy people, gathered from all nations, may serve Thee in unity of faith; through Jesus Christ, Thy Son, our Lord.

FOR THE JEWS

Almighty and everlasting God, who lovest to show mercy, hear the prayers which we offer unto Thee for Thine ancient people, that, acknowledging Jesus Christ, who is the Light of truth, they may be delivered from their darkness; through the same Jesus Christ, Thy Son, our Lord.

FOR THE HEATHEN

Almighty and everlasting God, who desirest not the death of a sinner, but wouldest have all men to repent and live, hear our prayers for the heathen, take away iniquity from their hearts, and turn them from their idols unto the living and true God and Thine only Son; and gather them into Thy holy Church, to the glory of Thy name; through the same Jesus Christ, Thy Son, our Lord.

FOR THE CIVIL AUTHORITIES

O merciful Father in heaven, who holdest in Thy hand all the might of man and who hast ordained the powers that be for the punishment of evildoers and for the praise of them that do well, and of whom is all rule and authority in the kingdoms of the world, we humbly beseech Thee, graciously regard Thy servants, [the President of the United States, the Governor of this state,] our Judges and magistrates, and all the rulers of the earth. May all that receive the sword as Thy ministers bear it according to Thy commandment. Enlighten and defend them by Thy name, O God. Grant them wisdom and understanding, that under their peaceable governance Thy people may be guarded and directed in righteousness, quietness, and unity. Protect and prolong their lives, O God of our salvation, that we with them may show forth the praise of Thy name; through Jesus Christ, Thy Son, our Lord.

For our Enemies
Forgive, we beseech Thee, O Lord, our enemies and them that despitefully use us, and so change their hearts that they may walk with us in meekness and peace; through Jesus Christ, Thy Son, our Lord.

[406] O almighty, everlasting God, who through Thine only Son, our blessed Lord, hast commanded us to love our enemies, to do good to them that hate us, and to pray for them that persecute us, we earnestly beseech Thee that by Thy gracious visitation they may be led to true repentance and may have the same love and be of one accord and of one mind and heart with us and with Thy whole Church; through the same Jesus Christ, Thy Son, our Lord.

In Time of National Calamity
O Lord God, heavenly Father, we humbly confess unto Thee that by our evil-doing and continual disobedience we have deserved these Thy chastisements; yet we earnestly beseech Thee, for Thy name's sake, to spare us; restrain the harmful power of the enemy and succor Thy suffering people that Thy Word may be declared faithfully and without hindrance and that we, amending our sinful lives, may walk obedient to Thy holy commandments; through Jesus Christ, Thy Son, our Lord.

Look mercifully, O Lord, we beseech Thee, on the affliction of Thy people, and let not our sin destroy us, but let Thine almighty mercy save us; through Jesus Christ, Thy Son, our Lord.

Most loving and gracious Lord God, who for our many grievous sins art justified to sorely punish us, we flee to Thy tender and fatherly compassion alone, beseeching Thee that, as a father pitieth his children, Thou wouldest pity us miserable sinners. Turn away Thy righteous wrath and give us not over to deserved death, but deliver us that we may now and evermore praise Thee, O gracious God and Father, who desirest not the death of a sinner, but rather that he may turn from his wickedness and live; through Jesus Christ, Thy Son, our Lord.

For Prisoners
Almighty God, who didst bring the Apostle Peter forth out of prison, have mercy upon all who are suffering unjust imprisonment and set them free from their bonds that we may rejoice in their deliverance and continually give praise to Thee; through Jesus Christ, Thy Son, our Lord.

FOR PEACE AND QUIETNESS
O Lord, we beseech Thee mercifully to hear the prayers of Thy church that we, being delivered from all adversities and serving Thee with a quiet mind, may enjoy Thy peace all the days of our life; through Jesus Christ, Thy Son, our Lord.

IN TIME OF AFFLICTION AND DISTRESS

Almighty and everlasting God, the Consolation of the sorrowful and the Strength of the weak, may the prayers of them that in any tribulation or distress cry to Thee, graciously come before Thee, so that in all their necessities they may mark and receive Thy manifold help and comfort; through Jesus Christ, Thy Son, our Lord.

Almighty and most merciful God, who hast appointed us to endure sufferings and death with our Lord Jesus Christ before we enter with Him into eternal glory, grant us grace at all times to subject ourselves to Thy holy will and to continue steadfast in the true faith unto the end of our lives and at all times to find peace and joy in the blessed hope of the resurrection of the dead and of the glory of the world to come; through Jesus Christ, Thy Son, our Lord. [407]

Almighty God, cast not away Thy people who cry to Thee in their tribulation, but for the glory of Thy name be pleased to help the afflicted; through Jesus Christ, Thy Son, our Lord.

FOR THE SICK
Almighty, everlasting God, the eternal Salvation of them that believe, hear our prayers in behalf of Thy servants who are sick, for whom we implore the aid of Thy mercy, that, being restored to health, they may render thanks to Thee in Thy church; through Jesus Christ, Thy Son, our Lord.

O Lord, look down from heaven, behold, visit, and relieve Thy servants for whom we offer our supplications; look upon them with the eyes of Thy mercy; give them comfort and sure confidence in Thee, defend them from the danger of the enemy, and keep them in perpetual peace and safety; through Jesus Christ, Thy Son, our Lord.

FOR MOTHERS
O almighty, everlasting God and Father, Creator of all things, who by Thy grace, through Thy Son, our Lord, who hath redeemed us from sin, makest

the anguish of our human birth a holy and salutary cross, we pray Thee, O gracious Father, Lord and God, that Thou wouldest preserve and guard the work of Thine own hand. Forsake not them who cry to Thee in sore travail, but deliver them out of all their pains, to their joy and to the glory of Thy goodness; through Jesus Christ, Thy Son, our Lord.

In Time of Great Sickness

Almighty and most merciful God, our heavenly Father, we, Thine erring children, humbly confess unto Thee that we have justly deserved the chastening which for our sins Thou hast sent upon us; but we entreat Thee, of Thy boundless goodness to grant us true repentance, graciously to forgive our sins, to remove from us, or to lighten, our merited punishment, and so to strengthen us by Thy grace that as obedient children we may be subject to Thy will and bear our afflictions in patience; through Jesus Christ, Thy Son, our Lord.

In Time of Drought

O God, most merciful Father, we beseech Thee to open the windows of heaven and to send a fruitful rain upon us, to revive the earth, and to refresh the fruits thereof, for all things droop and wither. Graciously hear our prayer in this our necessity that we may praise and glorify Thy name forever and ever; through Jesus Christ, Thy Son, our Lord.

Thanksgiving

O Lord God, heavenly Father, from whom without ceasing we receive exceeding abundantly all good gifts and who daily of Thy pure grace guardest us against all evil, grant us, we beseech Thee, Thy Holy Spirit that, acknowledging with our whole heart all this Thy goodness, we may now and evermore thank and praise Thy loving-kindness and tender mercy; through Jesus Christ, Thy Son, our Lord.

Almighty God, our heavenly Father, whose mercies are new unto us every morning and who, though we have in no wise deserved Thy goodness, dost abundantly provide for all our wants of body and soul, give us, we pray Thee, Thy Holy Spirit that we may heartily acknowledge Thy merciful goodness toward us, give thanks for all Thy benefits, and serve Thee in willing obedience; through Jesus Christ, Thy Son, our Lord.

Almighty and most merciful God, who in Thy fatherly wisdom hast chastened us on account of our sins that we might not continue in impenitence and vain confidence and thus perish with the ungodly, in the midst of wrath Thou hast remembered mercy and hast graciously delivered us out of our affliction. We give Thee therefore most hearty thanks and praise that Thou hast turned away from us Thy just anger and shown Thyself favorable toward us, Thine unworthy servants. Bless the Lord, O my soul; and all that is within me, bless His holy name. Bless the Lord, O my soul, and forget not all His benefits. Thou, Lord, art merciful and gracious, slow to anger and plenteous in mercy. Glory be to Thee, O God, forever; through Jesus Christ, Thy Son, our Lord.

Glory be to Thee, O God most holy. Glory be to Thee, O God most high. Glory be to Thee, O King of heaven and earth, who, as a father pitieth his children, pitiest us. Fill us with joy and gladness in the Holy Ghost that, when Thou shalt render to every man according to his works, we may be found acceptable before Thee; through Him who hath redeemed us from the shame and curse of sin, even Jesus Christ, Thy Son, our Lord.

For Special Gifts and Graces

For Protection During the Day (at Morning Prayer)
O Lord, our heavenly Father, almighty and everlasting God, who hast safely brought us to the beginning of this day, defend us in the same with Thy mighty power, and grant that this day we fall into no sin, neither run into any kind of danger, but that all our doings, being ordered by Thy governance, may be righteous in Thy sight; through Jesus Christ, Thy Son, our Lord.

For Protection During the Night
Lighten our darkness, we beseech Thee, O Lord; and by Thy great mercy defend us from all perils and dangers of this night; for the love of Thine only Son, our Savior, Jesus Christ.

For Grace to Use Our Gifts
O Lord God Almighty, who dost endue Thy servants with divers and singular gifts of the Holy Ghost, leave us not, we beseech Thee, destitute of Thy manifold gifts nor yet of grace to use them always to Thy honor and glory; through Jesus Christ, Thy Son, our Lord.

For Grace to Receive the Word
Blessed Lord, who hast caused all Holy Scriptures to be written for our learning, grant that we may in such wise hear them, read, mark, learn, and inwardly digest them that by patience and comfort of Thy holy Word we

may embrace, and ever hold fast, the blessed hope of everlasting life which Thou hast given us in our Savior Jesus Christ.

For Grace to be Led Into All Truth
Enlighten our minds, we beseech Thee, O God, by the Spirit which proceedeth from Thee, that, as Thy Son hath promised, we may be led into all truth; through the same Jesus Christ, Thy Son, our Lord.

For Spiritual Renewal
Almighty God, who hast given us Thine only-begotten Son to take our nature upon Him, grant that we, being regenerate and made Thy children by adoption and grace, may daily be renewed by Thy Holy Spirit; through Jesus Christ, Thy Son, our Lord.

For Penitence
Merciful Father, give us grace that we may never presume to sin; but if at any time we offend Thy divine majesty, may we truly repent and lament our offense and by a lively faith obtain remission of all our sins, solely through the merits of Thy Son, our Savior, Jesus Christ.

For Pardon
Hear, we beseech Thee, O Lord, the prayer of Thy suppliants and spare those who confess their sins unto Thee that Thou mayest bestow upon us both pardon and peace; through Jesus Christ, Thy Son, our Lord.

For Deliverance From Sin
We beseech Thee, O Lord, in Thy clemency to show us Thine unspeakable mercy that Thou mayest both set us free from our sins and rescue us from the punishments which, for our sins, we deserve; through Jesus Christ, Thy Son, our Lord.

For Grace to do God's Will
Almighty God, give us grace that we may cast away the works of darkness and put upon ourselves the armor of light, now in the time of this mortal life, in which Thy Son Jesus Christ came to visit us in great humility, that in the Last Day, when He shall come again in His glorious majesty to judge both the quick and the dead, we may rise to the life immortal; through the same Jesus Christ, Thy Son, our Lord.

[410]
For Grace to Love and Serve God
O God, who, through the grace of Thy Holy Spirit, dost pour the gifts of charity into the hearts of Thy faithful people, grant unto Thy servants health

both of mind and body that they may love Thee with their whole strength and with their whole heart perform those things which are pleasing unto Thee; through Jesus Christ, Thy Son, our Lord.

For Aid Against Temptation
O God, who justifiest the ungodly and who desirest not the death of the sinner, we humbly implore Thy majesty that Thou wouldest graciously assist by Thy heavenly aid, and evermore shield with Thy protection, Thy servants who trust in Thy mercy, that they may be separated by no temptations from Thee and without ceasing may serve Thee; through Jesus Christ, Thy Son, our Lord.

For Faith
Almighty and ever-living God, who hast given to them that believe exceeding great and precious promises, grant us so perfectly and without all doubt to believe in Thy Son Jesus Christ that our faith in Thy sight may never be reproved. Hear us, O Lord, through the same Savior, Thy Son, Jesus Christ.

For Divine Guidance and Help
Direct us, O Lord, in all our doings with Thy most gracious favor and further us with Thy continual help, that in all our works begun, continued, and ended in Thee we may glorify Thy holy name and finally, by Thy mercy, obtain everlasting life; through Jesus Christ, Thy Son, our Lord.

O almighty and everlasting God, vouchsafe, we beseech Thee, to direct, sanctify, and govern both our hearts and bodies in the ways of Thy laws and in the works of Thy commandments, that through Thy most mighty protection, both here and ever, we may be preserved in body and in soul; through our Lord and Savior Jesus Christ.

For Spiritual Illumination
Grant, we beseech Thee, almighty God, that the brightness of Thy glory may shine forth upon us and that the light of Thy light, by the illumination of the Holy Spirit, may stablish the hearts of all that have been born anew by Thy grace; through Jesus Christ, Thy Son, our Lord.

For Likeness to Christ
Almighty God, who hast given Thine only Son to be unto us both a sacrifice for sin and also an example of godly life, give us grace that we may always most thankfully receive this His inestimable benefit and also daily endeavor

ourselves to follow the blessed steps of His most holy life; through the same Jesus Christ, Thy Son, our Lord.

For a Right Knowledge of Christ

O almighty God, whom to know is everlasting life, grant us perfectly to know Thy Son, Jesus Christ, to be the Way, the Truth, and the Life, that following His steps, we may steadfastly walk in the way that leads to eternal life; through the same Jesus Christ, Thy Son, our Lord.

[411]
For the Holy Spirit

O Lord God, heavenly Father, who by the blessed light of Thy divine Word hast led us to the knowledge of Thy Son, we most heartily beseech Thee so to replenish us with the grace of Thy Holy Spirit that we may ever walk in the light of Thy truth and, rejoicing with sure confidence in Christ, our Savior, may in the end be brought unto everlasting salvation; through the same Jesus Christ, Thy Son, our Lord.

Almighty and everlasting God, who of Thy great mercy in Jesus Christ, Thy Son, dost grant us forgiveness of sin and all things pertaining to life and godliness, grant us, we beseech Thee, Thy Holy Spirit that He may so rule our hearts that we, being ever mindful of Thy fatherly mercy, may strive to mortify the flesh and to overcome the world and, serving Thee in holiness and pureness of living, may give Thee continual thanks for all Thy goodness; through Jesus Christ, Thy Son, our Lord.

For Purity

Almighty God, unto whom all hearts are open, all desires known, and from whom no secrets are hid, cleanse the thoughts of our hearts by the inspiration of Thy Holy Spirit that we may perfectly love Thee and worthily magnify Thy holy name; through Jesus Christ, Thy Son, our Lord.

For Innocency of Life

O God, whose strength is made perfect in weakness, mortify and kill all vices in us and so strengthen us by Thy grace, that by the innocency of our lives and the constancy of our faith, even unto death, we may glorify Thy holy name; through Jesus Christ, Thy Son, our Lord.

For Love to God

O God, who makest all things to work together for good to them that love Thee, pour into our hearts such steadfast love toward Thee that the pure desires which by Thy Spirit have been stirred up in us may not be turned aside by any temptation; through Jesus Christ, Thy Son, our Lord.

For Charity

O Lord, who hast taught us that all our doings without charity are worth nothing, send Thy Holy Spirit and pour into our hearts that most excellent gift of charity, the very bond of peace and all virtues, without which whosoever liveth is counted dead before Thee. Grant this for Thine only Son Jesus Christ's sake.

For Humility

O God, who resistest the proud and givest grace to the humble, grant unto us true humility, after the likeness in which Thine only Son hath revealed it in Himself, that we may never be lifted up and provoke Thy wrath, but in all lowliness be made partakers of the gifts of Thy grace; through Jesus Christ, Thy Son, our Lord.

For Patience [412]

O God, who by the meek endurance of Thine only-begotten Son didst beat down the pride of the old enemy, help us, we beseech Thee, rightly to treasure in our hearts what our Lord hath of His goodness borne for our sakes, that after His example we may bear with patience whatsoever things are adverse to us; through the same Jesus Christ, Thy Son, our Lord.

For a Happy Death

Confirm, we beseech Thee, almighty God, Thine unworthy servants in Thy grace, that in the hour of our death the adversary may not prevail against us, but that we may be found worthy of everlasting life; through Jesus Christ, Thy Son, our Lord.

For the Blessedness of Heaven

Almighty, everlasting God, who didst give Thine only Son to be a High Priest of good things to come, hereafter grant unto us, Thine unworthy servants, to have our share in the company of the blessed; through Jesus Christ, Thy Son, our Lord.

For Peace

O God, who art the Author of peace and Lover of concord, in knowledge of whom standeth our eternal life, whose service is perfect freedom, defend us, Thy humble servants, in all assaults of our enemies, that we, surely trusting in Thy defense, may not fear the power of any adversaries; through the might of Jesus Christ, Thy Son, our Lord.

For an Answer to Prayer

Almighty God, who hast given us grace at this time with one accord to make our common supplications unto Thee and dost promise that, when two or three are gathered together in Thy name, Thou wilt grant their requests, fulfill now, O Lord, the desires and petitions of Thy servants, as may be most expedient for them; granting us in this world knowledge of Thy truth and in the world to come life everlasting; through Jesus Christ, Thy Son, our Lord.

Almighty God, the Fountain of all wisdom, who knowest our necessities before we ask and our ignorance in asking, we beseech Thee to have compassion upon our infirmities; and those things which for our unworthiness we dare not, and for our blindness we cannot ask, vouchsafe to give us for the worthiness of Jesus Christ, Thy Son, our Lord.

Almighty God, who hast promised to hear the petitions of those who ask in Thy Son's name, we beseech Thee mercifully to incline Thine ears to us who have now made our prayers and supplications unto Thee; and grant that those things which we have faithfully asked according to Thy will may effectually be obtained to the relief of our necessity and to the setting forth of Thy glory; through Jesus Christ, Thy Son, our Lord.

[413]
For Special Events in Life

On a Birthday
Merciful God, Thou hast allowed *N.* to experience the day of *his/her* birth: continue to bless *him/her* in the new year of *his/her* life, and fill *him/her* with the power of Thy Spirit, that *he/she* may attain to eternal salvation; through Jesus Christ our Lord.

On a Baptismal Birthday
O Lord, Thou hast received *N.* into the covenant of Holy Baptism as Thine own: deliver *him/her* from all evil and temptations, that sin and death may be powerless against *him/her*; through Jesus Christ our Lord.

On the Anniversary of Ordination
O Lord, remember the authority Thou hast bestowed on Thy servant *N.* through holy ordination; look not upon his mistakes, but make him worthy of his calling; through Jesus Christ our Lord.

Prayer for the Church and Her Pastors

O Lord, merciful, eternal Father of our Lord Jesus Christ, who in time past wast gracious to Thy people and forgavest their sins; be gracious even now to Thy people: Renew Thy Church through the pure preaching of Thy holy Word, the right use of the venerable sacraments, and the comforting absolution. Enlighten all Thy servants, that they may be found faithful stewards of Thy mysteries and may exercise the holy office of the keys in truthfulness. Preserve them in all the attacks of the devil, comfort them through the forgiveness of their sins, and fill them with ardent love toward Thee and Thy congregation. From Thy faithful people call workers into Thy harvest, and give them teachers to instruct them in the right faith. Cause unity in the Spirit, in faith, and in confession to grow. Send Thy Holy Spirit to cleanse the hearts of all who love Thy name and remove from them false doctrine and human inventions. Take away from the souls of all who eat one bread and drink from one cup with us whatever hinders them from becoming one in Thy truth. Purify, cleanse, and strengthen our hearts, and give us moderation and wisdom, that we may not strive against Thy Spirit in impatience and, instead of building, destroy what living faith Thy mercy hath still preserved. To Thy grace I commend all the fathers and brethren bound to me in Christ: *(Here name those in need of special supplication).* Preserve them, Lord, in body and soul, and bless them with Thy gifts of grace, that they may serve Thee as faithful workers in Thy vineyard. O Lord, let me also be found ever faithful, and serve Thee always in the true humility with which Thy Son bore His own cross. O Lord, direct all our days and our deeds in Thy peace. Amen.

Psalms Appropriate for Life's Various Situations

The Course of the Day

In the Morning
Psalm 1; 3; 5; 19; 23; 25; 33; 57:7-11; 59:16-17; 63; 90; 92; 103; 104:23; 108; 121; 127:1-2; 143:8-11.

At Midday
Psalm 33:18-19; 104:27-31; 106:1-5; 119:73-80, 89-96, 169-176; 136:1, 25; 145:15-21; 147:7-11.

In the Evening
Psalm 3; 4; 8; 16; 17; 25:1-11; 31:1-6; 36:7; 63; 74:16; 91; 92; 119:54-65; 121; 127; 134; 138; 139; 141:1-2.

Psalms to Guide Prayer for

The Church and Her Pastors
   Psalm 3; 5; 28; 59; 64; 71; 74; 77; 79; 80; 83; 94; 112; 125; 134; 150.

Enemies of the Church
   Psalm 3; 7; 11; 19; 23; 26; 27; 33; 36; 42; 46; 47; 54; 56; 57; 62; 76; 124; 125; 126; 141.

Peace in the Church
   Psalm 60; 86; 137; 140.

The Divine Word
   Psalm 67; 69; 119

[414] **Spiritual Direction**
   Psalm 38; 59; 86; 90; 130; 141; 142.

For Rulers and for the Household
   Psalm 2; 20; 62; 82; 101; 125; 127; 128; 133; 144.

For Fear, Love, and Trust in God
   Psalm 1; 4; 15; 33; 41; 78; 81; 91; 92; 95; 96; 100; 112; 115; 131; 146; 148; 149.

Life's Events

Thankfulness for Bodily Gifts
   Psalm 24:1; 36:7-10; 50:14, 23; 64:9-10; 65; 67; 95:1-8; 100; 103; 104; 107; 111; 115:12-13; 116; 126:3; 144:13-15; 145; 146; 147.

Birthdays
   Psalm 9:1; 18:1-2; 23; 25; 34; 66:16; 91; 92; 103; 116; 118:24; 121; 126:3; 136; 139:13-18, 23-24; 145.

Weddings
   Psalm 37:5; 67; 91; 100; 101; 103; 121; 123; 125; 127; 128; 139; 143:10.

Job and Vocation
   Psalm 90:16-17; 121; 123; 127; 128; 143:10; 145.

Sickness
   Psalm 6; 23:4; 25:16-18; 27:1; 31; 38; 39; 40:11-13, 17; 41:1-4; 42; 50:14-15; 62:1-2; 68:1-20; 73:23-28; 80:3; 102; 118:17; 119:76.

Recovery from Sickness
   Psalm 30; 40:1-11; 50:14-15; 23; 56:12-13; 68:20; 103; 107; 116; 119:65-80.

Aging
   Psalm 71; 73:23-28; 90; 91:16; 92:12-15.

Preparation for Dying
   Psalm 16; 23:4; 27:1; 31; 39; 90.

DEATH AND BURIAL
    Psalm 16:10; 23:4; 39; 90; 103:13-18; 116; 139:16; 144:4; 146:4-5.
COMFORT FOR SURVIVORS
    Psalm 23; 39:9; 80:19; 103:13-18; 119:92; 126.
COMFORT FOR WIDOWS(ERS) AND ORPHANS
    Psalm 9:9-10, 12; 10:14-18; 23; 27; 37:5, 37; 39:9; 55:22; 68:4-5, 19; 70; 82:3-4; 89:26; 102:17; 103:13; 118:8; 146; 147:3.

SPIRITUAL LIFE

THANKFULNESS FOR SPIRITUAL BLESSINGS
    Psalm 2; 23; 33; 34; 50:23; 66; 95; 97; 100; 103; 116; 138; 146; 147.
BAPTISM
    Psalm 23; 111; 115:14; 121.
CONFIRMATION
    Psalm 1; 25:5; 37:37; 86:11; 119:1-19.
CONFESSION, PREPARATION FOR
    The Seven Penitential Psalms: 6; 32; 38; 51; 102; 130; 143
COMFORT OF ABSOLUTION
    Psalm 32; 34; 103
BEFORE RECEIVING THE LORD'S SUPPER   [415]
    Psalm 22:26; 23; 25; 34:8; 42; 90; 103; 111; 116; 118:14-29.
RESURRECTION, JUDGMENT, AND ETERNAL LIFE
    Psalm 2:12; 5:4; 16:10-11; 17:15; 49:14; 50; 73:19; 96:11-13; 98; 126.

TIMES OF DISTRESS

AFFLICTION IN GENERAL
    Psalm 13; 25; 30:5; 38; 39:7; 40:11-13; 42; 43; 46; 50:14-15; 55:17; 62:1; 66:8-13; 68:19-20; 71; 73:23-28; 77; 90; 91:14-15; 97:11-12; 102:17-21; 112:4; 119:65-80, 92, 94; 121; 124:8; 126; 130.
THANKFULNESS FOR SALVATION
    Psalm 18:4-6; 34; 40; 66:8-20; 94:17-19; 103; 107; 118; 119:22; 147.
TIMES OF MASS DEATHS
    Psalm 62:1-2; 68:19-20; 80:3; 85; 90; 91.
TIMES OF WAR
    Psalm 3; 10; 18; 20; 27; 33:16-20; 44; 46; 60:11-12; 76; 81:13-14; 91; 108; 124; 127:1; 138:7; 143:9; 147:10-11.
POVERTY AND FAMINE
    Psalm 4:7; 9:9-19; 13:5; 23:1; 27:14; 33:18-22; 34:9-10; 36:5-7; 37:3-5, 18-19, 25; 46:1; 52:9; 55:22; 60:3; 62:1, 8; 69:29-33; 73:23-28; 77:2; 82:3-4; 84:11-12; 85; 104:27-30; 111; 132:15; 145; 147:9.

AGAINST THE POPE AND ANTICHRIST
    Psalm 10; 12; 36; 44; 55; 69; 70; 94; 109; 120.
AGAINST THE ENEMIES OF THE CHURCH
    Psalm 7; 19; 26; 27; 42; 54; 56; 57; 62; 141.
FOR PEACE IN THE CHURCH
    Psalm 60; 86; 137; 140.

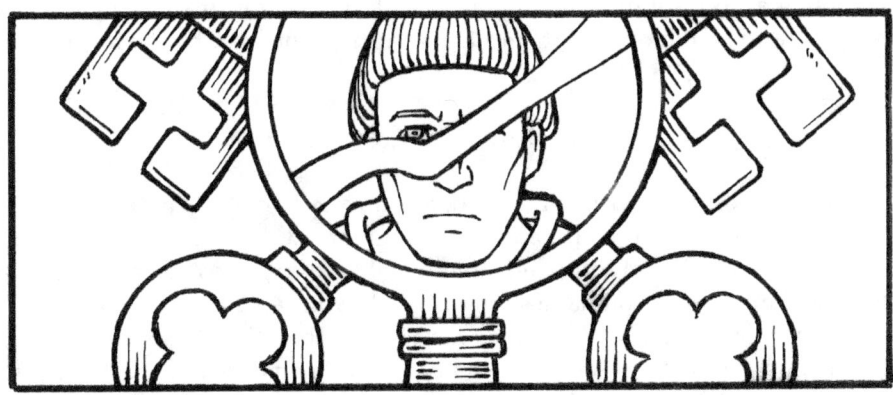

The Ten Commandments, Explanations, and Questions for Reflection and Self-Examination in Preparation for Private Absolution: A Confession Mirror (Beichtspiegel)

Introduction

Luther describes God as that to which we look for the greatest and highest good. From the time of the fall in the Garden of Eden, people have been constantly tempted to look inward for that good. Our selfish search for good within ourselves is the temptation of the old Adam in us. The Ten Commandments address this "self"-ish issue directly. We do not fear, love, and trust God above all things. On this earth we struggle against looking inward toward ourselves. In the questions below the common theme of selfishness is interwoven throughout. This constant breaking of the first commandment is a life-long struggle for Christians. No matter which of commandments 2-10 that we break, it is always an assault on having none other than God, the Father of our Lord Jesus Christ, as the center of our trust (faith). In the Ten Commandments there is a vertical relationship (we and God) and there is a horizontal relationship (we and our neighbors). The first table (Commandments 1-3) shows the vertical relationship, and the second table (Commandments 4-10) shows the horizontal. Even in the breaking of the horizontal relationships, however, we are offending against the vertical because it is God who has called us to live in harmony and love with our neighbor.

The *Small Catechism* urges us to consider our place in life according to the Ten Commandments. The Commandments act as a mirror to reflect our sinful thoughts, words, and deeds. This honest reflection, on account of God's holy Word working in us, will bear the fruit of repentance. In private confession and absolution we repent before our pastor of those sins which we know and feel in our heart, and he, in turn, grants us Christ's forgiveness individually.

What Belongs to Confession?

Confession is a return to God, a return to baptismal grace. The first part of confession is that I come into judgment with myself honestly and sincerely. I examine my life and must be able to say "yes" to the question: "Do you confess that you have sinned, and do you repent of your sins?" The second part of confession is that, as far as I am able, I try to set right what I have committed or omitted against my fellow man: I cannot ask God for forgiveness if I have not done this to my fellow man. The third part of confession is that I place my trust on the fact that Christ on the cross has paid also for my debt, for my guilt. I am asked: "Do you desire the forgiveness of your sins in the name of Jesus Christ?" and I must be able to speak my "yes" to this question. The fourth part of confession is that I resolve "in the power of the Holy Spirit to avoid the sins committed and to live in a Christian way." This I cannot do from my own ability, but only as far as the Spirit of God assists me. The fifth part of confession is that I confess my sins and accept the holy absolution as sure and certain before God in heaven. I must be able to say "yes" when I am asked whether I also believe that the forgiveness which the father confessor speaks to me in the name of God is God's forgiveness. The last part of confession, finally, is that I thank God. "For He has done great things for me" in the forgiveness of my guilt.

[417]
How do I Prepare for Confession?

Confession is not something one can take care of "in passing." There must be time for it, and the more time you take for it the better you will confess. At the very least you should prepare myself for it for about an hour.

1. Go into a quiet room where you can be alone, undisturbed. Radio, T.V., the telephone, other people, and all things which distract you must be excluded. If this cannot take place at home, then perhaps the church is the proper place of refuge.

2. Open the Holy Scriptures and pray one of the penitential Psalms slowly, word for word: Psalm 6, 32, 38, 51, 102, 130, 143 (perhaps Psalm 51 is the most suitable). Think for a moment over what God has to say to you in the Psalm.

3. Fold your hands for personal prayer: that God the Holy Spirit would show you what you have done wrong before God and men; how heavy your guilt lies; that you may confess sincerely and honestly; that you

may rejoice over the holy absolution with which all your sins are put to an end.

4. Take paper and pencil in hand and go through the following confession mirror, write your mistakes down (abbreviations are enough), so that you can set them forth in an orderly fashion and without stammering in private confession. (Destroy the "confession sheet" after confession is over. No one can read it except you.)

5. Try to make my confession as if it were the last one of your life. Do not mention any sin which you have not committed, but confess the sins committed without any excuse. No "perhaps," no "maybe," but only, "I have..." You should and may accuse only yourself—the names of others have no place in your confession.

Confession Mirror

In General: *Why does God give His holy Ten Commandments? What does He demand? All your heart, all your life should belong to Him! But every transgression of His will was a "no" to this demand. Have you walked the way that God calls you to? Have you tried to come nearer to Him? Have you lived according to His Word, or have you fallen into previous sins? Have you done that which your conscience previously told you was sin? Were your previous confessions in earnest? Have you delayed confession in order to sin further?*

The First Commandment
Thou shalt have no other gods.
What does this mean?
We should fear, love, and trust in God above all things.

To whom have I looked for the highest good? Have I doubted God's Word and thus committed idolatry by seeking my highest good from other sources? Which one was more important when I made my daily decisions: God or myself? What do I fear, what do I love, what do I trust more than my God? Have good times deluded me into thinking that I am in control? Am I tempted to think that I have God and everything I need when I have money and earthly goods? Have bad times caused me to despair and lose hope and trust in God? Have I doubted God's love for me when I have money problems, loss of possessions, sickness, or injury? Have I been discontent with what God has spoken of Himself in Jesus Christ and in the Scriptures? Have I put my own notions or the notions of others above what the Scriptures say about God?

[418]

To trust in God above all things is to have faith. Have I thought or done things that have weakened or hurt my faith in God? Have I denied the faith out of indifference or cowardice before acquaintances, relatives, friends, or those who believe differently?

I have God as my Lord over me. What contradicts Him in my life? Does my self-consciousness, my pride, my sensitivity, my temper, my dissatisfaction, my laziness, my "rights," my fearfulness, or weariness with my life contradict God in my life? Have I cursed God and His Church? Is it noticeable to others that I am a Christian: baptized, redeemed, made holy? Or have I been ashamed of my salvation?

Consider the things that you have done to weaken or hurt your faith according to the next nine commandments. Remember that your flesh is weak with sin and the old man in you must be killed daily.

The Second Commandment
Thou shalt not take the name of the Lord, thy God, in vain.
What does this mean?
We should fear and love God that we may not curse, swear, use witchcraft, lie, or deceive by His name, but call upon it in every trouble, pray, praise, and give thanks.

Have I called God "Father" with delight? Have I used holy words or holy names in a light-hearted way? Have I used them in anger, in mockery, thoughtlessly, or for superstitious reasons? Have I sworn carelessly or falsely? Have I taken oaths frivolously or even lied under oath intentionally? Have I kept my vows (baptismal vows, confirmation vows, marriage vows)? Have I received the holy absolution or the holy sacrament of the altar unworthily (mindless of the gift and my need for it)? Have I listened to and read God's Word diligently?

When the precious Name of Jesus is not used rightly, it is misused. Have I properly called on my heavenly Father through His only Son Jesus Christ and had faith that He hears and answers my prayer? Have I called on His Name wrongly through false worship?

God is one, and yet there are three persons, the Father, Son, and Holy Spirit. Have I desired to find salvation in any other name but the name of the Father, Son, and Holy Spirit? Have I wished that there were other paths to God outside of Christ, perhaps for the sake of others? Have I confirmed others in error and made conversion difficult for them by recognizing prayers to the gods of other religions as valid? Do I pray absent-mindedly or inattentively? Do I bring every worry, concern, and grief to God in prayer? Or do I neglect prayer altogether? Have I given thanks and praise to God for his promise to listen compassionately and unendingly to my supplications? Have I consulted astrologers, fortune-tellers, palm-readers, or spiritualists? Have I been led by superstitions? Have I been influenced by horoscopes? Have I done little or nothing to spread the Name of God? Have I supported preaching and the administration of the sacrament with my prayers, conversations, and tithe?

The Third Commandment
Thou shalt sanctify the holy-day.
What does this mean?
We should fear and love God that we may not despise preaching and His Word, but hold it sacred, and gladly hear and learn it.

Have I neglected the reading of the Bible thinking that hearing it on Sunday is enough? Do I let other daily activities take precedence over prayer and meditation on God's Word? Have I kept every day holy with the reading and meditation upon God's Word? Has the hearing and reading of God's Word become boring and meaningless to me? Have I despised the preaching of His Word by not coming to church as regularly as I should? Have I let my mind wander when I am at church and become distracted by my thoughts? Do I despise the reception of Holy Communion by not coming to receive it or by receiving it with no thought of the great price Jesus paid for my sin on the cross? Have I been an unfaithful witness to others in our congregation by my absence from or inattention in the Divine Service? Have I gone to church only out of habit, or because I was forced? Do I get bored with the sermon, the holy liturgy, or the celebration of the sacrament, when I should know that the Lord Jesus is present and wants to speak to me through them? Did I also reflect on the service and the sermon after it was over, or did I forget it all right away? Does my attendance to the Divine Service suffer because of my other weekend activities? Do I needlessly despise worship services that are offered during the week, not taking the opportunity to pray publicly with other members? Am I ready to learn from the sermon and make progress in Christianity? Have I destroyed the blessing of the Divine Service for myself and others with frivolous criticism? Have I stopped to consider that God will one day ask me what I have done with my Sundays and whether I have taken His Word and His Divine Service seriously? Have I observed the penitential seasons of the church year (Advent, Lent, Holy Week, days of humility and prayer) with requisite seriousness?

The Fourth Commandment
Thou shalt honor thy father and thy mother.
> *What does this mean?*
> We should fear and love God that we may not despise nor anger our parents or masters, but give them honor, serve, obey, and hold them in love and esteem.

For children: How have I behaved toward my parents? Have I been loveless, unfriendly, unthankful, rude, rebellious, disobedient, or full of pride? Have I hurt their feelings? Have I wished them evil or harm, despised them? Have I left them alone in danger, in sickness, in old age? Have I thanked them with my words and deeds? Have I helped them? Have I prayed that God would give my parents the strength, knowledge and desire to do what is best for me, even if I don't like it?

Have I loved and honored those people whom my parents have chosen to instruct me: my teachers and professors? Have I shown the proper respect and obedience to the civic leaders who have been given their position by God to govern this country, state, and city? Have I been hypocritical to my superiors and defamed them behind their backs? Have I prayed earnestly for the well-being of the leaders of government? Have I placed myself above the law, thinking it sometimes doesn't apply to me, perhaps when I know better? Have I treated my parents and other authorities as representatives of God for my sake?

For parents and superiors: Have I protected those entrusted to me from bad influences? Have I provided for them in all external things? Have I made time for them? Have I made time to think about them? Have I been a good example for them? Have I been impatient, hot-tempered, rude, or unfair? Have I shown preference to someone? Have I prayed for the Lord to guide my words and actions? Have I become exasperated and wished that I did not have children or responsibility for those whom God gave me?

How have you behaved toward your pastor or the church? Have you prayed for your parents, your superiors, and your pastor?

The Fifth Commandment
Thou shalt not kill.
> *What does this mean?*
> We should fear and love God that we may not hurt nor harm our neighbor in his body, but help and befriend him in every bodily need.

Some people imagine that because they have not killed anyone with their own hands or caused someone to die, that this commandment has been kept. However, there are many other ways to hurt and harm your neighbor or, in other words, to kill him.

Have I hurt or harmed my neighbor by physical hitting or by destructive words? Have I murdered my neighbor's reputation by speaking harmful words about him? Have I acted as though my neighbor is a treasured gift from God?

Simply leaving my neighbor alone does not fulfill this [421] commandment. Have I helped my neighbor in every physical need, or only when it was convenient, if at all? Have I passed up the opportunity to do good to my neighbor? Have I allowed hunger, temperature, or loneliness to kill my neighbor out of my laziness, comfort, indifference, or on purpose? Have I prayed for my friends and enemies alike, that nothing evil or bad would happen to them? Have I held grudges? Have I forgiven when I should have? Have I attempted to commit suicide or else tried to physically harm myself? Have I failed to help prevent my neighbor from committing suicide or hurting himself? Have I considered euthanasia to be an acceptable option for others, if they are really suffering, instead of leaving their life in God's hands? Do I overeat or drink too much? Have I encouraged or not aided my neighbor when he eats or drinks too much? Do I smoke in excess or allow my neighbor to smoke to his physical detriment? Have I neglected to properly care for animals, and thus been a poor steward of God's creation?

For rulers: Have I neglected to use the sword instituted by God to punish evil and protect innocent lives?

The Sixth Commandment
Thou shalt not commit adultery.
What does this mean?
We should fear and love God that we may lead a chaste and decent life in words and deeds, and each love and honor his spouse.

In this commandment God requires cleanness of me, even in thoughts and desires, and if I be unmarried, He requires the conscientious preservation of my body and my soul for the duty of marriage or for an unmarried life of service to Him.

Have I despised God's gift of sexuality by looking at other people around me for selfish pleasure? Do I look at others with indecency and lust? Have I spoken in a crude manner about sex or made light of the intimacy that God has given to a husband and wife? Have I injured my modesty with my behavior: my eyes, offensive clothing, looking at obscene pictures, or by listening to or telling crude jokes? Have I seduced myself or others to unchaste things? Have I striven sincerely for purity of thoughts, of speech, of body and of soul, or not striven at all? Have I considered my body as a temple of the Holy Spirit through holy Baptism? Do I pray, turn away, and fight against temptations? Have I done unchaste things with myself or with others?

If single, do I consider my unmarried state as coming from the hand of God?

[422] If married, have I made time for my spouse? Have I refused the blessing of children due to selfishness or a desire for comfort? Have I desired to break my marital fidelity? Have I actually broken it? Do I harbor intentions or have I even consented to divorce? Have I been concerned for the soul of my spouse?

Have I condoned homosexual relationships and failed to address it as a sinful act? Have I had sexual intercourse with a man or woman who is not my spouse? Have I read, viewed, or listened to immoral, suggestive or pornographic books, magazines, pictures, movies, music, dances, plays, or internet sites? Have I neglected to encourage others to be faithful to their spouses in the fear of God?

The Seventh Commandment
Thou shalt not steal.
What does this mean?
We should fear and love God that we may not take our neighbor's money or property, nor get them by false ware or dealing, but help him to improve and protect his property and business.

Have I been discontent with what God has or has not given me? Have I approved of stealing in certain situations, perhaps if my neighbor stole from me first? Have I stolen by neglecting to help take care of my neighbor's property, possessions, or earnings? Have I been lazy at work or school and not fulfilled my duties in a faithful manner? Do I accept pay even when I have not done a satisfactory job or not done the job at all? Have I been stingy with paying those who work under me? Do I demand unreasonable payment for poor work? Have I stolen information by plagiarism or cheating at work or school? Have I overcharged for the goods that I sell? Do I simply sell for my own gain, not caring for the needs of my neighbor? Have I wasted food by overeating or taking more than I should eat? Have I cheated on my taxes, or not reported income to the state? Have I supported my neighbor by all means available to me? Have I kept something that was borrowed or found? Have I damaged another person's property? Have I given offerings, as I was able, for the needy, for collections, for the church, and for missions? Have I kept stolen property for myself?

The Eighth Commandment
Thou shalt not bear false witness against thy neighbor.
> *What does this mean?*
> We should fear and love God that we may not deceitfully belie, betray, slander, or defame our neighbor, but defend him, speak well of him, and put the best construction on everything.

Have I spread rumors about my neighbor? Have I spoken poorly about my neighbor to other people? Have I murdered my neighbor's reputation by passing on harmful information even if it is true? — Just because something is true does not mean that you can spread it. It must be true, not harmful to someone else, *and* beneficial to others.

Have I told lies about my neighbor or to him? Have I given true witness to the truth, or have I lied in court or to other authorities such as parents, teachers, or policemen? Have I celebrated upon hearing hurtful news? Have I defended the reputation and feelings of my neighbor even when I do not like him? Do I look for the bad in someone instead of seeing the good? Have I failed to keep the private sins of others secret when they have confessed and repented of them? Have I helped him to confess them? Have I explained all things in a way that is complimentary to my neighbor? Where a sin is public, have I testified publicly against it, thereby giving faithful witness to the truth? Have I lied to harm someone? Have I lied to help someone? (That too, even if unavoidable, is sin.) Have I been nosey with the secrets of others? Have I cast doubt on the honor of others? Have I listened to gossip or even passed it on? Did I protect others and their reputation when I was able? Have I had the courage to privately show my neighbor his errors, which I have observed, before I spoke about it with others?

The Ninth Commandment
Thou shalt not covet thy neighbor's house.
> *What does this mean?*
> We should fear and love God that we may not craftily seek to get our neighbor's inheritance or house, and obtain it by a show of right, etc., but help and be of service to him in keeping it.

Do I look at the life of others and become bitter or dissatisfied with the life that God has given me? Do I get jealous that other people look happier than I do? Have I competed with others in order to have as much money and possessions as those around me? Have I engaged in lawsuits to

[423]

attempt to satisfy my greed? Have I tried to get my neighbor's land or house and made it appear legal?

The Tenth Commandment

Thou shalt not covet thy neighbor's wife, nor his man-servant, nor his maid-servant, nor his cattle, nor anything that is his.
What does this mean?
We should fear and love God that we may not estrange, force, or entice away our neighbor's wife, servants, or cattle, but urge them to stay and do their duty.

[424] Have I wanted my neighbor's spouse, workers, or his property to be mine? Have I tried to win the affections of my neighbor's spouse, children, or employees for my personal use? Have I been slow to give my neighbor what properly belongs to him? Have I failed to assist my neighbor at all times in keeping what is his?

What Does God Say of All These Commandments?

He says thus: I the Lord, thy God, am a jealous God, visiting the iniquity of the fathers upon the children unto the third and fourth generation of them that hate Me, and showing mercy unto thousands of them that love Me and keep My commandments." [Exodus 20:5-6]
What does this mean?
God threatens to punish all that transgress these commandments. Therefore we should dread His wrath and not act contrary to these commandments. But He promises grace and every blessing to all that keep these commandments. Therefore we should also love and trust in Him, and gladly do according to His commandments.

Have I looked at the Ten Commandments as a way to properly do good works in faith? Or have I made up my own seemingly good works? Have I depended on works for salvation? Have I failed to teach the Ten Commandments to my children or family? Have I tried to rely on my own power and strength to keep these Commandments? Do all of my actions proceed from a heart that fears God and looks to Him alone? Have I been proud or self-righteous, thinking I can do good works apart from faith in Jesus? Have my trust and faith rested and depended upon the works that I do?

Summary Questions

Have I worked at becoming a better Christian? Have I fought against my errors? Has terror of God's wrath against sin moved my heart?

Has the love of Christ, who let Himself be crucified for me, moved my heart? Am I indifferent about how God sees me and what His Son has done for me? Do I have a favorite sin? What sin is hardest for me to fight? What is it that must change with me? Where must I begin?

This confession mirror by no means contains all sins you could have committed. It is only meant to help you find the trail – you can then ask yourself further questions.

Do I believe that my sins are serious in the eyes of God and believe that Jesus Christ died for all of my sins and gives forgiveness to me through His Word and through the Sacraments?

If you believe this, my dear brother or sister in Christ, then come and unburden your conscience before your pastor who has been placed in the stead of Jesus for your comfort. Your confession does not need to be perfect, for the Absolution that Jesus gives is. [425]

Index of Psalm Tones

Tone	Canticles and Psalms
I	Tue-Mag.,Wed-Ben. || 1 Chr. 29:10-13, Is. 45:15-25 || 1, 2, 6, 9ii, 16, 18ii, 25i, 25ii, 26, 27, 31i, 32, 33i, 35i, 37iii, 38ii, 40, 42i, 46, 47, 48, 49i, 58, 59ii, 62, 68iii, 72, 73ii, 74iii, 77i, 78vi, 83, 101, 102ii, 104iii, 105i, 106i, 107i, 118i, 118ii, 119xiii-xvii, 124, 128, 133, 136i, 147i, 148
II	Is. 38:10-20 || 3, 9i, 11, 20, 21, 31iii, 35ii, 41, 49ii, 60, 63, 70, 73iii, 78iv, 86, 89ii, 96, 118iii, 129, 144i, 150
III	Compl-Nunc. || Sir. 36:1-16, Dan. 3:36-68 || 17, 19, 22iii, 84, 109ii, 111, 132, 136ii
IV	Fri-Mag. || Jer. 31:10-14, Hab. 3:2-11, Judt. 16:15-21 || 8, 12, 18i, 25iii, 28, 30, 31ii, 34i, 35iii, 37i, 44iii, 45, 54, 59i, 66ii, 69ii, 74ii, 78v, 81, 82, 85, 93, 95, 98, 99, 100, 103ii, 106ii, 106iii, 108, 113, 119vii-xii, 122, 140, 141, 145ii, 145iii, 146
V	Wed-Mag. || Ath. Creed || 15, 52, 61, 77ii, 80, 87, 88, 102iii, 109iii, 119i-vi, 125, 138
VI	Mon-Ben. || Deut. 32:1-8 || 7i, 22i, 23, 24, 43, 68ii, 75, 90, 92, 104i, 112, 117, 119xviii-xxii, 123, 144ii
VII	Sun-Ben., Tue-Ben., Thur-Ben., Thur-Mag., Sat-Mag. || 1 Sam. 2:1-10, Hab. 3:12-19, Tob. 13:1-7 || 7ii, 33ii, 51, 71ii, 89i, 107ii, 107iii, 110, 120, 126, 127, 135, 139i, 149
VIII	Mon-Mag., Fri-Ben., Sat-Ben. || Is. 12:1-6, Dan. 3:29-34, 67 || 4, 5, 10, 13, 14, 18iii, 22ii, 29, 34ii, 36, 37ii, 38i, 42ii, 44i, 44ii, 50i, 50ii, 53, 55, 56, 57, 65, 66i, 68i, 69i, 71i, 73i, 74i, 76, 78ii, 78iii, 79, 89iii, 91, 94, 97, 102i, 103i, 104ii, 105ii, 105iii, 109i, 116, 121, 130, 134, 137, 142, 143, 145i.
IX	Sun-Mag. || 114, 115
Irr.	Ex. 15:1-18, Deut. 32:19-43 || 39, 64, 67, 69iii, 78i, 131, 139ii, 147ii

Index of Hymn First Lines

All hymn texts and melodies included in this book are in the public domain and are taken from the following hymnals:
EH=The English Hymnal 1906; PHB=A Plainsong Hymnbook 1932;
TLH=The Lutheran Hymnal 1941.

A hymn of glory let us sing (EH)	466
Again the Lord's own day is here (PHB)	350
Almighty God, who from the flood (EH)	376
An image of that heavenly light (EH)	421
Be present, holy Trinity (EH)	482
Blessed city, heavenly Salem (EH)	566
Christ, in highest heaven enthroned (PHB)	561
Come, Holy Ghost, with God the Son (EH)	48
Come, Holy Ghost, Creator blest (EH)	473
Come, Thou Redeemer of the earth (EH)	403
Creator of the stars of night (EH)	392
Earth's mighty Maker, whose command (EH)	365
Eternal Glory of the sky (EH)	378
Eternal Monarch, King most high (EH)	464
Father, most holy, merciful and tender (EH)	481
Father, we praise Thee, now the night is over (EH)	350
From east to west, from shore to shore (EH)	404
He, whose confession God of old accepted (EH)	546, 558
High Word of God, who once didst come (EH)	391
His cheering message from the grave (EH)	455
Jesus, the Father's only Son (EH)	402
Jesus, the virgin's crown, do Thou (EH)	553
Jesus! The very thought is sweet (EH)	410
Jesus, the world's redeeming Lord (PHB)	75
Let the example of St. John remind us (EH)	513
Let the round world with songs rejoice (EH)	540
Lo! Golden light rekindles day (EH)	373
Lo, the blest cross is displayed (PHB)	524
Maker of man, who from Thy throne (EH)	382
Most holy Lord and God of heav'n (EH)	371
Now in holy celebration (EH)	518
Now is the healing time decreed (EH)	436
Now that the daylight (EH)	48
O blest Creator of the light (EH)	353
O boundless Wisdom, God most high (EH)	359

O Christ, our joy, to whom is giv'n (EH)	466
O Christ, the Father's Voice and His eternal Word (EH)	548
O Christ, who art the Light and Day (PHB)	74
O glorious King of martyr hosts (EH)	543, 546
O God of truth, O Lord of might (EH)	49
O God, Creation's secret force (EH)	49
O God, Thy soldiers' crown and guard (EH)	542
O kind Creator, bow Thine ear (EH)	430
O let the heart beat high with bliss (EH)	411
O Light of Light, by love inclined (EH)	422
O Savior, Lord, to Thee we pray (PHB)	73
O Splendor of God's glory bright (TLH)	355
O Thou whose all-redeeming might (EH)	550, 555
O Trinity of blessed light (EH)	387
O what their joy and their glory must be (PHB)	504
Portal of the world's salvation (EH)	517
Rejoice! The year upon its way (EH)	471
Servant of God, remember (PHB)	74
Sing, my tongue, the glorious battle (EH)	439
Son of a virgin, Maker of Thy mother (EH)	552
Sweet flow'rets of the martyr band (EH)	407
Te lucis ante terminum	81
Th' eternal gifts of Christ, the King (EH)	539
The cross, whereby the world is blessed (PHB)	524
The dawn is sprinkling in the east (EH)	384
The day draws on with golden light (EH)	454
The fast, as taught by holy lore (EH)	431
The glory of these forty days (EH)	436
The God whom earth and sea and sky (EH)	536
The Lamb's high banquet we await (EH)	456
The noble deeds of saints (EH)	543
The praises of that saint we sing (EH)	555
The royal banners forward go (EH)	441
The star proclaims the King is here (EH)	414
The winged herald of the day (EH)	361
Thee, O Christ, the Father's splendor (PHB)	527
Thirty years among us dwelling (EH)	440
To Thee, before the close of day (EH)	69
When Christ our Lord had passed once more (EH)	470
Ye choirs of new Jerusalem (EH)	456
Ye clouds and darkness, hosts of night (EH)	367

Index of Latin Hymn Names

A solis ortus cardine	404
Ad cenam Agni	456
Adesto, sancta Trinitas	482
Aeterna caeli gloria	378
Aeterna Christi munera	539
Aeterne Rex altissime	464
Ales diei nuntius	361
Antra deserti	513
Audi benigne Conditor	430
Aurora jam spargit polum	384
Aurora lucis rutilat	454
Beata nobis gaudia	471
Caelestis formam gloriae	421
Caeli Deus sanctissime	371
Chorus novae Jerusalem	456
Christe, qui lux es et dies	74
Christe, qui sedes Olympo	561
Christe, redemptor omnium	402
Clarum decus jejunii	436
Conditor alme siderum	392
Crux benedicta nitet	524
Crux mundi benedictio	524
Cultor Dei memento	74
Deus tuorum militum	542
Ecce tempus idoneum	436
En dies est dominica	350
Ex more docti mystico	431
Exultet caelum laudibus	540
Exultet cor praecordiis	411
Festum matris gloriosae	518
Fortem, virili pectore	555
Hostis Herodes impie	414
Hymnum canamus gloriae	466
Immense caeli Conditor	359
Iste confessor	546, 558
Jam Christus astra ascenderunt	470
Jam lucis orto sidere	48
Jesu, Corona virginum	553
Jesu, Redemptor omnium	550, 555

Jesu, Salvator saeculi	75
Jesus, dulcis memoria	410
Lucis Creator optime	353
Lustra sex qui jam peracta	440
Lux ecce surgit aurea	373
Magnae Deus potentiae	376
Mundi salus affutura	517
Nocte surgentes	350
Nox et tenebrae et nubila	367
Nunc Sancte nobis Spiritus	48
O Lux beata Trinitas	387
O nata Lux de lumine	422
O Pater sancte	481
O quanta qualia sunt illa sabbata	504
O qui perpetuus nos	548
Pange, lingua gloriosi praelium	439
Plasmator hominis	382
Quem terra, pontus sidera	536
Rector potens, verax Deus	49
Rerum Deus tenax vigor	49
Rex gloriose Martyrum	543, 546
Salvator mundi Domine	73
Salvete, flores martyrum	407
Sanctorum meritis	543
Sermone blando Angelus	455
Splendor paternae gloriae	355
Te lucis ante terminum	69, 81
Telluris ingens Conditor	365
Tibi, Christe, splendor Patris	527
Tu Christe nostrum gaudium	466
Urbs beata Jerusalem	566
Veni, Creator Spiritus, mentes	473
Veni, Redemptor gentium	403
Verbum supernum prodiens	391
Vexilla Regis prodeunt	441
Virginis Proles	552

www.ingramcontent.com/pod-product-compliance
Lightning Source LLC
Chambersburg PA
CBHW071947110526
44592CB00012B/1026